成人本科学士学位英语统考（英语三级）考试大纲与指南

本书编委会　编

北京大学出版社
PEKING UNIVERSITY PRESS

图书在版编目(CIP)数据

成人本科学士学位英语统考(英语三级)考试大纲与指南/本书编委会编. —北京：北京大学出版社，2011.1

ISBN 978-7-301-18060-0

Ⅰ.①成… Ⅱ.①本… Ⅲ.①英语－成人教育：高等教育－教学参考资料 Ⅳ.①H31

中国版本图书馆 CIP 数据核字（2010）第 218514 号

书　　名：成人本科学士学位英语统考(英语三级)考试大纲与指南
著作责任者：本书编委会　编
责 任 编 辑：叶　丹
封 面 设 计：肖　红
标 准 书 号：ISBN 978-7-301-18060-0/H・2689
出 版 发 行：北京大学出版社
地　　址：北京市海淀区成府路 205 号　100871
网　　址：http://www.pup.cn　电子信箱：zbing@pup.pku.edu.cn
电　　话：邮购部 62752015　发行部 62750672　编辑部 62754382　出版部 62754962
印 刷 者：北京虎彩文化传播有限公司
经 销 者：新华书店
787 毫米×1092 毫米　16 开本　20.5 印张　520 千字
2011 年 1 月第 1 版　2020 年 1 月第 3 次印刷
定　　价：39.80 元

前　　言

为了客观地测试成人本科毕业生申请学士学位人员的英语水平，确保学位授予质量，根据全国人大常委会通过的《中华人民共和国学位条例》、国务院批准的《中华人民共和国学位条例暂行实施办法》、国务院学位委员会制定的《关于授予成人高等教育本科毕业生学士学位暂行规定》和国务院学位委员会办公室《关于外国语达不到要求不能授予成人高等教育本科毕业生学士学位问题的复函》的精神和要求，通过成人本科学士学位英语统一考试，成为成人本科毕业生获得学士学位的必要条件。

成人本科学士学位英语，又称成人三级英语、成人英语三级。开展成人本科学士学位英语考试旨在加强国家对授予学士学位的宏观质量控制、规范管理，是国家组织的对申请学士学位人员进行外国语水平认定的重要环节。1994 年，北京市教委根据国家有关规定制定了《北京地区成人本科学士学位英语统一考试大纲》，1997 年进行了第一次修订。2003 年，北京市教委组织有关专家对考试大纲再次进行修订，并于 2003 年 11 月开始执行，一直沿用至今。各地的考试大纲与北京相比，考试内容基本一致。

按照这个考试大纲，我们组织北京大学、清华大学、北京师范大学、中国人民大学、中央广播电视大学等高校长期从事成人本科学士学位英语命题和教学工作的教师，编写了《成人本科学士学位英语统考(英语三级)考试大纲与指南》一书，作为各高校教学和辅导的教材，也可作为广大应试者复习备考之用。

本书编委会

目　　录

第一章　考试大纲与样题 …………………………………………………… (1)

第二章　阅读理解题解题技巧 …………………………………………… (10)

第三章　语法与词汇题解题技巧 ………………………………………… (36)

第四章　挑错题解题技巧 ………………………………………………… (88)

第五章　完形填空题解题技巧 …………………………………………… (110)

第六章　翻译题解题技巧 ………………………………………………… (154)

第七章　历年考试真题 …………………………………………………… (166)

附录　词汇表 ……………………………………………………………… (284)

第一章　考试大纲与样题

第一节　考 试 大 纲

自1991年以来，北京地区成人高等教育英语三级统一考试已经连续举行了13次。为使这一考试更加规范，也使广大考生能够熟悉英语三级考试的内容、题型、难度及记分办法，特制定本大纲。

成人英语三级统一考试的目的是为了检测本地区成人教育系列中非外语专业的英语教学水平，保证成人本科毕业生学士学位的授予质量。

成人英语教学的目的是培养学生具有较强的阅读能力，一定的英汉互译能力和初步的听力能力，使他们能以英语为工具，获取专业所需要的信息，并为进一步提高英语水平打下较好的基础。为此，本考试主要考核学生运用语言的能力，重点是考核学生的阅读能力以及对语法结构和词语用法的熟练程度。

本考试是一种标准化考试。由于尚不具备口试条件，目前暂只进行笔试。考试范围主要参照全日制文理科本科英语教学大纲所规定的一至三级除说的技能以外的大部分内容。在题型设计上，除英汉互译部分是主观性试题外，其余试题均采用客观性的多项选择题形式。待将来条件成熟时，再酌情增加听力及短文写作的内容。

本考试每年举行两次，分别在4月和11月，每次考试时间为两小时，即上午9:00—11:00。

考试内容：

本考试内容包括五个部分：分别是阅读理解、词语用法与语法结构、挑错、完形填空和英汉互译。全部题目按顺序统一编号，共85题。

第一部分：阅读理解(Part I Reading Comprehension)，共15题，考试时间40分钟。

要求考生阅读三篇短文，总阅读量不超过900个词。每篇文章后有五个问题，考生应根据文章内容从每题四个选择项中选出一个最佳答案。短文选材的原则是：

1. 题材广泛。包括人物传记、社会、文化、日常知识、热门话题及科普常识等。但所涉及的背景知识应能为学生所理解。

2. 体裁多样。包括叙述文、说明文、议论文等。

3. 文章的语言为中等难度。无法猜测而又影响理解的关键词，如超出全日制文理科教学大纲中词汇表一至三级的范围，则用汉语注明词义。

阅读理解部分主要测试考生的下述能力：

1. 掌握所读材料的主旨和大意；
2. 了解说明主旨和大意的事实和细节；
3. 既理解字面的意思，又能根据所读材料进行一定的判断和推论；
4. 既理解个别句子的意义，又能在一定程度上理解上下文的逻辑关系。

阅读理解部分主要考核学生通过阅读获取信息的能力，既要求准确，也要求有一定的速度。

第二部分：词语用法和语法结构(Part II Vocabulary and Structure)，共30题，考试时间25分钟。题目中50%的内容为词和短语的用法，50%为语法结构。要求考生从每题四个选项中选出一个最佳答案。

词语用法和语法结构部分主要考核学生运用词汇、短语及语法结构的能力。考试范围包括全日制文理科本科教学大纲中词汇表及语法结构表一至三级的主要内容。

第三部分：挑错(Part III Identification)，共10题，考试时间10分钟。挑错题由10个单句组成。每个句子含有标着A、B、C、D的四个划线部分，其中有一处是错误的，要求考生从四个划线部分中挑出其错误的部分。

挑错部分是词语用法和语法结构部分的延伸，目的是测试学生掌握词汇、短语及语法结构的熟练程度，其重点是固定搭配和句型。考试范围与第二部分相同。

第四部分：完形填空(Part IV Cloze)，共20题，考试时间15分钟。完形填空题是在一篇题材熟悉、难度适中的短文(约200词)中留有20个空白。每个空白为一题，每题有四个选项。要求考生在全面理解内容的基础上选出一个最佳答案，使短文的结构和意思恢复完整。填空的选项包括结构词和实义词，有些选项会涉及一些重要的语法内容。

完形填空部分主要考核学生综合运用语言的能力。

第五部分：翻译(Part V Translation)，共10题，考试时间30分钟。翻译试题由两部分组成。第一部分为英译汉，要求考生把前面阅读理解文章中划线的五个句子译成中文；第二部分为汉译英，要求考生把五个难度适中的中文句子译成英文。英译汉和汉译英的句子难度均低于课文的英语文章。评分标准要求译文达意，无重大语言错误。

翻译部分主要考核学生词汇、语法、句型等方面综合运用语言的能力。

答题及记分办法

客观性试题用机器阅卷，要求考生从每题四个选项中选出一个最佳答案，并在答题纸(Answer Sheet)上相应部分用铅笔在字母中间划一横线。每题只能选择一个答案，多选无效，该题按零分计。多项选择题记分只算答对的题数，答错不扣分。翻译类主观性试题按科学的评分标准评分，其答案必须写在另附的答题纸上。

整套试题共计100分，60分为及格标准。凡达到及格标准的考生均发给成人教育大学英语三级考试合格证书。

第二节 考试样题

北京地区成人本科学士学位英语统一考试

2019.11.9

Part I Reading Comprehension (30%)

Directions: There are three passages in this part. Each passage is followed by some questions or unfinished statements. For each of them there are four choices marked A, B, C and D. You should decide on the best choice and blacken the corresponding letter on the Answer Sheet.

Passage 1 Questions 1 to 5 are based on the following passage:

There are more species (种类) of beetles (甲虫) than any other form of life. About 380,000 species of beetles are known to exist, and more are discovered all the time. (76) There are several theories about why there are so many beetles, but evidence shows that beetles have the lowest extinction rates of any animal ever.

One of the reasons beetles survive so well is their body design. Most beetle species have two pairs of wings. The front pair of a beetle's wings are hard and thick. These protect the rear set of wings and the beetle's stomach region. They are not used for flying. Indeed, some species of beetles have lost the ability to fly, but they are still equipped with front wings.

Beetles can also eat a wide range of foods. Beetle species live all over the world, and they have many different types of food available to them. Most beetles are omnivores. That means they eat both plants and animals. The mixed diets help beetles adapt to many different environments.

Finally, beetles are good at moving quickly over long distances. Any change in animal's environment can be dangerous to it, but some species can avoid dangerous environment changes by migrating to a new place. Research shows that beetles respond quickly to shifts in temperature. They can migrate to safer environments.

Beetles' bodies and habits help give them anedge over other creatures. (77) They are unlikely to die out. As a result, beetles make up nearly one quarter of all animal species. There are more types of beetles on Earth than there are types of plants. Some types of beetles that exist today were around during the Permian period of history, 284 million years ago. Beetles, clearly, are here to stay.

1. What is the passage mainly about?
   A. Why beetles have two pairs of wings.
   B. Why there are so many species of beetles.
   C. Why there are different types of food for beetles.
   D. Why beetles are good at moving long distances.
2. Beetles survive better than other animals because of their ________.
   A. bodies and habits　　B. stomach and diets
   C. diets and ability to fly　　D. ability to fly and migrate
3. Which of the following is NOT TRUE of beetles?
   A. Some species have existed for 284 million years.
   B. They live all around the world.
   C. They have two pairs of wings to fly.
   D. They are unlikely to die out.
4. The wordedge in the last paragraph is closest in meaning to ________.
   A. evidence　　B. margin
   C. survival　　D. advantage
5. How many animal species are there according to the passage?
   A. Around 1.52 million.　　B. Around 380,000.
   C. Around 284 million.　　D. Not known.

Passage 2　Questions 6 to 10 are based on the following passage:

In today's extremely connected world, (78) people appear to have more chances to get into contact with one another than ever. Yet societies known as "uncontacted peoples" remain in parts of the world. These are communities with little contact with the wider world. It is estimated that about one hundred groups of uncontacted peoples exist today. In general, these groups remain uncontacted by choice; because of this, it is impossible to know much about their societies.

For example, North Sentinel Island in the Indian Ocean is home to a group that clearly wishes to stay separate from the rest of the world. They are referred to as the North Sentinelese. North Sentinel Island is one of the Andaman Islands, which are part of India. While groups on other Andaman Islands have slowly accepted tourism and development, the North Sentinelese fire warning arrows from their beaches at any boat that approaches their land. Over many decades, gifts and other efforts from outsiders have been rejected. From what little we know about their language, they have probably been isolated for tens of thousands of years.

Why might uncontacted peoples choose to remain isolated? Unfortunately, in many cases, these groups' past encounters with the outside world were violent. Former members of uncontacted groups have said that after friends and family were attacked or killed by outsiders, they avoided any kind of contact. Even peaceful contact can have disastrous effects. Many uncontacted groups have never been exposed to diseases, not even the common cold or flu. As a result, they often don't have immunity (免疫力) to these diseases, meaning that even minor contact with outsiders has resulted in deadly outbreaks. It's not surprising, then, that some groups prefer to keep to themselves.

6. What is the passage mainly about?
   A. Societies known as "uncontacted people".
   B. The North Sentinelese.
   C. Encounters with "uncontacted peoples".
   D. Contact with groups on the Andaman Islands.
7. What is TRUE of the majority of the Andaman Islands?
   A. They have developed contact with the wider world.
   B. They fire warning arrows at approaching boats.
   C. They reject gifts from outsiders.
   D. They are eager to develop tourism.
8. From which of the following do people know that the North Sentinelese have been separated for so many years?
   A. Peaceful contact. B. The warning arrows.
   C. Their language. D. Tourism.
9. How many reasons are given to explain the isolation of the "uncontacted peoples"?
   A. One. B. Two. C. Three. D. Four.
10. The expressionkeep to themselves in the last paragraph is closest in meaning to ________.
   A. stay separated B. guard secrets
   C. stick closely D. protect themselves

Passage 3 Questions 11 to 15 are based on the following passage:

(79) For more than 60 years, Lego (乐高) bricks have sparked children's imaginations. Now, a new version of these toys is in the works. They're Lego Braille Bricks, and they're being tested around the world.

Lego Braille Bricks are designed to help people learn Braille. That's a system of writing in which letters are represented by raised dots. People who are blind or visually impaired (弱视的) use their fingertips to read.

According to the World Health Organization, 36 million people worldwide are blind. In the United States, it's estimated that only 10% of blind children learn Braille. Lego Braille Bricks can help change that. The small knobs on the bricks are arranged as Braille letters. Blind children can use these knobs to learn Braille.

Lego plans to launch Braille Bricks next year. (80) For some schools and institutions, they will be free. Each set will contain about 250 bricks. Along with the alphabet, the bricks will feature numbers and math symbols.

The Danish Association of the Blind was the first organization to come up with the idea of using Lego bricks to teach Braille. Thorkild Olesen is the president of the group. Olesen is blind. He says many teachers don't have the tools and skills to help kids learn Braille. So they teach with audio (声音的) tools, such as audio books. "Like any other people, we need to express ourselves in writing. Audio can never replace Braille. Braille is the single most important tool for us to learn to spell correctly and write like sighted people."

"This is particularly critical when we know that Braille users often are more independent, have a higher level of education and better employment opportunities. We strongly believe," Olesen continues, "Lego Braille Bricks can help promote the level of interest in learning Braille."

11. Which of the following is the best title for the passage?
   A. Sparking Children's Imaginations B. Lego Braille Bricks

C. Teaching Blind Children Braille　　D. The Toy Industry

12. Lego Braille Bricks will be launched in ________.

A. 2019　　B. 2020　　C. 2021　　D. 2022

13. The phrasecome up with in Paragraph 5 probably means ________.

A. put forward　　B. turn out　　C. sum up　　D. take over

14. According to Olesen, which of the following statements is NOT TRUE?

A. Teachers often use audio books to teach blind children.

B. Braille users often have better employment prospects.

C. There's no need for blind children to learn Braille.

D. Audio is helpful, but can never replace Braille.

15. According to the passage, which of the following statements about Lego Braille Bricks is NOT TRUE?

A. The idea was first proposed by the Danish Association of the Blind.

B. They are currently undergoing testing around the world.

C. They will be distributed for free to all blind children.

D. There are about 250 bricks in each set.

Part II　Vocabulary and Structure (30%)

Directions: In this part there are 30 incomplete sentences. For each sentence there are four choices marked A, B, C and D. Choose the ONE answer that best completes the sentence. Then blacken the corresponding letter on the Answer Sheet.

16. The hotel is in a quiet ________ near the sea.

A. station　　B. situation　　C. location　　D. stop

17. It was too late to ________ the damage done to their relationship.

A. revisit　　B. repair　　C. rebuild　　D. retire

18. Jane was ________ a grown-up when her father died.

A. enough　　B. almost　　C. closely　　D. nicely

19. A hospital spokesman said the woman had suffered a ________ heart attack.

A. fatal　　B. sick　　C. hard　　D. neutral

20. —Are you going to wear the yellow shirt or the white shirt?

—I'm going to wear the white ________.

A. it　　B. that　　C. one　　D. two

21. —How ________ money do I need to take?

—About three hundred dollars.

A. more　　B. much　　C. many　　D. few

22. I really must go now; ________ I'll be late for school.

A. for　　B. then　　C. otherwise　　D. that

23. The real trouble lies ________ their lack of confidence in their own abilities.

A. in　　B. on　　C. about　　D. off

24. Henry and Kate have been ________ since 2002.

A. marries　　B. marry　　C. married　　D. marrying

25. Peter is going to a lake ________ he can go fishing.

A. here　　B. there　　C. whereas　　D. where

26. What a lovely party! It is worth ________ all my life.

A. remembering　　B. to remember

C. to be remembered　　D. being remembered

27. We cannot understand ________ he avoided speaking to us.

A. before　　B. that　　C. why　　D. after

28. If the whole operation ________ beforehand, a great deal of time and money would have been lost.
A. was not planned B. has not been planned
C. had not been planned D. were not planned
29. Young ________ he is, he knows what is the right thing to do.
A. that B. as C. although D. however
30. When and where the new hospital will be built ________ a mystery.
A. to remain B. remains C. remain D. is remaining
31. The teacher had John ________ for her at the gate for a few more minutes.
A. wait B. to wait C. waited D. waits
32. By the end of next month, I ________ enough money to buy a camera.
A. will earn B. have earned C. must earn D. will have earned
33. The reason he won the election is ________ he is honest and confident of himself.
A. why B. what C. that D. which
34. Tom used to live in California, ________?
A. used he B. did he C. wasn't he D. didn't he
35. When it ________ to American history, he knows little about it.
A. talks B. speaks C. comes D. tells
36. For two weeks, I have ________ every day looking after him.
A. taken B. cost C. spent D. paid
37. Much ________ our relief, he survived the terrible road accident.
A. to B. in C. for D. with
38. He cannot ________ a car, for he doesn't earn that much.
A. obtain B. get C. deserve D. afford
39. This morning our water supply was ________ because of the cold weather.
A. let down B. cut off C. taken up D. brought away
40. It occurred to her that she might ________ a homeless child.
A. adapt B. adopt C. adjust D. admit
41. —________ did you go during the vacation?
—I didn't go anywhere. I stayed home.
A. Why B. How C. When D. Where
42. They thought about the problem for a long time but came to no ________.
A. end B. purpose C. opinion D. conclusion
43. There is a good program ________ television. Let's watch it.
A. on B. in C. for D. with
44. His ________ is to look after the animals.
A. duty B. honor C. glory D. luck
45. He was 29 when the war broke ________.
A. for B. up C. out D. down

Part III Identification (10%)

Directions: Each of the following sentences has four underlined marked A, B, C and D. Identify the one that is not correct. Then blacken the corresponding letter on the Answer Sheet.

46. <u>There is</u> no point <u>to argue</u> with him, <u>since</u> he has already <u>made up</u> his mind.
A B C D
47. People do not <u>realize</u> the importance <u>of</u> good health <u>since</u> they have lost <u>it</u>.
A B C D

48. Mr. Smith is looking for an experienced secretary who is able of managing a sales office.
A B C D

49. Generally spoken, schools in the city provide better education for students than those in the countryside.
A B C D

50. Curiously, the struggle to survive has greatimproved her health.
A B C D

51. I'm just a ordinary, boring but normal guy.
A B C D

52. It is because she is very devoted to her students so she is respected by them.
A B C D

53. I havedecided to save my money in a trip to China next year.
A B C D

54. I was drove 55 miles per hourwhen the police officer stopped me.
A B C D

55. If we owned a bigger house, they can live with us.
A B C D

Part IV　Cloze (10%)

Directions: There are 20 blanks in the following passage, for each blank there are four choices marked A, B, C and D at the end of the passage. You should choose the ONE answer that best fits into the passage. Then blacken the corresponding letter on the Answer Sheet.

The founder of Vassar College, Mathew Vassar, was born in England in 1792, and four years later moved to America with his parents.

In those __56__, the English people thought that they couldn't __57__ without a yearly supply of home-made ale (麦芽啤酒). However, such a thing was unknown in the quiet community to __58__ they had come. __59__ there was no barley (大麦) in the new home, seed was imported __60__ England. The family once more was __61__ to enjoy their favorite drink. When neighbors paid a visit, they were, of course, __62__ to have a drink. Thus, the fame of Vassar's ale __63__ increased, until finally the father decided to make ale to sell. Mathew, for some reason, __64__ the idea. He left home for Newburg, __65__ he remained four years, learning to keep books, and __66__ his money. He then returned home, working in his father's establishment __67__ a book-keeper (记账员).

All __68__ well for some time, till a fire came, destroying all the property, ruining his father, and worst of all __69__ his brother's death. The father returned to a farm, but Mathew was __70__ to restart the business.

He began the business __71__ and old shed and its fame increased, making the ale of Vassar known far and near. From such a beginning, the business __72__ into an immense one, which he carried on __73__ over thirty years.

When he retired, Mathew decided to do __74__ with his money for the betterment of society. In 1861 Vassar Female College was __75__ up, and afterwards was changed to Vassar College. It was the first female college ever established in the US.

56. A. moments　B. days　C. weeks　D. months
57. A. live　B. visit　C. move　D. speak
58. A. when　B. that　C. where　D. which
59. A. Although　B. After　C. As　D. Until
60. A. from　B. beside　C. to　D. by
61. A. easy　B. able　C. hard　D. sorry

62. A. found	B. taught	C. invited	D. required
63. A. hardly	B. mainly	C. mostly	D. steadily
64. A. promised	B. discovered	C. planned	D. disliked
65. A. where	B. which	C. when	D. why
66. A. save	B. lose	C. saving	D. losing
67. A. on	B. as	C. in	D. of
68. A. left	B. went	C. flew	D. sent
69. A. meeting	B. reaching	C. causing	D. drawing
70. A. determined	B. decided	C. considered	D. opposed
71. A. on	B. with	C. of	D. in
72. A. protected	B. became	C. organize d	D. developed
73. A. in	B. above	C. for	D. between
74. A. nothing	B. anything	C. something	D. everything
75. A. set	B. got	C. picked	D. looked

Part V Translation (20%)

Section A

Directions*: *In this part there are five sentences which you should translate into Chinese. These sentences are all taken from the 3 passages you have just read in Reading Comprehension. You can refer back to the passages to identify their meanings in the context.

76. There are several theories about why there are so many beetles.
77. They are unlikely to die out.
78. People appear to have more chances to get into contact with one another than ever.
79. For more than 60 years, Lego bricks have sparked children's imaginations.
80. For some schools and institutions, they will be free.

Section B

Directions*: *In this part there are five sentences in Chinese. You should translate them into English. Be sure to write clearly.

81. 一有消息我就告诉你。
82. 今天他要参加一个重要的面试。
83. 买这部手机你花了多少钱?
84. 他喜欢玩电脑游戏。
85. 她激动得说不出话来。

参考答案

1—15 BACDA AACBA BBACC

16—45 CBBAC BCACD ACCBB ADCDC CADBB DDAAC

46—55 BCCAC BCCAC

56—75 BADCA BCDDA CBBCA DDCCA

76. 关于为何有这么多种的甲壳虫有一些理论。
77. 他们不大可能灭绝。
78. 与以往相比,他们有更多的机会彼此接触。
79. 六十多年来,乐高积木激发着孩子们的想象力。

80．一些学校和机构会免费得到这些积木。
81．I will tell you as soon as I get some information.
82．He is going to attend an important interview today.
83．How much did you spend on this cell phone?
84．He likes playing computer games.
85．She is too excited to say anything.
（样题为 2019 年 11 月北京地区成人本科学士学位英语统一考试试题）

第二章　阅读理解题解题技巧

第一节　成人本科学士学位英语考试对阅读理解的总体要求

北京地区成人本科学士学位英语考试大纲对阅读理解这样要求："成人英语教学的目的是培养学生具有较强的阅读能力，一定的英汉互译能力和初步的听力能力，使他们能以英语为工具，获取专业所需要的信息，并为进一步提高英语水平打下较好的基础。为此，本考试主要考核学生运用语言的能力，重点是考核学生的阅读能力以及对语法结构和词语用法的熟练程度。"

该考试第一部分就是阅读理解，共 15 题，考试时间 40 分钟。要求考生阅读三篇短文，总阅读量不超过 900 个词。每篇文章后有五个问题，考生应根据文章内容从每题四个选择项中选出一个最佳答案。

考试大纲规定短文选材的原则是：1. 题材广泛。包括人物传记、社会、文化、日常知识、热门话题及科普常识等。但所涉及的背景知识应能为学生所理解。2. 体裁多样。包括叙述文、说明文、议论文等。3. 文章的语言为中等难度。无法猜测而又影响理解的关键词，如超出全日制文理科教学大纲中词汇表一至三级的范围，则用汉语注明词义。

考试大纲还明确指出：阅读理解部分主要测试考生的下述能力：1. 掌握所读材料的主旨和大意；2. 了解说明主旨和大意的事实和细节；3. 既理解字面的意思，又能根据所读材料进行一定的判断和推论；4. 既理解个别句子的意义，又能在一定程度上理解上下文的逻辑关系。

根据以上要求，近几年在北京地区成人本科学士学位英语考试试卷中，阅读理解文章的难易程度起伏不大，基本保持了一贯的"中等"难度，但也有一些细微的变化，三篇文章中总有一篇文章越来越长、难度越来越大。文章中出现的一些超出大纲的生词，也不再全部都加中文注释。这说明，对考生阅读理解能力中"猜词"能力的考查，不仅体现在题目中，而且已经融入到阅读理解的过程之中了。某些文章中虽无生词，但句子较长，如果考生缺乏对复合句的理解能力，就会出现单词都认识，就是看不懂句子的现象。

本章要解决的，就是根据北京地区成人本科学士学位英语考试大纲的要求，帮助那些基础不是太好的考生熟悉阅读理解部分的常见题型，掌握解题策略和技巧，以不变应万变，力争做对更多的题目。

第二节　成人本科学士学位英语考试阅读理解的特点及趋势是什么？

2.1　近年来成人本科学士学位英语考试阅读理解的特点

考生在备战成人本科学士学位英语考试过程中，不能盲目复习，必须有针对性、有目标地各个突破。本书专门就大家最头疼，也是分数比例所占最多的阅读部分进行讲解，希望能使考生有所突破。首先我们必须了解什么是阅读。

阅读是从书面语言中获取信息的一种复杂的智力活动，是从书面语言中获得知识的心理过程。据统计，我们所得到的知识 50％来自于阅读。学英语也是如此。英语阅读的过程是考生理解作品的过程，考生在阅读中一边对读物进行推断、预测；一边进行验证、修改，利用背景知识去理解读物的内容和作者的意图。考生通过自己头脑里的知识系统对读物进行扫描、释码，然后重新编码构成新的知识系统。

英语阅读有助于扩大词汇量，丰富语言知识，了解英语语言国家的文化习俗，掌握阅读技巧，提高运用语言的能力。

对于迫切需要通过成人本科学士学位英语考试的考生来说，我们就必须从应试的角度来看待阅读。成人本科学士学位英语考试只有了解阅读理解考什么，怎么考，才能找到对付阅读理解的方法和策略。

下面我们以最近一套比较标准的试卷(2006 年 4 月考试)为例分析一下阅读理解的特点。

（一）增大了阅读量

这次考试的总阅读量超出了大纲规定的 900 个词，并且文章中各种复合句比较多。尽管这样，考生也不必紧张。因为词汇难度并不大，虽然有 authoritarian 和 discredited 这样的难词，但都加了汉语注释，绝大多数词汇还是比较简单的。单是从阅读量来说，考生是能够在 40 分钟之内完成的。

（二）有限增加阅读理解难度

其一，增加深层次理解词汇含义的试题，考查在特定语境中理解词汇的能力

近几年来成人本科学士学位英语考试对词汇题的考查多要求考生利用语境猜测一些生词，从而为顺利阅读铺平道路，这种试题只要求考生根据语境猜测生词的基本意义，而不需要准确理解其严格意义，这属于浅层次词汇考查题。这套试卷出现了两道这样的试题，其中“social”的理解比较难，相当多的考生选择了“concerned about social welfare”，而正确答案是“friendly with other people”。

其二，增加了全文结论题，考查考生深层次理解文章内容的能力

全文结论题属深层次理解题，它要求考生在通读全文的基础上，认真分析主人公特定心态、文章大意及作者写作意图，在此基础上，考生还应考虑两个原则：高度的概括性和准确的针对性。

所谓高度的概括性是指文章结论必须直接总结观点，它应当是对文章大意的高度概括和总结；所谓准确的针对性是指文章结论不能太过于概括而失去了直接指向该文主要特点。请看第 5 题。

From the passage, we can conclude that ________.

A. children should keep away from TV

B. TV programs should be improved

C. children's books should have pictures

D. TV has a deep influence on the young

解析：选 D。认真阅读文章可知，作者说现在的孩子和以前不太一样了，就是他们看电视很多，而电视又在强烈地影响着他们。电视改变了政治，电视广告诱使人们买各种各样的东西。显然，文章主要谈的不是电视带来的好处，主要谈的是坏处，因此很多考生选 A。A 与 D 的区别主要在主语，A 的主语是孩子，D 的主语是电视，文章主要谈的是电视对孩子的影响，因此选 D。

其三，增加了透过现象看本质的试题，考查考生去伪存真的深层次理解能力

这套试题的阅读理解不少题考的是言外之意，而这种言外之意往往决定着考生对作者意图等深层次的理解是否准确，若不深究其言外之意、透过现象看本质，就会作出错误判断。如第 13 题。

The author's attitude towards American education can be best described as ________.

A. favorable　　B. negative

C. tolerant　　D. unfriendly

解析：选 A。不少考生可能会误选 B 或者 D,因为文章第一段最后一句是这样的："The old authoritarian (要绝对服从的) methods of education were discredited (不被认可) rather a long time ago — so much so that many people now think that they have gone too far in the direction of trying to make children happy and interested rather than giving them actual instruction." 意思是"很多人觉得现在(宽容的)教育方法已经走过头了,还是应该给孩子们一些实际的指导。"所以考生就认为作者是反对现行教育体制的。这个句子针对本题来说其实是一个假象,作者是认为现在的教育方法太过宽容,但第二段又说了"but it is not fair to say that the educational system fails." 尤其是最后一句"It probably does succeed in making most people sociable and ready to help one another both in material ways and through kindness and friendliness."最终说明美国的教育方式成功地使大多数人愿意与人为善,乐于助人,因此作者是赞同这种教育方法的。所以答案应选 A。

从题材角度来看,这套试题三篇阅读理解文章和最近几年考试的基本一致。在文体上涵盖了教育、文化和社会现象,没有考到的是人物和科普(这两类文章一直是成人本科学士学位英语考试阅读理解的热门选择)。在题目设计上更加体现了对文章的深层次理解,主要设计成主旨大意、事实推断、猜测词义、推断主题、正误判断等几个方面。

2.2 未来几年成人本科学士学位英语考试阅读理解的趋势

通过对 2003 年至 2010 年北京地区成人本科学士学位英语考试阅读理解题的分析,我们可预测今后的阅读理解试题会有以下几个趋势。

第一,沿袭过去一贯的风格

题材广泛,主要是人物传记、社会、文化、日常知识、热门话题及科普常识等。体裁多样,主要有叙述文、说明文、议论文等。文章的难易程度中等。以上这些方面不会有大的变化。

第二,文章中会减少对生词的注释

为什么要减少对生词的注释？就是使阅读文章更贴近生活,因为我们平时获取信息的时候,很少有时间查字典,所以考试中减少生词的注释,是希望考生能够通过上下文猜测词义,或者根据自己的词汇知识,比如说构词法去猜测。

第三,加大信息量的处理

文章的复杂程度将会加大。但是单项选择试题里考语法的试题难度将降低。把我们所学的比较复杂的语法现象,放到阅读理解中去考察,要求大家对复杂的语法现象要能够理解和处理。

第四,文章内容更贴近生活

阅读题材会涉及一些热门话题、情感世界、人际关系等,这些可能在过去的课本里见的比较少,像能源、环保、体育等热门话题会经常出现。至于体裁,现在比较偏重议论文和说明文,将来很有可能出现应用文等文体。

从以上几个方面可以看出,成人本科学士学位英语考试阅读理解的难度在逐渐加大,考生应该了解以上这些趋势。一方面,应增强做好阅读理解题目的信心,相信只要认真对待,严格训练,掌握技巧,考试时是能够提高阅读理解题目的正确率的;另一方面,考生应加强对词汇的深层次理解、标题确定原则的理解、透过现象看本质方法的理解及灵活分析细节方法的理解,以提高正确率。接下来,我们就针对阅读理解的题材和体裁特点,和考生一起来分析,攻克阅读理解这一难关。

第三节　正确的阅读方法及理解技巧

3.1　正确的阅读方法与步骤

一、基本的阅读方法

阅读是理解的前提和手段；理解是分析、加工和处理信息，是阅读的目的和结果。因此，做阅读理解题时，考生可以先看题目，然后再看文章，这样带着问题去阅读就更有目的性；也可以先看完文章，然后再做题，从宏观上把握文章的大意；还可以将两者结合起来，边看边做，边做边看。至于哪一种方法更实用，考生可以根据自己的实际情况来选用。在这里，介绍几种阅读的方法，希望考生能从中获益。

（一）略读法

略读法是快速阅读的一种方法，通常又称为浏览。略读的关键是在能抓住文章要点的前提下，以个人最快的速度阅读，主要目的是获得足够的信息以便准确地回答有关文章主旨的问题。利用略读法做阅读理解题时，要特别注意文章的各段首句，尤其是文章第一段的首句。因为作者往往在此处点明文章的主题，或作者的意图。要学会寻找文章段落的主题句，这是高效省时抓住段落大意的一条捷径，同时也是准确理解全文大意的有效途径，因为把整篇文章的每段主题句的意思综合起来实际上就是全文的中心思想。文章的主题句往往就是各段的首句，考生必须运用略读法快速准确地找到它。

做阅读理解题时，首先应浏览一遍所提问题及其选项，然后带着这些问题有目的、有针对性地阅读文章。一方面，把较简单的客观理解题做好；另一方面，把与问题相关的词语、句子划出来，为准确理解难句、解答难题做好准备。在这里强调一下新大纲实施以后增加的英译汉对阅读理解的帮助。

有考生认为增加了英译汉使得成人本科学士学位英语考试难度大增，其实不然。很多时候我们把下划线的那句话看懂并且翻译出来就会间接甚至直接帮助做对一道或几道题。如 2003 年 11 月 A 卷第二篇文章划出来的第 78 题“<u>In the first place, television is not only a convenient source of entertainment, but also a comparatively cheap one.</u>”这是第二段的第一句，“首先，电视不仅是很方便的一种娱乐来源，而且还很便宜”。而第 7 题是这么设计的：

Television, as a source of entertainment, is ________.

A. not very convenient　　B. very expensive

C. quite dangerous　　D. relatively cheap

毫无疑问，答案选 D。

（二）对应法

在进行完略读、了解了文章大意后，较简单的试题往往能立即解决。但还有一些综合性较强、结构较复杂的试题，如果只看一遍文章很难对问题把握得准，需要对文章里面的细节、结构、生词的含义进行认真分析、推敲，才能选出正确答案。这时若通读全文就会耽误时间。我们就可利用对应法对相关词语及句子甚至段落进行复读、研究，从而选出答案。

利用技巧，可以不需要阅读整篇文章，而只需找出可能包含所需信息的部分进行阅读就行，这种方法就是对应法。对应法主要是获得具体的信息，回答相应的问题，即细节问题，它常常与 5W 和 1H，即 Who, What, When, Where, Why 和 How 有关，有时跟具体的数字如长度、宽度、高度、距离、大小、尺寸等有联系。考生在使用对应法时，应该注意文章的结构和顺序排列，文章的结构有的是按时间顺序排列,有的是按空间顺序排列,有的是按逻辑顺序排列。弄清楚文章的排列顺序能帮助考生在阅读和回答问题时高效省时,准确无误。要注意提高阅读的速度和解题效率,大家必须练就用眼睛扫读的本领,在最短的时间内找到所需要的信息,要把注意力集中在与所需信息直接相关的词语上,以便做出正确选择。

如 2006 年 4 月考试阅读理解的第 1 题:

In the past, many young people ________.

A. knew the effects of war

B. went in for politics

C. liked to save the wounded in wars

D. were willing to be soldiers

与之对应的就是文章第一句和第二句:"Television has opened windows in everybody's life. Young men will never again go to war as they did in 1914.""电视开启了每一个人的生活之窗。年轻人不会再去打仗了,就像 1914 年(第一次世界大战爆发)的人们那样。"这句话隐含着就是 1914 年的时候,人们会盲目地去当兵打仗。这层意思其实包含在"did"之中。

再看第 12 题:

Some Americans complain about elementary schools because they think ________.

A. children are reluctant to help each other

B. schools lay too much emphasis on co-operation

C. children should grow up with competitive ideas

D. schools give little actual instruction to children

与之相关的句子为短文第一段最后一句:"The old authoritarian (要绝对服从的) methods of education were discredited (不被认可) rather a long time ago — so much so that many people now think that they have gone too far in the direction of trying to make children happy and interested rather than giving them actual instruction."这句话中由于出现了两个生词 authoritarian、discredited,给考生造成了理解上的困难,再加上复杂的句子结构,很多考生没有看懂。但我们通过对 so much... that 这个句型的分析,就可以理解这句话的意思:很久以前,要学生绝对服从的教育方式就被摒弃了,但是很多人认为走过头了,现在的教育太注重孩子的高兴了,而忽视了对孩子的实际指导。因此正确答案是 D。

(三) 研读法

研读就是仔细阅读,以求获得具体的信息,对文章有深层次的理解。研读主要是指围绕文章后面的问题进行细读,包括理解支持主题句的细节,根据作者的意图和中心思想进行推论,借助语法知识对涉及问题的难句、长句进行分析,力争达到准确地理解,根据上下文猜测词义等。

上面谈到的三种方法是基本的阅读方法,是做阅读理解题必不可少的三个步骤。

(四) 根据上下文判断词义法

考生应该有意识地积累英语单词,没有一定量的英语单词作基础和保障,英语的听、说、读、写、译等各项技能都无从谈起。采取哪些方法来记单词呢?可以把一个生词放在具体的句子语境中记忆。还可以采用:转换法(同一个单词可能同时具备名词、动词、形容词、副词等词性)、词缀法(在某个单词前面或后面加一些词缀,可能改变单词的词性和词意,使之成为一个新单词)、派生法、合成法等,也可以从广播电影电视和报纸杂志中学习英语词汇。

(五) 同义互释法

所谓同义互释,就是在阅读的时候从备选项中找出与原文意思相同或相近的词、词组或短语，它们在意思上相同或相近，可以互相解释，互相替换。它是英语阅读理解的常见方法之一，在成人本科学士学位英语考试中有些深层理解或者判断推理的问题可以采用同义互释法。同义互释的考题在成人本科学士学位英语考试中多次出现，而且在大学四六级考试中也很常见。

（六）判断推理法

利用略读法、对应法和猜测词义法等能够解决答题中的许多问题。可是，在答题的时候，考生有时会发现所给的四个选项中，有不止一个选项可以作为答案项，即考生常常抱怨的：四选二容易而二选一难。这种困境往往在判断推理题时出现。在答题时，大家一旦发现有一个看似正确的选项，就立即把它作为正确答案的备选项，这是不明智的，正确的方法是再看一看其他选项中还有没有更完备的答案。如果有别的备选答案的话，就要根据文章的主旨和作者的意图，选择比较，去伪存真，做出深层理解和全面分析，进行合理的推理和判断，选出切合文章主旨和作者意图的最佳答案。

在成人本科学士学位英语考试中，阅读理解题中四个选项，有时有一个或两个与常识或我们在其他各学科中所学的知识不相符，我们可先将其排除，再对剩下的选项进行筛选就容易多了。如 2000 年考试阅读理解的第 3 题：

Advertisement is mainly paid for by ________.

A. the customer　　B. the producer

C. increased sales　　D. reduced prices

答案肯定不能选 D，价格减少了，怎么还能支付广告费呢？根据常识，羊毛出在羊身上，因此答案肯定选 A。在文章中也有对应，答案在第三段：it is clear that it is customer who pays for advertisement. 因此广告的费用主要是由顾客来付。

再如第 4 题：

Advertisement can increase demand ________.

A. all the time　　B. in any circumstances

C. in a growing market　　D. in a shrinking market

我们也可以迅速淘汰 D，因为 shrinking 是缩水的意思，市场都萎缩了，还怎么能做广告呢？A 和 B 也不能选，因为都犯了绝对化的错误。所以只能选 C。文章中的对应是在第四段：When the market is growing, advertisement helps to increase demand. 因此，如果市场扩大了，广告有助于增加需求。

由此可见，考生平时要注意各种知识和生活经验的积累，为排除错误选项提供依据。

在考试时，考生可以根据不同的阅读目的，采用不同的阅读方法。例如：要了解一篇文章的主题思想和段落大意，可以用略读法；要获得某些特定的信息，可以用对应法；要掌握确切的内容，深入理解文章，就要用研读法。

总之，做阅读理解，考生应该从整体上把握一篇文章的脉络，一定要明确每一段的大意，理解文章的中心思想和作者的行文思路，这是做阅读理解获取高分的基础和前提条件。阅读理解能力的提高，是一个渐进的过程。考生在掌握了基本的语言知识和正确的阅读方法的基础上，一定要多读书，以扩大知识面，这对提高阅读理解能力会有很大的帮助。只要考生在平时广泛阅读，注意养成良好的阅读习惯，掌握正确的阅读理解方法和技巧，提高阅读理解的素质和能力，考试时也就不会感到困难了。

二、怎样找出阅读理解题的答案

根据上面提到的几种阅读方法，建议大家在阅读时按照下面步骤完成阅读任务，会起到事半功倍的效果。

（一）通篇略读，了解全文大意

对全文通篇略读，舍弃无关紧要的细节，全力捕捉全文中心思想。要达到三个效果：

(1) 对文章有一个总的概念和印象，文章讲什么，有关什么方面的内容。

(2) 了解文章的中心思想和作者的基本观点、立场。

(3) 记住文中的信息方位，如什么地方是作者的观点，什么地方是作者所举的例子，什么地方是作者分析的原因，以便再读时查找。

通篇略读是为了在短时间内确定材料的中心大意或主题思想，因此考生要注意主要信息。如即使是新闻报道，也以某一事件作为报道的主要内容，将该事件的时间、地点、人物、原因、过程及结果等几方面叙述清楚，从而引起读者的普遍关注；议论文总有一个中心论题，可重点阅读第一段、结束段以及其他各段的第一句或末一句。在阅读过程中，目光要快速移动，千万不要停顿或复视，要对准关键词、句；同时要不断地对内容做预测，使大脑的逻辑思维、推理判断贯穿于整个阅读的始终。这样就节省了阅读时间，起到了“会当凌绝顶、一览众山小”的效果，迅速而准确地抓住了全文的大意。

（二）细读全文，注重关键词句

针对题目中的问题细读材料，可以缩小阅读范围，迅速找到与问题有关的信息，细读与题目相关联的词、句、段，对关键部分要透彻理解，仔细推敲。在这一过程中，对有关细节可放慢速度，精读有关部分，一边阅读一边归纳，加快做题速度，力求一次性选出正确答案。

考生在逐句阅读过程中，目光要瞄准文章中的实词，尤其是名词和动词。同时要抓住一些敏感的信息，如时间、地点、人物、事件、原因、结果以及某些词汇、词语等。一般说来，这些问题会在文章中有说明交代，运用对应法是不难找到线索的。

（三）透过表层，深入开拓，正确解题

在理解原文的基础上，对未知含义进行演绎、推断，并利用文章中出现的各种信息及所论述的观点、论证、作者的态度或评论等，进行综合性的概括，或者说进行推理。要熟练地识别各种线索，并对信息进行分析鉴别，区分哪些是主要信息，哪些是次要信息，哪些是主题思想，哪些是对主题的陈述，从而达到准确理解文章内涵的目的。

（四）先题目，后文章

如果遇到一篇文章一上来看了几行就难住了无法读下去，可以试着倒过来先去看题目，然后根据题目再去寻找文章中的有关信息，因为在一篇文章里并非每个句子都与题目有关，因此即使你对于一篇文章并未完全看懂，但也不至于会全军覆没。

（五）应考的几个小技巧

(1) 如果问的是文章中的一段的中心思想，则应重点读段首句和尾句，看是否有主题句。

(2) 如果文章中提到的事实多、涉及面广，可采取抓关键词的办法，记住文章中所谈及的各个方面，从而判断选取答案。

(3) 有时遇到看不懂的难句，读了几遍仍然不懂，可作记号，暂时放下，先做后面的题。等其他题都做完了，这道题的答案很可能会自然“浮现”。

（六）给自己的选择加“保险”

考生在阅读理解应试方面的难点之一在于对自己初选的答案没有把握，总是感觉几个备选项都言之有理，有时一念之差，可能就把答案改错了。

如何来判定自己的选择是否正确呢？考生可以利用以下技巧给自己的选择加上“五重保险”：

(1) 在遇到考察结论性观点，总结归纳思想的题目时，比较选项内容的全面概括性。一般来说，概括性全面、思路符合逻辑的选项是正确的。

(2) 将选项与原文线索句中重点词同义互释。两个表达意思相同的句子是可以通过语法和同义词转换实现统一的。能达到这个要求的就是正确选项。

(3) 在研究题目四个选项时，看选项中是否含绝对性的词语，有这类词的选项一般要排除。

(4) 遇到结论推断题时，一般来说，重复例证事实，就事论事的选项要排除。

(5) 最重要的一点是在做完每篇文章的题目时，对其进行贯通串联，如果逻辑上出现了错误或与原文中心意思相悖，就肯定是在某个环节上出了问题。

3.2 快速阅读的技巧

一、掌握正确的快速阅读方法

为了快速阅读全文，提高对文章理解的准确度，可根据阅读材料的特点，从以下几个方面入手。

(一) 弄清文章体裁，快速理解文章

快速阅读很重要的一点就是把握住文章的体裁及题材。关于文章的体裁和题材，在前面已经提到。不同体裁的文章，就要根据其体裁的特点，运用不同的方法快速阅读、正确理解。

记叙文往往一开始就交代人物(who)、时间(when)、地点(where)及事件(what)，然后再详细叙述事件发生的原因(why)。如1998年考试阅读理解中的Passage 2，时间(when)：Sunday, September 2nd, 1666；地点(where)：London；人物(who)：Pepys and his wife；事件(what)：London fire；原因(why)：The baker's house caught fire and the lane was narrow。如此弄清了这些问题，即5个W，文章也就弄明白了。

议论文中，作者先提出一个论点，再对此进行分析，或举例加以论证，得出结论。如2001年考试阅读理解中的Passage 2，作者提出Chinese acupuncture is worldwide这一论点，然后从历史发展的角度分析针灸的起源，再谈到今天中国医生依然致力于改进针灸方法。

说明文中，作者首先提出说明对象，然后从时间、空间、用途、方法、步骤等各个不同侧面加以说明。如2000年考试阅读理解的Passage 3中，作者先提出了Most people have had a dog or wanted one as their companion at some time in their lives这一现象，然后从如何收养小狗一直讲到如何培养宠物与主人的关系。

(二) 读首尾句，预测文中细节

在成人本科学士学位英语考试中，阅读理解的文章都是没有标题的。这就给总结文章中心思想带来了困难。然而，英语的写作特点告诉我们：一般情况下，英语文章多是按"总—分—总"这样一个思路写的。因此，研读首、尾句，对快速阅读理解文意具有重要的意义。我们不但由此可以总结出文章的内容，还可以揣测作者的态度、意图，从而进一步猜出作者所要写的细节。如：在2004年考试中的Passage 2，首句为：If the Europeans thought a drought—a long period of dry weather—was something that happened only in Africa, they know better now. 尾句为：It will take several years of unusually heavy winter rain, the experts say, just to bring existing water reserves up to their normal levels. 把它们联系起来一看就知道：在欧洲，干旱已经是现实，并且将持续很长一段时间。由此，我们可以预测作者在文章中肯定会叙述近年来欧洲干旱的具体细节，比如有哪些表现，都发生在哪些国家等等。事实上，文章后的题目设计就是按照这个思路展开的。

(三) 注意连接词，揣测作者意图

英语文章中，作者往往先叙述或介绍常人的观点，他人的态度、看法，然后再提出自己的想法或与之不同的观点，即作者本人的意图或事实真相及本文的主旨。两者之间常用 but、however、yet、in spite of、though、although、even though、even if 等连词，或 but in fact、on the contrary 等短语连接。在 2003 年考试的阅读理解中的 Passage 3，以及 2004 年考试阅读理解的 Passage 3，都是如此。

掌握了文章的阅读方法，就大大加快了阅读速度。同时理解的正确性也就大大提高了。

二、快速阅读的质量保证

英语阅读的质量包括两项硬指标：一是阅读的速度；二是理解的准确程度。读慢了，完成不了任务；而理解得不准确等于没读。只有快而准同时具备，才能提高阅读质量。因此平时就务必在这两方面下工夫，养成良好的阅读习惯。

在阅读过程中，生词、难句是在所难免的。如果一碰到生词、难句就追根刨底，孤立地去思考，甚至还想马上查字典把它译成汉语才能罢休，其结果不但影响了阅读速度，反而不能弄清其意。因此，应养成从文章的篇章结构入手，跨过少量生词、难句所造成的阅读障碍。领会文章的主题思想，理清文章的脉络层次，然后从整体上对词句进行推敲，攻克难关。最后又回到对全文进行归纳总结的良好阅读习惯，使阅读从感性认识进一步升华形成理性认识，从而加快阅读文章的速度，提高对文章理解的正确性。

三、快速阅读的注意事项

需要注意的是，在考试中进行快速阅读的目的是为了节省时间，做更多的题目或检查已经做过的题目，但是，强调了阅读速度，理解的准确程度往往会下降。很多考生在阅读的时候，往往是一目十行，大脑中却一片空白，根本不知文章所云。要解决阅读速度和准确理解这一对矛盾，考生在平时的阅读过程中需要多加训练。

一般来说，我们提倡的快速阅读必须是在对文章有较好理解的基础上进行的，也就是说，考生在平时的阅读训练中一开始不能图快，应该以求准确为主，什么时候读懂了什么时候结束。经过一段时间的训练，理解能力提高了，再逐步加快阅读速度。

当考生普遍了解了阅读方法与技巧后，感到有了长足的进步，但再往后就感到提高不是太大，这主要是因为头脑中的积累不够，因此在平时的学习过程中还应把握以下两个方面：

（一）掌握大纲要求的词汇，熟练掌握英语的语法及惯用法，在平时学习中注意对所学的语法知识加以归纳总结，做到熟练运用。

（二）进行有计划、有目的、大量的阅读实践。只有通过大量的阅读，才能建立语感，掌握正确的阅读方法，提高阅读技能。但应注意的是这种阅读不是盲目的，而是有计划、有目的的，平时应将精读和泛读的内容区分开，定期进行阅读效果总结。同时，还应扩大阅读面，看一些有关英、美等国社会文化背景的材料和科普读物，这对于提高理解能力是大有裨益的。

3.3 如何根据文章选材特点进行阅读

一、题材特点

成人本科学士学位英语考试大纲指出，阅读理解部分短文选材题材广泛，包括人物传记、社会、文化、文史知识、热门话题及科普常识等。

例如 1998 年考试阅读理解的 4 篇文章，Passage 1 是说明文，讲述了报纸的发展和人们阅读报纸习惯的形成；Passage 2 是记叙文，以 Pepys 夫妇的视角描述了发生在 1666 年著名的伦敦大火；Passage 3 篇是说明文，描述了人类人口增长的历史和对现实的压力；Passage 4 是一篇经济类的议论文，介绍了物价对人们消费行为的影响。

又如 2004 年 11 月考试的阅读理解，经过改革，2003 年 11 月以后的考试只有 3 篇阅读理解了。Passage 1 是历史类的说明文，讲述了美国农业机械的发展；Passage 2 是关于教育的议论文，讨论了学龄前儿童语言能力开发的两种观点，作者赞同父母要培养儿童主动回应的习惯，而不是仅仅被动地听父母阅读；Passage 3 依然谈的是美国，这是篇关于美国人体重超重的议论文，最后得出的结论是胖人不见得比瘦人吃得多。

二、常见题材应试指导

以上各类题材都以一定的文体形式出现，都有自己的特点。考生只有抓住各类文体的特点，才能较容易地做对各种阅读理解试题。根据不同的文体采用不同的阅读方法。下面主要介绍一下科普类文章的特点。

科普类文章在成人本科学士学位英语考试中越来越受到重视，几乎每年的考试都有关于对科普内容的考查。这类文章的特点是科技词汇较多，句子长并且结构复杂，理论性和逻辑性较强。通常文章所介绍的知识对于一些考生来说比较陌生。因此科普类文章是令考生比较头疼的一类题材。

下面结合一篇成人本科学士学位英语考试阅读理解文章，谈谈科普类文章的特点和解题思路。2004 年 4 月考试的 Passage 3：

How can we get rid of garbage（垃圾）? Do we have enough energy sources to meet our future energy needs?

These are two important questions that many people are asking today. Some people think that man might be able to solve both problems at the same time. They suggest using garbage as an energy source, and at the time it can save the land to hold garbage.

For a long time, people buried garbage or dumped（倾倒）it on empty land. Now, empty land is scarce. But more and more garbage is produced each year. However, garbage can be a good fuel to use. The things in garbage do not look like coal, petroleum, or natural gas; but they are chemically similar to these fossil(化石) fuels. As we use up our fossil-fuel supplies, we might be able to use garbage as an energy source.

(79) Burning garbage is not a new idea. Some cities in Europe and the United States have been burning garbage for years. The heat that is produced by burning garbage is used to boil water. The steam that is produced is used to make electricity or to heat nearby buildings. In Paris, France, some power plants burn almost 2 million metric tons of the cities garbage each year. The amount of energy produced is about the same as would be produced by burning almost a half million barrels of oil.

(80) Our fossil fuel supplies are limited. Burning garbage might be one kind of energy source that we can use to help meet our energy needs. This method could also reduce the amount of garbage piling up on the earth.

我们可以看出来科普类文章有这么几个特点：

（一）科普类文章中的词汇的意义比较专一、稳定、简明、不带感情色彩。纵观整篇文章，它没有文学英语中常采用的排比、比喻、夸张等修辞手段，一词多义的现象也不突出。

（二）句子结构较复杂，语法分析较困难。为了描述一个客观事物，严密地表达自己的思想，作者会经常使用集多种语法现象于一体的长句。例如 The things in garbage do not look like coal, petroleum, or natural gas; but they are chemically similar to these fossil（化石）fuels. 此句较长，是由两个并列句构成，关系为转折。其中有“煤炭”、“石油”、“天然气”、“相似”等词汇，考生理解起来有一定难度。

(三) 虚拟语气经常出现。因为科学家在对事物进行研究、探讨和论证时,为了更为客观,很多解释和陈述都用虚拟语气。

例如 Burning garbage might be one kind of energy source that we can use to help meet our energy needs. 燃烧的垃圾可能是我们能够利用的一种能源。

(四) 常使用被动语态。

例如 But more and more garbage is produced each year. 每年越来越多的垃圾被制造出来。

我们来分析一下这类文章的结构及解题思路。

科普类文章一般由标题(headlines)、导语(introductions)、背景(background)、主体(main body)和结尾(ends)五部分构成。

1. 标题是文章中心思想的精辟概括。成人本科学士学位英语考试中的文章一般不给标题,但让考生选择标题的题型却经常出现。如第 15 题:

The best title for the passage may be ________.

A. Garbage and the Earth　　B. Fossil Fuel and Garbage

C. Land and Garbage　　D. Garbage—Energy Source

这是一道主旨题。结合全文内容可推断 D 项为最佳答案。

2. 导语一般位于整篇的首段。如本篇中开头就用两个问句揭示了主题:How can we get rid of garbage (垃圾)? Do we have enough energy sources to meet our future energy needs? 因此抓住了导语即对叙述的内容有了大体把握,这对做阅读题至关重要。可以直接回答第 11 题:

What two problems can man solve by burning garbage?

A. The shortage of energy and air pollution.

B. The shortage of energy and the land to hold garbage.

C. Air pollution and the shortage of fossil fuel.

D. Air pollution and the shortage of land to hold garbage.

通读第一段的这两个问题,就可推断此题选 B。

3. 背景交代一个事实的起因。第一段的两个问题实际就是一个背景交代。

4. 主体则对导语概括的事实进行详细叙述。成人本科学士学位英语考试在主体部分设题最多。例如第 12 题:

Which of the following is NOT the result of burning garbage?

A. The garbage burned is turned into fossil fuels.

B. The heat produced is used to boil water.

C. The steam produced is used to make electricity

D. The steam produced is used to heat buildings.

例如第 13 题:

According to the passage, which of the following is NOT true?

A. About 2 million metric tons of garbage is burned in France each year.

B. In a modern society, more and more garbage is produced each year.

C. Using garbage is a good way to solve the problem of energy shortage.

D. It will be too expensive to use garbage as an energy source.

5. 结尾往往也是中心思想的概括并常常与导语相呼应,命题者也常在此处设题。

例如第 14 题:

What is the author's attitude?

A. Delighted.　　B. Sad.

C. Agreeing.　　D. Disagreeing.

文章最后一句 This method could also reduce the amount of garbage piling up on the earth. “这个方法也可以减少垃圾在地球上的堆放”。可以看出来，作者是欣赏这个方法的，因此选 C。

要做好科普类文章试题，首先要掌握这类文章的特点及结构，真正读懂并理解它。其次，多读些科普类文章，比如太空与海洋、保护环境、创造与发明、动物世界等。这样长期坚持，既开阔了视野，又能迅速地做好此类题目。

3.4 如何利用语境的褒贬性进行推断

阅读理解要求考生在掌握主旨大意的基础上弄清文章的事实和细节及上下文的逻辑关系。几乎每篇文章的语境都有一定的褒贬性，这种褒贬性反映了主人公的特定心理和情绪状态及作者的写作意图，因此利用好文章的语境褒贬性就能在把握主旨大意的基础上对文章进行准确的逻辑判断。如何利用语境的褒贬性对阅读理解题进行信息推断呢？

一、找出语境褒贬性的标志性词汇或句子

认真阅读原文，找出反映语境褒贬性的标志性词汇或句子，并进行逻辑判断。

2002 年考试阅读理解题 Passage 2，首句为：The market investigation is indispensable to sales promotion（市场调查对于产品推广来说是至关重要的）。这句话是文章的主题句，反映出文章的主旨大意，其中 indispensable 一词反应出了明显的赞同倾向。作者在首句谈了一个这么肯定的观点，下文必然会分析为什么重要，以及怎么去市场调查。因此第 9 题应选 D 选项。

Making market investigation is very important because ________.

A. in market, goods on sale are numerous

B. every producer is facing keen competition

C. it can greatly promote sales

D. all of the above

答案选 D。根据文章第二段的内容：“在国际市场上，来自世界各地的商品很多，商家面临着激烈的竞争。在这种情况下，他们要想尽一切办法来使自己熟悉市场，才能打开销路。”只有 D 最正面，最全面，看似绝对化，其实是正确答案。

二、语境的深层次理解

所谓深层次理解包括对英语背景知识的掌握。作为一门语言，只是知道 ABC 是不够的。尤其是阅读理解，经常谈到美国、英国这些国家的历史政治等知识，如果没有相关的背景知识，做阅读理解题目的时候就会比较吃力，甚至褒贬性都看不出来。

读完 2002 年 Passage 3 后，我们知道全文谈的是林肯总统，而且一开始就说他不受欢迎，因为第一段第四句说得很清楚：He was not at all popular. 很多考生第 11 题选对了。

In 1863, Abraham Lincoln was ________.

A. very critical　　B. unpopular

C. very popular　　D. very courteous

答案很明显选 B。

但最后一题，即第 15 题选错的很多。

Which of the following statements is NOT true according to the passage?

A. Lincoln's Gettysburg Address has deep meaning.

B. Lincoln's Gettysburg Address is simple in style.

C. Lincoln's Gettysburg Address is memorized by every American school child.

D. Lincoln's Gettysburg Address is the greatest speech ever delivered in the United States.

如果了解这段历史的话,知道林肯总统被美国人视为最伟大的总统之一,他在 Gettysburg 的演讲是千古名篇,那么就不会选 A 了,答案是 D。

第四节 阅读理解解题技巧及训练

4.1 主旨题:如何把握所读材料的主旨和大意

一、考点规律和应试技巧

主旨题的范围一般包括:短文标题、主题、大意或段落大意等。做这类题目,要迅速地剔除文中的细节事实、作者所使用的论据,找到各段的主题句,然后进行归纳、总结和概括。但要注意,概括出来的中心思想一定要能够覆盖全文或整个段落,不可离题太远、太笼统,或者只概括一段或几句话的意思。主旨题是用来测试考生是否理解整篇文章的主旨和大意,是否具有把握中心思想的能力,每次考试都会有这类题目出现。

找到主题句是解题的关键。主题句在文章中的位置要视文章的结构及体裁而定。下面介绍两个找主题句的方法。

(一) 根据位置找主题句

阅读理解的主题句往往在文章的第一句。因此,认真阅读文章第 1 段对理解整篇文章十分重要。还有,每一段的第一个句子对理解该段落十分重要。有时将每段的第一句综合起来就可以推断出该文章的主旨大意。

(二) 根据细节归纳出主题句

文章主题句出现的位置没有一定的规则,而且有些文章根本就没有明确的主题句。这时,上面所说的方法就行不通了。因此,考生还是要凭借对文章的理解来总结归纳出文章的主题。在无法确定主旨大意时,可以先做其他题目,因为对其他题目的解答有助于对文章进一步理解。如有些陈述、描写性段落无主题句,而读者可依据文章中细节的相互关系推断出主题句。

总之,考生要记住解主旨题的基本技巧:

1. 认真阅读文章的第一段或每段的第一个句子。

2. 作者往往有意识地反复论述文章的主题。

3. 文章或段落的主题句常常会出现在一些标志性的提示后。例如:

On the whole, in short, therefore...

I agree with the opinion that...

Given all these points above, I would support the idea that...

For all the reasons mentioned above, I would prefer...

做主旨题时考生易犯以下三种错误:

一是把主题的一部分看成是全文的中心思想。这样的选择太具体,不能准确地概括出整篇文章或段落的中心思想。

二是表达作者的中心思想时,词语概括范围太大,太笼统,超出了作者的本意。

三是选项本身是正确的,但只是片面地回答了问题。因此,在确定文章的中心思想时,选项的内容既不能太具体也不能太笼统。

二、主旨题的提问方式有以下几种

(1) The general idea of the passage is about ________.

(2) The main idea of the article is ________.

(3) The main purpose of this selection is ________.

(4) The passage suggests that ________.

(5) Which of the following best states the theme of the passage?

(6) In this passage the author discusses primarily ________.

(7) The passage is mostly about ________.

(8) The passage is mainly concerned about ________.

(9) Which of the following best states the main idea of the passage?

(10) What is the main point made in the passage?

(11) What is the main topic of the passage?

(12) What is the best title for the passage?

(13) Which of the following is the main topic of the passage?

(14) From the passage we may conclude that ________.

(15) This article mainly tells about the story of ________.

(16) The subject discussed in this text is ________.

4.2　态度题：如何领会作者的观点与态度

一、考点规律和应试技巧

理解作者意图，是属于深层次理解题。考生须具备能根据全文内容，尤其是根据文章的基调领悟作者意图、情感、弦外之音的能力。这离不开对文章中心思想的把握，以及透过现象看本质的能力。

作者在文章中不仅客观地进行叙述和说明，他还往往持有某种态度。如对某一观点或赞同或反对，或肯定或批评。作者的观点和态度除了直接表达外，还经常在文章中间接表达出来。有时通过全文的叙述，考生可从文章的主要内容去理解作者的观点，有时作者也会在文章中用特殊的词汇表达自己的思想感情。

下面以 1999 年考试 Passage 3 为例进行分析。

The young people who talk of the village as being "dead" are talking nothing but nonsense, as in their hearts they must surely know.

No, the village is not dead. There is more life in it now than there ever was. But it seems that "village life" is dead. Gone for ever. It began to decline (衰落) about a hundred years ago, when many girls left home to go into service in town many miles away, and men also left home in increasing number in search of a work, and home was where work was. There are still a number of people alive today who can remember. What "village life" meant the early years of the present century? It meant knowing and being known by everybody else in the village. It meant finding your entertainment in the village of within walking distance of it. It meant housewives tied to the home all day and every day. It meant going to bed early to save lamp-oil and coal.

Then came the First World War and the Second World War. After each war, new ideas, new attitudes, new trades and occupations were revealed to villagers. The long-established order of society was no longer taken for granted. Electricity and the motorcar were steadily operating to make "village life" and "town life" almost alike. Now with the highly developed science and technology and high-level social welfare for all, there is no point whatever in talking any longer about "village life". It is just life, and that a better life.

Finally, if we have any doubts about the future, or about the many changes, which we have seen in our lives, we have only to look in at the school playground any mid-morning; or see the children as they walk homeward in little groups. Obviously these children are better fed, better clothed, better educated, healthier, prettier and happier than any generation of children that ever before walked the village street.

15. From the passage we can see that the writer's attitude toward "village life" is ________.

A. positive B. negative C. neutral D. unclear

作者其实在一开始就表达了对乡村生活的态度:认为乡村生活"死"了的年轻人,连他们自己都不相信这一点。这说明作者是对乡村生活持正面态度的。然后,作者就分析了乡村生活的演变,尤其是两次世界大战造成的剧烈影响。之所以很多考生选错,就在于没有看懂最后一段。作者在最后一段描述了现在乡村生活的美好,以致于一些考生误以为作者认为过去不好,就选B。也有人选C,认为作者很中立。什么叫"中立"? 作者通篇没有一处说乡村生活不好,这明明就是肯定。因此答案选A。

总之,做理解作者态度(attitude)或语气(tone)这样的题,关键在于把握作者对全文主体事物(与主题有关)的态度。表达作者态度——褒义、中性和贬义的手段主要有:一是加入形容词定语;二是加入副词状语;三是特殊动词。英语中有些动词也表明说话者的正负态度,如:fail(未能)、ignore(忽视)、overestimate(过高估计)等动词表示一种负态度。确定作者态度,可以有两种思路:问全文主体事物的(包括主题),可以根据阐述主题或有关主体事物的相关句中的形容词、副词或动词确定作者的态度;如果问的是对某一具体事物的态度,则可以定位到具体相关句,然后确定答案。

二、态度题的提问方式有以下几种

(1) What is the author's attitude towards ________.

(2) In the passage the author's attitude towards "..." is ________.

(3) The author seems to think that ________.

(4) The writer is trying to present a point of view in ________.

(5) The author wants to appeal to ________.

(6) The author's style is ________.

(7) The author's tone would be best described as ________.

(8) What is the author's opinion of ________?

(9) The writer believes that ________?

(10) What is the author's main purpose in the passage?

(11) The main purpose of writing this text is ________?

(12) In the author's opinion, ________?

4.3　细节题：如何寻找文章中的事实和细节

一、考点规律和应试技巧

成人本科学士学位英语考试阅读理解试题一共有 15 道，有超过一半的试题考查的是对细节的理解。因此，考生必须掌握细节题的解法。一般的步骤是：首先阅读文章后面的问题，确定所需查找的细节及事实的范围，然后利用略读手法快速确定在文中的出处，并对其进行转换、加工，直至确定最佳答案。

有关细节的问题是以 what，who，which，when，where，how，why 等词引导的特殊疑问句，就文中某一个词语、某一句子、某一段落或某一细节或事实进行提问，要求考生回答。还有一种问法是填空式的。

细节题的命题特点是：所提问题一般可直接或间接从文章中找到答案，故解题原则是：忠实于原文，决不要主观臆断。其干扰项的特点是：偷梁换柱，即偷换概念，将正确的时间、地点、数量等做一些变化，从而对正确选项进行干扰。细节与中心内容的关系是辩证的，只有抓住中心才能正确理解有关细节。同时文章事实细节不是孤立的，所以只有注意上下文及全篇的逻辑关系，才能做出准确判断。此外，弄懂文章的组织结构对迅速捕捉所需信息也很重要。

（一）所谓细节题，是指原文提到了某事物、现象或理论，题干针对原文具体叙述本身发问。这类题的表现形式多种多样，不妨总结如下：

1. 是非题

出题形式：

(1) 三正一误(三项正确，只有一项不符合原文内容)

Which of the following is true except...

Which of the following is mentioned except...

(2) 三误一正(三项错误，只有一项符合原文内容)：

Which of the following is true?

解题方法：

(1) 定位法

根据题干或选项中的线索词回原文找相关句，与选项相比较确定答案。

(2) 固定思路

这种做题方法主要与三正一误的下列问法相联系：

Which of the following mentioned except...

Which of the following is not mentioned...

这种问题的正确选项所包含的信息通常连续出现在同一段，而且往往无列举标志词，如 first，second，third 等。做题时只需阅读有关段落，根据一个选项中的关键词在其前后找其他两个正确选项，剩下一个原文中未提到的，为正确答案。

2. 例证题

这类题的基本结构为 The author provides in line...(或 Paragraph...)an example in order to...，意思是问文中举出某现象或例子的目的。文章如果是说明文和议论文，文中举出一些例子无非是为了说明一定的道理。关键在于这个例子在原文出现的位置，但不管如何，这个例子之前或之后不远处通常都有一句总结说明性的话，这句话就是答案，即举例的目的。如果例子与全文主题有关，则例证主题，答案为主题句。如果例子与段落主题有关，就例证段落主题，则答案为段落主题句；此外，答案为例子前后总结说明性的话。

3. 其他形式的具体题

(1) 年代与数字

这个考点有几种出题方式,但不管以何种形式出现,只要题干问年代与数字,答案就对应于文章中的年代与数字。

(2) 比较

比较考点的表现形式主要有:

a. 比较级与含有比较意义的词汇手段和句型结构。

b. 表示绝对意义的字眼:first (第一),least(最不),uttermost (最)等。

c. 表示唯一性的词汇:only,unique 等。

阅读时最好能圈出表示最高级、唯一性和绝对意义的词汇,便于做题时对照原文定位。

(3) 原因

这种题的答案在原文通常有一些表示因果关系的词汇提示。

a. 表示因果关系的名词:result,reason。

b. 表示因果关系的动词:result in(结果),result from(由于,由),base... on...(以……为基础),be due to(由于)。

c. 表示因果关系的连词或介词:because,for,why。

d. 表示因果关系的副词:as a result,consequently 等。

阅读时对这些提示词应该予以注意。除了上述原文有因果关系提示词的显性原因考点之外,隐性原因(两个句子之间为因果关系,但无有关提示词)也是常见考点。不管是显性原因考点,还是隐性原因考点,原文相关句出现的格式都是先说原因,后说结果,而在题干中通常给出结果,就其原因提问。

(二) 一般来说,大部分细节题都能直接或间接从文章中找到答案。考生需注意的是根据问题和文章中的关键词迅速找到包含所需信息的句子或短语。回答这类题时最好采用对应法。需要注意的是,尽管大部分细节题都能直接或间接地在文章中找到答案,但正确选项很少用和原问一模一样的词汇,而多用不同的词语表达出来。

1. 直接事实题

在解答这类问题时考生要抓住题干文字信息,采用针对性方法进行阅读,因为这类题的答案在文章中可以直接找到。

例如 2000 年阅读理解 Passage 4 第 16 题:

The Americans go to the movies mainly because they want ________.

A. to enjoy a good story　　B. to experience an exciting life

C. to see the actors and actresses　　D. to escape their daily life

答案:D。文章第一段的第二句话说:They go to the movies to escape their normal everyday existence and to experience a life more exciting than their own. 后面又谈到 But the main reason why people go to the movies is to escape. 所以美国人去看电影的重要原因是逃避现实生活。A,B,C 只是原因之一,而不是主要原因。

2. 间接事实题

解此类题需要结合上下文提供的语境和信息进行简单概括和判断。

例如 2000 年阅读理解 Passage 4 第 18 题:

It is obvious that real life is ________.

A. less romantic than that in the movies　　B. more romantic than that in the movies

C. as romantic as that in the movies　　D. filled with romantic stories

答案：A。第一段的最后一句话：They are in a dream world where things often appear to be more romantic and beautiful than in real life. 电影是个梦幻世界，反过来说明现实生活没有电影浪漫。

细节题是测试考生对文章提供的信息的理解能力，因文章的细节是服务于中心思想的，而且相互之间是呼应的。因此，考生还需要弄清主旨和细节之间的关系，这有助于迅速在文章中寻找具体的信息。

二、细节题的提问方式有以下几种

(1) From the passage we know that ________.

(2) In the passage, the author states that ________.

(3) The writer mentions all of the items listed below except ________.

(4) Which of the following statements is correct according to the passage?

(5) Which of the following statement is NOT true?

(6) Which of the following is NOT mentioned in the third paragraph?

(7) When did the author begin to ________?

(8) From the text, we learn that ________.

4.4　词汇题：如何根据上下文判断词语的含义

一、考点规律和应试技巧

近年来，阅读理解中的词义猜测题已经成了成人本科学士学位英语考试题中的必考题。另外，在阅读中，我们会经常遇到一些生词，需要根据上下文猜测它们的词义。此类问题考查考生紧扣原文，根据上下文语境判断单词、短语或短句意义的能力。常见的题型有直接对生词进行解释；对多义词或短语在文章具体语言环境中的意义做出准确判断；对文中一些代词的指代对象做出界定。

在阅读中不可避免地会碰到生词，因此考生是否具有猜词能力十分关键。由于词义猜测题并不完全是检测词汇量，因此命题老师会尽量选择能够通过上下文推测出词义的词语来设题，不含任何技巧的词义猜测题比较少见。猜词技巧是阅读理解中不可缺少的一种技巧。一个人的猜词能力取决于他熟悉语言的程度、所具有的知识和经验、所具有的逻辑推理和判断能力。

在做此类题时，考生应紧扣原文，根据上下文语境进行判断，切记不要望文生义或断章取义，也不能只选择自己熟悉的意思。应利用上下文已知的逻辑关系——转折、因果、对比、定义等进行判断；有时可以根据修饰语大体判断要猜测的词指什么，然后再根据上下文做出判断；有时还要分析句子的语法结构，注意词与词之间的关系；有时也可以依靠已有的经验或常识进行判断；同时，要注意某些标点符号的作用，如破折号可以表示解释上文内容，分号可以表示并列或相反的内容等。

下面介绍几种解题方法：

（一）根据常识、经验猜生词

例如：My parents went out and bought a new TV. That afternoon my father put an antenna on the roof (屋顶) so that we could watch the pictures on TV clearly.

根据经验，我们可以判断出“antenna”是电视机的“天线”。

The old man put on his spectacles and began to read.

根据常识,我们可以猜出“spectacles”的意思是“眼镜”。

The door was so low that I hit my head on the lintel.

结合常识,我们可以猜出“lintel ”的意思是“门上方的门框”。

(二) 根据上下文解释做出判断

有时文章中出现一个需要猜测其意义的词或短语,下面接着出现其定义或解释,这就是判断该词或短语意义的主要依据。例如 2001 年考试 Passage 4 的第 19 题:

From the passage we can see “phased employment” means ________.

A. two or more women share the same job

B. women stay at home on weekdays and go to work on weekends or holidays

C. a woman should resign her job forever if she has a child

D. women are allowed to take leave from their jobs during their childbearing years

这个术语出现在文章的第四段的首句,接下来第二句就解释了:The theory suggests that a woman worker take leave from her job when she is seven months pregnant(妊娠) and stay off the job until her baby reaches the age of 3. 这告诉我们,妇女可以在怀孕七个月的时候请假,一直到孩子三岁的时候再来上班。因此妇女生育期间可以请假是正确的,答案选 D。

上下文包括以下几方面:

1. 根据文中的定义、解释猜生词

例如:Skimming means looking over a passage quickly to get the main idea before you begin to read it carefully.

从所给的定义,我们可以猜出“skimming”的意思是“快速阅读”或“略读”。

The harbor (港口) is protected by a jetty—a wall built out into the water.

根据定义,港口是由延伸到海水里的大墙保护的,所以,“jetty”的大概意思是“防波堤”。

2. 利用事例或解释猜生词

例如:The doctor is studying glaucoma and other diseases of the eye.

从 other diseases of the eye 可以判断出“glaucoma”指的是“一种眼睛的疾病”。

3. 利用重复解释的信息猜生词

例如:Mr. Smith always arrives home punctually, neither early nor late.

根据 neither early nor late 这一解释,可以推断出“punctually”的意思是“准时地,守时地”。

4. 根据同位关系进行判断

阅读中出现一些难词,有时后面就是一个同位语,对前面的词进行解释,这种解释有时也用连词“or”连接。

例如:The “Chunnel”, a tunnel(隧道) connecting England and France, is now complete.

此句中“a tunnel”是“chunnel”的同位语。因此,The “Chunnel”就是英法之间的海底隧道。

(三) 利用标点符号和提示词猜测词义

例如:One of the obstacles to false reading is vocalizing—saying the words to themselves in a low voice.

从破折号后的解释可猜出“vocalizing”指“低声对他们自己说”。

(四) 根据上下文的指代关系进行选择

文章中的代词 it,that,he,him 或 them 可以指上文提到的人或物,其中 it 和 that 还可以指一件事。有时代词指代的对象相隔较远,要认真查找;也有时需要对前面提到的内容进行总结,才能得出代词所指代的事。

例如 2004 年 11 月考试 Passage 1 第 1 题：

1. The word "here"(Para. 1, Line 4) refers to ________.

A. Europe　　B. America

C. New Jersey　　D. Indiana

原文："In Europe", said Thomas Jefferson, "the object is to make the most of their land, labor being sufficient; here it is to make the most of our labor, land being abundant."由此可以看出 here 与前面提到的 Europe 是相对的，那么肯定指的就是美国，就可以判断出答案为 B。

（五）根据构词法进行判断

在英语中，有很多词可以在前面加前缀(prefix)，在后面加后缀(suffix)，从而构成一个词，乍看起来，这个词可能是生词，但掌握了一定的构词法知识，就不难猜出它的词义。

例如：Market research shows that Gold and others who buy organic food can generally give clear reasons for their preferences but their knowledge of organic food is far from complete.

我们知道，prefer 的意思是"宁愿，愿意"，根据上下文可以判断 prefer 的名词形式 preference 的含义应是"偏爱，爱好"。

构词法主要包括：

1. 合成法

把两个或两个以上的词组合成一个词的构词方法叫合成法。由合成法而得来的词叫合成词。合成词在英语中非常活跃，而且数量很大。如果遇到的生词是合成词，可以把它还原成一个一个的独立词，看每部分是什么意思，再把各个意思综合起来，便可得到这个合成词的大概意思了。例如：

bed(床)＋room(房间)＝bedroom(卧室)

school(学校)＋mate(伙伴)＝schoolmate(校友)

2. 派生法

通过给一个词根加上前缀、后缀而构成一个新词的构词方法叫派生法。通常情况下，前缀只改变词义，而后缀既改变词义又改变词性。牢记一些常见的前缀、后缀的用法，可以猜出许多单词的词义。例如：

care(小心)＋ful(有……的)＝careful(小心的)

use(用处)＋ful(有……的)＝useful(有用的)

hope(希望)＋ful(有……的)＝hopeful(有希望的)

im(不)＋possible(可能的)＝impossible(不可能的)

im(不)＋polite(礼貌的)＝impolite(不礼貌的)

dis(不)＋like(喜欢)＝dislike(不喜欢)

3. 转化法

由一种词性转化成另一种词性的构词方法：例如：

hand(手)n. —hand(传递)v.

water(水)n. —water(给……浇水)v.

late(迟的)adj. —late(迟地)adv.

after(在……之后)prep. —after(在……之后)conj.

根据近年来成人本科学士学位英语考试阅读理解对考生提出的新要求，我们建议考生在以下几个方面加强自我训练：

1. 猜测熟词新含义

猜测熟词含义除了要求考生有较强的语境分析能力外，还要求考生有较宽的知识面，对常见有新含义的熟词要弄清其用法，并将这些词进行简要归纳整理。

2. 了解反映现代生活和科技知识的专业词语

近年来阅读理解题中出现了大量反映现代生活和科技知识的专业词语。比如 environmental safety(环境安全)、green products(绿色产品)、interactions(交往)等等，考生要尽可能地多了解这些词语。

当然，猜测词义的方法有很多，在此不一一赘述，希望考生在平时阅读中，具体情况具体分析，用不同的方法去处理阅读中的生词和短语，不断提高阅读的速度和效率。需要注意的是，在阅读中碰到生词时，如果该词无关大局，既不影响答题，又不影响正确理解文章的意思，就可以不去管它。如果该生词很关键，影响了对文章整体语义的理解，就应该设法运用正确的猜词方法，尽可能地把握该生词的意思。

二、词汇题的提问方式有以下几种

(1) The underlined word (phrase) in the passage means ________.

(2) The word "it (them)" in the first paragraph refers to ________.

(3) The underlined sentence in the last paragraph means ________.

(4) Which of the following is closest in meaning to the underlined word in the second paragraph?

(5) What does (do) the underlined word (words) refer to?

4.5　推理题：如何根据文章进行推理与判断

一、考点规律和应试技巧

推理题属于主观性极强的高难度阅读理解题。做这类题目时，要严格依据作者所陈述的细节、事实以及作者的措词，找出能够表露作者思想倾向和感情色彩的词语，然后利用自己已获得的相关知识进行推理判断，从而得出符合逻辑的结论。

阅读理解中对一篇文章的正确理解首先取决于看懂文章的具体内容，但由于篇幅或其他原因，作者常常对某些问题一带而过，有的只给出一些暗示，有些叙述得非常含蓄。这就要求考生不仅能够读懂原文，同时还要做到从文章的字里行间去体会作者虽未说明但欲表达的意思，即理解作者的言外之意。如："When the bell finally rang, Joe jumped from the edge of his chair and grabbed it." 乍一看，这句话意义清楚、明白。但仔细品味就知道：从 finally 折射出"等了好久"，from the edge of 说明"焦躁不安"，由此可知"这是一个非常重要的电话"。

推理题要求在理解原文表面文字信息的基础上，作出一定判断和推论，从而得到文章的隐含意义。推理题所涉及的内容可能是文中某一句话，也可是某几句话，但做题的指导思想都是以文字信息为依据，既不能做出在原文中找不到文字根据的推理，也不能根据表面文字信息做多步推理。所以，推理题的答案只能是根据原文表面文字信息一步推出的答案：即对原文某一句话或某几句话所作的同义改写(paraphrase)。

成人本科学士学位英语考试的推理题难度很小，并不涉及复杂的判断和推理。其主要做法是：根据题干中的关键词或选项中的线索找到原文的相关句，读懂后，比照选项，对相关句进行同义改写的选项为正确答案。做题时要注意题干的语言形式，如 According to the passage, It can be inferred from the passage that ________; It can be concluded from the passage that ________等，虽然从表面上看是问有关全文的题，但很多时候，只需要根据选项中的线索找到原文中与之相关的一句话或几句话，就可以得出答案。

针对推理题的不同形式，可以采取以下做法：

1. 假如题干中有具体线索，则根据具体线索找到原文相关句(一句话或几句话)，然后做出推理；

2. 假如题干中无线索，如 It can be inferred from the passage that ________; It can be concluded from the passage that ________等，先扫一下 4 个选项，排除不可能的选项，然后根据最可能的选项中的关键词找到原文相关句，做出推理；

3. 如果一篇文章中其他题都未涉及文章主旨，那么推理题，如 infer, conclude 题型，可能与文章主旨有关，考生应该定位到文章主题所在位置(如主题句出现处)；假如其他题已经涉及文章主旨，那么要求推断出来的内容可能与段落主题有关，如果如此，应该找段落主题所在处；如果不与段落主题有关，有时与全文或段落的重要结论有关，这时可以寻找与这些结论相关的原文叙述。

阅读理解测试中有关推理的问题要求考生在理解原文直接陈述的观点或描写的事实的基础上领会作者的言外之意，进行合乎逻辑的推理，得出合理的结论。大家虽然不能直接在文章中找到答案，但往往可以用可供推论的依据，准确判断作者的观点并得出合乎逻辑的结论。但应该注意的是：一定要严格按照作者提供的信息推论，不能凭借自己的主观想法，推理的依据应该能在文章中找到。

解推断题最最忌讳的是主观臆断、以偏概全。不能只注意表象，而要究其本质，要从文章本身的内容出发，认真分析词、句及段落间的逻辑关系。

推断题一般包括两大类：

(1) 暗指题：即作者的言外之意，一般只能从字里行间获得信息；

(2) 推理题：必须从文章本身出发，以事实为依据。

例如 2004 年 4 月考试 Passage 1 的第 4 题：

Which of the following is most unlikely for the author to do?

A. To talk to the students who have mental problems.

B. To help students develop a feeling of self-respect.

C. To keep a student from playing alone.

D. To announce a student's scores in public.

通过阅读全文，我们知道本文的主旨谈的是学生早期教育的问题。中心思想是要帮助学生建立自信，不能轻易打击和揭短，让孩子丧失前进的信心。因此，文章中虽然没有提及，但是我们依然可以轻松地选出正确答案 D。

二、推理题常见的设题方式有

(1) It can be inferred from the text that ________.

(2) From the text we know that ________.

(3) The story implies that ________.

(4) The paragraph following the passage will most probably be ________.

(5) The writer's attitude toward... is ________.

(6) The author implies (suggested) that...

(7) We can infer from the passage that...

(8) It may be concluded from the passage that...

(9) Which of the following statements does the passage support?

(10) According to the passage, which of the following is true (false)?

(11) With which of the following does the author agree?

(12) What does the passage say about...?

第五节 怎样避免阅读理解中的常见错误

一、两类常见错误

(一) 误解字面意思导致的错误

1. 词汇短语缺乏,理解句子能力差

2. 疏忽原文,偷换概念

例如:Living things must have air, water, and food. Some living things must have light. All these things are able to be got on the earth...

问:It is impossible for living things to exist on the earth ________.

A. unless there is no water

B. if there were no light at all

C. even if there were water and air

D. if there were nothing

可能会有考生选D。问题就在于忽视了原文,偷换了概念,试想如果把这里的 nothing 换成除 air, water, food 以外的东西,成立吗?显然是不可能成立的。

3. 理解不全,断章取义,以偏概全

(二) 误解深层意思导致的错误

1. 误选文章标题和中心思想

2. 缺乏合理想象,误解作者的写作意图

3. 盲目追求速度,理解不深导致特定细节理解错误

4. 脱离具体的语言环境,错误地推测意思

二、避免错误的对策

(一) 培养阅读兴趣,消除心理劣势

兴趣是我们学好英语的根本。建议考生通过阅读了解世界各国的风俗习惯、天文地理、政治经济等能激发学习兴趣的材料;另一方面,也要培养心理优势,心理学研究表明导致学生之间产生差距的主要原因并非智力本身,而是学习欲望、毅力、自信心等心理因素,消除畏难情绪,变"心理劣势"为"心理优势",主动地积极地进行阅读。

(二) 学习阅读方法,养成良好习惯

学习阅读方法是培养阅读能力的关键,首先要纠正不正确的阅读方法,如有声读、用笔或手指指着读,或一碰到生词就停下来查阅等读法。其次,要掌握正确的阅读方法,平时训练时要不出声、不回视,克服先把文字变成声音,再去想它的意思的不良习惯,良好的阅读方法一旦形成,对以后的工作、学习大有裨益。

(三) 训练阅读速度和阅读技能,提高阅读能力

阅读能力主要体现在阅读速度和阅读技能这两个方面:

1. 掌握正确的阅读方法,根据文章和问题选用相关的技巧进行阅读,阅读一结束马上进行阅读测试,如答题的正确率达到70%,就提速,如果达不到的话,就以原来的速度反复训练,这样持之以恒,阅读速度就会慢慢变快了。

2. 要经常进行限时定量的阅读练习，训练思维与速度，一般每40分钟做3篇有一定难度的阅读理解，做完即核对答案，然后认真统计分析出错的原因，阅读速度和阅读技能的提高，在通过一段时间训练后一定能实现。

第六节 如何理解阅读中的长句与难句

分析近几年成人本科学士学位英语考试英语阅读理解题，不难发现，篇幅长，信息量大，知识覆盖面广，并且掺杂了大量的长句、难句。有许多句子直接涉及考题，考生尽管认识单词，但由于长、难句的语法结构复杂，考生不易抓准主句，从而导致似懂非懂，容易丢分。

造成句子理解困难的主要原因有以下几点：

1. 句子的倒装

在这种句子中，通常为了突出句子的某一重要信息，该成分提到主语之前。由于这种句子与正常语序不同，往往加深了理解的难度。

例如：No less important than students' academic work are their extra-curricular activities. 下列哪个选项与其意义相同？

A. Academic work is less important than extra-curricular activities.

B. Extra-curricular activities are much more important than academic work.

C. Extra-curricular activities are equally important compared with academic work.

D. Academic work, no less than extra-curricular activities, is important.

本句的正常语序是：The students' extra-curricular actives are no less important than their academic activities. 由于句子不仅采用了倒装形式，而且还具有比较意义和双重否定，因而变得复杂。选择项中B与原句意思相反，A和D项为错误信息。正确选项为C。

2. 虚拟语气

虚拟语气是一个语法难点。因为其表示的内容与真实条件相反，加上其形式变化多种多样，读者容易产生误解。

例如：Had the announcement been made earlier, more people would have attended the lecture. 下列哪个选项与其意义相同？

A. Not many people came to hear the lecture because it was held so late.

B. The lecture was held earlier so that more people would attend.

C. Fewer people attended the lecture because of the early announcement.

D. Since the announcement was made late, fewer people came to hear the lecture.

本句为过去时的虚拟语气。由于从句省略了if，所以句子以倒装形式出现。其正常的语序应该是：The announcement had been made earlier, more people would have attended the lecture. 这句话所表示的与过去条件相反："要是早一点通知，听讲座的人数就会多些。"换句话说，由于通知的太晚，听讲座的人数不多。因而正确答案应该是D。

3. 比较级与最高级

比较级和最高级是增加句子难度的因素之一。由于句子中出现了其中一种形式或者两者兼而有之，句子的形式与结构不但显得复杂，理解难度也随之增大。

例如：There is hardly a concept more frequently mentioned by public spoken or in print than the concept of "freedom". 下列哪个选项与其意义相同？

A. Whether in speech or in publications, the most frequently mentioned concept is that of "freedom".

B. The concept of "freedom" is the only concept frequently mentioned either in speeches or in print.

C. The concept of "freedom" is the concept mentioned neither in speeches nor in print.

D. Along with other concepts, the concept of "freedom" is frequently mentioned by public speakers and writers.

本句中出现了 more... than 这一比较结构,并且还用了 hardly 这一表示否定意义的副词,这样,句子不仅结构复杂,语义也非常隐晦。B,C 和 D 三个选择项是三种不同释义,与原义相悖,A 项利用最高级对原句进行了正确的释义,故为正确答案。

4. 双重否定

有的句子含有形式上和语义上的双重否定,设置圈套干扰考生的思维,使考生上当。阅读此类句子时,我们不妨将其转换为肯定句。

例如:It is not unusual to see children doing the work of adults in great many rural areas. 下列哪个选项与其意义相同?

A. One rarely sees children working like adults in great rural areas.

B. Children often work adults occupations in many rural areas.

C. It is common for children to watch adults at work in numerous areas.

D. Adults hardly ever do work for their children in large areas.

本句中的 not unusual 为双重否定。我们完全可以理解为 very usual,即肯定形式。这样,句子的意义就非常明白了。我们就不难发觉本题的正确答案应为 B。

5. 语义隐晦

有些句子结构繁杂,通常从句套从句,句意含蓄,容易置人于云里雾里,难以作出正确判断。

例如:Rivers and water courses afford a very convenient and accessible source of supply; and one of the principal reasons for towns in older times having established by the banks, rivers is supposed to have been the facility with which, in such situation, an ample supply of water was secured. 下列哪个选项与其意义相同?

A. Rivers and water sources are secured.

B. Rivers and water courses are useful.

C. Rivers and water courses are convenient sources of water supply for towns.

D. The main support of ancient towns is needed.

这个句子结构复杂。整个句子由两个并列分句组成,前一分句意思较明晰,即"河流和水道提供了非常方便的水源"。第二个分句不仅结构复杂,而且语义也极为隐晦,其意思是:"过去的城镇建立在河流的岸边,河流能够供应充足的水源是主要的原因之一。"遇上这类难句,考生首先要弄清楚句子结构,即何为主干,何为枝叶:然后再一层一层地理解,最后得出整句的意义:从本题后面的四个选项来看,A 和 B 都太窄,D 为错误信息,唯有 C 比较全面体现了全句的含义。故 C 是正确答案。

6. 习惯用语

有时一个句子难以理解,是由于句子中的某一个习惯用语或固定词组引起的。如果读者不熟悉这一固定词组或习惯用语,整个句子的理解也就无从下手。因此,平时尽可能地多掌握一些固定词组和习惯用语是必要的。

例如:Harry was a capable lawyer, but it was difficult for him to live up to the reputation established by his more brilliant father. 下列哪个选项与其意义相同?

A. Harry was a capable lawyer, but it was a hard life for him to be with his father, who was brilliant and of great repute.

B. A capable lawyer as Harry was, he found it difficult to equal the reputation set by his more brilliant father.

C. Although Harry was a capable lawyer, his father, who was more brilliant, made it difficult for him to live by the reputation already established.

D. Despite the fact that he had a brilliant father with good reputation, Harry found it difficult to live his capability.

能否透彻理解这个句子,取决于是否了解"live up to"这个习惯用语。了解这个习惯用语的意思,整个句子的意思也就一目了然了。"live up to"是"做到、符合"的意思。整句话的意思为"尽管哈利是一个很有才干的律师,但是要达到比他更加才华横溢的父亲所获得的那种荣誉是很不容易的。"由此可见,B 是最佳选项。

第三章　语法与词汇题解题技巧

语法与词汇部分是成人本科学士学位英语考试的第二部分（Vocabulary and Structure），30小题，每题 1 分，共计 30 分。同时，对于第三部分挑错（Identification），第五部分翻译（Translation）——特别是其中的汉译英部分，语法与词汇都是基础。

根据对历次考试的真题进行分析，我们发现，成人本科学士学位英语考试关注的是考生运用英语最基本的能力，特别是语法与词汇部分，极少有偏、难、怪的题目出现。因此，我们只要熟悉了成人本科学士学位英语考试的命题规律，加强基础训练并辅之以相应的考试技巧，尤其是注重对历年真题的学习，通过考试甚至拿到高分并非难事。

在本章中，我们将逐一探讨成人本科学士学位英语考试中的重点难点语法现象——虚拟语气、从句、非谓语动词、反意疑问句、倒装以及主谓一致等，并提示词汇题的命题思路以及复习对策。

第一节　虚 拟 语 气

虚拟语气是成人本科学士学位英语考试的重点之一，许多考生谈之而色变。其实大可不必，因为虚拟语气规则性很强，结构是很清晰的。

在英语中，语气（mood）用于表明说话人的目的和意图。英语中有四种语气——陈述语气（I have a pen.）、疑问语气（Do you have a pen?）、祈使语气（Let me have the pen.）和虚拟语气（I wish I had the pen.）——而虚拟语气用来表示纯然假想的情况或主观愿望。为了把这种与事实不符的状态表现出来，英文中借助了一些形式符号，这是虚拟语气的重点。

1.1　虚拟语气在条件句中的用法

一、真实条件句和非真实条件句

含有条件状语从句的复合句叫条件句。它可分为真实条件句和非真实条件句。前者所描述的情况已经是事实或可能实现，比方说 If I have time, I will come over to see you. 而后者（也称为虚拟条件句）所假设的情况在过去或现在都不存在，将来也不大可能发生，即纯然假想，例如 If I were you, I would not stay here any longer.

在非真实条件句中，这个非真实的条件（从句）以及在这个非真实的条件之下所发生的结果（主句）通常都使用虚拟语气。

二、非真实条件句虚拟语气的基本形式：时态倒退

时间	从句谓语动词	主句谓语动词
现在时	did/were	would do #
将来时	should/did(were)/were to do *	would do #
过去时	had done	would have done #

* 假设情况的可能性从大到小。

\# 主句中的谓语动词有时也可以用 should, might, could 来构成。

我们套用以上表格，看看虚拟语气在不同时间框架下的具体应用。

1. 对现在的虚拟

If I *lived* near my office, I *would/should/could/might walk* to work.

如果我住得离办公室很近的话，我就走着去上班了。

2. 对将来的虚拟

If he *should come/came/were to* come, I *would/should/could/might ask* him about it.

如果他要是来的话，我就问问他这个事儿。

3. 对过去的虚拟

If I *had left* sooner, I *would/should/might/could have caught* the bus.

如果我(当时)早点离开的话，我就有可能赶上那班车了(实际情况是动身晚了，所以没赶上)。

上述表格是一切虚拟语气形式变化的基础。虽然考试中会偶尔涉及一些特殊形态，但万变不离其宗。只要熟练掌握了这个表格，就能够做到化难为易。

1.2 虚拟语气的特殊形态及难点

一、错综时间非真实条件句

一般情况下，非真实条件句的主句和从句所指的时间是一致的，但有时也有可能不一致，这种主句谓语和从句谓语在时间上不一致的句子被称为错综时间非真实条件句。我们只要根据含义弄清楚各自动作所发生的时间，再套用上面的表格来选择虚拟形式就可以了。例如：

If you *had taken* her advice, you *wouldn't be* in such a big trouble now.

如果你当时采纳了他的建议，现在就不会面对这么一个大麻烦了。

二、含蓄虚拟句

含蓄虚拟句指的是句中没有条件从句，但却通过上下文或某种其他方式来暗示虚拟的句子。例如：

To have told my secret would have given me away.

如果你当时把我的秘密泄露出去，你可就把我给卖了。

这句话相当于 If you had told my secret, you would have given me away.

在成人本科学士学位英语考试中，一旦遇到含蓄虚拟句，一定要用一些关键符号来标示：

or — He was ill, or he would have come.

without — Without electricity, there would be no modern industry.

如果没有电的话，就不会有现代工业。

but for — But for his help, I could not have finished it so early.

要不是因为他的帮助，我就不可能这么早就完工了。

三、条件句中省略 if 所引发的倒装

如果条件句中包含助动词 were，should 或 had，可以把 if 省略，然后把这几个词放到主语之前，形成部分倒装。例如：

Were I him, I would not do it.

(= If I were him, ...)

Were I to meet Jack tomorrow, I should ask him about the issue.

(= If I were to meet Jack tomorrow, ...)

Should you change your mind, no one would blame you.

(= If you should change your mind, ...)

Had he been more careful, he could have avoided such a terrible accident.

(= If he had been more careful, ...)

(四) 跳层虚拟

所谓跳层虚拟,指的是句子的一半是真实情况,不用虚拟;而另一半是非真实情况,需要虚拟。需要虚拟的部分,参考表格的变化原则。例如:

We didn't know his telephone number; otherwise we would have called him.

我们不知道他的电话号码(这是事实,不需要虚拟);否则我们就给他打电话了(事实上并没有打,因此要虚拟)。

1.3 虚拟语气在从句中的用法

一、虚拟语气在宾语从句中的用法

1. wish 后的宾语从句

(1) 表示与现在的事实相反:宾语从句的动词用过去式 did/were

I wish I knew his address.

I wish it were still summer.

(2) 表示与过去的事实相反:had done

I wish I hadn't spent so much money.

2. would rather 后的宾语从句:表示"希望、宁愿"

用 did 表示现在或将来;用 had done 表示过去

—Do you mind if I smoke here?

—I would rather you didn't.

I'd rather you hadn't told me about it.

3. 在某些表示命令、要求、建议的动词后面,宾语从句通常用 should do 来表示虚拟。

注意,should 可以省略,在成人本科学士学位英语考试中,这是常态。

这些动词常见的有:ask, demand, desire, propose, advise, order, require, request, suggest, insist 等等。例如 2004 年 4 月考试第 42 题:

The doctor advised her that she (should) get enough rest before going back to work.

注意:当 insist 当作"坚持认为",suggest 当作"表明、暗示"时,后边的宾语从句不用虚拟。例如:

He insisted that he was innocent.

The bloody shirt suggests that he might be involved in the murder.

4. 在含有以 it 为形式宾语的宾语从句中,表示命令、要求、建议,从句用 should do 来表示虚拟,should 可以省略。例如:

We consider it necessary that a meeting (should) be held immediately.

二、虚拟语气在同位语从句中的用法

在表示命令、建议、请求、计划等名词后面的同位语从句中,用 should do 来表示虚拟,should 可以省略。

这类名词常见的有 suggestion, proposal, demand, desire, order, requirement 等。例如 2001 年 6 月考试第 47 题:

Her suggestion that everybody (should) sing a song was not appreciated.

三、虚拟语气在某些以 it 为形式主语的主语从句中的用法

用 should do 来虚拟，should 可以省略。

1. 主句为“主—系—表”结构，表语为某些表示“重要、应当、合适、关键”的形容词，如：advisable，appropriate，better，best，crucial，desirable，essential，imperative，important，necessary 等，例如：

It is important that every member (should) be informed of these rules.

2. 主句的谓语是某些表示命令、要求、建议的动词的被动语态。例如：

It is proposed that the matter (should) be discussed at the next meeting.

3. 主句为“主—系—表”结构，表语为某些短语。这些短语与上述 1、2 中的词同根同源。例如：

It is of great importance that you (should) be here on time.

It is our demand that he (should) be sent here soon.

四、虚拟语气在表语从句中的用法

主句的主语是表示命令、建议、请求、计划等的名词，用 should do 来表示虚拟，should 可以省略。例如 2002 年 6 月考试第 48 题：

The general's command was that the soldiers (should) leave their fort and carry out more important tasks.

五、虚拟语气在状语从句中的用法

1. 让步状语从句

even if/even though 引导的让步状语从句发生虚拟，其形式为非真实条件句虚拟的基本形式(参考表格)。例如：

Even if my mother were here, I should say the same thing.（对现在的虚拟）

Even though it had been a rainy day, I should have gone to see him.（对过去的虚拟）

2. 方式状语从句

as if/as though 引导的方式状语从句也会发生虚拟，其形式为：从句用 did 表示从句与主句的动作同时发生，用 had done 表示从句的动作在主句的动作之前发生。例如：

He treats me as if I were a stranger.（从句和主句的动作同时发生）

Charles laughed, as though that were a joke.（从句和主句的动作同时发生）

He talks/talked about Rome as if he had been there himself.（从句的动作在主句的动作之前发生）

注意：如果表示可能的事实，那么方式状语从句中的谓语动词就不需要使用虚拟语气，而是使用一般的陈述语气。例如：

The milk smells as if it is sour.（牛奶完全有可能真的是酸了）

3. 目的状语从句

从句用 in case, for fear (that), lest 引导，表示否定目的，动词用 should do 来表示虚拟，同样，should 可以省略。例如：

He took an umbrella with him in case/for fear/lest he (should) be caught in the rain.

1.4　情态动词高频考点

通过以上对虚拟语气的学习，我们发现，在很大程度上，虚拟语气所表达的纯然假想或主观愿望，都是借助情态动词来表达的。或与虚拟语气结合考查，或单独考查，情态动词的用法都是成人本科学士学位英语考试的高频考点之一。

接下来,我们来分析一下历年成人本科学士学位英语考试中密度最高的情态动词考点,也就是情态动词+have done 的结构。

1. would have done：表示对已发生事情的可能猜测;多用于虚拟语气中。例如 2002 年 6 月考试第 47 题：

Something must have happened on their way here. Or they *would have arrived* by now.

2. may/might have done：表示对已发生事情的可能猜测,多于用单纯猜测中。例如 2003 年 11 月考试第 22 题：

I can't find the recorder in the room. It *may have been taken* by somebody.

3. must have done：表示对已发生事情的肯定猜测。例如 2004 年 11 月考试第 25 题：

Since the road is wet and slippery this morning, it *must have rained* last night.

4. can't have done：翻译成"不可能",表示对过去事情的否定判断。例如

You *can't have seen* her in the office last Friday; she's been out of town for two weeks.

5. should have done/ought to have done：表示应该做的事情没有做；

shouldn't have done/ought not to have done：表示不该做的事情却做了

用于对过去动作的责备和批评。例如：

You *should have checked* the time before we left.

You *shouldn't have trusted* him so readily.

6. could have done：对过去能做而没有做的事情表示遗憾、惋惜。例如 2003 年 4 月考试第 59 题：

He abandoned a career that *could have led to* his becoming one of the most influential people in the world.

7. needn't have done：表示"本不必"。例如：

You *needn't have come* in person — a letter would have been enough.

第二节 从 句

对句法知识,特别是从句知识的考查是成人本科学士学位英语考试语法与词汇部分最重要的考点之一。以 2006 年 4 月考试为例,30 道语法与词汇题目中,有 7 道题目就是直接针对句法进行的考查。此外,10 道挑错题目中,有 3 道也是直接考查考生对句法知识的理解和运用。同时,如果没有扎实的句法功底,在翻译环节拿到高分也是不太可能的。比如说第 82 题汉译英"无论多忙,你都应该抽时间看望父母",考查的就是对于让步状语从句 No matter how 的应用。因此,考生应把句法部分作为备考的重要任务来完成。

学习从句,首先要对英语的基本句法知识有一个清晰了解。

句子基本结构：根据谓语动词的性质,我们将英语的句子结构概括为五大基本句型。

其一,主语+不及物动词：动词本身就可以表达完整的意念,不需要宾语及补语,但可以有状语修饰。例如：

It rained (heavily last night).

其二,主语+系动词+表语：动词本身不能表达完整的含义,需要表语。例如：

She is a doctor.

I feel hungry.

除了 be 之外，常用的系动词还包括：

(1) 表示感觉：feel，look，sound，smell，taste，seem，appear

(2) 表示变成：become，go，run，get，turn，fall，come，grow

(3) 表示存在：remain，continue，stay，keep

其三，主语＋及物动词＋宾语：动词需要一个宾语才能使含义完整。例如：

We learn English.

其四，主语＋及物动词＋间接宾语＋直接宾语：动词需要两个宾语以使含义完整。例如：

He bought me a book.

其五，主语＋及物动词＋宾语＋宾语补足语：动词不仅需要一个宾语，还需要一个宾语补足语。例如：

They elected him President.

句子的基本分类：英语句子的分类标准不同，得出的分类结果也不同，比如说，按照使用目的来分，可以分为陈述句、疑问句、感叹句和祈使句。对考生而言，最重要的是要深入理解按照语法结构进行划分所得出的分类结果，这是一切句法考题命题的起点。

简单句：只包含一套主谓结构的句子。例如：It rained yesterday.

并列句：包含两套或两套以上主谓结构的句子，这些主谓结构之间要用并列连词来连接。例如：You have to go，or I will leave.

复合句：一个主句＋一个或多个从句，从句要由连接代词或连接副词来连接。例如：The man who's standing there is my boyfriend.

根据这种分类标准，我们就可以非常清晰地认定，汉语中"我的主意是我们乘车去哪儿"翻译成英文"My idea is we go there by bus"是错误的，因为如果认为这是一个简单句，但它却有两套主谓结构(idea is 和 we go)；而如果认为是一个并列句，却缺少并列连词；若是主从复合句，又缺少连接词(正确的写法是：My idea is that we go there by bus.)。再复杂的题目，也都是在这样简单结构的基础之上发展起来的。

根据句子所充当的成分，我们可以把从句分为名词性从句、定语从句和状语从句。

2.1　名词性从句的用法

一个名词在句子中可以充当主语、宾语、表语、同位语，因此，名词性从句也就主要包含主语从句、宾语从句、表语从句和同位语从句四大类。

(一) 主语从句

在句子中充当主语的从句称为主语从句。例如：

What I need urgently is some cash.

接下来，我们看看成人本科学士学位英语考试中关于主语从句要求考生掌握的要点。

1. 由连词 that，whether 引导的主语从句：that 和 whether 在从句中不担任成分，不能省略，多用 it 作形式主语。例如：

That the earth is round is true. (＝ It is true that the earth is round.)

2. 由连接代词 what，whatever，who，whoever 等和连接副词 when，where，how，why 等引导的主语从句：这些词在从句中担任主语、宾语、状语，不能省略；多用 it 作形式主语；ever 起强调作用。例如：

Who let out the news remained unknown. (＝ It remained unknown who let out the news.)

When we will start is not clear. (＝ It is not clear when we will start.)

(二) 宾语从句

1. 在句子中充当宾语的从句称为宾语从句。例如:

I know *she is coming*.

成人本科学士学位英语考试中针对宾语从句的主要考点如下:

宾语从句语序问题:陈述句的语序,即:

疑问代词/疑问副词 + 作主语的名词或代词 + 谓语动词

I don't *know who she is*.

Can you tell me *what he did* that made you so upset?

2. 介词后面的宾语从句:其实质与动词后的宾语从句没有区别,注意语言的完整性即可。

I am not at all interested in *where he has gone*.

高频考点:

in that 表示原因,翻译成"因为"。例如:

He is respected by all in that he cares about all.

except that 表示部分修正,翻译为"除了……"、"只可惜"。例如:

She is a talented singer except that she is too skinny.

3. if 和 whether:表示"是否"。只能用 whether,不能用 if 的情况:

(1) 后面跟不定式:He doesn't tell me whether to go or stay.

(2) 前面有介词:He raised the question of whether we could find the necessary money.

(3) 后面与 or not 连用:I wonder whether I'll catch the last bus or not.

(4) 引导主语从句:Whether they win or lose is all the same to me.

(三) 表语从句

在句子中充当表语的从句称为表语从句。例如:

All she desires is *that you stay longer with her*.

表语从句常用的连接词与主语从句相同。例如:

This is *what* he wants.

The question is *whether* we can finish our work by tomorrow morning.

(四) 同位语从句

在句子中充当同位语的从句称为同位语从句。例如:

When news came to us *that twenty teachers and students had been caught involved in cheating in the exam*, it was taken extremely seriously.

在成人本科学士学位英语考试中,考生应对如下内容熟练掌握:

1. 同位语从句经常出现在如下名词后:information, fact, idea, news, thought, belief, doubt, question, suggestion 等等。例如:

I have no *idea* that you were here.

2. 关于同位语从句的引导词:

(1) 连词 that 最常用,通常不省略

The suggestion *that* we invite him is quite good.

(2) 连词 whether

He put forward a problem *whether* we stay or leave.

(3) 连接代词 who, what

The question *who* will be the monitor is easy to answer.

(4) 连接副词 when, where, why, how

Have you an idea *how* the Dead Sea formed?

3. 定语从句和同位语从句的区别

看从句所修饰的名词与从句之间的关系：如果该名词与从句之间可以划等号,那就是同位语从句;如果不能划等号,这个名词只是后边从句的一部分,则是定语从句。例如：

The news that the leader will come here is not true.（同位语从句）

The news that you told me last week is not true.（定语从句,news 作 you told me 的直接宾语）

（五）名词性从句用法难点总结

1. 引导宾语从句的 that 可省略,引导主语、表语和同位语从句的 that 一般不可省略。例如：

The students are less interested in maths than in physics is obvious.（误）

That the students are less interested in maths than in physics is obvious.（正）

2. what, whatever, whoever, whomever 这四个词引导的名词性从句

首先,要明白这四个词的来历——其中任何一个其实都相当于两个词：

what ＝（the）thing that /（the）place that

whatever ＝ anything that（表强调）

whoever ＝ anyone who(表强调)

whomever ＝ anyone whom(表强调)

Whatever he says is true. ＝ Anything that he says is true.

Whoever wants to come is welcome. ＝ Anyone who wants to come is welcome.

其次,注意区别这些词的主格和宾格形式。what 和 whatever 是主格宾格同形,whoever 是主格,whomever 是宾格。选用主格还是宾格取决于这个词在从句中所起的语法作用,特别是在介词后面的宾语从句中,不要想当然认为一定是宾格,而要根据这个词在从句中的成分而定。

Give the book to whomever needs it.（误）

Give the book to whoever needs it.（正）

2.2 定语从句的用法

在句子中充当定语的从句称为定语从句。例如：

The boy *who she kissed in the party* finally fell in love with her.

首先,我们来认识一下定语从句的引导词。

关系代词：that, which, who, whom, whose

关系副词：when, where, why 等。

注意,what 不能引导定语从句。

（一）定语从句的常考考点及难点

1. 关系代词在定语从句中必定担当一个句子成分,因此,如果用了关系代词作从句中的主语,就不能再用其他名词或代词作主语,否则会造成主语重复。例如：

Pumas are large, cat-like animals *which they* are found in America.（误）

Pumas are large, cat-like animals *which* are found in America.（正）

2. 在一般情况下,关系代词和关系副词应紧跟在先行词之后。但在某些情况下,它们之间也有可能会被一些别的词分开。在这种情况下,要注意辨认哪一个词是真正的先行词,否则会引起关系代词的误用。例如：

The *time* will come to us *who* man can fly to the outer space freely.(误)

The *time* will come to us *when* man can fly to the outer space freely.(正)

3. 关系代词 that, which, who 所代替的先行词可以是单数的,也可以是复数的,如果它们在定语从句中作主语,那么从句中谓语动词的数要和先行词的数一致。例如:

Tourists have shown great interest in the *items* displayed in the room, which has been unearthed recently.(误)

Tourists have shown great interest in the *items* displayed in the room, which have been unearthed recently.(正)

4. 非限制性定语从句须用逗号和主句分开。如果先行词是物,那么从句要用 which 作关系代词,不能用 that;如果先行词是人,要用 who 或 whom。例如:

We visited the birthplace of the great pianist, that was located on the top of a small hill.(误)

We visited the birthplace of the great pianist, which was located on the top of a small hill.(正)

5. 在定语从句中作介词宾语的关系代词只能用 which(指物)或 whom(人),不能用 that 或 who。例如:

Dams can be very beneficial to the areas in that they are built.(误)

Dams can be very beneficial to the areas in which they are built.(正)

6. 关系代词 whose 在定语从句中作定语,修饰另一名词或代词,解释为"(先行词)……的"。先行词是人或物时,都用 whose(物时相当于 of which)。

They have found a new star, which origin and path are still a mystery.(误)

They have found a new star, whose origin and path are still a mystery.(正)

7. as 作关系代词,引导定语从句。例如:

We have such grapes *as* you have never seen.

He is a teacher, *as* is clear from his manner.

As was expected, he performed the task with success.

8. "名词(代词)+介词+关系代词"引出定语从句。例如:

We've tested three hundred types of boot, *none of which* is completely waterproof.

(二) 定语从句常见错误分析

在学习了定语从句的核心知识之后,我们认识一下在成人本科学士学位英语考试中常见的定语从句错误,这也是命题人经常在选项中给我们设置的障碍。

1. 从句中多宾语

The finger I dipped into the cup was not the one I put it into my mouth.(it 多余)

2. 从句中缺少主语

He is the professor ________ gave us a speech yesterday.(gave 缺少了 who/that 作主语)

3. 从句中主谓不一致

I, who *is* your friend, will try my best to help you.(误)

I, who *am* your friend, will try my best to help you.(正)

4. 搭配错误

Don't talk about *such* things *that* you do not understand.(误)

Don't talk about *such* things *as* you do not understand.(正)

在 such... as 结构中,as 所引导的是定语从句时,不能用其他关系代词代替。

5. 关系代词误用

(1) what 与 that 误用

All *what* he could do was to go back home.(误)

All *that* he could do was to go back home.（正）

正如我们所说，what 不引导定语从句。that 才引导定语从句，修饰 all。此外，我们在讲名词性从句的时候解释过，what 就等于 the thing that/all that，因此，上面的句子也可以写作一个主语从句：What he could do was to go back home.

(2) who 与 whom 误用

The citizens, most of *who* were workers, welcomed the mew mayor.（误）

The citizens, most of *whom* were workers, welcomed the mew mayor.（正）

(3) that 与 which 误用

Allen's dog, *that* was very old now, became ill and died.（误）

Allen's dog, *which* was very old now, became ill and died.（正）

(4) that 与 who 误用

They talked of things and persons *who* they knew in the school.（误）

They talked of things and persons *that* they knew in the school.（正）

注意：当先行词有多个，而且既有人又有物时，关系代词要用 that。

6. 关系代词与关系副词混淆

I have been to the city *where* you visited last week.（误）

I have been to the city *that* you visited last week.（正）

She would never forget the evening *that* she lost the beautiful necklace.（误）

She would never forget the evening *when* she lost the beautiful necklace.（正）

注意，当定语从句修饰代表地点、时间的先行词时，要看清楚关系词在从句中所作的成分。在上面的例 1 中，that 作及物动词 visit 的宾语；在例 2 中，when 作 she lost the beautiful necklace 的时间状语。

2.3 状语从句的用法

在句子中充当状语的从句称为状语从句。例如：

Someone stole my wallet *while I was sleeping*.

（一）状语从句的基本用法：

注意：状语从句的连接词不在句子中作任何语法成分。

1. 时间状语从句：常用连接词有 when, whenever, as(当……时), while(与……同时), before, after, until, till, (ever) since, once, the moment, as soon as, the minute, hardly... when, no sooner... than(一……就……)等等。除了对于基本连接词的考查，成人本科学士学位英语考试对于时间状语从句的关注点主要还有两个：

(1) 时间状语从句表示将来动作时，要用一般现在时态。例如 2003 年 11 月考试第 34 题：

—When are you going to visit your uncle in Chicago?

—As soon as we complete our work for tomorrow.

(2) 用 hardly... when, no sooner... than 表示"一……就……"，如果 hardly 或 no sooner 置于句首，会引发倒装变化。例如：

No sooner had he settled down than the storm came.

Hardly had he settled down when the storm came.

2. 条件状语从句：常用连接词有 if, as long as, provided(如果), unless(除非), on condition that(如果，条件是)等等。

同样,在从句表示将来动作时,要用一般现在时态。例如 2005 年 4 月考试第 34 题:

The doctor will not perform the operation *unless it is absolutely necessary*.

3. 原因状语从句:常用连接词有 because,表示必然的因果关系;since,表示一种间接或附带的原因;as,只是表示提一下。例如:

He cannot come to school *because he is ill*.

Everyone likes you *as you are both kind and honest*.

4. 让步状语从句:常用连接词有 though, although, even if, even though(就算), as(尽管), however(无论如何), whatever, wherever, whoever, whomever, no matter how/what/where/who/whom(无论……),while(尽管)等等。例如 2003 年 4 月考试第 29 题:

While I admit that there are problems, I don't agree that they cannot be solved.

注意一个难点:as 引导让步状语从句,被强调的部分放在句首,进行到装。例如:

Great as the author was, he proved a bad model.

5. 方式状语从句:常用 as(如,像),as if, as though(好像)来连接。例如:

I did as he asked.

6. 目的状语从句:常用连接词有:so that, in order that 表示肯定目的,做"为了、以便于"讲;for fear (that), in case, lest 表示否定目的,作"以免"讲。例如 2002 年 6 月考试第 27 题:

I wrote it down in case I should forget it.

7. 结果状语从句:通常用 so... that, such... that 来连接,要注意 such 修饰名词,so 修饰形容词副词。例如:

They are such hard-working students that I admire them a lot.

The students are so hard-working that I admire them a lot.

8. 比较状语从句:常用连接词有 as... as...,表示同级比较;more... than... 表示不同级比较。例如:

I love you as deeply as he (does).

I love you more than he (does).

(二) 状语从句常见错误分析

同样,在学习了状语从句的核心知识之后,我们再认识一下在成人本科学士学位英语考试中常见的状语从句错误,从而加以巩固和深化。

1. despite, in spite of 和 although, though

它们表达的含义都是"尽管",表示逻辑让步关系,但 despite 和 in spite of 是介词,后面加名词或名词性内容;而 although 或 though 是连词,后面跟从句。例如:

Although Jackie is short, he never gives up the hope for life.

Despite the fact that Jackie is short, he never gives up the hope for life.

2. during 是介词,不要当成时间状语的连接词

During he was working, I went out alone and did some shopping. (误)

While he was working, I went out alone and did some shopping. (正)

3. because of, thanks to 是介词,不要当成原因状语的连接词

Thanks to the teacher has given me a lot of help, I have made great progress. (误)

Thanks to the teacher's help, I have made great progress. (正)

Thanks to the teacher who has given me a lot of help, I have made great progress. (正)

4. 不要把表示结果的不定式结构 too... to... 和表示结果状语从句的 so... that... 混淆。例如：

I have been *too* busy *that* I don't have time to call you.（误）

I have been *too* busy *to* call you.（正）

I have been *so* busy *that* I don't have time to call you.（正）

5. since 的用法：

作连词，引导原因状语从句和时间状语从句。

作介词，后加时间用作时间状语；用作介词的 since 不能表示原因。例如：

Since being ill, he had to postpone the trip.（误）

Since he was ill, he had to postpone the trip.（正）

6. 同级比较的 as... as... 不要和不同级比较的 more... than 混淆。例如：

Our library has a *larger* collection of books *as* any other library in US.（误）

Our library has a *larger* collection of books *than* any other library in US.（正）

7. even 是副词，不能单独引导从句。例如：

Even no one took any interest in his experiment, he preserved and finally made an important discovery.（误）

Even though no one took any interest in his experiment, he preserved and finally made an important discovery.（正）

2.4 关系代词 that 用法小结

在名词性从句和定语从句中，我们都见到了连接词 that 的身影。许多考生由于对 that 的用法认识不系统、不深入，经常在成人本科学士学位英语考试中栽跟头。我们在此加以总结：

1. that 的省略问题

(1) that 作定语从句中动词的宾语，可省略。例如：

I am in complete agreement with everything (that) he said.

(2) that 紧跟先行词，作定语从句中介词的宾语，可省略。例如：

Here is the way (that) you have been looking for.

(3) that 作定语从句的表语时，可省略。例如：

Shanghai is no longer the city (that) it used to be.

2. 定语从句中 that 和 which 的用法区别：

(1) 只能用 which 的情况

a. 非限定性定语从句。例如：

Beijing, which is the capital of China, is a very beautiful city.

b. 在定语从句中作介词的宾语时，如果介词放在关系代词之前，只能用 which。例如：

This is the hotel in which you will stay.

I have the book (that/which) you are talking about.

(2) 只能用 that 的情况

a. 当先行词为 all, everything, nothing, something, anything, much, little 等不定代词时。例如：

He was trying to teach us all (that) he knew at this last lesson.

b. 先行词被序数词或形容词最高级修饰时。例如：

This is the best film that has been shown this year.

c. 先行词有两个或以上，而且既有人又有物，要用 that，不能用 which，who，whom。先行词被 the only，the very，the same，the last 所修饰时，也只能用 that。例如：

This is his only book that has sold so many copies.

2.5　强调句

基本结构：It is ＋ 强调的部分 ＋ that...

如果被强调的部分是人，可以用 who/whom。

可以强调句中的主语、宾语、状语等，但绝不用来强调谓语。成人本科学士学位英语考试的考查重点是对状语部分的强调。例如 2004 年 4 月考试第 16 题：

It is from my grandparents that I learned a lot.

第三节　非谓语动词

所谓非谓语动词，顾名思义，指的是从动词变化而来，但在句子中充当谓语以外其他句子成分的结构。非谓语动词有三大类：不定式、动名词和分词。在许多考生看来，非谓语动词由于形式变化丰富，在句子中充当的成分复杂，因此是成人本科学士学位英语考试语法部分最难啃的骨头。其实，对非谓语动词的恐惧大可不必。只要把握一个根本原则——不要生硬记忆语法条目，关键是要弄清动作发生的时间和主被动关系——绝大多数的成人本科学士学位英语考试题目都可以迎刃而解。

3.1　不定式

(一) 不定式的一般用法

1. 成分和形式

在句子中的语法成分：不作谓语。

带 to 和不带 to 的动词不定式：

不定式的基本形式是 to do，例如 I want to go home. 但有时也会出现不带 to 的情况，如情态动词后，I can go home now，或其他一些情况。

2. 不定式的时间和主被动关系

时间	主动形式	被动形式
一般时	to do	to be done
完成时	to have done	to have been done
进行时	to be doing	
完成进行时	to have been doing	

我们来看看 1999 年 6 月考试第 52 题：

The magnificent museum is said ________ about a hundred years ago.

A. to be built　　　　B. to have been built

C. to have built　　　　D. to have being built

根据对动作时间先后和主被动关系进行的分析，我们发现，A 选项没有交代时间，C 选项没有交代被动，D 选项出现了基本的语法错误。答案自然是 B，即表格中的“被动-完成”形式。

3. 不定式的否定

not ＋ to do

例如 1999 年 6 月考试第 59 题：

They have done things they *ought not to have done*.

4. 不定式的逻辑主语

所谓逻辑主语，指的是含义上该动作的发出者。例如：

She taught me to read.（me 是 read 的发出者）

I am glad to help you.（I 是 help 的发出者）

5. 不定式的被动形式

当不定式的逻辑主语是动作的接受者时，不定式就需要用被动形式。

She was sent to there to be trained as an astronaut.（she 是"被培训"）

（二）不定式的考查重点

1. 不定式的主被动关系

例如 1999 年 6 月考试第 39 题：

The ability ________ is very important for any speaker.

A. to hear clearly　　B. to be clearly heard

C. to hearing clearly　　D. to being clearly heard.

显然，speaker(演讲者)是"被听到"，所以一举选定 B 选项。

2. 不带 to 的动词不定式作宾语补足语

(1) 下列动词常用不带 to 的动词不定式作宾语补足语：

使役动词：make，have，let

感官动词：see，watch，notice，look at，hear，listen to，find

例如 2003 年 4 月第 25 题：

I'll *have you know* that I'm a qualified engineer.

注意：

a. 当主动句变被动句时，作主语补足语的不定式必须带 to。

例如 2004 年 11 月考试第 21 题：

Henry is *often seen to read* English aloud every morning in the classroom.

b. 感官动词＋ do 表示一般性动作，＋ doing 表示正在进行的动作。

例如 2005 年 4 月考试第 35 题：

Today the police can watch cars running on roads by radar.

(2) 下列短语之后的不定式也不带 to：

had better，would rather，prefer to do A rather than do B，can't but do，do nothing but 等。

例如 2003 年 11 月考试第 39 题：

I *cannot but admit* the truth of your words，although they go against my interests.

注意：如果 but(except)前面没有谓语动词 do，那么后面的 to 要还原出来。例如：

He had nothing to do but wait.

He wanted nothing but to stay here.

He did have no choice but to wait.（这里的 did 是助动词，表示强调）

3. have sb. do，have sb. doing，have sb./ sth. done 的区别

have sb. do 表示让某人干某事，一般性动作

have sb. doing 表示让某人正在干……

have sb./sth. done 让某人/某物被……

例如 2002 年 6 月考试第 50 题：

We are going to *have our office rearranged* to make room for a new engineer.

3.2 动名词

动名词是由动词转化为名词的词。和普通的名词一样，动名词可以在句子中充当主语、宾语、表语、定语和补语成分。

(一) 动名词的一般用法

1. 成分和形式

成分：和名词相同——主语、宾语、表语、定语和补语

形式：doing

否定形式：not doing

2. 动名词的时间和主被动关系

时间	主动形式	被动形式
一般时	doing	being done
完成时	having done	having been done

我们来看 2002 年 6 月考试第 56 题：

We all feel sorry for *having kept* you waiting for so long after your arrival. 正是上表中的“主动-完成”形式。

3. 只能用动名词，不能用不定式的情况

(1) 介词的宾语只能用动名词，不能用不定式：

She is fond of *playing* tennis.

(2) 下列动词的宾语：

advise，mind，finish，suggest，delay，enjoy，practice，quit，imagine，doubt，consider，mention，risk，deny，avoid，admit，miss，resist，appreciate，keep，postpone，excuse 等等。

例如 1998 年 6 月考试第 42 题：

We shall appreciate *hearing* from you soon.

(3) 下列短语的宾语：

can't help，it is no use，be worth，be busy，feel like，look forward，object to，be used to，be accustomed to，as to，with regard to，be devoted to，spend sth. doing，have a ... time doing，have trouble/difficulty doing 等等。

例如 2004 年 11 月考试第 43 题：

Do you feel like *having* something to eat today?

(4) 下列动词＋ sb. ＋ from doing：

protect，prevent，stop，prohibit，inhibit，discourage，ban 等等。

例如 2001 年 6 月考试第 46 题：

The medicine can prevent you from *getting* drunk.

4. 动名词的逻辑主语

当动名词的逻辑主语和主句主语一致时，其逻辑主语通常省略；若不一致，则逻辑主语必须用所属格的形式表示出来，例如：

She considers dancing on the stage her another life.

Nobody showed interest in his talking.

（二）动名词的考查重点：与不定式的区别

1. stop/go on doing 表示停下或继续正在做的事；stop/go on to do 表示停下来以便改做另外一件事，例如：

Man never stops searching for new ways of getting new energy.

He went on to clean the floor after washing blanket.

2. remember/forget doing 表示动作发生在过去，“记得/忘记干了某事”，remember/forget to do 表示动作尚未发生，“记得/忘记去干某事”，例如：

I remember having given the letter to him.

I forgot to give the letter to him.

3. regret doing 表示后悔干了某事，regret to say/tell 表示“很遗憾告诉……”，例如：

I regret letting the thief go.

I regret to tell you that I can't go with you.

4. try doing 表示试着干，很容易做到；try to do 表示设法干，费力

Try knocking at the door.

I will try to get you some money.

5. want/require/need ＋ doing 用主动形式表示被动含义。

例如 2000 年 6 月第 47 题：

My room is mess. It needs tidying up.（房屋是“被整理”。）

6. mean doing 表示意味着……；mean to do 表示想要干。

Wasting time means wasting life.

I didn't mean to hurt you.

7. like/love/hate doing 表示一般习惯；like/love/hate to do 表示当下情况

I like swimming, but I don't like to swim now.

3.3　分词

（一）分词的一般用法

1. 分词的种类

(1) 现在分词：doing，表示主动、进行；

(2) 过去分词：done，表示被动、完成。

2. 分词的否定形式：not doing/not done

3. 现在分词的时间和主被动关系

时间	主动形式	被动形式
一般时	doing	being done
完成时	having done	having been done

这是使用分词的关键。

4. 分词的语法功能

分词在句子当中可以充当表语、定语、状语、补语等成分。

(1) 作表语和补语

现在分词的"一般-主动"形式表示逻辑上的主谓关系;而过去分词强调逻辑上的动宾关系。例如:

The news sounds exciting.(消息"主动"使人兴奋,因此用现在分词)

I am excited at the news.(我是"为、被"消息所兴奋,因此用过去分词)

我们来看2004年11月考试第35题:

Pierre often makes himself ________ by gesturing with his hands.

A. to understand　　B. understanding

C. to be understood　　D. understood

首先,make是我们在前面所讲过的"使役动词",要加不带to的动词不定式,所以排除了A选项和C选项。接下来,Pierre是让别人理解他,他自己是"被理解",所以选定过去分词D。

(2) 作定语

现在分词的"一般-主动"形式表示它所修饰的名词和该分词是逻辑上的主谓关系。例如a moving film,a house facing south;现在分词的"一般-被动"形式表示一个正在进行的被动动作,例如a meeting being held now;而过去分词表示已经完成的被动动作,当然有时只强调被动或只强调完成。例如a meeting held yesterday(既表示完成也表示被动),a letter written in pen(表示被动),a developed country(表示完成)。

(3) 作状语

现在分词的各种形式和过去分词都能做句子的状语。在这里,我们要格外强调的是:过去分词往往只强调被动而不强调时间性,所以若要强调一个被动动作在谓语动词表示的动作之前发生,必须用现在分词的"完成-被动"形式。例如:

Having been given much help, the workers finished the project earlier than expected.

(二) 分词的考查重点

1. 主语的一致性:非谓语动词作状语修饰主句时,它们的逻辑主语必须和主句主语保持一致。例如:

To succeed at school, good scores are essential.(误)

To succeed at school, one needs good scores.(正)

我们再来看一道题:

Arriving at the bus stop, ________ waiting there.

A. he found a lot of people　　B. a lot of people were found

C. a lot of people found　　D. he was found a lot of people

arriving的逻辑主语(也就是这个动作的发出者)是he,因此,为了维护主语的一致性,我们排除了B和C;最后选定A选项,因为he是"主动发现"。

2. 独立主格结构:当分词的逻辑主语和主句主语不一致时,必须把分词的逻辑主语给补充完整。加上了逻辑主语的分词就叫做独立主格结构。

例如2004年11月考试第16题:

It being pretty late, we decided to leave at once, as we didn't want to risk missing the bus.

with结构:独立主格的发展变化,表示一种伴随状态。

例如 2004 年 4 月考试第 38 题：
With the flowers blooming everywhere, the park looks beautiful.

第四节　反意疑问句

在成人本科学士学位英语考试中，对反意疑问句的考查也频频出现。我们先介绍一般规则，再讲常考的重点。

4.1　基本用法：陈述句十附加问句

考查的重点是附加问句部分，其一般原则是：前肯定，后否定；前否定，后肯定；有情态动词就用情态动词，没有情态动词就用助动词；前后时态要一致。例如：

You are a teacher, aren't you?

You didn't do your work, did you?

此外，还要注意以下两个经常给考生制造麻烦的点：

1. have to 要用 do/does/did 来组织反意疑问句。

例如 2004 年 11 月考试第 42 题：

We had to wait a long time to get our passports, didn't we?

2. there be 句型的反意疑问句：用省略了主语的 there be 形式。例如：

There won't be any concert this evening, will there?

4.2　常考的重点

（一）含有否定词的反意疑问句

当陈述句部分已有表示否定含义的 no, nothing, nobody, hardly, never, scarcely, seldom, rarely 时，反问句要用肯定形式。

例如 2002 年 6 月考试第 53 题：

You *never* told me you have seen the film, *did* you?

（二）祈使句的反意疑问句

统一用肯定形式。例如：

Close the door, will you?

Don't close the door, will you?

注意成人本科学士学位英语考试常考的一个点：

Let us..., will you?（因为 let us 表达的是请求别人让己方干某事）

Let's..., shall we?（因为 let's 表达的是建议我们大家一起干某事）

（三）其他一些特殊用法

1. 主句主语是第一人称(I, we)，谓语是表示认为的动词(think, suppose, guess 等)，反问句部分的人称要和从句一致，肯、否定形式要和前面整句相反。例如：

I guess *he* is a teacher, isn't *he*?

I don't think *you*'ve heard of him before, have *you*?

2. 否定前缀不能视为否定词，其反意疑问句仍用和前面含义相反的形式。例如：

It is impossible, *isn't it*?

He *is not* unkind to his classmates, *is* he?

第五节　倒　　装

正常的英语句序是主语—谓语动词/系动词—宾语/表语。但在有些情况下，会发生谓语部分(包括动词和系动词)全部或部分提前到主语之前的现象。这种结构变化就称之为倒装。

所谓完全倒装，指的是整个谓语提到主语之前；而相应地，部分倒装则是助动词/情态动词/be 动词提到主语之前。部分倒装是考查重点。

接下来，我们看看成人本科学士学位英语考试常考的倒装变化。

5.1　否定副词置于句首

当这些表示否定含义的副词——not, nor, neither, never, hardly, scarcely, rarely, barely, seldom, little, not until, not only... (but also), no sooner... (than), by no means, under no circumstances 等等——出现在句首的时候，要发生部分倒装。

例如 2004 年 4 月考试第 44 题：

No sooner had he entered the house than the telephone rang.

5.2　only 引导的状语置于句首

only 引导的状语结构有很多种形式，在成人本科学士学位英语考试中出现过的包括：

1. only ＋ 副词。例如：Only then did he realize the fact.
2. only ＋ 介词短语。例如：Only through me can you understand the world.
3. only ＋ 状语从句。例如：Only when we catch the thief can we leave.

5.3　so 引导的句子

比如说我们非常熟悉的 He is a teacher and *so am I*. 此外，还有结果状语从句：*So high is the tree* that nobody can pick a pear from it.

5.4　虚拟语气省略 if

具体内容请参考虚拟语气部分。

5.5　as 引导的让步状语从句

正如我们在从句部分解释的那样，as 引导让步状语从句引发的倒装结构是：

名词(无冠词)＋as＋主语＋谓语。例如：*Kid as he is*, he solves the puzzle.

形容词＋as＋主语＋谓语。例如 2004 年 11 月考试第 34 题：

Busy as he was at Harvard, he began again to write his essay.

第六节　主 谓 一 致

顾名思义，主谓一致指的是在英语行文中，主语和谓语要保持单复数的一致性。考生所面临的难点是如何判断主语的单复数。这就是我们接下来要做的工作。

6.1　形式上复数、意义上单数的名词作主语，谓语动词用单数。例如：physics, maths, news, means 等我们看看 2000 年 6 月考试第 63 题挑错题：

The news coming from different parts of the world are often extremely discouraging these days.

很显然，主语 news 是单数，谓语 are 是复数，主谓不一致了。

6.2　主语为数个并列名词时，不管这些名词是单数、复数、可数、不可数，谓语动词一律用复数。例如：

Intelligence, education and experience all *help* shape management styles.

6.3　单个动名词、不定式、从句作主语时，谓语动词用单数。

例如 2002 年 6 月考试第 49 题：

How the fire in the dancing hall started *remains* a mystery.

上句中，主语是 How the fire in the dancing hall started，是一个从句。

6.4　a number of(＝many)后用复数动词，the number of 后用单数动词。例如 1998 年 6 月考试第 66 题挑错题：

A number of errors made by him was surprising.

A 应改为 The。

6.5　主语＋介词短语＋名词/代词，主谓一致关系不受介词后边的名词/代词影响。

成人本科学士学位英语考试中在这个结构里常考的介词有：with, along with, together with, as well as, including, except, but, besides, rather than, more than, accompanied by 等等。例如：

I together with some friends, *am* planning a party.

6.6　many a, more than one 修饰的单数名词作主语时，谓语动词用单数。例如：

Many a student/More than one student *is* interested in it.

6.7　分数、百分数，all, some, any, more, most, the rest, a lot of, the majority of, a large quantity of，如果后面跟的是单数名词或不可数名词，谓语动词用单数；如果后面跟的是复数名词，谓语动词用复数。例如：

Half of the *water is* wasted.

Six percent of their *goats were* killed by two wolves.

6.8　there be 句型，由 or, nor, not only... but also, not... but, either... or, neither... nor 等连接的并列主语的谓语动词，依据就近原则确定谓语动词的形式。也就是说，根据距离位于动词最近的那个名词或代词的数来判断。例如 2003 年 11 月考试第 35 题：

Neither John nor *I am* able to persuade Richard's grandfather to attend the wedding.

第七节　词　汇　题

7.1　词汇题的考查思路

纵观历年考试，词汇题占 30 分语法与词汇部分的 7 分—15 分，2003 年 11 月后，基本上是语法与词汇各占一半。经过分析，我们发现，成人本科学士学位英语考试的词汇题目主要是从以下几个角度来考查的：

（一）单个考查词汇

涉及的包括动词、名词、代词、形容词、介词等主要词类，以动词和名词为主。

例如2006年4月考试第21题：

Have you any ________ that you were not there at 9' o clock last night?

A. statement B. cause

C. words D. proof

statement含义为"陈述"，cause指"原因"，words则是"谈话"，而只有proof"证据"符合句子所表达的含义。

（二）形近词的考查

例如2006年4月考试第17题：

In teaching English we should not ________ our students of their mistakes all the time.

A. remind B. remember

C. remain D. remark

remind表示"提醒"，remember表示"记忆"，remain是"保持、仍然是"，remark则是"评估"。根据语境，选定remind。

（三）词语之间的搭配关系

这是词汇题考查的主要内容。比如说动词和介词、动词和副词、介词和名词、介词和形容词，以及动词短语和介词短语等等。还需要考生多积累、多练习。例如2006年4月考试第44题：

He asked her to go to a concert with him but she ________ his invitation ________ politely.

A. turned; down B. turned; out

C. turned; away D. turned; up

这是典型的动词短语题目，也就是同一个动词搭配不同的副词所表达的不同含义。turn out有"制造、生产、结果是"之义；turn away则是"走开、转过脸"；turn up义取up，表示"发现、出现"；只有turn down才表示"拒绝"的意思。

7.2 历年真题词汇题解析

下面，我们对历年考试的词汇部分逐题解读，可以发现词汇题考点设计的大致轮廓。尤其是2003年11月大纲修订后，词汇部分的试题保持了相对的稳定性。

Unit 1

31. The boy's laziness ________ his failure in the exams.

A. resulted from B. brought in C. resulted in D. led into

正确答案：C。

解析：result from：由……造成，起源于……；bring in：生产，产生；result in：导致，结果是……；lead into：引起，引入。

32. Only guests of the hotel enjoy the ________ of using the private beach.

A. privilege B. possibility C. favor D. advantage

正确答案：A。

解析：privilege：特权，优惠；possibility：可能，可能性；favor：喜好，恩惠；advantage：优点，有利条件。

33. Tom ________ more than twenty pounds for the dictionary.

A. spent B. paid C. cost D. took

正确答案：B。

解析：spend：花费，支付，通常与 in 或 on 搭配；pay：支付，付出，通常与 for 搭配；cost：花费，值，主语通常是物；take：花费，主语通常是物。

34. The governor had to ________ all his appointments for the day and rush to the train accident.

A. set off　B. pay off　C. see off　D. call off

正确答案：D。

解析：set off：出发，启程；pay off：偿清，得到好结果；see off：为……送行，向……告别；call off：取消，放弃。

35. One car went too fast and ________ missed hitting another car.

A. completely　B. greatly　C. narrowly　D. little

正确答案：C。

解析：completely：完全地，全然；greatly：非常，极大地；narrowly：勉强；little：毫不。

37. It took me a long time to ________ the disappointment of losing the match.

A. get over　B. get up　C. get into　D. get down

正确答案：A。

解析：get over：克服，从……中恢复；get up：起床，增强；get into：使陷入，卷入；get down：记下，着手进行。

38. All the reference books should be made ________ to the teachers and students in our university.

A. concerned　B. available　C. related　D. flexible

正确答案：B。

解析：concerned：关心的，有关的；available：可获得的，可用的；related：有关的，相关的；flexible：灵活的，易弯曲的。

39. He never thought the committee would ________ his proposal.

A. put up　B. object to　C. pass on　D. call on

正确答案：B。

解析：put up：支起，提出；object to：反对，不支持；pass on：传递，传给；call on：呼吁，号召。

46. The two men were arrested for breaking into that shop and have been ________ \$10,000.

A. committed　B. driven　C. charged　D. fined

正确答案：D。

解析：commit：从事，犯罪；drive：驱赶，驱使；charge：控告，控诉；fine：罚款，处罚。

47. The driver might have ________ the accident if he had had his headlights on.

A. missed　B. avoided　C. stopped　D. dismissed

正确答案：B。

解析：miss：错过，漏掉；avoid：避免，躲过；stop：停止，阻止；dismiss：解散，解除。

51. He was ________ enough to understand my questions from the gestures I made.

A. intelligent　B. efficient　C. proficient　D. diligent

正确答案：A。

解析：intelligent：聪明的，理解力强的；efficient：有效的，效率高的；proficient：熟练的，精通的;diligent:勤奋的,用功的。

52. If you ________ the speed limit, you will get into trouble with the police.

A. exclude B. exceed C. excuse D. execute

正确答案:B。

解析:exclude:排除,拒绝;exceed:超过,超越;excuse:原谅,劳驾;execute:实行,执行。

Unit 2

21. He knows little of English to say ________ of English culture.

A. something B. everything C. nothing D. anything

正确答案:C。

解析:something:某东西,某事;everything:每个东西,每件事;nothing:没有东西,没事;anything:任何东西,任何事。根据前面的"knows little of English"可知,选C。

22. Being ignorant of the law is no ________ of breaking the law.

A. reason B. excuse C. ground D. point

正确答案:B。

解析:reason:原因,理由;excuse:借口,藉口;ground:理由,根据;point:点,要点。

23. The new law, it is said, will be ________.

A. put into effect B. taken into account C. kept in sight D. brought to mind

正确答案:A。

解析:put into effect:实施,生效;take into account:考虑,顾及;keep in sight:保持在视线范围内;bring to mind:想起,回忆起。

30. The pain will go away ________.

A. by and by B. by chance C. all over D. at present

正确答案:A。

解析:by and by:逐渐,不久;by chance:碰巧,偶然;all over:遍及,到处;at present:现在,目前。

37. The Olympic Committee has drawn up strict rules for the sportsmen to ________.

A. go by B. go on C. go over D. go after

正确答案:A。

解析:go by:遵守,遵循;go on:继续,接着;go over:仔细检查,复习;go after:追逐,追求。

38. I'm far from ________ with what you have done.

A. pleased B. pleasing C. pleasure D. please

正确答案:A。

解析:pleased:高兴的,满意的,通常与 with 搭配;pleasing:愉快的,令人喜爱的;pleasure:高兴,愉快;please:请。

42. Are you serious in ________ such a view?

A. putting on B. putting off C. putting up D. putting forward

正确答案:D。

解析:put on:穿上,戴上;put off:推迟,延期;put up:举起,搭起;put forward:提出要求、建议等。

50. If you can provide the wine, I'll ________ the food.

A. see to　B. look at　C. ask for　D. think about

正确答案：A。

解析：see to：负责；look at：看，看待；ask for：要求，请求；think about：思考，考虑。

51. He was fully ________ of his own shortcomings.

A. sensitive　B. sensible　C. serious　D. sincere

正确答案：A。

解析：sensitive：敏感的，通常与 of 或 to 搭配；sensible：明理的，明智的；serious：严肃的，认真的；sincere：真诚的，诚挚的。

54. That mountain village can't be ________ by telephone yet.

A. reached　B. achieved　C. attached　D. arrived

正确答案：A。

解析：reach：（通讯）到达、抵达；achieve：完成，达到（目标等）；attach：附上，系上；arrive：到达（某地）。

55. Problems will ________ if you do it this way.

A. rise　B. arise　C. raise　D. arouse

正确答案：B。

解析：rise：升起，上升；arise：（问题等）出现、发生；raise：提高，提升；arouse：唤醒，激发。

Unit 3

25. Mary never tells anyone what she does for a ________.

A. job　B. work　C. profession　D. living

正确答案：D。

解析：for a living 是习惯搭配，意思是"谋生"。

30. The voters told the politician that he could ________ on their support in the next general elections.

A. expect　B. decide　C. count　D. doubt

正确答案：C。

解析：expect：期待，期望；decide：就……做出决定，决定要，与 on 搭配；count：期待，指望，与 on 搭配；doubt：怀疑，疑惑。

33. When she heard the bad news, she ________ completely.

A. broke away　B. broke up　C. broke down　D. broke out

正确答案：C。

解析：break away：改掉，放弃；break up：分解，解散；break down：崩溃，垮掉；break out：突然发生，爆发。

34. He ________ a large fortune from his business.

A. made　B. won　C. expected　D. gained

正确答案：A。

解析：make a fortune 是习惯搭配，意思是"赚大钱，发大财"。

36. He looked behind him to ________ he was not being followed.

A. believe　B. find　C. make sure　D. look

正确答案：C。

解析：believe：相信，认为；find：发现，找到；make sure：确信，确定；look：看，观察。

37. The car was repaired but not quite to my ________.

A. joy B. pleasure C. attraction D. satisfaction

正确答案：D。

解析：to one's satisfaction 是习惯搭配，意思是“令某人满意”。

38. Are you ________ spending more money on the space program?

A. in favor of B. by favor of C. in favor to D. out of favor

正确答案：A。

解析：in favor of：支持，赞成；by favor of：请面交；in favor to 搭配不当；out of favor：得不到别人的尊重。

39. Fortunately, the demonstration ________ to be quite peaceful.

A. turned in B. turned out C. showed off D. showed up

正确答案：B。

解析：turn out to be 是固定搭配，意思是“结果是，被证明是”。

41. Selfish people often take ________ of other people's kindness.

A. advantage B. care C. use D. profit

正确答案：A。

解析：take advantage of 是习惯搭配，意思是“利用”。

42. His business is growing so fast that he must ________ more workers.

A. take up B. take on C. take over D. take out

正确答案：B。

解析：take up：拿起，占据；take on：雇用，吸收；take over：接管，接替；take out：清除，除掉。

48. A great celebration is going to be held ________ the distinguished writer.

A. in spite of B. in honor of C. in favor of D. in the name of

正确答案：B。

解析：in spite of：虽然，尽管；in honor of：为了向……表示敬意；in favor of：支持，赞成；in the name of：以……的名义。

49. All the members in the jury agreed that the man was ________ of theft.

A. criminal B. charged C. guilty D. faulty

正确答案：C。

解析：criminal：可耻的，不道德的；charged：控告，控诉；guilty：有罪的，通常与 of 搭配；faulty：有缺点的，有毛病的。

50. Having finished the letter, he ________ it carefully and sealed the envelop with a kiss.

A. folded B. bent C. turned D. equipped

正确答案：A。

解析：fold：折，折叠；bent：弯曲，弯腰；turn：翻，转；equip：装备，配备。

51. The police were given an order that the stolen documents must be recovered at all ________.

A. accounts B. conditions C. payments D. costs

正确答案：D。

解析：at all costs 是习惯搭配，意思是“不惜任何代价”。

Unit 4

21. The ________ of the play is so great that many people want to see it.

A. attention　B. attraction　C. attempt　D. attack

正确答案：B。

解析：attention：注意，专心；attraction：吸引力，诱惑力；attempt：尝试，试图；attack：进攻，攻击。

22. Do you think they have ________ food for all these people here?

A. subsequent　B. beneficial　C. sufficient　D. average

正确答案：C。

解析：subsequent：随后的，继之而来的；beneficial：有利的，有利可图的；sufficient：足够的，充足的；average：平均的，普通的。

23. The old lady ________ on hearing his son's death.

A. broke in　B. broke down　C. broke out　D. broke away

正确答案：B。

解析：break in：打断，闯入；break down：崩溃，垮掉；break out：突然发生，爆发；break away：改掉，放弃。

24. I have to ________ my visit as I'll be very busy next week.

A. call for　B. call on　C. call off　D. call in

正确答案：C。

解析：call for：需要，要求；call on：号召，请求；call off：取消，停止；call in：来访，叫人进来。

25. He has been teaching for 2 years, but being a teacher is not his ________.

A. chance　B. character　C. attitude　D. choice

正确答案：D。

解析：chance：机会，时机；character：品质，特征；attitude：态度，看法；choice：选择，抉择。

26. This is a very ________ situation and we don't know how to face it yet.

A. comprehensive　B. compound　C. complicated　D. competent

正确答案：A。

解析：comprehensive：综合的，全面的；compound：复合的，混合的；complicated：复杂的；competent：有能力的，能胜任的。

32. Do you mean this is the ________ decision you have made after thinking for hours?

A. upright　B. ultimate　C. total　D. tight

正确答案：B。

解析：upright：正直的，诚实的；ultimate：最后的，最终的；total：全部的，完全的；tight：紧密的，紧凑的。

34. I gave John a present but he gave me nothing ________.

A. in return　B. in turn　C. in advance　D. in vain

正确答案：A。

解析：in return：作为报答，作为回报；in turn：轮流，依次地；in advance：预先，事先；in vain：白费地，徒劳。

35. I cannot tell the ________ difference between the twins.

A. slender B. single C. simple D. slight

正确答案：D。

解析：slender：苗条的，细长的；single：单个的，单独的；simple：简单的，容易的；slight：细微的，微小的。

36. Words ________ meaning, as we all know.

A. convince B. convey C. contribute D. conquer

正确答案：B。

解析：convince：使相信，使明白；convey：表达，传达；contribute：捐献，贡献；conquer：攻克，征服。

Unit 5

21. You should be able to ________ right from wrong.

A. perceive B. distinguish C. sight D. observe

正确答案：B。

解析：perceive：感觉，察觉；distinguish：区分，区别，通常与 from 搭配；sight：看见，发现；observe：观察，研究。

22. Any student who ________ his homework is unlikely to pass the examination.

A. reduces B. offends C. practices D. neglects

正确答案：D。

解析：reduce：降低，减少；offend：冒犯，触犯；practice：练习，训练；neglect：忽视，漏做。

24. Your sister has made an ________ for you to see the dentist at 3 this afternoon.

A. appointment B. interview C. opportunity D. assignment

正确答案：A。

解析：make an appointment 是习惯搭配，意思是"与……人预约、约会"。

25. The committee is expected to ________ a decision this evening.

A. reach B. arrive C. bring D. take

正确答案：A。

解析：reach a decision 是习惯搭配，意思是"作出决定"。

26. He spoke so quickly that I didn't ________ what he said.

A. make for B. make sure C. make over D. make out

正确答案：D。

解析：make for：走向，前往；make sure：确信，确定；make over：修改，改造；make out：理解，明白。

28. It is not that I do not like plays. The reason why I did not go to the theater last night was that I could not ________ the time.

A. offer B. leave C. afford D. manage

正确答案：C。

解析：offer：提供，供应；leave：离开，出发；afford：承担得起，负担得起；manage：设法，经营。could not afford 是习惯搭配，意思是"抽不出(钱、时间)，出不起钱等"。

29. The chemical factory was demolished ________ protecting the environment.

A. in spite of B. in honor of C. in favor of D. in the name of

正确答案：D。

解析：in spite of：虽然，尽管；in honor of：为了向……表示敬意；in favor of：支持，赞成；in the name of：以……的名义。

30. After a three-hour heated discussion, all the members in the jury reached the conclusions that the man was ________ of murder.

A. criminal　B. charged　C. guilty　D. faulty

正确答案：C。

解析：criminal：可耻的，不道德的；charged：控告，控诉；guilty：有罪的，通常与 of 搭配；faulty：有缺点的，有毛病的。

31. Having finished the letter, he ________ it carefully and sealed the envelop with a kiss.

A. folded　B. bent　C. turned　D. curved

正确答案：A。

解析：fold：折，折叠；bend：弯曲，弯腰；turn：翻，转；curve：使弯成弧形，使弄弯。

34. Just as a married man cannot leave his work, a poor man cannot ________ to get sick.

A. have　B. go　C. expect　D. afford

正确答案：D。

解析：can/could not afford 是习惯搭配，意思是"负担不起，承担不起"。

35. ________, we keep records on all the experiments so that we may have enough data.

A. As a whole　B. As a rule　C. On the average　D. By all means

正确答案：B。

解析：as a whole：总体来看，整体来看；as a rule：通常情况下，一般来说；on the average：平均地，一般地说；by all means：一定，务必。

36. Nobody but a young woman ________ the airplane crash.

A. endured　B. rejected　C. survived　D. lived

正确答案：C。

解析：endure：持续，忍受；reject：拒绝，谢绝；survive：幸存，活下来；live：生活，居住。

37. Professor Smith is always very ________ to the reaction of the audience when he gives lectures.

A. sentimental　B. sensitive　C. sensible　D. positive

正确答案：B。

解析：sentimental：伤感的，多愁善感的；sensitive：敏感的，灵敏的，通常与 of 或 to 搭配；sensible：明智的，理智的；positive：积极的，肯定的。

41. His few personal belongings made it possible for him to move from place to place ________.

A. in ease　B. at ease　C. with ease　D. with easiness

正确答案：C。

解析：in ease 搭配不当；at ease：安逸，自由自在；with ease：不费力地，轻而易举地；with easiness 搭配不当。

Unit 6

23. The teacher asked his students to leave enough ________ on the page for correction.

A. room　B. margin　C. place　D. paper

正确答案：B。

解析：room：空间，地方；margin：页边空白，页边线；place：地方，场所；paper：纸，纸张。

30. What may happen to you, if you ________ in your school work?

A. fall down B. fall apart C. fall off D. fall behind

正确答案：D。

解析：fall down：倒塌，跌倒；fall apart：散开，崩溃；fall off：跌落，滚落；fall behind：落后，跟不上。

31. She was ________ the top prize in the competition.

A. awarded B. rewarded C. received D. accepted

正确答案：A。

解析：award：授给，奖给；reward：酬谢，奖赏；receive：得到，获得；accept：接受，认可。

32. They have ________ many horrible crimes against the people.

A. done B. made C. committed D. had

正确答案：C。

解析：commit crime 是习惯搭配，意思是"犯罪"。

34. His failure to pay the debts ________ the suspicion that he was not to be trusted.

A. concerns B. confesses C. confuses D. confirms

正确答案：D。

解析：concern：关心，考虑；confess：承认，供认；confuse：混淆，弄混；confirm：证明，表明。

35. Having heard so much about Mr. Smith, they were ________ to meet and have a chat with him.

A. eager B. desperate C. urgent D. earnest

正确答案：A。

解析：eager：渴望的，希望的，通常与 to 搭配；desperate：不顾一切的，孤注一掷的；urgent：急迫的，紧迫的；earnest：郑重其事的，非常认真的。

36. We were deeply impressed by her important ________ to the success of the project.

A. work B. determination C. improvement D. contribution

正确答案：D。

解析：work：工作，劳动；determination：决心，决定；improvement：改善，改进；contribution：贡献，所起的作用。

37. I'd like to take ________ of this opportunity to thank you for your co-operation.

A. advantage B. occasion C. benefit D. profit

正确答案：A。

解析：take advantage of 是习惯搭配，意思是"利用"。

40. Bill doesn't ________ what people say about him.

A. concern B. matter C. care D. disturb

正确答案：C。

解析：concern：关心，认为有趣；matter：要紧，有关系；care：密切关注，审慎考虑；disturb：打搅，妨碍。

41. Mr. Wilson said that he did not want to ________ any further responsibilities.

A. take on B. get on C. put up D. look up

正确答案：A。

解析：take on：承担，承受；get on：继续，上车；put up：张贴，搭起；look up：仰望，查找。

47. The new English dictionary I bought yesterday ________ me almost twenty yuan.

A. spent　B. paid　C. cost　D. took

正确答案：C。

解析：spend 和 pay 的主语通常是人；cost 的主语是物；take 通常与 it 搭配。

49. They discussed the problem three or four times, but could come to no ________.

A. end　B. conclusion　C. result　D. judgment

正确答案：B。

解析：come to a/no conclusion 是习惯搭配，意思是"得出结论/没有得出结论"。

50. She is very careful. She ________ very few mistakes in her work.

A. does　B. takes　C. makes　D. gets

正确答案：C。

解析：make mistakes 是习惯搭配，意思是"犯错误"。

52. I'd like to ________ a special table for the coming Valentine's Day.

A. preserve　B. deserve　C. conserve　D. reserve

正确答案：D。

解析：preserve：保护，维持；deserve：应得，应受；conserve：保护，保存；reserve：预定，预留。

57. It ________ me as an uphill battle, simply because it is an awkward and time-consuming process.

A. appears　B. occurs　C. strikes　D. hits

正确答案：C。

解析：It strikes me that 是习惯句型，意思是"我觉得……，我的印象是……"。

60. I believe you have ________ some important points in the report.

A. left alone　B. left behind　C. left off　D. left out

正确答案：D。

解析：leave alone：不理，不管；leave behind：留下，丢弃；leave off：停止做，戒掉；leave out：遗漏，忽略。

Unit 7

16. Today books are ________ to everyone because they are no longer expensive.

A. available　B. preferable　C. reliable　D. actual

正确答案：A。

解析：available：能得到的，可获得的；preferable：更好的，更可取的；reliable：可靠的，可信赖的；actual：实际的，真实的。

18. The forest fire caused by the volcano is difficult to be ________.

A. put off　B. put away　C. put out　D. put up

正确答案：C。

解析：put off：推迟，延期；put away：收起来，放好；put out：扑灭，熄灭；put up：建造，搭起。

21. Robots have already ________ human tasks in the industrial field.

A. taken on B. taken out C. taken up D. taken over

正确答案：D。

解析：take on：呈现，雇用；take out：拿出，清除；take up：拿起，占去；take over：接替，接管。

23. He took the medicine, but it didn't have any ________.

A. answer B. cause C. effect D. work

正确答案：C。

解析：have effect 是习惯搭配，意思是“见效，开始发生作用”。

24. It is ________ that over one million Americans now live below the poverty line.

A. judged B. estimated C. calculated D. considered

正确答案：B。

解析：judge：判断，断定；estimate：估计，评估；calculate：计算，估算；consider：考虑，认为。

26. When there are small children around, it is necessary to put bottles of pills out of ________.

A. hand B. hold C. place D. reach

正确答案：D。

解析：out of hand：无法控制，失控；out of hold 搭配不当；out of place：不合适，不在适当的位置；out of reach：手够不着，达不到。

27. I hadn't seen him for years, but I ________ his voice on the telephone.

A. realized B. discovered C. recognized D. heard

正确答案：C。

解析：realize：认识到，了解；discover：发现，发觉；recognize：辨别出，识别出；hear：听到，听见。

28. This place, originally a small town, has been ________ into a modern city.

A. transported B. transferred C. transmitted D. transformed

正确答案：D。

解析：transport：运送，运输；transfer：转移，迁移；transmit：发射，播送；transform：改变，转变。

29. There was nobody ________ when we came round the corner.

A. out of sight B. at sight C. by sight D. in sight

正确答案：D。

解析：out of sight：看不见，在视野之外；at sight：一看到就；by sight 搭配不当；in sight：被看到，在视线之内。

31. They couldn't ________ him of his mistake.

A. advise B. convince C. persuade D. believe

正确答案：B。

解析：convince somebody of something 是习惯搭配，意思是“使某人相信、认识到某事”。

43. Since you won't take advice, there is no ________ in asking for it.

A. place B. point C. reason D. way

正确答案：B。

解析：there is no point in doing 是习惯句型，意思是“做……没有意义”。

Unit 8

20. Over ten people died and twenty people were ________ wounded in the train crash.

A. horribly　B. wrongly　C. bitterly　D. seriously

正确答案：D。

解析：horribly：可怕地，非常；wrongly：错误地，不正确地；bitterly：不痛快地，悲苦地；seriously：严重地，危险地。

21. Do you think Tommy is ________ the truth

A. saying　B. speaking　C. telling　D. talking

正确答案：C。

解析：tell the truth 是习惯搭配，意思是“说实话”。

22. It is so hot. You should put the food into the refrigerator now. Otherwise, it will ________ soon.

A. harm　B. hurt　C. spoil　D. damage

正确答案：C。

解析：harm：伤害，损害；hurt：伤害，使受伤；spoil：食物变质，腐烂；damage：损害，伤害。

24. It is important to remember the saying that ________ is better than cure.

A. prevention　B. promotion　C. permission　D. proportion

正确答案：A。

解析：prevention：预防，防止；promotion：促进，推销；permission：允许，许可；proportion：比例，均衡。

25. Winning or losing is temporary, but friendship ________.

A. expects　B. lives　C. remains　D. lasts

正确答案：D。

解析：expect：预期，期望；live：生活，居住；remain：保持，保留；last：延续，持续。

26. Peter, whom everyone suspected, ________ to be innocent.

A. turned out　B. turned off　C. turned up　D. turned over

正确答案：A。

解析：turn out to be 是习惯搭配，意思是“结果是，被证明是”。

28. So ________ is the weather in England that by lunchtime there could be thunder and lightening.

A. various　B. varies　C. variable　D. variation

正确答案：C。

解析：various：各种各样的，不同的；vary：变化，改变；variable：易变的，多变的；variation：变更，变异。

39. The shortage of energy is getting worse. It ________ an immediate solution.

A. calls off　B. calls up　C. calls for　D. calls at

正确答案：C。

解析：call off：取消，停止；call up：叫醒，打电话；call for：需要，要求；call at：拜访，停留。

40. The teacher spoke so fast that it was hard for the students to ________ what he was saying.

A. take in　B. take out　C. take up　D. take over

正确答案：A。

解析：take in：领会，理解；take out：拿出，取出；take up：拿起，占去；take over：接替，接管。

Unit 9

27. I believe that every crime, ________ the circumstance, should be severely punished.

A. in spite of　　B. because of　　C. instead of　　D. on account of

正确答案：A。

解析：in spite of：不管，尽管；because of：因为，由于；instead of：而不是，代替；on account of：由于，因为。

29. Yesterday Mr. Smith gave a vivid ________ of his recent visit to China.

A. dialogue　　B. idea　　C. tale　　D. account

正确答案：D。

解析：give an account of 是习惯搭配，意思是"描述……，说明……"。

36. The bridge was named ________ the hero who gave his life for the cause of the people.

A. after　　B. for　　C. because of　　D. before

正确答案：A。

解析：name after 是习惯搭配，意思是"以……来命名"。

37. There was a large crowd in the square ________ against the war.

A. protecting　　B. protesting　　C. preventing　　D. promoting

正确答案：B。

解析：protect：保护，保卫：protest：反对，抗议，通常与 against 搭配；prevent：防止：promote：促进，提高。

38. We have ________ to the government for a home improvement loan.

A. arranged　　B. approached　　C. applied　　D. appointed

正确答案：C。

解析：apply to 是习惯搭配，意思是"申请，要求"。

39. Tom ________ the shopkeeper with overcharging him for the articles he had bought.

A. accused　　B. charged　　C. blamed　　D. criticized

正确答案：C。

解析：accuse：指责，控告，通常与 of 搭配；charge：控告，控诉，通常与 with 搭配；blame：指责，责备，通常与 for 搭配；criticize：批评，批判，通常与 for 搭配。

40. The idea sounds very good but will it work in ________?

A. practice　　B. place　　C. advance　　D. company

正确答案：A。

解析：in practice：在实践中，在实际中；in place：在适当的位置，合适的；in advance：预先，事先；in company 搭配不当。

Unit 10

16. History is a record of mankind; different historians, ________, interpret it differently.

A. therefore　　B. on the contrary　　C. however　　D. consequently

正确答案：C。

解析：therefore：因此，所以；on the contrary：与此相反，正相反；however：然而，不过；consequently：因此，所以。

18. Before the child went to bed, the father asked him to ________ all the toys he had taken out.

A. put off B. put up C. put away D. put out

正确答案：C。

解析：put off：推迟，延期；put up：举起，搭起；put away：收起来，放好；put out：扑灭，熄灭。

28. Women all over the world are ________ equal pay for equal jobs.

A. calling on B. calling about C. calling off D. calling for

正确答案：A。

解析：call on：要求，号召；call about：找某人谈某事；call off：取消，停止；call for：使必要，需要。

31. The children lined up and walked out ________.

A. in place B. in condition C. in order D. in private

正确答案：C。

解析：in place：在适当的位置，合适的；in condition：健康，在可使用的状况；in order：按顺序，按次序；in private：私下地，私底下。

36. The little boy saw the plane ________ and burst into flames.

A. complete B. compel C. crash D. clutch

正确答案：C。

解析：complete：完成，结束；compel：强迫；crash：坠毁，撞毁；clutch：抓住，掌握。

38. From her conversation, I ________ that she had a large family.

A. deduced B. decided C. declared D. deceived

正确答案：A。

解析：deduce：推论，推断；decide：决定，决心；declare：宣布；deceive：欺骗，蒙骗。

39. This question is too hard, it is ________ my comprehension.

A. below B. beyond C. over D. without

正确答案：B。

解析：beyond one's comprehension 是习惯搭配，意思是"超出某人的理解力"。

40. In order to buy her house she had to obtain a ________ from the bank.

A. finance B. capital C. loan D. debt

正确答案：C。

解析：finance：财务，资金；capital：资本，资金；loan：贷款，借款；debt：债，债务。

43. You two have got a lot ________.

A. in general B. in common C. in all D. in any case

正确答案：B。

解析：get/have something in common 是习惯搭配，意思是"有共同的……"。

Unit 11

25. Take the medicine now. I believe it will ________ your pain.

A. release B. relive C. reject D. relieve

正确答案：D。

解析：release：释放，排放；relive：重过，再经历；reject：拒绝，谢绝；relieve：缓解，消除。

29. Each term our professors would ________ a list of books for us to read.

A. hand in B. give away C. pass out D. write out

正确答案：D。

解析：hand in：上交，呈送；give away：赠送，泄露；pass out：分配，分发；write out：写出。

31. I believe you have ________ your purse in the living-room.

A. left alone B. left behind C. left off D. left out

正确答案：B。

解析：leave alone：不管，不理；leave behind：忘带，留下；leave off：停止做，戒掉；leave out：遗漏，省略。

32. The results of the survey are interesting and they ________ more questions than they can answer.

A. bring about B. prohibit C. project D. benefit from

正确答案：A。

解析：bring about：带来，引发；prohibit：禁止，阻止；project：计划，投射；benefit from：得益于，受益于。

43. They have agreed that they will ________ to the policy and will not change it.

A. commit B. stick C. combine D. fall

正确答案：B。

解析：commit to：委托，托付；stick to：坚持，遵守；combine 和 fall 一般不与 to 搭配。

44. The company has to ________ the benefits against the costs in the last three months.

A. boast B. blame C. block D. balance

正确答案：D。

解析：boast：吹嘘，自夸；blame：指责，责备；block：阻碍，妨碍；balance：抵消，抵偿，通常与against 搭配。

45. We've ________ paper and ink. Ask Mrs. Edward to lend us some.

A. run away with B. run out of C. run off D. run down

正确答案：B。

解析：run away with：与……私奔；run out of：用完，耗光；run off：减轻体重，使流掉；run down：停止；诽谤。

Unit 12

20. The monitor ________ the examination papers to the class for his teacher.

A. delivered B. distributed C. reported D. presented

正确答案：B。

解析：deliver：递送，交付：distribute：分发，分给；report：报告，报道；present：赠与。

22. The children looked up as the planes passed ________.

A. overall　B. overhead　C. outward　D. forward

正确答案：B。

解析：overall：整体的，全部的；overhead：在头上，在空中；outward：外面的，表面的；forward：向前，前进。

23. Charles Dickens ________ many wonderful characters in his novels.

A. invented　B. discovered　C. uncovered　D. created

正确答案：D。

解析：invent：发明，创造；discover：发现，碰见；uncover：揭露，揭示；create：创作，创造。

24. Many young people find it harder to appreciate ________ music than pop music.

A. simple　B. light　C. ancient　D. classical

正确答案：D。

解析：light music：轻音乐；classical music：古典音乐。

25. If the wounded soldier had been given first ________, he would not have died.

A. help　B. aid　C. care　D. attention

正确答案：B。

解析：first aid 是固定搭配，意思是"急救"。

30. We all believe that it'd be hard for him to ________ extra responsibilities now.

A. take apart　B. take up　C. take on　D. take back

正确答案：C。

解析：take apart：拆开，拆卸；take up：拿起，占去；take on：承担，承受；take back：收回，使回忆起。

35. Since there isn't much time left, you can just tell us about it ________.

A. in detail　B. in short　C. in all　D. in brief

正确答案：D。

解析：in detail：详细地，详尽地；in short：简而言之，总之；in all：总计，总共；in brief：简单地，简明扼要地。

39. I don't think it appropriate to ________ such an issue at the meeting.

A. bring in　B. bring off　C. bring up　D. bring about

正确答案：A。

解析：bring in：提出，引入；bring off：使脱离险境，成功完成；bring up：教育，培养；bring about：造成，引起。

Unit 13

31. As Christmas was coming, the town began a ________ clearing on a large scale.

A. through　B. thorough　C. though　D. thought

正确答案：B。

解析：through：通过，凭借；thorough：彻底的，全面的；though：尽管，但是；thought：思想，想法。

33. It is a good idea for parents to monitor the ________ as well as the kind of television that their children watch.

A. number B. size C. amount D. screen

正确答案:C。

解析:number:数目,数量,通常接可数名词;size:尺寸,大小;amount:数量,数额,通常接不可数名词;screen:银屏,屏幕。

34. I'm afraid that there isn't ________ for you in my car.

A. place B. seat C. corner D. room

正确答案:D。

解析:place:地方,场所;seat:座位,席位;corner:角,角落;room:空间,地方。

35. It suddenly ________ to me that we could use a computer to do the job.

A. happened B. occurred C. agreed D. presented

正确答案:B。

解析:It occurs/occurred to somebody that 是习惯句型,意思是"……浮现在某人的脑海中,……被某人想到"。

36. The old people often raise ________ for the sake of companionship.

A. pets B. pipes C. pills D. pies

正确答案:A。

解析:pet:宠物;pipe:管道,管子;pill:药,药物;pie:饼。

37. The river here is very wide but ________, so you can walk across it.

A. narrow B. arrow C. shallow D. hollow

正确答案:C。

解析:narrow:狭窄的,狭小的;arrow:箭,箭状物;shallow:浅的,不深的;hollow:空的,空洞的。

38. The streets were empty ________ the policemen on duty.

A. besides B. except C. excepting D. except for

正确答案:D。

解析:besides:除了……外还有;except:除了,表示不包括在内;excepting:通常用于句首或 always, not, without 等后面,表示"除了",不包括在内;except for:除了,包括在内。

39. Don't leave matches or cigarettes on the table within the ________ of little children.

A. hand B. reach C. space D. distance

正确答案:B。

解析:within the reach of 是习惯搭配,意思是"伸手可及"。

44. I'm putting on weight. The doctor has warned me to ________ sugar.

A. keep up B. keep back C. keep off D. keep away

正确答案:C。

解析:keep up:保养,维持;keep back:隐瞒,扣留;keep off:禁食,不接近;keep away:不接近,缺席。

45. We were ________ for half an hour in the traffic and so we arrived late.

A. kept up B. held up C. cut up D. brought up

正确答案:B。

解析:keep up:保养,维持;hold up:耽搁,使停顿;cut up:切碎,切割;bring up:抚养,培养。

Unit 14

20. With oil prices keeping ________, people are hesitating whether to buy a car or not.

A. rising　B. arising　C. raising　D. arousing

正确答案：A。

解析：rise：上升，上涨；arise：出现，发生；raise：增加，提升；arouse：唤醒，激起。

22. We were very disappointed at the ________ to our advertisement, and our products didn't sell well.

A. replies　B. response　C. answers　D. words

正确答案：B。

解析：reply to：答复，回答；response to：反应，回应；answer to：……的答案；word 一般不与 to 搭配。

28. She is very ________ to ring me tonight. I can sense that.

A. liable　B. possible　C. likely　D. likeable

正确答案：C。

解析：liable to：易于……的，有……倾向的；possible：可能的，可能发生的，一般不与 to 搭配；likely to：可能的，有可能的；likeable 不与 to 搭配。

29. Small talk is a good way to kill time, make friends and ________ something with others.

A. argue　B. replace　C. share　D. match

正确答案：C。

解析：argue with：与……人争论、争吵；replace with：用……代替、替代；share with：与……分享、共享；match with：与……匹配。

30. Some people like drinking coffee, for it has ________ effects.

A. promoting　B. stimulating　C. enhancing　D. encouraging

正确答案：B。

解析：promoting：促进，提升；stimulating：刺激的，有刺激性的；enhancing：提高，增强；encouraging：鼓舞的，鼓励的。

38. The president spoke at the business meeting for nearly an hour without ________ his notes.

A. bringing up　B. referring to　C. looking for　D. trying on

正确答案：B。

解析：bring up：抚养；refer to：提及，涉及，参考，查阅；look for：寻找，寻求；try on：试穿，哄骗。

39. It is certain that he will ________ his business to his son when he gets old.

A. take over　B. think over　C. hand over　D. go over

正确答案：C。

解析：take over：接管，接替；think over：认真考虑，仔细考虑；hand over：让与，移交；go over：检查，考虑。

41. When climbing the hill, John was knocked unconscious by an ________ rolling stone.

A. untouched　B. unfamiliar　C. unexpected　D. unbelievable

正确答案：C。

解析：untouched：未触及的，原样的；unfamiliar：不熟悉的，陌生的；unexpected：没有想到的，意外的；unbelievable：不可信的，难以置信的。

42. Her brother ________ to leave her in the dark room alone when she disobeyed his order.

A. declared B. threatened C. warned D. exclaimed

正确答案：B。

解析：declare：宣布；threaten：威胁，恐吓；warn：警告，告诫；exclaim：呼喊，惊叫。

43. Alice trusts you. Only you can ________ her to give up the foolish idea.

A. suggest B. attract C. tempt D. persuade

正确答案：D。

解析：suggest：建议；attract：吸引，引起；tempt：引诱，诱惑；persuade：说服，劝告。

44. A man is being questioned in relation to the ________ murder.

A. advised B. attended C. attempted D. admired

正确答案：C。

解析：attempted murder 是习惯搭配，意思是“谋杀未遂”。

45. Modern plastics can ________ very high and very low temperatures.

A. stand B. hold C. carry D. support

正确答案：A。

解析：stand：忍受，经得起；hold：保持，把握；carry：携带，运输；support：支持，支撑。

Unit 15

16. When I mention the problem, I'm not ________ all of you.

A. talking about B. referring to C. listening to D. carrying out

正确答案：B。

解析：talk about：谈论，讨论；refer to：针对，有关；listen to：听；carry out：实施，贯彻。

17. Your idea seems to be good but it isn't ________.

A. practical B. possible C. plentiful D. precious

正确答案：A。

解析：practical：实用的，实际的；possible：可能的，潜在的；plentiful：丰富的，大量的；precious：珍贵的，宝贵的。

19. “Which do you want, the red one or the black one?”

“________. How about showing me another?”

A. Either B. Both C. Neither D. None

正确答案：C。

解析：either：两者之一；both：两个都；neither：两个都不；none：(三个以上)都不。

23. I hope the stove will ________ enough heat to warm the room.

A. get over B. give in C. get out D. give off

正确答案：D。

解析：get over：克制；give in：投降，让步；get out：出来，走开；give off：发出，放出。

26. Wait a moment, please. Richard will be back ________.

A. in no time B. at no time C. at times D. at a time

正确答案：A。

解析：in no time：立刻，马上；at no time：绝不，决不；at times：有时，间或；at a time：依次，逐一。

31. Alice trusts you；only you can ________ her to give up the foolish idea.

A. suggest　　B. attract　　C. tempt　　D. persuade

正确答案：D。

解析：suggest：建议；attract：吸引，引起；tempt：引诱，诱惑；persuade：说服，劝告。

33. He is a man who is always ________ fault with other people.

A. putting　　B. seeking　　C. finding　　D. looking for

正确答案：C。

解析：find fault with 是习惯搭配，意思是"找……的岔子，对……吹毛求疵"。

34. I am sure David will be able to find the library because he has a pretty good ________ of direction.

A. idea　　B. feeling　　C. experience　　D. sense

正确答案：D。

解析：have a sense of 是习惯搭配，意思是"有……感"。

35. They started off late and got to the airport with minutes to ________.

A. spare　　B. catch　　C. leave　　D. make

正确答案：A。

解析：to spare 是习惯搭配，意思是"剩下"。

36. The evening news comes on at seven o'clock and ________ only thirty minutes.

A. keeps　　B. continues　　C. finishes　　D. lasts

正确答案：D。

解析：keep：保留，保存；continue：继续，延续，后面一般不接时间；finish：完成，结束；last：持续，延续。

37. The factory had to ________ a number of employees because of the economic crisis in the country.

A. lay out　　B. lay off　　C. lay aside　　D. lay down

正确答案：B。

解析：lay out：设计，展开；lay off：暂时解雇；lay aside：积蓄；lay down：放下，规定。

38. People may have different opinions about Karen，but I admire her. ________，she is a great musician.

A. After all　　B. As a result　　C. In other words　　D. As usual

正确答案：A。

解析：after all：毕竟，究竟；as a result：结果，因此；in other words：换句话说，换言之；as usual：像往常一样。

Unit 16

17. The factory had to ________ a number of employees because of the economic decline in the country.

A. lay out　　B. lay off　　C. lay aside　　D. lay down

正确答案：B。

解析：lay out：设计，展开；lay off：暂时解雇；lay aside：留出；lay down：放下，规定。

18. His parents ________ his money, so he is in trouble now.

A. cut off B. cut through C. gave up D. brought down

正确答案：A。

解析：cut off：切断，削减；cut through：穿过，挤进；give up：放弃，认输；bring down：击败，使降低。

19. Can you ________ the difference ________ the two phrases?

A. tell, between B. speak, from C. say, of D. talk, between

正确答案：A。

解析：tell the difference between 是习惯搭配，意思是"辨别……之间的区别"。

20. If anyone happens to drop in while I am out, ________ him or her leave a message.

A. have B. get C. ask D. tell

正确答案：A。

解析：have someone do something 是习惯搭配，意思是"要求某人做某事"。

22. I ________ the boy to save money, but he wouldn't listen.

A. hoped B. suggested C. wanted D. made

正确答案：B。

解析：hope：希望，后面一般不接动词不定式；suggest：建议，提议；want：希望，想；make 后面接人时不接 to+动词原形。

23. I made a call to my parents yesterday. To my disappointment, ________ of them answered it.

A. either B. none C. neither D. nobody

正确答案：C。

解析：either：两者之一；none：(三个以上)都不；neither：两个都不；nobody：没有人。

25. The idea ________ to him in his dream and he decided to carry it out.

A. happened B. struck C. appeared D. occurred

正确答案：D。

解析：something occurs/occurred to somebody 是习惯搭配，意思是"……浮现在某人的脑海中，……被某人想到"。

31. It is no ________ talking to him; because he will never change his mind.

A. help B. use C. time D. way

正确答案：B。

解析：It is no use doing something 是习惯搭配，意思是"做……没有用"。

40. Don't worry me now. I will mend that coat ________.

A. by and by B. off and on C. back and forth D. now and then

正确答案：A。

解析：by and by：不久，马上；off and on：断断续续，有时；back and forth：来回地；now and then：有时，时而。

41. Please join us. We can easily make ________ for one more at this table.

A. seat B. place C. room D. space

正确答案：C。

解析：make room for 是习惯搭配，意思是“给……让出空间”。

45. Encouragement is sometimes much more ________ than criticism.

A. effective　B. efficient　C. executive　D. extensive

正确答案：A。

解析：effective：有效的，有用的；efficient：有能力的，效率高的；executive：执行的，行政的；extensive：广泛的，大量的。

Unit 17

16. Don't be too ________ about things you are not supposed to know.

A. strange　B. amusing　C. curious　D. conscious

正确答案：C。

解析：curious about 是习惯搭配，意思是“对……感到好奇”。

22. For the sake of her daughter's health, she decided to move to a warm ________.

A. weather　B. temperature　C. season　D. climate

正确答案：D。

解析：weather：天气；temperature：温度，气温；season：季节，季；climate：气候，天气。

23. Be careful when you cross this very busy street. If not, you may get ________ by a car.

A. run out　B. run over　C. run away　D. run after

正确答案：B。

解析：run out：用光，耗尽；run over：撞翻并从身上扎过，撞到；run away：逃跑，跑掉；run after：追赶，追求。

26. —You seem to show interest in cooking.

—What? ________, I'm getting tired of it.

A. On the contrary　B. To the contrary

C. On the other hand　D. To the other hand

正确答案：A。

解析：on the contrary：与之相反，正相反；to the contrary：相反的，有相反情况的；on the other hand：另一方面；to the other hand 搭配不当。

28. Time will ________ whether I made the right choice or not.

A. see　B. say　C. tell　D. know

正确答案：C。

解析：see：看见，看到；say：说，讲；tell：表明，显示；know：知道，了解。

30. It suddenly ________ to me how we could improve the situation.

A. occurred　B. feared　C. shook　D. struck

正确答案：A。

解析：something occurs/occurred to somebody 是习惯搭配，意思是“……浮现在某人的脑海中，……被某人想到”。

35. We stayed for the night at the foot of the mountain and ________ to climb it the next morning.

A. set about　B. set off　C. set up　D. set out

正确答案：D。

解析：set about：开始做，攻击；set off：出发，动身；set up：创立；set out：打算，计划。

37. "to put off something" means "to ________".

A. look for it　B. put it in place　C. postpone it　D. cancel it

正确答案：C。

解析：look for it：寻找……；put it in place：把……放在适当的位置；postpone it：推迟……；cancel it：取消……。

40. Some drivers always drive carelessly. There is some ________ danger while they are driving.

A. painful　B. potential　C. probable　D. primary

正确答案：B。

解析：painful：痛苦的，棘手的；potential：潜在的，可能的；probable：可能的，或有的；primary：首要的，基本的。

42. Can you ________ the three mistakes in this paragraph?

A. turn out　B. bring out　C. call out　D. pick out

正确答案：D。

解析：turn out：制造，培养；bring out：取出，出版；call out：调来，召集；pick out：挑出。

Unit 18

21. After 15 years in the United States, he has finally decided to ________ American citizenship.

A. concentrate on　B. apply for　C. look out for　D. appeal on

正确答案：B。

解析：concentrate on：关注于，集中于；apply for：申请，要求；look out for：搜寻，试图得到；appeal on：呼吁，恳求。

22. It is well known that teaching is a job ________ enough patience.

A. calling on　B. calling off　C. calling for　D. calling in

正确答案：C。

解析：call on：拜访，号召；call off：取消，停止；call for：需要，要求；call in：请来，来访。

23. Surely it doesn't matter where the clubs get their money; what ________ is what they do with it.

A. counts　B. applies　C. stresses　D. functions

正确答案：A。

解析：count：有价值，有意义；apply：应用，申请；stress：强调，重读；function：运行，起作用。

25. It doesn't make ________ to buy that expensive coat when these cheaper ones are just as good.

A. sense　B. opinion　C. use　D. program

正确答案：A。

解析：make sense 是习惯搭配，意思是"有意义"。

26. The task is too much for me, so I can't carry on ________ any longer. I must get some help.

A. singly　B. simply　C. alone　D. lonely

正确答案：C。

解析：singly：单个地，单身地；simply：简单地，简易地；alone：单独地，独自地；lonely：孤独的，寂寞的。

30. Without my glasses I can hardly ________ what has been written in the letter.

A. make for　B. make up　C. make out　D. make over

正确答案：C。

解析：make for：走向，前往；make up：编造，弥补；make out：辨认出，辨别出；make over：转让，移交。

31. Her heart ________ faster when she entered the exam hall.

A. jumped　B. sank　C. beat　D. hit

正确答案：C。

解析：jump：跳，跳跃；sink：下沉，沉下；beat：(心脏)跳动；hit：打，击打。

32. Would you mind keeping a(n) ________ on the house for us while we are away?

A. eye　B. look　C. hand　D. view

正确答案：A。

解析：keep an eye on 是习惯搭配，意思是“照看，看管”。

33. I am afraid that his phone number has slipped my ________ for the moment.

A. head　B. brain　C. mind　D. sense

正确答案：C。

解析：slip one's mind 是习惯搭配，意思是“忘了”。

34. It was the wealth of the ________ pioneer landowner John Harvard that made Harvard University possible.

A. precious　B. curious　C. anxious　D. prosperous

正确答案：D。

解析：precious：宝贵的，珍贵的；curious：好奇的，有求知欲的；anxious：焦急的，忧虑的；prosperous：成功的，富足的。

35. I am not sure whether we can give the right advice ________ emergency.

A. on account of　B. in case of　C. at the risk of　D. in spite of

正确答案：B。

解析：on account of：由于，因为；in case of：万一，以防；at the risk of：冒……的风险；in spite of：不管，尽管。

36. Vingo was released from prison ________ the successful efforts of his friends to prove his innocence.

A. according to　B. as a result of　C. for reasons of　D. with the help of

正确答案：B。

解析：according to：根据，按照；as a result of：由于……的结果，由于……的缘故；for reasons of：因为，由于；with the help of：在……的帮助下，借助于……。

Unit 19

18. This magazine is very ________ with young people, who like its content and style.

A. familiar　B. popular　C. similar　D. particular

正确答案：B。

解析：要填的词应该与后面的 with 搭配。familiar with：熟悉……；popular with：受到……的欢迎、好评；similar 和 particular 不与 with 搭配。

19. The art show was ________ being a failure; it was a great success.

A. far from　B. along with　C. second to　D. regardless of

正确答案：A。

解析：far from：远非；along with：除……之外；second to：紧次于；regardless of：不管，不顾。

20. Health problems are closely connected with bad eating habits and a ________ of exercise.

A. limit　B. lack　C. need　D. demand

正确答案：B。

解析：要填的词应该与 a...of 搭配。a limit of：一种……限制；a lack of：缺乏……；need 和 demand 一般不与 a...of 搭配。

21. In our daily life, everyone fails every now and then. It is how you react that makes a ________.

A. development　B. difference　C. progress　D. point

正确答案：B。

解析：make a difference 是固定搭配，意思是“有区别，有意义，紧要”。

23. Don't worry if you can't understand everything. The teacher will ________ the main points at the end.

A. recover　B. review　C. require　D. remember

正确答案：B。

解析：recover：恢复；review：回顾；require：需要；remember：记住。

24. It is reported that the police will soon look ________ the case of the two missing children.

A. upon　B. after　C. into　D. out

正确答案：C。

解析：look upon：显得不错；look after：照顾；look into：调查；look out：当心。

25. One of the best ways for people to keep fit is to ________ healthy eating habits.

A. grow　B. develop　C. increase　D. raise

正确答案：B。

解析：grow：发展；develop：培养，形成；increase：增加；raise：提高。

26. The company is starting a new advertising campaign to ________ new customers to its stores.

A. join　B. attract　C. stick　D. transfer

正确答案：B。

解析：join：加入；attract：吸引；stick：刺入；transfer：转移。

32. The college sports meet was ________ till next week because of the heavy rain.

A. put out　B. put on　C. put off　D. put up

正确答案：C。

解析：put out：扑灭；put on：穿上；put off：推迟；put up：张贴。

35. That big dictionary ________ Tom two hundred dollars.

A. spent　　B. paid　　C. cost　　D. took

正确答案：C。

解析：物体作主语，表示花费某人多少时间或金钱时，应该用 cost；spend 和 pay 的主语通常是人。

41. I was so tired then that I fell ________ in class.

A. asleep　　B. sleep　　C. sleeping　　D. slept

正确答案：A。

解析：fall asleep 是固定搭配，意思是“入睡，睡着”。

43. Given the choice between work and play, Tom would surely prefer the ________.

A. late　　B. later　　C. latter　　D. last

正确答案：C。

解析：指后者时应该用 the latter。

44. He began to work for a big company ________ an early age.

A. on　　B. at　　C. of　　D. with

正确答案：B。

解析：at... age 是习惯搭配，意思是“在……年龄时”。

Unit 20

16. It was hard for him to learn English in a family, in which ________ of the parents spoke the language.

A. none　　B. neither　　C. both　　D. each

正确答案：B。

解析：none 表示三者以上的都不；neither 表示两者都不；both 表示两者都。

18. This new machine is technically far ________ to the previous type.

A. superior　　B. junior　　C. senior　　D. equal

正确答案：A。

解析：要填的词应该与后面的 to 搭配。B 和 C 不与 to 搭配；superior to：优于……；equal to：与……相等。

20. She became the first woman to enter the school but withdrew after a few days ________ stress.

A. because of　　B. in spite of　　C. instead of　　D. in honor of

正确答案：A。

解析：because of：由于……；in spite of：尽管……；instead of：而不是；in honor of：为了对……表示敬意。

22. The discovery of these tombs is ________ for scholars' studying Chinese history.

A. of very important　　B. great significant

C. of great significance　　D. greatly importance

正确答案：C。

解析：of＋名词＝该名词的形容词意思。

23. Sean's strong love for his country is ________ in his recently published poems.

A. relieved　　B. reflected　　C. responded　　D. recovered

正确答案：B。

解析：relieve：解除；reflect：反映；respond：回答；recover：恢复。

25. The teacher stressed again that the students should not ________ any important details while retelling the story.

A. bring out B. let out C. leave out D. make out

正确答案：C。

解析：bring out：拿出，显示；let out：放出，释放；leave out：遗漏，省略；make out：拼凑，完成。

26. The man moved ________ forward and looked over the edge, shrinking his shoulders.

A. accurately B. cautiously C. brilliantly D. disappointedly

正确答案：B。

解析：accurately：正确地；cautiously：小心谨慎地；brilliantly：灿烂地；disappointedly：失望地。

27. The police are trying to find out the ________ of the woman, killed in the traffic accident.

A. evidence B. recognition C. identity D. status

正确答案：C。

解析：evidence：证据；recognition：识别；identity：身份；status：地位。

29. Climate change will greatly ________ wheat and rice production if nations don't take steps now.

A. fall B. leak C. lack D. reduce

正确答案：D。

解析：fall：落下；leak：泄露；lack：缺少；reduce：降低。

30. She always buys ________ my birthday.

A. something awful to B. anything awful to

C. something nice for D. anything nice for

正确答案：C。

解析："为……买东西"应该是 buy……for……，所以 A 和 B 不对；本句话是肯定句，不能用 anything，所以 D 也不对。

32. It is very ________ of you to arrange an early meeting between your boss and our team.

A. considerate B. considerable C. considering D. considered

正确答案：A。

解析：considerate：体谅的，考虑周到的；considerable：相当大的；considering：考虑；considered：经过深思熟虑的，受尊敬的。

34. The wind was so strong last night that it tore the ________ of the ship into two or three pieces.

A. mask B. mine C. sail D. satellite

正确答案：C。

解析：mask：面具；mine：矿，水雷；sail：帆；satellite：卫星。

38. ________ Hongkong, is often regarded as ________ international centre for business, finance and tourism.

A. /; an　　B. An; /　　C. The; /　　D. /; the

正确答案：A。

解析：Hongkong 是地名，不必加冠词；international centre 前面应该加 an，所以选 A。

39. They went ________ the schedule for the conference again and again until they felt satisfied with every detail of it.

A. out　　B. up　　C. over　　D. by

正确答案：C。

解析：要填的词 went 搭配。go out：出去；go up：上升；go over：查看，重温；go by：时光流失。

40. Schools should teach our kids various subjects, and moreover, teach them how to ________ right from wrong.

A. make　　B. take　　C. tell　　D. put

正确答案：C。

解析：tell right from wrong 是固定搭配，意思是“辨别是非”。

42. In time of trouble Charlie could always ________ a solution.

A. put aside　　B. look down upon　　C. break out　　D. come up with

正确答案：D。

解析：put aside：撇开，储备；look down upon：轻视，瞧不起；break out：爆发；come up with：提出，想出。

43. Before building a house, you will have to ________ the government's permission.

A. get from　　B. follow　　C. receive　　D. ask for

正确答案：D。

解析：要填的词应该与 permission 搭配，只有 ask for 与之搭配符合句意。

第八节 解题技巧

8.1 语法与词汇部分的 3 个命题特点

1. 考点覆盖面广

虽然语法与词汇部分才 30 道题，但考查的基础知识却十分广泛，如非谓语动词、名词性从句、定语从句、状语从句、虚拟语气、倒装句、强调句、主谓一致、反意疑问句、动词时态、情态动词、短语动词、动词辨析、名词、代词、形容词、副词等。

2. 突出动词重点

在 30 道题中一般有 8—12 题考查动词，突出了动词的重要性。动词的考点包括时态、语态、非谓语动词、情态动词、动词短语等，这些项目也正是成人本科考生英语学习的重点和难点。

3. 强调从句运用

除动词外，重点是考查各类从句，即名词性从句、状语从句、定语从句。强调从句的运用能力，是因为从句运用能力的强弱，体现着英语表达能力的高低。

命题者常常利用熟悉的句型结构，或者一些固定搭配来制造陷阱，误导考生得出错误的答案。针对这种情况，我们粗略归纳了常见陷阱题的类型并加以分析，希望能对考生在解题过程中巧识陷阱有所帮助。

8.2 识破单项填空的5类陷阱

1. 思维定势型

思维定势是指人们在长期的思维过程中所形成的一种固定的思维模式。它是一把双刃剑,如果运用得当,它可以帮助考生将考题内容与以前所学知识迅速联系起来,并在短时间内调集解决问题所需的相关知识进行分析、推理,并很快得出正确的结论;若运用不当,它便会误导考生掉入命题者所预设的陷阱,得出错误的结论。如:

例1 In order not to be disturbed, I spent three hours ________ in my study.

A. locking　　B. locked　　C. to lock　　D. to be locked

解析:答案为B,但考生易误选A,以为是考查spend...(in)doing结构。其实,不是"锁门"花去了三小时,而是"将自己锁在书房里度过了三小时",用过去分词短语作伴随状语。

2. 规则硬套型

指不从语言实际出发,不考虑特定的语言环境,而是机械地套用语法规则,生搬硬套语法的条条框框,从而错误地作出选择。如:

例2 He made up his mind to devote his life ________ pollution ________ happily.

A. to prevent; to live　　B. to prevent; from living

C. to preventing; to live　　D. to preventing; living

解析:答案为C,但易误选B,认为第一空应填的to是不定式符号,第二空是prevent...(from) doing sth.固定搭配。其实devote...to...(把……奉献给……)中的to是介词,后接动词的-ing形式;第二空也不是"防止污染过上幸福生活",而是"为了过上幸福生活而防止污染",用不定式作目的状语。

3. 母语干扰型

学外语最忌母语干扰,但由于母语在大脑中根深蒂固,所以常常会对外语学习者大脑中尚不牢固的外语知识产生负面影响。命题者也往往利用这一点制造陷阱。如:

例3 I'll come to see you if ________.

A. you're convenient　　B. it is convenient for you

C. you feel convenient　　D. it is convenient with you

解析:答案为B,但易误选A或C,因为按汉语意思,"如果你方便的话"易直译为if you are convenient或if you feel convenient。事实上,英语中表示"如果你方便的话",通常说if it is convenient for [to] you.

4. 插入隔离型

有时一个本来很简单的句子,在其中插入两个成分,或将某些成分从正常位置调入一个在考生看来属"非正常"的位置,则很有可能给考生的理解带来困难。如:

例4 He ran as fast as he could ________ the bus.

A. catch　　B. to catch　　C. catching　　D. caught

解析:答案为B,但易选A,以为情态动词could后要接动词原形。其实,这里的情态动词could后已省略了一个动词原形run,后面应用动词不定式表示目的。

5. 借用倒装型

英语句子的一般语序为"主语部分+谓语部分",如果把整个谓语或谓语的一部分放到主语前面,我们称之为倒装。命题者就利用这种"不正常"的句式跟你"绕圈子"。解类似的题目,关键是要熟悉倒装规则,学会识别倒装句。如:

例 5 ________ he followed my advice, he would have succeeded.

A. When B. If C. Had D. Has

解析：答案为 C，但易误选 B。若选 B，主句和从句的时态就会矛盾了，根据后面的谓语的形式，前面要用过去完成时 had followed 才对。其实，这里是 if 引导的虚拟条件句，if 被省略，将 had 提前了。

8.3 做语法与词汇部分的 13 种方法

1. 找准关键词语

有时题干中带有对解题起着关键作用的词语，如果能迅速找准这些词语，再结合各选项的意义和用法，就能很快选出正确答案。如：

例 1 It is ________ any wonder that his friend doesn't like watching television much.

A. no B. such C. nearly D. hardly

解析：此题的关键词是 any，因为 any 常用于疑问句、否定句或条件句中，而此句不是疑问句，也不是条件句，所以应该是否定句。能构成否定句的只有选项 A 和 D，而 no 本身就相当于 not any，于是排除 A。因此，正确答案是 D(hardly＝almost not)。

2. 分析句子结构

有些试题的考点本来十分简单，但命题者却通过使用定语从句，或者将我们熟悉的固定词组有意拆分、重新组合，使我们在结构上产生错觉，出现迷惑。这时，我们只要保持清醒的头脑，仔细分析句子的结构，就会拨开迷雾。如：

例 2 This is the main use that the scientists make ________ natural resources.

A. in B. up of C. from D. of

解析：科学家不可能是由自然资源做成或组成的，那该选哪个答案呢？其实只要分析一下句子结构，便知“that the scientists make...”是定语从句，关系代词 that 是代替先行词 use 的，将其置入定语从句之中，就得到“the scientists make use...”。显然是考查 make use of 这一词组的，正确答案是 D。

3. 适当转换句式

有时将题干的句式转换成自己更熟悉的句式，就能很容易选出正确答案。如：将疑问句、强调句、感叹句或倒装句改为陈述句，将被动句改为主动句、无序句调整为正常句。如：

例 3 —Mr Wang, whom would you rather ________ the important meeting?

—Tom.

A. have attend B. have attended C. having attend D. have to attend

解析：若将疑问句改为陈述句，就是 I would rather have Tom attend the important meeting. 其中 would rather 后必须接动词原形，have sb. do sth. 是“要某人做某事”。所以选 A。

4. 补全省略成分

口语中常常会使用一些省略句，做题时若将被省略的成分补充完整，答案就会一目了然。

例 4 —What do you think made Mary so upset?

—________ her new bike.

A. As she lost B. Lost C. Losing D. Because of losing

解析：将答句补全，就是________ her new bike made Mary so upset. 显然，只能选 C，用动名词短语作主语。

5. 删除干扰部分

就是将起干扰作用的定语从句、介词短语或插入语,如:I think/suppose/believe; do you think/suppose/believe; you know, of course 等删除,从而更容易地选出正确答案。如:

例 5 We agree to accept ________ they thought was the best tourist guide.

A. whichever B. whoever C. whatever D. whomever

解析:去掉插入语 they thought,可知宾语从句中缺主语,又能与 the best tourist guide 搭配的,只有选项 B。

6. 利用对称结构

就是在做题过程中要善于利用 and, but 等并列连词。若前面是个句子,后面也必定是个句子,反之亦然;若连接的是几个动词,这几个动词也必定是同一时态或同一形式。如:

例 6 —English has a large vocabulary, hasn't it?

—Yes. ________ more words and expressions and you will find it easier to read and communicate.

A. Know B. Knowing C. To know D. Known

解析:因为第二个 and 后面是一个句子,所以前面也必定是一个句子,但前面这个句子没有主语,只能选用动词原形,构成一个祈使句,因此,正确答案是 A。

例 7 On Saturday afternoon, Mrs. Green went to the market, ________ some bananas and visited her cousin.

A. bought B. buying C. to buy D. buy

解析:因为 and 后面是过去式 visited,前面也必定是动词的过去式,所以正确答案是 A。

7. 注意标点符号

标点有时对我们做题有提示作用,不同的标点可能导致选不同的答案,考生做题时,一定要小心。如:

例 8 There are eight tips in Dr. Roger's lecture on sleep, and one of them is: ________ to bed early unless you think it is necessary.

A. doesn't go B. not to go C. not going D. don't go

解析:此题很容易误选 B,认为它是用不定式作表语。其实,冒号已经表明后面是 Dr. Roger 讲的原话,这原话应当是个句子,只有选 D 才能构成一个否定形式的祈使句。

例 9 He is always really rude, ________ is why people tend to avoid him.

A. that B. it C. this D. which

解析:此题很容易误选 A,因为考生非常熟悉 that's why... 这个句型,而事实上此题的正确答案是 D,因为两个句子之间是逗号,又无连词,所以要用 which 引导一个非限制性定语从句。若将逗号改为分号或 and,答案就是 A 了。

8. 熟记固定搭配

在平时的学习中注意积累一些常见的固定句式、动词与副词的搭配、名词与形容词的搭配等等,这对做题十分有利。如:

例 10 Mr. Smith used to smoke ________ but he has given it up.

A. seriously B. heavily C. badly D. hardly

解析:因为指烟瘾或酒瘾很重,要用 heavy 或 heavily,所以要选 B。此外,雨、雪下得"大"、烟雾"浓"、交通"拥挤"、波涛"汹涌"等,也用 heavy。

9. 消除思维定势

有些试题的题干，看上去好像就是固定搭配，考生做题时，自以为十分有把握，结果却做错了。所以，越是遇到十分熟悉的所谓固定搭配时，越要从句子结构上或者句子意思上仔细分析，以免掉入命题人设计的陷阱。如：

例 11　Everyone here will thank the firefighters for the things they have done to prevent fires ________ the environment safer.

A. make　　B. to making　　C. to make　　D. n from making

解析：此题容易误选 D，以为是考查 prevent sb./sth. from doing 这一固定搭配的。其实，"使环境更安全"是"他们为防火所做的工作"的目的，所以用动词不定式，选 C。

10. 检查有无谓语

有时看似两个句子，于是就选连词，正好掉进命题人设计的陷阱。事实上，有时貌似句子的"句子"却没有谓语，其中的动词只是一个非谓语动词（多为分词）。如：

例 12　He wrote five novels, two of ________ translated into English.

A. it　　B. them　　C. which　　D. that

解析：此题很容易误选 C，同学们以为后面是非限制性定语从句。事实上，translated 是过去分词，而不是谓语动词，后面不是句子，无需连词，所以正确答案是 B。若在 translated 前加上 were，were translated 就是谓语，这时就选关系代词 which 了。

11. 查看有无连词

若经查实，前后的确是两个句子，就要看其中的一个分句是否已经用了连词。若已经有连词，一般不再用连词；若还没有用连词，就一定要选连词。如：

例 13　If Han excellent Chinese novel is translated into English, ________ means many more people in the world can enjoy it.

A. as　　B. which　　C. what　　D. that

解析：因为前句已经有连词 if，所以答案选 D，that 指前句所述内容。若没有 if，就选 B，which 引导一个非限制性定语从句。

12. 识别相似句型

有的句型十分相似，若不仔细分辨，便很容易出错。如：

例 14　________ is known to everybody, light travels much faster than sound.

A. It　　B. As　　C. That　　D. What

解析：此题选 B，as 引导一个非限制性定语从句，先行词是后面整个句子。若将逗号改为 that，就选 A，it 是形式主语，that 引导主语从句；若接着又在 that 前加上一个 is，则应选 D，what 引导的是主语从句，that 引导的是表语从句。

13. 正确把握语境

有时孤立地看留空格的那个句子，好像多个答案都可以，但与上下句的意思联系起来，就会发现问题。因此，做题时一定要正确把握语境。如：

例 15　I agree with most of what you said, but I don't agree with ________.

A. everything　　B. anything　　C. something　　D. nothing

解析：此题很容易误选 B。因为这是个否定句，若选 B，I don't agree with anything 就等于 I agree with nothing(of what you said)，这就与前一分句的意思发生矛盾了。正确答案应该是 A。

第四章　挑错题解题技巧

纵观历年成人本科学士学位英语考试试题，挑错题主要考查 16 个大的方向，有明显的规律。比如考主谓一致，划线错误通常出在动词的第三人称单数上；比如考强调句，强调句“it is＋非形容词性的词＋that/who/whom＋句子”，划线错误通常出在 that/who/whom 上；比如考倒装句，不该倒装时倒装了，该倒装时没有倒装，或者倒装的顺序不对；比如考并列结构，如果看到 and、but、then、or 以及 as 等词，那么后面句子的结构应该与前面的句子结构一致，否则就是错误的；比如考否定词，若句子中出现两个或两个以上的否定词，则划线的否定词有可能错误。另外，挑错题还常考反意疑问句、时态、比较级、虚拟语气、从句、非谓语动词、形容词与副词、代词与限定词、do 的用法、词义辨析、介词等。

下面对历年成人本科学士学位英语考试挑错部分逐题进行解析，就可以发现挑错题的规律。

Unit 1

61. The more frequent the child expresses his interest in an activity, the stranger it will become.
(A: frequent　B: interest　C: an　D: it)

正确答案：A。

解析：A 是修饰“expresses his interest”的，应该是副词，所以不对。

62. It is always easier to select a tool than to use them.
(A: It is　B: easier　C: select　D: use them)

正确答案：D。

解析：D 中指代的是“a tool”，应该是单数，所以不对。

63. During the discussion, Mr. Boyd remained silent when asking his opinion.
(A: During the discussion　B: remained silent　C: when　D: asking)

正确答案：D。

解析：Mr. Boyd 应该是被要求发表意见，应该用被动语态，所以 D 不对。

64. She sings too loudly, the same as what her teacher does.
(A: too loudly　B: same　C: as　D: what)

正确答案：D。

解析：本句话比较的是唱歌音量的高低程度，应该是副词，所以 D 不对。

65. He asked what had the weather been like during my holidays and I said that it had been awful.
(A: He asked what　B: had the weather been　C: I said　D: it had been awful)

正确答案：B。

解析：B 与前面的 what 一起构成宾语从句，引导词 what 后面应该接主语，所以不对。

66. A number of errors made by him was surprising.
(A: A　B: errors　C: made　D: surprising)

正确答案：A。

解析：a number of 接可数名词复数形式构成复数，表示“大量的……”；the number of 接可数名词复数构成单数，表示“……的数量”，所以 A 不对。

67. She stood there for a while with her hands risen.
(A: for a while　B: with　C: her　D: risen)

正确答案：D。

解析：她的手举着是主动语态，不是被动，所以 D 不对。

68. It is on each individual effort which the safety and happiness of the whole depend.
A B C D

正确答案：B。

解析：本句话是一个强调句型，强调的是“each individual effort”，应该用 that 引导，所以 B 不对。

69. Our history professor is such a knowledgeable person that it seems that there isn't nothing which he does not know.
A B C D

正确答案：C。

解析：C 与前面的“there isn't”构成双重否定，与句子的意思相反，所以不对。

70. I feel like to take a long walk. Would you like to go with me?
A B C D

正确答案：A。

解析：“feel like”后面通常接动名词，所以 A 不对。

Unit 2

61. This morning I got up late, so I came to school ten minutes later.
A B C D

正确答案：D。

解析：本句话中并没有比较，不能用比较级，所以 D 不对。

62. A good artist like a good engineer learns as many from his mistakes as from successes.
A B C D

正确答案：C。

解析：C 是修饰 learn 的，表示的是知识，应该是不可数名词，所以不对。

63. This is the sportsman whom everyone says will win the first prize at the Winter Olympic Games.
A B C D

正确答案：D。

解析：表示“在 the Winter Olympic Games”应该用 in 或 during，所以 D 不对。

64. Unlike Americans who seem to prefer coffee, the English drinks a great deal of tea.
A B C D

正确答案：C。

解析：the English 指的是所有英国人，应该是复数，所以 C 不对。

65. Convincing that they were trying to poison him, he refused to eat anything.
A B C D

正确答案：D。

解析：anything 通常用在否定句或疑问句中，而 refuse 并不表示否定，所以 D 不对。

66. Would you mind waiting a moment for me? My work will be finished at no time.
A B C D

正确答案：D。

解析：“at no time”的意思是“决不”，与句子的意思不符，所以 D 不对。

67. He will not borrow you the money even if you ask.
A B C D

正确答案：B

解析：borrow 表示“从……借来”，与句子的意思相反，所以 B 不对。

68. It is important that she goes to see the doctor immediately.
A B C D

正确答案：C。

解析：“It is important that”后面的句子应该用虚拟语气，动词用(should)＋ 动词原形，所以 C 不对。

69. You have heard from him since last month, have you?
A B C D

正确答案：D。

解析：前面的句子是肯定形式，后面的反意问句应该用否定形式，所以 D 不对。

70. Walking in the street, the cars and buses are running like streams.
A B C D

正确答案：A。

解析：A 与后面句子的主语搭配不当，所以不对。

Unit 3

61. If you happen to come across Jack, please tell him to come and see me when he will be free.
A B C D

正确答案：D。

解析：后面的 when 引导的是状语从句，应该用一般现在时态表示将来，所以 D 不对。

62. The United States is composed of fifty states, two of those are separated from the others by land or water.
A B C D

正确答案：B。

解析：B 应该是引导句子修饰前面的 states，应该用“two of which”，所以不对。

63. The news coming from different parts of the world are often extremely discouraging these days.
A B C D

正确答案：C。

解析：news 是不可数名词，所以 C 不对。

64. We had lived in this house for three years while my father decided to have us move to a new neighborhood.
A B C D

正确答案：B。

解析：B 前面的句子用的是过去完成时态，B 后面的句子用的是一般过去时态，说明 B 前面的句子发生在后面的句子之前，所以 B 不对。

65. I don't think I can understand this book, the subject it deals with is not familiar with me.
A B C D

正确答案：D。

解析：“be familiar with”的意思是“对……熟悉”，而本句话要表达的是为我所熟悉，应该是

"be familiar to",所以 D 不对。

66. Nancy had a great deal of trouble to concentrate on her work because of the noise in the next room.
A: a great deal of　B: to concentrate on　C: because of　D: in

正确答案：B。

解析："have trouble"后面通常接动名词,所以 B 不对。

67. The course would have been offered this term, but it cancelled because too few students had registered before registration closed.
A: have been offered　B: cancelled　C: had registered　D: closed

正确答案：B。

解析：the course 被取消应该是被动语态,所以 B 不对。

68. Even though she looks very young, she is twice older than my twenty-year-old sister.
A: Even though　B: young　C: twice older than　D: twenty-year-old

正确答案：C。

解析："是……的两倍"用 twice 表示应该是"twice as... as",所以 C 不对。

69. In the days when coal was so widely used, no one realized how soon and how complete oil would replace it.
A: widely　B: no one　C: complete　D: it

正确答案：C。

解析：C 是修饰 replace 的,应该是副词,所以不对。

70. Those of us who work in chemical laboratories should have their lungs checked quite regularly.
A: Those of　B: laboratories　C: their　D: checked

正确答案：C。

解析：C 指代的应该是前面的"those of us",所以不对。

Unit 4

61. The meeting was interesting to some people, and to me it was boring.
A: interesting　B: to　C: and　D: boring

正确答案：C。

解析：前后句子的意思应该是相反的,所以 C 不对。

62. Ever since the world began, nations have difficulty in keeping peace with their neighbors.
A: Ever since　B: began　C: have difficulty　D: in keeping

正确答案：C。

解析："ever since"引导的句子的主句应该用完成时态,所以 C 不对。

63. Mary showed the customs officer her passport, then John showed him his one.
A: customs　B: then　C: him　D: his

正确答案：D。

解析：his 与后面的 one 搭配不当,所以 D 不对。

64. I was just falling sleep last night when I heard a knock at the door.
A: falling　B: sleep　C: when　D: at

正确答案：B。

解析：表示"入睡"应该是"fall asleep",所以 B 不对。

65. She was angry, went out, and slamming the door behind her.
A B C D

正确答案：C。

解析：C 表达的动作应该与前面的"went out"连贯,所以不对。

66. Bats are able to guide them by producing sound waves too high for us to hear.
A B C D

正确答案：B。

解析：本句话应该表达的是"引导它们自己",应该用反身代词,所以 B 不对。

67. The boy denied to have seen anyone in the building when being questioned by the teacher shortly after the incident.
A B C D

正确答案：A。

解析：deny 后面接动词时通常用动名词形式,所以 A 不对。

68. I could not speak the language, neither had my friends nor acquaintances in the town.
A B C D

正确答案：C。

解析：前面句子用的是 could,后面的句子也应该用 could,所以 C 不对。

69. The salesman told me that a good pair of glasses were supposed to last at least 3 to 4 years.
A B C D

正确答案：B。

解析：were 应该用 was,原因是主语为 a good pair of glasses,谓语动词用单数,所以 B 不对。

70. You had better return to your dormitory and to enjoy the company of your roommates instead of wasting time with me.
A B C D

正确答案：C。

解析：C 动作应该与 B 并列,应该用原形,所以不对。

Unit 5

61. At no time and under no circumstances China will be the first to use nuclear weapons.
A B C D

正确答案：B。

解析：否定词放在句首时句子应该倒装,所以 B 不对。

62. Neither John and his father was able to wake up early enough to catch the morning train.
A B C D

正确答案：A。

解析：neither 通常与 nor 搭配,所以 A 不对。

63. The development of industry has also brought about large numbers of problems which have to solve.
A B C D

正确答案：D。

解析：问题应该是被解决,是被动语态,所以 D 不对。

64. As time went on, he suffered such heavy losses that he was forced giving up his business.
A B C D

正确答案：D。

解析："被迫做……"应该是"be forced to do"，所以 D 不对。

65. Mary found it difficult to talk calmly about which she had experienced at the station.
A B C D

正确答案：C。

解析：C 不仅要引导后面的句子，还要在句子中作宾语，只有用 what 可以这样，所以 C 不对。

66. Some people find swimming more enjoyable than to sit at home reading.
A B C D

正确答案：B。

解析：本句话比较的是两个动作，B 应该与前面的 swimming 形式一样，所以不对。

67. The law I am referring to requires that everyone who owns a car has accident insurance.
A B C D

正确答案：D。

解析：require 后面的宾语从句应该用虚拟语气，动词应该用(should)＋ 动词原形，所以 D 不对。

68. The responsibility of the manager in such a large international enterprise is far greater than his typist.
A B C D

正确答案：D。

解析：本句话比较的是两个人的责任，前后的形式应该一样，所以 D 不对。

69. The course would have been offered this term. But it cancelled because too few students had registered before registration closed.
A B C D

正确答案：B。

解析：the course 被取消应该是被动语态，所以 B 不对。

70. In the days when coal was so widely used, no one realized how soon and how complete oil would replace it.
A B C D

正确答案：C。

解析：C 应该是修饰 replace 的，应该是副词，所以不对。

Unit 6

61. A student is allowed to enter into this room only if a teacher has given permission.
A B C D

正确答案：B。

解析：enter 本身就是"进入"之意，不必加 into，所以 B 不对。

62. He jumped over the fence, ran across the field, and disappearing into the woods.
A B C D

正确答案：D。

解析：D表示的动作与前面的C连贯，形式应该与A一样，所以不对。

63. Find answers to these questions is something like a detective story.
A B C D

正确答案：A。

解析：动词做主语时通常用动词不定式形式或者动名词形式，所以A不对。

64. Even though Sedat has been studying English for three years before came to the United States, it is still difficult for him to express himself.
A B C D

正确答案：B。

解析：B表示的动作应该在来美国之前，应该是过去完成时态，所以不对。

65. A number of foreign visitors were taken to the industrial exhibition which they saw many new products.
A B C D

正确答案：C。

解析：C引导的从句应该是修饰"the industrial exhibition"，应该是地点，所以不对。

66. It is driving on the left what causes visitors to Britain the most trouble.
A B C D

正确答案：C。

解析：本句话是一个强调句型，应该用it is... that句型表达，所以C不对。

67. When she came back from Hollywood, she wanted to tell everybody about all the stars and exciting people who she had seen.
A B C D

正确答案：D。

解析：D引导的先行词all the stars and exciting people作see的宾语，应该用whom引导，所以不对。

68. Many of the society's wealth is controlled by large corporations and government agencies.
A B C D

正确答案：A。

解析：wealth是不可数名词，所以A不对。

69. The simplest kind of plant, alike the simplest kind of animal, consists of only one cell.
A B C D

正确答案：B。

解析："就像……"应该是介词，所以B不对。

70. Despite they are small, the horses are strong and have great energy.
A B C D

正确答案：A。

解析：despite后面一般接词或短语，不能接句子，所以A不对。

Unit 7

46. I'm old enough not to let my troubles to interfere with my work.
A B C D

正确答案：C。

解析：let后面的动词应该用原形，所以C不对。

47. It was in the primary school where my teacher introduced me to computers.
A　B　C　D

正确答案：C。

解析：本句话是一个强调句型，应该用“it was... that”句型表示，所以 C 不对。

48. Where did the accident in which your friend was hurt took place?
A　B　C　D

正确答案：D。

解析：前面已经用了 did，后面的动词应该用原形，所以 D 不对。

49. There are twelve people take part in the experiment, four working as a group.
A　B　C　D

正确答案：B。

解析：B 引导的短语是修饰 people 的，不能用动词原形，所以不对。

50. Red and green light, if mixing, in the right proportion, will give us yellow.
A　B　C　D

正确答案：B。

解析：颜色是被人们混合，应该用被动语态，所以 B 不对。

51. We strongly suggest that Smith is told about his physical condition as soon as possible.
A　B　C　D

正确答案：C。

解析：suggest 后面的宾语从句应该用虚拟语气，动词应该用(should)＋ 动词原形，所以 C 不对。

52. Nearly three quarters of the surface of the earth are covered with water, and there would be even less land if the polar icecaps were melt.
A　B　C　D

正确答案：B。

解析：“three quarters of the surface of the earth”表达的是单数，所以 B 不对。

53. The seventeenth century was one which many significant advances were made in both science and philosophy.
A　B　C　D

正确答案：A。

解析：A 引导的从句修饰的是时间，应该用 when，所以不对。

54. No matter whatever happens, we're determined to do our best and make the experiment a success.
A　B　C　D

正确答案：A。

解析：whatever 与 no matter 重复，所以 A 不对。

55. Let's not waste time on matters of no important. We have other vital problems to deal with.
A　B　C　D

正确答案：B。

解析：of 后面应该接名词，应该用 importance，所以 B 不对。

Unit 8

46. Individual freedom does not in any sense mean that you can do what you like at your free will.
A B C D

正确答案：D。

解析："随心所欲地"应该是"at one's own will"，所以 D 不对。

47. When we finally finished the tiring journey, we could not hardly move a step further.
A B C D

正确答案：C。

解析：could not 和 hardly 构成双重否定，与句子的意思相反，所以 C 不对。

48. Arriving for the lecture early is better than to take the chance of being late.
A B C D

正确答案：C。

解析：本句话比较的是两个动作，C 应该与前面的 arriving 形式相同，所以不对。

49. These part-time students expect to offer some jobs on campus during the coming summer vacation.
A B C D

正确答案：A。

解析：工作机会是被提供给学生的，应该是被动语态，所以 A 不对。

50. He was so excited after hearing the news and he could not fall asleep immediately.
A B C D

正确答案：B。

解析：B 应该与前面的 so 搭配引导从句，应该用 that，所以不对。

51. You will not able to pass the examination unless you work harder than you do now.
A B C D

正确答案：A。

解析：able 是形容词，不能接在 will 之后，应该用"be able to"短语，所以 A 不对。

52. Only when it started to rain he noticed that he had left his raincoat somewhere.
A B C D

正确答案：B。

解析：only 放在句首时句子应该倒装，所以 B 不对。

53. The waste, according to the people there, has already found their way into the drinking water.
A B C D

正确答案：C。

解析：C 应该是指代 waste，而它应该是单数，所以不对。

54. If you try to learn too many things at a time you may get confusing.
A B C D

正确答案：D。

解析：D 是修饰人的，而 confusing 是修饰物的，所以不对。

55. After his graduation from the university, he has worked in a famous computer company.
A B C D

正确答案：A。

解析：后面的句子用的是完成时态，那么前面的短语应该用表示完成时态的介词，所以 A 不对。

Unit 9

46. It is(A) in(B) his spare time when(C) Robert teaches himself(D) English and Japanese.

正确答案：C。

解析：本句话是一个强调句型，应该用"it was... that"句型表示，所以C不对。

47. People complain that the cost(A) of setting up(B) a company are(C) so great that only the rich can afford to run(D) a company in that country.

正确答案：C。

解析：后面句子的主语是cost，是单数，所以C不对。

48. Between you and I(A), we have had(B) an eye on(C) him for some time, and he might be(D) a runaway.

正确答案：A。

解析：between是介词，表示"我"应该用me，所以A不对。

49. At(A) school Li Ming ran into(B) many problems, such as choosing(C) classes and to handle(D) his time.

正确答案：D。

解析：D做such as的宾语，应该与choosing的形式一样，所以不对。

50. Comparing(A) with the weather of(B) last winter, it is much(C) milder and more pleasant this winter(D).

正确答案：A。

解析：天气应该是被比较，应该用被动语态，所以A不对。

51. Advertising(A) gives useful information about which(B) products(C) to buying(D).

正确答案：D。

解析："要买的产品"应该是将来时态，应该用to + 动词原形表示，所以D不对。

52. In Hawaii(A), people are friendly(B) and always warmly(C) welcomed(D) visitors.

正确答案：D。

解析：根据前面的"are friendly"可知，本句话用的是一般现在时态，所以D不对。

53. Mara Dona will face(A) a possible prison term if(B) finding(C) guilty on(D) the shooting charges.

正确答案：C。

解析：Mara Dona是被认定有罪，应该用被动语态，所以C不对。

54. Having returned(A) from Berlin(B), he received no telephone call(C), neither(D).

正确答案：D。

解析：句尾的"也没有"应该用either，所以D不对。

55. "I am looking(A) forward to(B) receive(C) your letter!" she said happily(D).

正确答案：C。

解析：look forward to后面应该接动名词，所以C不对。

Unit 10

46. It was in this school where he had studied for four years.
A B C D

正确答案：C。

解析：本句话是一个强调句型，应该用“it was... that”句型表示，所以 C 不对。

47. Being felt that she had done something wonderful, she sat down to rest.
A B C D

正确答案：A。

解析：她觉得怎么样应该是主动语态，所以 A 不对。

48. Jane had a great deal of trouble to concentrate on her study because of the noise in the next room.
A B C D

正确答案：B。

解析：have trouble 后面应该接动名词，所以 B 不对。

49. The way which different kinds of rock lie on one another helps to tell the story of long ago.
A B C D

正确答案：D。

解析：of 后面应该接名词或代词，所以 D 不对。

50. We were young men when we first met in London, poor, struggle, full of hope and ideas.
A B C D

正确答案：C。

解析：C 应该与前面的 poor 形式一样，所以不对。

51. Of the two lectures, the first was by far the best one, partly because the person who delivered it had such a pleasant voice.
A B C D

正确答案：B。

解析：两者之间不能用最高级，所以 B 不对。

52. According to our estimate, only one out of three company managers have been trained in the field of management.
A B C D

正确答案：C。

解析：one out of three 应该是单数，所以 C 不对。

53. Today we have made great achievements, but tomorrow we shall win still great victories.
A B C D

正确答案：D。

解析：still 后面应该接比较级，所以 D 不对。

54. Lewis had to travel by bus as his car had been damaged in an accident some days before and he was failed to get it repaired.
A B C D

正确答案：D。

解析：Lewis 没能做什么应该是主动语态，所以 D 不对。

55. Collecting toy cars as a hobby becomes increasingly popular during the past fifty years.
A B C D

正确答案：B。

解析：根据后面的“during the past fifty years”可知，本句话应该用完成时态，所以 B 不对。

Unit 11

46. How could you make such a little child to help you carry the big box?
(A: could; B: such; C: to help; D: carry)

正确答案：C。

解析：用 make 表示“使、要某人做某事”时，后面的动词应该用原形，所以 C 不对。

47. As soon as we've finished supper, we'll all go to downtown to see the Sound of Music.
(A: As soon; B: we've finished; C: we'll all; D: to)

正确答案：B。

解析：B 表示的时态与后面的“we'll all go”不符，所以不对。

48. I really appreciate you recommended me to that company in time.
(A: appreciate; B: you recommended; C: that; D: in time)

正确答案：B。

解析：appreciate 后面应该接名词、代词或动名词，所以 B 不对。

49. He will not do it had he known how serious the outcome would be.
(A: will not do; B: had he known; C: serious; D: would be)

正确答案：A。

解析：根据 B 可知，本句话是虚拟语气，所以 A 不对。

50. Her name sounds familiar with me but I can't tell who she is at the moment.
(A: sounds; B: with; C: can't; D: who)

正确答案：B。

解析：“be familiar with”的意思是“对……熟悉”，而本句话要表达的是为我所熟悉，应该是“be familiar to”，所以 B 不对。

51. Rice has been a basically food for millions of people for hundreds of years.
(A: has been; B: basically; C: millions of; D: hundreds of)

正确答案：B。

解析：B 是修饰 food 的，应该是形容词，所以不对。

52. The director and manager of the department are very strict with the employees.
(A: The director; B: manager; C: are; D: with)

正确答案：C。

解析：A 和 B 指的是同一个人，应该是单数，所以 C 不对。

53. Research shows that employees whose obtain satisfaction from their jobs are more productive.
(A: Research shows; B: whose; C: satisfaction; D: productive)

正确答案：B。

解析：B 引导的句子修饰 employees，不是指他们的什么，所以不对。

54. Looking from another angle, the painting would show something different.
(A: Looking; B: angle; C: would; D: something)

正确答案：A。

解析：图画是被人们观看，应该是被动语态，所以 A 不对。

55. “Never I have heard such a thing in my life!” said the old man.
(A: Never; B: I have heard; C: a thing; D: said)

正确答案：B。

解析：never 放在句首时句子应该倒装，所以 B 不对。

Unit 12

46. This morning I heard on the radio (A) which (B) the steel industry has decided to give (C) its employees a 10% raise (D) in pay.

正确答案：B。

解析：B 引导的句子作 heard 的宾语从句，所以 B 不对。

47. Not knowing (A) the language and having no (B) friends in the country, he found impossible (C) to get (D) a job.

正确答案：C。

解析：后面的句子表示“觉得找到工作不可能”，C 中缺宾语，所以不对。

48. Once giving (A) a set of (B) instructions, a computer can gather a wide range (C) of information for different purposes (D).

正确答案：A。

解析：计算机是被给指令，应该用被动语态，所以 A 不对。

49. The old man will never (A) forget the event, that (B) has changed (C) his life ever since (D).

正确答案：B。

解析：B 引导的是非限定性定语从句，修饰 event，只能用 which，所以不对。

50. Little children will listen (A) what (B) people say and try to (C) imitate what (D) they hear.

正确答案：A。

解析：listen 后应加 to，所以不对。

51. We should start at once (A) and not waste too (B) much time to argue (C) about (D) the procedure.

正确答案：C。

解析：waste time 后面的动词应该用动名词，所以 C 不对。

52. “Shall I (A) give you a cheque for \$10? (B)” “I'd rather you give (C) me \$10 in notes (D).”

正确答案：C。

解析：I'd rather 后面的句子是虚拟语气，所以 C 不对。

53. After driving (A) twenty miles, he suddenly realized (B) that he has been (C) driving (D) in a wrong direction.

正确答案：C。

解析：根据 B 可知，本句话为过去时态，所以 C 不对。

54. We will have (A) to put off (B) our departure in the case (C) it rains (D).

正确答案：C。

解析：引导从句的“以防，以免”应该是 in case，所以 C 不对。

55. The girl her father is a famous pianist learned to play the piano when she was a small child.
A B C D

正确答案：A。

解析：A 引导的句子修饰 girl，应该用 whose，所以不对。

Unit 13

46. He didn't dare to leave the house for fear someone would recognize him soon.
A B C D

正确答案：C。

解析：for fear 引导短语或词组，for fear that 才引导从句，所以 C 不对。

47. You can see the whole city for miles from here in a clear day.
A B C D

正确答案：D。

解析：在确切日子前面应该用 on，而不是 in，所以 D 不对。

48. He wished he didn't tell her the truth that brought her so much pain.
A B C D

正确答案：B。

解析：wish 后面的句子是虚拟语气，wish 用的是一般过去时，那么 B 应该用过去完成时，所以不对。

49. The room, which window faces the south, is the nicest one of all on this floor.
A B C D

正确答案：A。

解析：A 引导的句子修饰 room，表示该房间的窗子，应该用 whose，所以不对。

50. He is a true friend of mine, whom I can always depend whenever I get into trouble.
A B C D

正确答案：C。

解析："信赖、依赖"应该用 depend on 表示，所以 C 不对。

51. Let's go and watch that new movie at eight tonight, won't we?
A B C D

正确答案：D。

解析：Let's 引导的句子的反意问句应该用 shall we，所以 D 不对。

52. It is very important that the students' voice is heard by the authorities of all our schools.
A B C D

正确答案：D。

解析：D 用法重复，所以不对。

53. This is such a beautiful day that everyone around us feel like going out for a walk.
A B C D

正确答案：C。

解析：everyone 是单数，一般现在时的动词要变形，所以 C 不对。

54. We saw a big dog that was fierce and felt frightened in our way home.
A B C D

正确答案：C。

解析："在回家的路上"应该是"on one's way home"，所以 C 不对。

55. You will feel inconvenient in Japan if you can either speak Japanese nor English.
A B C D

正确答案：C。

解析：根据前面的"feel inconvenient"可知，后面的句子应该表示否定，所以 C 不对。

Unit 14

46. He invited me to go to a party and I did not want to join him that evening.
A B C D

正确答案：C。

解析：C 引导的句子与前面句子的意思转折，所以 C 不对。

47. The information which she was injured in the accident was given by Liz.
A B C D

正确答案：A。

解析：A 引导的从句修饰 information，应该用 that，所以不对。

48. Look at the beautiful flowers here! How wonderful they are smelling.
A B C D

正确答案：D。

解析：smell 一般不用进行时态，所以 D 不对。

49. Dear Helen, please forgive him for his rudeness, can you?
A B C D

正确答案：D。

解析：前面是 please 引导的祈使句，后面的反意问句应该用 will，所以 D 不对。

50. Did anyone inform you with the change of the schedule that had been decided yesterday?
A B C D

正确答案：C。

解析："告知、通知某人某事"应该是"inform someone of something"，所以 C 不对。

51. Despite his old age, he is still very healthful and often works in the field.
A B C D

正确答案：D。

解析："健康的"应该是"healthy"，所以 D 不对。

52. This equipment is based upon advanced technique and it is highly reliable.
A B C D

正确答案：C

解析：technique 作"技术，技能，工艺"解释时，为可数名词，C 应该加 s。

53. It is about time that we go to supper, for we still have a meeting to attend this evening.
A B C D

正确答案：B。

解析："It is about time that"后面的句子应该用一般过去时态，所以 B 不对。

54. Every now and then he would come here paying a visit to his old aunt, who lived all alone in a small house.
A B C D

正确答案：D。

解析："独自一人"用 alone 表示即可，D 显得累赘，所以不对。

55. The passengers saw the thief stole on the bus, but they didn't say anything.
A B C D

正确答案：B。

解析："看见某人在做某事"应该是"see somebody doing something"，所以 B 不对。

Unit 15

46. Have you noticed her coat is wet? She must be caught in the rain.
A B C D

正确答案：C。

解析：前面的句子用的是完成时态，说明 C 也应该用完成时态，所以不对。

47. Teenagers always long for the time which they are able to be independent.
A B C D

正确答案：B。

解析：B 引导的句子修饰 time，应该用 when，所以不对。

48. Since the injury is bad, the doctors will operate him immediately.
A B C D

正确答案：C。

解析："给某人做手术"应该是"operate on somebody"，所以 C 不对。

49. Let's hurry up and try to get to the railway station in time, can we?
A B C D

正确答案：D。

解析：Let's 引导的句子的反意问句应该用 shall we，所以 D 不对。

50. He refused joining us last Saturday night. Don't you think it strange?
A B C D

正确答案：B。

解析：refuse 后面应该接 to do，所以 B 不对。

51. Some old beautiful Italian oil paintings are being displayed in the exhibition hall.
A B C D

正确答案：A。

解析：修饰名词时，描述性形容词应该放在新旧形容词之前，所以 A 不对。

52. If you had been there, I'm sure you would have enjoyed to see the Chinese Team win.
A B C D

正确答案：C。

解析：enjoy 后面接动词时应该用动名词形式，所以 C 不对。

53. On seeing the boy fell into the river, she sprang to her feet and went to the rescue.
A B C D

正确答案：B。

解析："看见某人干什么"应该是"see somebody doing something"，所以 B 不对。

54. Traditionally, work determines our way of life. But if 98 percent of us don't need to work, what are we going to do with oneself?
A B C D

正确答案：D。

解析：D 指代的应该是 we，所以不对。

55. Only by practice will you be able to improve your speaking English and gradually speak fluently.
A B C D

正确答案：C。

解析:“英语口语”应该是“spoken English”,所以 C 不对。

Unit 16

46. Two woman teachers and four girl students were praised at the meeting yesterday.
A B C D

正确答案:A。

解析:woman 与其他词一起构成复数时应该改成 women,所以 A 不对。

47. After she got married, Lily went to see her mother each other week.
A B C D

正确答案:D。

解析:“每隔一个星期”应该是“every other week”,所以 D 不对。

48. There will be more than three hundreds students taking part in the sports meet.
A B C D

正确答案:B。

解析:hundred 表示“几百”时,不能用复数形式,只有在与 of 搭配时才用复数形式,所以 B 不对。

49. While shopping, people sometimes can't help persuading into buying something they don't really need.
A B C D

正确答案:B。

解析:B 表示的是被动意思,与本句话的意思不符,所以不对。

50. We are all for your proposal that the discussion is to be put off.
A B C D

正确答案:D。

解析:proposal 后面的从句应该是虚拟语气,动词应该用(should)+ 动词原形,所以 D 不对。

51. Factory workers had to work very hard before, so had farmers.
A B C D

正确答案:D。

解析:so 后面应该接助动词 did,所以 D 不对。

52. He finds it easier to do the cooking himself than teaching his wife to cook.
A B C D

正确答案:C。

解析:C 应该是与 to do the cooking 相比较,动词形式应该一样,所以不对。

53. There was too much dust that we couldn't see what was happening.
A B C D

正确答案:B。

解析:B 应该与后面的 that 一起引导从句,应该用 so,所以不对。

54. The boy did not have to leave the next day because he got his visa extending.
A B C D

正确答案:D。

解析:get 后面接某物再接动词时,该动词应该用过去分词,所以 D 不对。

55. What does Mr. Johnson like? He's a friendly sort of man. I like to work with him.
A B C D

正确答案:A。

解析：句中的 like 是形容词，所以 A 不对。

Unit 17

46. The reporter was very pleased when the chairman allowed him to ask few questions.
A B C D

正确答案：D。

解析：few 表示否定，与句子的意思相反，所以 D 不对。

47. He tried to learn Greek but soon got tired of it and gave up it.
A B C D

正确答案：D。

解析：give up 后面接代词时应该放在它们中间，所以 D 不对。

48. With the sun setting, we stopped working, putting away our tools and were going to go home.
A B C D

正确答案：C。

解析：C 表示的动作应该与 stopped working 并列，应该用过去时，所以不对。

49. Polite manners in China demand that a person stands up when anyone enters a room or when anyone hands him something.
A B C D

正确答案：B。

解析：demand 后面的从句应该是虚拟语气，动词应该用(should)＋ 动词原形，所以 B 不对。

50. This is the sportsman whom everyone says will win the gold medal at the Winter Olympic Games.
A B C D

正确答案：B。

解析：sportsman 在后面从句中作主语，所以 B 不对。

51. I heard that you really had a wonderful time at John's birthday party, hadn't you?
A B C D

正确答案：D。

解析：后面反意问句应该用助动词，所以 D 不对。

52. E-mail as well as mobile telephones are becoming more and more popular in daily communication.
A B C D

正确答案：B。

解析：句子的主语是 E-mail，是单数，所以 B 不对。

53. They are going to have the servicemen installed an electric fan in the office tomorrow.
A B C D

正确答案：C。

解析：用 have 表示"要某人做某事"时，后面的动词应该用原形，所以 C 不对。

54. Two woman teachers and four girl students were praised at the meeting yesterday.
A B C D

正确答案：A。

解析：woman 与其他词一起构成复数时应该改成 women，所以 A 不对。

55. Lesson Three is the most difficult lesson, but it isn't the most difficult lesson in Book
A B C D

Four.

正确答案：A。

解析：前面的句子没有比较范围，不应该用最高级，所以 A 不对。

Unit 18

46. A(A) container weighs(B) more after air is put(C) in it(D) proves that air has weight.

正确答案：A。

解析：本句话中的 container 是特指，所以 A 不对。

47. The young man, to make(A) several attempts to beat(B) the world record in high jumping, decided(C) to have another try(D).

正确答案：A。

解析：动词不定式一般表示目的，此处应改为动名词 having made。

48. Of(A) the two coats, I'd choose(B) the cheapest(C) one to spare some money for(D) a book.

正确答案：C。

解析：两者之间不能用最高级，所以 C 不对。

49. The protection of(A) our environment is(B) not nothing(C) to be left to the government. Everyone should be concerned(D).

正确答案：C。

解析：not 与 nothing 构成双重否定，与句子的意思相反，所以 C 不对。

50. There are(A) moments in life where(B) you miss someone so much that(C) you just want to(D) pick them up from dreams and hug them for real.

正确答案：B。

解析：B 引导的句子修饰的是 moments，是时间，所以不对。

51. None of us(A) had the final say(B) in this matter, and therefore(C) it was recommended that we waited(D) for the authorities.

正确答案：D。

解析："it was recommended that"后面的句子是虚拟语气，动词应该用(should)＋ 动词原形，所以 D 不对。

52. After(A) her two-week vacation was over(B), Dorothy regretted to spend(C) so much money for so little pleasure(D).

正确答案：C。

解析：regret 后面的动词一般用动名词形式，所以 C 不对。

53. Don't make(A) Helen's remarks too seriously(B). She is so upset(C) that I don't think she really knows what she is saying(D).

正确答案：A。

解析："认真考虑某事"应该是"take something seriously"，所以 A 不对。

54. Workers newly arrive from the south or rural areas perform their job differently from
A B C
those from other sections of the city.
D

正确答案：A。

解析：A 引导的短语是修饰 workers 的，应该用分词形式，所以不对。

55. While remembered mainly for the invention of the telephone, Alexander Graham Bell
A B C
devoted his life to help the deaf.
D

正确答案：D。

解析："devote one's life to"后面的动词应该是动名词，所以 D 不对。

Unit 19

46. How an interesting role she played in the film! No wonder she has won an Oscar.
A B C D

正确答案：A。

解析：引导感叹句时，how 后面应该接形容词或副词，what 后面应该接名词短语，所以 A 不对。

47. The famous scientist, in his honor a dinner party will be held tonight, is to arrive
A B C D
soon.

正确答案：B。

解析："为了表示敬意"应该是"in honor of ＋ 某人"，所以 B 不对。

48. The old man was so angry and spoke so fast that none of his children understood that
A B C D
he meant.

正确答案：D。

解析：D 不仅要引导从句，还要在从句中作宾语，只有 what 可以，所以 D 不对。

49. The young man, to make several attempts to beat the world record in high jumping,
A B C
decided to have another try.
D

正确答案：A。

解析：动词不定式一般表示目的，此处应改为动名词 having made。

50. In the town was found many old people who badly needed money and care.
A B C D

正确答案：B。

解析：本句话是一个倒装句，句子的主语是 many old people，所以用 was 不对。

51. As early as the 12th century boys in England enjoyed to play football.
A B C D

正确答案：D。

解析：enjoy 后面接动词时通常用-ing 形式，所以 D 不对。

52. So absorbed she was in her work that she didn't realize it was time that she picked up
A B C D

her daughter.

正确答案：B。

解析：so 放在句首时句子要倒装，所以 B 不对。

53. In big cities(A) there is(B) an increasingly(C) need for(D) cheap apartments for the lower middle class.

正确答案：C。

解析：C 修饰的是 need，而 need 在句中是名词，所以 C 不对。

54. The price(A) of(B) meat was much more higher(C) than expected(D).

正确答案：C。

解析：high 是单音节词，其比较级不必加 more，所以 C 不对。

55. Joe's father has died(A) ten years ago, so(B) he has lived(C) with his mother since then(D).

正确答案：A。

解析：ten years ago 是一个过去的时间，不能用在完成时态的句子中，所以 A 不对。

Unit 20

46. When you've finished(A) with that book, don't(B) forget to put it back(C) on the shelf, won't you(D)?

正确答案：D。

解析：反义疑问句的前面句子是否定时，后面句子应该用肯定，所以 D 不对。

47. The workers(A) in the factory demanded(B) that their pay would be(C) raised by(D) 20 percent.

正确答案：C。

解析：demand 后面的从句应该是虚拟语气，谓语动词用 should＋动词原形，should 可以省略。所以 C 不对。

48. It remains(A) to see(B) whether Jim will be(C) fit enough to play(D) in the finals.

正确答案：B。

解析：it 指的是后面的句子，是一件事，应该用被动语态，所以 B 不对。

49. I invited(A) Joe and Linda as well as(B) Tom to dinner(C), but neither of(D) them came.

正确答案：D。

解析：前面提到三个人，而 neither 只能表示两者不，所以不对。

50. Over the past(A) 20 years, the Internet has helped change(B) our world in either(C) way or another for the better(D).

正确答案：C。

解析：in one way or another 是习惯搭配，意思是“以这种或那种方式”，所以 C 不对。

51. How and why(A) this language has(B) survived for more than a thousand years, while spoke(C) by very few, is hard to explain(D).

正确答案：C。

解析：语言是被说，所以用 spoke 不对。

52. Nearly(A) half of Americans aged(B) 25 and old(C) take part in some form(D) of continuing education.

正确答案：C。

解析：C 应该表示"比 25 岁大"之意，所以用 old 不对，应用比较级。

53. Many parents feel they need to(A) keep a closer eye to(B) their children because of(C) concerns about(D) crime and school violence.

正确答案：B。

解析：keep an eye on 是固定搭配，意思是"关注，注意"，所以 B 不对。

54. For(A) married mothers, the time spend(B) on child care increased(C) to an average(D) of 12.9 hours a week in 2009.

正确答案：B。

解析：time 作主语表示花时间时应该是被动语态，所以 B 不对。

55. There is an increasingly(A) amount of evidence that(B) more and more young people are taking(C) an active interest in(D) politics.

正确答案：A。

解析：A 是修饰 amount 的，应该是形容词，所以不对。

第五章　完形填空题解题技巧

第一节　完形填空的规律

1.1　完形填空的4个显著特点

1. 短文特点

以故事性较强的记叙文或者夹叙夹议的文体为主，难度低于阅读理解中的短文。一般来讲，故事类文章情节多有曲折，结尾出人意料，常常是幽默所在，也是“包袱”所在；议论类文章结构严谨，层次分明，语句中有较多的“对仗”现象。

2. 设空特点

短文的首句通常不设空。考生通过首句可以迅速确定文章的主题和故事发生的背景，把握文章的发展方向。

3. 选项特点

每题的四个选项均属于同一词类或同一语法形式，而且往往都和设空前后的单词形成某种搭配，这样便形成了很强的迷惑性和干扰性，其区别在于语境意义的不同。有时单独看某一句，可能用哪个选项都正确，没有语法错误，但根据对文章的整体理解和上下文语境，却只有一个语义正确的选项。

4. 语境特点

语境就是指上下文，若空格的答案由上文决定叫前制性设空，空格的答案由下文决定叫后制性设空，空格的答案需要综合上下文而定的则为语篇性设空。成人本科学士学位英语考试完形填空通常以后制性设空和语篇性设空为主。语篇性设空可分为三个层次：① 句子层次，空格的答案由所处的那一个句子决定；② 句组层次，空格的答案由相邻不远的一组句子决定；③ 语篇层次，空格的答案由语篇内容综合决定。成人本科学士学位英语考试完形填空按句组层次和语篇层次设空的题居多，这种设题方式体现了“突出语篇”的命题思路。

1.2　完形填空的8个考点

1. 考查语法规则

考查考生运用语法知识的能力。近年来，完形填空中单纯考查语法知识的题一般不多，只是偶尔有个别考题。如：

例1　On May 27, 1995, our life was suddenly changed. It happened a few minutes past three, __56__ my husband, Chris, fell from his horse...

56. A. since　　B. before　　C. when　　D. while

解析：因 a few minutes past three 是“我丈夫”从马上掉下来的时间，应是定语从句的先行词，所以用 when 引导定语从句，正确答案是 C。

2. 考查固定搭配

动词与名词的搭配，动词与介词或副词的搭配，介词与名词的搭配，句式结构的固定搭配，等等，这类搭配在成人本科学士学位英语考试完形填空中时有出现。如：

例 2　... The former __57__ every possible effort to avoid being discovered... It was not long __60__ a customer who had seen him arrive hurried in to inform him...

57. A. do　B. take　C. make　D. try

60. A. when　B. after　C. until　D. before

解析：因 make every effort（尽力）是固定词组，It was not long before...（不久以后就）是固定句式，所以这两题的正确答案分别是 C 和 D。

3. 考查词语辨析

考查考生在特定语境中区别近义词的能力。几个选项的词性相同，意义相近，要求考生在特定的语境中区分它们之间的细微差别。一般说来，其中的两个选项容易排除，难辨的是另两个。如：

例 3　Scott and his companions were terribly disappointed. When they got to the South Pole, they found the Norwegians（挪威人）had __66__ them in the race to be the first ever to reach it.

66. A. hit　B. fought　C. won　D. beaten

解析：由第一句的 disappointed 可知，挪威人已经"胜过了"Scott 和他的同伴们，很容易排除选项 A 和 B；而其余两个选项都有"胜过"之意，这就要求我们知道它们之间的细微差别：win 的宾语通常是比赛、奖品或荣誉等，而 beat 的宾语则是竞赛或竞争的对手。所以正确答案是 D。

4. 考查行文逻辑

考查考生对上下文逻辑关系的理解，如转折关系、让步关系、因果关系、递进关系、增补关系、比较关系、对比关系等。若四个选项都是表示文章的起承转合、上下连贯等逻辑关系的词语，则必须弄清句子前后的逻辑关系，才可作出正确选择。如：

例 4　You are near the front line of a battle. Around you shells are exploding; people are shooting from a house behind you. What are you doing there? You aren't a soldier. You aren't __62__ carrying a gun. You're standing in front of...

62. A. simply　B. really　C. merely　D. even

解析：因为第 62 空这句话与前句是递进关系，"你不是士兵，甚至连枪也没有带"，所以正确答案是 D。

5. 考查经验常识

考查考生在日常的学习和生活中所积累的经验和基本生活常识以及一些基本的科学常识。如：

例 5　But we run so much that, afterwards, we had trouble __58__.

58. A. speaking　B. moving　C. sleeping　D. breathing

解析：跑得太多，其结果当然是上气不接下气，即呼吸困难了，我们一般都会有这样的生活经历，所以正确答案是 D。

6. 考查文章结构

考查考生对文章脉络层次的把握能力。如：

例 6　First of all, I respected his devotion to teaching... __59__, I admired the fact that he would talk to students outside the classroom or talk... Finally, I was attracted by his lively sense of humor.

59. A. Later　B. Secondly　C. However　D. Therefore

解析：本文的写作结构很清楚：开篇点题——难忘的哲学教授，然后逐条陈述为什么难忘：前有 First of all 提起，后有 Finally 落脚，那么中间只有用 Secondly 来过渡了，所以正确答案是 B。

7. 考查逻辑推理

考查考生根据题意和所掌握的知识经验进行简单的逻辑推理来确定答案的能力。如：

例 7　The Greek myth that explains why there are changes of seasons is about Demeter, the goddess of the harvest. She had a daughter, Persephone, whom she loved very much. Hades, god of the underworld, fell in love with Persephone, and he asked Zeus, the __68__ of the gods, to give Persephone to him as his wife. Zeus did not want either to disappoint Hades or to upset Demeter, so...

68. A. winner　B. ruler　C. advisor　D. fighter

解析：冥王海地斯(Hades)要求宙斯(Zeus)把农业女神得墨忒耳(Demeter)的女儿珀尔塞福涅 (Persephone)赐给(give)他做妻子，谁能行使如此大权？不难推知，只有众神之统领(ruler)了，所以正确答案是 B。

8. 考查前后语境

考查考生根据上下文提供的信息进行分析及推理的能力。成人本科学士学位英语考试的完形填空题中绝大多数属这种题型。有的根据上文，有的根据下文，有的要结合上下文，甚至要理解全文才能作出正确的选择。如：

例 8　One afternoon, I was out exploring... and saw a new kind of cactus(仙人掌). I crouched (蹲) down for a closer look. "You'd better not __57__ that."

I turned around to see an old woman.

...

"Would you like to come to my home tomorrow? Someone should teach you which plant you should and shouldn't touch."

57. A. move dig　B. 不填　C. pull　D. touch

解析：此题若不读到最后一段的最后一句的最后一个单词，则很难选出正确答案 D。

1.3　完形填空的 4 个解题步骤

1. 通读全文，理解大意

因为成人本科学士学位英语考试的完形填空题以后制性设空和语篇性设空为主，所以千万不要看一句填一空。而要首先利用首句，跳过空格，浏览全文，从整体上感知全文，理解文章大意，了解故事发展情节，然后再进行试填。这是做好完形填空的前提，万万不可省略。如：

例 1　In Renee Smith's classroom, attendance is up, trips to the headmaster's office are down and students are handing in assignments on time. The Springfield High School teacher says she has seen great __65__ since adding a few new students to her class—five Labrador puppies and their father.

65. A. promotion B. progress　C. disturbance　D. disappointment

解析：从首句可知，作者直截了当地给考生交代了所要叙述的事情的结果：在 Renee Smith 的班上，听课的学生人数增多了，违纪的人数减少了。分析第 65 空可知，该句是从正面的角度阐述了导致这一结果的原因，同时又是下文所陈述内容的总结句。故选 B。

2. 瞻前顾后,避难就易

在理解文章大意的情况下,结合各选项的意义和用法,遵循先易后难的原则,先解决那些自己有把握的问题。对少数难题,暂时跳过,或许在上文中难以判断的题在下文中就有暗示或者明显的提示,或许一个在前面不能解的题在填出了另一空后会令你豁然开朗。

3. 复读全文,解决"残敌"

借助已经补全的空白,我们对全文有了更清楚的理解,可以集中解决所遗留的少数疑难问题。我们根据短文中句与句、段与段的逻辑关系进行判断,采用排除法或其他方法去逐步缩小范围,最终得出正确答案。对于实在无从下手的个别题目,我们则完全可以凭语感来确定:把几个选项逐一放在空格内念两遍,哪个念起来顺口、舒服就选哪个。如:

例 2　I've __65__ to tell every girl I know to do something that people don't think girls can do. It's part of being human to advance to new __66__, so shouldn't it be expected that girls should step up and start __67__ the limits of things boys and men used to dominate(主宰)?

65. A. chosen　B. tried　C. learned　D. promised
66. A. levels　B. points　C. steps　D. parts
67. A. reading　B. accepting　C. pushing　D. setting

解析:从语法角度看,第 65 题的四个选项都正确,但从上下句子之间的语境及逻辑角度推测,只有 B 才能说出作者当时的心理状态。第 66 题为四个名词,与上下文似乎没有多大关系,只有根据作者的心理活动及对句意的推断,方可作出正确选择,说明女孩能做人们认为不能做的事,这是人们应该达到的一种新的思想境界,故选 A。第 67 题是较难的一个小题,考生只有通过分析本句句意,经过认真推敲,才能选出"pushing the limits of things..."意为"摆脱男人们过去主宰的事情的限制",故选 C。

4. 再次读题,弥补疏漏

做完题后,考生务必要结合自己所选择的答案重新阅读短文内容,注意围绕文章中心,查看文章内容是否通顺、结构是否完整、搭配是否有误等,切忌死抠语法或断章取义。要着眼于全局,从宏观上考虑。

1.4　完形填空的 3 个解题原则

根据近年成人本科学士学位英语考试完形填空题的特点,要正确解答完形填空题,我们必须遵循下列三项原则。

1. 上下求索:寻信息

有的空格的提示信息很可能在文章的前面出现,有的空格的提示信息也可能在后面出现,有的空格的提示信息在前面和后面都有出现,需要综合起来考虑。

2. 左顾右盼:找搭配

答题时,眼睛不能只盯在空格上或盯在一个句子上,一定要"左顾右盼",弄清前后的固定搭配。

3. 思前想后:通全文

选择答案时,一定要考虑到此选项不但在本句中是可以的,而且要在全文中讲得通。但在具体的解答过程中,还需要对以下解题技巧加以关注。

1.5 完形填空的10个解题技巧

1. 根据首句信息

完形填空题所采用的短文一般不给标题,但首句往往不设空,通常是个完整的句子,它是了解全文的窗口,由此可判断文章的大意或主题。除重视首句信息外,我们在做题前还必须跳过空格,快速浏览全文,整体把握文章大意。

2. 根据行文逻辑

当选项是表示文章的起承转合、上下连贯等逻辑关系的词语时,就要求我们正确判断上下文的逻辑关系,如转折关系、让步关系、因果关系、递进关系、增补关系、比较关系、对比关系等,从而选择恰当的选项。

3. 根据语篇标志

它指能表明各个句群或段落之间的内在联系的词语语篇标志。如表示结构层次的语篇标志词有：firstly, secondly, thirdly, finally 等；表示逻辑关系的词语有：therefore, so, thus, but, however 等；表示递进关系的词语有：even, besides, what's more 等；表示时间关系的词语有：before, after, so far 等；表示选择关系的有：or, whether... or 等等。根据这些语篇标志,我们可以迅速弄清上下文的关系,理清文章的脉络层次,从而作出正确的选择。

4. 根据习惯搭配

就是根据词语的习惯搭配或固定句式等来选择答案。习惯搭配包括动词与名词的搭配、动词与介词或副词的搭配、介词与名词的搭配等。

5. 根据逻辑推理

就是根据文章意思和我们原有的生活经验及科普常识等进行简单的逻辑推理来确定答案。

6. 根据语法分析

在完形填空中单纯考查语法知识的题极少,但借助语法分析来理解句子、推测语境、判断搭配却是必不可少的。语法主要涉及各类从句的引导词、主谓一致、动词时态和语态、倒装结构和虚拟语气等等。

7. 根据语言结构

就是根据对比或对照结构、排比结构、类似结构等语言结构形式来判断和选择答案。

8. 根据词语辨析

一般说来,四个选项中,在联系上下文的情况下,考生很容易能将两个选项排除,剩下两项,需要对上下文再进行细致的推敲和对所剩两选项的词义进行细微的辨析才能确定正确答案。

9. 根据词语复现

有时为了使语篇中的句子相互衔接和连贯,作者会以原词、同义词或近义词、概括性词语等形式重复出现在同一语篇中。有时根据这样的复现词语也可选出正确答案。

10. 根据前后语境

成人本科学士学位英语考试完形填空中绝大多数题是要通过上下文才能作出正确选择的。有的根据上文,有的根据下文,有的要结合上下文,甚至看完通篇并理解才能作出正确的选择。其中根据下文选择的题最多,考生要特别注意。

以上10个技巧需要综合考虑,灵活运用。一个小题可能需要运用其中的两个或几个技巧才能解答,也可能运用不同的技巧都能解答同一个小题。

第二节　历年试题解析

Unit 1

Once upon a time a poor farmer taking a sack of wheat to the mill did not know __71__ to do when it slipped from his horse and fell __72__ the road. The sack was __73__ heavy for him to __74__, and his only hope was that __75__ someone would come riding by and __76__ a hand.

It was not long __77__ a rider appeared, but the farmer's heart sank when he __78__ him, for it was the great man who lived in a castle near by. The farmer __79__ have dared to ask __80__ farmer to help, or any poor man who might have come __81__ the road, but he could not beg a __82__ of so great a man.

__83__, as soon as the great man came up he got __84__ his horse, saying, "I see you've had bad luck, friend. How good it is __85__ I'm here just at the __86__ time." Then he took one __87__ of the sack, the farmer the other, and between them they lifted it on the horse.

"Sir," asked the farmer, "how can I pay you?"

"Easily enough," the great man __88__. "Whenever you see __89__ else in trouble, __90__ the same for him."

71. A. how	B. what	C. which	D. whether
72. A. on	B. in	C. off	D. onto
73. A. so	B. very	C. quite	D. too
74. A. pick	B. lift	C. take	D. leave
75. A. presently	B. immediately	C. generally	D. quickly
76. A. lend	B. present	C. borrow	D. put
77. A. before	B. until	C. after	D. since
78. A. knew	B. understood	C. remembered	D. recognized
79. A. ought	B. should	C. would	D. could
80. A. one	B. other	C. some	D. another
81. A. across	B. along	C. through	D. alone
82. A. favor	B. support	C. hand	D. help
83. A. Nevertheless	B. However	C. Moreover	D. Although
84. A. off	B. from	C. down	D. out of
85. A. when	B. which	C. then	D. that
86. A. exact	B. same	C. right	D. good
87. A. piece	B. end	C. part	D. edge
88. A. referred	B. responded	C. reflected	D. replied
89. A. someone	B. everyone	C. anyone	D. one
90. A. make	B. create	C. do	D. perform

参考译文

从前，有一个穷苦的农夫拿着一袋麦子到磨坊去磨麦子，可是那袋麦子从马上滑到了路上，他不知道该做什么才好。那袋麦子非常重，他搬不到马上去，他的唯一希望就是不久有人骑着马路过这里，帮助他把麦子抬到马上。

不久，一个骑马的人过来了，但是，当他认出那个人时，他的心沉下去了，因为那是一个住在附近城堡的大人物。农夫本来想求别的农夫帮助他，或者求任何路过的穷人帮助他，但他不能求这样的一个大人物帮忙。

不过，那个人一过来，就从马上下来，对农夫说，"朋友，我发现你的运气不好。我来得正是时候，真是不错。"接着，他抬起袋子的一端，农夫抬起另一端，两个人把袋子抬到了马上。

农夫问，"先生，我怎么报答您呢？"

那个大人物答道，"很简单，以后你无论什么时候看到任何人遇到麻烦，就为他做同样的事情。"

解析

71. 本题测试语法。后面的句子说，袋子太重，他搬不到马上去，希望有人帮忙，说明是做的事情，所以应该选 B。

72. 本题测试介词。所填的词与 fell... the road(落到……路)搭配，只有选 D 符合文章的意思。

73. 本题测试语法。此处只有用否定意思才符合文章的意思，too... to...（太……以至于不能……）是否定意思，所以应该选 D。

74. 本题测试动词。pick 的意思是捡起，lift 的意思是举起、抬起，take 的意思是拿，leave 的意思是遗留。袋子是从马上掉下来的，应该是抬回或搬回马上去，并且根据后面的 they lifted it on the horse 可知，应该选 B。

75. 本题测试副词。presently 的意思是不久，immediately 的意思是立刻，generally 的意思是通常，quickly 的意思是迅速地。根据后面的 someone would come 可知，本句话表示将来，所以应该选 A。

76. 本题测试搭配。lend (sb.) a hand 是习惯搭配，意思是"给(某人)帮助"。

77. 本题测试语法。until 与 not 搭配的意思是直到……才，与文章的意思不符；since 的意思是自从……，其主句通常用完成时态；选 B 不符合文章的意思。应该选 A。

78. 本题测试动词。know 的意思是认识，understand 的意思是理解，remember 的意思是记得，recognize 的意思是认出。前面的句子说他的心沉下去了，后面的句子说那是一个住在附近城堡的大人物，说明所填的词应该表示认出人，所以应该选 D。

79. 本题测试语法。根据后面的 any poor man who might have come 可知，本句话表示虚拟。A 的表达不对；B 用的人称不对；D 表示的是可能性，与文章的意思不符。只有选 C。

80. 本题测试限定词。one 强调数量是一个，other 后面通常接复数词，some 后面通常接复数词，another 的意思是另外的、别的。根据后面的 any poor man 可知，此处不是特指某个农夫，所以应该选 D。

81. 本题测试介词。across 的意思是越过……，along 的意思是沿着……，through 的意思是通过……，通常指从一处穿越到另一处，alone 的意思是独自地。所填的词的宾语是 road，所以应选 B。

82. 本题测试搭配。ask/beg a favor of 是习惯搭配，意思是"请求……的帮忙"。

83. 本题测试语法。nevertheless 表示转折，通常不放在句首，however 表示转折，通常用逗号与其他部分隔开，moreover 表示递进，although 表示让步，通常引导句子。后面的句子说，那个人一过来就从马上下来，说明出乎农夫的意料之外，表示转折，所以应该选 B。

84. 本题测试搭配。所填的词与 got 搭配。get off 的意思是下来，get from 搭配不当，get down 的意思是降下，get out of 的意思是避免。所填的词的宾语是 his horse，所以应该选 A。

85. 本题测试语法。所填的词引导句子，所以 C 不对；when 引导时间状语或宾语从句，which 引导定语从句，that 引导主语、宾语或定语从句。本句话中的 it 只是形式主语，真正的主语是所填的词引导的句子，所以应该选 D。

86. 本题测试形容词。exact 的意思是准确的，主要指只允许很小的误差余地的，same 的意思是相同的，right 的意思是合适的，主要指就情况而言是最佳的，good 的意思是不错的。所填的词修饰 time，所以应该选 C。

87. 本题测试搭配。piece 的意思是块、片，end 的意思是端头、末端，part 的意思是部分，edge 的意思是边缘。所填的词修饰 sack(袋子)，根据后面的 the farmer the other 可知，应该选 B。

88. 本题测试搭配。前面的句子是农夫的一句问话，那么后面的句子就应该是答句，说明 A 和 C 不对；respond 通常不指出回答的内容，而 reply 通常指出回答的内容，所以应该选 D。

89. 本题测试搭配。所填的词与 else 搭配，所以 B 和 D 不对；本句话指的是随便什么人，所以应该选 C。

90. 本题测试搭配。make 的意思是制作，create 的意思是创造，do 的意思是做，perform 的意思是履行。所填的词与 the same 搭配，就是指大人物所做的事情，所以应该选 C。

Unit 2

For thousands of years, people thought of glass as something beautiful to look at. Only recently __71__ come to __72__ something look through. Stores __73__ their goods in large glass windows. Glass bottles and jars __74__ food and drink allow us __75__ the contents. Glass __76__ spectacles(眼镜), microscopes, telescopes, and __77__ very useful and necessary objects, __78__ glasses, are used by people who cannot see __79__ or by people who want to protect their eyes __80__ bright light. Microscopes make tiny things larger __81__ we can examine them. Telescopes __82__ objects that are far away appear __83__ closer to us.

__84__ in recent years plastics have replaced glass __85__ conditions where glass might be __86__ broken, there are new uses __87__ for glass that were never imagined in the __88__. Perhaps the greatest __89__ of glass is that its constituent(形成的) parts are inexpensive and can be found __90__ over the world.

71.	A. they	B. do they	C. they have	D. have they
72.	A. think it	B. think if of	C. think it as	D. think of it as
73.	A. protect	B. hide	C. display	D. set aside
74.	A. hold	B. held	C. that hold	D. that holding
75.	A. see	B. to see	C. seeing	D. seen
76.	A. used to make	B. is used to make	C. is used to making	D. used to making
77.	A. many others	B. many other	C. else	D. another
78.	A. and	B. as well	C. or	D. either
79.	A. perfectly	B. perfect	C. perfection	D. perfected
80.	A. from	B. in	C. with	D. beyond
81.	A. so as	B. as that	C. so that	D. such that
82.	A. let	B. watch	C. get	D. make
83.	A. ever	B. rather	C. more	D. much
84.	A. Because of	B. Despite	C. However	D. Although
85.	A. under	B. below	C. within	D. on
86.	A. hardly	B. easily	C. nearly	D. almost
87.	A. being developed	B. be developed	C. be developed	D. to be developed
88.	A. ancient	B. past	C. old	D. aged
89.	A. goodness	B. advance	C. advantage	D. progress
90.	A. all	B. around	C. anywhere	D. wholly

参考译文

几千年来，人们认为玻璃是某种看起来很美丽的东西。只是到了最近，人们才开始认为它是某种可以透视的东西。商店把它们的商品放在大玻璃橱窗里面展示。盛有食物和饮料的玻璃瓶和玻璃罐可以让我们看见里面的东西。玻璃被用来制作眼镜、显微镜、望远镜以及其他许多非常有用也必需的东西，眼镜要么被那些不能看得很清晰的人使用，要么被那些希望保护眼睛免受强光照射的人使用。显微镜使微型物变得更大，以便我们可以观察它们。望远镜使得遥远的东西变得离我们近得多。

近几年,在玻璃很轻易被打破的情况下,虽然塑料代替了玻璃,但是,人们正在开发玻璃的新用途,这些用途在过去是从来没有想象过的。也许,玻璃的最大优势就是,它所制作的东西不贵,可以在全世界见到。

解析

71. 本题测试语法。本句话是由 only 引导的倒装句,后面的主、谓语应该倒装,所以 A 和 C 不对;后面的句子用的是一般现在时态,所以 D 也不对。应选 B。

72. 本题测试语法。所填的词应该与前面句子中的 thought of glass as something beautiful 结构类似,所以应选 D。

73. 本题测试动词。protect 的意思是保护,hide 的意思是隐藏,display 的意思是展示,set aside 的意思是留出。所填的词的宾语是 goods,根据后面的 in large glass windows 可知,应该选 C。

74. 本题测试语法。所填的词修饰 glass bottles and jars,是物体,应该用被动语态,所以应该选 B。

75. 本题测试语法。allow 允许某人(某物)后面应该接动词不定式,所以应该选 B。

76. 本题测试语法。本句话的主语是 glass,是物体,应该用被动语态,所以 A 和 D 不对;is used to make 的意思是被用来制作,is used to making 的意思是习惯于制作。应选 B。

77. 本题测试限定词。many others 后面不必接名词;C 修饰 useful and necessary objects 明显不对;前面的句子只提到了玻璃的一个好处,那么用 D 修饰 useful and necessary objects 也不对。只有选 B。

78. 本题测试搭配。所填的词与后面的 or... 搭配,只有 either 可以与之搭配。

79. 本题测试修饰词。所填的词修饰前面的 see,只有选 A。

80. 本题测试搭配。prevent... from... 是习惯搭配,意思是"防止……免受……"。

81. 本题测试语法。显微镜把微型物放大是为了我们可以观察微型物,说明后面是目的状语,所以应选 C。

82. 本题测试语法。后面的动词用的是原形,并且是物体,只有选 let。

83. 本题测试修饰词。所填的词修饰 closer,所以 A、B 和 C 都不对,应该选 D。

84. 本题测试语法。所填的词引导句子,只有 D 可以引导句子。

85. 本题测试搭配。on condition 是习惯搭配,意思是"在……情况下"。

86. 本题测试搭配。hardly 的意思是几乎不;easily 的意思是轻易,nearly 的意思是几乎,almost 的意思是差不多。句子的主语是 glass,所填的词修饰 broken,所以应该选 B。

87. 本题测试语法。所填的词修饰 use(用途),所以 B 和 C 不对;A 表示现在的动作,D 表示将来的动作。本文用的是一般现在时态,所以应该选 A。

88. 本题测试搭配。in the past 是习惯搭配,意思是"过去"。

89. 本题测试名词。goodness 的意思是仁慈、善良,advance 的意思是进步、前进,advantage 的意思是优势、有利条件,progress 的意思是进步、前进。前面的句子提到了玻璃的许多好处,后面的句子还是在讲玻璃的好处,所以应该选 C。

90. 本题测试搭配。all over the world 是习惯搭配,意思是"在全世界"。

Unit 3

Tourism has become a very big __71__. For Spain, Italy and Greece it is the largest __72__ of foreign exchange, and __73__ for Britain, it is the fourth. Faced __74__ this huge income, no government can afford to look __75__ on the business: questions of hotel bath rooms, beach umbrellas and ice-cream sales are now __76__ by ministers of tourism with solemn expertise. Before the Second World War the tourist industry was widely __77__ as being unmanly and stupid. But __78__ has become a new industry, as trade business used __79__; in Spain, Italy, Greece and much of Eastern Europe, new road __80__ have opened up in the country, first to tourists, and __81__ to industry and locals.

__82__ of tourism is a nationalized industry, a __83__ part of national planning. In a place west of Marseilles, the French government is killing mosquitoes and __84__ six big vacation places to __85__ nearly a million tourists. In Eastern Europe, a whole new seaside __86__ has sprung up; __87__ the last few years the governments have greatly __88__ when tourists from the West __89__ from half a million four years __90__ to nearly two million last year.

71. A. firm	B. business	C. company	D. affair
72. A. factor	B. resource	C. source	D. cause
73. A. even	B. yet	C. also	D. ever
74. A. in front of	B. of	C. with	D. for
75. A. up	B. at	C. for	D. down
76. A. determined	B. discussed	C. argued	D. sold
77. A. regarded	B. said	C. talked	D. spread
78. A. agriculture	B. war	C. tourism	D. education
79. A. be done	B. done	C. to do	D. to doing
80. A. types	B. styles	C. buildings	D. systems
81. A. than	B. later	C. then	D. latter
82. A. Many	B. All	C. None	D. Much
83. A. key	B. minor	C. linking	D. questioning
84. A. built	B. building	C. to be built	D. have built
85. A. attract	B. pull	C. hold	D. contain
86. A. civilization	B. culture	C. writing	D. book
87. A. over	B. for	C. after	D. beyond
88. A. suffered	B. lost	C. invested	D. benefited
89. A. added	B. divided	C. reduced	D. multiplied
90. A. since	B. before	C. ago	D. after

参考译文

旅游业成为一个很大的产业。对于西班牙、意大利以及希腊来说,它是最大的外汇来源,甚至对于英国来说,它也是第四大外汇来源。面对这笔巨大的收入,没有哪国政府可以轻视这个产业;现在,具有严谨的专门知识的旅游部长们正在讨论旅店的浴室、海滨的太阳伞以及冰淇淋的销售问题。第二次世界大战之前,人们普遍认为旅游业是一个丢人、无聊的产业。但是,旅游业已经成为一个新的产业,正如曾经的贸易业那样;在西班牙、意大利、希腊以及东欧的大部分地区,乡村的新公路体系已经建立,首先是为旅游者服务,其次才为工业和当地人服务。

大多数旅游业都是国有产业,是国家计划的一个主要部分。在马赛的西部地区,法国政府正在灭蚊,正在兴建6个大型度假区,以便吸引近百万旅游者。在东欧,一个全新的海滨文化正在兴起;过去几年,政府已经获得了极大利益——西欧来的旅游者从4年前的50万增加到去年的200万。

解析

71. 本题测试名词。firm 的意思是公司、商号,business 的意思是商业、行业,company 的意思是公司、陪伴,affair 的意思是事务、事情。根据后面的 no government can afford to look... on the business 可知,应选 B。

72. 本题测试名词。factor 的意思是因素、要素,resource 的意思是资源、财力,source 的意思是来源、源极,cause 的意思是原因、动机。foreign exchange 修饰所填的词,根据后面的 this huge income 可知,应选 C。

73. 本题测试语法。前面句子提到旅游业对于西班牙、意大利以及希腊的意义重大,本句话提到英国,说旅游业是其第四大外汇来源,说明本句话是在强调。只有 even 可以表示强调。

74. 本题测试搭配。face 通常与 with 搭配,意思是“面对……”。

75. 本题测试搭配。look down upon/on 是习惯搭配,意思是“轻视、看不起……”。

76. 本题测试搭配。determine 的意思是决定,discuss 的意思是讨论,argue 的意思是争论, sell 的意思是销售。所填的词的宾语是 questions,所以 A 和 D 不对;discuss 主要指与他人就……问题交换意见,argue 主要是指陈述事实或理由来支持别人所反对的观点,所以应选 B。

77. 本题测试搭配。所填的词与后面的 as 搭配,只有 regard 可以与之搭配,意思是“把……看成是,认为……是……”。

78. 本题测试语法。前面的句子说的是二战前人们对旅游业的看法,本句话转折说的是旅游业的现状,所以应选 C。

79. 本题测试语法。used to+动词原形的意思是“过去常……”,be used to+动名词的意思是“习惯于……”,所以应选 C。

80. 本题测试名词。type 的意思是类型、典型,style 的意思是风格、时尚,building 的意思是建筑物、营造物,system 的意思是体系、系统。road 与所填的词搭配作 open up(建立、建设)的宾语,只有选 D 符合文章的意思。

81. 本题测试语法。前面句子提到 first to tourists,本句话提到的是 to industry and locals,应该是递进,所以应该选 then。

82. 本题测试语法。tourism 是不可数名词,所以 A 不对;选 C 与文章的意思相反;B 太绝对,与事实不符。只有选 D 符合文章的意思。

83. 本题测试形容词。key 的意思是主要的,minor 的意思是次要的,linking 的意思是连接的,questioning 的意思是质疑的。前面的句子提到,旅游业是一个很大的产业,它是一些国家的最大外汇来源,说明旅游业是国家经济的重要部分,所以应该选 A。

84. 本题测试语法。根据前面的 and 可知,所填的词应该与前面句子的时态一致,所以应选 B。

85. 本题测试动词。attract 的意思是吸引、招引,pull 的意思是吸引、引诱,hold 的意思是容纳、保持,contain 的意思是包含、容纳。前面的句子说兴建了大型度假区,后面的句子说游客从 50 万增长到 200 万,说明所填的词表示吸引之意,所以 C 和 D 不对;attract 主要指引起……的兴趣、注意等,pull 主要指招揽观众,所以应选 A。

86. 本题测试名词。civilization 的意思是文明,culture 的意思是文化,writing 的意思是写作,book 的意思是书本。所填的词与 seaside 搭配作 spring up(兴起)的宾语,所以 C 和 D 不对;civilization 主要指人类社会知识、文化和物质发展的高级阶段,culture 主要指某一时期的行为方式、艺术、信仰或风俗等的特点和产物,所以应该选 B。

87. 本题测试搭配。over 加一段过去的时间,表示“在过去的某段时期”。

88. 本题测试动词。suffer 的意思是遭受、受损, lose 的意思是损失、失去,invest 的意思是投资、投入,benefit 的意思是获利、受益。后面的句子说,旅游者从以前的 50 万增长到去年的 200 万,说明政府获得了很大的利益,所以应选 D。

89. 本题测试搭配。add 的意思是增加,通常与 to 搭配,divide 的意思是划分,通常与 into 搭配,reduce 的意思是减少,multiply 的意思是增加,通常与 from... to 搭配。应该选 D。

90. 本题测试语法。表示几年前应该用 ago。

Unit 4

Television broadcasts are __71__ to an area that is within the __72__ of the sending station or its relay (中转站). __73__ television relays are often placed on hills and mountains so that they can __74__ a wider region, they still can not cover more land than one from the hilltop __75__ a clear day.

However, the rays also go out into the atmosphere, __76__ there is a relay station on a satellite that __77__ around the earth, it can send the pictures to any point on the earth from which the satellite is __78__. Three satellites __79__ turning around over the equator (赤道)

send any television program to any part of the earth. __80__ makes it possible for world __81__ of newspapers to give the news in all countries at the same time. __82__ it may be possible for a subscriber（订户）to a televised newspaper to __83__ a button and see a newspaper page __84__ his television screen. He could also decide when he wants the page __85__, __86__, by dialing different such as __87__ on a telephone dial, he could choose the language or the edition of the paper he wants to read.

It seems strange to think that, even today, methods of the __88__ are not entirely useless. For example, sometimes __89__ agencies which use radio and Telstar also use pigeons to __90__ messages between offices in large cities because the pigeons are not bothered by traffic problems.

71. A. prohibited	B. bounded	C. limited	D. shifted
72. A. range	B. view	C. miles	D. distance
73. A. Even	B. Although	C. Unless	D. Whenever
74. A. cover	B. spread	C. help	D. pass
75. A. in	B. during	C. on	D. at
76. A. and then	B. by far	C. when	D. and if
77. A. spins	B. revolves	C. jumps	D. circles
78. A. watched	B. visible	C. spotted	D. protected
79. A. always	B. temporarily	C. permanently	D. periodically
80. A. This	B. That	C. What	D. Which
81. A. population	B. editions	C. articles	D. reports
82. A. The other day	B. At the future	C. Someday	D. One day
83. A. touch	B. press	C. suppress	D. thumb
84. A. at	B. in	C. on	D. by
85. A. turn	B. to turn	C. turning	D. to be turned
86. A. also	B. moreover	C. and	D. then
87. A. what	B. these	C. those	D. ones
88. A. passed	B. past	C. old days	D. out-of-date
89. A. press	B. conference	C. newspapers	D. books
90. A. bring	B. take	C. distribute	D. send

参考译文

电视广播被局限于发射台或中转站可以覆盖的区域。虽然电视台的中转站通常安置在山上，以便它们可以覆盖一个更广的范围，但是，它们覆盖的范围仍然比不上在晴朗的天气安放在山顶的中转站。

不过，信号也会辐射到太空，如果一颗环绕地球运转的卫星上有中转站，那么这个中转站就可以从可视的卫星上传播到地球的任何一个地方。三颗始终在赤道上空盘旋的卫星可以向地球的任何一个地方发送电视节目。这使得报纸的世界版本可以同时在世界各国发布新闻。将来有一天，订户可以订阅由电视播送的报纸，按一下按钮，就可以在其电视屏幕上看报纸。他还可以决定何时翻页面，并且，通过调不同的频道，就像电话拨号那样，他可以挑选他希望看的文字或报纸版面。

甚至就在目前，认为以前的方法完全没有用似乎很奇怪。比如，利用广播和通讯卫星的新闻报道机构有时也利用鸽子在大城市的办公室之间传播信息，因为鸽子不会受交通问题的困扰。

解析

71. 本题测试动词。prohibit 的意思是禁止，bound 的意思是限制，limit 的意思是限制，shift 的意思是转移。根据 television broadcasts 与 sending station(发射台)、relay 中转站之间的关系可知，television broadcasts 受到限制，所以 A 和 D 不对；bound 主要指组成界限或限制，limit 主要指限制或限定在某一范围之内，所以应选 C。

72. 本题测试搭配。within the range of 是习惯搭配，意思是“在……范围内”。

73. 本题测试语法。所填的词引导从句，所以 A 不对；although 引导让步状语从句，unless 引导条件状语从句，whenever 引导时间状语从句。根据后面的 they still can not cover 可知，后面的句子表示转折，所以应选 B。

74. 本题测试动词。句子的主语是 television relays，根据后面的 they still can not cover 可知，应选 A。

75. 本题测试搭配。在确定日子前面应该用 on。

76. 本题测试语法。所填的词引导句子，所以 B 和 C 不对；后面的句子与前面的句子并列，并且引导从句，所以应选 D。

77. 本题测试动词。spin 的意思是旋转，revolve 的意思是旋转，jump 的意思是跳跃，circle 的意思是循环。句子的主语是 satellite，所以 C 不对；spin 主要指快速旋转、自旋，revolve 主要指绕中心点运行，circle 主要指环绕……作圆周运动。根据后面的 around the earth 可知，应选 B。

78. 本题测试修饰词。所填的词修饰 satellite。watched 的意思是观察的，visible 的意思是可见的，spotted 的意思是有污点的，protected 的意思是被保护的。根据前面的 can send the pictures to any point on the earth 可知，应选 B。

79. 本题测试限定词。所填的词修饰 turning around over the equator。always 通常不修饰动词，temporarily 的意思是暂时地，permanently 的意思是不变地，永恒地，periodically 的意思是周期性地。根据后面的 send any television program to any part of the earth 可知，应选 C。

80. 本题测试语法。所填的词指代前面句子的内容，所以 C 和 D 不对；就近的用 this，远的用 that，所以应选 A。

81. 本题测试搭配。newspaper 修饰所填的词。population 的意思是人口，edition 的意思是版面、版本，article 的意思是文章，report 的意思是报道。根据后面的 give the news 可知，应该选 B。

82. 本题测试语法。本句话讲的是未来的事情，所以 A 不对；B 的表达不对；someday 主要指将来某个不确定的时候，one day 主要指某一天、总有一天，所以选 C 符合文章的意思。

83. 本题测试搭配。所填的词与 button 搭配。press button 是习惯搭配，意思是“按按钮”。

84. 本题测试搭配。screen 通常与 on 搭配。

85. 本题测试语法。want 加某人或某物后面应该接动词不定式，所以 A 和 C 不对；D 的语态不对。应选 B。

86. 本题测试语法。后面的句子与前面的句子意思连贯，所以所填的词表示并列，应该选 C。

87. 本题测试语法。本句话是说，通过调不同的频道，可以挑选希望看的文字或报纸版面，就像电话拨号那样，说明所填的词指代“不同的频道”，所以应选 C。

88. 本题测试搭配。“过去”通常用 the past 表示。

89. 本题测试名词。press 的意思是新闻报道，conference 的意思是会议，newspaper 的意思是报纸，book 的意思是书本。根据后面的 use radio and Telstar 可知，应该选 A。

90. 本题测试搭配。所填的词的宾语是 messages，根据后面的 between offices in large cities 可知，应该选 send。

Unit 5

Can you imagine how you would feel if you fell dangerously ill and could not reach or call a doctor? Millions of people __71__ the world are in this unfortunate __72__, living in distant places __73__ there are no railways, no proper roads and no telephones. Thousands of __74__ are lost every year __75__ could have been saved if medical attention __76__ in time.

__77__ today help could be brought quickly and easily __78__ many of these people

__79__ full advantage was taken __80__ the aeroplane. __81__ country has proved this __82__ than Australia. The Australians __83__ greater use of the aeroplane than any __84__ people in the world. In no other country __85__ the total number of miles flown by the __86__ person so high. In fact, it has been __87__ that Australians jump into planes __88__ people in other countries jump into trains and buses. It is not surprising, __89__ that Australia should have been the first country __90__ a Flying Doctor Service.

71. A. on B. through C. all over D. within
72. A. society B. world C. way D. position
73. A. where B. because C. although D. which
74. A. people B. children C. families D. lives
75. A. when B. in which C. which D. they
76. A. had been provided B. had been paid more C. was given D. was provided
77. A. Even B. But C. Finally D. So
78. A. from B. with C. in D. to
79. A. but B. if only C. and D. unless
80. A. of B. from C. about D. on
81. A. One B. Any C. Not D. No
82. A. better B. worse C. more D. less
83. A. made B. did C. were making D. make
84. A. of B. else C. other D. Japanese
85. A. of B. in C. are D. is
86. A. living B. average C. brave D. medical
87. A. suggested B. estimated C. worked out D. said
88. A. when B. while C. as D. but
89. A. therefore B. in a way C. perhaps D. accordingly
90. A. of B. to develop C. made up D. into

参考译文

如果你病得很重却又联系不到医生,你能想象你的感受吗? 全世界数百万人就处于这种不幸的境地,他们生活在没有铁路、没有专门的公路以及电话的地方。每年,成千上万人失去了生命,如果提供了及时的医治,这些生命本来是可以被挽救的。

但如今,只要充分利用飞机的优势,就可以迅速、便捷地给许多这样的人提供帮助。没有哪个国家提供的这种帮助比澳大利亚更好。澳大利亚人比世界上任何其他国家的人都更广泛地利用飞机。没有哪个国家的普通人乘飞机的总里程有如此长。事实上,据说,澳大利亚人乘飞机就像其他国家的人坐火车和公共汽车。因此,澳大利亚是世界上第一个开办乘飞机出诊医生的国家就不足为奇了。

解析

71. 本题测试搭配。all over the world 是习惯搭配,意思是"在全世界"。

72. 本题测试名词。society 的意思是社会,world 的意思是世界,way 的意思是方法,position 的意思是境地。前面的句子说,你病得很重却又联系不到医生,这讲的是一种状况,并且 unfortunate 修饰所填的词,所以应选 D。

73. 本题测试语法。所填的词引导从句修饰 places,是地点,只有选 where。

74. 本题测试搭配。所填的词作 lost 和 save 的宾语,只有 D 与之搭配符合文章的意思。

75. 本题测试语法。所填的词引导从句修饰 lives,只有选 C。

76. 本题测试语法。根据前面的 could have been saved 以及 if 可知,本句话是虚拟语气,所以 C 和 D 不对;本句话并没有进行比较,所以 B 不对。应选 A。

77. 本题测试语法。根据该段第一句话中的 today help could be brought quickly and easily 可知,本句话讲的是现在状况的改善,说明本段意思转折,所以应选 B。

78. 本题测试介词。"给某人提供……"中的"给"应该用 to。

79. 本题测试语法。所填的词引导的是条件状语,所以 A 和 C 不对;如果选 D,则与文章的意思相反。应选 B。

80. 本题测试语法。所填的词应该是连接 full advantage 和 the aeroplane,所以应选 A。

81. 本题测试语法。根据后面的 The Australians... greater use of the aeroplane than any people in the world newspaper 可知,本句话应该表示否定,所以 A 和 B 不对;not 修饰 country 不对。应该选 D。

82. 本题测试语法。根据后面的 than 可知,本句话是在比较,并且后面的句子都是在讲澳大利亚取得的成就,所以应选 A。

83. 本题测试语法。本段讲的是现在的情况,应该用一般现在时态,所以应选 D。

84. 本题测试修饰词。所填的词修饰 people in the world,只有选 C。

85. 本题测试语法。本句话是一个倒装句,句子的主语是 the total number of miles,是一个单数,so high 是句子的表语,所以只有选 D。

86. 本题测试修饰词。后面的句子说,澳大利亚人乘飞机就像其他国家的人坐火车和公共汽车,说明这讲的是澳大利亚人的普遍情况,所以应选 B。

87. 本题测试语法。后面的句子并没有给数据,所以 B 和 C 不对;A 的意思是暗示,与文章的意思不符。应选 D。

88. 本题测试语法。所填的词引导的从句修饰前面整句话,只有 as 可以引导定语从句。

89. 本题测试语法。前面的句子都是在讲澳大利亚取得的成就,本句话是在做总结,所以 B 和 C 不对;accordingly 通常放在句首或句尾,而 therefore 可以放在句中。应选 A。

90. 本题测试语法。所填的词与 a Flying Doctor Service 搭配修饰 the first country,只有选 B。

Unit 6

In China it is relatively usual to ask people their age, but in the west this question is generally regarded as impolite. This is particularly true __71__ women, and even more __72__ if the inquirer (问者) is a man.

However, it is very __73__ to ask children their age, and some adults may not mind being asked __74__. In fact, some elderly people are quite happy to __75__ the age, especially if they feel they look young __76__ their age. Nevertheless, it is not very wise to ask a __77__ question like "How old are you?" If elderly people want to talk about their age, and perhaps receive a compliment(恭维话) on how young they look, they may easily bring __78__ the topic themselves and ask the other to __79__ how old they are. __80__ such a situation, it is quite acceptable to discuss age __81__. They normally expect to be complimented on their youthfulness, rather than __82__ that they look very old.

__83__ Westerners do not usually ask people directly how old they are, this does not __84__ that they are not interested to know how old other people are. They may ask __85__ for the information, __86__ they may try to __87__ the topic indirectly, sometimes discussions about educational __88__ and the number of years of working experience may provide some __89__, but this is not always the __90__. Of course, individuals also vary in what they are interested or willing to talk about.

71. A. with	B. for	C. of	D. to
72. A. that	B. than	C. such	D. so
73. A. average	B. normal	C. expected	D. unusual
74. A. too	B. also	C. neither	D. either
75. A. reveal	B. reflect	C. release	D. remark
76. A. to	B. with	C. for	D. at
77. A. open	B. strange	C. impolite	D. direct
78. A. about	B. up	C. along	D. to
79. A. guess	B. know	C. learn	D. predict
80. A. For	B. With	C. In	D. On
81. A. free	B. with freedom	C. freely	D. in a free way
82. A. being told	B. told	C. to tell	D. to be told
83. A. Even	B. Though even	C. Even that	D. Even though
84. A. include	B. intend	C. mean	D. conclude
85. A. no one else	B. anyone else	C. someone else	D. everyone else
86. A. still else	B. or else	C. so else	D. rather else
87. A. approach	B. solve	C. address	D. discuss
88. A. background	B. level	C. knowledge	D. systems
89. A. topics	B. clues	C. evidences	D. suggestions
90. A. case	B. truth	C. reality	D. fact

参考译文

在中国,询问人们的年龄很平常,但在西方,问这个问题通常被认为不礼貌。对于女性来说尤其如此,如果询问者是一个男性更是如此。

不过,询问孩子的年龄非常正常,有些成人也可能不介意被问这个问题。事实上,有些老年人非常乐意公开自己的年龄,尤其是如果他们觉得在他们那个年龄他们还显得年轻时更是如此。但是,直接问别人像“你多大年龄了?”这样的问题很不明智。如果老年人希望谈论他们的年龄,也许在你说“他们显得年轻”这样的恭维话后,他们自己可能会一下子就提出这个话题,要别人猜他们多大年龄了。在这种情况下,随意讨论年龄就是可以接受的。他们通常希望别人恭维他们的年轻,而不是被告知他们显得非常老。

即使西方人通常不直接询问别人有多大年龄,但这并不意味着他们对于了解别人有多大不感兴趣。他们可能询问别人这方面的信息,要不然,他们可能试着直接涉及这个话题,有时,有关教育背景的讨论以及工作经历的年限可以提供一些线索,但情况并不总是这样。当然,人们感兴趣的方面或喜欢谈论的方面也不尽相同。

解析

71. 本题测试介词。“对于……来说……”通常用 to。

72. 本题测试语法。所填的词指代前面句子的内容,所以选 D 符合文章的意思。

73. 本题测试形容词。average 的意思是一般的,normal 的意思是正常的,expected 的意思是期望的,unusual 的意思是不寻常的。所填的词应该与前面句子 it is relatively usual to ask people their age 中的 usual 的意思相近,所以应选 B。

74. 本题测试语法。所填的词放在句尾,只有 A 和 D 可以放在句尾;A 表示肯定,D 表示否定,所以应选 D。

75. 本题测试动词。reveal 的意思是公开, reflect 的意思是表现,release 的意思是释放,通常指从囚禁、约束或痛苦中解放,remark 的意思是谈论,通常要与 on 或 upon 搭配使用。所填的词的宾语是 the age,所以应选 A。

76. 本题测试搭配。与 age 搭配的介词通常是 at。

77. 本题测试形容词。open 的意思是公开的,strange 的意思是奇怪的,impolite 的意思是不礼貌的,direct

的意思是直接的。后面的句子说,也许在你说"他们显得年轻"这样的恭维话后,他们自己可能会一下子就谈到年龄这个话题,所以应选 D。

78. 本题测试搭配。bring about 的意思是使发生、致使,bring up 的意思是提出、引出,bring along 的意思是使发展、引来,bring to 的意思是停止、阻碍。所填的词的宾语是 the topic,所以应选 B。

79. 本题测试动词。guess 的意思是猜测,know 的意思是知道,learn 的意思是了解,predict 的意思是预测。本文主要讨论的是询问别人年龄的问题,所以应选 A。

80. 本题测试搭配。situation 通常与 in 搭配。

81. 本题测试修饰词。所填的词修饰 discuss age,所以应选 C。

82. 本题测试语法。rather than 后面通常接动词原形,所以 A 和 B 不对;所填的词的语态应该与 to be complimented 相同,所以应选 D。

83. 本题测试语法。所填的词引导从句,只有 D 可以引导从句。

84. 本题测试固定句型。It/this does not mean that 是固定句型,意思是"这并不意味着……"。

85. 本题测试语法。选 A 则与文章的意思相反;B 和 D 太绝对,与文章的意思不符。只有选 C 符合文章的意思。

86. 本题测试语法。选项中只有 B 的表达正确,意思是"要不然,否则"。

87. 本题测试动词。approach 的意思是接近、涉及,solve 的意思是解决、解答,address 的意思是发表演说、致辞,discuss 的意思是讨论、谈论。所填的词的宾语是 the topic,说明 B 和 C 不对;后面的句子说,有关教育问题的讨论以及工作经历的年限可以提供一些有关年龄的蛛丝马迹,说明并不是直接讨论年龄这个话题,所以应选 A。

88. 本题测试搭配。所填的词与 educational 搭配,指的是一个人接受教育的情况,只有选 A 符合文章的意思。

89. 本题测试名词。topic 的意思是话题,clue 的意思是线索,evidence 的意思是证据,suggestion 的意思是建议。前面的句子提到,也许在你说"他们显得年轻"这样的恭维话后,他们自己可能会一下子就提出这个话题,要别人猜他们多大年龄了,说明有关教育背景的讨论以及工作经历的年限可以提供的是一些线索,不可能是证据,所以应选 B。

90. 本题测试固定句型。It/this is not always the case 是固定句型,意思是"并不总是如此"。

Unit 7

What do we mean by a perfect English pronunciation? In one __56__ there are as many different kinds of English as there are speakers of it. __57__ two speakers speak in exactly the same __58__. We can always hear differences __59__ them, and the pronunciation of English __60__ a great deal in different geographical __61__. How do we decide what sort of English to use as a __62__? This is not a question that can be __63__ in the same way for all foreign learners of English. __64__ you live in a part of the world __65__ India or West Africa, where there is a long __66__ of speaking English for general communication purpose, you should __67__ to acquire a good variety of the pronunciation of this area. It would be __68__ in these circumstances to use as a model BBC English or __69__ of the sort. On the other hand, if you live in a country __70__ there is no traditional use of English, you must take __71__ your model some form of __72__ English pronunciation. It does not __73__ very much which form you choose. The most __74__ way is to take as your model the sort of English you can __75__ most often.

56. A. meaning B. sense C. case D. situation
57. A. Not B. No C. None D. Nor
58. A. type B. form C. sort D. way
59. A. between B. among C. of D. from

60. A. changes	B. varies	C. shifts	D. alters
61. A. areas	B. parts	C. countries	D. spaces
62. A. direction	B. guide	C. symbol	D. model
63. A. given	B. responded	C. satisfied	D. answered
64. A. Because	B. When	C. If	D. Whether
65. A. as	B. in	C. like	D. near
66. A. custom	B. use	C. tradition	D. habit
67. A. aim	B. propose	C. select	D. ten
68. A. fashion	B. mistake	C. nonsense	D. possibility
69. A. everything	B. nothing	C. anything	D. things
70. A. where	B. that	C. which	D. wherever
71. A. to	B. with	C. on	D. as
72. A. practical	B. domestic	C. native	D. new
73. A. care	B. affect	C. trouble	D. matter
74. A. effective	B. sensitive	C. ordinary	D. careful
75. A. listen	B. hear	C. notice	D. find

参考译文

谈到"正确的英语发音",我们指的是什么？从某种意义上来说,有多少说话者,就有多少种不同的发音。没有哪两个说话者以完全相同的方式讲英语。我们通常可以听出他们之间的区别,地理位置不同,英语的发音就有很大的区别。我们怎样确定哪种英语才能作为标准(英语)使用呢？对于所有学习英语的外国人来说,这个问题不能以同样的方式回答。

如果你生活在像印度或西非这样的地方——长久以来,这些地方的人有为了交流的目的而讲英语的传统,你的目的就应该是了解该地区的不同发音。在这种状况下,讲像 BBC 那样的标准英语或任何类似的英语是一种错误。相反,如果你生活在没有讲英语的传统的国家,你就应该把某种本土英语发音当作标准。你选择哪种发音没有太大的关系。最有效的方式就是把你能最常听到的那种英语作为标准。

解析

56. 本题测试习惯搭配。in a/one sense 是习惯搭配,意思是"从某种意义上来说"。

57. 本题测试语法。A 和 C 修饰 two speakers 不对;前面的句子并不是否定,所以 D 也不对。应选 B。

58. 本题测试搭配。in... way 是习惯搭配,意思是"以……方式"。

59. 本题测试搭配。difference 后面通常接 between 或 in。

60. 本题测试搭配。所填的词应该与后面的 in different geographical... 搭配,只有 vary 可以与 from... to... 和 in... 搭配。

61. 本题测试搭配。所填的词与 geographical(地理的)搭配,只有 area 与之搭配符合文章的意思。

62. 本题测试名词。direction 的意思是方向,guide 的意思是指南,symbol 的意思是符号,model 的意思是标准、模板。根据后面的 take as your model the sort of English 可知,应选 D。

63. 本题测试搭配。所填的词的宾语是 question,所以 A 和 C 不对;respond 主要是指作出答复,通常不指出回答的内容,answer 主要指对某个问题的口头或书面的回答,所以应选 D。

64. 本题测试语法。所填的词引导条件状语从句,所以 A 和 D 不对;when 也可以引导条件状语,但强调的是时间,而 if 引导的从句强调的是条件,所以应选 C。

65. 本题测试介词。所填的词与 India or West Africa situation 搭配,修饰 a part of the world,所以应选 C。

66. 本题测试名词。custom 的意思是习惯、风俗,主要指某人的习惯性做法或某一特定群体或地区的人们所遵循的惯例,use 的意思是使用、用法,tradition 的意思是传统、惯例,主要指某民族一直遵守的一种思想或行为方式,habit 的意思是习惯、习性,主要指某人的习惯性的举止或做法。所填的词指的是像印度或西非这些地方人们的普遍习惯,所以应选 C。

67. 本题测试动词。aim 的意思是以……为目标、目的是……,propose 的意思是计划、打算,select 的意思是选择、挑选,turn 的意思是转向、翻到。根据句中的 you should... 可知,本句话表示目的,所以应选 A。

68. 本题测试名词。fashion 的意思是时尚,mistake 的意思是错误,nonsense 的意思是胡说,possibility 的意思是可能性。前面的句子说,在有讲英语传统的国家,你的目的就应该是了解该地区的不同发音,说明讲标准英语不对,所以应选 B。

69. 本题测试不定代词。本句话指的是任何像 BBC 标准英语的发音,所以选 C 符合文章的意思。

70. 本题测试语法。所填的词引导从句修饰 country,是地点,所以应选 A。

71. 本题测试介词。根据后面的 take as your model the sort of English 可知,应选 D。

72. 本题测试形容词。practical 的意思是实际的,domestic 的意思是国内的,主要指国家内部的,native 的意思是本土的,主要指出生地的,new 的意思是新的。根据前面的 On the other hand 可知,后面的句子意思与前面句子对应,也就是应该把讲英语母语者的发音作为标准音,所以应选 C。

73. 本题测试固定句型。It does (not) matter 是固定句型,意思是"有(没有)关系"。

74. 本题测试搭配。effective 的意思是有效的,sensitive 的意思是敏感的,ordinary 的意思是普通的,careful 的意思是认真的。所填的词修饰 way(方法),所以选 A 符合文章的意思。

75. 本题测试搭配。listen 的意思是听,与 to 搭配才能跟听到的内容,hear 的意思是听见,notice 的意思是注意到,find 的意思是发现。所填的词的宾语是 the sort of English,所以应选 B。

Unit 8

People used to say, "The hand that rocks the cradle rules the world." And "__56__ every successful man there's a woman."

__57__ these saying mean the same thing. Men __58__ the world, but their wives rule them.

Most of the American women like __59__ their husbands and __60__ successful, __61__ some of them want __62__ for themselves. They want __63__ jobs. When they work they want to be __64__ paid. They want to be as successful as __65__.

The American women's liberation(解放)movement was started by women who don't want to __66__ successful men. They want to stand __67__ men, with the same chance for success. They don't want to be told that certain jobs or offices are __68__ to them. They refuse to work side by side with men who do the same work for __69__ pay.

A __70__ woman must be __71__ of being a woman and have confidence(自信)in __72__. If somebody says to her, "You've come a long way, baby." She'll smile and answer, "Not nearly as __73__ as I'm going to go, baby!"

This movement is quite new, and __74__ American women do not agree. But it has already made some important changes in women's __75__ and in men's lives, too.

56. A. Behind　　B. Beside　　C. Before　　D. Under
57. A. Neither　　B. All　　C. Both　　D. Either
58. A. manage　　B. have　　C. control　　D. rule
59. A. forcing　　B. to make　　C. waiting　　D. looking
60. A. fathers　　B. mothers　　C. sons　　D. daughters
61. A. so　　B. but　　C. thus　　D. or
62. A. more　　B. little　　C. everything　　D. nothing

63. A. light	B. heavy	C. no	D. good
64. A. nice	B. fairly	C. continuously	D. endlessly
65. A. husbands	B. others	C. men	D. other women
66. A. walk beside	B. move behind	C. go before	D. stand behind
67. A. beside	B. for	C. behind	D. against
68. A. opened	B. closed	C. open	D. close
69. A. a different	B. the same	C. a higher	D. a high
70. A. good	B. free	C. working	D. liberated
71. A. able	B. kind	C. proud	D. fond
72. A. her heart	B. herself	C. her position	D. her husband
73. A. far	B. farther	C. long	D. distant
74. A. some	B. all	C. few	D. many
75. A. lives	B. world	C. society	D. position

参考译文

人们常说,“摇摇篮的手统治世界。”他们还说,“每一个成功的男士背后都有一个女性。”

这两种说法都表示同一个意思。男性统治世界,但他们的妻子统治他们。

大多数美国女性都乐意使她们的丈夫和儿子成功,但其中的有些人却为自己要求的更多。她们希望得到好工作。工作时,她们希望得到公平的报酬。她们希望像男性那样成功。

美国的女性解放运动是由那些不愿意站在成功男士后面的女性发起的。她们希望与男性平起平坐,有相同的成功机会。她们不想被告知某些工作或办公室不适应她们。她们拒绝与工作相同但报酬不同的男性一起工作。

一个被解放的女性应该为自己是一名女性感到骄傲,应该对自己有信心。如果有人对她说,“宝贝,你有点落伍了。”她会笑着回答,“还不至于那么过分,宝贝!”

这场运动还很时新,许多美国女性也不赞同这场运动。但是,这场运动不仅给女性的生活而且给男性的生活带来了一些重大变化。

解析

56. 本题测试固定句型。Behind every successful man there's a woman. 是一个固定说法,意思是“每一个成功的男士背后都有一个女性。”

57. 本题测试语法。前面段落讲了两句话,所以 B 和 D 不对;选 A 则与文章的意思相反。应选 C。

58. 本题测试动词。所填的词应该与后面 their wives rule them 中的 rule 意思相近,所以应选 D。

59. 本题测试语法。所填的词应该与后面的 successful 搭配,只有 make 后面可以接形容词。

60. 本题测试语法。所填的词应该与 husbands 属于同类,所以 B 和 D 不对;选 A 与文章的意思不符。只有选 C。

61. 本题测试语法。前面的句子讲的是大多数女性的做法,而本句话讲的是某些女性的做法,并且意思与前面句子对应,所以应选 B。

62. 本题测试语法。根据后面的 they want... they want to be... they want to be... 可知,应选 A。

63. 本题测试搭配。所填的词的修饰 jobs,所以应选 D。

64. 本题测试修饰词。所填的词修饰 paid,所以 A 不对;选 C 和 D 与文章的意思不符。应选 B。

65. 本题测试语法。本句话是女性与男性之间的比较,所以应选 C。

66. 本题测试短语。walk beside 的意思是和……并肩走,move behind 的意思是在……背后移动,go before 的意思是走在前面,stand behind 的意思是站在……的背后、做后援。前面的段落说,有些女性希望像男性那样成功,说明她们不愿意做幕后工作,所以应选 D。

67. 本题测试语法。本句话与前面句子的意思相反,所以应选 A。

68. 本题测试语法。根据前面的 They don't want to be told 可知,选 A 和 C 与文章的意思相反;本句话的主语是 certain jobs or offices,是物,所以应该用被动语态。应选 B。

69. 本题测试语法。根据前面的 They refuse to work side by side 可知,选 B 与文章的意思相反;根据前面的 with the same chance for success 可知,所填的词应该与 the same 意思相反。只有选 A。

70. 本题测试语法。前面的段落提到了女性的解放运动,本段讲的就是这些女性的行为,所以应选 D。

71. 本题测试搭配。所填的词与 of 搭配,所以 A 不对;be kind of 的意思是好心肠的,be proud of 的意思是对……感到骄傲的,be fond of 的意思是喜欢……。只有选 C 符合文章的意思。

72. 本题测试搭配。本句话表示对……人有信心,所以 A 和 C 不对;选 D 与文章的意思不符。应选 B。

73. 本题测试语法。as... as 中间应该接原级,所以 B 不对;前面提到的是 a long way,说明指的是远近问题,所以应选 A。

74. 本题测试语法。前面句子提到,这场(女性解放)运动还很时新,说明很多人还不了解它,所以应选 D。

75. 本题测试语法。所填的词应该与后面 in men's lives 中的 lives 意思相同,只有选 A。

Unit 9

Can authority be criticized? In __56__ of the world, authority is not __57__ either out of respect or out of __58__. In such countries children are not expected to __59__ their teachers in school and __60__ young scholars or __61__ industrial men are hampered (受阻) in technical research because they don't feel free to __62__ with their superiors. Clever researchers may be considered too __63__ to have "any fight" to present __64__ that are different from knowledge and wisdom of men of old ages.

__65__, the American is __66__ from childhood to question, analyze and search. School tasks are __67__ to encourage the use of a __68__ range of materials. A composition topic like "Write a paper __69__ the world's supply of sugar" will send even __70__ in search of completely unfamiliar ideas. __71__ in the primary grades, children are taught to __72__ libraries, and to search for __73__ ideas of various sorts. __74__ the time they are 14, 15 and 16, many young scholars are making original and __75__ contributions in all fields of science.

56. A. much B. any C. such D. many
57. A. accepted B. claimed C. isolated D. challenged
58. A. hate B. mercy C. fear D. sympathy
59. A. question B. ask C. change D. charge
60. A. famous B. brilliant C. employed D. curious
61. A. imaginative B. sensible C. original D. affective
62. A. disagree B. complain C. link D. cooperate
63. A. young B. brave C. old D. nervous
64. A. functions B. awards C. rewards D. findings
65. A. Secondly B. Then C. Therefore D. However
66. A. treated B. trained C. traced D. transformed
67. A. done B. designed C. fulfilled D. neglected
68. A. wide B. limited C. moderate D. various
69. A. of B. on C. for D. to
70. A. a child B. a boy C. a girl D. an adult

71. A. Since B. As C. If D. Even
72. A. organize B. manage C. clean D. use
73. A. conventional B. same C. new D. familiar
74. A. When B. Since C. During D. By
75. A. precious B. valuable C. worth D. priceless

参考译文

权威可以批评吗？在世界的许多地方，权威要么是出于尊敬、要么是出于憎恨而没有受到挑战。在这样的国家，人们不希望孩子在学校质疑老师，求知的年轻学者或有想像力的产业人士在技术研究上受到阻碍，因为他们觉得与其上级合作时不自由。人们认为，聪明的研究人员可能太嫩，不可能有“任何斗志”来提出与年长研究人员的知识和智慧不同的研究发现。

不过，美国人从孩提时期起就开始被教育去质疑、分析与探索。学校的任务被设计用来鼓励应用广泛的素材。像“写一篇有关世界食糖供应的文章”这样的作文题会促使孩子追求全新的观念。甚至在小学阶段，老师就教孩子去利用图书馆，去追求各种各样的新观念。从14、15和16岁开始，许多年轻学者就在各个科学领域做出独创、非常宝贵的贡献。

解析

56. 本题测试语法。“在……的许多地方”通常用 much 表示。

57. 本题测试动词。accept 的意思是接受，claim 的意思是声称，isolate 的意思是隔离，challenge 的意思是挑战。前面的句子说，权威可以批评吗？所填的词的宾语是 authority，并且本句话是否定意思，所以应选 D。

58. 本题测试语法。根据句中的 either... or... 可知，所填的词应该与 respect 的意思对应，所以应选 A。

59. 本题测试动词。question 的意思是质疑，ask 的意思是询问，change 的意思是改变，charge 的意思是指控。根据前面的 authority is not challenged 可知，应选 A。

60. 本题测试形容词。famous 的意思是著名的，brilliant 的意思是才华横溢的，employed 的意思是受雇的，curious 的意思是求知的。所填的词修饰 young scholars，后面的句子提到，这些人在技术研究上受到阻碍，所以选 D 符合文章的意思。

61. 本题测试形容词。imaginative 的意思是有想象力的，sensible 的意思是有感觉的，original 的意思是独创的，affective 的意思是有情感的。所填的词修饰 industrial men，并且后面提到了技术研究，所以应选 A。

62. 本题测试搭配。所填的词与 with 搭配，所以 B 不对；disagree with 的意思是“与……意见不同”，link with 的意思是“与……联合”，cooperate with 的意思是“与……合作”。所填的词的宾语是 their superiors，根据前面的 they don’t feel free 可知，应选 D。

63. 本题测试形容词。所填的词放在 too... to 之间，表示否定意思，根据后面的 have “any fight”可知，应选 A。

64. 本题测试名词。function 的意思是功能，award 的意思是奖品，reward 的意思是奖金，finding 的意思是发现。句子的主语是 clever researchers，根据后面的 are different from knowledge and wisdom of men of old ages 可知，应选 D。

65. 本题测试语法。前面的段落讲的是许多地方的人不挑战权威，而本段讲的是美国人鼓励挑战权威，说明本段的意思转折，所以应选 D。

66. 本题测试动词。treat 的意思是对待，train 的意思是教育、培养，trace 的意思是追踪，transform 的意思是转换。后面的句子提到学校的任务，所以应选 B。

67. 本题测试动词。do 的意思是做，design 的意思是设计，fulfill 的意思是完成，neglect 的意思是忽视。所填的词的宾语是 school tasks，所以 A 和 D 不对；文中并没有提到是否完成任务的问题，所以选 B 符合文章的意思。

68. 本题测试搭配。a wide range of 是习惯搭配，意思是“范围广泛的……”。

69. 本题测试介词。"有关……的文章"通常用 on。

70. 本题测试语法。前面的句子提到 from childhood,后面又提到老师教育孩子使用图书馆,所以应选 A。

71. 本题测试语法。A 和 C 不能与 in the primary grades 搭配;本句话并不是比较,所以 B 也不对。应选 D。

72. 本题测试搭配。所填的词的宾语是 libraries,根据后面的 to search for... ideas of various sorts 可知,应选 D。

73. 本题测试形容词。所填的词修饰 ideas,前面提到了 in search of completely unfamiliar ideas,所以应选 C。

74. 本题测试语法。A 不能与 the time they are 14, 15 and 16 搭配使用;选 B 则句子应该用完成时态;选 C 表示在此期间做的事情,与文章的意思不符。前面的句子讲的是小学阶段的事情,而本句话讲的是少年时期,所以应选 by。

75. 本题测试形容词。precious 的意思是宝贵的,主要指价钱或价值很高的,valuable 的意思是有价值的,主要指具有可观的用来使用或交换的货币或物质价值的,worth 的意思是值得的,主要指具有……的价值的,priceless 的意思是非常珍贵的,主要指拥有无法估价的价值的。所填的词修饰 contributions(贡献),应该选 D。

Unit 10

About a month ago I was present at a serious occasion with the reading of a will. I can remember one passage that particularly struck me. It ran something __56__ this.

"And I direct that $10,000 be __57__ to old William B, whom I have wished to help for many years, __58__ always put off doing so." It __59__ the last words of a dying man. But the story does not __60__ there. When the lawyers came to __61__ out the bequest (遗赠), they discovered that old William B had __62__, too, and so the __63__ deed was lost.

I felt rather __64__ about that. It seemed to me a most regrettable __65__ that William should not have had his $10,000 just __66__ somebody kept putting __67__ giving it to him. And from __68__ accounts, William could have done with the __69__. But I am sure __70__ there are thousands of kindly little deeds waiting to be __71__ today, which are being put off "__72__ later."

George Herbert, in praise of good intentions, __73__ that "One of these days is better than __74__ of these days." But I say that __75__ is better than all.

56. A. about B. for C. like D. of
57. A. consumed B. paid C. cost D. devoted
58. A. but B. or C. still D. and
59. A. has been B. were C. is D. was
60. A. remain B. end C. finish D. appear
61. A. find B. point C. put D. carry
62. A. died B. disappeared C. escaped D. hidden
63. A. invaluable B. identical C. good D. historic
64. A. exciting B. sorry C. faithful D. happy
65. A. matters B. dream C. task D. thing
66. A. because B. for C. as though D. till
67. A. off B. into C. in D. on
68. A. every B. some C. any D. all
69. A. payment B. money C. regrets D. expense
70. A. whether B. of C. that D. often

71.	A. protected	B. done	C. made	D. rewarded
72.	A. until	B. still	C. too	D. toward
73.	A. implies	B. marked	C. regrets	D. says
74.	A. some	B. any	C. all	D. none
75.	A. Morning	B. Spring	C. Today	D. Time

参考译文

大约一个月以前,我出席了一个解读遗嘱的严肃场合。我还记得,其中的一个段落给我印象特别深刻。这段话像是这样说的。

"我规定,10,000美元赠给老威廉·B,我希望帮助他许多年了,但我总是推迟这么做。"这是一个垂死的人说的最后几句话。但是,故事到此还没有结束。当律师来执行遗赠时,他们发现,老威廉·B也已经去世了,因此,这一善举也就失去意义了。

我对此感到非常的难过。就我看来,最可惜的事情是,威廉没有得到这10,000美元,只是因为某人一直推迟给他这笔钱。并且,从各个方面来说,威廉本可以利用这笔钱的。但是,我确信,现在有成千上万小善举等着人们去做,这些善举一直推迟到"很晚"才实施。

为了赞扬好意,乔治·赫伯特说,"这些日子中的一天比所有这些日子都有意义。"但我说,现在比所有日子都有意义。

解析

56. 本题测试固定句型。It/the story ran like this是固定句型,意思是"它(故事)是这么说的……"。选C。

57. 本题测试动词。consume的意思是消费,pay的意思是付给,cost的意思是花费,devote的意思是赠给、献给。根据后面提到的the bequest(遗赠)可知,应选D。

58. 本题测试语法。根据后面的always put off doing so可知,本句话与前面的句子意思转折,所以应选A。

59. 本题测试语法。本句话讲的是过去的事情,并且主语是单数,所以应选D。

60. 本题测试动词。remain的意思是保留,end的意思是结束,finish的意思是完成,appear的意思是出现。句子的主语是the story,并且后面的句子还是讲遗嘱的事情,所以应选B。

61. 本题测试搭配。所填的词与out搭配。find out的意思是找出、查明,point out的意思是指出、引向,put out的意思是放出、伸出,carry out的意思是执行、实行。所填的词的宾语是the bequest(遗赠),所以应选D。

62. 本题测试动词。前面提到,这是一个垂死人的话,本句话中用了too,根据后面的the deed was lost可知,本句话表示威廉也已经去世了,所以应选A。

63. 本题测试形容词。invaluable的意思是无价的,identical的意思是同样的,good的意思是善良的,historic的意思是历史上著名的。所填的词修饰deed,根据后面的there are thousands of kindly little deeds可知,应选C。

64. 本题测试形容词。exciting的意思是令人兴奋的,sorry的意思是难过的、遗憾的,faithful的意思是忠实的,happy的意思是高兴的。根据后面的It seemed to me a most regrettable...可知,应选B。

65. 本题测试搭配。regrettable(可惜的)修饰所填的词。根据前面的a most可知A不对;本句话并不是讲理想和任务,所以B和C不对。只有选D。

66. 本题测试语法。"威廉没有得到钱"与"有人一直推迟给他钱"这两者之间是因果关系,所以C和D不对;for不能与just搭配使用。应选A。

67. 本题测试搭配。所填的词与put搭配,表达的意思应该与前面的put off doing so的意思相近,只有选A。

68. 本题测试搭配。from all accounts是习惯搭配,意思是"从各个方面来看"。

69. 本题测试名词。payment的意思是付款,money的意思是钱,regret的意思是遗憾,expense的意思是费用。前面的句子提到,威廉本可以得到这笔钱,所以应选B。

70. 本题测试语法。所填的句子引导从句,所以B和D不对;后面的句子是陈述句,所以A也不对。应选 C。

71. 本题测试搭配。所填的词的宾语是 deeds，所以应选 B。

72. 本题测试搭配。所填的词的与 put off 搭配。只有选 A 符合文章的意思。

73. 本题测试动词。imply 的意思是暗示，mark 的意思是做标记，regret 的意思是遗憾，say 的意思是说，主要指有说话内容的说。本句话是在引用别人的话，应该用一般现在时态，所以 B 不对；根据后面引号里面的内容可知，应选 D。

74. 本题测试语法。根据后面的 is better than all 可知，本句话是在比较一个和所有，所以应选 C。

75. 本题测试语法。本句话是在比较日子，所以 A、B 和 D 都不对。应该选 C。

Unit 11

In every cultivated language there are two great classes of words, which make up the whole vocabulary. First, there are those words __56__ which we become familiar in daily conversation, which we __57__, that is to say, from the __58__ of our own family and from our friends, and __59__ we should know and use __60__ we could not read or write. They __61__ the common things of life with all the people who __62__ the language. Such words may be called "popular", since they belong to the people __63__ and are not excluded __64__ a limited class.

On the other hand, our language __65__ a large number of words which are comparatively __66__ used in ordinary conversation. Their meanings are known to every educated person, but there is little __67__ to use them at home or in the market-place. Our __68__ acquaintance (熟悉) with them comes not from our mother's __69__ or from the talk of our schoolmates, __70__ from books that we read, lectures that we __71__, or the more __72__ conversation of highly educated speakers who are discussing some particular __73__ in a style properly higher above the habitual __74__ of everyday life. Such words are called "learned", and the __75__ between them and the "popular" words is of great importance to a right understanding of language study process.

56. A. at B. with C. by D. through
57. A. study B. imitate C. stimulate D. learn
58. A. mates B. relatives C. members D. fellows
59. A. which B. that C. those D. ones
60. A. even B. despite C. even if D. in spite of
61. A. mind B. concern C. care D. relate
62. A. hire B. apply C. adopt D. use
63. A. in public B. at most C. at large D. at best
64. A. in B. from C. with D. on
65. A. consists B. consists of C. makes D. composes
66. A. seldom B. much C. greatly D. often
67. A. possibility B. way C. reason D. necessity
68. A. primary B. first C. principal D. prior
69. A. tips B. mouth C. ears D. tongue
70. A. besides B. and C. yet D. but
71. A. hear of B. attend C. hear from D. listen
72. A. former B. formula C. formal D. forward

73. A. theme	B. topic	C. idea	D. point
74. A. border	B. link	C. degree	D. extent
75. A. relation	B. distinction	C. connection	D. similarity

参考译文

任何文明语言中，都有两大类词语，这两大类词语构成了总词汇。首先，有一些词语是我们日常交谈中熟悉的词语，就是说，是我们向家庭成员和朋友学来的词语，是我们应该知道并且使用的词语，即使我们不会读或写。这些词语涉及所有使用该语言的人们生活的普通事情。这类词语可以被称作"流行词语"，因为这些词语大多属于人民，没有受到一个有限阶层的排除。

其次，我们的语言包含大量在日常交谈中很少使用的词语。只有受过教育的人才知道这些词的意思，但却没有必要在家里或市场上使用。我们对这些词语的主要了解不是源于母亲的语言，或者与同学的交谈，而是源于我们阅读的书本，源于我们听的报告，或者源于接受高等教育者之间的更正式交谈，这些人以远高于日常生活习惯范畴的方式讨论着某个特别主题。这类词语被称作"学习词语"，它们与"流行词语"之间的区别对于正确理解语言的研究过程至关重要。

解析

56. 本题测试搭配。be/become familiar with 是习惯搭配，意思是"熟悉……"。

57. 本题测试搭配。所填的词与后面的 from 搭配，只有 learn 可以与之搭配，意思是"向……学习"。

58. 本题测试名词。mate 的意思是配偶，relative 的意思是亲戚，member 的意思是成员，fellow 的意思是伙伴。our own family 修饰所填的词，并且后面的句子提到了从母亲那里学习语言，所以应选 C。

59. 本题测试语法。根据 and 可知，本句话与前面的句子并列，所以所填的词引导定语从句，修饰 words。应选 A。

60. 本题测试语法。所填的词引导句子，只有选 C。

61. 本题测试搭配。mind 的意思是介意，concern 的意思是涉及，care 的意思是关心，relate 的意思是与……有关。句子的主语是 They(词语)，所填的词的宾语是 the common things of life(生活的普通事情)，所以应选 B。

62. 本题测试动词。hire 的意思是雇用，apply 的意思是应用，主要指把……投入或应用于某个特定用途，adopt 的意思是采用，use 的意思是使用，主要指把某物当作工具使用，以满足需要或达到目的。所填的词的宾语是 language，所以应选 D。

63. 本题测试短语。in public 的意思是公开，at most 的意思是至多、大多，at large 的意思是详细，at best 的意思是最多。所填的词修饰 belong to，所以应选 B。

64. 本题测试搭配。exclude 通常与 from 搭配，意思是"排除……"。

65. 本题测试动词。前面一段介绍了第一类词语的内容，本段介绍的是第二类词语的内容，说明所填的词应该与 which make up the whole vocabulary 中的 make up (构成)的意思相近。只有选 B。

66. 本题测试语法。根据后面的 Their meanings are known to every educated person 可知，这种词语使用的范围小，所以应选 A。

67. 本题测试固定句型。there is little /no necessity to do something 是固定句型，意思是"没有必要做……"

68. 本题测试形容词。primary 的意思是主要的，主要指在质量或重要性上处于首要的，first 的意思是第一的，principal 的意思是主要的，主要指在程度上处于首要的，prior 的意思是优先的。所填的词修饰 acquaintance with them(了解词语)，所以应选 C。

69. 本题测试名词。tip 的意思是暗示，mouth 的意思是嘴，ear 的意思是耳朵，tongue 的意思是舌头、语言。根据后面的 or from the talk of our schoolmates 可知，所填的词应该指语言，所以应选 D。

70. 本题测试语法。not... but... 是强调句式，意思是"不是……而是……"。

71. 本题测试搭配。hear of 的意思是听说，attend 的意思是倾听，hear from 的意思是收到来信，listen 的意思是听，listen to 后面才能接宾语。所填的词的宾语是 lectures，所以应选 B。

72. 本题测试搭配。所填的词修饰 conversation，所以 B 不对；former 的意思是以前的，formal 的意思是正式的,forward 的意思是前进的。根据后面的 highly educated speakers 可知,应选 C。

73. 本题测试搭配。theme 的意思是主题,主要指谈话、论文、文章等的题目,topic 的意思是话题、主题,主要指讨论或交谈的主题,idea 的意思是想法,point 的意思是要点,主要指一个概念或叙述的主要观点。句子的主语是 highly educated speakers,所填的词作 discussing 的宾语,所以应选 B。

74. 本题测试名词。border 的意思是边界,link 的意思是连接,degree 的意思是程度,主要指存在、行动或联系的范围,extent 的意思是范畴,主要指事物延展的范围或高度。habitual(习惯的)和 everyday life 修饰所填的词,所以应选 D。

75. 本题测试搭配。所填的词语后面的 between 搭配,只有 distinction 可以与之搭配,意思是"……之间的区别"。

Unit 12

In China it is relatively usual to ask people their age, but in the West this question is generally regarded as impolite. This is particularly true __56__ women, and even more __57__ if the inquirer is a man.

However, it is very __58__ to ask children their age, and some adults may not mind __59__ either. In fact, some elderly people are quite happy to __60__ their age, especially if they feel they look young __61__ their age. Nevertheless, it is not very wise to ask a(n) __62__. question like "How old are you?". If elderly people want to talk about-their age, and perhaps receive a compliment on how young they look, they may easily __63__ the topic themselves, and ask the other person to __64__ how 01d they are. __65__ such a question, it is quite acceptable to discuss age __66__. They normally expect to be complimented on their youthfulness, though rather than __67__ that they look very old!

__68__ Westerners do not usually ask people directly how old they are, this does not __69__ that they are not interested to know how old other people are. They may ask someone else __70__ the information, __71__ they may try to __72__ the topic indirectly. Sometimes discussions about educational __73__ and the number of years of working experience may provide some __74__, but this is not always the __75__.

56. A. to	B. for	C. in	D. of
57. A. that	B. such	C. than	D. so
58. A. average	B. normal	C. expected	D. unusual
59. A. being asked	B. asking	C. to ask	D. to be asked
60. A. release	B. reflect	C. reveal	D. remark
61. A. to	B. with	C. for	D. at
62. A. open	B. strange	C. impolite	D. direct
63. A. bring about	B. bring up	C. bring along	D. bring to
64. A. guess	B. know	C. learn	D. predict
65. A. For	B. With	C. In	D. On
66. A. free	B. freedom	C. freely	D. in a free way
67. A. being told	B. told	C. to tell	D. to be told
68. A. Though even	B. Even	C. Even that	D. Even though
69. A. include	B. intend	C. mean	D. conclude
70. A. about	B. of	C. with	D. for
71. A. rather than	B. or else	C. so else	D. still else

72. A. approach	B. solve	C. address	D. take
73. A. background	B. level	C. knowledge	D. experience
74. A. knowledge	B. clues	C. evidence	D. suggestions
75. A. truth	B. case	C. reality	D. fact

参考译文

在中国，询问人们的年龄很平常，但在西方，问这个问题通常被认为不礼貌。对于女性来说尤其如此，如果询问者是一个男性更是如此。

不过，询问孩子的年龄非常正常，有些成人也可能不介意被问这个问题。事实上，有些老年人非常乐意公开自己的年龄，尤其是如果他们觉得在他们那个年龄他们还显得年轻时更是如此。但是，直接问别人像“你多大年龄了?”这样的问题很不明智。如果老年人希望谈论他们的年龄，也许在你说“他们显得年轻”这样的恭维话后，他们自己可能会一下子就提出这个话题，要别人猜他们多大年龄了。在这种情况下，随意讨论年龄就是可以接受的。他们通常希望别人恭维他们的年轻，而不是被告知他们显得非常老。

即使西方人通常不直接询问别人有多大年龄，但这并不意味着他们对于了解别人有多大不感兴趣。他们可能询问别人有关这方面的信息，要不然，他们可能试着直接涉及这个话题，有时，有关教育背景的讨论以及工作经历的年限可以提供一些线索，但情况并不总是这样。当然，人们感兴趣的方面或喜欢谈论的方面也不尽相同。

解析

56. 本题测试介词。“对于……来说……”通常用 to。

57. 本题测试语法。所填的词指代前面句子的内容，而 A 通常不与 more 搭配，只有选 D 符合文章的意思。

58. 本题测试形容词。average 的意思是一般的，normal 的意思是正常的，expected 的意思是期望的，unusual 的意思是不寻常的。所填的词应该与前面句子 it is relatively usual to ask people their age 中的 usual 的意思相近，所以应选 B。

59. 本题测试语法。mind 后面的动词应该改为动名词，所以 C 和 D 不对；B 的语态不对。应选 A。

60. 本题测试搭配。release 的意思是释放，通常指从囚禁、约束或痛苦中解放，reflect 的意思是表现，reveal 的意思是公开，remark 的意思是谈论，通常要与 on 或 upon 搭配使用。所填的词的宾语是 the age，所以应选 C。

61. 本题测试搭配。与 age 搭配的介词通常是 at。

62. 本题测试形容词。open 的意思是公开的，strange 的意思是奇怪的，impolite 的意思是不礼貌的，direct 的意思是直接的。后面的句子说，也许在你说“他们显得年轻”这样的恭维话后，他们自己可能会一下子就谈到年龄这个话题，所以应选 D。

63. 本题测试搭配。bring about 的意思是使发生、致使，bring up 的意思是提出、引出，bring along 的意思是使发展、引来，bring to 的意思是停止、阻碍。所填的词的宾语是 the topic，所以应选 B。

64. 本题测试动词。guess 的意思是猜测，know 的意思是知道，learn 的意思是了解，predict 的意思是预测。本文主要讨论的是询问别人年龄的问题，所以应选 A。

65. 本题测试搭配。situation 通常与 in 搭配。

66. 本题测试修饰词。所填的词修饰 discuss age，所以应选 C。

67. 本题测试语法。rather than 后面通常接动词原形，所以 A 和 B 不对；所填的词的语态应该与 to be complimented 相同，所以应选 D。

68. 本题测试语法。所填的词引导从句，只有 D 可以引导从句。

69. 本题测试固定句型。It/this does not mean that 是固定句型，意思是“这并不意味着……”。

70. 本题测试搭配。所填的词与 ask 搭配，所以 C 不对；ask about 的意思是打听、询问，ask of 的意思是要求、问……问题，ask for 的意思是请求、寻求。所填的词的宾语是 the information，所以应选 A。

71. 本题测试短语。C 和 D 的表达不对；rather than 的意思是胜过、而不是，or else 的意思是要不然、否则。只有选 B 与文章的意思符合。

72. 本题测试搭配。approach 的意思是接近、涉及,solve 的意思是解决、解答,address 的意思是发表演说、致辞,take 的意思是拿走、取。所填的词的宾语是 the topic,说明 B 和 C 不对;后面的句子说,有关教育问题的讨论以及工作经历的年限可以提供一些有关年龄的蛛丝马迹,说明并不是直接讨论年龄这个话题,所以应选 A。

73. 本题测试搭配。所填的词与 educational 搭配,指的是一个人接受教育的情况,只有选 A 符合文章的意思。

74. 本题测试名词。knowledge 的意思是知识,clue 的意思是线索,evidence 的意思是证据,suggestion 的意思是建议。前面的句子提到,也许在你说"他们显得年轻"这样的恭维话后,他们自己可能会一下子就提出这个话题,要别人猜他们多大年龄了,说明有关教育背景的讨论以及工作经历的年限可以提供的是一些线索,不可能是证据,所以应选 B。

75. 本题测试固定句型。It/this is not always the case 是固定句型,意思是"并不总是如此"。

Unit 13

In most cultures, when you meet acquaintances for the first time during a day, it is normal to greet them. The main purpose of this greeting is to __56__ a good relationship between the people __57__, and each language usually has __58__ set phrases which can be used for this purpose. Sometimes, though, there can be __59__ differences in the type of phrases which can be used, and cultural misunderstandings can easily __60__. The following is a true example.

A young British woman went to Hong Kong to work, and at the time of her __61__ she knew nothing about the Chinese culture or language. __62__ her way to school one day, she went to the bank to get some money. __63__, the bank clerk asked her if she had had her lunch. She was extremely surprised __64__ such a question because in the British culture it would be __65__ an indirect invitation to lunch. Between unmarried young people it can also __66__ the young man's interest in dating the girl. __67__ this bank clerk was a complete stranger __68__ the British girl, she was very much taken aback (生气), and hastily commented that she had eaten __69__. After this she __70__ to school and was even more surprised when one of the teachers asked the same question. By now she __71__ that it could not be an invitation, but was puzzled __72__ why they asked it. __73__ the following days she was asked the same question again and again. Only much later __74__ that the question had no real meaning __75__, it was merely a greeting.

56. A. build on B. build up C. build into D. build out
57. A. concerned B. concern C. concerning D. to concern
58. A. a number of B. the number of C. the amount of D. an amount of
59. A. considered B. considering C. considerable D. considerate
60. A. raise B. arise C. arouse D. lead
61. A. arrive B. arrived C. arrives D. arrival
62. A. In B. To C. By D. On
63. A. To her disappointment B. In her disappointment
    C. To her surprise D. In her surprise
64. A. on B. at C. to D. with
65. A. regarded as B. defined as C. looked as D. thought as
66. A. reflect B. intend C. release D. indicate
67. A. Since B. That C. Far D. With

68. A. with　B. by　C. to　D. at
69. A. yet　B. already　C. too　D. at all
70. A. processed　B. produced　C. provided　D. proceeded
71. A. released　B. relieved　C. realized　D. regretted
72. A. with regards　B. as to　C. as if　D. as far as
73. A. In　B. On　C. At　D. For
74. A. she discovered　B. she did discover
C. did she discover　D. does she discover
75. A. above all　B. after all　C. in all　D. at all

参考译文

在大多数文化中，当你在一天中第一次见到熟人时跟他打招呼是正常的。这种问候的主要目的是增进相关人员之间的良好友谊，每种语言通常都有许多固定短语用于这个目的。但有时，可用短语的类型可能有很大的差异，就可能轻易产生文化上的误解。下面就是一个真实的例子。

一名年轻的英国女士到香港去工作，到香港时，她不了解中国文化或语言。有一天，在去学校的路上，她到银行去取钱。令她感到奇怪的是，银行的职员问她是否吃了午饭。她对这样一个问题感到非常惊奇，因为，在英国文化中，这被看成是非正式地邀请你去吃午饭。如果在两个未婚的年轻人之间，这还可能表示那个年轻人有意约会那个女孩。由于这个银行职员对于那个英国女孩来说完全是陌生人，所以她非常生气，连忙说她已经吃过午饭了。过后，她继续往学校去，当一名教师问她同样的问题时，她感到更奇怪。至此，她意识到这不是一种邀请，但还是对人们为什么问这样的问题感到迷惑。在接下来的日子里，人们反复问她同样的问题。只是很久之后她才发现，这个问题根本没有什么意思，只是一种问候。

解析

56. 本题测试搭配。build on 的意思是建立于、指望，build up 的意思是增进、增大，build into 的意思是嵌在墙上、使成为组成部分，build out 的意思是扩建、增建。所填的词的宾语是 a good relationship，所以应选 B。

57. 本题测试语法。所填的词修饰 people，只有 concerned 可以作后置定语。

58. 本题测试短语。D 的表达不对；a number of 的意思是许多、大量，通常接可数名词的复数，the number of 的意思是……的数量，是一个单数概念，the amount of 的意思是……的数量，后面接不可数名词。根据后面的 set phrases 可知，应选 A。

59. 本题测试修饰词。considered 的意思是考虑过的、被尊重的，considering 的意思是鉴于、考虑到，是介词，considerable 的意思是相当大的、不少的，considerate 的意思是考虑周到的、体贴的。所填的词修饰 differences，所以应选 C。

60. 本题测试搭配。raise 的意思是提高、唤起，arise 的意思是产生、引起，主要指由……而引起、导致，arouse 的意思是唤起、引起，主要指激起别人的兴趣与爱好，lead 的意思是引导、导致，通常与 to 搭配使用。所填的词的宾语是 misunderstandings，所以应选 B。

61. 本题测试语法。her 修饰所填的词，说明所填的词应该是名词，所以应选 D。

62. 本题测试搭配。“在去……的路上（途中）”通常用 on the way to 表示。

63. 本题测试短语。B 和 D 的表达不对；To her disappointment 的意思是令她失望的是，To her surprise 的意思是令她奇怪的是。根据后面的 She was extremely surprised 可知，应选 C。

64. 本题测试搭配。be surprised at 是习惯搭配，意思是“对……感到惊奇”。

65. 本题测试短语。regarded as 的意思是被看成是……，defined as 的意思是被定义为……，looked as 搭配不当，thought as 的意思是被认为是……。所填的词的宾语是 an indirect invitation，所以选 A 符合文章的意思。

66. 本题测试动词。reflect 的意思是表明，主要指作为某人行动的结果而显示出，intend 的意思是打算，release 的意思是释放，indicate 的意思是表示，主要指作为一种标志、症状或象征。根据后面的 the young man’s

interest in dating the girl 可知,应选 D。

67. 本题测试语法。所填的词引导句子,所以 C 和 D 不对;前面的句子是从句,后面的句子才是主句,所以 B 也不对。应选 A。

68. 本题测试介词。"对……人来说"应该用 to。

69. 本题测试修饰词。所填的词修饰 eaten,所以 D 不对;A 一般用于否定句中;C 只有在前面提到同样动作时才能用。只有选 B 符合文章的意思。

70. 本题测试搭配。process 的意思是加工、处理,produce 的意思是生产、制造,provide 的意思是供应、供给,proceed 的意思是继续进行、前进,通常与 to 搭配使用。根据后面的 to school 可知,应选 D。

71. 本题测试动词。release 的意思是释放,relieve 的意思是解除,realize 的意思是认识到、意识到,主要指完全地或正确地理解……,regret 的意思是后悔。根据后面的 it could not be an invitation 可知,这是一个结果,所以应选 C。

72. 本题测试短语。with regards 的表达不对,应该是 with regard to(至于、关于),as to 的意思是至于、关于,as if 的意思是好像、似乎,as far as 的意思是至于、远到。puzzle 通常与 about 搭配,意思是"对……感到迷惑",只有 as to 相当于 about。

73. 本题测试搭配。in the following days 是习惯搭配,意思是"在接下来的日子里"。

74. 本题测试语法。only 在句首时句子通常要倒装,所以 A 和 B 不对;D 的时态不对。应选 C。

75. 本题测试搭配。above all 的意思是最重要,after all 的意思是毕竟,in all 的意思是总共,at all 的意思是根本。只有 D 可以与前面的 not 搭配,意思是"一点也不、没有"。

Unit 14

When I was 16 years old, I made my first visit to the United States, it wasn't the first time I had been __56__. Like most English children I learned French at school and I had often __57__ to France, so I was used __58__ a foreign language to people who did not understand __59__. But when I went to America I was really looking forward to __60__ a nice easy holiday without any __61__ problems.

How wrong I was! The misunderstanding began at the airport. I was looking for a __62__ telephone to give my American friend Danny a __63__ and tell her I had arrived. A friendly old man saw me __64__ lost and asked __65__ he could help me. "Yes," I said, "I want to give my friend a ring." "Well, that's __66__." he exclaimed. "Are you getting __67__? But aren't you a bit __68__?" "Who is talking about marriage?" I replied. "I __69__ want to give a ring to tell her I've arrived. Can you tell me where there's a phone box?" "Oh!" he said, "There's a phone downstairs."

When at last we __70__ meet up, Danny __71__ the misunderstandings to me. "Don't worry," she said to me. "I had so many __72__ at first. There are lots of words which the Americans __73__ differently in meaning from __74__. You'll soon get used to __75__ things they say. Most of the time British and American people understand each other!"

56. A. out　　B. aboard　　C. away　　D. abroad
57. A. gone　　B. been　　C. got　　D. come
58. A. to speak　　B. for speaking　　C. to speaking　　D. to speaking of
59. A. English　　B. French　　C. Russian　　D. Latin
60. A. having　　B. buying　　C. giving　　D. receiving
61. A. time　　B. human　　C. money　　D. language
62. A. perfect　　B. popular　　C. public　　D. pleasant

63. A. ring	B. letter	C. word	D. message
64. A. to look	B. looking like	C. looking	D. feeling like
65. A. that	B. if	C. where	D. when
66. A. well	B. strange	C. nice	D. funny
67. A. to marry	B. marrying	C. to be married	D. married
68. A. small	B. smart	C. little	D. young
69. A. very	B. just	C. so	D. just now
70. A. did	B. could	C. do	D. can
71. A. described	B. explained	C. talked	D. expressed
72. A. trouble	B. difficulties	C. fun	D. things
73. A. write	B. speak	C. use	D. read
74. A. us British	B. British us	C. us Britain	D. we British
75. A. such	B. these	C. some	D. all the

参考译文

16 岁时，我第一次游览美国，这不是我第一次出国。就像大多数英国孩子一样，我在学校学法语，经常去法国，所以，我习惯于对那些不懂英语的人讲外语。但是，当我到美国时，我确实期望过一个没有语言障碍的愉快假日。

我是多么的错误！误解从机场开始。我当时正在寻找一个公用电话，准备给我的美国朋友丹尼打电话，告诉她我已经到了美国。一位友好的老人看我像是迷路了，便问我是否可以帮助我。我说，"是的，我想给我的朋友打电话。"他大声说道，"啊，真奇怪。""你准备结婚吗？但是你难道不有点小吗？"我答道，"谁在谈论结婚？我只是想打电话告诉她我已经到了。你可以告诉我哪里有电话亭吗？"他说，"啊！楼下有电话。"

我们最后碰面时，丹尼给我解释了这场误会。她说，"别担心，我起初也遇到很多困难。有很多词美国人用的意思与我们英国人不同。你不久就会习惯他们说的这样的话的。大部分时间里，英国人和美国人是相互理解的！"

解析

56. 本题测试修饰词。前面的句子提到第一次到美国，后面的句子提到，他经常与法国，说明他出过国，所以应选 D。

57. 本题测试语法。have been to 某地不能与 often 搭配使用，所以 B 不对；说话者并不在法国，所以 D 不对；get to 某地的意思是到达某地，与文章的意思不符。应选 A。

58. 本题测试语法。用 use 表示习惯于……应该用 be used to＋动名词这种结构，所以 A 和 B 不对；speak of 的意思是谈及、说起，与文章的意思不符。应选 C。

59. 本题测试名词。本文没有提到过俄罗斯或拉美国家的人，所以 C 和 D 不对；根据前面的 Like most English children 可知，作者是英国人，所以应选 A。

60. 本题测试搭配。所填的词与 holiday 搭配，只有选 A 符合文章的意思。

61. 本题测试名词。后面的段落讲的是造成的语言误解，所以应选 D。

62. 本题测试修饰词。perfect 的意思是完美的，popular 的意思是流行的，public 的意思是公共的，pleasant 的意思是愉快的。所填的词修饰 telephone，后面的句子说他想给朋友打电话，所以应选 C。

63. 本题测试名词。前面的句子提到他在寻找电话，并且后面的句子提到 give my friend a ring，所以应选 A。

64. 本题测试语法。"看见某人干什么"应该是 see someone＋动名词，所以 A 不对；look like 的意思是好像是……，feel like 的意思是想要……。lost 的意思是迷路的，所以应选 B。

65. 本题测试语法。所填的词引导的句子作 ask 的宾语从句，只有选 B 符合文章的意思。

66. 本题测试动词。根据后面的问话可知,那个老人感觉奇怪,所以应选 B。

67. 本题测试语法。“结婚”应该是 be/get married,所以应选 D。

68. 本题测试形容词。前面句子提到老人觉得奇怪,以为他要结婚,所填的词形容人,只有选 D 才能表现出奇怪的意思。

69. 本题测试修饰词。所填的词修饰 want to give a ring,只有选 B 符合文章的意思。

70. 本题测试语法。本文讲的是一个故事,用的是一般过去时态,所以 C 和 D 不对;用 A 表示强调,用 B 表示能力。只有选 A 符合文章的意思。

71. 本题测试搭配。describe 的意思是描述,explain 的意思是解释, talk 的意思是谈论,express 的意思是表达。所填的词语后面的 to me 搭配,只有 explain 可以与 to 搭配,表示“向……人解释……”之意。

72. 本题测试语法。so many 后面应该接可数名词的复数,所以 A 和 C 不对;前面的句子提到了误解,后面的句子提到了词的用法不同,说明遇到的是语言困难,所以应选 B。

73. 本题测试搭配。前面的句子提到了误解,并且 differently in meaning 修饰所填的词,所以应选 C。

74. 本题测试语法。“我们什么人”应该是 us+哪国人,所以 B 和 D 不对;Britain 的意思是英国,不是英国人,所以应选 A。

75. 本题测试语法。文中并没有明确指出说的什么话,所以 B 和 C 不对;D 太绝对,与文章的意思不符。只有选 A 符合文章的意思。

Unit 15

A king once __56__ seriously ill. His doctors and wise men tried cure __57__ cure, but nothing __58__. They were ready to __59__ hope, when the king's old servant spoke up. He said, "If you can find a happy man, take the shirt from his back and __60__ it on the king, then he will __61__." So the king's officials rode __62__ throughout the kingdom; yet nowhere __63__ a happy man, No one seemed __64__; everyone had some complaints. If a man was rich, he never had enough. If he was not rich, it was someone else's __65__. If he was __66__, he had a bad mother-in-law. If he had a good mother-in-law, he was catching a cold. Everyone had something to complain about. __67__, one night the king's own son was passing a small cottage __68__ he heard someone say, "Thank you. I've finished my daily labor, and helped my fellow man. My family and I have eaten our fill, and now we can __69__ and sleep in peace. __70__ more could I want?" The prince was very happy __71__ a happy man at last. He gave __72__ to take the man's shirt to the king, and pay the __73__ as much money as he __74__. But when the king's officials went into the cottage to take the happy man's shirt __75__ his back, they found he had no shirt at all.

56. A. fell B. felt C. feel D. fall
57. A. to B. by C. for D. after
58. A. played B. worked C. operated D. affected
59. A. give off B. give out C. give up D. give in
60. A. place B. put C. dress D. wear
61. A. recover B. relax C. relieve D. remove
62. A. off and on B. back and forth C. up and down D. far and wide
63. A. had they found B. should they find C. could they find D. did they find
64. A. content B. contrary C. concrete D. complete
65. A. fault B. mistake C. error D. shortage
66. A. helpful B. heavy C. healthy D. high

67.	A. Consequently	B. Finally	C. Lately	D. Fortunately
68.	A. while	B. which	C. whenever	D. when
69.	A. lay	B. lie	C. laid	D. lain
70.	A. Which	B. Who	C. When	D. What
71.	A. to having found	B. to have been found	C. to have found	D. to find
72.	A. orders	B. messages	C. words	D. letters
73.	A. official	B. owner	C. servant	D. master
74.	A. advised	B. said	C. asked	D. wished
75.	A. from	B. out of	C. off	D. down

参考译文

从前,一个国王生病了。他的御医和贤明之士尝试了一个又一个治疗方法,但没有一种方法有效。他们开始绝望了,这时,国王的一个老仆人发话了。他说,"如果你们能够找到一个愉快的人,脱掉他的衬衣穿在国王的身上,国王就会康复。"国王手下的官员来回在全国各地奔波,但他们到处都没能找到一个愉快的人,没有人看起来心满意足,每个人都有一些抱怨。如果一个人富有,那么他的财富从来都不够。如果他不富有,那么这应该是其他某个人的过错。如果他健康,那么他就会有一个坏继母。如果他有一个好继母,那么他就会得感冒。每个人都会有抱怨的事情。幸运的是,一天晚上,国王的儿子在经过一间小农舍时听到有人在说,"谢谢你。我已经干完了我日常的工作,并且帮助了我的同事。我和我的家人已经吃饱了,我们现在可以躺下来安详地睡觉了。我还能希望得到更多什么呢?"王子非常高兴他终于找到了一个快乐的人。他下令把这个人的衬衣拿给国王,尽可能多地给了这个人他想要的钱。但是,当国王手下的官员走进农舍去从那个快乐者身上取衬衣时,他们发现,他根本就没有衬衣。

解析

56. 本题测试搭配。fall ill 是习惯搭配,意思是"生病"。应选 A。

57. 本题测试搭配。cure after cure 是习惯搭配,意思是"一个又一个治疗方法"。应选 D。

58. 本题测试对上下文的理解。前面的句子提到尝试了许多种治疗方法,本句话还是指治疗方法,所以应该表示是否有效的意思。应选 B。

59. 本题测试搭配。所填的词与后面的 hope 搭配,只有选 C 才符合文章的意思。

60. 本题测试搭配。所填的词的宾语是 shirt,并且与后面的 on the king 搭配,只有选 B 才符合文章的意思。

61. 本题测试对上下文的理解。前面的句子提到了治疗国王疾病的方法,所以所填的词应该表示"康复"之意。应选 A。

62. 本题测试搭配。off and on 的意思是"断断续续地",back and forth 的意思是"来来回回地",up and down 的意思是"上下地,前后地",far and wide 的意思是"广泛地"。所填的词与 rode(奔波)搭配,所以应选 B。

63. 本题测试语法。本句话表示的是一种能力,所以应选 C。

64. 本题测试搭配。本句话的主语是人,所填的词作 seem 的表语,所以应选 A。

65. 本题测试词义辨析。fault 的意思是"过失,责任",指对过错应承担的责任、小过失;mistake 的意思是"错误,过错",指由于有缺陷的判断而造成的错误;error 的意思是"失误,差错",指由于理解或认识的不正确而导致的错误;shortage 的意思是"缺乏,不足",指缺少……东西。所填的词作 someone else's 的宾语,所以 D 不对;一个人是否富有与认识或理解是否正确没有关系,所以 B 和 C 不对。应选 A。

66. 本题测试搭配。句子的主语是人,所以 D 不对;根据后面的 If he had a good mother-in-law, he was catching a cold. 可知,应 C。

67. 本题测试语法。前面的句子提到,所有人都有抱怨,而本句话提到的是例外情况,因此只有选 D 才符合文章的意思。

68. 本题测试语法。所填的词引导时间状语从句,所以 B 不对;C 的表达不对;表示一个动作发生时另一个动作正在发生一般用 when,表示一个动作正在发生时另一个动作发生了一般用 while,应选 D。

69. 本题测试语法。所填的词跟 can 后面,所以 C 和 D 不对;根据后面的 and sleep 可知,应选 B。

70. 本题测试语法。本句话是一个特殊疑问句,所填的词作 want 的宾语,只有选 D。

71. 本题测试语法。A 的表达不对;句子的主语是 the prince,发现人应该是主动语态,B 不对;D 的时态不对。应选 C。

72. 本题测试搭配。give words to 是固定搭配,意思是"下令,发话"。

73. 本题测试对上下文的理解。前面句子提到拿了那个人的衬衣,本句话说的是给钱的问题,所以应选 B。

74. 本题测试搭配。所填的词的宾语是 money,只有选 C 才符合文章的意思。

75. 本题测试对上下文的理解以及搭配。根据前面的 take the shirt from his back 可知,应选 A。

Unit 16

A young woman was driving through the __56__ countryside. It was dark and raining. Suddenly she saw an old woman __57__ the side of the road, __58__ her hand out as if she wanted __59__. "I can't __60__ her out in this weather," the woman said to herself, so she stopped the car and opened the door.

"Do you want a lift?" she asked. The old woman __61__ and climbed into the car. After a __62__, she said to the old woman, "Have you been waiting for a long time?" The old woman shook her head. "__63__," thought the young woman. She __64__ again. "Bad weather for the time of the year." she said. The old woman nodded. No matter __65__ the young woman said the hitchhiker(搭便车的人) gave no answer __66__ a nod of the head.

Then the young woman __67__ the hitchhiker's hands, which were large and hairy. Suddenly she __68__ that the hitchhiker was __69__ a man! She stopped the car. "I can't see out of the rear screen," she said, "Would you mind __70__ it for me?" The hitchhiker nodded and opened the door. __71__ the hitchhiker was out of the car, the frightened young woman __72__.

When she got to the next village she __73__ to a stop. She noticed that the hitchhiker had __74__ his handbag __75__. She picked it up and opened it. She gave a gasp; inside the bag was a gun!

56. A. lovely	B. lonely	C. noisy	D. crowded
57. A. at	B. beside	C. by	D. near
58. A. holding	B. to hold	C. to be holding	D. to be held
59. A. an aid	B. a taxi	C. a car	D. a lift
60. A. permit	B. leave	C. allow	D. order
61. A. answering	B. shook	C. nodded	D. smiles
62. A. while	B. moment	C. time	D. period
63. A. Curious	B. Interesting	C. Strange	D. Wonderful
64. A. told	B. did	C. made	D. tried
65. A. when	B. which	C. how	D. what
66. A. except for	B. apart from	C. other than	D. more than
67. A. saw	B. noticed	C. watched	D. observed
68. A. recognized	B. realized	C. recovered	D. remembered
69. A. practically	B. basically	C. actually	D. probably
70. A. clear	B. cleared	C. to clear	D. clearing

71. A. As long as	B. As far as	C. As soon as	D. As well as
72. A. raced off	B. ran away	C. fell down	D. moved on
73. A. pulled	B. picked	C. pushed	D. paused
74. A. lift	B. lost	C. laid	D. left
75. A. beneath	B. behind	C. backwards	D. afterwards

参考译文

一名年轻女人正驱车穿过偏僻的乡村。天色开始变暗,并且在下雨。突然,她看见一个老妇人站在路边,手伸着,好像要搭便车。“我不能在这种天气把她留在这里,”这名年轻女人自言自语道,因此,她便停下车打开了车门。

“你想搭便车吗?”她问道。那个老妇人点了点头,然后爬进了车。过了一会儿,那名年轻女人对老妇人说,“你等了很长时间吗?”老妇人摇了摇头。“真奇怪,”年轻女人想到。她又试了试。“这是一年中最糟糕的天气。”她说。老妇人点了点头。无论那名年轻女人说什么,搭便车的人除了点点头,不作任何回答。

后来,那名年轻女人注意到了搭便车者的手,那双手又大,毛发又浓密。突然,她意识到,这个搭便车者其实是一个男人!她停下车。“我看不清后视镜,”她说,“你介意为我把它擦干净吗?”搭便车者点了点头,打开了车门。搭便车者一下车,那名惊恐的年轻女人就飞车而去。

当她到达下一个村庄时,她停下了车。她发现,搭便车者把他的手提包遗留在了车上。她捡起提包打开一看,吓得直喘气,包里面是一把枪。

解析

56. 本题测试搭配。所填的词修饰 countryside,所以应选 lonely(偏僻的)。

57. 本题测试搭配。at the side of 是习惯搭配,意思是“在……旁边”。

58. 本题测试语法。所填的词引导短语作伴随状语,只有用-ing 形式。应选 A。

59. 本题测试对上下文的理解。根据后面的 Do you want a lift? 可知,应选 D。

60. 本题测试搭配。leave out 是习惯搭配,意思是“遗留”。

61. 本题测试语法。所填的词应该与后面的 climbed into the car 时态一致,所以 A 和 D 不对;选 B 则与 climbed into the car 搭配不当。应选 C。

62. 本题测试搭配。after a while 是固定搭配,意思是“过了一会”。

63. 本题测试对上下文的理解。前面的句子提到,那名搭便车者只是点头或摇头,并不回答问题,说明其行为奇怪,所以应选 C。

64. 本题测试对上下文的理解。前面的句子提到搭便车者行为的奇怪,后面的句子提到她又提出的问题,说明所填的词表示尝试、检验之意,所以应选 D。

65. 本题测试语法。所填的词既要引导句子,还要作 said 的宾语,只有选 D。

66. 本题测试短语辨析。except for 的意思是“除了……之外”,不包括后面的内容,而 apart from 的意思是“除……之外”,包括后面的内容,other than 的意思是“不同于”,more than 的意思是“胜过”。只有选 A 才符合文章的意思。

67. 本题测试词义辨析。所填的词的宾语是 hands,根据后面的 which were large and hairy 可知,这是注意观察的结果,所以应选 B。

68. 本题测试对上下文的理解。前面的句子提到,搭便车者的手又大,毛发又浓密,导致那名女人发现了问题,所以应选 B。

69. 本题测试词义辨析。所填的词修饰整个句子,强调事情的真相,所以应选 C。

70. 本题测试语法。mind 后面的动词应该变成-ing 形式。

71. 本题测试语法。所填的词引导的是时间状语从句,所以应选 C。

72. 本题测试对上下文的理解。文章谈论的是一名年轻女人开车时遇到的情况,只有选 A 才符合文章的意思。

73. 本题测试搭配。pull to a stop 是习惯搭配,意思是"停车"。

74. 本题测试搭配。leave sth. behind 是习惯搭配,意思是"把……遗留在……地方"。

75. 同上。

Unit 17

Scientists say that something very serious is happening to the earth. It will begin to get __56__ in the following years. There will be major changes in __57__ in the new century. Coastal waters will have a __58__ temperature. This will have a __59__ effect on agriculture. In northern areas, the __60__ season will be ten days longer by the year 2010. However, in warmer areas, it will be too dry. The __61__ of water could __62__ by eighty percent. This would __63__ a large decrease in agriculture production.

World temperature could __64__ two degrees centigrade by the year 2040. However, the increase could be three times as great in the Arctic and Antarctic areas. This could cause the __65__ sheets to melt and raise the __66__ of the oceans __67__ one to two meters. Many coastal cities would be __68__ water.

Why is this happening? There is too __69__ carbon dioxide in the air. __70__ oil, gas and coal burn, they create large amounts of carbon dioxide. This carbon dioxide lets __71__ enter the earth's atmosphere and __72__ the earth. However, it doesn't let as much heat __73__ the atmosphere and enter space. It's like a blanket. The heat __74__ the sun can pass through the blanket to warm the earth. The heat __75__ there and can't escape through the blanket again.

Scientists call this the green-house effect.

56. A. warmer　B. colder　C. better　D. worse
57. A land　B. agriculture　C. climate　D. weather
58. A. lower　B. higher　C. normal　D. proper
59. A. good　B. general　C. serious　D. useful
60. A. getting　B. playing　C. taking　D. growing
61. A. much　B. many　C. amount　D. number
62. A. fall　B. decrease　C. refuse　D. rise
63. A. lead　B. keep　C. make　D. cause
64. A. increase　B. drop　C. lift　D. realize
65. A. water　B. rain　C. stone　D. ice
66. A. degree　B. level　C. coast　D. area
67. A. by　B. to　C. of　D. with
68. A. above　B. under　C. below　D. over
69. A. little　B. many　C. few　D. much
70. A. If　B. Because　C. When　D. Why
71. A. sunlight　B. air　C. rain　D. gas
72. A. cold　B. protect　C. hurt　D. heat
73. A. enter　B. get　C. leave　D. reach
74. A. through　B. by　C. from　D. on
75. A. stores　B. arrives　C. stands　D. stays

参考译文

科学家指出,地球正在发生某些严重的事情。在未来几年,地球将开始变暖。在新世纪,地球的气候将发生巨大变化。近海的水温将变得更高。这将对农业产生普遍影响。到2010年时,北部地区的生长期将比现在长10天。不过,在更暖的地区,气候会变得非常干燥。水量可能增加80%。这可能导致农业生产的大幅度减产。

到2040年时,世界的温度可能升高两度。不过,北极和南极地区的温度可能是现在的三倍。这可能导致冰盖融化,提高海平面一到两米。许多沿海城市将会被海水淹没。

为什么会发生这种事情呢?因为空气中有太多的二氧化碳。当石油、天然气以及煤炭燃烧时,它们就会产生大量的二氧化碳。这些二氧化碳使得阳光进入大气层,使得地球升温。但是,二氧化碳又不会让同样的高温散发出大气层进入太空。这就像一个毯子。来自于太阳的高温可以穿过毯子,使得地球变暖。而高温只能停留在地球,不能再穿过毯子散发。

科学家称之为"温室效应"。

解析

56. 本题测试根据上下文进行推理。本段的后面提到"the season will be ten days longer by the year 2010. It will be too dry",这说明地球的温度将更高,所以应选A。

57. 本题测试根据上下文进行推理。本段后面讲的是海水的温度将升高,生长期将变得更长,说明本题是指气候,所以应选C。

58. 本题测试根据上下文进行推理。根据下面段落中的第一、二句话可知应选B。

59. 本题测试修饰词。本题后面的句子讲的是生长期更长、气候会更干燥、水量会增加等问题,说明这是产生的普遍影响,所以应选B。

60. 本题测试搭配。growing season是固定搭配,意思是"生长期"。

61. 本题测试语法。本题指的是水量,所以A和B不对;amount后面接不可数名词,number后面接可数名词,所以应选C。

62. 本题测试搭配。所填的词要与后面的by搭配,只有选D。

63. 本题测试语法。本题前面讲的是现象,后面应该是由此产生的结果,所以B和C不对;lead to才表示结果。应选D。

64. 本题测试根据上下文进行推理。根据后面的句子"the increase could be three times as great in the Arctic and Antarctic areas."可知,应选A。

65. 本题测试搭配。ice sheet是固定搭配,意思是"冰盖,冰帽"。

66. 本题测试搭配。sea level和ocean level是固定搭配,意思是"海平面"。

67. 本题测试搭配。与rise和raise等具有"提高、增长"之意的词搭配的介词是by。

68. 本题测试根据上下文进行推理。前面的句子提到海平面会提高两米左右,说明海水会淹没沿海城市,所以应选B。

69. 本题测试搭配。要填的词应该与前面的too搭配,修饰后面的carbon dioxide(二氧化碳),是不可数名词,所以应选D。

70. 本题测试语法。燃烧物体产生二氧化碳是同时进行的,应该是时间状语,所以应选C。

71. 本题测试根据上下文进行推理。后面的句子具体讲解了温室效应,所以应选A。

72. 本题测试根据上下文进行推理。根据后面的"it doesn't let as much heat"可知,应选D。

73. 本题测试根据上下文进行推理。根据后面的"and can't escape through the blanket again"可知,应选C。

74. 本题测试搭配。"来自于……"应该是from。

75. 本题测试根据上下文进行推理。根据前面的"it doesn't let as much heat leave the atmosphere and enter space"可知,应选D。

Unit 18

Conversation begins almost the moment we come into contact with another and continues throughout the day __56__ the aid of cell phones and computers. However, we are so often absorbed in conversation that we __57__ sight of its true purpose and value.

One important __58__ of a good conversation is that the words are __59__ used to express thoughts and feelings. We are __60__ deep thoughts and strong emotions, yet our vocabularies are not __61__ for this expression, and many __62__ little effort to expand that. Perhaps you see a movie that __63__ you deeply, yet you have the following conversation: "So, what did you think of the film?" "Oh, my God, it was so sad, I swear. I went through __64__ a box of tissues(面巾纸). I was in tears." This dialogue is __65__ an effective way of expressing feelings. It gives no __66__ of how or why the movie truly __67__ you. Such commonly-used phrases are certainly not enough to describe a deeply moving experience. However, not only __68__ try to avoid overused words, you must __69__ be careful in your selection. The purpose of expanding vocabulary is not to use the __70__ or most impressive words, but to find those best suited.

What is lacking in many conversations is the ability to talk to another rather than just talking with that person. A __71__ person will find that even in the most ordinary conversations. There are a thousand questions __72__ to be asked if you have courage and a desire for exchange. Good conversations should not be __73__ nonsense, but of a meeting of two __74__ the human condition. It should bring a better understanding of others and offer a release of emotions more than drive away __75__ thoughts or kill time.

56. A. for	B. at	C. under	D. with
57. A. lose	B. have	C. win	D. miss
58. A. issue	B. problem	C. aspect	D. question
59. A. funny	B. careful	C. only	D. properly
60. A. lack of	B. short of	C. fond of	D. full of
61. A. short	B. enough	C. much	D. bad
62. A. take	B. make	C. get	D. try
63. A. teaches	B. pushes	C. touches	D. directs
64. A. using up	B. to use	C. used up	D. using off
65. A. partly	B. actually	C. hardly	D. truly
66. A. sign	B. model	C. pattern	D. fact
67. A. infected	B. infects	C. affects	D. affected
68. A. you will	B. must you	C. you must	D. will you
69. A. too	B. never	C. also	D. yet
70. A. bigger	B. biggest	C. big	D. important
71. A. careless	B. efficient	C. thoughtful	D. able
72. A. waiting	B. wait	C. waited	D. waits
73. A. make up for	B. made up of	C. make up of	D. made up for
74. A. are sharing	B. shared	C. sharing	D. shares
75. A. clever	B. pleasant	C. unpleasant	D. happy

参考译文

一旦我们开始接触到别人，我们就开始利用手机和电脑进行交流，并且会持续一整天。不过，我们通常太专注于交流了，以至于我们忘记了交流的真正意图和价值。

适度交流的一个重点就是，人们适当运用言语来表达自己的想法和感受。我们有太多深刻的想法，用太多丰富的感受，因此，我们的词汇不足以表达这些想法和感受，许多人也不努力去扩展这些词汇。也许你看过一部深深打动你的电影，但你还是会有如下的交流："那么，你认为这部电影怎么样？""噢，天哪，太悲伤了。到看完时我用光了整整一盒面巾纸。我泪流满面。"这种交谈不是一种表达情感的有效方法。它没有具体说明那部电影如何以及为什么真正触动了你。这类普遍运用的语句肯定不足以描述一段深受感动的体验。不过，你不仅要尽量避免过度运用词句，你还要尽量认真斟酌。扩展词汇的目的不是要用最多或最感人的词语，而是要用那些最贴切的词语。

许多交谈中所缺乏的是同别人交谈的能力，而不只是与那个人交谈而已。一个善于思考的人甚至会在最平常的交谈中发现这一点。如果你有勇气，并且有交流的愿望，那么你就会有许多问题要问。适度的交谈不应该有废话，而是应该表达两个兴趣相投的人相见的感受。它应该使别人更进一步的了解你，提供一个释放情感的机会，而不是谈论一些不愉快的想法，或者浪费时间。

解析

56. 本题测试搭配。with the aid of 是固定搭配，意思是"利用……，借助于……，凭借……"。应选 D。

57. 本题测试搭配。lose sight of 是固定搭配，意思是"忽视……，忘记……"。应选 A。

58. 本题测试名词。issue 的意思是"问题"；problem 的意思是"问题"；aspect 的意思是"方面，点"；question 的意思是"问题"。本句话谈的是适度交谈的重点，所以应选 C。

59. 本题测试语法。要填的词修饰 used，应该是副词，所以 A 和 B 不对；根据前面的 good conversation 可知，应选 D。

60. 本题测试根据上下文进行推理。根据后面的"yet our vocabularies are not..."可知，本题表示"多的"意思，应选 D。

61. 本题测试根据上下文进行推理。根据前面的"We are full of deep thoughts and strong emotions..."可知，应选 B。

62. 本题测试搭配。make efforts to 是固定搭配，意思是"努力做……"。

63. 本题测试搭配。要填的词应该与后面的 deeply 搭配，只有 touch 与之搭配符合题意。

64. 本题测试语法。go through 后面应该接 doing，所以 B 和 C 不对；use off 搭配不当。应选 A。

65. 本题测试语法。根据后面的"It gives no... of how or why the movie truly..."可知，本题表示否定意思，所以应选 C。

66. 本题测试搭配。give fact of 是习惯搭配，意思是"具体说明……"。

67. 本题测试根据上下文进行推理。根据前面的"you see a movie that touches you deeply..."可知，应选 C。

68. 本题测试语法。not only 放在句首时句子应该倒装，所以 A 和 C 不对；根据后面的"you must"可知，应选 B。

69. 本题测试搭配。只有 also 才能与 not only 搭配。

70. 本题测试语法。根据后面的"most impressive words"可知，应选 B。

71. 本题测试修饰词。根据后面的"will find that even in the most ordinary conversations"可知，应选 C。

72. 本题测试语法。要填的词引导短语修饰 questions，表示主动，所以应选 A。

73. 本题测试语法。要填的词跟在 be 后面，应该表示被动，所以 A 和 C 不对；B 的意思是"由……构成、组成"，D 的意思是"弥补……"。应选 B。

74. 本题测试语法。要填的词引导短语修饰 a meeting of two，表示主动，所以应选 C。

75. 本题测试修饰词。根据前面的"bring a better understanding of others and offer a release of emotions more than..."可知，本题应该表示否定意思。应选 C。

Unit 19

There ___56___ a king who had twelve beautiful daughters. They ___57___ in twelve beds all in one room and when they went to bed, the ___58___ were shut and locked up. ___59___, every morning ___60___ shoes were found to be quite worn through as if they had been danced in all night. Nobody could ___61___ how it happened, or ___62___ the princesses had been.

So the king made it ___63___ to all that if any person could discover the ___64___ and find out where it was that the princesses danced in the ___65___, he would have the ___66___ he liked best to take as his wife, and would be king ___67___ his death. But whoever tried and did not succeed, after three days and nights, would be ___68___ to death.

A prince from a nearby country soon came. He was well entertained, and in the evening was taken to the chamber (大房间) next ___69___ the one where the princesses lay in their twelve ___70___. There he was to sit and ___71___ where they went to dance; and, in order ___72___ nothing could happen without him hearing it, the door of his ___73___ was left open. But the prince soon went to sleep; and when he ___74___ in the morning he found that the princesses had all been dancing, ___75___ the soles of their shoes were full of holes.

56. A. was	B. were	C. is	D. are
57. A. did	B. slept	C. washed	D. kicked
58. A. chairs	B. desks	C. doors	D. roofs
59. A. So	B. Therefore	C. Then	D. However
60. A. their	B. your	C. our	D. her
61. A. make out	B. take out	C. find out	D. speak out
62. A. when	B. what	C. why	D. where
63. A. know	B. knowing	C. knows	D. known
64. A. story	B. secret	C. news	D. idea
65. A. night	B. day	C. afternoon	D. morning
66. A. one	B. it	C. some	D. that
67. A. before	B. after	C. of	D. below
68. A. made	B. passed	C. put	D. handed
69. A. by	B. to	C. at	D. on
70. A. boxes	B. buckets	C. sofas	D. beds
71. A. notice	B. keep	C. watch	D. hit
72. A. that	B. which	C. who	D. whose
73. A. kitchen	B. classroom	C. chamber	D. restaurant
74. A. ate	B. awoke	C. slept	D. ran
75. A. for	B. so	C. but	D. though

参考译文

从前,有一个国王,他有12个美丽的女儿。她们都睡在一间屋子里,当她们上床睡觉时,房门就会被锁上。不过,每天早上都会发现她们的鞋穿破了,好像她们整晚都在跳舞。没有人知道这是怎么回事,也不知道公主们都去过哪里。

因此,国王通告全国,如果有人能够发现这个秘密,查明公主们晚上跳舞的地点,他就可以娶他最喜欢的一个公主为妻,并且在国王死后继承王位。但是,如果经过三天的努力而没有成功,无论是谁,都会被处死。

不久,附近一个王国的王子来到该国。他受到很好的款待,到了晚上,他被带到公主睡觉的房间隔壁的一个大房间就寝。在那里，他要坐等着观察公主们会到哪里去跳舞；为了避免错过任何发生的事情，他房间的门一直开着。但是，王子不久就睡着了，等到他第二天早上醒来时，他发现，公主们整个晚上一直在跳舞，因为她们的鞋跟满是裂口。

解析

56. 本题测试语法。本文是在讲一个故事，所以 C 和 D 不对；后面的 a king 说明 B 也不对。应选 A。

57. 本题测试搭配。根据后面的 in twelve beds 可知，应选 B。

58. 本题测试搭配。根据后面的 shut and locked up 可知，应选 C。

59. 本题测试语法。前面的句子讲"公主们的房门被锁上了"，后面的句子说"每天早上都会发现鞋子穿破了"，说明前后句子意思转折，所以应选 D。

60. 本题测试根据上下文进行推理。前面的句子都是讲公主们，说明本题应该是指公主们的鞋。应选 A。

61. 本题测试搭配。make out：声称；take out：取出；find out：发现，知晓；speak out：无保留地说出。根据后面的 how it happened 可知，应选 C。

62. 本题测试根据上文进行推理。前面句子说公主们好像整晚在跳舞，但没人知道是怎么回事，说明本题是指跳舞的地点，所以应选 D。

63. 本题测试语法。make 后面接物时，后面的动词通常用过去分词。

64. 本题测试根据上下文进行推理。前面段落提到没有人知道公主们在何处跳舞之事，所以本题应该是指这件事。应选 B。

65. 本题测试根据上下文进行推理。前面提到公主们是在晚上跳舞，所以应选 A。

66. 本题测试语法。本题是指一个公主，所以应选 A。

67. 本题测试根据上下文进行推理。只有在该国王死后才可能继承王位，所以应选 B。

68. 本题测试搭配。put to death 是固定搭配，意思是"处死"。

69. 本题测试搭配。next to 是固定搭配，意思是"隔壁"。

70. 本题测试搭配。lay 只有与 bed 搭配才符合文章的意思。

71. 本题测试搭配。notice：注意到；keep：保持；watch：观察；hit：击打。根据后面的 where they went to dance 可知，应选 C。

72. 本题测试搭配。in order that 是固定搭配，意思是"为了"。

73. 本题测试根据上下文进行推理。根据前面的句子可知，王子应该是开自己所住房间的房门，所以应选 C。

74. 本题测试根据上下文进行推理。前面句子提到王子睡着了，本题说的第二天早上的事情，所以应选 B。

75. 本题测试语法。本题是在讲原因，所以应选 A。

Unit 20

Of all the websites, one that has attracted attention recently is myspace. com. Most of this attention has come from the media and tells every reason. __56__ the website should be __57__. The threat of Internet predators (窃掠者) is indeed a tough reality, __58__ shutting down the site is not the answer. If myspace. com __59__ shut down, another site would quickly __60__ its place. Therefore, the right way is to teach teens how to use the site safely and educate them __61__ who may be predators and how to __62__ them.

The key to __63__ safe on the Internet is to make sure that your profile (个人资料) is secure. The __64__ way is to change the privacy setting on your profile to "private", which protects your information __65__ only the people on your friend list can view it. Although this is __66__, it is not perfect. Predators can find ways to view your profile if they really want to, __67__ through hacking in (黑客入侵) or figuring out their way onto your friend list. Thus, you should never post too much personal __68__. Some people actually post their home and school addresses, date of birth, and so on, often __69__ predators know exactly where they will be and __70__.

The most information that is safe is your first name and province. Anything more is basically __71__ a predator into your life.

Another big problem is photos. I suggest __72__ skipping photos and never posting a photo of a friend online without his or her __73__.

Most important, never, __74__ any circumstances, agree to a real-life meeting with anyone you meet online, __75__ how well you think you know this person. There are no guarantees that they have told the truth.

56. A. what	B. how	C. why	D. which
57. A. shut down	B. open up	C. get into	D. turn on
58. A. but	B. even	C. despite	D. since
59. A. is	B. are	C. was	D. were
60. A. get	B. make	C. take	D. push
61. A. as	B. about	C. for	D. in
62. A. avoid	B. get	C. benefit	D. hide
63. A. stay	B. be staying	C. stayed	D. staying
64. A. difficult	B. simplest	C. simple	D. most difficult
65. A. as to	B. no matter	C. so that	D. because
66. A. efficient	B. interesting	C. effective	D. impressive
67. A. if	B. whether	C. however	D. whatever
68. A. information	B. documents	C. fries	D. messages
69. A. let	B. make	C. allow	D. letting
70. A. what	B. why	C. when	D. how
71. A. introducing	B. inviting	C. investing	D. interrupting
72. A. partly	B. mostly	C. lastly	D. completely
73. A. favor	B. rule	C. information	D. permission
74. A. above	B. under	C. below	D. at
75. A. no matter	B. even if	C. unless	D. also

参考译文

在所有网站中,最近引人关注的是 myspace. com 网站。主要的关注来自媒体,并且详尽解释了该网站为什么应该被关闭的原因。互联网窃掠者的威胁的确是一个不争的事实,但关闭网站不是解决问题的办法。如果 myspace. com 网站被关闭了,那么另一个网站很快就会取代它的位置。因此,正确的方法是告诉青少年如何安全使用网站,教导他们有关哪些人可能是窃掠者、如何避免接触他们等方面的知识。

要想在互联网上使自己安全,就必须确保自己的个人资料安全。最简单的方法就是将你个人资料上的隐私保护设定为"私有的",这样会保护你的资料,以便只有在你好友名单中的人才能查看你的资料。这种方法虽然有效,但不完美。如果窃掠者真想查看你的资料,他们就能找到方法——要么通过黑客入侵,要么设法进入你好友的名单。因此,你永远都不要发布太多个人信息。有些人竟然发布其家庭和学校地址、自己的生日等方面的信息,这时常使得窃掠者能够准确得知这些人将去何处、什么时候去。

大多数安全的信息就是你的名字和你所处的省份。更多的问题主要是邀请窃掠者进入你的生活所导致的。

另一个大问题就是照片。我建议,彻底略去照片,并且未经好友的许可绝不在网上发布他们的照片。

最重要的是，无论何种情况，永远都不要同意与你在网上相识的任何人进行现实约会，无论你自认为多么了解他。你不能担保这些人告诉你了实情。

解析

56. 本题测试语法。根据前面的 every reason 可知，后面的句子应该是讲原因，所以应选 C。

57. 本题测试词组。shut down：关闭；open up：开张；get into：进入；turn on：打开（电视、灯等）。根据后面的 shutting down the site is not the answer 可知，应选 A。

58. 本题测试语法。本句话表示转折，只有选 A。

59. 本题测试语法。根据后面的 another site would quickly 可知，本句话表示虚拟，应选 D。

60. 本题测试搭配。take one's place 是固定搭配，意思是"取代……的位置"。

61. 本题测试介词。"教导某人……知识"应该用介词 about。

62. 本题测试动词。avoid：避开，避免；get：得到，获得；benefit：有益于，得益；hide：隐藏，躲藏。前面句子提到互联网窃掠者的威胁，所以应选 A。

63. 本题测试语法。the key to 后面如接动词时应该用-ing 形式，所以应选 D。

64. 本题测试语法。要填的词前有 the，说明应该是最高级，所以 A 和 C 不对；选 D 与句意相反。应选 B。

65. 本题测试语法。要填的词引导目的状语从句，只有选 C。

66. 本题测试形容词。efficient：有能力的，效率高的；interesting：有趣的，有吸引力的；effective：有效的，效果不错的；impressive：给人印象深刻的，感人的。本句话的主语是前面提到的方法，根据后面的 it is not perfect 可知，应选 C。

67. 本题测试语法。根据后面的 or 可知，本句话表示选择，所以应选 B。

68. 本题测试名词。前面句子是在讲保护个人资料的问题，所以应选 A。

69. 本题测试语法。要填的词表示伴随状语，动词应该用-ing 形式，并且根据后面的 predators know 可知，只有选 D。

70. 本题测试语法。根据前面的 their home and school addresses, date of birth 可知，应选 C。

71. 本题测试动词。introduce：介绍；invite：邀请；invest：投资；interrupt：打断。根据后面的 into your life 可知，应选 B。

72. 本题测试副词。partly：部分地；mostly：主要地；lastly：最后；completely：彻底，完全地。根据后面的 never posting a photo of a friend online 可知，应选 D。

73. 本题测试搭配。without one's permission 是固定搭配，意思是"未经某人的许可"。

74. 本题测试搭配。under any circumstances 是固定搭配，意思是"无论何种情况"。

75. 本题测试搭配。no matter how 是习惯搭配，意思是"无论如何……"。

第六章　翻译题解题技巧

第一节　英译汉技巧

1.1　英语与汉语的区别

1. 英语习惯用被动语态，而汉语习惯用主动语态。汉语句子时常没有主语，而英语句子除了个别特殊情况（如祈使句、感叹句）以外，不能没有主语。所以，在翻译时，一定要把握英汉两种语言的不同表达习惯，既要忠实于原文，又要符合汉语的表达习惯。

例如：Something must be done to protect our environment from further pollution.

（必须采取措施，使我们的环境免受进一步的污染。）

2. 英语习惯用从句（长句），而汉语习惯用单句（短句）。在考试中要善于运用分译法，用汉语的短句来表达英语长句的内容。

例如：In warmer areas primitive man could use branches to make a framework which was then covered with leaves.（在气候较为温暖的地方，原始人类能用树枝搭建屋架，外面用树叶遮盖。）

3. 英语习惯用名词表示行为动作，汉语则往往相反。

例如：He paid a visit to an exhibition of advanced science and technology on Sunday.

（星期天他参观了一个高科技展览。）

4. 表达时间、空间时，英语习惯先小后大，汉语则往往相反。

例如：He was born in an out-of-way mountain village in South China at 2 a. m. on May 6, 1968.（他于1968年五月六日凌晨两点出生于中国南部一个偏僻的小山村里。）

1.2　通过语境吃透句子

词语的理解离不开上下文，这是我们在翻译中必须时刻牢记的一条。英语中一词一义的情况极为罕见，只有通过上下文才能了解单词的确切的含义。在翻译中，要特别注意以下三个问题：

1. 认真把握多义词在语境中的特定含义

例如：What you said sounds reasonable.（你的话听起来有道理。）

　　His father gave him a sound beating.（他爸爸痛打他一顿。）

2. 注意习惯用语的理解

英语历史悠久，拥有极为丰富的习语，对习语的掌握程度往往决定一个学习者的真实语言水平。因而，考试经常涉及这方面的内容。例如：

I know this fellow from A to Z.（这家伙我非常了解。）

3. 确定代词在上下文中的指代关系

代词的理解更是离不开一定的语境，代词、代名词或者代动词在句中指代的是什么，只有在特定的语境中才能确定。对于代词的考查是英译汉常考之内容。在翻译中，有时代词只是照字面译为“这、那”是远远不够的，须将代替的部分加以重述。

We have 365 days in a year.（一年有365天。）

A big nation had its problems, a small nation has its advantages.（大国有大国的问题，小国有小国的有利条件。）

1.3 翻译技巧

1. 词类的转译

名词、动词、形容词往往根据需要转译为其他词类。例如：

My admiration for him grew more.（我对他越来越敬佩。）（*n.* —*v.*）

He acted as if he were a teacher.（他的举止像个教师。）（*v.* —*n.*）

2. 词的增补

在翻译过程中，经常遇到这种情况：英文原文中某些词语，无法用一般字典中相对应的汉语释义表达出来。翻译时考生应根据原文的意思，用地道的汉语表达出来。有时要根据英语动词时态形式增补时间修饰语，有时要增补原文中的省略部分，有时要把代词还原为所指的对象，有时要增补连接词以加强修辞效果。例如：

They are working on my bike.（他们正在修理我的自行车。）

We found him at his book in the library.（我们发现他在图书馆看书。）

3. 定语从句的翻译

英语和汉语的定语都有前置、后置之分。但不同的是，英语以定语后置为主；汉语则以前置为主，极少用后置。所以在翻译过程中，后置定语的翻译是一大难题，尤其是定语从句的翻译。通常有两种译法：一是译作前置定语；一是采用分译法。

限制性定语从句一般可按前置修饰语译作“……的”。

例如：This is the reason why an airplane sometimes must taxi a long way before taking off.（这就是为什么飞机在起飞之前有时必须滑行一段长路的原因。）

非限制性定语从句大多在句中起补充说明的作用，翻译时不改变其语序，而是根据其作用区别处理，有时通过重复先行词将定语从句译为并列句或独立句，有时加上连接词语，译为转折、目的、结果、原因、让步、条件、时间等状语从句。

例如：In Southern France a solar furnace has been built, where temperature reach more than 3,000 centigrade.（在法国南部已经建造了一座太阳炉，炉温高达摄氏3000度以上。）

1.4 做题步骤

考生要遵循三个基本要求，即“忠实、通顺、易懂”。译文要力求忠实原文，能直译则直译。也就是说如果直译出来的汉语通顺就直译，不便于直译的英语句子在处理时，要力求在忠实于原文的基础上，使译文通顺。

英译汉做题的步骤应该是：

1. 了解句子大意

先了解句子大意，先思考，再动笔，不要反复涂改。有的考生往往是拿到试卷就开始翻译，“只见树木，不见森林”，等译不下去了再回读，那样做既费时间又影响情绪。

2. 理解和表达

这是英译汉应试中的实质性阶段。鉴于试题具有一定的难度,尤其是长句的翻译,要在准确理解的基础上,按照汉语的表达习惯,用地道的汉语表达出来。

3. 校改

考试过程中,考生不能像平时那样从容不迫,初译时往往侧重于理解,容易忽视译文的连贯性,从而译出英语式的汉语句子。所以,译完后要回过来看一看译文是否通顺连贯。还有一个不可忽略的问题是书写,一份整洁的答卷会取悦于判卷老师,也等于成功了一半。

第二节 汉译英技巧

2.1 汉译英应试技巧

1. 事先筹划,再来做题

在翻译每一个句子时,一定要事先筹划:先要想好译成什么样的英语句子结构,是简单句还是复合句,或者是强调句、倒装句。假如选用了复合句,那么要明确哪部分是主句,从句采用的形式,是定语从句、状语从句还是其他的从句。在一个句子内,主语是什么,谓语用什么时态,是主动还是被动,要不要虚拟语气,这些都要事先筹划好。

然后动笔进行翻译。遣词造句过程中,要格外注重一些细节问题:仔细斟酌、选用最能确切表达原文意思的英文单词或词组;名词的复数形式,动词的不规则变化,主谓语的一致性,单词的拼写,标点符号,大小写,冠词的使用等。任何一个细节注意不到都可能出错丢分。

2. 灵活处理,提高把握

在翻译过程中,有时可能碰到一些英语单词不会写,这时千万不能灰心丧气,甚至放弃整个句子。这时可以寻找意思相近而自己熟知的词或词组来代替。无论如何不要把那个词空着,更不要用汉字去替代。对句子的结构同样也可以灵活处理,有些没把握的结构,可以用比较有把握的结构来代替。例如,复合句没有把握,可以用两个简单句来表示;分词做状语没有把握,可以用状语从句来代替等等。

3. 注重书写和卷面整洁

这个问题经常被考生忽略。有的考生在考试中信手写来,一些不良的书写习惯也带了进来,例如 r、V 不分,i、I 不分,有的经常遗忘标点符号,从而造成不必要的丢分。

在对此题进行备考复习时,首先对以往做过的汉译英作业进行复习,凡是作业中的错误之处,要进行思考,以求提高水平和技巧。另外,进行语法复习、阅读复习、单词复习过程中,对一些重点句、重点语法现象,除了记忆之外也要往汉译英方面想一想,自己给自己提问题:若要考汉译英,这部分可能出什么类型题?这样就会印象更深。

2.2 重点汉译英句型

1. 动词

例如:这篇文章的目的是告诉学生怎样培养良好的学习习惯。

本句话的谓语动词是"是","告诉学生怎样培养良好的学习习惯"动词不定式短语作表语。

参考译文:The purpose of this article is to tell the students how to develop good study habits.

2. 形式主语

例如：对护士来说，坚持这项规定是很重要的。

本句话的主语是“坚持这项规定”，由于主语较长，因此用 it 作形式主语。

参考译文：It is very important for nurses to stick to this rule.

3. nothing but...

例如：艾米过去除了咖啡什么都不喝。

“除了……不”短语通常译成“nothing but...”。

参考译文：Amy used to drink nothing but coffee.

4. 发现(看见、听见)某人做……

例如：亚当斯先生发现他 13 岁的儿子正从他的皮夹子里偷钱时大为震惊。

“发现某人做……”通常译成 find someone doing something。

参考译文：Mr. Adams was greatly shocked to find his 13-year-old son stealing money from his wallet.

5. 动词不定式的否定式

例如：他努力控制住自己的感情，假装没有听见那个令人悲痛的消息。

“假装”后面的“没有听见”是动词不定式的否定形式。

参考译文：He tried hard to hold himself in and pretended not to have heard the sad news.

6. 表示手段

例如：作者想通过这篇文章向读者传达她对赞扬与批评的看法。

“通过这篇文章”作方式状语，表示手段。

参考译文：Through the article the author wants to convey to the readers his view on praise and criticism.

7. 比较结构

例如：我们常常发现，运用一个规律比懂得它要难得多。

本句话的后半部分是一个比较结构，比较的是动作。

参考译文：We often find it much more difficult to apply a rule than to know it.

8. can't help doing something

例如：她读这部小说时，不禁想起了她在农村度过的那五年。

“不禁……，忍不住……”通常用 can't help＋动名词结构翻译。

参考译文：When she read the novel, she couldn't help thinking of the five years she had spent in the countryside.

9. 连续性动词

例如：我正忙着做一种新的捕鼠装置时，马克走来拖着我出去看花展了。

“走来拖”是连续行动作。

参考译文：I was busy making a new device for catching rats when Mark came and dragged me to a flower show.

10. before 的用法

例如：美国许多父母在孩子出生之前就为他们的教育留出一笔专款。

本句话中的“出生之前”应该用“... before...”翻译。

参考译文：Many parents in the United States set aside a fund for their children's education before they are born.

11. 引导词+不定式短语

例如:小男孩急于想减轻那位妇人的痛苦,但不知道该怎么办。

“不知道该怎么办”应该用引导词+不定式短语结构翻译,译成 not know what to do。

参考译文:The young boy was eager to make the woman less unhappy, but he did not know what to do.

12. 太……以致于不……

例如:南希虽然很想参加辩论,但腼腆得不敢开口。

“太……以致于不……”短语通常用“too... to”结构翻译。

参考译文:While she felt like joining in the argument, Nancy was too shy to open her mouth.

13. 一……就……

例如:这项建议在会上一宣布,她就站起来提出异议。

“一……就……”通常用“as soon as”或“no sooner... than”翻译。

参考译文:No sooner had the proposal been announced at the meeting than she got to her feet to protest.

14. 强调句

例如:很明显,是他的年轻助手在经营这家书店。

本句话是一个强调句式,强调的是“他的年轻助手”。

参考译文:It is obvious that it is his young assistant who is running the book store.

15. 插入语

例如:你觉得什么时候最有可能在家里找到他?

本句话中的“你觉得”是插入语。

参考译文:What do you think is the likeliest time to find him at home?

16. 使某人做某事

例如:他这次考试失败使他意识到定期复习功课是多么重要。

“使某人做某事”通常用“make somebody+动词原形”翻译。

参考译文:He failed in the exam, which has made him realize the importance of reviewing his lessons regularly.

17. 存在的,有

例如:有迹象表明,不少工厂正面临着十分困难的局面。

本句话中的“有迹象”是存在的有,通常用“there be”句型翻译。

参考译文:There are indications that numerous factories are faced with a very difficult situation.

18. 从句

(1) 状语从句

例如:不管有多困难,我们都不能放弃自己的目标。

本句话中包含一个让步状语从句。

参考译文:No matter how difficult it is, we should never give up our goals.

(2) 定语从句

例如:几天前,由三位医生和两名护士组成的医疗队到山区去了。

本句话中的“由三位医生和两名护士组成的”是定语从句,修饰医疗队。

参考译文：The medical team which was composed of three doctors and two nurses set off for the mountain area a few days ago.

(3) 主语从句

例如：在我访问你们那个地方时，给我印象最深的是你们那儿的人对我们的友谊。

本句话中的“给我印象最深的”是主语从句。

参考译文：What impressed me most during my visit in your country was the friendship your people have for our people.

(4) 同位语从句

例如：我相信比较高级的动物是由比较低级的动物进化而来的这一学说。

本句话中的“比较高级的动物是由比较低级的动物进化而来的”这句话是“学说”的同位语从句。

参考译文：I believe in the theory that the higher animals developed from the lower ones.

(5) 表语从句

例如：他那句话的含义是他想在政府部门找个工作。

本句话中的“他想在政府部门找个工作”是表语从句。

参考译文：The implication of his statement is that he'd like to find a job in a government department.

2.3 历年汉译英试题解析

Unit 1

81. 他们想出一个解决这个问题的办法。

They came up with a solution to the problem.

解析：本句话的谓语动词是“想出”，“解决问题的办法”应该用 a solution to 这个短语。

82. 你离开教室时，别忘了关灯。

Don't forget to turn off the lights when you leave the classroom.

解析：本句话的主句是一个祈使句的否定句，when 引导的是时间状语从句。

83. 他喜欢一边做作业，一边听音乐。

He likes to listen to music while doing his homework.

解析：本句话的谓语动词是“喜欢”，while 引导的是一个短语，也可引导从句。

84. 我已了解清楚，他的结论是以事实为依据。

I have known that his conclusion is based on facts.

解析：“他的结论是以事实为依据”是“了解”的宾语从句。

85. 对于年轻人来说，独立思考问题的能力很重要。

As for the young, the ability to think on their own is important.

解析：本句话的主语是“独立思考问题的能力”，谓语动词是“是”，“对于年轻人来说”是状语。

Unit 2

81. 今年他们建造的房子跟去年一样多。

They have built as many houses this year as they did last year.

解析：本句话中有一个比较结构，比较的是建造的房子多少。

82.对不起,我忘了把你要的书带来了。

I am sorry I forgot to bring the book you want.

解析:"我忘了把你要的书带来了"是宾语从句,其中的"你要的"是定语从句,修饰"书"。

83.这项工作太难了,你干不了。

The work is too difficult for you to do.

解析:"太……以致于不……"短语通常用"too... to..."结构翻译。

84.无论多么困难,我也不会失去信心。

No matter how difficult it is, I will never lose my faith.

解析:"无论多么困难"是一个让步状语从句。

85.物体离我们越远,看起来就越小。

The farther an object is away from us, the smaller it looks.

解析:本句话中有一个比较结构,比较的是物体的远近对视觉的影响。

Unit 3

81. 我们的新产品非常受欢迎,对此我们感到十分自豪。

Our new products are very popular, so we are proud of it.

解析:本句话的谓语动词是"be"动词,"我们感到十分自豪"是结果状语从句。

82. 您能说话大声点好让每个人都听得见吗?

Could you speak aloud so that everyone can hear you?

解析:"好让每个人都听得见"是目的状语从句。

83. 除了英语,你最好再学一门外语。

Besides English, you'd better study another foreign language.

解析:本句话中的"除了……还"应该用"besides"翻译,"you'd better"后面应该接动词原形。

84. 在教育孩子方面,表扬要比批评有效得多。

For teaching children, praising is better than criticizing.

解析:本句话中有一个比较结构,比较的是表扬与批评的效果好坏。

85. 每个人都知道,学习对一个人的成长是至关重要的。

As we all know, learning is vital to one's growing-up.

解析:本句话的谓语动词是"是","每个人都知道"是一个定语从句,修饰整个句子。

Unit 4

81. 使我感到惊奇的是,他的英语说得如此的好。

What surprised me is that he could speak English so well.

解析:本句话的谓语动词是"是","使我感到惊奇"是主语从句,"他的英语说得如此的好"是表语从句。

82. 开会的时间到了,咱们把收音机关了吧。

It is time for meeting. Let's turn off the radio.

解析:前面句子是固定句型"It is time for",后面是一个由"Let's"引导的祈使句。

83. 尽管有许多困难,我们仍然决心执行我们的计划。

Although there are a lot of difficulties, we are still determined to carry out our plan.

解析：本句话的谓语动词是“决心”,“尽管有许多困难”是让步状语从句。

84. 我们居住的地球是一个大球体。

The earth we are living is a big sphere.

解析：“我们居住的”是定语从句,修饰地球。

85. 我们向李先生学习,因为他有丰富的工作经验。

We learn from Mr. Li because he is rich in working experiences.

解析：本句话的谓语动词是“向……学习”,“因为他有丰富的工作经验”是原因状语从句。

Unit 5

81. 正是那棵树在洪水中救了他们的命。

It is that tree that saved their lives in the flood.

解析：本句话是一个强调句式,强调的是那棵树。

82. 我们无法想象在那个遥远的星球上存在什么东西。

We can't imagine what may exit in that remote star.

解析：本句话的谓语动词是“无法想象”,“在那个遥远的星球上存在什么东西”是宾语从句。

83. 他今早上学又迟到了。昨晚他肯定是睡得太晚了。

He was late for school again this morning. He must have slept too late last night.

解析：前面句子的谓语动词是“be”动词,后面句子中的“肯定睡得太晚”应该用“情态动词+完成时态”结构表示。

84. 父母没有预料到孩子的问题这样难回答。

The parents did not expect that their child's question was too hard to answer.

解析：“孩子的问题这样难回答”是宾语从句,其中有一个“too... to...”结构。

85. 然而,在那个国家还有成千上万的年轻人却很难找到工作。

However, there are still thousands of young people in that country who have trouble in finding a job.

解析：本句话中的“有成千上万的年轻人”是存在的“有”,通常用“there be”句型翻译,后面的“很难找到工作”是定语从句,修饰“年轻人”。

Unit 6

81. 他起得很早为的是赶上第一班公共汽车。

He got up early so as to catch the first bus.

解析：“为的是赶上第一班公共汽车”是目的状语,用“so as to...”或“in order to...”短语翻译。

82. 直到昨天晚上他才改变了他的主意。

It was not until yesterday that he changed his mind.

解析：本句话是一个强调句式,强调的是“昨天晚上”。

83. 同意这项建议的请举手。

Whoever agrees on this suggestion please put up your hands.

解析：本句话是一个祈使句。

84. 无论多忙,你都应该抽时间看望父母。

No matter how busy you are, you should spend some time visiting your parents.

解析:“无论多忙”是让步状语从句。

85. 每次访问他们都会发现这个城市呈现出新的面貌。

Each time they visit this city, they can notice that it is taking on a new look.

解析:“每次访问”是时间状语从句,“这个城市呈现出新的面貌”是宾语从句。

Unit 7

81. 她的工作是照看这些老人。

Her job is to look after these old people.

解析:本句话的谓语动词是“是”,不定式短语做表语。

82. 学生应该在上课之前完成家庭作业。

The students should finish their homework before class.

解析:本句话中的“上课之前”应该用“before”翻译。

83. 这些老人养成了每天早上锻炼的习惯。

These old people have developed the habit of doing exercise every morning.

解析:本句话的谓语动词是“养成”,应该用完成时态。

84. 如果到处都太拥挤,旅行会令人很不愉快。

If it is too crowded everywhere, the travel will be very unpleasant.

解析:本句话的谓语动词是“be”动词,“如果到处都太拥挤”是条件状语从句。

85. 我不知道你那奇怪的想法来自何处。

I do not know where your strange ideas come from.

解析:“你那奇怪的想法来自何处”是宾语从句。

Unit 8

81. 事实上,水污染的危害远不止这点。

In fact, the dangers of water pollution are far beyond this.

解析:本句话的谓语动词是“be”动词,“事实上”是插入语。

82. 这个问题不像我们最初想象的那么复杂。

This problem is not so complicated as we imagined at first.

解析:本句话中有一个比较结构,比较的是想象的复杂性,应该用“not so... as...”结构翻译。

83. 如果你那时没有及时离开,我无法想象会发生什么情况。

If you had not left in time then, I could not imagine what would have happened.

解析:“如果你那时没有及时离开”是条件状语从句,表示虚拟语气。

84. 他们发现在下午6点前不可能完成这项工作。

They found it impossible to finish this job before 6 p.m.

解析:本句话中的“发现不可能完成工作”应该用“find+it+形容词+动词不定式”结构翻译,“it”是形式宾语。

85. 由于我没有读过这本书,所以我无法对此作出评论。

Because I have not read the book, I am not able to make comment on it.

解析:“由于我没有读过这本书”是原因状语从句。

Unit 9

81. 每个人都喜欢受表扬而不是被批评。

Everyone likes to be praised rather than to be criticized.

解析：本句话的谓语动词是"喜欢","而不是"短语应该用"rather than"或"instead of"短语翻译。

82. 人们抱怨当地政府在处理污染问题上力度不够。

People complain that the local government hasn't taken enough measure to deal with pollution.

解析：本句话的谓语动词是"抱怨","当地政府在处理污染问题上力度不够"是宾语从句。

83. 只要你尽力而为,即使将来失败也没人会指责你。

As long as you try your best, nobody will blame you even if you fail in future.

解析："只要你尽力而为"和"即使将来失败"都是条件状语从句,

84. 他告诉我要慢慢来,没有必要提前完成这项工作。

He told me to take my time and it was unnecessary to complete the job in advance.

解析：后面句子的形式主语是"it",真正的主语是"提前完成这项工作",应该用"it is ＋ 形容词 ＋ 动词不定式"结构翻译。

85. 我们推迟了这个会议,以便能够更好地应付紧张的局势。

We put off this meeting so as to cope with the tense situations better.

解析："以便能够更好地应付紧张的局势"是目的状语。

Unit 10

81. 如果我是他,我就会尽最大努力按时完成任务。

If I were him, I would try my best to complete the task on time.

解析："如果我是他"是条件状语从句,表示虚拟语气。

82. 我不记得曾经在哪里见过他。

I don't remember where I have ever been met him.

解析："在哪里见过他"是宾语从句。

83. 这所大学提供了他所期望的一切。

The university has provided everything he expected.

解析：本句话的谓语动词是"提供","他所期望的"是定语从句,修饰"一切"。

84. 我们一得出结论就通知你。

We will inform you as soon as we come to conclusion.

解析："一……就……"通常用"as soon as..."或"no sooner... than"翻译。

85. 你们应该充分利用每个机会说英语。

You should make full use of every chance to speak English.

解析：本句话的谓语动词是"应该充分利用"。

Unit 11

81. 我想说的是,在奥运会上做志愿者(volunteer)对于年轻人是有意义的事。

What I want to say is that it is significant for young people to be volunteers in Olympic Games.

解析：“我想说的是”是主语从句，后面的句子是表语从句，“it”是形式主语，真正的主语是“在奥运会上做志愿者”。

82. 简而言之，每个人都该为自己的行为负责。

In short, everyone should be responsible for his behavior.

解析：本句话的谓语动词是“be”动词，“简而言之”是插入语。

83. 我下决心一个月内在功课上要赶上同学们。

I am determined to catch up with my classmates in one month.

解析：本句话的谓语动词是“下决心”。

84. 在我看来，他们很难掩盖事实真相。

As for me, it is difficult for them to cover the truth.

解析：本句话的形式主语是“it”，真正的主语是后面的“掩盖事实真相”，“在我看来”是状语。

85. 直到会议结束那位经理一直保持沉默不语。

The manager kept silent till the meeting was over.

解析：“直到会议结束”是时间状语从句。

Unit 12

81. 他们5年前搬走了，但我们还保持联系。

They moved 5 years ago, but we still keep in touch with each other.

解析：“但我们还保持联系”表示转折，“保持联系”应该用“keep in touch with each other”翻译。

82. 看起来这封信是在匆忙中写成的。

It seems that the letter was finished in a hurry.

解析：本句话的谓语动词是“是”，“这封信是在匆忙中写成的”是表语从句。

83. 在得到更多细节之前，我想避免跟他说话。

I hoped to avoid talking to him before I got more details.

解析：本句话中的“在得到更多细节之前”应该用“before”翻译。

84. 每当听到这首歌时，我就会想起你。

Every time I listen to the song, it reminds me of you.

解析：“每当听到这首歌”是时间状语从句。

85. 由于很多学生缺席，我们不得不将会议延期。

We had to put off the meeting because many students were absent.

解析：“由于很多学生缺席”是原因状语从句，“不得不”表示客观因素，应该用 have to 翻译。

Unit 13

81. 我们期待和你一起工作。

We are looking forward to working with you.

解析：本句话的谓语动词是“期待”，用进行时态。

82. 他一到上海就给我打了一个长途电话。

He gave me a long-distance call as soon as he arrived at Shanghai.

解析：“一……就……”通常用“as soon as...”或“no sooner...than”翻译。

83. 你知道会议开始的确切时间吗？

Do you know exactly when the meeting will start?

解析："会议开始的时间"是宾语从句。

84. 她将成功归因于努力工作。

She owes her success to hard work.

解析：本句话的谓语动词是"归因于"，用"owe... to..."短语翻译。

85. 村里的每个人都喜欢他，因为他对人很友好。

Everyone in the village liked him because he was very friendly to them.

解析："因为他对人很友好"是原因状语从句。

Unit 14

81. 今天早上他起床晚了，所以没有赶上火车。

He got up so late this morning that he missed the train.

解析："所以没有赶上火车"是结果状语从句，通常用"so... that"翻译。

82. 你们昨天的会议得出什么结论了吗？

Did you arrive at any conclusion in yesterday's meeting?

解析：本句话的谓语动词是"得出结论"。

83. 我在回家的路上，买了一本英汉词典。

I bought an English-Chinese dictionary on my way home.

解析：本句话的谓语动词是"买"，"我在回家的路上"是状语。

84. 一直到12月下旬，他们才让我加入他们小组。

They didn't allow me to join their group until late December.

解析："直到……才……"通常用"not... until"短语翻译。

85. 我父亲在找工作，我母亲在医院照看外祖母。

My dad is looking for a job while my mother is looking after my grandmother in hospital.

解析：本句话的谓语动词是"寻找"，"我母亲在医院照看外祖母"是时间状语从句。

第七章　历年考试真题

北京地区成人本科学士学位英语统一考试(A)

2003.11

Part I　Reading Comprehension (30%)

Passage 1　Questions 1 to 5 are based on the following passage:

After a busy day of work and play, the body needs to rest. Sleep is necessary for good health. During this time, the body recovers from the activities of the previous day. (76) The rest that you get while sleeping enables your body to prepare itself for the next day.

There are four levels of sleep, each being a little deeper than the one before. As you sleep, your muscles relax little by little. Your heart beats more slowly, and your brain slows down. After you reach the fourth level, your body shifts back and forth from one level of sleep to the other.

Although your mind slows down, from time to time you will dream. Scientists who study sleep state that when dreaming occurs, your eyeballs begin to move more quickly (although your eyelids are closed). This stage of sleep is called REM, which stands for rapid eye movement.

(77) If you have trouble falling asleep, some people recommend breathing very slowly and very deeply. Other people believe that drinking warm milk will help make you drowsy. There is also an old suggestion that counting sheep will put you to sleep!

1. A good title for this passage is ________.

   A. Sleep　　B. Good　　C. Dreams　　D. Work and Rest

2. The word "drowsy" in the last paragraph means ________.

   A. sick　　B. stand up　　C. asleep　　D. a little sleepy

3. This passage suggests that not getting enough sleep might make you ________.

   A. dream more often　　B. have poor health　　C. nervous　　D. breathe quickly

4. During REM, ________.

   A. your eyes move quickly　　B. you dream

   C. you are restless　　D. both A and B

5. The average number of hours of sleep that an adult needs is ________.

   A. approximately six hours　　B. around the hours

   C. about eight hours　　D. not stated here

Passage 2　Questions 6 to 10 are based on the following passage:

Obviously television has both advantages and disadvantages.

(78) In the first place, television is not only a convenient source of entertainment, but also a comparatively cheap one. With a TV set in the family people don't have to pay for expensive seats at the theatre, the cinema, or the opera. All they have to do is to push a button or turn a knob, and they can see plays, films, operas and shows of every kind. Some people, however, think that this is where the danger lies. The television viewers need do nothing. He does not even have to use his legs if he has a remote control. He makes no choice and exercises, no judgment. He is completely passive and has everything to him without any effort on his part.

Television, it is often said, keeps one informed about current events and the latest developments in science and politics. The most distant countries and the strangest customs are brought right into one's sitting room. It could be argued that the radio performs this service as well; but on television everything is much more living, much more real. Yet here again there is a danger. The television screen itself has a terrible, almost physical charm for us. (79) We get so used to looking at the movements on it, so dependent on its pictures, that it begins to control our lives. People are often heard to say that their television sets have broken down and that they have suddenly found that they have far more time to do things and that they have actually begun to talk to each other again. It makes one think, doesn't it?

There are many other arguments for and against television. We must realize that television itself is neither good nor bad. It is the uses that it is put to that determine its value to society.

6. What is the major function of paragraph 1?
   A. To arouse the reader's concern.
   B. To introduce the theme of the whole passage.
   C. To summarize the whole passage.
   D. To state the primary uses of TV.
7. Television, as a source of entertainment, is ________.
   A. not very convenient　　B. very expensive
   C. quite dangerous　　D. relatively cheap
8. Why are some people against TV?
   A. Because TV programs are not interesting.
   B. Because TV viewers are totally passive.
   C. Because TV prices are very high.
   D. Because TV has both advantages and disadvantages.
9. One of the most obvious advantages of TV is that ________.
   A. it keeps us informed　　B. it is very cheap
   C. it enables us to have a rest　　D. it controls our lives
10. According to the passage, whether TV is good or not depends on ________.
    A. its quality　　B. people's attitude towards it
    C. how we use it　　D. when we use it

Passage 3　Questions 11 to 15 are based on the following passage:

Too often young people get themselves employed quite by accident, not knowing what lies in the way of opportunity for promotion, happiness and security. As a result, they are employed doing jobs that afford them little or no satisfaction. (80) Our school leavers face so much competition that they seldom care what they do as long as they can earn a living. Some stay long at a job and learn to like it; others quit from one to another looking for something to suit them. The young graduates who leave the university look for jobs that offer a salary up to their expectation.

Very few go out into the world knowing exactly what they want and realizing their own abilities. The reason behind all this confusion is that there never has been a proper vocational guidance in our educational institution. Nearly all grope (摸索) in the dark and their chief concern when they look for a job is to ask what salary is like. They never bother to think whether they are suited for the fob or, even more important, whether the job suits them. Having a job is more than merely providing yourself and your dependants with daily bread and some money for leisure and entertainment. It sets a pattern of life and, in many ways, determines social status in life, selection of friends, leisure and interest.

In choosing a career you should first consider the type of work which will suit your interest. Nothing is more pathetic than taking on a job in which you have no interest, for it will not only discourage your desire to succeed in life but also ruin your talents and ultimately make you an emotional wreck (受到严重伤害的人) and a bitter person.

11. The reason why some people are unlikely to succeed in life is that they ________.

A. have ruined their talents B. have taken on an unsuitable job
C. think of nothing but their salary D. are not aware of their own potential

12. The difficulty in choosing a suitable job lies mainly in that ________.
A. much competition has to be faced
B. many employees have no working experience
C. the young people only care about how much they can earn
D. schools fail to offer students appropriate vocational guidance

13. Which of the following statements is most important according to the passage?
A. Your job must suit your interest. B. Your job must set a pattern of life.
C. Your job must offer you a high salary. D. Your job must not ruin your talents.

14. The best title for this passage would be ________.
A. What Can A Good Job Offer B. Earning A Living
C. Correct Attitude On Job-hunting D. How To Choose A Job

15. The word "pathetic" in Paragraph 3 most probably means ________.
A. splendid B. miserable C. disgusted D. touching

Part II Vocabulary and Structure(30%)

16. Today books are ________ to everyone because they are no longer expensive.
A. available B. preferable C. reliable D. actual

17. We shall ask for samples ________ and then we can make our decision.
A. to be sent B. being sent C. to set D. to have been sent

18. The forest fire caused by the volcano is difficult to be ________.
A. put off B. put away C. put out D. put up

19. It was not ________ midnight that they discovered the children were not in their beds.
A. before B. at C. after D. until

20. The girl's not happy at the new school. She has ________ friends there.
A. few B. a few C. little D. quite a few

21. Robots have already ________ human tasks in the industrial field.
A. taken on B. taken out C. taken up D. taken over

22. I can't find the recorder in the room. It ________ by somebody.
A. must have taken B. may have taken
C. may have been taken D. should have been taken

23. He took the medicine, but it didn't have any ________.
A. answer B. cause C. effect D. work

24. It is ________ that over one million Americans now live below the poverty line.
A. judged B. estimated C. calculated D. considered

25. He left ________ an important detail in his account.
A. off B. over C. behind D. out

26. When there are small children around, it is necessary to put bottles of pills out of ________.
A. hand B. hold C. place D. reach

27. I hadn't seen him for years, but I ________ his voise on the telephone.
A. realized B. discovered C. recognized D. heard

28. This place, originally a small town, has been ________ into a modern city.
A. transported B. transferred C. transmitted D. transformed

29. There was nobody ________ when we came round the corner.
A. out of sight B. at sight C. by sight D. in sight

30. We'll be only too glad to attend your party ________ we can get a baby-sitter.

A. so far as　　B. provided that　　C. unless　　D. except that

31. They couldn't ________ him of his mistake.
A. advise　　B. convince　　C. persuade　　D. believe

32. The old gentleman never fails to help ________ is in need of his help.
A. whom　　B. who　　C. whoever　　D. whomever

33. ________ under a microscope, a fresh snowflake has a delicate six-pointed shape.
A. Seeing　　B. Seen　　C. To see　　D. To be seen

34. "When are you going to visit you uncle in Chicago?"
"As soon as ________ our work for tomorrow."
A. we're complete　　B. we'd complete　　C. we'll complete　　D. we complete

35. Neither John nor I ________ able to persuade Richard's grandfather to attend the wedding.
A. am　　B. are　　C. are to be　　D. is

36. You ought ________ the matter to the manager the day before yesterday.
A. to report　　B. to have reported　　C. to reporting　　D. have reported

37. We look forward to ________ to the opening ceremony.
A. invite　　B. be invited　　C. having been invited　　D. being invited

38. Excuse me, but it is time to have your temperature ________.
A. taking　　B. taken　　C. took　　D. take

39. I cannot ________ the truth of your words, although they go against my interests.
A. but admit　　B. but admitting　　C. help but to admit　　D. help but admitting

40. When I went to visit Mrs. Smith last week, I was told she ________ two days before.
A. has left　　B. was leaving　　C. would leave　　D. had left

41. The boat will not arrive ________ forty-four hours.
A. in　　B. at　　C. for　　D. by

42. In winter, animals have a hard time ________ anything to eat.
A. to find　　B. to finding　　C. to find out　　D. finding

43. Since you won't take advice, there is no ________ in asking for it.
A. place　　B. point　　C. reason　　D. way

44. ________ is know to all, too much smoking will cause lung cancer.
A. That　　B. It　　C. As　　D. What

45. They have developed techniques which are ________ to those used in most factories.
A. more　　B. better　　C. greater　　D. superior

Part III　Identification (10%)

46. I 'm <u>old enough</u> (A) <u>not to</u> (B) let my troubles <u>to interfere</u> (C) <u>with</u> (D) my work.

47. <u>It was</u> (A) <u>in the primary school</u> (B) <u>where</u> (C) my teacher introduced me <u>to</u> (D) computers.

48. <u>Where</u> (A) did the accident <u>in which</u> (B) your friend <u>was hurt</u> (C) <u>took place</u> (D)?

49. <u>There are</u> (A) twelve people <u>take part in</u> (B) the experiment, four <u>working</u> (C) <u>as a</u> (D) group.

50. <u>Red and green</u> (A) light, <u>if mixing</u> (B), <u>in</u> (C) the right proportion, <u>will give</u> (D) us yellow.

51. We <u>strongly</u> (A) suggest <u>that</u> (B) Smith <u>is told</u> (C) about <u>his</u> (D) physical condition as soon as possible.

52. Nearly <u>three quarters of the surface</u> (A) of the earth <u>are</u> (B) covered with water, and <u>there</u> (C) would be eve less land <u>if</u> (D) the polar icecaps were melt.

53. The seventeenth century was one which(A) many significant advances(B) were made(C) in both(D) science and philosophy.

54. No matter whatever happens(A), we're determined to do our best(B) and make(C) the Experiment a success(D).

55. Let's not(A) waste time on matters of no important(B). We have other vital(C) problems to deal with(D).

Part IV Cloze (10%)

What do we mean by a perfect English pronunciation? In one __56__ there are as many different kinds of English as there are speakers of it. __57__ two speakers speak in exactly the same __58__. We can always hear differences __59__ them, and the pronunciation of English __60__ a great deal in different geographical __61__. How do we decide what sort of English to use as a __62__? This is not a question that can be __63__ in the same way for all foreign learners of English. __64__ you live in a part of the world __65__ India or West Africa, where there is a long __66__ of speaking English for general communication purpose, you should __67__ to acquire a good variety of the pronunciation of this area. It would be __68__ in these circumstances to use as a model BBC English or __69__ of the sort. On the other hand, if you live in a country __70__ there is no traditional use of English, you must take __71__ your model some form of __72__ English pronunciation. It does not __73__ very much which form you choose. The most __74__ way is to take as your model the sort of English you can __75__ most often.

56. A. meaning B. sense C. case D. situation
57. A. Not B. No C. None D. Nor
58. A. type B. form C. sort D. way
59. A. between B. among C. of D. from
60. A. changes B. varies C. shifts D. alters
61. A. areas B. parts C. countries D. spaces
62. A. direction B. guide C. symbol D. model
63. A. given B. responded C. satisfied D. answered
64. A. Because B. When C. If D. Whether
65. A. as B. in C. like D. near
66. A. custom B. ue C. tradition D. habit
67. A. aim B. propose C. select D. ten
68. A. fashion B. mistake C. nonsense D. possibility
69. A. everything B. nothing C. anything D. things
70. A. where B. that C. which D. wherever
71. A. to B. with C. on D. as
72. A. practical B. domestic C. native D. new
73. A. care B. affect C. trouble D. matter
74. A. effective B. sensitive C. ordinary D. careful
75. A. listen B. hear C. notice D. find

Part V Translation (20%)

Section A

76. The rest that you get while sleeping enables your body to prepare itself for the next day.
77. If you have trouble falling asleep, some people recommend breathing very slowly and very deeply.
78. In the first place, television is not only a convenient source of entertainment, but also a comparatively cheap one.
79. We get so used to looking at the movements on it, so dependent on its pictures, that it begins to control our lives.

80. Our school leavers face so much competition that they seldom care what they do as long as they can earn a living.

Section B

81. 他们想出一个解决这个问题的办法。
82. 你离开教室时，别忘了关灯。
83. 他喜欢一边做作业，一边听音乐。
84. 我已了解清楚，他的结论是以事实为依据。
85. 对于年轻人来说，独立思考问题的能力很重要。

参考答案

1—15 ACBDD BDBAC BDACB
16—45 ABCDA DCCBD DCDDB BCBDA BDBAD ADBCD
46—55 CCDBB CBAAB
56—75 BBDAB ADDCC CABCA DCDAB
76. 睡眠时得到的休息，能够使(你的)身体为第二天的活动做好准备。
77. 如果难于入睡，有人建议(此时)进行缓慢的深呼吸。
78. 首先，电视不仅是(一种)便捷的、而且是廉价的娱乐来源。
79. 我们习惯盯着屏幕上的一举一动、如此依赖它的画面，电视开始控制我们的生活。
80. 我们毕业生面对的竞争如此激烈，他们不大在意从事什么工作，只要能养家糊口就行。
81. They are trying to come up with a solution to the problem.
82. Don't forget to turn off the lights when you leave the classroom.
83. He likes to listen to music while doing his homework.
84. I have made sure that his conclusion is based on facts.
85. As for the young, the ability to think on their own is important.

北京地区成人本科学士学位英语统一考试(A)

2004.4

Part I Reading Comprehension (30%)

Passage 1 Questions 1 to 5 are based on the following passage:

A youngster's social development has a profound effect on his academic progress. Kids who have trouble getting along with their classmates can end up behind academically as well and have a higher chance of dropping out (退学). In the early grades especially, experts say, youngsters should be encouraged to work in groups rather than individually so that teachers can spot children who may be having problems making friends. "When children work on a project", says Lillian Kate, an educational professor at the Illinois University, "they learn to work together, to disagree, to think, to take turns and lighten tensions. These skills can't be learned through lecture. We all know people who have wonderful technical skills but don't have any social skills. Relationships should be the first R".

At a certain age, children are also learning to judge themselves in relation to others. For most children, school marks the first time that their goals are not set by an internal clock but by the outside world. Just as the 1-year-old struggling to walk, the 6-year-old is struggling to meet adult expectations. Young kids don't know how to distinguish early-childhood education for the state of New Jersey, "(76) if they try hard to do something and fail, they may conclude that they will never be able to accomplish a particular task". "The effects are serious", says Hills, "a child who has had his confidence really damaged needs a rescue operation".

1. The author seems to think that a kid's poor relationship with his classmates would ________.

A. have negative effects on his study
B. develop his individualism but limit his intelligence
C. eventually lead to his leaving school
D. have nothing to do with his achievements in a course

2. In the first paragraph, the word spot means ________.
A. teach B. help C. find D. treat

3. For most children, school makes them understand ________.
A. that it is society rather than individual that decides one's future
B. that they can meet the social needs
C. that one's effort and one's ability can be two quite different matters
D. that social needs and individual needs have nothing in common

4. Which of the following is most unlikely for the author to do?
A. To talk to the students who have mental problems.
B. To help students develop a feeling of self-respect.
C. To keep a student from playing alone.
D. To announce a student's scores in public.

5. Which of the following is the major concern of the passage about a student's needs?
A. Individualism and cooperation.
B. Academic success and independent thinking.
C. Socialization and feeling of competence.
D. Intelligence and respect.

Passage 2 Questions 6 to 10 are based on the following passage:

If the Europeans thought a drought—a long period of dry weather—was something that happened only in Africa, they know better now. After four years of below-normal rainfall (in some cases only 10 percent of annual average), vast areas of France, Spain, Portugal, Belgium, Britain and Ireland are dry and barren (贫瘠). (77) Water is so low in the canals of northern France that waterway traffic is forbidden except on weekends. Oyster (牡蛎)grows in Brittany report a 30 percent drop in production because of the loss of fresh water in local rivers necessary for oyster breeding. In southeastern England, the rolling green hills of Kent have turned so brown that officials have been weighing plans to pipe in water from Wales. In Portugal, farmers in the southern Alentejo region have held prayer meeting for rain. So far, in vain.

(78) Governments in drought-spread countries are taking severe measures. Authorities in hard-hit areas of France have banned washing cars and watering lawns. In Britain, water will soon be metered, like gas and electricity. "The English have always taken water for granted," says Graham Warren, a spokesman of Britain's National Rivers Authority. "Now they're putting a price on it." Even a sudden end to the drought would not end the misery in some areas. It will take several years of unusually heavy winter rain, the experts say, just to bring existing water reserves up to their normal levels.

6. What does the author mean by saying "they know better now?"
A. They know more about the causes of the drought.
B. They have a better understanding of the drought in Africa.
C. They have realized that the drought in Europe is the most serious one.
D. They have realized that droughts hit not only Africa but also Europe.

7. The drought in Europe has brought about all the following problems except ________.
A. below-normal rainfall B. difficult navigation
C. a sharp drop in oyster harvest D. bone-dry hills

8. The British government intends to ________.
A. forbid the car-washing service B. increase the price of the water used

C. end the misery caused by the drought　　D. charge fees for the use of the water

9. Which of the following statements is true according to the passage?
   A. Germany is the only country free from the drought.
   B. Water reserves are at their lowest level in years due to drought.
   C. The drought is more serious in Britain than in France.
   D. Europe will not have heavy rain until several years later.
10. Which of the following is the most appropriate title for the passage?
   A. Europe in Misery　　B. Drought Attacks Europe
   C. Be Economical With Water　　D. Europe, a Would-be Africa

Passage 3　Questions 11 to 15 are based on the following passage:

How can we get rid of garbage? Do we have enough energy sources to meet our future energy needs?

These are two important questions that many people are asking today. Some people think that man might be able to solve both problems at the same time. They suggest using garbage as an energy source, and at the time it can save the land to hold garbage. For a long time, people buried garbage or dumped it on empty land. Now, empty land is scarce. But more and more garbage is produced each year. However, garbage can be a good fuel to use. The things in garbage do not look like coal, petroleum, or natural gas; but they are chemically similar to these fossil fuels. As we use up our fossil-fuel supplies, we might be able to use garbage as an energy source.

(79) Burning garbage is not a new idea. Some cities in Europe and the United States have been burning garbage for years. The heat that is produced by burning garbage is used to boil water. The steam that is produced is used to make electricity or to heat nearby buildings. In Paris, France, some power plants burn almost 2 million metric tons of the cities garbage each year. The amount of energy produced is about the same as would be produced by burning almost a half million barrels of oil.

(80) Our fossil fuel supplies are limited. Burning garbage might be one kind of energy source that we can use to help meet our energy needs. This method could also reduce the amount of garbage piling up on the earth.

11. What two problems can man solve by burning garbage?
   A. The shortage of energy and air pollution.
   B. The shortage of energy and the land to hold garbage.
   C. Air pollution and the shortage of fossil fuel.
   D. Air pollution and the shortage of land to hold garbage.
12. Which of the following is NOT the result of burning garbage?
   A. The garbage burned is turned into fossil fuels.
   B. The heat produced is used to boil water.
   C. The steam produced is used to make electricity.
   D. The steam produced is used to heat buildings.
13. According to the passage, which of the following is NOT true?
   A. About 2 million metric tons of garbage is burned in France each year.
   B. In a modern society, more and more garbage is produced each year.
   C. Using garbage is a good way to solve the problem of energy shortage.
   D. It will be too expensive to use garbage as an energy source.
14. What is the author's attitude?
   A. Delighted.　　B. Sad.　　C. Agreeing.　　D. Disagreeing.
15. The best title for the passage may be ________.
   A. Garbage and the Earth　　B. Fossil Fuel and Garbage
   C. Land and Garbage　　D. Garbage—Energy Source

Part II Vocabulary and Structure(30%)

16. It is from my grandparents ________ I learned a lot.
A. who B. whom C. that D. which
17. The writer has published many books, ________ are well received by the readers.
A. none of whom B. all of which C. neither of who D. one of which
18. Classes ________, the students left for home without delay.
A. were over B. being over C. are over D. over
19. This is the dictionary ________ I depend a lot whenever I have problems with new words.
A. with which B. in which C. on which D. for which
20. Over ten people died and twenty people were ________ wounded in the train crash.
A. horribly B. wrongly C. bitterly D. seriously
21. Do you think Tommy is ________ the truth?
A. saying B. speaking C. telling D. talking
22. It is so hot. You should put the food into the refrigerator now. Otherwise, it will ________ soon.
A. harm B. hurt C. spoil D. damage
23. Don't forget to write to me, ________?
A. will you B. didn't you C. are you D. don't you
24. It is important to remember the saying that ________ is better than cure.
A. prevention B. promotion C. permission D. proportion
25. Winning or losing is temporary, but friendship ________.
A. expects B. lives C. remains D. lasts
26. Peter, whom everyone suspected, ________ to be innocent.
A. turned out B. turned off C. turned up D. turned over
27. Isn't that ________ they call peace and friendship?
A. which B. this C. what D. where
28. So ________ is the weather in England that by lunchtime there could be thunder and lightening.
A. various B. varies C. variable D. variation
29. All the arrangements should have been completed prior ________ our departure.
A. in B. to C. by D. before
30. I must tell you how ________ a letter from you.
A. pleased I was to receive B. pleased I was to receiving
C. was I pleased to receive D. pleased I was receiving
31. I am considering ________ my job as I'm not getting on well with my boss.
A. changing B. to change C. changed D. to be changed
32. ________ the advice of his friends, he would not have suffered such a heavy loss in his business.
A. If he took B. If he should take C. Were he to take D. Had he taken
33. John, ________ the bet, had to pay for the dinner.
A. lost B. having lost C. losing D. having loss
34. Do not trust such men ________ often like to praise you to your face.
A. who B. that C. as D. they
35. We have a desperate need ________ practice strict economy in every department.
A. to B. of C. for D. about
36. But for my classmates' help, I ________ the work in time.
A. did not finish B. could not finish
C. will not finish D. would not have finished
37. ________ is known to us all, the earth moves around the sun.
A. Because B. For C. So D. As

38. With the flowers ________ everywhere, the park looks beautiful.
A. to bloom　B. blooming　C. be blooming　D. to be blooming
39. The shortage of energy is getting worse. It ________ an immediate solution.
A. calls off　B. calls up　C. calls for　D. calls at
40. The teacher spoke so fast that it was hard for the students to ________ what he was saying.
A. take in　B. take out　C. take up　D. take over
41. Some pop singers have much influence ________ the young people.
A. to　B. for　C. onto　D. on
42. The doctor advised her that she ________ enough rest before going back to work.
A. to get　B. get　C. gets　D. got
43. I think I will do it myself ________ asking him for help.
A. rather than　B. other than　C. instead of　D. in place of
44. No sooner had she entered the house ________ the telephone rang.
A. when　B. than　C. as　D. while
45. Mary said to me, "Had I seen your bag, I ________ it to you."
A. will return　B. must return
C. could return　D. would have returned

Part III　Identification (10%)

46. Individual freedom does not in any sense (A) mean that (B) you can do what (C) you like at your free-will (D).
47. When we finally (A) finished the tiring (B) journey, we could not hardly (C) move a step further (D).
48. Arriving for (A) the lecture early is better (B) than to take (C) the chance of being late (D).
49. These part-time students expect to offer (A) some jobs on (B) campus during (C) the coming (D) summer vacation.
50. He was so (A) excited after hearing the news and (B) he could not (C) fall asleep immediately (D).
51. You will not able (A) to pass the examination unless (B) you work harder (C) than you do (D) now.
52. Only when it started (A) to rain he noticed (B) that he had left (C) his raincoat somewhere (D).
53. The waste, according to (A) the people there, has already (B) found their (C) way into the (D) drinking water.
54. If you try to (A) learn too (B) many things at a time (C) you may get confusing (D).
55. After (A) his graduation (B) from (C) the university, he has worked (D) in a famous computer company.

Part IV　Cloze (10%)

People used to say, "The hand that rocks the cradle rules the world." And "__56__ every successful man there's a woman."

__57__ these saying mean the same thing. Men __58__ the world, but their wives rule them.

Most of the American women like __59__ their husbands and __60__ successful, __61__ some of them want __62__ for themselves. They want __63__ jobs. When they work they want to be __64__ paid. They want to be as successful as __65__.

The American women's liberation(解放)movement was started by women who don't want to __66__ successful men. They want to stand __67__ men, with the same chance for success. They don't want to be told that certain jobs or offices are __68__ to them. They refuse to work side by side with men who do the same work for __69__ pay.

A __70__ woman must be __71__ of being a woman and have confidence (自信) in __72__. If somebody says to her, "You've come a long way, baby." She'll smile and answer, "Not nearly as __73__ as I'm going to go, baby!"

This movement is quite new, and __74__ American women do not agree. But it has already made some important changes in women's __75__ and in men's lives, too.

56. A. Behind	B. Beside	C. Before	D. Under
57. A. Neither	B. All	C. Both	D. Either
58. A. manage	B. have	C. control	D. rule
59. A. forcing	B. to make	C. waiting	D. looking
60. A. fathers	B. mothers	C. sons	D. daughters
61. A. so	B. but	C. thus	D. or
62. A. more	B. little	C. everything	D. nothing
63. A. light	B. heavy	C. no	D. good
64. A. nice	B. fairly	C. continuously	D. endlessly
65. A. husbands	B. others	C. men	D. other women
66. A. walk beside	B. move behind	C. go before	D. stand behind
67. A. beside	B. for	C. behind	D. against
68. A. opened	B. closed	C. open	D. close
69. A. a different	B. the same	C. a higher	D. a high
70. A. good	B. free	C. working	D. liberated
71. A. able	B. kind	C. proud	D. fond
72. A. her heart	B. herself	C. her position	D. her husband
73. A. far	B. farther	C. long	D. distant
74. A. some	B. all	C. few	D. many
75. A. lives	B. world	C. society	D. position

Part V Translation (20%)

Section A

76. If they try hard to do something and fail, they may conclude that they will never be able to accomplish a task.
77. Water is so low in the canals of northern France that waterway traffic is forbidden except on weekends.
78. Governments in drought-spread countries are taking severe measures. Authorities in hard-hit areas of France have banned washing cars and watering lawns.
79. Burning garbage is not a new idea. Some cities in Europe and the United States have been burning garbage for years.
80. Our fossil fuel supplies are limited. Burning garbage might be one kind of energy source that we can use to help meet our energy needs.

Section B

81. 今年他们建造的房子跟去年一样多。
82. 对不起,我忘了把你要的书带来了。
83. 这项工作太难了,你干不了。
84. 无论多么困难,我也不会失去信心。
85. 物体离我们越远,看起来就越小。

参考答案

1—15 ACADC DADBB BADCD

16—45 CBBCD CCAAD ACCBA ADBCA DDBCA DBCBD
46—55 DCCAB ABCDA
56—75 ACDBC BADBC DABAD CBADA
76. 如果他们试图做什么事，却没有做成，他们可能会得出这样的结论：他们永远也不能完成某一特定的任务。
77. 法国北商运河河水的水位是如此之低，以至除周末外，船只禁止航行。
78. 在旱灾蔓延的国家，各级政府正在采取严厉的措施。法国遭受旱灾较重的地区的地方当局已禁止用水洗车和浇草坪。
79. 燃烧垃圾并非什么新想法。多年来，一些欧洲和美国的城市一直都在这么做。
80. 我们的矿物燃料供应有限。燃烧垃圾可能会提供一种有助于满足我们能源需求的能源。
81. They have built as many houses this year as they did last year.
82. I am sorry. I forgot to bring the book you want.
83. The work (job) is too difficult for you to do.
84. No matter how difficult it is, I will never lose my faith.
85. The farther an object (a body) is away from us, the smaller it looks.

北京地区成人本科学士学位英语统一考试(B)

2004.11

Part I Reading Comprehension (30%)

Passage 1 Questions 1 to 5 are based on the following passage:

(76) The agriculture revolution in the nineteenth century involved two things: the invention of labor-saving machinery and the development of scientific agriculture. Labor-saving machinery naturally appeared first where labor was scarce. "In Europe", said Thomas Jefferson, "the object is to make the most of their land, labor being sufficient; here it is to make the most of our labor, land being abundant". It was in America, therefore, that the great advances in nineteenth-century agricultural machinery first came. At the opening of the century, with the exception of a crude (粗糙的) plow, farmers could have carried practically all of the existing agricultural tools on their backs.

(77) By 1860, most of the machinery in use today had been designed in an early form, the most important of the early inventions was the iron plow. As early as 1850 Charles Newbolt of New Jersey had been working on the idea of a cast-iron plow and spent his entire fortune in introducing his invention. The farmers, however, would home none of it, claiming that the iron poisoned the soil and made the weeds grow. Nevertheless, many people devoted their attention to the plow, until in 1869, James Oliver of South Bend, Indiana, turned out the first chilled-steel plow.

1. The word "here"(Para. 1, Line 4) refers to ________.
   A. Europe　B. America　C. New Jersey　D. Indiana
2. Which of the following statement is NOT true?
   A. The need for labor helped the invention of machinery in America.
   B. The farmer rejected Charles Newbolt's plow for fear of ruin of their fields.
   C. Both Europe and America had great need for farm machinery.
   D. It was in Indiana that the first chilled-steel plow was produced.
3. The passage is mainly about ________.
   A. the agriculture revolution　B. the invention of labor-saving machinery
   C. the development of scientific agriculture　D. the farming machinery in America
4. At the opening of the nineteenth-century, farmers in America ________.
   A. preferred light tools　B. were extremely self-reliant (自给的)
   C. had many tools　D. had very few tools
5. It is implied but not stated in the passage that ________.

A. there was a shortage of workers on American farms

B. the most important of the early invention was the iron plow

C. after 1869, many people devoted their attention to the plow

D. Charles Newbolt had made a fortune by his cast-iron plow

Passage 2 Questions 6 to 10 are based on the following passage:

By adopting a few simple techniques, parents who read to their children can greatly increase their children's language development. It is surprising but true. (78) How parents talk to their children makes a big difference in the children's language development. If a parent encourages the child to actively respond to what the parent is reading, the child's language skills increase.

A study was done with 30 three-year-old children and their parents. Half of the children participated in the experimental study; the other half acted as the control group. In the experimental group, the parents were given a two-hour training session in which they were taught to ask open-ended questions rather than yes-or-no questions. For example, the parent should ask, "What is the doggie doing?" rather than "Is the doggie running away?" (79) The parents in the experimental group were also instructed in how to help children find answers, how to suggest alternative possibilities and how to praise correct answers.

At the beginning of the study, the children did not differ in measures of language development, but at the end of one month, the children in the experimental group showed 5.5 months ahead of the control group on a test of verbal expression and vocabulary. Nine months later, the children in the experimental group still showed an advance of 6 months over the children in the control group.

6. Which of the following can be inferred from the passage?

A. Children who talk a lot are more intelligent.

B. Parents who listen to their children can teach them more.

C. Active children should read more and be given more attention.

D. Verbal ability can easily be developed with proper methods.

7. What does "it" in line 2 can most probably be replaced by?

A. Parents increasing children's language development.

B. Reading techniques being simple.

C. Parents reading to children.

D. Children's intelligence development.

8. According to the author, which of the following questions is the best type to ask children about?

A. Do you see the elephant? B. Is the elephant in the cage?

C. What animals do you like? D. Shall we go to the zoo?

9. The difference between the control group and the experimental group was ________.

A. the training that parents received B. the age of the children

C. tile books that were read D. the number of the children

10. The best conclusion we can draw from the passage is that ________.

A. parents should be trained to read to their children

B. the more children read, the more intelligent they will become

C. children's language skills increase when they are required to respond actively

D. children who read actively seem six months older

Passage 3 Questions 11 to 15 are based on the following passage:

In the United States, 30 percent of the adult population has a "weight problem". To many people, the cause is obvious: they eat too much. But scientific evidence does little to support this idea. Going back to the America of the 1910s, we find that people were thinner than today, yet they ate more food. In those days people worked harder physically, walked more, used machines much less and didn't watch television.

Several modern studies, moreover, have shown that fatter people do not eat more on the average than thinner people. In fact, some investigations, such as the 1979 study of 3,545 London office workers, report that, on balance, fat people eat less than slimmer people.

Studies show that slim people are more active than fat people. A study by a research group at Stanford University School of Medicine found the following interesting facts:

The more the men ran, the more body fat they lost.

The more they ran, the greater amount of food they ate.

(80) Thus, those who ran the most ate the most, yet lost the greatest amount of body fat.

11. The physical problem that many adult Americans have is that ________.
    A. they are too slim　B. they work too hard
    C. they are too fat　D. they lose too much body fat
12. According to the article, given 500 adult Americans, ________ people will have a "weight problem".
    A. 30　B. 50　C. 100　D. 150
13. Is there any scientific evidence to support that eating too much is the cause of a "weight problem"?
    A. Yes, there is plenty of evidence.
    B. Of course, there is some evidence to show this is true.
    C. There is hardly any scientific evidence to support this.
    D. We don't know because the information is not given.
14. In comparison with the adult American population today, the Americans of the 1910s ________.
    A. ate more food and had more physical activities
    B. ate less food but had more activities
    C. ate less food and had less physical exercise
    D. had more weight problems
15. Modem scientific researches have reported to us that ________.
    A. fat people eat less food and are less active
    B. fat people eat more food than slim people and are more active
    C. fat people eat more food than slim people but are less active
    D. thin people run less, but have greater increase in food intake

Part II　Vocabulary and Structure(30%)

16. ________, we decided to leave at once, as we didn't want to risk missing the bus.
    A. As it being pretty late　B. It being pretty late
    C. It was being pretty late　D. Being pretty late
17. ________ was once regarded as impossible has now become a reality.
    A. What　B. That　C. Which　D. As
18. Mr. Smith, together with his wife and children, ________ going to the party this weekend.
    A. am　B. is　C. are　D. will
19. Would you mind ________ the computer game in your room?
    A. him playing　B. his playing　C. him to play　D. him play
20. By next year he ________ in New York for five years.
    A. has worked　B. has been working　C. works　D. will have worked
21. Henry is often seen ________ English aloud every morning in the classroom.
    A. read　B. reads　C. reading　D. to read
22. Without heat and sunlight, plants on the earth ________ well.
    A. would not grow　B. will not grow　C. had not grown　D. would not be grown
23. Only recently ________ to deal with the environmental problems.
    A. something has done　B. has something done

C. has something been done D. something has been done

24. The question ________ at the meeting tomorrow is very important.
A. to discuss B. being discussed C. to be discussed D. will be discussed

25. Since this road is wet and slippery this morning, it ________ last night.
A. must rain B. was raining C. must have rained D. may rain

26. The mother didn't know ________ to blame for the broken glass as it happened while she was out.
A. who B. when C. how D. what

27. I believe that every crime, ________ the circumstance, should be severely punished.
A. in spite of B. because of C. instead of D. on account of

28. The workers are busy ________ models for the exhibition.
A. to make B. with making C. being making D. making

29. Yesterday Mr. Smith gave a vivid ________ of his recent visit to China.
A. dialogue B. idea C. tale D. account

30. The definition leaves ________ for disagreement.
A. a small room B. much room C. great deal room D. not so big a room

31. By the time you arrive this evening, ________ for two hours.
A. I will study B. I will have been studied
C. I had studied D. I will have been studying

32. I would have joined him in a picnic, but I ________ his company.
A. will not like B. didn't like C. had not liked D. might not like

33. Let's finish our homework in a few seconds; it's time we ________.
A. played football B. will play football C. play football D. are playing football

34. ________ at Harvard, he began again to write his essay.
A. Busy was as he B. Busy as was he C. Busy as he was D. As was he busy

35. Pierre often makes himself ________ by gesturing with his hands.
A. to understand B. understanding C. to be understood D. understood

36. The bridge was named ________ the hero who gave his life for the cause of the people.
A. after B. for C. because of D. before

37. There was a large crowd in the square ________ against the war.
A. protecting B. protesting C. preventing D. promoting

38. We have ________ to the government for a home improvement loan.
A. arranged B. approached C. applied D. appointed

39. Tom ________ the shopkeeper with overcharging him for the articles he had bought.
A. accused B. charged C. blamed D. criticized

40. The idea sounds very good but will it work in ________?
A. practice B. place C. advance D. company

41. He got a job so that he could be independent ________ his parents.
A. on B. in C. of D. from

42. We had to wait a long time to get our passports, ________?
A. won't we B. don't we C. didn't we D. shouldn't you

43. Do you feel like ________ today?
A. having something eaten B. having something to eat
C. to have something eaten D. to have something to eat

44. It's vital that enough money ________ collected to get the project started.
A. is B. be C. must be D. can be

45. We consider ________ the instrument be adjusted each time it is used.
A. that it necessary B. it necessary that C. necessary that D. necessary of it that

Part III Identification (10%)

46. It is in his spare time when Robert teaches himself English and Japanese.
A B C D

47. People complain that the cost of setting up a company are so great that only the rich can afford to run a company in that country.
A B C D

48. Between you and I, we have had an eye on him for some time, and he might be a runaway.
A B C D

49. At school Li Ming ran into many problems, such as choosing classes and to handle his time.
A B C D

50. Comparing with the weather of last winter, it is much milder and more pleasant this winter.
A B C D

51. Advertising gives useful information about which products to buying.
A B C D

52. In Hawaii, people are friendly and always warmly welcomed visitors.
A B C D

53. Mara Dona will face a possible prison term if finding guilty on the shooting charges.
A B C D

54. Having returned from Berlin, he received no telephone call, neither.
A B C D

55. "I am looking forward to receive your letter!" she said happily.
A B C D

Part IV Cloze (10%)

Can authority be criticized? In __56__ of the world, authority is not __57__ either out of respect or out of __58__. In such countries children are not expected to __59__ their teachers in school and __60__ young scholars or __61__ industrial men are hampered in technical research because they don't feel free to __62__ with their superiors. Clever researchers may be considered too __63__ to have "any right" to present __64__ that are different from knowledge and wisdom of men of old ages.

__65__, the American is __66__ from childhood to question, analyze and search. School tasks are __67__ to encourage the use of a __68__ range of materials. A composition topic like "Write a paper __69__ the world's supply of sugar" will send even __70__ in search of completely unfamiliar ideas. __71__ in the primary grades, children are taught to __72__ libraries, and to search for __73__ ideas of various sorts. __74__ the time they are 14, 15 and 16, many young scholars are marking original and __75__ contributions in all fields of science.

56. A. much B. any C. such D. many
57. A. accepted B. claimed C. isolated D. challenged
58. A. hate B. mercy C. fear D. sympathy
59. A. question B. ask C. change D. charge
60. A. famous B. brilliant C. employed D. curious
61. A. imaginative B. sensible C. original D. affective
62. A. disagree B. complain C. link D. cooperate
63. A. young B. brave C. old D. nervous
64. A. functions B. awards C. rewards D. findings
65. A. Secondly B. Then C. Therefore D. However
66. A. treated B. trained C. traced D. transformed
67. A. done B. designed C. fulfilled D. neglected
68. A. wide B. limited C. moderate D. various
69. A. of B. on C. for D. to
70. A. a child B. a boy C. a girl D. an adult
71. A. Since B. As C. If D. Even

72. A. organize	B. manage	C. clean	D. use
73. A. conventional	B. same	C. new	D. familiar
74. A. When	B. Since	C. During	D. By
75. A. precious	B. valuable	C. worth	D. priceless

Part V Translation (20%)

Section A

76. How parents talk to their children makes a big difference in the children's language development. If a parent encourages the child to actively respond to what the parent is reading, the child's language skills increase.
77. The parents in the experimental group were also instructed in how to help children find answers, how to suggest alternative possibilities and how to praise correct answers.
78. The agriculture revolution in the nineteenth century involved two things: the invention of labor-saving machinery and the development of scientific agriculture.
79. By 1860, most of the machinery in use today had been designed in an early form.
80. Thus, those who ran the most ate the most, yet lost the greatest amount of body fat.

Section B

81. 我们的新产品非常受欢迎,对此我们感到十分自豪。
82. 您能说话大声点好让每个人都听得见吗?
83. 除了英语,你最好再学一门外语。
84. 在教育孩子方面,表扬要比批评有效得多。
85. 每个人都知道,学习对一个人的成长是至关重要的。

参考答案

1—15 BCBDA DACAC CDCAA
16—45 BABBD CACCC AADDB DBACD ABCBA CCBBB
46—55 CCADC DCCDC
56—75 DDAAD ADADD BCABA DDCDB
76. 父母对孩子谈话方式的不同导致孩子在语言能力发展上截然不同。如果父母鼓励孩子对其所读内容作出积极反应,孩子的语言能力就可以明显提高。
77. 教实验组的父母如何帮助孩子寻找答案、如何引导孩子思考其他答案的可能性,以及如何鼓励孩子得出正确答案。
78. 19世纪的农业革命主要包括省力农具的发明和科学农业的发展。
79. 大部分今天所使用的机械,在1860年就设计出了它的雏形。
80. 于是,那些运动量愈大的人吃得就愈多,从而消耗的体内脂肪也就愈多。
81. We take pride in the fact that our new products meet the market very well.
82. Could you raised your voice so as to be beard?
83. Besides English, you'd better study another language.
84. For teaching children, praising is better than criticizing.
85. As we all know, learning is vital to one's growing-up.

北京地区成人本科学士学位英语统一考试(B)

2005.4.23

Part I Reading Comprehension (30%)

Passage 1 Questions 1 to 5 are based on the following passage:

When we talk about intelligence, we do not mean the ability to get good scores on certain kinds of tests or even the ability to do well in school. By intelligence we mean a way of living and behaving, especially in a new or upsetting situation. If we want to test intelligence, we need to find out how a person acts instead of how much he knows what to do.

(76) For instance, when in a new situation, an intelligent person thinks about the situation, not about himself or what might happen to him. He tries to find out all he can, and then he acts immediately and tries to do something about it. He probably isn't sure how it will all work out, but at least he tries. And, if he can't make things work out right, he doesn't feel ashamed that he failed; he just tries to learn from his mistakes. An intelligent person, even if he is very young, has a special outlook on life, a special feeling about life, and knows how he fits into it.

If you look at children, you'll see great difference between what we call "bright" children and "not-bright" children. They are actually two different kinds of people, not just the same kind with different amount of intelligence. For example, the bright child really wants to find out about life—he tries to get in touch with everything around him. (77) But, the unintelligent child keeps more to himself and his own dream-world; he seems to have a wall between him and life in general.

1. According to this passage, intelligence is ________.
   A. the ability to study well　B. the ability to do well in school
   C. the ability to deal with life　D. the ability to get high scores on some tests
2. In a new situation, an intelligent person ________.
   A. knows more about what might happen to him　B. is sure of the result he will get
   C. concentrates on what to do about the situation　D. cares more about himself
3. If an intelligent person failed, he would ________.
   A. try not to feel ashamed　B. learn from his experiences
   C. try to regret as much as possible　D. make sure what result he would get
4. Bright children and not-bright children ________.
   A. are two different types of children　B. are different mainly in their degree of cleverness
   C. have difference only in their way of thinking　D. have different knowledge about the world
5. The author of this passage will probably continue to talk about ________.
   A. how to determine what intelligence is　B. how education should be found
   C. how to solve practical problems　D. how an unintelligent person should be taught

Passage 2　Questions 6 to 10 are based on the following passage:

Human needs seem endless. (78) When a hungry man gets a meal, he begins to think about an overcoat, when a manager gets a new sports car, a big house and pleasure boats dance into view.

The many needs of mankind might be regarded as making up several levels. When there is money enough to satisfy one level of needs, another level appears.

The first and most basic level of needs involves food. Once this level is satisfied, the second level of needs, clothing and some sort of shelter, appears. By the end of World War II, these needs were satisfied for a great majority of Americans. Then a third level appeared. It included such items as automobiles and new houses.

By 1957 or 1958 this third level of needs was fairly well satisfied. Then, in the late 1950s, a fourth level of needs appeared: the "life-enriching" level. (79) While the other levels involve physical satisfaction, that is, the feeding, comfort, safety, and transportation, this level stresses mental needs for recognition, achievement, and happiness. It includes a variety of goods and services, many of which could be called "luxury" items. Among them are vacation trips, the best medical and dental care, and recreation. Also included here are fancy goods and the latest styles in clothing.

On the fourth level, a lot of money is spent on services, while on the first three levels more is spent on goods. Will consumers raise their sights to a fifth level of needs as their income increases, or will they continue to demand luxuries and personal services on the fourth level?

A fifth level would probably involve needs that can be achieved best by community action. Consumers may be spending more on taxes to pay for government action against disease, ignorance, crime, and prejudice. After filling our stomachs, our clothes closets, our garages, our teeth, and our minds, we now may seek to ensure the health, safety, and leisure to enjoy more fully the good things on the first four levels.

6. According to the passage, man will begin to think about such needs as housing and clothing only when ________.
   A. he has saved up enough money
   B. he has grown dissatisfied with his simple shelter
   C. he has satisfied his hunger
   D. he has learned to build houses
7. It can be inferred from the passage that by the end of World War II, most Americans ________.
   A. were very rich　　B. lived in poverty
   C. had the good things on the first three levels　　D. did not own automobiles
8. Which of the following is NOT related to "physical satisfaction"?
   A. A successful career.　　B. A comfortable home.
   C. A good meal.　　D. A family car.
9. What is the main concern of man on the fourth level?
   A. The more goods the better.　　B. The more mental satisfaction the better.
   C. The more "luxury" items the better.　　D. The more earnings the better.
10. The author tends to think that the fifth level ________.
   A. would be little better than the fourth level
   B. may be a lot more desirable than the first four
   C. can be the last and most satisfying level
   D. will become attainable before the government takes actions

Passage 3　Questions 11 to 15 are based on the following passage:

We use both words and gestures to express our feelings, but the problem is that these words and gestures can be understood in different ways.

It is true that a smile means the same thing in any language. So does laughter or crying. There are also a number of striking similarities in the way different animals show the same feelings. Dogs, tigers and humans, for example, often show their teeth when they are angry. This is probably because they are born with those behavior patterns.

Fear is another emotion that is shown in much the same way all over the world. (80) In Chinese and in English literature, a phrase like "he went pale and begin to tremble" suggests that the man is either very afraid or he has just got a very big shock. However, "he opened his eyes wide" is used to suggest anger in Chinese whereas in English it means surprise. In Chinese "surprise" can be described in a phrase like "they stretched out their tongues!" Sticking out your tongue in English is an insulting gesture or expresses strong dislike.

Even in the same culture, people differ in ability to understand and express feelings. Experiments in America have shown that women are usually better than men at recognizing fear, anger, love and happiness on people's faces. Other studies show that older people usually find it easier to recognize or understand body language than younger people do.

11. According to the passage, ________.
   A. we can hardly understand what people's gestures mean
   B. we can not often be sure what people mean when they describe their feelings in words or gestures
   C. words can be better understood by older people
   D. gestures can be understood by most of the people while words can not
12. People's facial expressions may be misunderstood because ________.
   A. people of different ages may have different understanding
   B. people have different cultures
   C. people of different sex may understand a gesture in a different way
   D. people of different countries speak different languages
13. In the same culture, ________.

A. people have different ability to understand and express feelings
B. people have the same understanding of something
C. people never fail to understand each other
D. people are equally intelligent

14. From this passage, we can conclude ________.
A. words are used as frequently as gestures
B. words are often found difficult to understand
C. words and gestures are both used in expressing feelings
D. gestures are more efficiently used than words

15. The best title for this passage may be ________.
A. Words and Feelings B. Words, Gestures and Feelings
C. Gestures and Feelings D. Culture and Understanding

Part II Vocabulary and Structure (30%)

16. History is a record of mankind; different historians, ________, interpret it differently.
A. therefore B. on the contrary C. however D. consequently

17. It was not until it got dark ________ working.
A. that they stopped B. when they stopped
C. did they stop D. that they didn't stop

18. Before the child went to bed, the father asked him to ________ all the toys he had taken out.
A. put off B. put up C. put away D. put out

19. Thinking that you know ________ in fact you don't is not a good idea.
A. what B. that C. when D. which

20. "________ does Mr. Johnson go to London on business?""At least once a month."
A. How many B. How long C. How often D. How

21. Helen was much kinder to her youngest child than she was to the others, ________, of course, made the others jealous.
A. who B. what C. that D. which

22. Evidence came up ________ specific speech sounds are recognized by babies as young as 6 months old.
A. where B. that C. which D. what

23. He ________ when the bus came to a sudden stop.
A. was almost hurt B. was almost to hurt himself
C. was almost hurt himself D. was almost hurting himself

24. I suppose you are not serious, ________?
A. do I B. don't I C. are you D. aren't you

25. This composition is good ________ some spelling mistakes.
A. except B. besides C. except that D. except for

26. When I say that someone is in Shanghai for good, I mean that he is there ________.
A. to find a good job B. for tile time being
C. to live a happy life D. for ever

27. Rubber differs from plastics ________ it is produced naturally and not in file lab.
A. at that B. in that C. for that D. with that

28. Women all over the world are ________ equal pay for equal jobs.
A. calling on B. calling about C. calling off D. calling for

29. With the bridge ________, there was nothing for it but to swim.
A. was destroyed B. destroying C. being destroyed D. destroyed

30. Having no money but ________ to know, he simply said he would go without dinner.
A. not to want anyone B. wanted no one
C. not wanting anyone D. to want no one

31. The children lined up and walked out ________.
   A. in place B. in condition C. in order D. in private
32. The teacher, as well as all his students, ________ by the dancer's performance.
   A. was impressed B. had impressed C. impressed D. were impressed
33. ________ is well known, the key to success lies in hard work.
   A. As B. That C. Which D. What
34. The doctor will not perform the operation ________ it is absolutely necessary.
   A. so B. if C. for D. unless
35. Today the police can watch cars ________ on roads by radar.
   A. run B. to run C. running D. to be run
36. The little boy saw the plane ________ and burst into flames.
   A. complete B. compel C. crash D. clutch
37. Beijing is well ________ its beautiful scenery and the Great Wall.
   A. known as B. known to C. known about D. known for
38. From her conversation, I ________ that she had a large family.
   A. deduced B. decided C. declared D. deceived
39. This question is too hard, it is ________ my comprehension.
   A. below B. beyond C. over D. without
40. In order to buy her house she had to obtain a ________ from the bank.
   A. finance B. capital C. loan D. debt
41. Some cities have passed laws that allow coal and oil ________ only if their sulfur content is low.
   A. burning B. to burn C. being burned D. to be burned
42. Space vehicles were launched into outer space ________ search of another living planet.
   A. to B. at C. in D. for
43. You two have got a lot ________.
   A. in general B. in common C. in all D. in any case
44. It is time to ________ fields in which they are just as capable as men.
   A. keep women's B. stop to keep women out
   C. keep women away D. stop keeping women out of
45. Frank's lessons were too hard for him, and he soon fell ________ the rest of the class.
   A. behind B. down C. off D. away from

Part III Identification (10%)

46. It was (A) in this school (B) where (C) he had studied for four years (D).
47. Being felt (A) that she had done (B) something wonderful (C), she sat down to rest (D).
48. Jane had a great deal of (A) trouble to concentrate on (B) her study because of (C) the noise in the next (D) room.
49. The way which (A) the different kinds of rock lie on (B) one another (C) helps to tell the story of long ago (D).
50. We were young men when (A) we first met (B) in London, poor, struggle (C), full of (D) hope and ideas.
51. Of the two lectures, the first (A) was by far the best one (B), partly because the person who delivered it (C) had such (D) a pleasant voice.
52. According to (A) our estimate, only one out of (B) three company managers have been (C) trained in the field of (D) management.
53. Today we have made great achievements (A), but tomorrow we shall (B) win (C) still great victories (D).

54. Lewis had to travel by bus as(A) his car had been damaged(B) in an accident some days before(C) and he was failed(D) to get it repaired.

55. Collecting(A) toy cars as a hobby becomes(B) increasingly(C) popular during the past(D) fifty years.

Part IV Cloze (10%)

About a month ago I was present at a serious occasion with the reading of a will. I can remember one passage that particularly struck me. It ran something __56__ this.

"And I direct that $10,000 be __57__ to old William B, whom I have wished to help for many years, __58__ always put off doing so." It __59__ the last words of a dying man. But the story does not __60__ there. When the lawyers came to __61__ out the bequest (遗赠), they discovered that old William B had __62__, too, and so the __63__ deed was lost.

I felt rather __64__ about that. It seemed to me a most regrettable __65__ that William should not have had his $10,000 just __66__ somebody kept putting __67__ giving it to him. And from __68__ accounts, William could have done with the __69__. But I am sure __70__ there are thousands of kindly little deeds waiting to be __71__ today, which are being put off "__72__ later."

George Herbert, in praise of good intentions, __73__ that "One of these days is better than __74__ of these days." But I say that __75__ is better than all.

56. A. about	B. for	C. like	D. of
57. A. consumed	B. paid	C. cost	D. devoted
58. A. but	B. or	C. still	D. and
59. A. has been	B. were	C. is	D. was
60. A. remain	B. end	C. finish	D. appear
61. A. find	B. point	C. put	D. carry
62. A. died	B. disappeared	C. escaped	D. hidden
63. A. invaluable	B. identical	C. good	D. historic
64. A. exciting	B. sorry	C. faithful	D. happy
65. A. matters	B. dream	C. task	D. thing
66. A. because	B. for	C. as though	D. till
67. A. off	B. into	C. in	D. on
68. A. every	B. some	C. any	D. all
69. A. payment	B. money	C. regrets	D. expense
70. A. whether	B. of	C. that	D. often
71. A. protected	B. done	C. made	D. rewarded
72. A. until	B. still	C. too	D. toward
73. A. implies	B. marked	C. regrets	D. says
74. A. some	B. any	C. all	D. none
75. A. morning	B. spring	C. today	D. time

Part V Translation (20%)

Section A

76. For instance, when in a new situation, an intelligent person thinks about the situation, not about himself or what might happen to him.

77. But, the unintelligent child keeps more to himself and his own dream-world; he seems to have a wall between him and life in general.

78. When a hungry man gets a meal, he begins to think about an overcoat, when a manager gets a new sports car, a big house and pleasure boats dance into view.

79. While the other levels involve physical satisfaction, that is, the feeding, comfort, safety, and

transportation, this level stresses mental needs for recognition, achievement, and happiness.

80. In Chinese and in English literature, a phrase like "he went pale and begin to tremble" suggests that the man is either very afraid or he has just got a very big shock.

Section B

81. 使我感到惊奇的是,他的英语说得如此得好。
82. 开会的时间到了,咱们把收音机关了吧。
83. 尽管有许多困难,我们仍然决心执行我们的计划。
84. 我们居住的地球是一个大球体。
85. 我们向李先生学习,因为他有丰富的工作经验。

参考答案

1—15 CCBAD CDABB BBACB

16—45 CACAC DBACD DBDDC CAADC CDABC DCBDA

46—55 CABDC BCDDB

56—75 CDADB DACBD AADBC BADCC

76. 比如,当身处一个新环境时,聪明人就会考虑情况,而不是考虑他自己,或者什么会发生在他身上。
77. 但是,一个不聪明的孩子更加封闭,沉迷于自己的梦中世界;在他和周围的生活之间似乎有堵墙。
78. 当一个饥饿的人吃饱后,他开始想外套,当一个经理得到一辆新跑车后,大房子和游艇就进入他的视野了。
79. 其他几个层次都和身体满意度相关,比如,饮食,舒适度,安全和交通,而这个层次强调精神需要,比如认同,成就和幸福。
80. 在中国和英国文学当中,这样的习语比如"他脸色苍白,浑身颤抖"表示他很害怕或者受到很大的打击。
81. What surprised me is that she could speak English so well.
82. It is time for meeting. Let's turn off the radio.
83. Although there are a lot of difficulties, we are still determined to carry out our plan.
84. The earth we are living is a big sphere.
85. We learn from Mr. Li, because he is rich in working experiences.

北京地区成人本科学士学位英语统一考试(A)

2005.11

Part I Reading Comprehension (30%)

Passage 1 Questions 1 to 5 are based on the following passage:

Languages are remarkably complex and wonderfully complicated organs of culture. (76) They contain the quickest and the most efficient means of communicating within their respective culture. To learn a foreign language is to learn another culture. In the words of a poet and philosopher, "As many languages as one speaks, so many lives one lives." A culture and its language are as necessary as brain and body; while one is a part of the other, neither can function without the other. In learning a foreign language, the best beginning would be starting with the non-language elements of the language: its gestures, its body language, etc. Eye contact is extremely important in English. Direct eye contact leads to understanding, or, as the English saying goes, seeing eye-to-eye. We can never see eye-to-eye with a native speaker of English until we have learned to look directly into his eyes.

1. The best title for this passage is ________.

A. Organs of Culture　　B. Brain and Body

C. Looking into his eyes　　D. Language and Culture

2. According to this passage, the best way to learn a foreign language is ________.

A. to read the works of poets and philosophers

B. to find a native speaker and look directly into his eyes

C. to begin by learning its body language
D. to visit a country where you can study

3. According to this passage, gestures are ________.
A. spoken words B. a non-language element
C. pictures in a language D. written language

4. "As many languages as one speaks, so many lives..."means ________.
A. if one learns many foreign languages, one will have a better understanding of his own language
B. life is richer and more interesting if one knows several languages
C. no matter how many languages one knows, one can never know more than one's own culture
D. if a person speaks only one language, he will live a very happy life

5. Which of the following doesn't share the same meaning with the others?
A. signs B. gestures C. efficient D. body language

Passage 2 Questions 6 to 10 are based on the following passage:

Trees are useful to man in three very important ways: they provide him with wood and other products; they give him shade; and they help to prevent droughts (干旱) and floods.

Unfortunately, man has not realized that the third of these services is the most important. Two thousand years ago a rich and powerful country cut down its trees to build warships, with which to gain itself an empire (帝国). It gained the empire, but, without its trees, its soil became hard and poor. When the empire fell to pieces, the home country found itself faced by flood and starvation.

(77) Even though a government realizes the importance of a plentiful supply of trees, it is difficult for it to persuade villagers to see this. The villagers want wood to cook their food with; and they can earn money by selling wood. They are usually too lazy to plant and look after the trees. (78) So, unless the government has a good system of control, or can educate the people, the forests will slowly disappear.

This does not only mean that the villagers' children and grandchildren will have fewer trees. The results are even more serious, for where there are trees their roots break the soil up allowing the rain to sink in—and also bind the soil, thus preventing its being washed away easily; but where there are no trees, the rain falls on hard ground and flows away from the surface, causing flood.

6. What is the most important function of trees?
A. Providing fuel. B. Offering shade.
C. Preventing natural disaster. D. Providing wood.

7. What eventually happened to the empire in the paragraph?
A. Its people died of hunger. B. It fell to pieces.
C. It became a giant empire. D. It built many ships with wood.

8. It is implied in the passage that the villagers ________.
A. want a plentiful supply of trees B. want firewood badly
C. just want to get money D. don't realize the importance of trees

9. The role of trees is to ________.
A. loosen soil B. keep soil in position C. harden soil D. both A and B

10. What is the passage mainly concerned with?
A. The benefits of trees. B. Trees and soil protection.
C. The various uses of trees. D. Different attitudes toward trees.

Passage 3 Questions 11 to 15 are based on the following passage:

Adam Smith was the first person to see the importance of the division of the labor. He gave us an example of the process by which pins were made in England.

"One man draws out the wire, another strengthens it, a third cuts it, a fourth points it, and a fifth gives it a head. Just to make the head requires two or three different operations. The work of making pins is divided into about eighteen different operations, which in some factories are all performed by different people, though in others the same man will sometimes perform two or three of them."

Ten men, Smith said, in this way, turned out twelve pounds of pins a day or about 4800 pins a worker. (79) But if all of them had worked separately and independently without division of labor, they certainly could not have made twenty pins in a day and not even one.

There can be no doubt that division of labor is an efficient way of organizing work. Fewer people can make more pins. Adam Smith saw this, (80) but he also took it for granted that division of labor is itself responsible for economic growth and development and it accounts for the difference between expanding economies and those that stand still. But division of labor adds nothing new, it only enables people to produce more of what they already have.

11. According to the passage, Adam Smith was the first person to ________.
   A. take advantage of the physical labor
   B. introduce the division of labor into England
   C. understand the effects of the division of labor
   D. explain the bad causes of the division of labor
12. Adam Smith saw that the division of labor ________.
   A. enabled each worker to design pins more quickly
   B. increased the possible output per worker
   C. increased the number of people employed in factories
   D. improved the quality of pins produced
13. Adam Smith mentioned the number 4800 in order to ________.
   A. show the advantages of the old labor system
   B. stress how powerful the individual worker was
   C. show the advantages of the division of labor
   D. stress the importance of increased production
14. According to the writer, Adam Smith's mistake was in believing that the division of labor ________.
   A. was an efficient way of organizing work
   B. was an important development in methods of production
   C. finally led to economic development
   D. increased the production of existing goods
15. According to the writer, which one of the following is NOT true?
   A. Division of labor can enable fewer people to make more pins.
   B. Division of labor helps people to produce more of what they already have.
   C. Division of labor is by no means responsible for economic growth.
   D. Division of labor is an efficient way of organizing work.

Part II Vocabulary and Structure(30%)

16. He spent ________ collecting materials for his article.
   A. a half year　　B. half year　　C. half a year　　D. half of a year
17. To succeed in a scientific experiment, ________.
   A. one needs being patient person　　B. patience is to need
   C. one needs to be patient　　D. patience is what needed
18. English is used by more people than is ________ language except Chinese.
   A. any　　B. any other　　C. other　　D. all other
19. The dish ________ terrible! I don't like it at all.
   A. tastes　　B. tasted　　C. will taste　　D. is tasted
20. She ________ be ill because I saw her playing tennis just now.
   A. can't　　B. couldn't　　C. mustn't　　D. may not
21. Sorry, officer. I ________ at 80 miles but I didn't see any sign in the area telling people how fast they can drive.

A. should not drive　　B. shouldn't have driven
C. mustn't drive　　D. can't drive

22. Why not ________ Professor Li for help? He is kind-hearted and willing to help.
A. ask　　B. you ask　　C. to ask　　D. your asking

23. It is not easy ________ the answer to the difficult math problem.
A. to figure out　　B. figuring out　　C. figure out　　D. being figured out

24. The tsunami (海啸) ________ over 160, 000 people were killed was a terrible disaster for human beings.
A. of that　　B. among which　　C. during that　　D. in which

25. Take the medicine now. I believe it will ________ your pain.
A. release　　B. relive　　C. reject　　D. relieve

26. How can you ________ her offer? I'm afraid she will feel hurt.
A. turn out　　B. turn up　　C. turn down　　D. turn away

27. She apologized for ________ to attend the meeting.
A. her being not able　　B. her to be not able
C. her not to be able　　D. her not being able to

28. This new coat cost me ________ the last one I bought two years ago.
A. three times　　B. three times as much as
C. three times as much　　D. three times much as

29. Each term our professors would ________ a list of books for us to read.
A. hand in　　B. give away　　C. pass out　　D. write out

30. I ________ my wallet when I was shopping in the store.
A. must have dropped　　B. should have dropped
C. could drop　　D. ought to have dropped

31. I believe you have ________ your purse in the living-room.
A. left alone　　B. left behind　　C. left off　　D. left out

32. The results of the survey are interesting and they ________ more questions than they can answer.
A. bring about　　B. prohibit　　C. project　　D. benefit from

33. He abandoned a career that ________ to his becoming one of the most influential people in the world.
A. could have led　　B. would lead　　C. should have led　　D. must lead

34. The doctor's advice was that the patient ________ at once.
A. to be operated　　B. being operated　　C. be operated　　D. operated

35. ________ by the look on her face, she didn't catch what I meant.
A. Judging　　B. Judged　　C. Judge　　D. To judge

36. By no means ________ our mistakes.
A. we ought ignore　　B. we ought to ignore
C. ought we ignore　　D. ought we to ignore

37. The teacher has his students ________ a composition every other week.
A. to write　　B. written　　C. writing　　D. write

38. Give the books to ________ needs them for the English class and the writing class.
A. whomever　　B. whom　　C. who　　D. whoever

39. A solid is different from a liquid ________ the solid has its definite shape.
A. in that　　B. in which　　C. in what　　D. because of which

40. It is because he is kind and modest ________ he wins the respect of others.
A. what　　B. which　　C. why　　D. that

41. Your mother told me that you overslept this morning, ________?
A. didn't she　　B. didn't you　　C. did she　　D. did you

42. ________, he felt tired out after the long journey for eight hours.
A. Strong as he is　　B. The stronger he is
C. Strong man that he is　　D. For he is strong

43. They have agreed that they will ________ to the policy and will not change it.
A. commit B. stick C. combine D. fall

44. The company has to ________ the benefits against the costs in the last three months.
A. boast B. blame C. block D. balance

45. We've ________ paper and ink. Ask Mrs. Edward to lend us some.
A. run away with B. run out of C. run off D. run down

Part III Identification (10%)

46. How could you make such a little child to help you carry the big box?
(A: could; B: such; C: to help; D: carry)

47. As soon as we've finished supper, we'll all go to downtown to see the Sound of Music.
(A: As soon; B: we've finished; C: we'll all; D: to)

48. I really appreciate you recommended me to that company in time.
(A: appreciate; B: you recommended; C: that; D: in time)

49. He will not do it had he known how serious the outcome would be.
(A: will not do; B: had he known; C: serious; D: would be)

50. Her name sounds familiar with me but I can't tell who she is at the moment.
(A: sounds; B: with; C: can't; D: who)

51. Rice has been a basically food for millions of people for hundreds of years.
(A: has been; B: basically; C: millions of; D: hundreds of)

52. The director and manager of the department are very strict with the employees.
(A: The director; B: manager; C: are; D: with)

53. Research shows that employees whose obtain satisfaction from their jobs are more productive.
(A: Research shows; B: whose; C: satisfaction; D: productive)

54. Looking from another angle, the painting would show something different.
(A: Looking; B: angle,; C: would; D: something)

55. "Never I have heard such a thing in my life!" said the old man.
(A: "Never; B: I have heard; C: a thing; D: said)

Part IV Cloze (10%)

In every cultivated language there are two great classes of words, which makes up the whole vocabulary. First, there are those words __56__ which we become familiar in daily conversation, which we __57__, that is to say, from the __58__ of our own family and from our friends, and __59__ we should know and use __60__ we could not read or write. They __61__ the common things of life with all the people who __62__ the language. Such words may be called "popular", since they belong to the people __63__ and are not excluded __64__ a limited class.

On the other hand, our language __65__ a large number of words which are comparatively __66__ used in ordinary conversation. Their meanings are known to every educated person, but there is little __67__ to use them at home or in the market-place. Our __68__ acquaintance (熟悉) with them comes not from our mother's __69__ or from the talk of our schoolmates, __70__ from books that we read, lectures that we __71__, or the more __72__ conversation of highly educated speakers who are discussing some particular __73__ in a style properly higher above the habitual __74__ of everyday life. Such words are called "learned", and the __75__ between them and the "popular" words is of great importance to a right understanding of language study process.

56. A. at B. with C. by D. through
57. A. study B. imitate C. stimulate D. learn
58. A. mates B. relatives C. members D. fellows
59. A. which B. that C. those D. ones
60. A. even B. despite C. even if D. in spite of
61. A. mind B. concern C. care D. relate
62. A. hire B. apply C. adopt D. use
63. A. in public B. at most C. at large D. at best
64. A. in B. from C. with D. on

65. A. consists	B. consists of	C. makes	D. composes
66. A. seldom	B. much	C. greatly	D. often
67. A. possibility	B. way	C. reason	D. necessity
68. A. primary	B. first	C. principal	D. prior
69. A. tips	B. mouth	C. ears	D. tongue
70. A. besides	B. and	C. yet	D. but
71. A. hear of	B. attend	C. hear from	D. listen
72. A. former	B. formula	C. formal	D. forward
73. A. theme	B. topic	C. idea	D. point
74. A. border	B. link	C. degree	D. extent
75. A. relation	B. distinction	C. connection	D. similarity

Part V Translation (20%)

Section A

76. They contain the quickest and the most efficient means of communicating within their respective culture.
77. Even though a government realizes the importance of a plentiful supply of trees, it is difficult for it to persuade the villagers to see this.
78. So, unless the government has a good system of control, or can educate the people, the forests will slowly disappear.
79. But if all of them had worked separately and independently without division of labor, they certainly could not have made twenty pins in a day and not even one.
80. But he also took it for granted that division of labor is itself responsible for economic growth and development and it accounts for the difference between expanding economies and those that stand still.

Section B

81. 正是那棵树在洪水中救了他们的命。
82. 我们无法想象在那个遥远的星球上存在什么东西。
83. 他今早上学又迟到了。昨晚他肯定是睡得太晚了。
84. 父母没有预料到孩子的问题这样难回答。
85. 然而,在那个国家还有成千上万的年轻人很难找到工作。

参考答案

1—15 DCBBC CBDDB CBCCC
16—45 CCBAA BAADD CDBDA BAACB DDDAD BABDB
46—55 CBBAB BCBAB
56—75 BDCAA BDBBB ADCDD BCBDB
76. 它们包含着各自文化当中最迅速和最有效的交流方式。
77. 即使一个政府意识到了大量树木存在的重要性,要劝说村民们也看到这点却是困难的。
78. 所以,除非有好的控制体系,或者能教育好民众,否则,森林将会缓慢地消失。
79. 但是如果他们分散工作,没有劳动分工,他们肯定不可能一天生产出 20 个大头针,也许一个也生产不出来。
80. 但是他想当然地认为劳动分工本身就可以促进经济增长和发展并且以此来解释为什么有些经济体经济快速增长,而有些则停滞不前。
81. It is that tree that saved their lives in the flood.
82. It is beyond our imagination what exits in that star which is so far away.
83. He was late again this morning. He must have slept too late last night.
84. The parents did not expect that their child's question was too hard to give a reply.
85. However, there are still thousands of young people who are hard to find a job in that country.

北京地区成人本科学士学位英语统一考试(A)

2006.4.22

Part I Reading Comprehension (30%)

Passage 1 Questions 1 to 5 are based on the following passage:

Television has opened windows in everybody's life. Young men will never again go to war as they did in 1914. Millions of people now have seen the effects of a battle. And the result has been a general dislike of war, and perhaps more interest in helping those who suffer from all the terrible things that have been shown on the screen.

Television has also changed politics. The most distant areas can now follow state affairs, see and hear the politicians before an election. Better informed, people are more likely to vote, and so to make their opinion count.

Unfortunately, television's influence has been extremely harmful to the young. (76) Children do not have enough experience to realize that TV shows present an unreal world; that TV advertisements lie to sell products that are sometimes bad or useless. They believe that the violence they see is normal and acceptable. All educators agree that the "television generations" are more violent than their parents and grandparents.

Also, the young are less patient. (77) Used to TV shows, where everything is quick and interesting, they do not have the patience to read an article without pictures; to read a book that requires thinking; to listen to a teacher who doesn't do funny things like the people on children's programs. And they expect all problems to be solved happily in ten, fifteen, or thirty minutes. That's the time it takes on the screen.

1. In the past, many young people ________.
   A. knew the effects of war　　B. went in for politics
   C. liked to save the wounded in wars　　D. were willing to be soldiers
2. Now with TV people can ________.
   A. discuss politics at an information center　　B. show more interest in politics
   C. make their own decisions on political affairs　　D. express their opinions freely
3. The author thinks that TV advertisements ________.
   A. are not reliable on the whole　　B. are useless to people
   C. are a good guide to adults　　D. are very harmful to the young
4. Which is NOT true according to the passage?
   A. People have become used to crimes now.
   B. With a TV set some problems can be solved quickly.
   C. People now like to read books with pictures.
   D. The adults are less violent than the young.
5. From the passage, we can conclude that ________.
   A. children should keep away from TV　　B. TV programs should be improved
   C. children's books should have pictures　　D. TV has a deep influence on the young

Passage 2 Questions 6 to 10 are based on the following passage:

Nonverbal (非语言的) communication has to do with gestures, movements and closeness of two people when they are talking. (78) The scientists say that those gestures, movements and so on have meaning which words do not carry.

For example, the body distance between two speakers can be important. North Americans often complain that South Americans are unfriendly because they tend to stand close to the North American when speaking, while the South American often considers the North American to be "cold""or "distant" because he keeps a greater distance between himself and the person he is speaking to. The "eye contact" provides another example of what we are calling nonverbal communication. Scientists have observed that there is more eye contact between people who like each other than there is between people who don't like each other. (79) The length of time that the person whom you are speaking to looks at your eyes indicates the amount of interest he has in the things you are talking about.

On the other hand, too long a gaze can make people uncomfortable. The eyes apparently play a great part in nonverbal communication. Genuine warmth or interest, shyness or confidence can often be seen in the eyes. We do not always consider a smile to be a sign of friendliness. Someone who is always smiling, and with little apparent reasons, often makes us uneasy.

6. According to the passage, nonverbal communication ________.
   A. is a method often used by people who cannot speak
   B. can tell something that words cannot
   C. can be used to talk with people who cannot bear
   D. is less used than words
7. The South American ________.
   A. tends to keep a distance between himself and the person he is speaking to
   B. usually stands close to the person he is talking to
   C. is often unfriendly when spoken to
   D. is often cold and distant when speaking
8. Which of the following is NOT true?
   A. Less eye contact suggests distance in relation.
   B. The longer one looks at you, the more interest he has in you.
   C. There is more eye contact between people who like each other.
   D. Shorter eye contact shows more interest in what one is talking about.
9. Too long a gaze ________.
   A. may upset people being looked at　　B. shows one's great confidence
   C. indicates one's interest in the talk　　D. tells you how friendly one is
10. Constant smiling without apparent reason ________.
   A. is a sign of one's friendliness　　B. is a sign of one's unfriendliness
   C. makes people feel happy　　D. makes people feel uncomfortable

Passage 3　Questions 11 to 15 are based on the following passage:

In the United States elementary education begins at the age of six. At this stage nearly all the teachers are women, mostly married. (76) The atmosphere is usually very friendly, and the teachers have now accepted the idea that the important thing is to make the children happy and interested. The old authoritarian（要绝对服从的）methods of education were discredited（不被认可）rather a long time ago — so much so that many people now think that they have gone too far in the direction of trying to make children happy and interested rather than giving them actual instruction.

The social education of young children tries to make them accept the idea that human beings in a society need to work together for their common good. So the emphasis is on co-operation rather than competition throughout most of this process. This may seem curious, in view of the fact that American society is highly competitive; however, the need for making people sociable in this sense has come to be regarded as one of the functions of education. Most Americans do grow up with competitive ideas, and obviously quite a few as criminals, but it is not fair to say that the educational system fails. It probably does succeed in making most people sociable and ready to help one another both in material ways and through kindness and friendliness.

11. According to the passage, the U. S. elementary education is supposed to make children ________.
   A. sensible and sensitive　　B. competitive and interested
   C. curious and friendly　　D. happy and co-operative
12. Some Americans complain about elementary schools because they think ________.
   A. children are reluctant to help each other
   B. schools lay too much emphasis on co-operation
   C. children should grow up with competitive ideas

D. schools give little actual instruction to children

13. The author's attitude towards American education can be best described as ________.
A. favorable B. negative C. tolerant D. unfriendly

14. The American educational system emphasizes ________.
A. material wealth B. competition C. co-operation D. personal benefit

15. The word "sociable" most probably means ________.
A. fond of talking freely B. friendly with other people
C. concerned about social welfare D. happy at school

Part II Vocabulary and Structure (30%)

16. Since he left the university, he ________ in an accounting company.
A. has been working B. had worked C. had been working D. was working

17. The weather in China is different from ________.
A. America B. in America C. that in America D. one in America

18. It was not until dawn ________ their way out of the forest.
A. when they found B. that they found C. did they find D. that they didn't lind

19. ________ he says or does won't make me change my mind at all.
A. Whatever B. However C. Which D. How

20. We all believe that it'd be hard for him to ________ extra responsibilities now.
A. take apart B. take up C. take on D. take back

21. He was very rude to the customs officer, ________ of course made things even worse.
A. who B. whom C. what D. which

22. The goods ________ when we arrived at the airport.
A. were just unloading B. were just been unloading
C. had just unloaded D. were just being unloaded

23. All things ________, the planned trip had to be called off.
A. considered B. be considered C. considering D. having considered

24. ________ purpose did you say their team would beat ours?
A. For which B. What C. For what D. Which

25. Since there isn't much time left, you can just tell us about it ________.
A. in detail B. in short C. in all D. in brief

26. People appreciate ________ with him because he has a good sense of humor.
A. to work B. working C. to have worked D. have working

27. The little village hasn't changed much ________ a new road and two more stores.
A. except B. besides C. except that D. except for

28. Let's start working on the project, ________?
A. shall we B. will we C. don't we D. aren't we

29. I don't think it appropriate to ________ such an issue at the meeting.
A. bring in B. bring off C. bring up D. bring about

30. In fact, I would rather have left for the countryside ________ at home.
A. by staying B. than staying C. than to stay D. than have stayed

31. ________ a teacher, one must first be a pupil.
A. Being B. Having been C. To be D. To have been

32. ________, a form must be filled in.
A. If you want to get this job B. In order to get this job
C. Making request for this job D. To ask for this job

33. ________ in a company, Miss Li will become a famous pop singer.
A. It is an employee that B. She was an employee
C. An employee before D. Once an employee

34. He asked her to go to a concert with him but she ________ his invitation ________ politely.
A. turned; down B. turned; out C. turned; away D. turned; up

35. ________ Japanese, she has to study another foreign language.
A. Except B. Except for C. In addition to D. Beside

36. It was while she was sleeping in her bedroom ________ a thief broke into the house.
A. which B. that C. where D. than

37. In learning English we should not ________ our students of their mistakes all the time.
A. remind B. remember C. remain D. remark

38. These three teachers vary ________ their manner of teaching.
A. between B. from C. with D. in

39. Who can it be? I'm quite ________ a loss to guess.
A. of B. on C. in D. at

40. The monitor ________ the examination papers to the class for his teacher.
A. delivered B. distributed C. reported D. presented

41. Have you any ________ that you were not there at 9 o'clock last night?
A. statement B. cause C. words D. proof

42. The children looked up as the planes passed ________.
A. overall B. overhead C. outward D. forward

43. Charles Dickens ________ many wonderful characters in his novels.
A. invented B. discovered C. uncovered D. created

44. Many young people find it harder to appreciate ________ music than pop music.
A. simple B. light C. ancient D. classical

45. If the wounded soldier had been given first ________, he would not have died.
A. help B. aid C. care D. attention

Part III Identification (10%)

46. This morning I heard on the radio (A) which (B) the steel industry has decided to give (C) its employees a 10% raise (D) in pay.

47. Not knowing (A) the language and having no (B) friends in the country, he found impossible (C) to get (D) a job.

48. Once giving (A) a set of (B) instructions, a computer can gather a wide ranger (C) of information for different purposes (D).

49. The old man will never (A) forget the event, that (B) has changed (C) his life ever since (D).

50. Little children will listen (A) what (B) people say and try to (C) imitate what (D) they hear.

51. We should start at once (A) and not waste too (B) much time to argue (C) about (D) the procedure.

52. "Shall I (A) give you a cheque for (B) $10?" "I'd rather you give (C) me $10 in notes. (D)"

53. After driving (A) twenty miles, he suddenly realized (B) that he has been (C) driving (D) in a wrong direction.

54. We will have (A) to put off (B) our departure in the case (C) it rains (D).

55. The girl her (A) father is (B) a famous pianist learned (C) to play the (D) piano when she was a small child.

Part IV Cloze (10%)

In China it is relatively usual to ask people their age, but in the West this question is generally regarded as impolite. This is particularly true __56__ women, and even more __57__ if the inquirer is a man.

However, it is very __58__ to ask children their age, and some adults may not mind __59__ either. In fact, some elderly people are quite happy to __60__ their age, especially if they feel they look young __61__ their age. Nevertheless, it is not very wise to ask a(n) __62__ question like "How old are you?" If elderly people want to talk about their age, and perhaps receive a compliment on how young they look, they may easily __63__ the topic themselves, and ask the other person to __64__ how old they are. __65__ such a question, it is quite acceptable to discuss age __66__. They normally expect to be complimented on their youthfulness, though rather than __67__ that they look very old!

__68__ Westerners do not usually ask people directly how old they are, this does not __69__ that they are not interested to know how old other people are. They may ask someone else __70__ the information, __71__ they may try to __72__ the topic indirectly. Sometimes discussions about educational __73__ and the number of years of working experience may provide some __74__, but this is not always the __75__.

56. A. on B. for C. in D. of
57. A. that B. such C. than D. so
58. A. average B. normal C. expected D. unusual
59. A. being asked B. asking C. to ask D. to be asked
60. A. release B. reflect C. reveal D. remark
61. A. to B. with C. for D. at
62. A. open B. strange C. impolite D. direct
63. A. bring about B. bring up C. bring along D. bring to
64. A. guess B. know C. learn D. predict
65. A. For B. With C. In D. On
66. A. free B. freedom C. freely D. in a free way
67. A. being told B. told C. to tell D. to be told
68. A. Though even B. Even C. Even that D. Even though
69. A. include B. intend C. mean D. conclude
70. A. about B. of C. with D. for
71. A. rather than B. or else C. so else D. still else
72. A. approach B. solve C. address D. take
73. A. background B. level C. knowledge D. experience
74. A. knowledge B. clues C. evidence D. suggestions
75. A. truth B. case C. reality D. fact

Part V Translation (20%)

Section A

76. Children do not have enough experience to realize that TV shows present an unreal world; that TV advertisements lie to sell products that are sometimes bad or useless.
77. Used to TV shows, where everything is quick and interesting, they do not have the patience to read an article without pictures; to read a book that requires thinking; to listen to a teacher who doesn't do funny things like the people on children's programs.
78. The scientists say that those gestures, movements and so on have meaning which words do not carry.
79. The length of time that the person whom you are speaking to looks at your eyes indicates the mount of interest he has in the things you are talking about.
80. The atmosphere is usually very friendly, and the teachers have now accepted the idea that the important thing is to make the children happy and interested.

Section B

81. 他起得很早为的是赶上第一班公共汽车。
82. 直到昨天晚上他才改变了他的主意。
83. 同意这项建议的请举手。
84. 无论多忙,你都应该抽时间看望父母。

85. 每次访问他们都会发现这个城市呈现出新的面貌。

参考答案

1—15　DBDBD　BBDAD　DDACB

16—45　ACBAC　DDACD　BDACD　CADAC　BADDB　DBDDB

46—55　BCABA　CCCCA

56—75　BABAA　CDAAC　CDDCD　DAABB

76. 孩子们没有足够的经验来判断电视呈现的现实其实是不真实的；电视广告为了卖产品而欺骗宣传，这是很糟糕并且无益的。

77. 孩子们适应了电视节目，在那里面，一切都是迅速和有趣的，他们没有耐心读没有图片的文章，也没有耐心读需要自己思考的图书，也没有耐心聆听老师，因为老师不能像儿童节目里的人物一样做一些滑稽的事情。

78. 科学家们说，这些姿态、行为等，有着话语所不能承载的含义。

79. 从和你说话的人凝视你的时间长短就可以判断他对你们所讨论事情的感兴趣程度。

80. 气氛通常非常友好，老师们也接受了这个观念，即重要的是让学生们感到快乐和有兴趣。

81. He got up early so as to catch the first bus.

82. It was not until yesterday that he changed his mind.

83. Please raise your hands whoever agree on this suggestion.

84. No matter how busy you are, you should spend some time visiting your parents.

85. Each time they visit this city, they can notice that it is taking on a new look.

北京地区成人本科学士学位英语统一考试(A)

2006. 11. 25

Part I　Reading Comprehension (30%)

Passage 1　Questions 1 to 5 are based on the following passage:

One study shows that Americans prefer to answer with a brief "Yes", "No", "Sure", or the very popular "Yeah" rather than with a longer reply. (76) But brief replies do not mean Americans are impolite or unfriendly to some extent. Very often, Americans are in a hurry and may greet you with a single word "Hi", indeed; this is a greeting you will hear again and again during your stay in the United States. It is used by everyone, regardless of rank, agent occupation. However, those who are accustomed to longer greetings may require a little more time before they feel comfortable with American simple talk.

Americans sometimes use plain talk when they are uncomfortable. (77) If people praise them or thank them in an especially polite way, they may become uncomfortable and not know what to say in reply. They don't want to be impolite or rude, you can be sure that they liked what was said about them. Except for certain holidays, such as Christmas, Americans don't usually give gifts. Thus, you will find Americans embarrassed as they accept gifts, especially if they have nothing to give in return. They are generally a warm but informal people.

1. The fact that Americans like shorter answers tells us ________.

A. they reply very quickly in a hurry　　B. they choose words too carefully

C. they like replying briefly　　D. they want to be as polite as they can

2. Those who like using beautiful or formal words ________.

A. need more time to get used to American simple greeting

B. need no time to get familiar with American greeting

C. do not very much like American way of greeting

D. think Americans are not polite at all

3. Which of the following is NOT true?

A. Americans often answer with the words like "sure","yeah".

B. They are not impolite with brief replies.

C. Americans in high ranks must use formal words in greeting.

D. Americans are a warm but informal people.

4. The Americans like others' praise but if in a polite way ________.

A. they don't know what to say in reply B. they feel somewhat uneasy

C. they don't want to reply D. both A and B

5. The passage indicates that ________.

A. Americans exchange gifts the first time they meet.

B. Americans seldom give gifts except for some holidays.

C. Americans often bring some gifts to their friends.

D. Americans only want to get gifts from others.

Passage 2 Questions 6 to 10 are based on the following passage:

(78) The advantages and disadvantages of a large population have long been a subject of discussion among economists(经济学家). It has been argued that the supply of good land is limited. To feed a large population, inferior land must be cultivated and the good land worked intensively. Thus, each person produces less and this means a lower average income than could be obtained with a smaller population. Other economists have argued that a large population gives more scope for specialization and the development of facilities such as ports, roads and railways, which are not likely to be built unless there is a big demand to justify them.

One of the difficulties in carrying out a world-wide birth control program lies in the fact that official attitudes to population growth vary from country to country depending on the level of industrial development and the availability of food and raw materials. In the developing country where a vastly expanded population is pressing hard upon the limits of food, space and natural resources, it will be the first concern of government to place a limit on the birthrate, whatever the consequences may be. In the highly industrialized society the problem may be more complex. A decreasing birthrate may lead to unemployment because it results in a declining market for manufactured goods. (79) When the pressure of population on housing declines, prices also decline and the building industry is weakened. Faced with considerations such as these, the government of a developed country may well prefer to see a slowly increasing population, rather than one which is stable or it decline.

6. A smaller population may mean ________.

A. higher productivity, but a lower average income

B. lower productivity, but a higher average income

C. lower productivity, and a lower average income

D. higher productivity, and a higher average income

7. According to the passage, a large population will provide a chance for developing ________.

A. agriculture B. transport system C. industry D. national economy

8. In a developed country, people will perhaps go out of work if the birthrate ________.

A. goes up B. is decreasing C. remains stable D. is out of control

9. According to the passage slowly rising birthrate perhaps is good for ________.

A. a developed nation B. a developing nation

C. every nation with a big population D. every nation with a small population

10. It is no easy job to carry out a general plan for birth control throughout the world because ________.

A. there are too many underdeveloped countries in the world

B. underdeveloped countries have low level of industrial development

C. different governments have different views about the problem

D. even developed countries may have complex problems

Passage 3 Questions 11 to 15 are based on the following passage:

To us it seems so natural to put up an umbrella to keep the water off when it rains. But actually the umbrella was not invented as protection against rain. It was first used as a shade against the sun.

Nobody knows who first invented it, but the umbrella was used in very ancient times. Probably the first to use it were the Chinese, way back in the eleventh century B. C..

We know that the umbrella was also used in ancient Egypt and Babylon as a sunshade. And there was a strange thing connected with its use; it became a symbol of honor and authority. In the Far East in ancient times, the umbrella was allowed to be used only by royal people or by those in high office.

In Europe, the Greeks were the first to use the umbrella as a sunshade. And the umbrella was in common use in ancient Greece. But it is believed that the first persons in Europe to use the umbrellas as protection against the rain were the ancient Romans.

During the Middle Ages, the use of the umbrella practically disappeared. Then it appeared again in Italy in the 16th century. And again it became a symbol of power and authority.

Umbrellas have not changed much in style during all this time, though they have become much lighter in weight. (80) It wasn't until the twentieth century that women's umbrellas began to be made in a variety of colors.

11. The first use of umbrellas was as ______.
    A. protection against rain　　B. a shade against the sun
    C. a symbol of power　　D. a symbol of honor
12. ______ were regarded as the people who first used umbrellas.
    A. Romans　　B. Greeks　　C. Chinese　　D. Europeans
13. The umbrella was used only by royal people or those in high office ______.
    A. in Europe in the eighteenth century　　B. in ancient Egypt and Babylon
    C. in the Far East in ancient times　　D. during the Middle Ages
14. According to the passage, which of the following is NOT true?
    A. Women enjoy using umbrellas with various kinds of colors.
    B. The inventor of the umbrella is unknown.
    C. Once ordinary people had no right to use umbrellas.
    D. Umbrellas were popular and cheap in the ancient times.
15. Which of the following may be the best title for the passage?
    A. When Was the Umbrella Invented　　B. The Role of Umbrellas in History
    C. The Colors and Shapes of Umbrella　　D. Who Needed Umbrellas First

Part II　Vocabulary and Structure (30%)

16. The news quickly spread through the village ______ the war had ended.
    A. which　　B. what　　C. that　　D. where
17. We hurried to the station ______ find ourselves three hours earlier for the train.
    A. only to　　B. in order to　　C. so as to　　D. such as to
18. I meant ______ you, but I'm afraid I forgot.
    A. ringing　　B. being ringing　　C. to ringing　　D. to ring
19. We live in a time ______, more than ever before in history, people are moving about.
    A. what　　B. when　　C. which　　D. where
20. Is there any possibility of getting the price ______ further?
    A. reduced　　B. reduce　　C. reducing　　D. be reduced
21. ______ you feel too ill to go out, I would rather not stay at home tonight.
    A. Because　　B. Although　　C. Unless　　D. If
22. Because of many mistakes, she was made ______ these letters again.
    A. type　　B. to typing　　C. typed　　D. to type
23. It is hot and dry; the flowers need ______.
    A. being watered　　B. be watered　　C. to water　　D. to be watered
24. He began by showing us where the country was and went on ______ us about its climate.
    A. telling　　B. to tell　　C. to telling　　D. to be told
25. Our failure ______ ourselves to modern life often causes us trouble in our work.
    A. to adopt　　B. to apply　　C. to adapt　　D. to act
26. Once ______ of the necessity of a move, he worked hard to find a new home.

A. convinced B. be convinced C. convincing D. having convinced

27. So many representatives ________, the conference had to be put off.
A. were absent B. to be absent C. being absent D. had been absent

28. In no case ________ the students from exploring new ideas.
A. we should prevent B. we could prevent
C. should we prevent D. shouldn't we prevent

29. I don't think it advisable that Tom ________ to the job since he has no experience.
A. be assigned B. is assigned C. will be assigned D. has been assigned

30. With all this work on hand, she ________ to the dance party last night.
A. oughtn't to go B. hadn't gone C. shouldn't have gone D. mustn't have gone

31. As Christmas was coming, the town began a ________ clearing on a large scale.
A. through B. thorough C. though D. thought

32. E-mail writing has became the usual means of communication ________ people some distance away.
A. for B. on C. to D. with

33. It is a good idea for parents to monitor the ________ as well as the kind of television that their children watch.
A. number B. size C. amount D. screen

34. I'm afraid that there isn't ________ for you in my car.
A. place B. seat C. corner D. room

35. It suddenly ________ to me that we could use a computer to do the job.
A. happened B. occurred C. agreed D. presented

36. The old people often raise ________ for the sake of companionship.
A. pets B. pipes C. pills D. pies

37. The river here is very wide but ________, so you can walk across it.
A. narrow B. arrow C. shallow D. hollow

38. The streets were empty ________ the policemen on duty.
A. besides B. except C. excepting D. except for

39. Don't leave matches or cigarettes on the table within the ________ of little children.
A. hand B. reach C. space D. distance

40. —How did you pay the workers?
—As a rule, they were paid by ________.
A. the hour B. an hour C. hour D. the time

41. ________ of the students in our class are from the north.
A. Two ninth B. Second ninth C. Second nines D. Two ninths

42. My father has classes ________ day: Mondays, Wednesdays and Fridays.
A. each other B. every other C. this and the other D. all other

43. This morning Jack came to school late ________.
A. than usual B. as usual C. like usual D. like usually

44. I'm putting on weight. The doctor has warned me to ________ sugar.
A. keep up B. keep back C. keep off D. keep away

45. We were ________ for half an hour in the traffic and so we arrived late.
A. kept up B. held up C. cut up D. brought up

Part III Identification (10%)

46. He didn't dare (A) to leave (B) the house for fear (C) someone would recognize him (D) soon.

47. You can see (A) the whole city for miles (B) from here (C) in (D) a clear day.

48. He wished (A) he didn't tell (B) her the truth that (C) brought her so much (D) pain.

49. The room, which (A) window faces (B) the south, is the nicest (C) one of all on (D) this floor.
50. He is a true (A) friend of mine (B), whom I can always depend (C) whenever I get into (D) trouble.
51. Let's (A) go and watch (B) that new movie at eight tonight (C), won't (D) we?
52. It is very (A) important that the students' voice is heard (B) by the authorities (C) of all our (D) schools.
53. This is such a (A) beautiful day that everyone around (B) us feel like (C) going out (D) for a walk.
54. We saw (A) a big dog that was fierce and felt frightened (B) in (C) our way (D) home.
55. You will (A) feel inconvenient in Japan if (B) you can either (C) speak (D) Japanese nor English.

Part IV　Cloze (10%)

In most cultures, when you meet acquaintances for the first time during a day, it is normal to greet them. The main purpose of this greeting is to __56__ a good relationship between the people __57__, and each language usually has __58__ set phrases which can be used for this purpose. Sometimes, though, there can be __59__ differences in the type of phrases which can be used, and cultural misunderstandings can easily __60__. The following is a true example.

A young British woman went to Hong Kong to work, and at the time of her __61__ she knew nothing about the Chinese culture or language. __62__ her way to school one day, she went to the bank to get some money. __63__, the bank clerk asked her if she had had her lunch. She was extremely surprised __64__ such a question because in the British culture it would be __65__ an indirect invitation to lunch. Between unmarried young people it can also __66__ the young man's interest in dating the girl. __67__ this bank clerk was a complete stranger __68__ the British girl, she was very much taken aback (生气), and hastily commented that she had eaten __69__. After this she __70__ to school and was even more surprised when one of the teachers asked the same question. By now she __71__ that it could not be an invitation, but was puzzled __72__ why they asked it. __73__ the following days she was asked the same question again and again. Only much later __74__ that the question had no real meaning __75__ — it was merely a greeting.

56. A. build on	B. build up	C. build into	D. build out
57. A. concerned	B. concern	C. concerning	D. to concern
58. A. a number of	B. the number of	C. the amount of	D. an amount of
59. A. considered	B. considering	C. considerable	D. considerate
60. A. raise	B. arise	C. arouse	D. lead
61. A. arrive	B. arrived	C. arrives	D. arrival
62. A. In	B. To	C. By	D. On
63. A. To her disappointment	B. In her disappointment	C. To her surprise	D. In her surprise
64. A. on	B. at	C. to	D. with
65. A. regarded as	B. defined as	C. looked as	D. thought as
66. A. reflect	B. intend	C. release	D. indicate
67. A. Since	B. That	C. Far	D. With
68. A. with	B. by	C. to	D. at
69. A. yet	B. already	C. too	D. at all
70. A. processed	B. produced	C. provided	D. proceeded
71. A. released	B. relieved	C. realized	D. regretted
72. A. with regards	B. as to	C. as if	D. as far as
73. A. In	B. On	C. At	D. For
74. A. she discovered	B. she did discover	C. did she discover	D. does she discover
75. A. above all	B. after all	C. in all	D. at all

Part V Translation (20%)

Section A

76. But brief replies do not mean Americans are impolite or unfriendly to some extent.
77. If people praise them or thank them in an especially polite way, they may become uncomfortable and not know what to say in reply.
78. The advantages and disadvantages of a large population have long been a subject of discussion among economists(经济学家).
79. When the pressure of population on housing declines, prices also decline and the building industry is weakened.
80. It wasn't until the twentieth century that women's umbrellas began to be made in a variety of colors.

Section B

81. 她的工作是照看这些老人。
82. 学生应该在上课之前完成家庭作业。
83. 这些老人养成了每天早上锻炼的习惯。
84. 如果到处都太拥挤,旅行会令人很不愉快。
85. 我不知道你那奇怪的想法来自何处。

参考答案

1—15 CACDB DBBAC BCCDB
16—45 CADBA CDDBC ACCAC BDCDB ACDBA DBBCB
46—55 CDBAC DBCCC
56—75 BAACB DDCDA DACBD CBACD
76. 但是某种程度上简短回答并不意味着美国人不礼貌或不友好。
77. 如果人们以特别礼貌的方式表扬或感谢他们,他们可能会变得不舒服和不知道该说什么作为回答。
78. 人口庞大的利弊一直是经济学家讨论的话题。
79. 当人口增长对住房的压力减少,房价降了下来,建筑业就会衰退。
80. 直到二十世纪妇女们用的伞才开始被制造成五颜六色的。
81. Her job is to look after these aged people.
82. The students should finish their homework before they go to class.
83. These aged people have developed the habit of morning exercise everyday.
84. If too crowded everywhere, the travelling will be very unpleasant.
85. I do not know where your strange ideas come from.

北京地区成人本科学士学位英语统一考试(A)

2007. 4. 21

Part I Reading Comprehension (30%)

Passage 1 Questions 1 to 5 are based on the following passage:

Many a young person tells me he wants to be a writer. (76) I always encourage such people, but I also explain that there's a big difference between "being a writer" and writing. In most cases these individuals are dreaming of wealth and fame, not the long hour alone at a typewriter. "You've got to want to write," I say to them, "not want to be a writer."

The reality is that writing is a lonely, private and poor-paying affair. For every writer kissed by fortune there are thousands more whose longing is never rewarded. When I left a 20-year career in the U. S. Coast Guard to become a freelance (自由栏目) writer, I had no prospects at all. What I did have was a friend who found me my room in a New York apartment building. It didn't even matter that it was cold and had no bathroom. I immediately bought a used manual typewriter and felt like a genuine writer.

After a year or so, however, I still hadn't gotten a break and began to doubt myself. It was so hard to sell a story that I barely made enough to eat. But I knew I wanted to write, I had dreamed about it for years. I wasn't going to be one of those people who die wondering: What if ? (77) I would keep putting my dream to the test even though it meant living with uncertainty and fear of failure. This is the **shadowland** of hope, and anyone with a dream must learn to live there.

1. The passage is meant to ________.
   A. warn young people of the hardships that a successful writer has to experience
   B. advise young people to give up their idea of becoming a professional writer
   C. show young people it's unrealistic for a writer to pursue wealth and fame
   D. encourage young people to pursue a writing career
2. What can be concluded from the passage?
   A. Genuine writers often find their work interesting and rewarding.
   B. A writer's success depends on luck rather than on efforts.
   C. Famous writers usually live in poverty and isolation.
   D. The chances for writer to become successful are small.
3. Why did the author begin to doubt himself after the first year of his writing career?
   A. He wasn't able to produce a single book.
   B. He hadn't seen anything for the better.
   C. He wasn't able to have a rest for a whole year.
   D. He though that he lacked imagination.
4. "... people who die wondering: What if ?"(Lin3-4, Para3) refers to "those ________."
   A. who think too much of the dark side of life
   B. who regret giving up their career halfway
   C. who think a lot without making a decision
   D. who are full of imagination even upon death
5. "Shadowland" in the last sentence refers to ________.
   A. the wonderland one often dreams about
   B. the bright future that one is looking forward to
   C. the state of uncertainty before one's final goal is reached
   D. a world that exists only in one's imagination

Passage 2 Questions 6 to 10 are based on the following passage:

Man is a land animal, but he is also closely tied to the sea. Throughout history the sea has served the needs of man. The sea has provided man with food and a convenient way to travel to many parts of the world. Toady, experts believe that nearly two-thirds of the world's population live within eighty kilometers of the seacoast.

(78)In the modern technological world the sea offers many resources to help mankind survive. Resources on land are beginning to grow less. The sea, however, still offers hope to supply many of man's needs in the future.

The riches of the sea yet to be developed by man's technology are impressive. Oil and gas explorations have existed for nearly thirty years. Valuable amounts of minerals such as iron, copper and so on exist on the ocean floor.

Besides oil and gas, the sea may offer new sources of energy. For example, warm temperature of the ocean can be used as the steam in a steamship. Sea may also offer a source of energy as electricity for mankind.

Technology is enabling man to explore even deeper under the sea. It is obvious that the technology to harvest the sea continues to improve. (79) By the 2050, experts believe that the problems to explore the food, minerals and energy resources of the sea will have been largely solved.

6. What is the best title for the passage?
   A. Needs of Man B. Sea Harvest and Food

C. Sea and Sources of Energy D. Sea Exploring Technology

7. It can be inferred from the passage that ________.

A. man hasn't completely made use of the riches of the sea

B. technology for exploring the sea has been solved

C. harvesting rice in the sea will be made possible

D. in the near future man can live on the ocean floor

8. Why does the author mention a steamship?

A. To illustrate that man can make use of sources of energy from the sea.

B. To show that a steamship is better than other kinds of ships.

C. To argue that man should use steamships.

D. To indicate that it is warmer in the ocean than on land.

9. According to the author, technology is important because ________.

A. resources on land are running short in ten years

B. man can use it to explore the deeper sea

C. it is a lot of fun diving into the sea

D. ancient people used it to explore the sea

10. According to the author, when will the problems to explore the deeper sea largely be solved?

A. In the next generation. B. By the end of the 20th century.

C. In the near future. D. By the middle of the 21st century.

Passage 3 Questions 11 to 15 are based on the following passage:

Today, cigarette smoking is a common habit. About forty-three percent of the adult men and thirty-one percent of the adult women in the United States smoke cigarettes regularly. It is encouraging to see that millions of people have given up smoking.

It is a fact that men as a group smoke more than women. Among both men and women the age group with the highest proportion of smokers is 24—44.

Income, education, and occupation all play a part in determining a person's smoking habit. City people smoke more than people living on farms. Well-educated men with high incomes are less likely to smoke cigarettes than men with fewer years of schooling and lower incomes. On the other hand, if a well-educated man with a higher income smoked at all, he is likely to smoke more packs of cigarettes per day.

The situation is somewhat different for women. (80) There are slightly more smokers among women with higher family income and higher education than among the lower income and lower educational groups. These more highly educated women tend to smoke more heavily.

Among teenagers the picture is similar. There are fewer teenaged smokers from upper-income, well-educated families, and fewer from families living in farm areas. Children are most likely to start smoking if one or both of their parents smoke.

11. What do we know from the first paragraph?

A. More and more people take up the habit of smoking.

B. There are more smoking women than smoking men in USA.

C. It is good news that more people have given up smoking.

D. The U. S. has more smoking people than any other country.

12. What factors determine a person's smoking habits?

A. Age, income and education. B. Age, sex and income.

C. Occupation, income and sex. D. Occupation, income and education.

13. Which of the following is true according to the passage?

A. City people are less likely to smoke.

B. People in rural areas are more likely to smoke.

C. Men with higher income tend to smoke.

D. Well-educated men with high incomes are generally less likely to smoke.

14. What is the smoking situation for women?

A. The situation is quite the same for women as for men.

B. Better-educated women are likely to smoke heavily.

C. There are more women smokers with low incomes.

D. Women with higher incomes and higher education do not tend to smoke.

15. What can we say about teenaged smokers?

A. The picture about the teenage smokers is similar to that of women smokers.

B. The situation among teenagers is quite the same with men.

C. High school students are more likely to smoke than college students.

D. Farmers' children tend to smoke more.

Part II Vocabulary and Structure (30%)

16. If you go to the movie tonight, so ________ I.

A. will　B. do　C. am　D. can

17. You don't know about the difficulty I had ________ the work then at all.

A. done　B. to do　C. for doing　D. in doing

18. ________ is well-known, the environment in China is badly in need of improvement.

A. It　B. That　C. As　D. What

19. Charles Babbage is generally considered ________ the first computers.

A. to invent　B. inventing　C. to have invented　D. having invented

20. With oil prices keeping ________, people are hesitating whether to buy a car or not.

A. rising　B. arising　C. raising　D. arousing

21. I walked out of the cinema, ________ to return to see the wonderful film the next Sunday.

A. determine　B. being determined　C. determined　D. to be determined

22. We were very disappointed at the ________ to our advertisement, and our products didn't sell well.

A. replies　B. response　C. answers　D. words

23. My suggestion yesterday was that a meeting ________ to discuss the matter.

A. should hold　B. must be held　C. would be held　D. be held

24. Before the guests come, I must get the glasses ________.

A. washed　B. to be washed　C. being washed　D. to wash

25. Who would you rather have ________ the computer, Mr. Lin or Mr. Chen?

A. repaired　B. repair　C. repairing　D. to repair

26. It turned out that the man was an excellent policeman working in New York, ________ had contributed a lot to the case.

A. that　B. which　C. who　D. where

27. ________ you don't know the rule won't be a sufficient excuse for your failure.

A. It is　B. That　C. Because　D. What

28. She is very ________ to ring me tonight. I can sense that.

A. liable　B. possible　C. likely　D. likeable

29. Small talk is a good way to kill time, make friends and ________ something with others.

A. argue　B. replace　C. share　D. match

30. Some people like drinking coffee, for it has ________ effects.

A. promoting　B. stimulating　C. enhancing　D. encouraging

31. ________ you're early you can't be sure of getting a seat.

A. If　B. Unless　C. When　D. Because

32. John likes Chinese food, but he ________ eating with chopsticks.

A. doesn't used to　B. doesn't use to　C. isn't used to　D. used not to

33. His wife had the front door painted green yesterday, ________ she?

A. did B. didn't C. had D. hadn't

34. After the war, a new school building was put up ________ there had once been a theatre.
A. that B. where C. which D. when

35. It shames me to say it, but I told a lie when ________ at the meeting by may boss.
A. questioning B. having questioned C. questioned D. to be questioned

36. A modern city has been set up in ________ was a wasteland ten years ago.
A. what B. which C. that D. where

37. Professor Smith, along with his assistants, ________ on the project day and night to meet the deadline.
A. work B. working C. is working D. are working

38. The president spoke at the business meeting for nearly an hour without ________ his notes.
A. bringing up B. referring to C. looking for D. trying on

39. It is certain that he will ________ his business to his son when he gets old.
A. take over B. think over C. hand over D. go over

40. The Internet has brought ________ big changes in the way we work.
A. about B. out C. back D. up

41. When climbing the hill, John was knocked unconscious by an ________ rolling stone.
A. untouched B. unfamiliar C. unexpected D. unbelievable

42. Her brother ________ to leave her in the dark room alone when she disobeyed his order.
A. declared B. threatened C. warned D. exclaimed

43. Alice trusts you. Only you can ________ her to give up the foolish idea.
A. suggest B. attract C. tempt D. persuade

44. A man is being questioned in relation to the ________ murder.
A. advised B. attended C. attempted D. admired

45. Modern plastics can ________ very high and very low temperatures.
A. stand B. hold C. carry D. support

Part III Identification (10%)

46. He invited(A) me to go(B) to a party and(C) I did not want to join him(D) that evening.

47. The information which(A) she was injured(B) in the accident(C) was given(D) by Liz.

48. Look(A) at the beautiful flowers(B) here! How(C) wonderful they are smelling(D).

49. Dear Helen, please forgive(A) him for(B) his rudeness(C), can you(D)?

50. Did(A) anyone inform(B) you with(C) the change of the schedule that had been decided(D) yesterday?

51. Despite(A) his old age(B), he is still very(C) healthful(D) and often works in the field.

52. This equipment(A) is based upon(B) advanced technique(C) and it is highly reliable(D).

53. It is about time(A) that we go to supper(B), for(C) we still have a meeting to attend(D) this evening.

54. Every now and then(A) he would come(B) here paying a visit to(C) his old aunt, who lived all alone(D) in a small house.

55. The passengers saw(A) the thief stole(B) on the bus(C), but they didn't say(D) anything.

Part IV Cloze (10%)

When I was 16 years old, I made my first visit to the United States, it wasn't the first time I had been __56__. Like most English children I learned French at school and I had often __57__ to France, so I was used

__58__ a foreign language to people who did not understand __59__. But when I went to America I was really looking forward to __60__ a nice easy holiday without any __61__ problems.

How wrong I was! The misunderstanding began at the airport. I was looking for a __62__ telephone to give my American friend Danny a __63__ and tell her I had arrived. A friendly old man saw me __64__ lost and asked __65__ he could help me. "Yes," I said, "I want to give my friend a ring." "Well, that's __66__." he exclaimed. "Are you getting __67__? But aren't you a bit __68__?" "Who is talking about marriage?" I replied. "I __69__ want to give a ring to tell he I've arrived. Can you tell me where there's a phone box?" "Oh!" he said, "There's a phone downstairs."

When at last we __70__ meet up, Danny __71__ the misunderstandings to me. "Don't worry," she said to me. "I had so many __72__ at first. There are lots of words which the Americans __73__ differently in meaning from __74__. You'll soon get used to __75__ things they say. Most of the time British and American people understand each other!"

56. A. out B. aboard C. away D. abroad
57. A. gone B. been C. got D. come
58. A. to speak B. for speaking C. to speaking D. to speaking of
59. A. English B. French C. Russian D. Latin
60. A. having B. buying C. giving D. receiving
61. A. time B. human C. money D. language
62. A. perfect B. popular C. public D. pleasant
63. A. ring B. letter C. word D. message
64. A. to look B. looking like C. looking D. feeling like
65. A. that B. if C. where D. when
66. A. well B. strange C. nice D. funny
67. A. to marry B. marrying C. to be married D. married
68. A. small B. smart C. little D. young
69. A. very B. just C. so D. just now
70. A. did B. could C. do D. can
71. A. described B. explained C. talked D. expressed
72. A. trouble B. difficulties C. fun D. things
73. A. write B. speak C. use D. read
74. A. us British B. British us C. us Britain D. we British
75. A. such B. these C. some D. all the

Part V Translation (20%)

Section A

76. I always encourage such people, but I also explain that there's a big difference between "being a writer" and writing.
77. I would keep putting my dream to the test even though it meant living with uncertainty and fear of failure.
78. In the modern technological world the sea offers many resources to help mankind survive.
79. By the year 2050, experts believe that the problems to explore the food, minerals and energy resources of the sea will have been largely solved.
80. There are slightly more smokers among women with higher family incomes and higher education than among the lower income and lower educational groups.

Section B

81. 事实上,水污染的危害远不止这点。
82. 这个问题不像我们最初想象的那么复杂。
83. 如果你那时没有及时离开,我无法想象会发生什么情况。
84. 他们发现在下午6点前不可能完成这项工作。

85. 由于我没有读过这本书，所以我无法对此作出评论。

参考答案

1—15 ADBCC DAABD CDDBB

16—45 ADCCA ABDAB CBCCB BCBBC ACBCA CBDCA

46—55 CADDC DCBDB

56—75 DACAA DCABB BDDBA BBCAA

76. 我总是鼓励这些人，但是我也会向他们解释“当作家”和“写作”是有很大不同的。

77. 尽管这意味着要生活在不确定和失败的恐惧中，但我依然坚持我的梦想，愿意接受考验。

78. 在当今科技时代，海洋提供了很多资源帮助人类生存。

79. 到2050年，专家相信开发海洋食品、矿产和能源的问题将会在很大程度上得到解决。

80. 和收入较低、文化程度不高的女性比起来，家庭收入更高、教育程度更高的女性有更多一些的人抽烟。

81. In fact, the dangers of water pollution are far beyond this.

82. This issue is not so complicated as I imagined at first.

83. If you had not left in time then, I could not imagine what would have happened.

84. They found out that it was impossible to finish this job before 6 pm.

85. Because I have not read the book, I can not make comment on it.

北京地区成人本科学士学位英语统一考试(A)

2007.11.17

Part I Reading Comprehension (30%)

Passage 1 Questions 1 to 5 are based on the following passage:

Scientists find that hard-working people live longer than average men and women. Career women are healthier than housewives. Evidence shows that the jobless are in poorer health than job holders. An investigation shows that whenever the unemployment rate increases by 1%, the death rate increases by 2%. All this comes down to one point, work is helpful to health.

Why is work good for health? It is because work keeps people busy away from loneliness. Researches show that people feel unhappy, worried and lonely when they have nothing to do. Instead, the happiest are those who are busy. (76) Many high achievers who love their careers feel that they are happiest when they are working hard. Work serves as a bridge between man and reality. By work people come into contact with each other. By collective activity they find friendship and warmth. This is helpful to health. The loss of work means the loss of everything. It affects man spiritually and makes him ill.

Besides, work gives one a sense of fulfillment and a sense of achievement. Work makes one feel his value and status in society. When a writer finishes his writing or a doctor successfully operates on a patient or a teacher sees his students grow, they are happy beyond words.

(77) From the above we can come to the conclusion that the more you work the happier and healthier you will be. Let us work hard and study hard and live a happy and healthy life.

1. The underlined word "average" in Paragraph 1 means ________.

   A. healthy　　B. lazy　　C. ordinary　　D. poor

2. The reason why housewives are not as healthy as career women is that ________.

   A. housewives are poorer than career women

   B. housewives have more children than career women

   C. housewives have less chance to communicate with others

   D. housewives eat less food than career women

3. Which of the following statements is TRUE according to Paragraph 2?

   A. Busy people have nothing to do at home.　　B. High achievers don't care about their families.

   C. There is no friendship and warmth at home.　　D. A satisfying job helps to keep one healthy.

4. We can infer from the passage that those who do not work ________.
   A. are likely to live a shorter life
   B. will lose everything at home
   C. can live as long as those who work
   D. have more time to make new friends
5. The best title for this passage may be ________.
   A. People Should Find a Job
   B. Working Hard Is Good for Healthy
   C. People Should Make More Friends by Work
   D. The Loss of Work Means the Loss of Everything

Passage 2 Questions 6 to 10 are based on the following passage:

A study of art history might be a good way to learn more about a culture than is possible to learn in general history classes. Most typical history courses concentrate on politics, economics and war. But art history focuses on much more than this because art reflects not only the political values of a people, but also religious beliefs, emotions and psychology. In addition, information about the daily activities of our ancestors can be provided by art. (78) In short, art expresses the essential qualities of a time and a place, and a study of it clearly offers us a deeper understanding than can be found in most history books.

In history books, objective information about the political life of a country is presented; that is, facts about politics are given, but opinions are not expressed. Art, on the other hand, is subjective(主观的): it reflects emotions and opinions. The great Spanish painter Francisco Goya was perhaps the first truly "political" artist. In his well-known painting "The Third of May, 1808," he criticized the Spanish government for its abuse (滥用) of power over people.

In the same way, art can reflect a culture's religious beliefs. For hundreds of years in Europe, religious art had been almost the only type of art that existed. Churches and other religious buildings were filled with paintings that described people and stories from the Bible. Although most people couldn't read, they could still understand the Bible stories in the pictures on church walls. By contrast, one of the main characteristics of art in the Middle East was (and still is) its absence of human and animal images. This reflects the Islamic belief that statues (雕像) are not holy.

6. More can be learned about a culture from a study of art history than general history because ________.
   A. art history shows us nothing but the political values
   B. general history only focuses on politics
   C. art history gives us an insight (洞察力) into the essential qualities of a time and a place
   D. general history concerns only religious beliefs, emotions and psychology
7. Art is subjective in that ________.
   A. a personal and emotional view of history is presented through it
   B. it only reflects people's anger or sadness about social problems
   C. it can easily arouse people's anger about the government
   D. artists were or are religious, who reflect only the religious aspect of the society
8. Which of the following statements is TRUE according to the passage?
   A. In history books political views of people are entirely presented.
   B. Francisco Goya expressed his religious belief in his painting "The Third of May, 1808."
   C. In the Middle East, you can hardly find animal or human figures on palaces or other buildings.
   D. For centuries in Europe, painters had only painted on wails of churches or other religious buildings.
9. The passage mainly discusses ________.
   A. the development of art history
   B. the difference between general history and art history
   C. what we can learn from art
   D. the influence of artists on art history
10. It can be concluded from the passage that ________.
   A. Islamic artists only paint images of plants, flowers or objects in their paintings

B. it is more difficult to study art history than general history
C. a history teacher must be quite objective
D. artists painted people or stories from the Bible to hide their political beliefs

Passage 3 Questions 11 to 15 are based on the following passage:

Blind people can "see" things by using other parts of their bodies. This fact may help us to understand our feelings about colon if blind people can sense color differences, then perhaps we, too, are affected by color unconsciously(无意识地).

(79) Manufacturers(生产商) have discovered by experience that sugar sells badly in green wrappings, that blue foods are considered unpleasant, and that cosmetics (化妆品) should never be packaged in brown. These discoveries have grown into a branch of color psychology.

Color psychology now finds application in everything from fashion to decoration. Some of our preferences are clearly psychological. Dark blue is the color of the night sky and therefore associated with calm, while yellow is a day color with associations of energy and incentive (刺激). For a primitive man, activity during the day meant hunting and attacking, while he soon saw red as the color of blood and anger and the heat that came with effort. And green is associated with passive defense and self-protection.

(80) Experiments have shown that colors, partly because of their psychological associations, also have a direct psychological effect. People exposed to bright red show an increase in breath, in heartbeat and in blood pressure; red is exciting. Similar exposure to pure blue has exactly the opposite effect; it is a calming color. Because of its exciting meaning, red is chosen as the signal for danger, but closer analysis shows that a vivid yellow can produce a more basic state of alarm. So fire engines and ambulances in some advanced communities are now rushing around in bright yellow colors that stop the traffic dead.

11. Our preferences for certain colors are ________ according to the passage.
A. associated with the time of the day
B. dependent on our personalities
C. are linked with our ancestors
D. partly due to psychological factors

12. If people are exposed to bright red, which of the following things does NOT happen?
A. They breathe faster.
B. They feel satisfied.
C. Their blood pressure rises.
D. Their hearts beat faster.

13. Which of the following statements is NOT true according to the passage?
A. Color probably has an effect on us which we are not conscious of.
B. Yellow fire engines have caused many bad accidents in some advanced communities.
C. People exposed to pure blue start to breathe more slowly.
D. The psychology of color is of some practical use.

14. Which of the following statements is TRUE according to the passage?
A. Manufacturers often sell sugar in green wrappings.
B. Dark blue can bring people the feeling of being energetic.
C. Primitive people associated heat and anger with red.
D. Green and yellow are associated with calm and passive defense.

15. Which of the following could be the most suitable title for the passage?
A. The Branch of Color Psychology
B. Color and its Meanings
C. The Practical Use of Color Psychology
D. Color and Feelings

Part II Vocabulary and Structure (30%)

16. When I mention the problem, I'm not ________ all of you.
A. talking about
B. referring to
C. listening to
D. carrying out

17. Your idea seems to be good but it isn't ________.
A. practical
B. possible
C. plentiful
D. precious

18. We were tired and nervous ________ the constant tension.
A. from
B. for
C. with
D. off

19. "Which do you want, the red one or the black one?"
"________. How about showing me another?"
A. Either　B. Both　C. Neither　D. None
20. "What makes her so unhappy?" "________ one of her favorite books."
A. Because she lost　B. Because of her losing　C. She lost　D. Her losing
21. "I usually sleep with the windows closed at night, even in summer." "You can never be ________ careful."
A. very　B. much　C. too　D. so
22. "________ is your nationality, Miss Green?" "Australian."
A. What　B. Where　C. Which　D. Who
23. I hope the stove will ________ enough heat to warm the room.
A. get over　B. give in　C. get out　D. give off
24. You look tired. Do you ________ a rest?
A. like having　B. feel like having　C. like have　D. feel like to have
25. ________ the price is, they are prepared to pay.
A. However　B. Whichever　C. Whatever　D. Wherever
26. Wait a moment, please. Richard will be back ________.
A. in no time　B. at no time　C. at times　D. at a time
27. ________ I accept that the plan is not perfect, I do actually like it.
A. When　B. Since　C. While　D. Unless
28. She says she'd rather he ________ tomorrow instead of today.
A. leaves　B. left　C. leave　D. would leave
29. I don't think Mary understood what you said, ________?
A. do I　B. didn't she　C. did you　D. did she
30. You ________ not have seen her yesterdays for she was abroad.
A. must　B. should　C. could　D. would
31. Alice trusts you; only you can ________ her to give up the foolish idea.
A. suggest　B. attract　C. tempt　D. persuade
32. The Internet has brought ________ big changes in the way we work.
A. about　B. out　C. back　D. up
33. He is a man who is always ________ fault with other people.
A. putting　B. seeking　C. finding　D. looking for
34. I am sure David will be able to find the library because he has a pretty good ________ of direction.
A. idea　B. feeling　C. experience　D. sense
35. They started off late and got to the airport with minutes to ________.
A. spare　B. catch　C. leave　D. make
36. The evening news comes on at seven o'clock and ________ only thirty minutes.
A. keeps　B. continues　C. finishes　D. lasts
37. The factory had to ________ a number of employees because of the economic crisis in the country.
A. lay out　B. lay off　C. lay aside　D. lay down
38. People may have different opinions about Karen, but I admire her. ________, she is a great musician.
A. After all　B. As a result　C. In other words　D. As usual
39. They had a pleasant chat ________ a cup of coffee.
A. for　B. with　C. during　D. over
40. Was it in 1969 ________ the American astronaut succeeded ________ landing on the moon?
A. when; on　B. that; on　C. which; in　D. that; in
41. The comments which he made ________ marketing bothered his boss greatly.
A. being concerned　B. concerned　C. be concerned　D. concerning
42. The news reporters hurried to the airport, only ________ the film stars had left.
A. to tell　B. to be told　C. telling　D. told

43. Mrs. White became a teacher in 1985. She ________ for twenty years by next summer.
A. will teach B. would have taught
C. has been teaching D. will have been teaching

44. After the new technique was introduced, the factory produced ________ cars in 2002 as the year before.
A. as many twice B. as twice many C. twice many as D. twice as many

45. There were dirty marks on her trousers ________ she had wiped her hands.
A. where B. when C. that D. what

Part III Identification (10%)

46. Have you noticed her coat is wet? She must be caught in the rain.
A: noticed B: is wet C: must be caught D: in

47. Teenagers always long for the time which they are able to be independent.
A: long for B: which C: are able to be D: independent

48. Since the injury is bad, the doctors will operate him immediately.
A: Since B: is bad C: will operate D: immediately

49. Let's hurry up and try to get to the railway station in time, can we?
A: Let's hurry up B: get to C: in time D: can we

50. He refused joining us last Saturday night. Don't you think it strange?
A: refused B: joining C: Don't D: it strange

51. Some old beautiful Italian oil paintings are being displayed in the exhibition hall.
A: old beautiful Italian B: are being C: displayed D: exhibition hall

52. If you had been there, I'm sure you would have enjoyed to see the Chinese Team win.
A: had been B: would have enjoyed C: to see D: win

53. On seeing the boy fell into the river, she sprang to her feet and went to the rescue.
A: On B: fell C: sprang D: went to

54. Traditionally, work determines our way of life. But if 98 percent of us don't need to work, what are we going to do with oneself?
A: Traditionally, B: way C: need to work D: oneself

55. Only by practice will you be able to improve your speaking English and gradually speak fluently.
A: Only B: will you C: speaking D: speak

Part IV Cloze (10%)

A king once __56__ seriously ill. His doctors and wise men tried cure __57__ cure, but nothing __58__. They were ready to __59__ hope, when the king's old servant spoke up. He said, "If you can find a happy man, take the shirt from his back and __60__ it on the king, then he will __61__." So the king's officials rode __62__ throughout the kingdom; yet nowhere __63__ a happy man. No one seemed __64__; everyone had some complaints. If a man was rich, he never had enough. If he was not rich, it was someone else's __65__. If he was __66__, he had a bad mother-in-law. If he had a good mother-in-law, he was catching a cold. Everyone had something to complain about. __67__, one night the king's own son was passing a small cottage __68__ he heard someone say, "Thank you. I've finished my daily labor, and helped my fellow man. My family and I have eaten our fill, and now we can __69__ and sleep in peace. __70__ more could I want?" The prince was very happy __71__ a happy man at last. He gave __72__ to take the man's shirt to the king, and pay the __73__ as much money as he __74__. But when the king's officials went into the cottage to take the happy man's shirt __75__ his back, they found he had no shirt at all.

56. A. fell B. felt C. feel D. fall
57. A. to B. by C. for D. after
58. A. played B. worked C. operated D. affected
59. A. give off B. give out C. give up D. give in
60. A. place B. put C. dress D. wear
61. A. recover B. relax C. relieve D. remove
62. A. off and on B. back and forth C. up and down D. far and wide

63. A. had they found	B. should they find	C. could they find	D. did they find
64. A. content	B. contrary	C. concrete	D. complete
65. A. fault	B. mistake	C. error	D. shortage
66. A. helpful	B. heavy	C. healthy	D. high
67. A. Consequently	B. Finally	C. Lately	D. Fortunately
68. A. while	B. which	C. whenever	D. when
69. A. lay	B. lie	C. laid	D. lain
70. A. Which	B. Who	C. When	D. What
71. A. to having found	B. to have been found	C. to have found	D. to find
72. A. orders	B. messages	C. words	D. letters
73. A. official	B. owner	C. servant	D. master
74. A. advised	B. said	C. asked	D. wished
75. A. from	B. out of	C. off	D. down

Part V Translation (20%)

Section A

76. Many high achievers who love their careers feel that they are happiest when they are working hard.
77. From the above we can come to the conclusion that the more you work, the happier and healthier you will be.
78. In short, art expresses the essential qualities of a time and a place, and a study of it clearly offers us a deeper understanding than can be found in most history books.
79. Manufacturers have discovered by experience that sugar sells badly in green wrappings, that blue foods are considered unpleasant, and that cosmetics should never be packaged in brown.
80. Experiments have shown that colors, partly because of their psychological associations, also have a direct psychological effect.

Section B

81. 每个人都喜欢受表扬而不是被批评。
82. 人们抱怨当地政府在处理污染问题上力度不够。
83. 只要你尽力而为，即使将来失败也没人会指责你。
84. 他告诉我要慢慢来，没有必要提前完成这项工作。
85. 我们推迟了这个会议，以便能够更好地应付紧张的局势。

参考答案

1—15　CCDAB　CACBA　DBBCC
16—45　BACCD　CADBC　ACBDC　DACDA　DBADD　DBDDA
46—55　CBCDB　ACBDC
56—75　ADBCB　ABCAA　CDDBD　CCBCA
76. 很多取得卓越成功的人热爱自己的职业生涯，他们认为当他们努力工作的时候他们是最幸福的。
77. 通过以上所述可以得出这样的结论，越辛勤工作，越幸福，就越健康。
78. 简而言之，艺术表现了当时和当地的本质的东西，对艺术的研究，很清楚的给我们提供了更深的理解，比什么更深呢？比我们能在大多数的历史教材中能发现的更多。
79. 厂商通过经验发现，糖用绿色包装卖的不好，蓝色的食品被认为是不讨人喜欢的，化妆品绝对不能用褐色来包装。
80. 实验表明，颜色部分是由于心理联系，对心理造成直接的影响。
81. Everyone likes to be praised not to be criticized.
82. It is complained that the local government hasn't taken enough measure to deal with pollution.
83. As long as you try your best, nobody will blame you even if you fail in future.
84. He told me to take my time and it was unnecessary to complete the job in advance.

85. We put off this meeting so as to cope with the tense situations better.

北京地区成人本科学士学位英语统一考试(A)

2008. 04. 19

Part I Reading Comprehension (30%)

Passage 1 Questions 1 to 5 are based on the following passage:

Looking back on my childhood, I am convinced that naturalists are born and not made. Although we were brought up in the same way, my brothers and sisters soon abandoned their pressed (紧抱的) flowers and insects. Unlike them, I had no ear for music and languages. I was not an early reader and I could not do mental arithmetic.

Before World War I we spent our summer holidays in Hungary. I have only the dim memory of the house we lived in, of my room and my toys. (76) Nor do I recall clearly the large family of grandparents, aunts, uncles and cousins who gathered next door. But I do have a crystal-clear memory of the dogs, the farm animals, the local birds and above all, the insects.

I am a naturalist, not a scientist. I have a strong love of the natural world, and my enthusiasm has led me into varied investigations. I love discussing my favorite topics and enjoy burning the midnight oil, reading about other people's observations and discoveries. Then something happens that brings these observations together in my conscious mind. Suddenly you fancy you see the answer to the riddle (谜), because it all seems to fit together. This has resulted in my publishing 300 papers and books, which some might honor with the rifle of scientific research.

But curiosity, a keen eye, a good memory and enjoyment of the animal and plant world do not make a scientist; one of the outstanding and essential qualifies required is self-discipline, a quality I lack. A scientist can be made. A naturalist is born. If you can combine the two, you get the best of both worlds.

1. According to the author, a born naturalist should first of all be ________.
   A. full of enthusiasm B. self-disciplined
   C. full of ambition D. knowledgeable
2. The first paragraph tells us that the author ________.
   A. lost his hearing when he was a child
   B. didn't like his brothers and sisters
   C. was born to a naturalist's family
   D. was interested in flowers and insects in his childhood
3. The author says that he is a naturalist rather than a scientist probably because he thinks he ________.
   A. just reads about other people's observations and discoveries
   B. comes up with solutions in most natural ways
   C. has a great deal of trouble doing mental arithmetic
   D. lacks some of the qualities required of a scientist
4. The author can't remember his relatives clearly because ________.
   A. he was fully occupied with observing nature
   B. he didn't live very long with them
   C. the family was extremely large
   D. he was too young when he lived with them
5. Which of the following statements is true?
   A. The author believes that a born naturalist cannot be a scientist.
   B. The author's brothers and sisters were good at music and languages.
   C. The author read a lot of books about the natural world and the oil industry.
   D. The author spent a lot of time working on riddles.

Passage 2 Question 6 to 10 are based on the following passage:

If you have a chance to go to Finland, you will probably be surprised to find how "foolish" the Finnish people are.

Take the taxi drivers for example. Taxis in Finland are mostly high-class Benz with a fare of two US dollars a kilometer. You can go anywhere in one, tell the driver to drop you at any place, say that you have some business to attend to, and then walk off without paying your fare. The driver would not show the least sign of anxiety.

The dining rooms in all big hotels not only serve their guests, but also serve outside diners. Hotel guests have their meals free, so they naturally go to the free dining rooms to have their meals. The most they would do to show their good faith is to wave their registration card to the waiter. With such a loose check, you can easily use any old registration card to take a couple of friends to dine free of charge.

The Finnish workers are paid by the hour. (77) They are very much on their own as soon as they have agreed with the boss on the rate. From then on they just say how many hours they have worked and they will be paid accordingly.

With so many loopholes(漏洞) in everyday life, surely Finland must be a heaven to those who love to take "petty advantages". But the strange thing is, all the taxi passengers would always come back to pay their fare after they have attended to their business; not a single outsider has ever been found in the free hotel dining rooms. And workers always give an honest account of the exact hours they put in. As the Finns always act on good faith in everything they do, living in such a society has turned everyone into a real "gentleman". (78) In a society of such high moral practice, what need is there for people to be on guard against others?

6. While taking a taxi in Finland, ________.
   A. a passenger can go anywhere without having to pay the driver
   B. a passenger pays two US dollars for a taxi ride
   C. a passenger can never be turned down by the taxi driver wherever he wants to go
   D. a passenger needs to provide good faith demonstration before they leave without paying
7. We know from the passage that big hotels in Finland ________.
   A. provide meals for only those who live in the hotels B. provide meals for any diners
   C. provide free wine and charge for food D. are mostly poorly managed
8. Which of the following is NOT true according to the passage?
   A. The workers in Finland are paid by the hour.
   B. The bosses in Finland are too busy to check the working hours of their employees.
   C. The workers are always honest with their working hours.
   D. The workers and their bosses will make an agreement in advance about the pay.
9. The word "those" in the last paragraph probably refers to ________.
   A. people who often take taxis B. people who often have meals in big hotels
   C. people who are dishonest D. people who are worthy of trust
10. It can be concluded that ________.
    A. Finnish people are not smart enough in daily life
    B. Finland has been a good place for cheats
    C. the Finnish society is of very high moral level
    D. all the Finns are rich

Passage 3 Questions 11 to 15 are based on the following passage:

There are many factors which may have an influence on adults and children being able to lead a healthy life.

Nowadays, people are very busy. Often, both parents work outside the home. Children are expected to take on more responsibility at home to help their parents. They also have sporting and leisure activities as well as school expectations.

The business also adds another factor: the need to use cars to get from one place to another quickly.

Today, society places a lot of emphasis on technology. Computers, DVDs, CDs, television, Play Stations and Xboxes have become major leisure activities, rather than traditional more active pursuits. This has led to a more sedentary lifestyle.

The media provide entertainment and information. (79) Unfortunately, they also promote fast food which fits easily into busy lifestyles. It is much more convenient at times to buy a quick take, away rather than prepare a meal. The media constantly bombard (轰炸) their audience with "perfect" body images, the need to buy the most fashionable clothes, the most up-to-date computer games, the best places to visit and the best things to do.

Environments vary. We may be exposed to pollution, such as cigarette smoke. This can be harmful to people who suffer from breathing difficulties. (80) Environments where passive smoking is unavoidable make it difficult to lead a healthy life.

It is important for everyone to be accepted and cared about by family and friends. Both of these groups can influence people—positively and negatively. Negative feelings can lead people to adopt an unhealthy lifestyle.

Perhaps the most important factor influencing healthy lifestyles is motivation, or the desire to be healthy. Any person who wants to be healthy will find a way to be healthy—if he/she is motivated enough!

11. The passage is mainly about ________.
A. benefits of a healthy lifestyle
B. demands of daily life
C. factors affecting a healthy lifestyle
D. a positive approach to healthy living

12. The word "sedentary" in Paragraph 4 probably means ________.
A. having a lot of things to do
B. involving little exercise or physical activity
C. being isolated from the outside world
D. experiencing a lot of stress

13. Which of the following is NOT mentioned in the passage as a factor leading to the popularity of fast food?
A. Cheap price.
B. The media.
C. Busy lifestyle.
D. Convenience.

14. Which is NOT listed as a factor influencing the ability to have a healthy lifestyle?
A. Pollution.
B. Economic factors.
C. Dependence upon cars.
D. Influence of family or friends.

15. According to the author, ________ may be the most important factor influencing healthy lifestyles.
A. technology
B. cultural background
C. environment
D. the desire to be healthy

Part II Vocabulary and Structure (30%)

16. Heating the gunshot, all the birds flew ________ every direction.
A. in
B. on
C. to
D. toward

17. The factory had to ________ a number of employees because of the economic decline in the country.
A. lay out
B. lay off
C. lay aside
D. lay down

18. His parents ________ his money, so he is in trouble now.
A. cut off
B. cut through
C. gave up
D. brought down

19. Can you ________ the difference ________ the two phrases?
A. tell, between
B. speak, from
C. say, of
D. talk, between

20. If anyone happens to drop in while I am out, ________ him or her leave a message.
A. have
B. get
C. ask
D. tell

21. There is no doubt ________ you will pass the exam this time. You have worked so hard in the past months.
A. whether
B. that
C. if
D. what

22. I ________ the boy to save money, but he wouldn't listen.
A. hoped
B. suggested
C. wanted
D. made

23. I made a call to my parents yesterday. To my disappointment, ________ of them answered it.
A. either
B. none
C. neither
D. nobody

24. No matter ________ he is able to come to the party or not, we will invite him.
A. when
B. whether
C. how
D. why

25. The idea ________ to him in his dream and he decided to carry it out.

A. happened B. struck C. appeared D. occurred

26. He would have paid ________ for the house if the salesgirl had insisted because he really wanted it.
A. twice as much B. much as twice C. as much twice D. twice much as

27. They decided to chase the cow away ________ it did more damage.
A. unless B. until C. before D. although

28. We wanted a new table for dinner, so my father bought ________ from a furniture store yesterday.
A. itself B. one C. himself D. another

29. A library with five thousand books ________ to the nation as a gift.
A. is offered B. has offered C. are offered D. have offered

30. ________ is often the case, we have worked out the production plan.
A. Which B. When C. What D. As

31. It is no ________ talking to him; because he will never change his mind.
A. help B. use C. time D. way

32. The way I thought of ________ the animal was of great value.
A. protecting B. protect C. being protected D. to protect

33. In another year or so, you ________ all about it.
A. forget B. would forget C. have forgotten D. will have forgotten

34. No one here believes the reason ________ he gave for his lateness.
A. that B. why C. for which D. what

35. The novel I bought last week is worth ________, I think.
A. reading B. being read C. to read D. to be read

36. After the fire, ________ would otherwise be a cultural centre is now reduced to a pile of ashes.
A. that B. it C. which D. what

37. Did you notice the little boy ________ away?
A. took the candy and run B. taking the candy and run
C. take the candy and run D. who taking the candy and running

38. ________ gives people more knowledge of the society than literature.
A. Anything B. Nothing C. Something D. Everything

39. If Mary catches ________ her diary, she'll be angry.
A. you reading B. yours reading C. you read D. you to read

40. Don't worry me now. I will mend that coat ________.
A. by and by B. off and on C. back an forth D. now and then

41. Please join us. We can easily make ________ for one more at this table.
A. seat B. place C. room D. space

42. You may depend on ________ he will not repeat his mistakes.
A. it that B. that C. him that D. which that

43. "That latest car must have cost you a pretty penny." "Oh, no, ________."
A. it didn't B. it mustn't C. it hasn't D. it must haven't

44. ________ the first to use nuclear weapons.
A. At no time China will be B. Never China will be
C. Will China never be D. At no time will China be

45. Encouragement is sometimes much more ________ than criticism.
A. effective B. efficient C. executive D. extensive

Part III Identification (10%)

46. Two woman (A) teachers and four girl (B) students were (C) praised at (D) the meeting yesterday.

47. After (A) she got married (B), Lily went to (C) see her mother each other week (D).

48. There will be more than three hundreds students taking part in the sports meet.
A B C D

49. While shopping, people sometimes can't help persuading into buying something they don't really need.
A B C D

50. We are all for your proposal that the discussion is to be put off.
A B C D

51. Factory workers had to work very hard before, so had farmers.
A B C D

52. He finds it easier to do the cooking himself than teaching his wife to cook.
A B C D

53. There was too much dust that we couldn't see what was happening.
A B C D

54. The boy did not have to leave the next day because he got his visa extending.
A B C D

55. What does Mr. Johnson like? He's a friendly sort of man. I like to work with him.
A B C D

Part IV Cloze (10%)

A young woman was driving through the __56__ countryside. It was dark and raining. Suddenly she saw an old woman __57__ the side of the road, __58__ her hand out as if she wanted __59__. "I can't __60__ her out in this weather," the woman said to herself, so she stopped the car and opened the door.

"Do you want a lift?" she asked. The old woman __61__ and climbed into the car. After a __62__, she said to the old woman, "Have you been waiting for a long time?" The old woman shook her head. "__63__," thought the young woman. She __64__ again. "Bad weather for the time of the year." she said. The old woman nodded. No matter __65__ the young woman said, the hitchhiker(搭便车的人) gave no answer __66__ a nod of the head.

Then the young woman __67__ the hitchhiker's hands, which were large and hairy. Suddenly she __68__ that the hitchhiker was __69__ a man! She stopped the car. "I can't see out of the rear screen," she said, "Would you mind __70__ it for me?" The hitchhiker nodded and opened the door. __71__ the hitchhiker was out of the car, the frightened young woman __72__.

When she got to the next village she __73__ to a stop. She noticed that the hitchhiker had __74__ his handbag __75__. She picked it up and opened it. She gave a gasp; inside the bag was a gun!

56. A. lovely B. lonely C. noisy D. crowded
57. A. at B. beside C. by D. near
58. A. holding B. to hold C. to be holding D. to be held
59. A. an aid B. a taxi C. a car D. a lift
60. A. permit B. leave C. allow D. order
61. A. answering B. shook C. nodded D. smiles
62. A. while B. moment C. time D. period
63. A. Curious B. Interesting C. Strange D. Wonderful
64. A. told B. did C. made D. tried
65. A. when B. which C. how D. what
66. A. except for B. apart from C. other than D. more than
67. A. saw B. noticed C. watched D. observed
68. A. recognized B. realized C. recovered D. remembered
69. A. practically B. basically C. actually D. probably
70. A. clear B. cleared C. to clear D. clearing
71. A. As long as B. As far as C. As soon as D. As well as
72. A. raced off B. ran away C. fell down D. moved on
73. A. pulled B. picked C. pushed D. paused
74. A. lift B. lost C. laid D. left
75. A. beneath B. behind C. backwards D. afterwards

Part V Translation (20%)

Section A

76. Nor do I recall clearly the large family of grandparents, aunts, uncles and cousins who gathered next door.
77. They are very much on their own as soon as they have agreed with the boss on the rate.
78. In a society of such high moral practice, what need is there for people to be on guard against others?
79. Unfortunately, they also promote fast food which fits easily into busy lifestyles.
80. Environments where passive smoking is unavoidable make it difficult to lead a healthy life.

Section B

81. 如果我是他，我就会尽最大努力按时完成任务。
82. 我不记得曾经在哪里见过他。
83. 这所大学提供了他所期望的一切。
84. 我们一得出结论就通知你。
85. 你们应该充分利用每个机会说英语。

参考答案

1—15 ADDAB DBBCC CBABD

16—45 ABAAA BBCBD ACBAD BDDAA DCBAA CAADA

46—55 ADBBD DCBDA

56—75 BAADB CACDD ABBCD CAADB

76. 我也不能清晰地记得爷爷奶奶、姑妈、叔叔以及堂兄妹们等一大家子在门外欢聚的场景。
77. 他们和老板就工资一达成协议，他们就非常独立了。
78. 在这样一个充满高尚道德行为的社会，人与人之间还有什么必要彼此防范呢？
79. 然而，他们也宣传适应繁忙生活方式的快餐。
80. 在被动吸烟不可避免的环境下，人们很难有健康的生活方式。
81. If I were him, I would try my best to complete the task on time.
82. I don't remember where I have ever been met him.
83. The university has provided everything he expected.
84. As soon as we come to conclusion, we will inform you.
85. You should make full use of every chance to speak English.

北京地区成人本科学士学位英语统一考试(A)

2008.11.22

Part I Reading Comprehension (30%)

Passage 1 Questions 1 to 5 are based on the following passage:

Scientists in India have invented a new way to produce electricity. Their invention does not get its power from oil, coal or other fuels, it produces electricity with the power of animals. India has about eighty million bullocks. They do all kinds of jobs. They work in the fields. They pull vehicles through the streets. They carry water containers. (76) Indian energy officials have been seeking ways to use less imported oil to provide energy. Scientists at the National Institute for Industrial Engineering in Bombay(孟买)wondered whether the millions of bullocks could help. Many villages in India lack electricity, but they have many bullocks. And often the animals are not working. One job done by bullocks is to pump water out of the well. The animals do this by walking around and around in a circle. As they walk, they turn a heavy stick that makes the pump move. **This simple technology is centuries old.** Scientists thought that the same technology could be used to produce electricity. Bullocks walk in a circle only two or three times a minute. This is much too slow to produce electricity, but it can create enough power to turn a series of gears(齿轮). A large gear sits next to a smaller gear. As the large gear turns it causes the smaller gear to turn. That gear turns an even smaller one. Each gear moves faster because it is a little smaller. The smallest gear may turn extremely fast. (77) clocks operate with gears. So do cars and so does the device invented by he Indian scientists to produce electricity.

According to the officials in the United Nations, the idea is being tested at several places in India. The device is easy to operate and repair. And it can be moved easily. It costs about three hundred and seven dollars now to make such a device, but production of large numbers of them could cut the cost of each to about two hundred dollars.

1. Who first thought of using bullocks to provide energy?
   A. Indian energy officials.
   B. Scientists in India
   C. Officials in the United Nations
   D. Researchers in Europe
2. Which kind of job that the bullocks do is NOT mentioned in the passage?
   A. Pulling vehicles.
   B. Plowing fields
   C. Pumping water out of wells
   D. Carrying food baskets.
3. Why are bullocks used to provide energy in India?
   A. Because bullocks have long been used by Indian people
   B. Because bullocks walk slowly and are easy to control.
   C. Because there are few non-working bullocks in India
   D. Because there is not enough oil in India.
4. In the sentence "This simple technology is centuries old" in Paragraph One, "This simple technology" refers to ________.
   A. using bullocks to produce energy
   B. using pumps to draw water out
   C. having bullocks walk around to make the pump move
   D. connecting gears of different sizes to produce electricity
5. Which of the following is true about the device mentioned in the passage?
   A. It has a large gear and a smaller gear.
   B. It's easy to use, but difficult to move.
   C. It's quite cheap.
   D. It's still being tested.

Passage 2 Questions 6 to 10 are based on the following passage:

On-the-job smoking is a hot issue for both smokers and non-smokers, and many managers now see smoking as a productivity(生产力) problem. Although some people question whether smoking really affects one's productivity, it has, in fact been proven that a smoker costs a company more than a non-smoker. According to professor William Weis, a smoking employee costs his or her employer about $5,700 more a year than a never-smoker. These costs include medical care, lost earnings and insurance. And absence due to smoking breaks is one of the productivity problems, yet it accounts for a great deal of employer costs.

(78) When the issue of smoking at the workplace is discussed, perhaps the most important problem is the health risk that smoking causes to both smokers and never-smokers. It has long been proven that smoking is linked to lung cancer. Now many health experts warn that passive smoking can cause lung cancer and other illnesses in healthy never-smokers. Passive smoking can be defined as exposure to second-hand tobacco smoke in enclosed areas. Anyone who has been with smokers indeed knows that their smoke can cause eye irritation(刺激), coughing, headaches and throat soreness. While eye irritation may seem a small thing to some smokers, it nevertheless is a problem that occurs every workday in offices and break-rooms and can lead to greater health problems. Employees who do not smoke should not be subjected(遭受) to the risks of passive smoking and need to be able to work in a safe environment. Surgeon General Koop states that the right of the smoker stops at the point where his or her smoking increases the disease risk of those occupying the same environment.

6. All the following cases are on-the-job smoking except that ________.
   A. an employer smokes while working in the office
   B. A taxi driver smokes while driving the car
   C. A worker smokes while working in the workshop
   D. a worker smokes while reading in the train

7. According to the passage, on-the-job smoking affects an employee's performance in the office in that ________.
A. he can't concentrate on what he is doing while smoking
B. he often goes away from his desk to smoke in the break-room
C. he often asks for sick leave as a result of too much smoking
D. he takes a rest from time to time because of eye irritation
8. Many managers do not seem to be in favor of on-the-job smoking mainly because it ________.
A. reduces productivity of the company to a certain degree
B. does harm to the health of never-smokers of the company
C. affects the relationship between smokers and non-smokers
D. makes the break-rooms more crowded and more polluted
9. Passive smoking means ________.
A. never-smokers take up the habit of smoking unwillingly
B. never-smokers have to put up with the active smokers
C. never-smokers share an enclosed area with smokers
D. never-smokers share an open area with smokers
10. In the second part of the passage, the author suggests banning (禁止) on-the-job smoking so as to ________.
A. cut down costs of medical care and insurance
B. create a healthy and safe working environment
C. prevent eye irritation from becoming a big health problem
D. improve the smoking employees' work efficiency

Passage 3 Questions 11 to 15 are based on the following passage:

Not all memories are sweet. Some people spend all their lives trying to forget bad experiences. Violence and traffic accidents can leave people with terrible physical and emotional scars. Often they relive these experiences in nightmares(恶梦).

(79) Now American researchers think they are close to developing a pill, which will help people forget bad memories. The pill is designed to be taken immediately after a frightening experience. They hope it might reduce, or possibly erase(抹去) the effect of painful memories.

In November, experts tested a drug on people in the US and France. The drug stops the body releasing chemicals that fix memories in the brain. (80) So far the research has suggested that only the emotional effects of memories may be reduced, not that the memories are erased.

The research has caused a great deal of argument. Some think it is a bad idea, while others support in.

Supporters say it could lead to pills that prevent or treat soldiers troubling memories after war. They say that there are many people who suffer from terrible memories.

"Some memories can ruin people's lives. They come back to you when you don't want to have them in a daydream or nightmare they usually come with very painful emotions," said Roger Pitman, a professor of psychiatry at Harvard Medical School. "this could relieve a lot of that suffering."

But those who are against the research say that it is very dangerous to change memories because memories give us our identity(特质). They also help us all avoid the mistakes of the past.

"All of us can think of bad events in our lives that were horrible at the time but make us who we are, I'm not sure we want to wipe those memories out," said Rebecca Dresser, a medical ethicist.

11. The passage is mainly about ________.
A. a new medical invention
B. a new research on memories
C. a way of erasing painful memories
D. an argument about the research on the pill
12. The drug tested on people can ________.

A. cause the brain to fix memories
B. stop people remembering their experiences
C. prevent body producing certain chemicals
D. wipe out the emotional effects of memories

13. We can infer from the passage that ________.
A. people doubt the effects of the pills.
B. the pill will stop people's and experiences.
C. taking the pill will do harm to people's health
D. the pill has probable been produced in America

14. Which of the following does Rebecca Dresser agree with?
A. Some memories can ruin people's lives.
B. people want to get rid of bad memories.
C. Experiencing bad events makes us different from others.
D. The pill will reduce people's suffering from bad memories.

15. The word "scars" in Paragraph One is close in meaning to ________.
A. good stories B. pains C. experiences D. memories

Part II Vocabulary and Structure(30%)

16. Don't be too ________ about things you are not supposed to know.
A. strange B. amusing C. curious D. conscious

17. He's got himself into a dangerous situation ________ he is likely to lose control over the plane.
A. where B. which C. while D. why

18. In order to change attitudes ________ employing women. The government is bringing in new laws.
A. about B. of C. towards D. on

19. The fact came up ________ specific speech sounds are recognized by babies as young as 6 months old.
A. what B. which C. that D. whose

20. It is generally believed that teaching is ________ it is a science.
A. an art much as B. much an art as
C. as an art much as D. as much an art as

21. ________ I have to put it away and focus my attention on study this week.
A. However the story is amusing B. No matter amusing the story is
C. However amusing to story is D. No matter how the story is amusing

22. For the sake of her daughter's health, she decided to move to a warm ________.
A. weather B. temperature C. season D. climate

23. Be careful when you cross this very busy street. If not, you may get ________ by a car.
A. run out B. run over C. run away D. run after

24. ________ some famous scientists have the qualities of being both careful and careless.
A. Strangely enough B. Enough strangely C. Strange enough D. Enough strange

25. Having a trip abroad is certainly good for the old couple. But it remains ________ whether they will enjoy it.
A. to see B. to be seen C. seeing D. seen

26. —You seem to show interest in cooking.
—What? ________ I'm getting tired of it.
A. On the contrary B. To the contrary
C. On the other hand D. To the other hand

27. These wild flowers are so special that I would do ________ I can to save them.
A. whatever B. that C. which D. whichever

28. Time will ________ whether I made the right choice or not.
A. see B. say C. tell D. know

29. Suddenly, a tall man driving a golden carriage ________ he girl and took her away, ________ into the woods.
A. seizing; disappeared　B. seized; disappeared
C. seizing; disappearing　D. seized; disappearing
30. It suddenly ________ me how we could improve the situation.
A. occurred　B. feared　C. shook　D. struck
31. Was it because he was ill ________ he asked for leave?
A. so　B. when　C. why　D. that
32. John likes Chinese food. But he ________ eating with chopsticks.
A. is used to　B. used to　C. isn't used to　D. didn't used to
33. Fujian Province lies ________ the east of China and Taiwan is ________ the east of Fujian.
A. in; in　B. to; in　C. to; to　D. in; to
34. For John this was the beginning of a new life, ________ he thought he would never see.
A. what　B. that　C. one　D. it
35. We stayed for the night at the foot of the mountain and ________ to climb it the next morning.
A. set about　B. set off　C. set up　D. set out
36. We should do as much as we can ________ our country better and more beautiful.
A. make　B. to make　C. makes　D. making
37. "to put off something" means "to ________."
A. look for it　B. put it in place　C. postpone it　D. cancel it
38. ________, he'll make a first-class tennis player.
A. Giving time　B. To give Time　C. Given time　D. Being given time
39. —Did you see her off the day before yesterday?
—No, but I wish I ________.
A. were　B. did　C. had　D. would
40. Some divers always drive carelessly. There is some ________ danger while they are driving.
A. painful　B. potential　C. probable　D. primary
41. You have stayed at home for two days. It's time you ________ for a walk.
A. go out　B. went out　C. will go out　D. would go out
42. Can you ________ the three mistakes in this paragraph?
A. turn out　B. bring out　C. call out　D. pick out
43. This is much ________ to the one I bought last week.
A. worse　B. lower　C. inferior　D. equal
44. ________ their country has plenty of oil, ours has none.
A. While　B. Where　C. When　D. Unless
45. There at the door stood a girl about the same height ________.
A. as me　B. as mine　C. with mine　D. with me

Part III　Identification (10%)

46. The reporter was very pleased when the chairman allowed him to ask few questions.
(A: very; B: when; C: allowed; D: few questions)
47. He tried to learn Greek but soon got tired of it and gave up it.
(A: tried to; B: soon; C: tired of it; D: gave up it)
48. With the sun setting, we stopped working, putting away our tools and were going to go home.
(A: setting; B: working; C: putting; D: going)
49. Polite manners in China demand that a person stands up when anyone enters a room or when anyone hands him something.
(A: Polite manners; B: stands up; C: enters; D: hands)
50. This is the sportsman whom everyone says will win the gold medal at the Winter Olympic Games.
(A: This; B: whom; C: says; D: at)

51. I heard that you really had a wonderful time at John's birthday Party, hadn't you?
A B C D

52. E-mail as well as mobile telephones are becoming more and more popular in daily communication.
A B C D

53. They are going to have the servicemen installed an electric fan in the office tomorrow.
A B C D

54. Two woman teachers and four girl students were praised at the Meeting yesterday.
A B C D

55. Lesson Three is the most difficult lesson, but it isn't the most difficult lesson in Book Four.
A B C D

Part IV Cloze (10%)

Scientists say that something very serious is happening to the earth. It will begin to get __56__ in the following years. There will be major changes in __57__ in the new century. Coastal waters will have a __58__ temperature. This will have a __59__ effect on agriculture. In northern areas, the __60__ season will be ten days longer by the year 2010. However, in warmer areas, it will be too dry. The __61__ of water could __62__ by eighty percent. This would __63__ a large decrease in agriculture production.

World temperature could __64__ two degrees centigrade by the year 2040. However, the increase could be three times as great in the Arctic and Antarctic areas. This could cause the __65__ shects to melt and raise the __66__ of the oceans __67__ one to two meters. Many coastal cities would be __68__ water.

Why is this happening? There is too __69__ carbon dioxide in the air. __70__ oil, gas and coal burn, they create large amounts of carbon dioxide. This carbon dioxide lets __71__ enter the earth's atmosphere and __72__ the earth. However, it doesn't let as much heat __73__ the atmosphere and enter space. It's like a blanket. The heat __74__ the sun can pass through the blanket to warm the earth. The heat __75__ there and can't escape through the blanket again.

Scientists call this the green-house effect.

56. A. warmer B. colder C. better D. worse
57. A. land B. agriculture C. climate D. weather
58. A. lower B. higher C. normal D. proper
59. A. good B. general C. serious D. useful
60. A. getting B. playing C. taking D. growing
61. A. much B. many C. amount D. number
62. A. fall B. decrease C. refuse D. rise
63. A. lead B. keep C. make D. cause
64. A. increase B. drop C. lift D. realize
65. A. water B. rain C. stone D. ice
66. A. degree B. level C. coast D. area
67. A. by B. to C. of D. with
68. A. above B. under C. below D. over
69. A. little B. many C. few D. much
70. A. If B. Because C. When D. Why
71. A. sunlight B. air C. rain D. gas
72. A. cold B. protect C. hurt D. heat
73. A. enter B. get C. heave D. reach
74. A. through B. by C. from D. on
75. A. stores B. arrives C. stands D. stays

Part V Translation (20%)

Section A

76. Indian energy officials have been seeking ways to use less imported oil to provide energy.

77. Clocks operate with gears. So do cars and so does the device invented by the Indian scientists to produce electricity.
78. When the issue of smoking at the workplace is discussed, perhaps the most important problem is the health risk that smoking causes to both smokers and never-smokers.
79. Now American researchers think they are close to developing a pill, which will help people forget bad memories.
80. So far the research has suggested that only the emotional effects of memories may be reduced, not that the memories are erased.

Section B

81. 我想说的是，在奥运会上做志愿者(volunteer)对于年轻人是有意义的事。
82. 简而言之，每个人都该为自己的行为负责。
83. 我下决心一个月内在功课上要赶上同学们。
84. 在我看来，他们很难掩盖事实真相。
85. 直到会议结束那位经理一直保持沉默不语。

参考答案

1—5 BDDCD DBACB DDDCB
16—45 CACCD CDBAB AACDD DCDCD BCCCB BDCAB
46—55 DDCBB DBCAA
56—75 ACBBD CDDAD BABDC ADCCD
76. 印度主管能源的官员一直在寻找减少进口石油的方法，并用其他方法来提供能源。
77. 钟表是用齿轮带动的，小汽车如此，印度科学家发电的装置也是如此。
78. 涉及工作场所抽烟的问题，最重要的问题恐怕就是抽烟给吸烟者以及不吸烟者带来的健康风险。
79. 现在美国研究者认为他们马上会开发一种新药，帮助人们忘记不好的记忆。
80. 到目前为止，研究表明记忆的情感后果可能被消弱但是决不会被抹掉。
81. What I want to say is that to be a volunteer in Olympic games is significant to young people.
82. In short, everyone should be responsible for his behavior.
83. I am determined to catch up with my classmates in one month.
84. As far as I am concerned, it is difficult for them to cover the truth.
85. Until the end of the meeting, the manager kept silent.

北京地区成人本科学士学位英语统一考试(A)

2009.4.18

Part I Reading Comprehension (30%)

Passage 1 Questions 1 to 5 are based on the following passage:

I hear many parents complain that their teenage children are rebelling. I wish it were so. At your age you ought to be growing away from your parents. You should be learning to stand on your own feet. But take a good look at the present rebellion. It seems that teenagers are all taking the same way of showing that they disagree with their parents. Instead of striking out boldly on their own, most of them are holding one another's hands for reassurance (放心).

They claim they want to dress as they please. But they all wear the same clothes. They set off in new directions in music. But they all end up listening to the same record. Their reason for thinking or acting in such a way is that the crowd is doing it. They have come out of their cocoon (茧) into a larger cocoon.

(76) It has become harder and harder for a teenager to stand up against the popularity wave and to go his or her own way. Industry has firmly carved out a market for teenagers. These days every teenager can learn from the advertisements what a teenager should have and be. This is a great barrier for the teenager who wants to find his

or her own path.

But the barrier is worth climbing over. The path is worth following. You may want to listen to classical music instead of going to a party. You may want to collect rocks when everyone else is collecting records. You may have some thoughts that you don't care to share at once with your classmates. Well, go to it. Find yourself. Be yourself. Popularity will come—with the people who respect you for who you are. That's the only kind of popularity that really counts.

1. The author's purpose in writing this passage is to tell ________.
   A. readers how to be popular with people around
   B. teenagers how to learn to make a decision for themselves
   C. parents how to control and guide their children
   D. people how to understand and respect each other
2. According to the author, many teenagers think they are brave enough to act on their own, but in fact most of them ________.
   A. have much difficulty understanding each other
   B. lack confidence
   C. dare not cope with any problems alone
   D. are very much afraid of getting lost
3. Which of the following is NOT true according to the passage?
   A. There is no popularity that really counts.
   B. Many parents think that their children are challenging their authority.
   C. It is not necessarily bad for a teenager to disagree with his or her classmates.
   D. Most teenagers are actually doing the same.
4. The author thinks of advertisements as ________ to teenagers.
   A. inevitable B. influential C. instructive D. attractive
5. The main idea of the last paragraph is that a teenager should ________.
   A. differ from others in as many ways as possible
   B. become popular with others
   C. find his real self
   D. rebel against his parents and the popularity wave

Passage 2 Questions 6 to 10 are based on the following passage:

(77) Much unfriendly feeling towards computers has been based on the fear of widespread unemployment resulting from their introduction. Computers are often used as part of automated (自动化) production systems requiring a least possible number of operators, causing the loss of many jobs. This has happened, for example, in many steelworks.

On the other hand, computers do create jobs. **They** are more skilled and better paid, though fewer in number than those they replace. Many activities could not continue in their present form without computers, no matter how many people are employed. Examples are the check clearing (交换) system of major banks and the weather forecasting system.

When a firm introduces computers, a few people are usually employed in key posts (such as jobs of operations managers) while other staff are re-trained as operators, programmers, and data preparation staff. (78) After the new system has settled down, people in non-computer jobs are not always replaced when they leave, resulting in a decrease in the number of employees. This decrease is sometimes balanced by a substantial increase in the activity of the firm, resulting from the introduction of computers.

The attitudes of workers towards computers vary. There is fear of widespread unemployment and of the takeover of many jobs by computer-trained workers, making promotion for older workers not skilled in computers more difficult.

On the other hand, many workers regard the trend toward wider use of computers inevitable. They realize that computers bring about greater efficiency and productivity, which will improve the condition of the whole economy, and lead to the creation of more jobs. This view was supported by the former British Prime Minister, James Callaghan in 1979, when he made the point that new technologies hold the key to increased productivity, which will benefit the economy in the long run.

6. The unfriendly feeling towards computers is developed from ________.
   A. the possible widespread unemployment caused by their introduction
   B. their use as part of automated production systems
   C. the least possible number of operators
   D. the production system in steelworks
7. The underlined word **"They"** (Line 1, Par. 2) refers to ________.
   A. computers　B. jobs　C. activities　D. systems
8. According to Paragraph 2, without computers ________.
   A. human activities could not continue
   B. there could not be weather forecasting systems
   C. many activities would have to change their present form
   D. banks would not be able to go on with check clearing
9. According to the passage, what results from the introduction of computers?
   A. After re-training, all employees in the firm get new jobs.
   B. A considerable proportion of people are employed in key posts.
   C. The firm keeps all of its original staff members.
   D. The decrease in staff members may be balanced by the increase of firm activities.
10. James Callaghan's attitude towards computers can be best described as ________.
   A. doubtful　B. regretful　C. unfriendly　D. supportive

Passage 3　Questions 11 to 15 are based on the following passage:

The vitamins necessary for a healthy body are normally supplied by a good mixed diet (饮食), including a variety of fruits and green vegetables. (79) It is only when people try to live on a very restricted diet that it is necessary to make special provision to supply the missing vitamins.

An example of the dangers of a restricted diet may be seen in the disease known as "beri-beri". (80) It used to distress large numbers of Eastern peoples who lived mainly on rice. In the early years of this century, a scientist named Eijkman was trying to discover the cause of "beri-beri". At first he thought it was caused by a germ. He was working in a Japanese hospital, where the patients were fed on polished rice which had the outer husk (外壳) removed from the grain. It was thought this would be easier for weak and sick people to digest.

Eijkman thought his germ theory was confirmed when he noticed the chickens in the hospital yard, which were fed on leftovers(剩饭) from the patients' plates, were also showing signs of the disease. He then tried to isolate the germ, but his experiments were interrupted by a hospital official, who declared that the polished rice, even though left over by the patients, was too good for chickens. It should be recooked for the patients, and the chickens should be fed on cheap rice with the outer layer still on the grain.

Eijkman noticed that the chickens began to recover on the new diet. He began to consider the possibility that eating unpolished rice somehow prevented or cured "beri-beri"—even that a lack of some element in the husk might be the cause of the disease. Indeed this was the case. The element needed to prevent "beri-beri" was shortly afterwards isolated from rice husks and is now known as vitamin B. Nowadays, this terrible disease is much less common thanks to our knowledge of vitamins.

11. A good mixed diet ________.
   A. normally contains enough vitamins　B. still needs special provision of vitamins
   C. is suitable for losing weight　D. is composed of fruits and vegetables
12. The disease "beri-beri" ________.
   A. kills large numbers of Eastern peoples　B. is a vitamin deficiency (缺乏) disease
   C. is caused by diseased rice　D. can be caught from diseased chickens
13. The chickens Eijkman noticed in the hospital yard ________.

A. couldn't digest the polished rice
B. proved "beri-beri" is caused by germs
C. were later cooked for the patients' food
D. were suffering from"beri-beri"

14. According to Eijkman, polished rice ________.
A. was cheaper than unpolished rice
B. was less nourishing (有营养的) than unpolished rice
C. was more nourishing than unpolished rice
D. cured "beri-beri"

15. The chemical substance missing from polished rice ________.
A. was vitamin
B. did not affect the chickens
C. was named the Eijkman vitamin
D. has never been accurately identified

Part II Vocabulary and Structure(30%)

16. By no means ________ to move to a new place far away from her workplace, because it isn't convenient for her family and herself.
A. Jane will agree B. will Jane agree C. Jane will disagree D. will Jane disagree

17. You can, ________ the sky is clear, see as far as the old temple on top of the mountain, but not today.
A. when B. where C. though D. because

18. With everything she needed ________ she went out of the shop, with her hands full of shopping bags.
A. bought B. to buy C. buying D. buy

19. Having taken our seats, ________.
A. the professor began the lecture
B. the lecture began in no time
C. we were attracted by the lecturer immediately
D. the bell announced the beginning of the lecture

20. In recent years many football clubs ________ as business to make a profit.
A. have run B. have been run C. had been run D. will run

21. After 15 years in the United States, he has finally decided to ________ American citizenship.
A. concentrate on B. apply for C. look out for D. appeal on

22. It is well known that teaching is a job ________ enough patience.
A. calling on B. calling off C. calling for D. calling in

23. Surely it doesn't matter where the clubs get their money; what ________ is what they do with it.
A. counts B. applies C. stresses D. functions

24. I didn't expect to receive a postcard from you! It's really ________ my wildest imagination.
A. behind B. beyond C. except D. through

25. It doesn't make ________ to buy that expensive coat when these cheaper ones are just as good.
A. sense B. opinion C. use D. program

26. The task is too much for me, so I can't carry on ________ any longer. I must get some help.
A. singly B. simply C. alone D. lonely

27. Americans eat ________ vegetables per person today as they did in 1910.
A. more than twice
B. as twice as many
C. twice as many
D. more than twice as many

28. The two girls are getting on very well and share ________ with each other.
A. little B. much C. some D. none

29. The taxi driver was put in ________ prison because his car had knocked down a child. His wife went to ________ prison to see him twice a month.
A. /; / B. the; the C. /; the D. the; /

30. Without my glasses I can hardly ________ what has been written in the letter.
A. make for B. make up C. make out D. make over

31. Her heart ________ faster when she entered the exam hall.

A. jumped B. sank C. beat D. hit

32. Would you mind keeping a(n) ________ on the house for us while we are away?
A. eye B. look C. hand D. view

33. I am afraid that his phone number has slipped my ________ for the moment.
A. head B. brain C. mind D. sense

34. It was the wealth of the ________ pioneer landowner John Harvard that made Harvard University possible.
A. precious B. curious C. anxious D. prosperous

35. I am not sure whether we can give the right advice ________ emergency.
A. on account of B. in case of C. at the risk of D. in spite of

36. Vingo was released from prison ________ the successful efforts of his friends to prove his innocence.
A. according to B. as a result of C. for reasons of D. with the help of

37. Some of the meat came from Canada. How about ________?
A. another B. the other C. others D. the rest

38. The man has a special talent for art and is ________ of a musician.
A. anybody B. anything C. somebody D. something

39. I know Jonathan quite well and never doubt ________ he can do a good job of it.
A. whether B. that C. when D. what

40. How many more decades will have to pass ________ scientists succeed in providing a cure for cancer?
A. when B. before C. since D. until

41. The engineer is not happy with the project, and ________ is her boss.
A. neither B. so C. either D. as

42. ________ for a long time, but he tried his best to catch up with his classmates.
A. Having been ill B. Being ill C. Though he was ill D. He was ill

43. How close parents are to their children ________ a strong influence on the development of the children's character.
A. have B. has C. having D. had

44. He changed his name, ________ that nobody would find out what he had done before.
A. having thought B. to think C. thinks D. thinking

45. There is so much work ________ today. Would you be kind enough to lend me a hand?
A. having done B. to be done C. being done D. will be done

Part III Identification (10%)

46. <u>A</u> container <u>weighs</u> more after air <u>is put</u> in, <u>it</u> proves that air has weight.
A B C D

47. The young man, <u>to make</u> several attempts <u>to beat</u> the world record in high jumping, <u>decided</u> to have <u>another try</u>.
A B C D

48. <u>Of</u> the two coats, <u>I'd choose</u> <u>the cheapest</u> one to spare some money <u>for</u> a book.
A B C D

49. The protection <u>of</u> our environment <u>is</u> not <u>nothing</u> to be left to the government. Everyone should <u>be concerned</u>.
A B C D

50. <u>There are</u> moments in life <u>where</u> you miss someone so much <u>that</u> you just <u>want to</u> pick them up from dreams and hug them for real.
A B C D

51. <u>None of us</u> had <u>the final say</u> in this matter, and <u>therefore</u> it was recommended that we <u>waited</u> for the authorities.
A B C D

52. <u>After</u> her two-week vacation was <u>over</u>, Dorothy regretted <u>to spend</u> so much money for <u>so little pleasure</u>.
A B C D

53. Don't <u>make</u>Helen's remarks too <u>seriously</u>. She is so <u>upset</u> that I don't think she really knows <u>what she is saying</u>.
A B C D

54. Workers newly <u>arrive</u> from the south <u>or</u> rural areas perform their job <u>differently</u> from those from <u>other sections</u> of the city.
A B C D

55. While(A) remembered(B) mainly for the invention(C) of the telephone, Alexander Graham Bell devoted his life to help(D) the deaf.

Part IV Cloze (10%)

Conversation begins almost the moment we come into contact with another and continues throughout the day __56__ the aid of cell phones and computers. However, we are so often absorbed in conversation that we __57__ sight of its true purpose and value.

One important __58__ of a good conversation is that the words are __59__ used to express thoughts and feelings. We are __60__ deep thoughts and strong emotions, yet our vocabularies are not __61__ for this expression, and many __62__ little effort to expand that. Perhaps you see a movie that __63__ you deeply, yet you have the following conversation: "So, what did you think of the film?" "Oh, my God, it was so sad, I swear. I went through __64__ a box of tissues(面巾纸). I was in tears." This dialogue is __65__ an effective way of expressing feelings. It gives no __66__ of how or why the movie truly __67__ you. Such commonly-used phrases are certainly not enough to describe a deeply moving experience. However, not only __68__ try to avoid overused words, you must __69__ be careful in your selection. The purpose of expanding vocabulary is not to use the __70__ or most impressive words, but to find those best suited.

What is lacking in many conversations is the ability to talk to another rather than just talking with that person. A __71__ person will find that even in the most ordinary conversations. There are a thousand questions __72__ to be asked if you have courage and a desire for exchange. Good conversations should not be __73__ nonsense, but of a meeting of two __74__ the human condition. It should bring a better understanding of others and offer a release of emotions more than drive away __75__ thoughts or kill time.

56. A. for	B. at	C. under	D. with
57. A. lose	B. have	C. win	D. miss
58. A. issue	B. problem	C. aspect	D. question
59. A. funny	B. careful	C. only	D. properly
60. A. lack of	B. short of	C. fond of	D. full of
61. A. short	B. enough	C. much	D. bad
62. A. take	B. make	C. get	D. try
63. A. teaches	B. pushes	C. touches	D. directs
64. A. using up	B. to use	C. used up	D. using off
65. A. partly	B. actually	C. hardly	D. truly
66. A. sign	B. model	C. pattern	D. fact
67. A. infected	B. infects	C. affects	D. affected
68. A. you will	B. must you	C. you must	D. will you
69. A. too	B. never	C. also	D. yet
70. A. bigger	B. biggest	C. big	D. important
71. A. careless	B. efficient	C. thoughtful	D. able
72. A. waiting	B. wait	C. waited	D. waits
73. A. make up for	B. made up of	C. make up of	D. made up for
74. A. are sharing	B. shared	C. sharing	D. shares
75. A. clever	B. pleasant	C. unpleasant	D. happy

Part V Translation (20%)

Section A

76. It has become harder and harder for a teenager to stand up against the popularity wave and to go his or her own way.
77. Much unfriendly feeling towards computers has been based on the fear of widespread unemployment resulting from their introduction.

78. After the new system has settled down, people in non-computer jobs are not always replaced when they leave, resulting in a decrease in the number of employees.
79. It is only when people try to live on a very restricted diet that it is necessary to make special provision to supply the missing vitamins.
80. It used to distress large numbers of Eastern peoples who lived mainly on rice.

Section B

81. 他们5年前搬走了,但我们还保持联系。
82. 看起来这封信是在匆忙中写成的。
83. 在得到更多细节之前,我想避免跟他说话。
84. 每当听到这首歌时,我就会想起你。
85. 由于很多学生缺席,我们不得不将会议延期。

参考答案

1—15　BCABC　ABCDD　ABDBA
16—45　BAACB　BCABA　CCBCC　CACDB　BCBBB　ADBDB
46—55　DACCB　DCAAD
56—75　DACDD　BBCAC　DCBCB　CABCC
76. 青少年要想保持自己的行事原则,不追逐潮流越来越难了。
77. 很多人对计算机的敌对情绪缘于担心计算机的应用会导致他们失业。
78. 在新的系统引进后,没有从事计算机相关工作的人员在离职后不再进行补充,从而导致员工人数下降。
79. 只有在人们饮食比较单一的情况下,才有必要补充饮食中缺失的维生素。
80. 以大米为主食的东方人常患有这种疾病。
81. They moved 5 years ago, but we still keep in touch.
82. It seemed that the letter was finished in a hurry.
83. I tried to avoid talking to him before I got more details.
84. The song reminds me of you every time I listen to it.
85. We have to put off the meeting because many students are absent.

北京地区成人本科学士学位英语统一考试(A)

2009.11.21

Part I　Reading Comprehension (30%)

Passage 1　Questions 1 to 5 are based on the following passage:

According to a recent survey, employees in many companies today work longer hours than employees did in 1979. They also take shorter vacations than employees in 1979. It seems that Americans are working harder today than ever before. Or are they? A management consultant, Bill Meyer, decided to find out. For three days, he observed an investment banker hard at work. Meyer wrote down everything the banker did during his long workday. At the end of the three-day period, Meyer reviewed the banker's activities with him. What did they find out? They discovered that the man spent 80 percent of his time doing unnecessary work. For example, he attended unnecessary meetings, made redundant (多余的) telephone calls, and spent time packing and unpacking his two big brief cases.

(76) Apparently many people believe that the more time a person spends at work, the more he or she accomplishes. When employers evaluate employees, they often consider the amount of time on the job in addition to job performance. Employees know this. Although many working people can do their job effectively during a regular 40-hour work week, they feel they have to spend more time on the job after normal working hours so that the people who can promote them see them.

A group of headhunters (猎头) were asked their opinion about a situation. They had a choice of two candidates for an executive position with an important company. The candidates had similar qualifications for the job. For example, they were both reliable. One could do the job well in a 40-hour work week. The other would do the same job in an 80-hour work week just as well. According to a headhunting expert, the 80-hour-a-week candidate would get the job. The time this candidate spends on the job may encourage other employees to spend more time at work, too. Employers believe that if the employees stay at work later, they may actually do more work.

However, the connection between time and productivity (生产率) is not always positive. (77) In fact, many studies indicate that after a certain point, anyone's productivity and creativity begin to decrease. Some employees are not willing to spend so much extra, unproductive time at the office. Once they finish their work satisfactorily, they want to relax and enjoy themselves. For these people, the solution is to find a company that encourages people to do both.

1. What is the main idea of this passage?
   A. Many people work long hours but do not always do a lot of work.
   B. Most people can get more work done by working longer hours.
   C. Most Americans work 80 hours a week, and some work even longer.
   D. People can make more money by working longer hours.
2. The management consultant wanted to find out ________.
   A. how hard the investment banker worked during his work hours
   B. when people spent time doing unnecessary work in their office
   C. if people needed vacation after working hard for a certain period of time
   D. whether Americans were really working harder than they had done before
3. Which of the following statements is TRUE?
   A. The more time a person spends at work, the more he or she accomplishes.
   B. Employers do not judge their employees' job performance according to the amount of working time.
   C. Some people work more than 40 hours a week in the hope of getting promotion.
   D. All employees are willing to spend extra time at work.
4. The 80-hour-a-week candidate would get the job because employers believe ________.
   A. that he is more reliable
   B. his example would lead other employees to work longer hours
   C. he has better qualifications
   D. he could encourage other employees to do a better job
5. The expression "to do both" in the last paragraph is ________.
   A. to finish their work satisfactorily and relax and enjoy themselves
   B. to pay attention to both performance and productivity
   C. to work long hours and have short vacations
   D. to relax and enjoy themselves quite frequently

Passage 2 Questions 6 to 10 are based on the following passage:

Many private institutions of higher education around the country are in danger. Not all will be saved, and perhaps not all deserve to be saved. There are low-quality schools just as there are low-quality businesses. We have no obligation to save them simply because they exist. But many thriving institutions that deserve to continue are threatened. They are doing a fine job educationally, but they are caught in a financial difficulty, with no way to reduce rising costs or increase revenues (收入) significantly. Raising fees doesn't bring in more revenue, for each time fees go up, the enrollment (注册人数) goes down, or the mount that must be given away in student aid goes up. (78) Schools are bad businesses, whether public or private, not usually because of bad management but because of the nature of the business. They lose money on every customer, and they can go bankrupt either from too few students or too many students. Even a very good college is a very bad business.

It is such colleges, thriving but threatened, that I worry about. Low enrollment is not their chief problem. Even with full enrollments, they may go under. Efforts to save them, and preferably to keep them private, are a national necessity. (79) There is no basis for arguing that private schools are bound to be better than public schools. There are plentiful examples to the contrary. Anyone can name state universities and colleges that rank as the finest in the nation and the world. It is now inevitable that public institutions will be dominant, and therefore diversity (多样性) is a national necessity. Diversity in the way we support schools tends to give us a healthy diversity in the forms of education. In an imperfect society such as ours, uniformity of education throughout the nation could be dangerous; in an imperfect society, diversity is a positive good. Eager supporters of public higher education know the importance of keeping private higher education healthy.

6. In the passage, the author asks the public to support ________.
   A. private higher education in general
   B. public higher education in general
   C. high-quality private universities and colleges
   D. high-quality state universities and colleges
7. According to the passage, schools are bad businesses because of ________.
   A. the nature of school　　B. poor teachers
   C. bad management　　D. too few students.
8. The phrase "go under" in the second paragraph is closest in meaning to ________.
   A. have low fees　　B. get into difficulties
   C. do a bad job educationally　　D. have low teaching standards
9. Which of the following statements is TRUE?
   A. There are many cases indicating that private schools are superior to public schools.
   B. The author thinks diversity of education is preferable to uniformity of education.
   C. A high-quality university is always a good business.
   D. Each time fees are raised, the enrollment goes up.
10. In the author's opinion, the way that can save private schools lies in ________.
   A. full enrollment　　B. raising fees
   C. reducing student aid　　D. national support

Passage 3　Questions 11 to 15 are based on the following passage:

The fourth-graders at Chicago's McCormick Elementary School don't know Chinese is supposed to be hard to learn. For most, who speak Spanish at home, it's becoming their third language. They've been hearing and using Chinese words since nursery, and it's natural to give a "ni hao" when strangers enter the classroom. "It's really fun!" says Miranda Lucas, taking a break from a lesson that includes a Chinese interview with Jackie Chan. "I'm teaching my mom to speak Chinese."

The classroom scene at McCormick is unusual, but it may soon be a common phenomenon in American schools, where Chinese is rapidly becoming the hot new language. Government officials have long wanted more focus on useful languages like Chinese, and pressure from them — as well as from business leaders, politicians, and parents — has produced a quick growth in the number of programs.

Chicago city officials make their best effort to include Chinese in their public schools. Their program has grown to include 3,000 students in 20 schools, with more schools on a waiting list. Programs have also spread to places like Los Angeles, New York City, and North Carolina. Supporters see knowledge of the Chinese language and culture as an advantage in a global economy where China is growing in importance. "This is an interesting way to begin to engage with the world's next superpower," says Michael Levine, director of education at the Asia Society, which has started five new public high schools that offer Chinese. "Globalization has already changed the arrangements in terms of how children today are going to think about their careers. The question is when, not whether, the schools are going to adjust."

(80) The number of students learning Chinese is tiny compared with how many study Spanish or French. But one report shows that before-college enrollment (报名人数) nearly quadrupled between 1992 and 2002, from 6,000 to 24,000. Despite the demand, though, developing programs isn't easy. And the No. one difficulty, everyone agrees, is having enough teachers. Finding teacher "is the challenge," says Scott McGinnis, an academic

adviser for a language institute and a Chinese teacher for 15 years at the college level. "Materials are easy comparison. Or getting schools funded."

11. The best title for this passage might be ________.
    A. Next Hot Language to Study: Chinese
    B. Next Hot Language to Study: Spanish
    C. Next Hot Language to Study: French
    D. Chicago Is the Place to Learn Chinese
12. The most difficult thing to do is finding ________.
    A. enough textbooks for the Chinese programs
    B. enough money for the Chinese programs
    C. enough teachers for the Chinese programs
    D. enough students for the Chinese programs
13. We learn from the passage that ________.
    A. Scott McGinnis has been a Chinese teacher for 15 years
    B. Jackie Chan is a Chinese teacher at McCormick Elementary School
    C. Chicago officials ire required to learn Chinese
    D. Scott McGinnis is good at giving his opinions on everything
14. According to the passage, all the following statements are true EXCEPT ________.
    A. the number of students learning Chinese is small
    B. Chinese programs have found their way in several major Cities in the U.S.
    C. government officials don't like the pressure from business leaders and parents to start Chinese programs
    D. China is becoming more and more influential in the world
15. The word "quadrupled" in the last paragraph is close in meaning to "multiplied by ________."
    A. three times B. four times
    C. five times D. six times

Part II Vocabulary and Structure (30%)

16. The driver was at ________ loss when ________ word came that he was forbidden to drive for speeding.
    A. a; / B. a; the C. the; the D. /; /
17. My uncle's house in the downtown area is much smaller than ours, but it is twice ________ expensive.
    A. as B. so C. too D. very
18. This magazine is very ________ with young people, who like its content and style.
    A. familiar B. popular C. similar D. particular
19. The art show was ________ being a failure; it was a great success.
    A. far from B. along with C. second to D. regardless of
20. Health problems are closely connected with bad eating habits and a ________ of exercise.
    A. limit B. lack C. need D. demand
21. In our daily life, everyone fails every now and then. It is how you react that makes a ________.
    A. development B. difference C. progress D. point
22. The hotel was awful! ________, our room was far too small. Then we found that the shower didn't work.
    A. To begin with B. After all C. In reality D. As a whole
23. Don't worry if you can't understand everything. The teacher will ________ the main points at the end.
    A. recover B. review C. require D. remember
24. It is reported that the police will soon look ________ the case of the two missing children.
    A. upon B. after C. into D. out
25. One of the best ways for people to keep fit is to ________ healthy eating habits.
    A. grow B. develop C. increase D. raise
26. The company is starting a new advertising campaign to ________ new customers to its stores.
    A. join B. attract C. stick D. transfer

27. Over the past decades, sea ice in the Arctic(北极) as a result of global warming ________.
A. had decreased　　B. will decrease
C. has been decreasing　　D. is decreasing

28. ________ twice, the postman refused to deliver our letters unless we chained our dog.
A. Being bitten　　B. Bitten　　C. Having bitten　　D. To be bitten

29. He ________ have completed his work; otherwise, he wouldn't be enjoying himself by the seaside.
A. should　　B. must　　C. wouldn't　　D. can't

30. Many children, ________ parents are away working in big cities, are taken good care of in the village.
A. their　　B. whose　　C. of them　　D. with whom

31. If it ________ tomorrow, we will stay indoors to have our training class.
A. rains　　B. rain　　C. will rain　　D. rained

32. The college sports meet was ________ till next week because of the heavy rain.
A. put out　　B. put on　　C. put off　　D. put up

33. Lord Jim ________ a private school five years ago with the money he earned through hard work.
A. finds　　B. found　　C. founds　　D. founded

34. When Bob and his friends came, we ________ our supper then.
A. had　　B. were having　　C. have　　D. are having

35. That big dictionary ________ Tom two hundred dollars.
A. spent　　B. paid　　C. cost　　D. took

36. It was in 2005 ________ we began to introduce this new technique into our company.
A. which　　B. then　　C. when　　D. that

37. He ________ the maths examination if he had worked hard enough, but he didn't.
A. would pass　　B. has passed　　C. would have passed　　D. passed

38. Since it is already midnight, we ________ now.
A. had better leaving　　B. had better leave
C. had better to leave　　D. had better have left

39. Rabbits are quiet animals, ________ they are able to make 20 different sounds.
A. how　　B. in spite of　　C. because of　　D. even though

40. There are two rooms in the house, ________ serves as a kitchen.
A. the smaller of which　　B. the smaller of that
C. the smallest of which　　D. the smallest of that

41. I was so tired that I fell ________ in class.
A. asleep　　B. sleep　　C. sleeping　　D. slept

42. I can only stay here for a while, but I'll come again in ________ days.
A. a few　　B. few　　C. a little　　D. little

43. Given the choice between work and play, Tom would surely prefer the ________.
A. late　　B. later　　C. latter　　D. last

44. He began to work for a big company ________ an early age.
A. on　　B. at　　C. of　　D. with

45. James doesn't like pop music, ________ does his sister.
A. so　　B. also　　C. either　　D. neither

Part III　Identification (10%)

46. <u>How</u> an interesting role she <u>played</u> in the film! <u>No wonder</u> she <u>has won</u> an Oscar.
(A: How; B: played; C: No wonder; D: has won)

47. <u>The</u> famous scientist, <u>in his honor</u> a dinner party <u>will be held</u> tonight, <u>is to</u> arrive soon.
(A: The; B: in his honor; C: will be held; D: is to)

48. The old man <u>was so</u> angry and spoke so <u>fast</u> that <u>none of</u> his children understood <u>that</u> he meant.
(A: was so; B: fast; C: none of; D: that)

49. The young man, to make several attempts to beat the world record in high jumping, decided to have another try.
(A: to make; B: attempts to; C: world; D: decided to)

50. In the town was found many old people who badly needed money and care.
(A: In; B: was; C: who; D: needed)

51. As early as the 12th century boys in England enjoyed to play football.
(A: As early as; B: the 12th century; C: in; D: to play)

52. So absorbed she was in her work that she didn't realize it was time that she picked up her daughter.
(A: So; B: she was; C: that; D: it was)

53. In big cities there is an increasingly need for cheap apartments for the lower middle class.
(A: cities; B: is; C: increasingly; D: for)

54. The price of meat was much more higher than expected.
(A: price; B: of; C: more higher; D: expected)

55. Joe's father has died ten years ago, so he has lived with his mother since then.
(A: has died; B: so; C: he has lived; D: since then)

Part IV Cloze (10%)

There __56__ a king who had twelve beautiful daughters. They __57__ in twelve beds all in one room and when they went to bed, the __58__ were shut and locked up. __59__, every morning __60__ shoes were found to be quite worn through as if they had been danced in all night. Nobody could __61__ how it happened, or __62__ the princesses had been.

So the king made it __63__ to all that if any person could discover the __64__ and find out where it was that the princesses danced in the __65__, he would have the __66__ he liked best to take as his wife, and would be king __67__ his death. But whoever tried and did not succeed, after three days and nights, would be __68__ to death.

A prince from a nearby country soon came. He was well entertained, and in the evening was taken to the chamber (大房间) next __69__ the one where the princesses lay in their twelve __70__. There he was to sit and __71__ where they went to dance; and, in order __72__ nothing could happen without him hearing it, the door of his __73__ was left open. But the prince soon went to sleep; and when, he __74__ in the morning he found that the princesses had all been dancing, __75__ the soles of their shoes were full of holes.

56. A. was	B. were	C. is	D. are
57. A. did	B. slept	C. washed	D. kicked
58. A. chairs	B. desks	C. doors	D. roofs
59. A. So	B. Therefore	C. Then	D. However
60. A. their	B. your	C. our	D. her
61. A. make out	B. take out	C. find out	D. speak out
62. A. when	B. what	C. why	D. where
63. A. know	B. knowing	C. knows	D. known
64. A. story	B. secret	C. news	D. idea
65. A. night	B. day	C. afternoon	D. morning
66. A. one	B. it	C. some	D. that
67. A. before	B. after	C. of	D. below
68. A. made	B. passed	C. put	D. handed
69. A. by	B. to	C. at	D. on
70. A. boxes	B. buckets	C. sofas	D. beds
71. A. notice	B. keep	C. watch	D. hit
72. A. that	B. which	C. who	D. whose
73. A. kitchen	B. classroom	C. chamber	D. restaurant
74. A. ate	B. awoke	C. slept	D. ran
75. A. for	B. so	C. but	D. though

Part V Translation (20%)

Section A

76. Apparently, many people believe that the more time a person spends at work, the more he or she accomplishes.
77. In fact, many studies indicate that after a certain point, anyone's productivity and creativity begin to decrease.
78. Schools are bad businesses, whether public or private, not usually because of bad management but because of the nature of the business.
79. There is no basis for arguing that private schools are bound to be better than public schools.
80. The number of students learning Chinese is tiny compared with how many study Spanish or French.

Section B

81. 我们期待和你一起工作。
82. 他一到上海就给我打了一个长途电话。
83. 你知道会议开始的确切时间吗?
84. 她将成功归因于努力工作。
85. 村里的每个人都喜欢他,因为他对人很友好。

参考答案

1—15 ADCBA CABBD ACACB
16—45 AABAB BABCB BCBBB ACDBC DCBDA AACBD
46—55 ABDAB DBCCA
56—75 ABCDA CDDBA ABCBD CACBA
76. 显然,很多人认为一个人花在工作上的时间越多,他完成的工作就越多。
77. 事实上,许多研究结果表明在工作到一定程度后,任何人的生产力和创造力都会开始下降。
78. 学校经营不善,无论是公立学校还是私立学校,原因并不在于管理糟糕,而在于学校经营本身。
79. 私立学校一定好于公立学校这一说法并无依据。
80. 与学习西班牙语和法语的学生数量相比,学习中文的学生还很少。
81. We are looking forward to working with you.
82. He gave me a long-distance calls upon his arrival at Shanghai.
83. Do you know when exactly the meeting is to begin?
84. She owes her success to hard work.
85. Everyone in the village liked him because he was very friendly people.

北京地区成人本科学士学位英语统一考试(A)

2010.05.08

Part I Reading Comprehension (30%)

Passage 1 Questions 1 to 5 are based on the following passage:

The multi-billion-dollar Western pop music industry is **under fire**. It is being blamed by the United Nations for the dramatic rise in drug abuse worldwide. "The most worrying development is a culture of drug-friendliness," says the UN's International Narcotics Control Board in a report released last year.

The 74 page study says that pop music, as a global industry, is by far the most influential trend setter for young people of most cultures. "Some songs encourage people to take drugs. (76) <u>Certain pop stars make statements and set examples as if the use of drugs for non-medicinal purposes were a normal and acceptable part of a person's lifestyle</u>," the study says.

Surprisingly, says the Board, the effect of drug-friendly pop music seems to survive despite the occasional shock of death by overdose (过量用药). "Such incidents tend to be seen as an occasion to mourn (哀悼) the loss of a role model, and not an opportunity to face the deadly effect of drug use," it notes. Since the 1970s, several internationally famous singers and movie stars—including Elvis Presley, Janice Joplin, John Belushi, Jimi Hendrix, Jonathan Melvin and Andy Gibbs—have died of either drug abuse or drug related illnesses. With the globalization of popular music, messages promoting, drug abuse are now reaching beyond their countries of origin. "In most countries, the names of certain POP stars have become familiar to the members of every household," the study says.

The UN study also blames the media for its description of certain drug incidents, which encourages rather than prevents drug abuse. "Over the past years, we have seen how drug abuse is increasingly regarded as being acceptable or even attractive," says Hamid Ghodse, president of the Board. "Powerful pressure groups and political campaigns aimed at legalizing controlled drugs," he says. Ghodse also points out that all the developments have created an environment which is tolerant(容忍的) of or even favorable to drug abuse and spoils international drug prevention efforts currently under way.

The study focuses on demand reduction and prevention within an environment that has become tolerant of drug abuse. The Board calls on governments to do their legal and moral duties, and to act against the pro-drug (赞成吸毒) messages of the youth culture to which young people increasingly are being exposed.

1. Which of the following statements does the author tend to agree with?
   A. The use of drugs for non-medicinal purposes is, an acceptable part of a person's lifestyle.
   B. The spreading of pop music may cause drug abuse to go beyond country boundaries.
   C. No efforts have been made to prevent the spreading of drug abuse.
   D. Governments have no ability to act against the pro-drug messages of the youth culture.
2. The expression "**under fire**" in the first paragraph means ________.
   A. in an urgent situation　　B. facing some problems
   C. being criticized　　D. in trouble
3. From the third paragraph, we learn that the youth ________.
   A. tend to mourn the pop stars who died of overdose as role models
   B. are shocked to know even pop stars may abuse drugs
   C. try to face the deadly effect of drug use
   D. may stop abusing drugs
4. Which of the following is not mentioned as tolerant of drug abuse?
   A. The spreading of pop music.
   B. The media.
   C. Political campaigns run by powerful pressure groups.
   D. The low price of some drugs.
5. According to the passage, pop music ________.
   A. has a great influence on young people of most cultures
   B. attracts a small number of young people
   C. is not a profitable industry
   D. is alone responsible for drug abuse

Passage 2　Questions 6 to 10 are based on the following passage:

There are many older people in the world and there will be many more. A little-known fact is that over 60 percent of the older people live in developing countries. According to the World Health Organization, by 2020 there will be 1 billion, with over 700 million living in developing countries.

It is a surprising fact that the population ageing is particularly rapid in developing countries. For example, it took France 115 years for the proportion of older people to double from 7 percent to 14 percent. It is estimated to take China a mere 27 years to achieve this same increase.

What are the implications of these increased numbers of older folk? (77) One of the biggest worries for governments is that the longer people live, the more likelihood there is for diseases and for disability(残疾).

Attention is being paid to the need to keep people as healthy as possible, including during old age, to lessen the financial burden on the state.

(78) Another significant problem is the need for the younger generations to understand and value the older people in their society. In some African countries, certainly in Asia, older people are respected and regarded as the ones with special knowledge. Yet traditions are fading away daily, which does not ensure the continued high regard of older people. As society changes, attitudes will change.

Much needs to be done to get rid of age discrimination (歧视) in employment. Life-long learning programs need to be provided to enable older people to be active members in a country's development.

Social security policies need to be established to provide adequate income protection for older people. Both public and private schemes are vital in order to build a suitable safety net.

To achieve equality in such matters will take considerable time and effort. One thing is sure: there is no time to be lost.

6. The proportion of older people ________.
   A. is bigger in developed countries than in developing countries
   B. is one-seventh of the population in developing countries
   C. will increase much faster in China than in France
   D. will be sixty percent in developing countries by 2020
7. According to the passage, which of the following are governments most worried about?
   A. The diseases and disability of older people.
   B. The longer life and good health of people.
   C. The loss of taxes on older people.
   D. The increasing respect for older people.
8. It is stated directly in the passage that older people should ________.
   A. be treated differently in different cultures
   B. enjoy a similar lifestyle
   C. be ignored as society changes
   D. be valued by the younger generations
9. Which of the following measures is NOT mentioned to solve the population ageing problem?
   A. Getting rid of age discrimination in employment.
   B. Ensuring adequate income protection for older people.
   C. Providing free health care for sick older people.
   D. Supplying life-long learning programs to older people.
10. The author concludes in the last paragraph that ________.
   A. governments have spent lots of time in solving the ageing problem
   B. population ageing is a hard problem, but it needs to be solved urgently
   C. people are too busy to solve the population ageing problem
   D. much time and effort will be lost in solving the ageing problem

Passage 3 Questions 11 to 15 are based on the following passage:

(79) Extensive new studies suggest that the world has, made extraordinary progress in reducing poverty in recent decades. The research suggests that the pace of economic progress has been rapid and continued for decades, built on the foundations of relative political stability, rising trade, and economic liberalization (自由化) after two world wars. One new study, published recently by the Institute for International Economics in Washington, finds that the proportion of the 6.1 billion people in the world who live on $1 a day or less shrank from 63 percent in 1950 to 35 percent in 1980 and 12 percent in 1999. By some other measures, the progress has been more modest. Still, economists agree that poverty has **plunged** in key nations such as India and especially China, thanks to slowing population growth as well as economic freedom. "This is a huge success for the world as a whole," says Harvard University economist Richard Cooper. "We are doing something right."

The news comes as the World Bank is about to open its annual meeting in Washington, an event that has been troubled in recent years by protests that the Bank and its sister institution, the International Monetary Fund (IMF 国际货币基金组织), have done too little for the world's poor. (80) The new economic research will not put an end to that dispute. Vast populations remain poor, and many still question the wisdom of World Bank policies. Nonetheless, the research findings are helpful to understand what policies should be followed by these institutions and hundreds of other development groups working very hard to hasten the pace of world economic progress. If dramatic gains are under way, the present policies-calling for open markets, free business activities, and tight monetary control are working and correct.

But critics of **IMF** and World Bank policies maintain that such economic success stories as Japan, China, South Korea and Singapore are rooted in more than just "free" markets. These nations have managed to grow rapidly, and thereby reduce poverty, by limiting imports when their domestic industries were young, pushing exports to rich nations, and putting controls on purely international financial flows. They have been open to foreign-owned factories, but have often insisted that those investors share the knowledge and skill on modern technologies.

11. The word **"plunged"** in the first paragraph means ________.
A. decreased B. climbed C. increased D. dropped into water
12. From the passage, we learn that ________.
A. World Bank has done nothing to help the poor in the world
B. IMF only helps the rich in the world
C. World Bank controls all the banks in the world
D. there are some demonstrations against World Bank in recent years
13. According to this passage, in ________, the world had the largest number of poor people.
A. 1999 B. 1980 C. 1950 D. 1990
14. According to the author, the economy of East Asian countries grew very fast because of the following measures EXCEPT ________.
A. encouraging export B. opening up to foreign investments
C. limiting international financial flows D. controlling import
15. The best title for this passage might be ________.
A. China's Contribution to the Reduction of Poverty in the World
B. World Bank's Extraordinary Progress in Recent Decades
C. India's Leading Role in Reducing Global Poverty
D. Global Progress in Reducing Poverty

Part II Vocabulary and Structure (30%)

16. It was hard for him to learn English in a family, in which ________ of the parents spoke the language.
A. none B. neither C. both D. each
17. You'd better go there by train. The train ticket is ________ the plane ticket.
A. as cheap three times as B. as three times cheap as
C. three times as cheap as D. cheaper three times than
18. This new machines technically far ________ to the previous type.
A. superior B. junior C. senior D. equal
19. There is a great deal of evidence ________ that music activities engage different parts of the brain.
A. indicate B. indicating C. indicated D. to be indicating
20. She became the first woman to enter the school but withdrew after a few days ________ stress.
A. because of B. in spite of C. instead of D. in honor of
21. ________ is known to us all is that the 2012 Olympic Games will be held in London.
A. It B. What C. As D. Which
22. The discovery of these tombs is ________ for scholars' studying Chinese history.
A. of very important B. great significant
C. of great significance D. greatly importance

23. Sean's strong love for his country is ________ in his recently published poems.
A. relieved B. reflected C. responded D. recovered
24. Would you please keep silent? The weather report ________ and I want to listen.
A. is broadcast B. is being broadcast C. has been broadcast D. had been broadcast
25. The teacher stressed again that the students should not ________ any important details while retelling the story.
A. bring out B. let out C. leave out D. make out
26. The man moved ________ forward and looked over the edge, shrinking his shoulders.
A. accurately B. cautiously C. brilliantly D. disappointedly
27. The police are trying to find out the ________ of the woman killed in the traffic accident.
A. evidence B. recognition C. identity D. status
28. By no means ________ to her parents.
A. this is the first time has she lied B. this is the first time does she tell a lie
C. is this the first time she has lied D. is this the first time she was lying
29. Climate change will greatly ________ wheat and rice production if nations don't take steps now.
A. fall B. leak C. lack D. reduce
30. She always buys ________ my birthday.
A. something awful to B. anything awful to
C. something nice for D. anything nice for
31. He failed to live up to ________ had been expected of him.
A. what B. which C. that D. all
32. It is very ________ of you to arrange an early meeting between your boss and our team.
A. considerate B. Considerable C. considering D. considered
33. I would have told him about the change of time for the class, ________ to class last time.
A. did he come B. he came C. had he come D. he had come
34. The wind was so strong last night that it tore the ________ of the ship into two or three pieces.
A. mask B. mine C. sail D. satellite
35. ________ all the money people here spend eating out, restaurants' profit is still below five percent.
A. Despite B. Thanks to C. Since D. Like
36. Many a man ________ life is meaningless without a purpose.
A. thinks B. thinking C. have thought D. think
37. John left home twenty minutes ago. It is usually half an hour's drive from his home to the office here. So he ________ soon.
A. should have arrived B. need arrive C. must have arrived D. may arrive
38. ________ Hongkong, is often regarded as ________ international Centre for business, finance and tourism.
A. /; an B. An; / C. The; / D. /; the
39. They went ________ the schedule for the conference again and again until they felt satisfied with every detail of it.
A. out B. up C. over D. by
40. Schools should teach our kids various subjects, and moreover, teach them how to ________ right from wrong.
A. make B. take C. tell D. put
41. By the time you finish your homework, all of us ________ ours at hand, I'm sure.
A. will finish B. will have finished
C. have finished D. have been finishing
42. In time of trouble Charlie could always ________ a solution.
A. put aside B. look down upon C. break out D. come up with
43. Before building a house, you will have to ________ the government's permission.
A. get from B. follow C. receive D. ask for

44. The director had her assistant ________ some hot dogs for the staff members.

A. picked up　　B. picks up　　C. pick up　　D. picking up

45. ________ their hats into the air, the fans of the winning team let out loud shouts of victory.

A. To throw　　B. Thrown　　C. Throwing　　D. Being thrown

Part III　Identification (10%)

46. When you've finished with that book, don't forget to put it back on the shelf, won't you?
A B C D

47. The workers in the factory demanded that their pay would be raised by 20 percent.
A B C D

48. It remains to see whether Jim will be fit enough to play in the finals.
A B C D

49. I invited Joe and Linda as well as Tom to dinner, but neither of them came.
A B C D

50. Over the past 20 years, the Internet has helped change our world in either way or another for the better.
A B C D

51. How and why this language has survived for more than a thousand years, while spoke by very few, is hard to explain.
A B C D

52. Nearly half of Americans aged 25 and old take part in some form of continuing education.
A B C D

53. Many parents feel they need to keep a closer eye to their children because of concerns about crime and school violence.
A B C D

54. For married mothers, the time spend on child care increased to an average of 12.9 hours a week in 2009.
A B C D

55. There is an increasingly amount of evidence that more and more young people are taking an active interest in politics.
A B C D

Part IV　Cloze (10%)

Of all the websites, one that has attracted attention recently is myspace. com. Most of this attention has come from the media and tells every reason. __56__ the website should be __57__. The threat of Intemet predators (窃掠者) is indeed a tough reality, __58__ shutting down the site is not the answer. If myspace. com __59__ shut down, another site would quickly __60__ its place. Therefore, the right way is to teach teens how to use the site safely and educate them __61__ who maybe predators and how to __62__ them.

The key to __63__ safe on the Internet is to make sure that your profile (个人资料) is secure. The __64__ way is to change the privacy setting on your profile to "private", which protects your information __65__ only the people on your friend list can view it. Although this is __66__, it is not perfect. Predators can find ways to view your profile if they really want to, __67__ through hacking in (黑客入侵) or figuring out their way onto your friend list. Thus, you should never post too much personal __68__. Some people actually post their home and school addresses, date of birth, and so on, often __69__ predators know exactly where they will be and __70__.

The most information that is safe is your first name and province. Anything more is basically __71__ a predator into your life.

Another big problem is photos. I suggest __72__ skipping photos and never posting a photo of a friend online without his or her __73__.

Most important, never, __74__ any circumstances, agree to a real-life meeting with anyone you meet online, __75__ how well you think you know this person. There are no guarantees that they have told the truth.

56. A. What　　B. How　　C. Why　　D. Which

57. A. shut down　　B. open up　　C. get into　　D. turn on

58. A. but　　B. even　　C. despite　　D. since

59. A. is	B. are	C. was	D. were
60. A. get	B. make	C. take	D. push
61. A. as	B. about	C. for	D. in
62. A. avoid	B. get	C. benefit	D. hide
63. A. stay	B. be staying	C. stayed	D. staying
64. A. difficult	B. simplest	C. simple	D. most difficult
65. A. as to	B. no matter	C. so that	D. because
66. A. efficient	B. interesting	C. effective	D. impressive
67. A. if	B. whether	C. however	D. whatever
68. A. information	B. documents	C. fries	D. messages
69. A. let	B. make	C. allow	D. letting
70. A. what	B. why	C. when	D. how
71. A. introducing	B. inviting	C. investing	D. interrupting
72. A. partly	B. mostly	C. lastly	D. completely
73. A. favor	B. rule	C. Information	D. permission
74. A. above	B. under	C. below	D. at
75. A. no matter	B. even if	C. unless	D. also

Part V Translation (20%)

Section A

76. Certain pop stars make statements and set examples as if the use of drugs for non-medicinal purposes were a normal and acceptable part of a person's lifestyle...
77. One of the biggest worries for governments is that the longer people live, the more likelihood there is for diseases and for disability (残疾).
78. Another significant problem is the need for the younger generations to understand and value the older people in their society.
79. Extensive new studies suggest that the world has made extraordinary progress reducing poverty in recent decades.
80. The new economic research will not put an end to that dispute.

Section B

81. 今天早上他起床晚了，所以没有赶上火车。
82. 你们昨天的会议得出什么结论了吗？
83. 我在回家的路上，买了一本英汉词典。
84. 一直到 12 月下旬，他们才让我加入他们小组。
85. 我父亲在找工作，我母亲在医院照看外祖母。

参考答案

1—15 BCADA CADCB ADCBD
16—45 BCABA BCBBC BCCDC AACCA ADACC BDDCC
46—55 DCBDC CCBBA
56—75 CAADC BADBC CBADC BDDBA
76. 某些流行歌手和影星发表了一些言论并且树立了这样一些典范，仿佛非医疗用途服用药物是一个人生活当中最为正常不过并且可以被接受的方面。
77. 政府最为头疼的事情之一在于，人们的寿命越长，就会出现越多的疾病和残疾。
78. 另外一个重要的问题在于，要让年轻人理解和尊重老年人在社会上的价值。
79. 最近的新型研究显示，我们的社会已经在最近几十年中，在减少贫困人口方面做出了很大贡献。
80. 新型的经济研究，也不会将这一争论进行终结。
81. He got up so late this morning that he missed the train.

82. Did you draw any conclusion at yesterday's meeting?
83. I bought an English-Chinese dictionary on my way home.
84. They didn't allow me to join their group until the end of December.
85. My dad is looking for a job while my mother is looking after my grandmother.

北京地区成人本科学士学位英语统一考试

2016.11.05

Part I Reading Comprehension(30%)

Directions: There are three passages in this Part. Each passage is followed by some questions or unfinished statements. For each of them there are four choices marked A, B, C and D. You should decide on the best choice and blacken the corresponding letter on the Answer Sheet.

Passage 1 Questions 1 to 5 are based on the following passage:

If the Dakota Access Pipeline(输油管道) is completed, it will carry nearly half a million barrels of oil across four states every day. Energy Transfer Partners (ETP), a Texas-based company behind the $3.8 billion project, hopes to finish construction this year. But the Standing Rock Sioux, an American Indian tribe (部落), is determined to stop the 1,172-mile pipeline from being built. (76) Both sides show no signs of backing down.

The Dakota Access Pipeline was announced in 2014. A section of it will run near the Standing Rock Sioux reservation. A reservation is an area of land set aside for American Indians. The tribe says the construction threatens to destroy historical areas and ancient burial sites. They also say the pipeline could pollute their main water source, the Missouri River. In April, the Standing Rock Sioux began a protest against the project. They camped at the construction site. Since then, thousands of people, including people from other American Indian tribes, have traveled to the site to join the protest.

ETP says that the pipeline will have built-in safety measures to protect against oil leaks. Workers will also monitor it remotely, and will be able to close valves(阀) within three minutes if leaks are detected.

American Indians have been staging a nonviolent protest for months. The protest took a turn last week when police were called to keep the peace between protesters and armed security guards hired by the company.

(77) Twenty-eight people have been arrested since then and charged with interfering with the pipeline construction.

1. Which of the following is the main idea of the passage?
   A. The Dakota Access Pipeline will create more markets for oil and gas.
   B. The Dakota Access Pipeline will create many job opportunities.
   C. American Indians oppose the construction of an oil pipeline.
   D. American Indians fight for equal voting rights.
2. ETP hopes to finish this project in ________.
   A. 2016 B. 2017 C. 2018 D. 2019
3. Why do American Indians protest against the construction of this pipeline?
   A. Because it will cost up to $3.8 billion.
   B. Because it threatens the region's water supply.
   C. Because it will make many people lose their jobs.
   D. Because it will force many people to leave their homes.
4. According to the passage, the workers can ________ in case of pipeline leaks.
   A. report it to the local government B. ask people to leave the leak affected areas
   C. call 911 D. close valves
5. According to the passage, which of the following statements is NOT TRUE?
   A. This pipeline will cross four states.
   B. This pipeline is 1,172 miles long.

C. All the protesters are from the Standing Rock Sioux.

D. Neither side of the dispute is willing to compromise.

Passage 2 Questions 6 to 10 are based on the following passage:

As the National Park Service celebrates its 100th anniversary (周年纪念), President Barack Obama has announced the establishment of one new national monument, and the expansion (扩大) of another, in Maine, more than 87,500 acres of forest will become government-protected parkland for the first time. In Hawaii, a national monument created by President George W. Bush in 2006 will expand to about 582,578 square miles, four times its current size.

Obama has now created or enlarged 26 national monuments during his presidency. As a result, his administration Says, Obama has protected more of the nation's land than any other president has. But some residents and officials, in both Maine and Hawaii, object to the plans. (78) They say their local economies depend on the use of these areas.

In establishing this monument, Obama took the side of conservationists (自然资源保护者) who want laws to protect wild lands. Creating a national park usually requires the approval of Congress. But a 1906 federal law allows the president to establish national monuments on his own.

The land's new status as a monument means that mining and drilling operations are forbidden there. (79) It may also severely limit activities such as logging, road-building, and hunting. Some of Maine's politicians who want to protect the state's loggin industries say Obama should not have acted alone. They say Washington should not tell the states how to use their land, especially when people's jobs are **at stake.** Maine politician Susan Collins said the president should have listened to Maine lawmakers and residents, as well as to the U. S. Congress, before making his decision.

However, those who support the president's decision say the establishment of the new monument will lead to new jobs through tourism.

6. Which of the following is the best title for the passage?

A. Creating New Jobs B. Protecting Wild Animals

C. Stimulating Local Economies D. Creating New National Monuments

7. Obama has established or enlarged ________ national monuments during his two terms.

A. 19 B. 20 C. 26 D. 30

8. In national monuments, ________ is forbidden.

A. logging B. hunting C. mining D. road-building

9. The phrase **at stake** in Paragraph 4 is closest in meaning to ________.

A. in return B. in danger C. at present D. by chance

10. According to the passage, which of the following statements is NOT TRUE?

A. The national monument in Hawaii was created by President Bush.

B. There is no ~objection to President Obama's decision.

C. President Obama made this decision on his own.

D. The establishment of the new monument will lead to new jobs.

Passage 3 Questions 11 to 15 are based on the following passage:

Toronto's third City Hall, now known as Old City Hall, was designed by Edward James Lennox and declared open on Sept. 18, 1899.

Created to provide more space for city officials, it turned out to be the largest building in the city and the largest city building in North America at the time.

Lennox took three years to design the City Hall and it took 11 years to build it. Contemporaries believe that the odd carvings (雕刻) above the Queen Street entrance were actually caricatures (漫画) of councilors at the time.

Lennox even included himself in the caricatures, on the west side of the central arch(拱门), and left a strange signature in the stonework of the link portions of the building.

The third City Hall was originally used as councilors' offices and legal offices, but it is used only as a courthouse today.

When the fourth City Hall (the one we know today) was declared open in 1965, Old City Hall was threatened to be pulled down. It was saved by a group of people called the "Friends of Old City Hall."

The clock tower stands parallel with the middle of Bay Street, rather than with the center of the building. The bells in the tower were not installed until the building opened. Old City Hall was declared a historical site in 1989.

(80) The entire structure cost more than $2.5 million to build at the time. This is equal to $53 million today.

11. Toronto's third City Hall came into use in ________.
A. the 18th century B. the 19th century
C. the 20th century D. the 21st century

12. Old City Hall was constructed in years.
A. 3 B. 7 C. 9 D. 11

13. The third City Hall is now used as a ________.
A. middle school B. hospital C. cinema D. courthouse

14. From the passage we learn that ________.
A. Toronto spends lots of money yearly developing the city
B. some local residents showed a great interest in protecting the city's cultural Site
C. the City Council of Toronto hasn't paid sufficient attention to the protection of the city's culture
D. the City Hall is still the largest city building in North America today

15. Which of the following statements is TRUE according to the passage?
A. To build a structure like the City Hall will cost $2.5 million today.
B. The clock tower stands parallel with the centre of the City Hall.
C. Old City Hall was once pulled down in the development of the city.
D. Old City Hall is now a historical site.

Part II Vocabulary and Structure(30%)

Directions: In this part there are 30 incomplete sentences. For each sentence there are four choices marked A, B, C and D. Choose the ONE answer that best completes the sentence. Then blacken the corresponding letter on the Answer Sheet.

16. Shanghai is ________ biggest city in ________ China in terms of population.
A. the; the B. the; / C. /; the D. /; /

17. When Jenny came to my place, I ________ breakfast with James.
A. have B. had C. have had D. was having

18. ________ I in your position, I would not accept the job.
A. Were B. Was C. Am D. Been

19. I got ________ money with me, so I wasn't able to buy even a bottle of water!
A. any B. some C. few D. little

20. —Must we send in our plan this week?
—No, ________; you can send it in next week.
A. you needn't B. you mustn't C. you can't D. you shouldn't

21. Would you mind ________ me some bread on your way home?
A. buy B. to buy C. buying D. bought

22. I can't finish the work in time ________ you help me translate the texts.
A. unless B. if C. where D. but

23. The driver ________ the passengers off at the supermarket and then went to the next stop.
A. feil　B. sank　C. dropped　D. stepped
24. That restaurant has a good ________ in the community for its delicious food and friendly service.
A. mood　B. mirror　C. reputation　D. report
25. The manager at once lost his ________ when he learnt that his secretary was late again for the meeting.
A. mind　B. temper　C. passion　D. way
26. The young soldier was ________ wounded in the war and died a few days later.
A. generously　B. lonely　C. fatally　D. slightly
27. Professor Simpson ________ the project carefully and made a few corrections.
A. went up　B. went down　C. went after　D. went over
28. When I go to heat the milk, please ________ the baby.
A. keep an eye on　B. set foot on
C. make a guess at　D. look forward to
29. Mr. and Mrs. Wright have got nine children—it's really a big ________.
A. home　B. family　C. house　D. room
30. Neither Bill nor his parents ________ at home.
A. is　B. are　C. has　D. have
31. The summer vacation ________ over, they then got down to their work again.
A. were　B. was　C. being　D. had been
32. He failed in his exam, ________ proves that he hadn't worked hard enough.
A. what　B. that　C. which　D. such
33. ________ is known to all, too much stress can cause disease.
A. Which　B. That　C. It　D. As
34. It was not until he came back ________ I left the office.
A. then　B. which　C. that　D. when
35. Only When he finished his homework ________ that he had made a mistake.
A. he then realized　B. did he realize　C. before he realized　D. he realized
36. If it ________ rain tomorrow, we'll have the party outside.
A. wouldn't　B. doesn't　C. didn't　D. won't
37. This is the dictionary you're looking for, ________?
A. isn't this　B. isn't that　C. isn't it　D. isn't there
38. It's going to rain. You'd better ________ an umbrella with you.
A. bring　B. take　C. carry　D. fetch
39. Mary never tells anyone what she does for a ________.
A. life　B. work　C. profession　D. living
40. I saw a car in the distance, but I couldn't ________ whether it was red or not.
A. make out　B. work on　C. look out　D. take in
41. There were a ________ number of students on the playground.
A. few　B. little　C. short　D. small
42. Students are expected to ________ lectures regularly.
A. present　B. go　C. attend　D. follow
43. The lecture was so ________ that everyone went to sleep.
A. boring　B. bored　C. interesting　D. interested
44. We can see a lot of people doing morning exercises in the park even ________ a cold morning.
A. on　B. in　C. at　D. during
45. The grade walked so fast that most of the tourists could not ________ him.
A. go in for　B. keep up with　C. follow up　D. pass on

Part III Identification(10%)

Directions: Each of the following sentences has four underlined parts marked A, B, Cand D. Identify the one that is not correct. Then blacken the corresponding letter on the Answer Sheet.

46. Professor Morison has never been to China, nor does Dr. Jones.
A B C D

47. As early as the 12th century, boys in England enjoyed to play football.
A B C D

48. Nobody allows to smoke here because smoking indoors is against the law.
A B C D

49. When a water is heated, it changes into vapor.
A B C D

50. He has come to work for a local newspaper about ten years ago, when he graduated from Peking University.
A B C D

51. One of the two chairs is mine; the another is my brother's.
A B C D

52. The more quickly you get there, the soon you will be able to relax.
A B C D

53. I ought have invited her to the party but I didn't know her Well.
A B C D

54. He was seriously ill for days, and now he looks strong and healthy.
A B C D

55. Although Jim has lived in Beijing for five years, but he doesn't speak Chinese well.
A B C D

Part IV Cloze (10%)

Directions: There are 20 blanks in the following passage, and for each blank there are 4 choices marked A, B, C and D at the end of the passage. You should choose ONE answer that best fits into the passage. Then blacken the corresponding letter on the Answer Sheet.

Green sea turtles (海龟) are the world's largest species of hard-shelled sea turtle, while most individuals weigh about 136 to 181 kilograms, some can be __56__ heavy as 204 kilograms. These turtles are found nesting (筑巢) along the coastline of more than 80 countries, with the largest nesting populations __57__ in Costa Rica and Australia.

Green sea turtles spend most of their lives underwater, __58__ they can rest for up to five hours' at a time before 59 up for air. When active, they typically stay underwater for a few minutes and swim up to the' surface to __60__ air for a few seconds. Green Sea turtles also bathe in the sun __61__ land.

Unlike most other sea turtles, adult green sea turtles eat primarily plant-based foods __62__ of Seaweed and sea grass. Scientists believe these green foods __63__ the sea turtle's fat its green color.

Similar to other sea turtles, green sea turtles travel long distances __64__ their feeding grounds and their nesting sites, with recorded distances __65__ than 2,600 kilometers. They have strong flippers (鳍形肢) that help them __66__ in the water.

Female green sea turtles leave the water in __67__ to lay eggs on the beach and will choose the same nesting __68__ as where they were born. A female will dig __69__ a nest with her flippers and lay about 115 eggs. Then she'll cover the eggs __70__ sand and return to the sea. After about two months, the babies will use a special "egg tooth" to break their shells and hatch (孵化) from their eggs.

The first few years of a green sea turtle's life are spent __71__ at sea, where they feed on tiny animals and plants __72__ live in the surface layer of the sea. AS they grow older, the turtles move to __73__ waters along the coast, where they fmd sea grass to eat.

Adult green sea turtles face many threats, primarily from humans, including injuries from passing boats, being __74__ in fishing nets and pollution. Newly hatched sea turtles are also at __75__ of being hunted by other animals as they move from their nests out to the sea.

56. A. at B. for C. in D. as
57. A. gone B. moved C. found D. knocked
58. A. where B. which C. that D. when
59. A. join B. come C. joining D. coming
60. A. breathe B. draw C. hold D. attract
61. A. for B. at C. on D. in
62. A. putting B. making C. containing D. consisting
63. A. take B. give C. taken D. given
64. A. among B. within C. between D. beyond
65. A. longer B. deeper C. richer D. higher
66. A. arrive B. swim C. reach D. jump
67. A. way B. place C. method D. order
68. A. lawn B. street C. level D. spot
69. A. out B. away C. above D. below
70. A. of B. with C. out D. for
71. A. float B. think C. floating D. thinking
72. A. when B. that C. what D. where
73. A. negative B. careful C. shallow D. polite
74. A. caught B. dropped C. grown D. reached
75. A. risk B. sight C. visit D. death

Part V Translation (20%)

Section A

Directions: In this part there are five sentences which you should, translate into Chinese. These sentences are all taken from the 3 passages you have just read in Reading Comprehension. You can refer back to the passages to identify their meanings in the context.

76. Both sides show no signs of backing down.
77. Twenty-eight people have been arrested since then and charged with interfering withn the pipeline construction.
78. They say their local economies depend on the use of these areas.
79. It may also severely limit activities such as logging, road-building, arid hunting.
80. The entire structure cost more than $2.5 million to build at the time.

Section B

Directions: In this part there are five sentences in Chinese. You should translate them into English. Be sure to write clearly.

81. 他在这所学校任教多久了?
82. 我希望我们的演出会成功。
83. 春天是游览这个城市的最佳季节。
84. 他们在打篮球。
85. 他十年前搬到这儿的。

参考答案

1—15 CABDC DCCBB BDDBD

16—45 BDADA CACCB CDABB CCDCB BCCDA DCAAB
46—55 CDAAA CCACC
56—75 DCADA CDBDA BDDAB CBCAA
76. 双方都没有表现妥协的迹象。
77. 之后有 28 人被捕,并被指控妨碍了输油管道的建设。
78. 他们说他们当地的经济依赖于这些地区的土地使用。
79. 这会严重限制诸如伐木、修建道路和狩猎这样的活动。
80. 当时整个建筑花费了 250 万加元。
81. How long has he been teaching in this school?
82. I hope our performance will be a success.
83. The best season to go around this city is in spring.
84. They are playing basketball.
85. He moved here 10 years ago.

北京地区成人本科学士学位英语统一考试

2017.05.06

Part I Reading Comprehension(30%)

Directions: There are three passages in this Part. Each passage is followed by some questions or unfinished statements. For each of them there are four choices marked A, B, C and D. You should decide on the best choice and blacken the corresponding letter on the Answer Sheet.

Passage 1 Questions 1 to 5 are based on the following passage:

People say that money cannot buy happiness. This was true for Howard Hughes. (76) He was one of the richest and most powerful men of his time. He had everything: good looks, success, power, and a lot of money. But he didn't have love or friendship because he couldn't buy them. All his life he used his money to control everything and everyone around him. In the end, he lost control of everything, even himself.

Howard Hughes was born in 1905 in Houston, Texas. His father started the Hughes Tool Company. He was a workaholic (工作狂) and made a lot of money. He bought everything he wanted. He even gave money to schools so Howard could get into them. From his father, Howard learned to be a successful but merciless businessman. Hughes's mother, Allene also had a big influence on his life. Howard was her only child. She protected him and gave him everything. Unfortunately, Allene had mental problems. (77) She was afraid of germs and diseases. She was **obsessed** with Howard's health, and he became obsessed with it too.

Allene died when Howard was 16 years old. Two years later his father died. Hughes inherited the Hughes Tool Company. Then he married Ella Rice. He and Ella moved to Los Angeles, California. It was there that Howard Hughes began to become a legend (传奇人物). Hughes began to invest his money in movies. He became an important producer soon after he moved to California. He worked hard, but he also played hard. He became obsessed with power and control. When he couldn't get something legally, he gave money to politicians and businessmen so they would help him. He owned a lot of businesses, including airplane companies, a movie studio (制片厂), Las Vegas hotels, gold and silver mines, and radio and television stations. Once he bought a television studio so he could watch movies all night. He also bought a hotel because he wanted to stay in his favorite room for one weekend.

1. According to the passage, Howard Hughes was not ________.
   A. good-looking B. wealthy C. friendly D. powerful
2. Which of the following about Hughes' father is NOT TRUE
   A. He started the Hughes Tool Company. B. He liked to spend money.
   C. He worked hard. D. He drank alcohol a lot.

3. Howard Hughes' parents died ________.

A. when he was 16 years old B. before he was 19 years old

C. after he got married D. after he moved to California

4. The word obsessed in paragraph 2 probably means ________.

A. troubled B. reduced C. related D. informed

5. From the passage, we learn what Mr. Hughes lacked in his life was

A. education B. love C. money D. good looks

Passage 2 Questions 6 to 10 are based on the following passage:

Half of the world's coral reefs (珊瑚礁) have died in the last 30 years. Now scientists are racing to ensure that the rest survive. Even if global warming were to stop right now, scientists predict that more than 90% 0f corals will die by 2050. If no major steps are taken to **address** the problem, the reefs may be headed for total extinction (灭绝).

(78) The planet's health depends on the survival of coral reefs. They are often described as "the rainforests of the sea" , because they provide shelter for a wide variety of sea life. In addition, the reefs serve as barriers that protect coastlines from the full force of powerful storms.

Corals are used in medical research for cures to diseases. They are key to local economies as well, since the reefs attract tourists, the fishing industry, and other businesses, bringing in billions of dollars.

(79) Corals are particularly sensitive to changes in temperature. A rise of just 1 to 2 degrees can force the corals to drive out the algae (水藻). Then the corals mm white in a process called "bleaching". Corals can recover from short-term bleaching, but long-term bleaching can cause permanent damage. In 1998, when sea surface temperatures were the highest in recorded history, coral reefs around the world suffered the most severe bleaching. It is estimated that even under the best of conditions, many of these coral reefs will need decades to recover.

Although reefs face other threats from pollution, industrial activities, and overfishing, it is global climate change that most concerns scientists. Scientists remain hopeful that it's not too late to save the reefs, and some are moving ahead on experiments to accomplish that goal.

6. Which of the following is the best title for the passage?

A. Rising Global Temperatures B. Rainforests Are in Danger

C. Coral Reefs Face Extinction D. Global Climate Change

7. The word address in Paragraph i is closest in meaning to ________.

A. break down B. stick to C. go over D. deal with

8. Why are coral reefs called "the rainforests of the sea"?

A. Because they are home to a wide variety of sea life.

B. Because they can protect our coasts from storms.

C. Because they might supply natural medicines.

D. Because they look like rainforests.

9. The corals turn ________ in the process of "bleaching".

A. red B. black C. green D. white

10. According to the passage, ________ is the biggest threat to coral reefs.

A. pollution B. overfishing

C. industrial activity D. climate change

Passage 3 Questions 11 to 15 are based on the following passage:

Over the years, college students have stood together for what they believe in, from civil rights to anti-war policies to the more recent protests against the unequal distribution of wealth. But nowhere in history have students banned (禁止) bottled water. Until now.

The bottled water ban, which started on just a few campuses, has now spread nationwide to more than 20 universities. The colleges have either completely banned the use of plastic bottles altogether, or some have taken a more limited approach with partial bans.

Many people believe that producing and using bottled water wastes money and harms the environment. They say that bottled water is unnecessary because public water supplies in the U. S. are among the best in the world. Water fountains and reusable bottles with easy access (获取) to filling stations are a better choice.

An organization called Ban the Bottle raises awareness about the economic and environmental costs of using plastic bottles. The group claims that eight glasses of' water a day costs each person 49 cents annually, while drinking from plastic containers costs $1,400 per year. Plastic bottles contain antimony—a chemical that in low doses causes depression, but in large doses can even lead to death.

The **controversy** over bottled or tap is not limited to the students and college administrations. The makers of bottled water see the movement as a threat. <u>(80) They argue that plastic bottles make up a small portion of the nation's total waste.</u> It's unfair to single out (单独挑出) their product when so many other items are packaged in plastic containers. Plus, water is a healthy choice compared to some sodas and juices that are also sold at school.

11. Which of the following is the main idea of the passage?
    A. Many universities ban or restrict the sale of bottled water.
    B. Many states ban or restrict the sale of bottled water.
    C. The bottled water industry is concerned about its decreasing sales.
    D. Many people are opposed to the bottled water ban.
12. According to Ban the Bottle, drinking bottled water costs ________ dollars per year.
    A. 8　　B. 20　　C. 49　　D. 1400
13. The Word controversy in Paragraph 5 is closest in meaning to ________.
    A. choice　　B. control　　C. argument　　D. statement
14. What does the bottled water industry use in its own defense?
    A. Bottled water is much cleaner than tap water.
    B. Students should have freedom of choice.
    C. The bottles are made in a more environment-friendly way.
    D. Water is healthier than some sodas and juices.
15. According to the passage, which of the following statements is TRUE?
    A. All the universities have banned the sale of bottled water.
    B. Plastic bottles may do harm to people's health.
    C. The purchase of soft drinks will increase.
    D. Bottled water is cheap and environment-friendly.

Part II Vocabulary and Structure(30%)

Directions: In this part there are 30 incomplete sentences. For each sentence there are four choices marked A, B, C and D. Choose the ONE answer that best completes thesentence. Then blacken the corresponding letter on the Answer Sheet.

16. They have decided to put the meeting ________ till next Monday.
    A. up　　B. on　　C. off　　D. forward
17. If you get into difficulties, don't hesitate to ask ________ advice.
    A. of　　B. out　　C. after　　D. for
18. While we were on holiday, our neighbor took ________ our house.
    A. notice of　　B. care of　　C. after　　D. on
19. Students are expected to ________ their classes regularly.
    A. come　　B. go　　C. attend　　D. follow
20. I was trying to get into the ________ bus when I heard a voice from behind.

A. crowd　B. crowding　C. crowds　D. crowded

21. Honesty is the most important a man should have.

A. effort　B. habit　C. quality　D. question

22. That student ________ his hand every time I asked a question.

A. made up　B. put up　C. rose　D. arose

23. He spoke English so well that I took it for ________ that he was an American.

A. good　B. certain　C. sure　D. granted

24. I am very ________ to you for your help.

A. grateful　B. agreeable　C. capable　D. enjoyable

25. The two girls look exactly ________ in appearance.

A. same　B. alike　C. like　D. same one

26. The children ________ happily in the classroom when the teacher came in.

A. talk　B. are talking　C. were ta'ddng　D. had talked

27. In the road accident the other day three people ________, including the driver.

A. killed　B. were killed　C. are killed　D. have killed

28. Jim's job is to keep his boss ________ of the latest development of that product in Europe.

A. inform　B. to inform　C. informed　D. informing

29. The young man ________ visited our school this morning is Maria's brother.

A. who　B. which　C. whose　D. what

30. I'm awfully tired and can't goany farther, Ted. Let's have a rest, ________?

A. shall we　B. will you　C. can you　D. may I

31. ________ the manager will come or not doesn't matter much.

A. Whether　B. That　C. if　D. What

32. The American and the British ________ a large number of social customs.

A. join　B. take　C. share　D. make

33. Martin, when you go to the meeting tomorrow, ________ your iPad with you.

A. bring　B. take　C. fetch　D. put

34. It is a three-storey house and the kitchen is on the ________ floor.

A. ground　B. earth　C. soil　D. land

35. The kids were especially ________ the coming Christmas because they would get lots of presents from their parents and uncles.

A. coming up with　B. looking forward to

C. making up for　D. getting rid of

36. The used car I bought cost four ________ pounds.

A. thousands　B. thousand of　C. thousands of　D. thousand

37. What's the matter with you? You ________ so pale.

A. are looking　B. look　C. have looked　D. looked

38. With the guide ________ the way, we set off on foot into the dark night.

A. leading　B. to lead　C. led　D. being led

39. I tore open the box, only ________ that some papers were missing.

A. discovering　B. to discover　C. discovered　D. discover

40. Either my parents or my elder brother ________ going to water the garden.

A. are　B. is　C. has　D. have

41. Can you imagine why ________?

A. did the boy say that　B. the boy said that

C. did the boy say　D. the boy said

42. Although it is raining hard, ________.

A. Tom still wants to go out B. and Tom still wants to go out
C. that Tom still wants to go out D. but Tom still wants to go out

43. I went to ________ Shanghai yesterday, On ________ train I met a famous pop star.
A. the; / B. /; the C. the; the D. /; /

44. ________ of the two brothers are fond of classical music.
A. Both B. All C. Each D. Either

45. There are not ________ students in Class One as in Class Two.
A. so many B. so much C. more D. much more

Part III Identification(10%)

Directions: Each of the following sentences has four underlined parts marked A, B, Cand D. Identify the one that is not correct. Then blacken the corresponding letter on the Answer Sheet.

46. The puzzle was so difficult that I gave up it in the end.
A B C D

47. In March when spring is already here, we usually plant many young trees on both side of the street.
A B C D

48. You'd better to go home now because it's going to rain in no time.
A B C D

49. After they reached the top of the mountain, they felt extremely hungrily and thirsty.
A B C D

50. Tom's father, as well as his mother, ask him to stay in New York for a few more days.
A B C D

51. After living a few weeks with him, I felt sorry for to be so unfriendly to him at ftrst.
A B C D

52. Robert is a great basketball fan and love Kobe Bryant very much.
A B C D

53. Hardly I had sat down when I heard someone knock at the door.
A B C D

54. Nobody believed that his excuse for being late was why his car broke down on his way to work.
A B C D

55. I wish I finished writing the essay yesterday, but I was too busy.
A B C D

Part IV Cloze (10%)

Directions: There are 20 blanks in the following passage, and for each blank there are 4 choices marked A, B, C and D at the end of the passage. You should choose ONE answer that best fits into the passage. Then blacken the corresponding letter on the Answer Sheet.

When I was young, I spent my summer vacations on my grandparents' farm. The summer that I graduated from college, I __56__ my grandparents once again. When I arrived, I discovered that there was a family __57__ in progress.

Grandpa's dog and hunting partner, Rusty, had taken on a very bad __58__ in his old age. He had begun __59__ into the chicken coop (鸡笼) and eating eggs. In the eyes of the local farmers, __60__ dogs started stealing eggs, there was no __61__ to cure them. They knew there was only one thing to be done __62__ such a dog-you had to shoot it and the sooner the __63__.

Rusty and Grandpa were old friends. Grandpa certainly didn't __64__ to shoot Rusty, but he knew it needed to be done. The "egg money" was Grandma's private income, so you can imagine __65__ she felt about the problem. __66__ the inexperienced confidence of youth, I told Grandpa that I thought I could "cure" the egg-stealing dog. I wanted to at least have a __67__ to save Rusty's life, and save Grandpa from the sadness of __68__ Rusty.

The next morning, I broke open six fresh eggs and put them in Rusty's bowl __69__ at the door to the chicken coop. Rusty came __70__ and noticed the eggs. He quickly __71__ the eggs and happily walked off for his nap (打盹). The following morning I did the __72__ thing. I put the eggs a few feet away from the chicken coop, toward the back door of the farmhouse __73__ Grandma usually fed Rusty. The next day I again moved the bowl closer to the house, and added some dog food to the eggs. Every day I moved the bowl closer to the back door, mixing more dog food and __74__ eggs. By the time the bowl reached the door, it was all dog food and no eggs. Rusty had again become __75__ to looking for his food at the back door of the house, and never again went into the chicken coop.

56. A. watched	B. noticed	C. invited	D. visited
57. A. peace	B. stress	C. crisis	D. miracle
58. A. habit	B. pattern	C. custom	D. crime
59. A. to throw	B. to break	C. throwing	D. breaking
60. A. once	B. before	C. while	D. although
61. A. desire	B. route	C. way	D. idea
62. A. in	B. at	C. for	D. with
63. A. wider	B. better	C. happier	D. calmer
64. A. care	B. start	C. Want	D. feel
65. A. how	B. when	C. what	D. which
66. A. In	B. With	C. On	D. At
67. A. rate	B. space	C. pity	D. chance
68. A. losing	B. helping	C. worrying	D. keeping
69. A. next	B. right	C. behind	D. beside
70. A. befom	B. after	C. along	D. from
71. A. saw	B. found	C. left	D. ate
72. A. specific	B. same	C. kind	D. different
73. A. what	B. which	C. where	D. when
74. A. fewer	B. more	C. little	D. few
75. A. accustomed	B. related	C. interested	D. depressed

Part V Translation (20%)

Section A

Directions: In this part there are five sentences which you should, translate into Chinese. These sentences are all taken from the 3 passages you have just read in Reading Comprehension. You can refer back to the passages to identify their meanings in the context.

76. He was one of the richest and most powerful men of his time.
77. She was afraid of germs and diseases.
78. The planet's health depends on the survival of coral reefs.
79. Corals are particularly sensitive to changes in temperature.
80. They argue that plastic bottles make up a small portion of the nation's total waste.

Section B

Directions: In this part there are five sentences in Chinese. You should translate them into English. Be sure to write clearly.

81. 不要放弃希望。
82. 我会去火车站接你。

83. 我不能去聚会,因为要准备考试。
84. 我们刚才去散步了。
85. 你喜欢流行音乐吗?

参考答案

1—15 CDBCB CDADD ADCDB
16—45 CDBCD CBDAB CBCAA ACAAB DBABB BABAA
46—55 CDACB CCACB
56—75 DCADA CDBCA BDABC DBCAA
76. 他是那个时代最富有、最有权势的人。
77. 她害怕病菌、害怕疾病。
78. 珊瑚礁的生存关乎地球是否处于健康状态。
79. 珊瑚礁特别对温度的变化感到敏感。
80. 他们为自己争辩说塑料污染只占全国垃圾污染的一小部分。
81. Don't give up hope.
82. I will pick you up at the railway station.
83. I can't attend the party, for I have to prepare for the examination.
84. We took a walk just now.
85. Do you like/care for pop music?

北京地区成人本科学士学位英语统一考试

2017.11.04

Part I Reading Comprehension(30%)

Directions: There are three passages in this Part. Each passage is followed by some questions or unfinished statements. For each of them there are four choices marked A, B, C and D. You should decide on the best choice and blacken the corresponding letter on the Answer Sheet.

Passage 1 Questions 1 to 5 are based on the following passage:

In 2014, older Americans fell 29 million times, leading to 7 million injuries, according to a report published last week. About 2.8 million cases were treated in emergency departments, and approximately 800,000 seniors went on to be hospitalized. More than 27,000 falls led to death. (76) And the problem is getting more and more serious.

"Older adult falls are increasing and, sadly, often indicate the end of independence," said Dr. Tom Frieden. The falls are preventable, Frieden stressed. He said individuals, families and health care providers can take steps to resist the trend.

Dr. Wolf-Klein is a medical professor in New York, She said one concern is that seniors who have experienced a fall alone at home don't tell anyone. When that happens, prevention efforts don't begin and they're at risk for additional falls that lead to broken bones and brain injuries.

"Elderly patients tend not to report falls to their families, or even doctors. A fall is a very frightening thing that you keep quiet about. They think if they mention it, they are afraid that they will move to a nursing home or need assistants to help out in the house," said Wolf-Klein.

It's also a status issue and may make someone feel that they're weaker than they really are, she explained. When someone does fall and hurt themselves, they are often neier the same, Wolf-Klein said. "You can develop chronic (慢性的) problems. After a fall, a percentage of the population will never return to walking around. People used to taking the subway, now they're in a wheelchair, or they may need help going to the bathroom. They become frailer and lose independence," she said.

1. Which of the following Is TRUE?
   A. In 2014, older adult falls caused 7 million injuries.
   B. In 2016, Americans fell 29 million times.
   C. Last year, 2. 8 million Americans had emergency treatment.
   D. Last month, more than 27,000 older Americans were hospitalized.
2. From the passage we learn that older adult falls ________.
   A. are decreasing
   B. can't be avoided
   C. must be treated in hospitals
   D. usually imply the end of independence
3. The wordfrailer in Paragraph 5 probably means ________.
   A. lonelier B. weaker C. smarter D. better
4. According to the passage, which of the following is TRUE?
   A. A fall is a very terrible thing that you keep quiet about.
   B. After a fall elderly people will not develop chronic problems.
   C. To prevent falls elderly people should move to a nursing home.
   D. Elderly patients tend to tell their families about their falls.
5. What is the main idea of this passage?
   A. Older adult falls are on the rise.
   B. People should keep quiet about their falls.
   C. Older adults are losing their independence.
   D. Older adult falls cause brain injuries.

Passage 2 Questions 6 to 10 are based on the following passage:

Marley Dias loves nothing more than getting lost in a book. But the books she was reading at school were starting to get on her nerves. She enjoyed *where the Red Fern Grows* and *The Shiloh Series*, but those classics, found in so many primary school classrooms, were all about white boys or dogs—or white boys and their dogs. Black girls, like Marley, were almost never the main character.

What she was noticing is actually a much bigger issue: fewer than 10 percent of children's books released in 2015 had a black person as the main character, according to a yearly analysis by the Cooperative Children's Book Center. In November 2015, Marley set out to gather 1,000 books with black girls as protagonists(主角)? Her campaign called "#1000BiackGirlBooks" was a big success. (77) She far exceeded her goal and collected more than 10,000 books! "Through my campaign, I want to give kids a stronger sense of identity." Marley says. (78) "The biggest thing I've learned is that kids' voices need to be heard."

In the future? Dias wants to be the editor(编辑)of her own magazine. She is already making the steps toward having a successful and meaningful career. At 11, she's aware of the racism in the publishing industry.

Like the television and movies, the publishing industry does not represent black girls or other people of coior in positive ways. The whitewashing (漂白) in this industry extends beyond not having people of color as characters. In 2012, white men wrote 88% of the book reviews. In 2013, only about 2% of the books were about black characters. Then if there are people of color in the books, the publishers attempt to whitewash people of color on the covers.

However, Dias is making it a little easier for other black girls searching for a character that is just like them. Her project is a positive step toward young black girls seeing and experiencing their lives in books.

6. Which of the following is the best title for the passage?
   A. Main Characters of Popular Books
   B. The # 1000BlackGirlBooks Campaign
   C. Whitewashing in the Publishing Industry

D. Further Reading for Kids and Teenagers

7. The phrase "get on her nerves" in Paragraph 1 is closest in meaning to ________.

A. make her ill B. make her excited

C. make her annoyed D. make her frightened

8. Marley started the #1000BlackGirlBooks campaign because ________.

A. she wanted to give some books to African children

B. she wanted to encourage children to read more books

C. she noticed the lack of black girls as main characters in the books

D. she didn't like the black girls described in the books she read for class

9. The original goal of the project was to collect ________ books.

A. 1000 B. 2015 C. 5000 D. 10,000

10. According to the passage, which of the following statements is NOT TRUE?

A. Marley Dias is a black girl.

B. Marley Dias doesn't like reading.

C. Marley Dias wants to become an editor in the future.

D. Movies seldom represent black people in positive ways.

passage 3 Questions 11 to 15 are based on the following passage:

The science behind solar (太阳的) energy is not new. But Sheridan Community Schools is the first school district in Indiana to be completely solar-powered. The district finished installing solar panels (太阳能板) for all three of its schools in 2016. Some of the panels can turn to follow the sun across the sky.

Sheridan's solar push is part of a trench In 2008, fewer than 1,000 schools used solar power. By 2014, there were 3,727 schools with solar panels in the US. This data comes from a report by the Solar Foundation, an organization that promotes the use of solar power. Roxie Brown, a program director there, says that the number of schools with solar panels has continued to rise since 2014.

(79) Solar power has some obvious advantages over other energy sources. Sunlight is a renewable (可再生的) resource, which means it won't run out. Solar panels don't harm the environment. Also, sunlight is free. So by using solar power, schools can save money on energy costs over time.

But switching to solar power isn9t always easy. Solar panels can be expensive to install. Sheridan Community Schools had to borrow money to pay for its solar transition. (80) The panels also take up space. But for many schools, going solar is worth it.

The use of solar energy can also help students learn about electricity and environmental issues. Teachers at schools that use solar power often incorporate it into their science lessons. The kids talk about it in the classroom. Then they can look at it in action. According to Brown, the educational impact of solar panels is "the most compelling reason" for schools to install them.

Brown hopes the panels will give Sheridan students a global perspective. "The world is bigger than the boundaries of their school district," he says. "They're doing things to help the world as a whole."

11. Sheridan Community Schools consists of ________ schools.

A. two B. three C. four D. five

12. According to the passage, solar energy has the following benefits EXCEPT that ________.

A. it creates no pollution B. it can save money

C. solar panels are easy to maintain D. solar energy is renewable

13. The wordincorporate in Paragraph 5 is closest in meaning to ________.

A. reach B. improve C. turn D. include

14. According tothe passage, which of the following statements is NOT TRUE?

A. Solar panels are vexy expensive to install.

B. Sheridan Community Schools is completely solar-powered.

C. In 2014, fewer than 13000 schools used solar power in the US.

D. More and more schools are switching to solar power to cut costs.

15. Which of the following is the best title for the passage?

A. Solar Power　　B. Schools Go Solar

C. Cheap Energy Sources　　D. A Global Perspective

Part II　Vocabulary and Structure(30%)

Directions: In this part there are 30 incomplete sentences. For each sentence there are four choices marked A, B, C and D. Choose the ONE answer that best completes the sentence. Then blacken the corresponding letter on the Answer Sheet.

16. ________ Hong Kong is one ofbusiest seaports in the world.

A. The; the　　B. /;/　　C. The;/　　D. /;the

17. The old mandead in the snow the next morning.

A. found　　B. was found　　C. was finding　　D. had found

18. It's time that weto take care of our own house.

A. begin　　B. will begin　　C. have begun　　D. began

19. ________ city do you prefer, Shanghai or London?

A. What　　B. Which　　C. Who's　　D. Whose

20. Mr Jones enjoys ________ his children out for long walks.

A. take　　B. takes　　C. to take　　D. taking

21. He ________ from college three years ago, but now he is the boss of a large business.

A. graduate　　B. graduates　　C. graduated　　D. has graduated

22. Henry waved to his sister, ________ was just getting off a bus.

A. who　　B. that　　C. which　　D. whose

23. Mark's coming to the meeting this afternoon, ________?

A. Doesn't he　　B. won't he　　C. isn't he　　D. shan't he

24. It was ________ dark that we could hardly see the faces of each other.

A. very　　B. quite　　C. so　　D. too

25. The car ________ halfway on the road, so we had to walk home.

A. broke up　　B. broke off　　C. broke out　　D. broke down

26. The bank charges 6 per cent ________ on all money borrowed from it.

A. salary　　B. pay　　C. income　　D. interest

27. The doctor kept him ________ on a life-support machine.

A. tidy　　B. alive　　C. gentle　　D. proud

28. Katy can think clearly when she is not under ________.

A. straw　　B. space　　C. stress　　D. surface

29. Last weekend lots of T-shirts were ________ here and the cheapest cost only one dollar.

A. at work　　B. on sale　　C. in practice　　D. out of sight

30. He decided to devote all his time and effort ________ scientific investigation.

A. in　　B. on　　C. from　　D. to

31. He fell in love with her at first ________.

A. scene　　B. sight　　C. view　　D. look

32. I have promised to help you and I'll ________ my word.

A. hold　　B. follow　　C. stick　　D. keep

33. If you have high blood pressure, you should ________ eating too much salty food.

A. escape　　B. suggest　　C. avoid　　D. relax

34. During the past ten years, there have been ________ changes in the country.

A. lasting B. dramatic C. powerful D. imaginary

35. I should like to rent a house, modem, comfortable and ________, in a quiet place.
A. after all B. all over C. above all D. first of all

36. We have always thought very ________ of him.
A. highly B. well C. greatly D. enough

37. He told his friends that he was going to Japan ________.
A. on duty B. on business C. on board D. on the spot

38. It's no use ________ for a doctor. It's too late already.
A. to send B. sending C. by sending D. having sent

39. I now you're planning to travel this summer, but do you know ________?
A. how much cost it will be B. how much has it cost
C. how much it will cost D. how much will it cost

40. Childish ________ she may be, she is kind and friendly.
A. if B. although C. as D. however

41. —Tom, is there ________ wrong with the car?
—Yeah, the engine refuses to start.
A. anything B. one thing C. nothing D. none

42. ________ succeed in doing anything.
A. Only by working hard we can B. By only working hard we can
C. Only by working hard can we D. Only we can by working hard

43. By the end of next month, you ________ here for three years.
A. will have studied B. study
C. will study D. have studied

44. Your temperature has dropped, so you ________ take the medicine.
A. don't B. mustn't C. needn't D. can't

45. ________, everything would have been all right.
A. He had been there B. Here he had been
C. Been here he had D. Had he been here

Part III Identification(10%)

Directions: Each of the following sentences has four underlined parts marked A, B, Cand D. Identify the one that is not correct. Then blacken the corresponding letter on the Answer Sheet.

46. When(A) Uncle Tom will come(B) back, please tell me(C)immediately(D).

47. I have lived in(A) this city thirty years ago(B), so(C) I know it quite well(D).

48. The background(A) music in(B) the little cafe sounds softly(C) and sweet to(D) me.

49. A news(A) of his arrest(B) traveled quickly(C)among(D) his friends.

50. I couldn't help to laugh(A)when(B) I saw the little boy in(C)his father's(D) overcoat.

51. After driving(A) for twenty miles, he suddenly realized(B) that he has been driving(C) in the wrong(D) direction.

52. Mary, together with(A) her classmates, are(B) in the lobby, waiting(C) to discuss with you the plans for the coming(D) sports meet.

53. Of the two students, one is named Tom and another named Fred.
A B C D

54. In their house there are four rooms, the largest of that is used as a drawing room.
A B C D

55. We have come to the conclusion when this summer will be much hotter than before.
A B C D

Part IV Cloze (10%)

Directions: There are 20 blanks in the following passage, and for each blank there are 4 choices marked A, B, C and D at the end of the passage. You should choose ONE answer that best fits into the passage. Then blacken the corresponding letter on the Answer Sheet.

My friend Jane once found a weasel (鼬鼠) when he was very young. As she was fond of pets, she thought she would bring him up.

Of course he had to be taught: all young things have to, and this weasel knew __56__? The good lady first began with __57__ some milk into her hand and __58__ him drink from it. Very soon, he would not take milk __59__ any other way. After his dinner, he would run to a soft blanlcet that was __60__ in Jane's bedroom. He slept there __61__ one or two hours.

This was all very well in the day, but Jane did not feel __62__ in leaving him loose during the night. Thus, whenever she went to bed, she __63__ the weasel up in a little cage that stood __64__ by. If she __65__ to wake up early? she would open the cage, and the weasel would come into her bed and go to sleep again __66__ next to her. If she was already dressed when he was let __67__, he would jump all about her, and would never once miss __68__ on her hands.

All his ways were pretty and gentle. He would stand __69__ Jane's shoulder and give little soft pats to her chin. He would run over a whole room __70__ of people at the mere sound of her voice. He was very fond of the sun and would roll about whenever it __71__ on him. The little weasd was rather a thirsty animal, but he would not drink much at a __72__. Baths were quite new to him, and he could not __73__ up his mind to them. Because of his dislike for baths, he suffered a good deal on __74__ days. His nearest approach to bathing was a __75__ cloth wrapped, round him, and this evidently gave him great pleasure.

56. A. anything	B. nothing	C. something	D. everything
57. A. pulling	B. linking	C. pouring	D. moving
58. A. ordering	B. asking	C. telling	D. letting
59. A. on	B. in	C. for	D. at
60. A. made	B. built	C. spread	D. paid
61. A. for	B. on	C. beyond	D. beside
62. A. angry	B. safe	C. risky	D. serious
63. A. shut	B. hit	C. sent	D. went
64. A. short	B. far	C. long	D. close
65. A. remembered	B. resolved	C. happened	D. occurred
66. A. laying	B. lying	C. lay	D. lie
67. A. up	B. out	C. down	D. away
68. A. sitting	B. sit	C. visiting	D. visit
69. A. in	B. beside	C. on	D. under
70. A. deep	B. proud	C. wide	D. full
71. A. dropped	B. shone	C. found	D. floated
72. A. time	B. moment	C. minute	D. place
73. A. take	B. detect	C. make	D. decide
74. A. quiet	B. noisy	C. busy	D. hot
75. A. wet	B. dry	C. flat	D. sharp

Part V Translation (20%)

Section A

Directions: In this part there are five sentences which you should, translate into Chinese. These sentences are all taken from the 3 passages you have just read in Reading Comprehension. You can refer back to the passages to identify their meanings in the context.

76. And the problem is getting more and more serious.
77. She far exceeded her goal and collected more than 10,000 books!
78. The biggest thing I've learned is that kids' voices need to be heard.
79. Solar power has some obvious advantages over other energy sources.
80. The panels also take up space.

Section B

Directions: In this part there are five sentences in Chinese. You should translate them into English. Be sure to write clearly.

81. 你昨天早上几点起床的?
82. 我们认识有十年了。
83. 这部电影让她想起了她的童年。
84. 他每天必须处理许多问题。
85. 经理不在时,这个商店由他负责。

参 考 答 案

1—15 ADBAA BCCAB BCDCB
16—45 DBDBD CACCD DBCBD BDCBC ABBCC ACACD
46—55 BBCAA CBDDB
56—75 BCDBC ABADC BBACD BACDA
76. 而且这个问题正变得越来越严重。
77. 她大大地超过了她的目标,收集了1万本书。
78. 我学到的最重要的是人们需要倾听孩子们的声音。
79. 太阳能比其他能源有明显的优势。
80. 太阳能板占用空间。
81. When did you get up yesterday morning?
82. We have known each other for 10 years.
83. This movie reminded her of her childhood.
84. He has to deal with a lot of problems every day.
85. When the manager is not here, he is in charge of this store.

北京地区成人本科学士学位英语统一考试

2018.05.12

Part I Reading Comprehension (30%)

Directions: There are three passages in this Part. Each passage is followed by some questions or unfinished statements. For each of them there are four choices marked A, B, C and D. You should decide on the best choice and blacken the corresponding letteron the Answer Sheet.

Passage 1 Questions 1 to 5 are based on the following passage:

In 1866, sailors on a German ship called Paula threw a bottle with a message into waters hundreds of miles off the western coast of Australia. One hundred and thirty-one years later, (76) the bottle was found on an

Australian island.

It's believed to be the oldest-known message in a bottle, in terms of the amount of time that has passed between when it was written and when it was found. Before this discovery, Guinness(吉尼斯)World Records said that the oldest was 108 years old, found in Germany in 2015. Australian and German researchers worked together to check whether the note is real or not.

Tonya Illman was walking on the beach in January when she spotted the old bottle. "I picked it up thinking it might look nice on display in my home," Illman says, according to an account on her husband's website. (77) The bottle was partially filled with wet sand. Shortly after, Illman's son's girlfriend poured out the contents and found a tightly rolled note covered in a piece of string.

Toodamp to open initially, according to the account, the group waited for it to dry and were amazed to see that it was carefully handwritten in German. "The first thing that caught my eye was the year 1866," said Illman's husband Kym. "It seemed totally unlikely to us that the note and bottle could have lasted that long."

The pair reached out to the Western Australia Museum, which set out to study the document. "Extraordinary finds need extraordinary evidence to support them, so we contacted colleagues in Germany for help to find more information." Ross Anderson, who is in charge of works of art in the museum, said in a statement.

But this message is no SOS or love letter.

1. According to Guinness World Records, the second oldest message was found ________.

A. in 2014 B. in 2015 C. in 2017 D. in 2016

2. Which of the following is TRUE?

A. A sailor named Paula threw the old bottle into waters in 1866.

B. Kym found the old bottle first.

C. This oldest message was found in Germany.

D. The oldest message was 131 years old.

3. From the passage, we learn that ________.

A. Tonya found the bottle first

B. Tonya and Kym contacted researchers in Germany for help

C. Illman's son broke the bottle to take out what was inside

D. the note was written in English

4. The word damp in Paragraph 4 is closest in meaning to ________.

A. wet B. dry C. cool D. hot

5. Which of the following is probably the best title for this passage?

A. Theoldest-known Message Found in Australia

B. The Oldest-known Message Found in Germany

C. An Extraordinary Evidence of History

D. A Guinness Beer Bottle

Passage 2 Questions 6 to 10 are based on the following passage:

A handwritten note from Albert Einstein sold for more than $1.5 million at an auction(拍卖会). He gave the note to a hotel porter in Japan in 1922. Einstein was not carrying money when the porter came to his room. (78) He was unable to give a cash tip, as a guest normally would. Instead, he gave a tip on how to live life.

"A calm and modest life brings more happiness than the pursuit of success combined with constant restlessness," Einstein wrote. The note was written in German.

It was written on notepaper from the Imperial Hotel in Ginza, Tokyo, where Einstein was delivering a series of lectures.

He was traveling to Asia when news that he had won the Nobel Prize for Physics reached him via telegraph. Einstein was unable to attend the prize-giving ceremony in Stockholm.

Gal Wiener is head of the auction house in Jerusalem, Israel, where the note was sold. He said Einstein told the hotel porter to keep the note since it "will probably be worth more than a regular tip."

Bidding (拍卖中的出价)onnote began at $2,000. It was expected to sell for no more than $8,000. But 25 minutes later, the auction house made the major sale.

(79) A second Einstein note was also sold at the auction. It went for more than $200,000. "where there's a will, there's a way," the note says.

Theidentity of the person or group that sold the notes has not been made public. Nor has that of the buyer or buyers.

6. The wordtip in Line 4, Paragraph 1 probably means ________.
   A. advice B. trick C. news D. trend
7. The note was written in ________.
   A. English B. Janpanese C. Germans D. French
8. Albert Einstein went to Janpan to ________.
   A. visit some friends B. do some sightseeing
   C. Receive the Nobel Prize D. give a series of lectures
9. The estimated sale value of the first note is about ________.
   A. $2,000 B. $8,000 C. $200,000 D. $1.5 million
10. According to the passage, which of the following statements is NOT TRUE?
   A. Einstein gave the porter the note instead of a tip.
   B. The buyer of the second note was a Japanese businessman.
   C. Einstein learned that he had won the Nobel Prize during his trip to Japan.
   D. Einstein told the porter to keep the note since it might become valuable.

Passage 3 Questions 11 to 15 are based on the following passage:

In 1950, Helena Rubinstein was one of the richest women in the world. She started with nothing. She had no money, no education, and no one to help her. All she had were12 jars of face cream and a lot of energy and ambition. She turned these into a multimillion-dollar cosmetics (化妆品)empire.

Helena Rubinstein was born in 1870 in krakow, Poland. She was the oldest of eight girls. Helena's mother thought that beauty was very important. She used a special skin cream that a foreign chemist made for her. Helena's mother made all of her daughters use it too.

Helena's father wanted her to be a doctor. But she hated medicine and left school.

Her father was very angry. Then he wanted her to get married, but she refused. In 1902, she went to Melbourne, Australia, to live with a cousin and an uncle. She took only her clothes and 12 jars of the face cream.

Helena didn't speak English. She had no money and no plans. After she arrived, everyone noticed her beautiful skin. In Australia, the hot and dry weather is very bad for the skin. When she told some of the women about the face cream, they all wanted some. Helena sold them her cream and then ordered more.

Helena borrowed $1,550 and opened a shop to sell the cream. (80) She worked 18 hours a day, seven days a week. She lived simply and saved all of her profits. She also learned how to make different kinds of creams and showed women how to take care of their skin. It was the first shop of this kind in the world.

In less than two years, Rubinstein had paid back her loan and saved $50,000. She made more and more money every year. All this time, she thought only of work and success. A newspaper reporter named Edward Titus was in love with her. But she was not interested in him. She left Australia andEurope to learn more about the science of beauty.

11. Which of the following is TRUE?
   A. Helena Rubinstein became the richest person in the world in 1950.
   B. Helena's father helped Her to start her business.
   C. Helena was an energetic and ambitious person.
   D. Helena's mother supposed her with valuable business ideas.

12. From the passage, we learn that ________.
   A. Helena had 8 sisters
   B. Helena was born in Poland
   C. Helena's mother made skin cream for her daughters
   D. Helena's father was a doctor
13. Which of the following is TRUE?
   A. Helena went to Australia to study medicine.
   B. Helena went to Australia to do business.
   C. Helena's uncle and cousin worked for her.
   D. The weather in Australia is very bad for the skin.
13. Which of the following is NOT TRUE?
   A. Helena was a hardworking businesswoman.
   B. Helena saved all the money she made.
   C. Helena could make a variety of creams.
   D. Helena was in love with Edward Titus.
15. Which of the following is probably the best title for this passage?
   A. The Science of Beauty　　B. The Story of Helena
   C. A Story of Love　　D. A Business Empire

Part II　Vocabulary and Structure(30%)

Directions: In this part there are 30 incomplete sentences. For each sentence there are four choices marked A, B, C and D. Choose the ONE answer that best completes the sentence. Then blacken the corresponding letter on the Answer Sheet.

16. She is more beautiful than ________ in the class.
   A. Any girl　　B. any other girl　　C. all the girls　　D. any girls
17. Please don't come here today. I would rather you ________ tomorrow.
   A. came　　B. will come　　C. come　　D. are coming
18. Tom and John seldom go to the library in the evening, ________?
   A. do they　　B. don't they　　C. are they　　D. aren't they
19. It was in this room ________ they had a meeting yesterday.
   A. which　　B. there　　C. that　　D. where
20. ________ it is very late now, the researchers are still working jn the lab.
   A. As　　B. when　　C. If　　D. Although
21. ________ and you will make it next time.
   A. Work hard　　B. To Work hard　　C. working hard　　D. worked hard
22. Written in great haste, ________.
   A. Jim made a1ot of mistakes in the report
   B. There are plenty of mistakes in the report
   C. we found several mistakes in the report
   D. the report is full of mistakes
23. The number of primary schools in the rural areas ________ doubling in the past 50 years.
   A. are　　B. is　　C. have been　　D. has been
24. The key ________ success is hard work and persistence.
   A. on　　B. to　　C. for　　D. of
25. The train starts ________ 6:20, so you'd better get there before 6.
   A. on　　B. at　　C. in　　D. of
26. In the past we had only a day off for the whole week: we worked every day ________ Sunday.

A. besides B. beside C. except D. on top of

27. Though Thomas is very busy, he ________ one evening a week to play with his kids.

A. sets aside B. goes after C. sees through D. makes out

28. The top of that mountain is always covered ________ snow.

A. of B. by C. with D. on

29. He does morning exercises every day ________ make himself strong.

A. In order that B. in order to C. so that D. such that

30. The girl was not happy at the new school because she had ________ friends there.

A. few B. a few C. little D. a little

31. Beijing, as the capital of ________ People's Republic of China, enjoys ________ diverse range of people and cultures.

A. the; the B. a; a C. the; a D. a; the

32. Now I ________ to work by bike instead of by car as there are too many cars on the road in rush hours.

A. go B. went C. am gone D. was going

33. Generally, snakes won't attack humans ________ they are threatened with danger.

A. if B. since C. unless D. while

34. An old man got badly ________ in the road accident yesterday.

A. injure B. to injure C. injured D. injuring

35. Would you mind ________ James that his father is coming to see him this weekend.

A. tell B. to tell C. telling D. told

36. David left ________ raincoat in the room and went out.

A. his B. him C. theirs D. them

37. This is by far ________ of the games I have ever watched.

A. the exciting B. the more exciting C. the most exciting D. as exciting

38. I can easily ________ him at golf.

A. hit B. strike C. win D. beat

39. Janet ________ "Good morning!" to the teacher and then came in.

A. said B. spoke C. told D. talked

40. Lucy doesn't like outdoor activities. Her only ________ is listening to classical music.

A. custom B. hobby C. attitude D. tradition

41. These facts ________ show that he's not to be trusted.

A. single B. sole C. alone D. lonely

42. The room was not tiny. Shoes, socks and books were seen ________ on the floor.

A. now and then B. here and there C. hand in hand D. side by side

43. She ________ her finger to her lips as a sign for silence.

A. rose B. raised C. elevated D. arose

44. ________ coffee is coffee that you can prepare very quickly, for example by just adding hot water.

A. Imaginary B. Instant C. Impatient D. Intentional

45. Even if parents no longer live together, they each continue to be ________ for their children in the eye of the law.

A. reluctant B. tough C. responsible D. modest

Part III Identification(10%)

Directions: Each of the following sentences has four underlined parts marked A, B, Cand D. Identify the one that is not correct. Then blacken the corresponding letter on the Answer Sheet.

46. If you <u>had studied</u>(A) the problem carefully <u>yesterday</u>(B), you <u>won't have</u>(C) any difficulty <u>now</u>(D).

47. Hardly they had got to the bus stop when bus suddenly pulled away.
A B C D

48. The mountain was really very high, but I tried hardly to climb it.
A B C D

49. The reason I didn't attend the lecture was simply because I caught a bad cold that day.
A B C D

50. Dr. Bell gave some lectures, visited the Great Wall and going shopping downtown in Beijing.
A B C D

51. The first man swim across the river will receive a prize.
A B C D

52. In the morning I got on the train, which arrived Shanghai at night.
A B C D

53. Henry is not used to live in a noisy and crowded community thought he grew up in New York.
A B C D

54. Do you know the old English saying that a apple a day keeps the doctor away?
A B C D

55. The harder he worked, the most troubles he had in his early days as a scientist.
A B C D

Part IV Cloze (10%)

Directions: There are 20 blanks in the following passage, and for each blank there are 4 choices marked A, B, C and D at the end of the passage. You should choose ONE answer that best fits into the passage. Then blacken the corresponding letter on the Answer Sheet.

During a trip to observe wild animals in Africa, I encountered the least brave animal on earth, the wildebeest (角马). I sat on a riverbank for three hours watching a group of thousands build __56__ the courage to drink water.

More than a million wildebeests __57__ northward into the wetlands. It is a long, dry and difficult journey. Frequently, the only available water is the Grumeti River, __58__ represents both life and death. Unlike some creatures that can take moisture __59__ the grass they eat, wildebeests must drink from the river to live. The river supports other wildlife, including __60__ that kill and eat other animals. Though thirsty __61__ traveling, the wildebeests stand back from the water, sensing possible danger.

Moving slowly toward the bank can __62__ hours, as an individual wildebeest steps forward, steps back and then carefully steps forward again. More wildebeests gather together and advance, gradually pushing the leaders to the river, __63__ they want to go or not. It's been a long time __64__ they drink last time, and you feel their anxiety for water.

Lions are possibly on the __65__, saving energy as they wait for an opportunity for lunch. Once the large group moves to the river, lions could __66__, making the group running in a wild and uncontrolled __67__. The mad rush would raise a dust cloud that blocks the __68__ of the wildebeests nearby. A kill is almost guaranteed.

Sitting on that riverbank, I noticed that a young wildebeest finally stepped ahead and drank while the __69__ adults held back. Soon, others began drinking. But __70__ lining up along the bank, taking turns, they gathered and pushed. Some had to walk farther into the water than they were __71__ to go. Those pushed farther in water got frightened and in __72__ frightened the others. They all retreated hastily and returned to their route. Only the few that were __73__ enough got a drink. The others went __74__. There was no danger that day. Only the wildebeests' fear and __75__ of courage kept them from drinking.

56. A. up	B. out	C. in	D. over
57. A. visit	B. travel	C. see	D. swim
58. A. that	B. which	C. where	D. when

59. A. above	B. under	C. from	D. over
60. A. this	B. those	C. that	D. them
61. A. among	B. above	C. from	D. between
62. A. take	B. pay	C. spend	D. charge
63. A. when	B. where	C. what	D. whether
64. A. before	B. because	C. since	D. though
65. A. watch	B. sight	C. shout	D. walk
66. A. rescue	B. join	C. attack	D. visit
67. A. solution	B. way	C. method	D. role
68. A. fear	B. shout	C. jump	D. view
69. A. fearful	B. confident	C. pleasant	D. happy
70. A. Regardless of	B. instead of	C. in case of	D. in spite of
71. A. interesting	B. pleasant	C. willing	D. reluctant
72. A. hope	B. story	C. step	D. turn
73. A. short	B. bold	C. kind	D. small
74. A. thirst	B. hunger	C. thirsty	D. hungry
75. A. show	B. grasp	C. look	D. lack

Part V　Translation (20%)

Section A

Directions: In this part there are five sentences which you should, translate into Chinese. These sentences are all taken from the 3 passages you have just read in Reading Comprehension. You can refer back to the passages to identify their meanings in the context.

76. The bottle was found on an Australian island.
77. The bottle was partially filled with wet sand.
78. He was unable to give a cash tip, as a guest normally would.
79. A second Einstein note was also sold at the auction.
80. She worked 18 hours a day, seven days a week.

Section B

Directions: In this part there are five sentences in Chinese. You should translate them into English. Be sure to write clearly.

81. 法国以葡萄酒而闻名。
82. 你离开教室的时候,请把灯关上。
83. 我每天六点起床。
84. 我们刚刚吃过午饭。
85. 学生们正在打扫教室。

参考答案

1—15　BDAAA　ACDBB　CBDDB

16—45　BAACD　ADDBB　CACBA　CACCC　ACDAB　CBBBC

46—55　CADCC　BCACB

56—75　ABBCB　CADCA　CBDAB　CDBCD

76. 人们在澳大利亚的一个岛屿上发现了这个瓶子。
77. 这个瓶子装着部分湿的沙子。
78. 不能够像其他客人所做的那样,他无法给搬运工小费。

79. 爱因斯坦写的第二个纸条也在这个拍卖会上拍卖。
80. 她每周工作七天，每天工作十八个小时。
81. France is famous for its wine.
82. Please turn off the lights when you leave the classroom.
83. I get up at 6 every day.
84. We had lunch just now.
85. The students are cleaning the classroom.

北京地区成人本科学士学位英语统一考试

2018.11.10

Part I Reading Comprehension (30%)

Directions: There are three passages in this part. Each passage is followed by some questions or unfinished statements. For each of them there are four choices marked A, B, C and D. You should decide on the best choice and blacken the corresponding letteron the Answer Sheet.

Passage 1 Questions 1 to 5 are based on the following passage:

Flores Colque celebrated her 118th birthday last month. She is the oldest woman in Bolivia (玻利维亚). Following the death of a woman in Japan earlier this year, Flores Colque may now be the oldest person in the world. Her national paper says Flores Colque was born on October 26, 1900 in the mountains of Bolivia.

During her long life, Flores Colque has seen two world wars. Her home country of Bolivia had a major revolution. And the town where she is from has grown from 3,000 people to 175,000. But right now, Flores Colque seems mostly interested in her dogs and cats. She has not heard of the Guinness Book of World Records, and she does not care whether experts confirm she is the oldest person alive.

"She's always been active, easygoing and fun," says her grandniece, who lives with her in a simple home with a dirt floor. Government officials have paid for some improvements to the house, adding a brick path and railings (栏杆) so Flores Colque can walk safely. The mayor's office calls Flores Colque part of the country's living history.

On the day a reporter visited, Flores Colque was playing a small guitar and singing old songs in her native language. "If you would have told me you were coming, I'd have remembered all the songs," she joked.

When she was growing up, Flores Colque herded sheep in the Bolivian highlands. (76) Then she moved to a valley, where she sold fruits and vegetables. Those fruits and vegetables became her main food, and she still eats a healthy diet—except for a piece of cake and a glass of soda sometimes. She never married and does not have children. She cannot hear very well, but she is alert(机敏的). Flores Colque's age would make her interesting anywhere, but it is especially notable in Bolivia. The United Nations says the country has one of the South America's highest levels of death.

1. Which of the following is TRUE?
   A. The oldest person in Japan was born in 1901.
   B. Flores Colque is the oldest person in Bolivia.
   C. The oldest person in Japan knew Flores Colque.
   D. Flores Colque has read the Guinness Book of World Records.
2. According to the passage, Flores Colque lives in ________ now.
   A. Japan　B. North America　C. Europe　D. South America
3. The word herded in the last paragraph can probably be replaced by ________.
   A. made animals move along as a group
   B. fed animals as a group
   C. kept animals from hurting each other
   D. made sure animals did not follow one another

4. From the passage we learn that Flores Colque once ________.
A. sang to make a living　　B. fought in World War Two
C. sold fruits and vegetables　　D. worked as an animal doctor
5. Which of the following statements about Flores Colque is NOT TRUE?
A. She is easygoing.　　B. She keeps pets.
C. She remains single allher life.　　D. She lives alone.

Passage 2　Questions 6 to 10 are based on the following passage:

Playing video games can be a fun way to unwind or spend time with friends. In schools, teachers use games like Minecraft to encourage teamwork and critical thinking.

(77) But for some players, gaming has become an unhealthy habit. Late at night, they are glued to a screen. Schoolwork suffers. The video-game world seems a friendlier place than the real one.

Mental health experts have taken notice. In June, the World Health Organization (WHO) added gaming disorder to its list of diseases and health conditions. A person may have the disorder if gaming has damaged his or her relationships with family and friends, and if it has affected his or her daily activities.

Not all experts agree that excessive gaming should be called a disorder. They say people hooked on video games may be suffering from other mental health problems that should be treated first.

Others think WHO made the right call. Psychiatrist(精神科医生) Clifford Sussman treats gaming addiction (上瘾). (78) He says kids often have feelings of anxiety and loneliness. They get angry when a parent asks them to stop playing video games.

What makes video games addictive? Playing excites the brain's reward center. After a while, the brain becomes numb (麻木的) to pleasure. You feel bored without a controller in your hand. So you play even more.

One key to healthy gaming is to track how long you play. Sussman recommends taking at least an hour-long break after every hour of play. That gives the brain time to recover.

Young gamers who think they might have a problem should seek help from an adult. Sussman suggests you first answer a simple question: "Are you in control, or is the game in control?"

6. Which of the following is the best title for the passage?
A. Mental Health Problems　　B. Excessive Gaming
C. Unhealthy Habits　　D. Teamwork Training
7. The wordunwind in Paragraph 1 is closest in meaning to ________.
A. match　　B. meet　　C. retreat　　D. relax
8. Clifford Sussman's attitude to WHO's recognition of excessive gaming as a disorder is ________.
A. supportive　　B. doubtful　　C. neutral　　D. critical
9. Sussman advises game players to ________.
A. quit playing video games
B. play sports instead of video games
C. go to the hospital to get medical treatment
D. rest for at least an hour after every hour of play
10. According to the passage, which of the following statements is NOT TRUE?
A. Video games are addictive.
B. Video games are never used in classroom teaching.
C. Excessive gaming may affect a person's daily activities.
D. Some experts don't think excessive gaming should be called a disorder.

Passage 3　Questions 11 to 15 are based on the following passage:

Jayden Hairston was very disappointed. More than anything in the world, he wanted to learn how to sing. His school in Yonkers—just north of New York City— didn't offer the music instruction he needed. So he begged his parents to sign him up for after-school lessons.

Jayden's mother wanted to help her son follow his passion. (79) But private lessons were too expensive. Jayden, then 6 years old, knew exactly what to do. He took out his iPad. Then he began researching after-school arts programs. He soon came across the website for Harlem School of the Arts (HSA), in New York City. There, he could take voice and dance lessons. It was a bit far from Yonkers. But he convinced his parents to take him for a visit.

That was three years ago. Now Jayden is one of HSA's most active students. He takes singing, dancing, or theater lessons almost every day after school. (80) Last year, he performed in seven productions.

Like Jayden, students in many communities across the United States have limited access (使用的机会或权利) to arts instruction in schools. HSA is one of many nonprofit groups that bridges this gap by offering affordable arts classes. Groups like HSA are funded by donations (捐赠) and state grants. Many also receive money from the federal government's National Endowment (基金)for the Arts (NEA).

The NEA was established in 1965. Its goal is to promote access to the arts for all Americans. Some people, however, believe if's not the responsibility of the federal government to provide arts funding. President Donald Trump's 2019 proposal calls on Congress to reduce NEA funding and eventually eliminate the agency. The Trump administration argues that "private and other public sources" already provide funding for the arts. Congress has yet to make a decision.

Supporters of arts education say cutting the NEA is a bad idea. It could leave many children unable to participate in the arts. That's because 40% of the agency's grants go to high-poverty neighborhoods.

11. Which of the following is the best title for the passage?

A. Arts Education Is Expensive

B. Jaden Has Great Musical Talent

C. Some Students Have Limited Access to Arts Instruction

D. Trump Calls on Congress to Reduce Arts Funding

12. Jayden got the information about HSA from ________.

A. his mother B. his music teacher C. the Internet D. the newspaper

13. Jayden Hairston is ________ years old now.

A. 6 B. 7 C. 8 D. 9

14. The wordeliminate in Paragraph 5 is closest in meaning to ________.

A. criticize B. remove C. rebuild D. run

15. According to the passage, which of the following statements is TRUE?

A. HSA is a nonprofit group established in 1965.

B. Congress agrees to Trump's proposal to cut the NEA.

C. Arts instruction directly affects students5 academic success.

D. Jay den takes singing, dancing, and theater lessons at HSA.

Part II Vocabulary and Structure (30%)

Directions: In this part there are 30 incomplete sentences. For each sentence there are four choices marked A, B, C and D. Choose the ONE answer that best completes the sentence. Then blacken the corresponding letter on the Answer Sheet.

16. If Peter ________ to the office tomorrow, tell him the news please.

A. come B. comes C. came D. willcome

17. Yesterday Mr Smith bought ________ English dictionary while I got a Russian novel in the bookstore.

A. a B. an C. the D. /

18. Every day ________ water is wasted here though we are badly short of it.

A. any B. a number of C. a lot of D. these

19. Lucy got to the station ________ late to catch the train, so she had to wait for the next one.

A. enough B. very C. too D. rather

20. There are not ________ students in Class One as in Class Two.

A. many as B. as many C. more as D. as more

21. Your hard work has made the project a success. Without your work it ________ a complete failure.

A. was B. were C. be D. would have been

22. She speaks English ________ than her brother does.

A. best B. better C. good D. well

23. —Must we hand in our ________ exercise books today?

—Yes, ________.

A. you will B. you must C. you do D. you can

24. They will have learned Russian for 7 years by the time they ________ from the university next year.

A. will graduate B. will have graduated

C. graduate D. are going to graduate

25. —Why did you sell the old car at such a low price?

—I did it only because I was made ________ it.

A. do B. to do C. doing D. done

26. On his way home, he suddenly heard his name ________.

A. calling B. called C. to call D. call

27. There was an ________ look on his face when the actress appeared on the stage.

A. excited B. excite C. exciting D. excitedly

28. Under no circumstance ________ to tell lies to parents.

A. children are allowed B. are children allowed

C. children will allow D. will children allow

29. Lily ________ have known the truth, or she would have told us.

A. mustn't B. shouldn't C. can't D. needn't

30. George applied for the position three times ________ he finally got it.

A. before B. until C. when D. after

31. The best way to ________ this goal is to introduce new advanced technology.

A. cross B. perform C. achieve D. complete

32. The man who was accused ________ stealing the car said that he was not guilty.

A. for B. with C. of D. about

33. If you want to treat your friends to dinner in a good restaurant at the weekend, you'd better book a table ________.

A. in front B. before C. ahead of D. in advance

34. Can you do the job alone, or do you want someone to ________ you?

A. affect B. assist C. apply D. arrange

35. But for her mother's sudden illness, she would never think of breaking this ________ with you.

A. review B. interview C. movement D. appointment

36. When my American friends talk about China, they will always ________ it with the Great Wall.

A. advertise B. associate C. attach D. combine

37. The company is starting a new advertising campaign to ________ new customers to its stores.

A. attend B. attract C. stick D. transfer

38. It's wrong to judge people only according to their family ________.

A. basis B. area C. task D. background

39. Joe's friends all have a new bicycle, and he ________ wants one, too.

A. badly B. very C. rather D. barely

40. Although they plant trees in this area every year, the tops of some hills are still ________.

A. blank B. bare C. hollow D. vacant

41. —What has ________ the boy who fell off the bike?

—Nothing serious. The doctor says that he can come back to school in a day or two.

A. become of B. happened with C. occurredof D. become with

42. It's bad ________ for a man to smoke in the public places.

A. behavior B. action C. movement D. belief

43. I was shocked ________ the president's words.

A. with B. at C. in D. for

44. The United States has long been ________ to be among the best places in the world for higher education.

A. proposed B. read C. considered D. old

45. In recent years, several companies have developed new English language tests that are low-cost and ________ to use.

A. easy B. glad C. happy D. well

Part III Identification (10%)

Directions: Each of the following sentences has four underlined parts marked A, B, C and D. Identify the one that is not correct. Then blacken the corresponding letter on the Answer Sheet.

46. Hardly had he entered the office that he realized that he had left his report behind.

A B C D

47. Alice is fond of playing the piano while Henry is interested in listening to the music.

A B C D

48. The boy sitting by the window is the only one of the students who are from the countryside in our school.

A B C D

49. They can read such stories what have been rewritten in simple English.

A B C D

50. Excuse me, could you please tell me when is the sports meet going to be held?

A B C D

51. On addition, more than one-third of Americans over the age of 25 have a college degree or higher.

A B C D

52. Scientists have long struggle with how to measure the effects of climate change on wildlife.

A B C D

53. Florida's busiest airport will be the firstin the country to scan face of all passengers.

A B C D

54. Americans are not very creatingwhen it comes to breakfast.

A B C D

55. Parents today are concerned that their children are spending too many time on a computer or other electronic devices.

A B C D

Part IV Cloze (10%)

Directions: There are 20 blanks in the following passage, and for each blank there are 4 choices marked A, B, C and D at the end of the passage. You should choose ONE answer that best fits into the passage. Then blacken the corresponding letter on the Answer Sheet.

Walking through the woods alone can be a frightening prospect for a kid, but not for 7-year-old Matthew of Portland, Oregon. He doesn't have a backyard to __56__ in, so the woods behind his house serve the same __57__. He spends hours out there: swinging on a swing, __58__ across the valley to a friend's house, and __59__ garden knives to cut a path. He lays __60__ sticks to form a bridge across the small stream. And he does all of this alone.

Matthew's mom, Laura Randall, wants her son to gain skills and confidence that only __61__ with doing things alone. But she didn't just __62__ her 7-year-old outside the door with garden tools one day. They worked up to it gradually with what Randall calls "experiments in independence."

"Just those moments, increasingly longer moments, where he can choose to be __63__ his own," Randall explains. Randall knows this isn't the __64__ for today's parenting style. Gone are the days __65__ kids ride their bikes alone until the streetlights come on.

Randall has met people who think she's a __66__ parent. Once, an off-duty police officer started yelling at her when she left Matthew alone in the car __67__ a few minutes while she ran into a shop.

Randall knows that parents in several states have been arrested for __68__ their kids walk to the park alone, or even __69__ them to walk to school. And so she was a bit __70__ about what this man might do.

Anyway, they talked it out, and the man walked __71__. Randall felt confident about __72__ her parenting, partly __73__ she had connected with a group __74__ Free Range Kids. This group __75__ childhood independence, and gives families the information they need to push back against a culture of overprotection.

56. A. swim B. play C. move D. live
57. A. road B. path C. target D. purpose
58. A. walking B. arriving C. reaching D. speaking
59. A. use B. enjoy C. using D. enjoying
60. A. out B. away C. down D. off
61. A. put B. come C. react D. pay
62. A. forbid B. order C. treat D. leave
63. A. at B. in C. with D. on
64. A. standard B. freedom C. relation D. reflection
65. A. when B. which C. where D. what
66. A. kind B. good C. bad D. sick
67. A. with B. for C. on D. at
68. A. accompanying B. asking C. encouraging D. letting
69. A. forbid B. allow C. forbidding D. allowing
70. A. excited B. moved C. worried D. pleased
71. A. away B. across C. up D. out
72. A. persuading B. defending C. arguing D. offering
73. A. although B. before C. because D. until
74. A. describe B. call C. described D. called
75. A. responds B. opposes C. provides D. promote

Part V Translation (20%)

Section A

Directions: In this part there are five sentences which you should translate into Chinese. These sentences are all taken from the 3 passages you have just read in Reading Comprehension. You can refer back to the passages to identify their meanings in the context.

76. Then she moved to a valley, where she sold fruits and vegetables.
77. But for some players, gaming has become an unhealthy habit.
78. He says kids often have feelings of anxiety and loneliness.
79. But private lessons were too expensive.
80. Last year, he performed in seven productions

Section B

Directions: In this part there are five sentences in Chinese. You should translate them into English. Be sure to write clearly.

81. 由于下大雨，到处都出现了交通拥堵。
82. 如果不能来开会，请告诉我。
83. 我们刚才去超市了。
84. 早餐我通常吃面包和鸡蛋。
85. 外面太嘈杂了，我无法集中精力。

参考答案

1—15 BDACD BDADB CCDBD
16—45 BBCCB DBBCB BABCA CCDBD BBDAB AABCA
46—55 BDCBC ABDBC
56—75 BDACC BDDAA CBDDC ABCDD
76. 然后她搬到山谷中，在哪里她卖水果和蔬菜。
77. 但是对于一些游戏者来说，打游戏已成为一种不健康的习惯。
78. 他说孩子们总是有这种焦虑的感受。
79. 但是私人的课程是非常昂贵的。
80. 去年，他在西部演出中有所表演。
81. There was a traffic jam everywhere because of the heavy rain.
82. If you can't come for the meeting, please tell me.
83. We went to the supermarket just now.
84. I usually have some bread and eggs for breakfast.
85. I can't concentrate because it is too noisy outside.

北京地区成人本科学士学位英语统一考试

2019.5.11

Part I Reading Comprehension (30%)

Directions: There are three passages in this part. Each passage is followed by some questions or unfinished statements. For each of them there are four choices marked A, B, C and D. You should decide on the best choice and blacken the corresponding letter on the Answer Sheet.

Passage 1 Questions 1 to 5 are based on the following passage:

On July 20, 1969, Neil Armstrong became the first person to walk on the moon. The spacesuit Armstrong wore on his mission has come to symbolize courage and human achievement. In 1971, the Smithsonian's National Air and Space Museum (NASM) acquired Armstrong's suit. It stood proudly on display for visitors to admire, until there were changes in the suit's appearance. "Over time, the suit started to show signs of deterioration (变坏)," Lisa Young says. She works at NASM and her job is to preserve historical and cultural treasures.

Plastics are tricky to preserve. They tend to degrade (降解) over time. Neoprene is one type of plastic in Armstrong's suit. The material can turn brittle and break into tiny pieces. <u>(76) This would ruin the spacesuit.</u> NASM, seeking ways to preserve this historical treasure, removed it from display in 2006.

Yet history can still be saved. Sunlight, water, humidity, and dust can cause plastics to degrade. Scientists have found that storing plastics in cooler temperatures, with lower humidity levels, can slow degradation. Young says Armstrong's suit is currently in storage at a temperature of 63°F and a lower relative humidity of 30%. These conditions will be maintained when Armstrong's suit returns to a museum display case in time for this year's 50th anniversary (周年纪念日) of the moon landing.

Plastic degradation affects art, too. Artist Claes Oldenburg created False Food Selection in 1966. (77) It consists of plastic food displayed in a wooden box. The plastic food used to look real. Now, some of it has flattened and yellowed. The artwork's wooden box produces an acidic gas that eats away at the plastic, which speeds up the degradation process. But Young is motivated to preserve this artwork and others like it. "Plastics are a part of our history," she says. "It's important to preserve them so that future generations can understand the journey we've taken."

1. Which of the following is the best title for the passage?
   A. Landing on the Moon B. Preserving Plastics
   C. Neil Armstrong's Spacesuit D. Application of Plastics
2. The wordbrittle in Paragraph 2 probably means ________.
   A. well established B. heavily loaded
   C. easily upset D. easily broken
3. In 2006, NASM removed Armstrong's spacesuit from display to ________.
   A. put it on sale B. return it to Armstrong
   C. give it to another museum D. look for ways to preserve it
4. In Claes Oldenburg's False Food Selection, the wooden box ________ the plastic degradation.
   A. slows down B. leads to
   C. accelerates D. doesn't play any role in
5. According to the passage, which of the following statements is NOT TRUE?
   A. Sunlight, water and dust contribute to plastic degradation.
   B. Armstrong's spacesuit is currently on public display at NASM.
   C. NASM acquired Armstrong's spacesuit in 1971.
   D. Claes Oldenburg is an artist.

Passage 2 Questions 6 to 10 are based on the following passage:

A little boy in South Carolina got to celebrate his birthday twice: After only one friend showed up to his birthday party, the local fire department decided to throw him another one.

The City of Beaufort Fire Department shared the story of a party the fire department held for a local boy named Cooper, who was disappointed when only one of his classmates showed up to his 6th birthday party. But after a community member gave the local fire department a call, (78) the members were quick to come to his rescue.

"We jumped on board and said we'll do whatever we can to make sure he has a great birthday and that more than one child shows up," Beaufort firefighter Ross Vezin says. "We made arrangements to pick him up from school along with his mom and brother, and we brought him to a bowling alley (保龄球场) along with a biker group."

The fire department was also able to bring nearly 75 other kids from school to celebrate alongside Cooper, whose mother, Nicoala Shiflet, said he has difficulty making friends because he suffers from autism (自闭症).

"They had cake and presents and got to do some bowling," Vezin continues, adding that the party came to be known as "Cooper's Birthday 2.0".

From riding in a fire truck to seeing the motorcycles from the biker group and even being welcomed by so many new friends, Cooper loved his celebration. And it won't be the last time that the little boy gets to hang out with the fire department responsible for it.

"We're also going to have him up next week," Vezin says. "We're going to give him a fire department T-shirt and a tour of our fire station."

6. Who did the most to make Cooper's second birthday party a great success?
   A. Firefighters from Beaufort Fire Department.
   B. Men from the biker group.

C. Community members.

D. Cooper's parents.

7. Which of the following statements is NOT TRUE according to the passage?

A. About 75 kids showed up at Cooper's second birthday party.

B. Cooper's mother and brother were at his second birthday party.

C. Those joining the second birthday party did some bowling.

D. Cooper got a T-shirt from the fire department at his second birthday party.

8. The phrasehave him up in the last paragraph is closest in meaning to ________.

A. invite him as a guest　　B. meet him by chance

C. take care of him　　D. make friends with him

9. Only one kid went to Cooper's first birthday party because ________.

A. Cooper was not good at making friends

B. other kids were busy with their classes then

C. Cooper liked to play with grown-ups

D. Cooper didn't invite his classmates

10. We learn from the passage that Cooper was ________ the second birthday party.

A. disappointed with　　B. satisfied with

C. frightened by　　D. angry about

Passage 3　Questions 11 to 15 are based on the following passage:

There was once a tree in South Africa so wide that it could fit 60 people inside its hollow trunk. The tree reached 62 feet into the sky. It was more than 1,100 years old. But recently, that tree and others like it have died. (79) Scientists are wondering why.

The tree was a baobab. A baobab looks like a giant oak (橡树) turned upside down. Its branches resemble roots reaching toward the sky. It grows in Africa and is called the Tree of Life. Baobab trees tend to live a long time. One of the oldest stood for more than 2,400 years. Various baobabs have been used as a shop, a prison, a house, and a bus shelter.

In 2005, scientists began a survey to determine the age of more than 60 baobabs. (80) During the process, they noticed that several of the trees had died. Their results, recently published *in Nature Plants*, show that nine of the 13 oldest baobab trees and five out of six of the largest died in the 12-year study period.

Stephan Woodborne conducted the baobab study with six other scientists. They say more research is needed to know why the trees died, but they think climate change may be to blame. That's because the trees showed no evidence of disease. Plus, many were in national parks, so they would have been protected from human harm. Also, Woodborne says, the most affected baobabs are on the outer edge of their ideal habitat (栖息地). Increasing heat and shifting rainy seasons have made it harder for baobabs in these areas to thrive.

Smaller and younger baobabs are dying too. "The big ones and the old ones caught the attention of the media," Woodborne says. "But it's not just those. It's unprecedented (空前的) that they should be dying across the age spectrum. We've got to do a reality check on our own footprints in terms of the way we live our lives. If we all changed what we did a little bit, it would start to make a difference."

11. Which of the following is the best title for the passage?

A. Die-off of Africa's Baobabs　　B. National Parks in Africa.

C. Africa Rainy Seasons　　D. Strange-Looking Baobabs

12. The baobab study lasted ________.

A. 6 years　　B. 9 years　　C. 12 years　　D. 13 years

13. According to Stephan Woodborne, the baobab trees died mainly because of ________.

A. human damage　　B. disease

C. climate change　　D. the attack of insects

14. The word spectrum in the last paragraph is closest in meaning to ________.
A. point B. range C. edge D. team
15. According to the passage, Which of the following statements is NOT TRUE?
A. Further research is needed to know why the Baobabs died.
B. Baobab trees can live a long time.
C. The researchers found that only old baobab trees died.
D. The baobab study involved more than 60 baobabs.

Part II Vocabulary and Structure (30%)

Directions: In this part there are 30 incomplete sentences. For each sentence there are four choices marked A, B, C and D. Choose the ONE answer that best completes the sentence. Then blacken the corresponding letter on the Answer Sheet.

16. Becoming ________ American citizen takes a lot of work.
A. / B. an C. a D. the
17. She was the only member of her family ________ spoke English.
A. that B. whom C. what D. which
18. ________ he walked, he looked carefully at the ice in front of him.
A. If B. As C. Since D. Whether
19. At about twelve o'clock, the man decided ________ to eat his lunch.
A. being stopped B. stopping
C. to be stopped D. to stop
20. He threw stones at the birds but could not hit ________.
A. him B. her C. it D. them
21. Peter is going to a lake ________ he can fish with his friends.
A. which B. here C. where D. there
22. They ________ into the dormitory already.
A. have moved B. moving C. move D. having moved
23. Everyone is getting old, but you look ________ than ever.
A. younger B. youngest C. the youngest D. young
24. —Do you enjoy your present job?
—________. I just do it for a living.
A. Of course B. Not really C. Not likely D. Not a little
25. They ________ have arrived at lunchtime but their flight was delayed.
A. will B. can C. must D. should
26. If you ________ smoke, please go outside.
A. can B. should C. must D. may
27. The police officers in our city work hard ________ the rest of us can live a safe life.
A. in case B. as if C. in order that D. only if
28. No matter how ________, it is not necessarily lifeless.
A. a desert may be dry B. dry may a desert be
C. may a desert be dry D. dry a desert may be
29. The girl glanced over her shoulder and found herself ________ by a young man in black.
A. was followed B. had been followed
C. following D. followed
30. They made a great effort to prepare the exhibition, ________ to achieve a big success.
A. hoped B. hoping C. to hope D. hope
31. I have been looking for this book for several weeks, and ________ I have found it.

A. at least　B. in no time　C. at last　D. at present

32. Thousands of people ________ the funeral.

A. cared　B. attended　C. devoted　D. appeared

33. I'm afraid you have no ________ but to come along with us.

A. possibility　B. permission　C. choice　D. selection

34. The old man got into the ________ of storing money under the bed.

A. habit　B. tradition　C. use　D. custom

35. She is so ________ that she cried for days when her pet cat died.

A. sensible　B. sensitive　C. imaginative　D. impressive

36. After dinner the minister made a short ________ to the guests.

A. delivery　B. speech　C. pronunciation　D. conversation

37. Jean is one of those modem girls who always ________ the latest fashions.

A. put up with　B. come up with　C. keep up with　D. get along with

38. The room was so quiet that she could hear the ________ of her heart.

A. hitting　B. beating　C. tapping　D. knocking

39. This watch is ________ to all the other watches in the store.

A. superior　B. advantageous　C. super　D. beneficial

40. The ________ of the valley was very wet.

A. head　B. basis　C. top　D. bottom

41. The sun ________ in the east.

A. rises　B. raises　C. increases　D. goes

42. When you have kids, you won't have time to go to parties ________.

A. further　B. still more　C. anymore　D. no more

43. They hid themselves ________ a tree.

A. off　B. after　C. behind　D. before

44. The protests were not ________ to New York.

A. balanced　B. ended　C. limited　D. attended

45. He has never recovered from the ________ of his brother's death.

A. aim　B. shock　C. plan　D. opinion

Part III　Identification（10%）

Directions: Each of the following sentences has four underlined parts marked A, B, C and D. Identify the one that is not correct. Then blacken the corresponding letter on the Answer Sheet.

46. He doesn't want to spend many time shoppingin New York.
　　A　B　C　D

47. If he were more experienced, I willvote for him.
　　A　B　C　D

48. Taking a train is most comfortable than taking an airplane.
　　A　B　C　D

49. I used to swam in high school but I don't have time now.
　　A　B　C　D

50. I hopethe weathermust be sunny Friday.
　　A　B　C　D

51. Jim sold most of his things. He has hardly nothing left in the house.
　　A　B　C　D

52. The new stadium being built for the next Asian Games will be three times as bigger as the present one.
　　A　B　C　D

53. After the long journey, the three of them went back home, hungry and tiredly.
A B C D

54. Surprising and happy, Tony stood up and accepted the prize.
A B C D

55. We tried hard, and eventually, we were able to get Mike lent us his car just for a day.
A B C D

Part IV Cloze (10%)

Directions: There are 20 blanks in the following passage, and for each blank there are 4 choices marked A, B, C and D at the end of the passage. You should choose ONE answer that best fits into the passage. Then blacken the corresponding letter on the Answer Sheet.

In the summer of 1838, John Wannamaker was born in Philadelphia. His father was a brick-maker. Whenever he was not __56__ school, John was engaged in turning bricks which were laid in the sun to __57__. Thus, the quality of working __58__ was instilled (灌输) into the young man. __59__ his own diligence, he later became the merchant prince of Philadelphia.

A few years later, school was __60__ and he worked in a store four miles away __61__ his home. He walked eight miles every day, going to work in the morning and __62__ back home in the evening. He __63__ only $1.25 for the entire week's work. Afterwards he was __64__ as a clerk in a law office, and later he worked in a clothing store at a __65__ of $1.50 per week. Here he seemed to find the calling __66__ suited his taste, and he developed a pleasing disposition (性格). People __67__ to trade with the young clerk. It was not long __68__ he was called to responsible positions.

In 1861, he already saved several hundred dollars. As he had __69__ a reputation for honesty and ability, he was able to start in business on his own account. This firm of Wannamaker & Brown was situated __70__ the comer of Sixth and Market streets. As the business __71__, other stores were opened. John Wannamaker, the poor clerk—after a __72__ of twenty years of hard work, pushed by energy, controlled a force of 6,000 employees. Not only did the firm handle clothing, but also articles that could be generally __73__ in retail (零售) stores.

The fecret of his great success is his tireless diligence, and a __74__ mastery of his business. He was one of the most successful merchants in history who were extremely good at thinking of new business ideas and __75__ them successful.

56. A. at B. with C. for D. about
57. A. work B. see C. fly D. dry
58. A. quite B. hard C. shortly D. easily
59. A. Beyond B. Along C. By D. In
60. A. absorbed B. announced C. abandoned D. advanced
61. A. for B. through C. with D. from
62. A. coming B. came C. leaving D. left
63. A. captured B. received C. combined D. returned
64. A. employed B. consumed C. followed D. displayed
65. A. service B. number C. salary D. course
66. A. where B. which C. when D. what
67. A. worried B. hated C. permitted D. liked
68. A. although B. after C. because D. before
69. A. earned B. reached C. pushed D. repaired
70. A. above B. below C. at D. with
71. A. followed B. divided C. increased D. dropped
72. A. justice B. period C. recall D. misery

73. A. visited　B. caught　C. produced　D. found
74. A. thorough　B. public　C. normal　D. recent
75. A. put　B. made　C. putting　D. making

Part V　Translation (20%)

Section A

Directions*: *In this part there are five sentences which you should translate into Chinese, These sentences are all taken from the 3 passages you have just read in Reading Comprehension. You can refer back to the passages to identify their meanings in the context.

76. This would ruin the spacesuit.
77. It consists of plastic food displayed in a wooden box.
78. The members were quick to come to his rescue.
79. Scientists are wondering why.
80. During the process, they noticed that several of the trees had died.

Section B

Directions*: *In this part there are five sentences in Chinese. You should translate them into English. Be sure to write clearly.

81. 他每天坐公共汽车上班。
82. 整个早晨我都在打篮球。
83. 这部电影值得看。
84. 今天比昨天热得多。
85. 飞机马上就要起飞了。

参考答案

1—15　BDDCB　ADAAB　ACCBC
16—45　BABDD　CAABD　CCDDB　CBCAB　BCBAD　ACCCB
46—55　BCBAC　CCDAD
56—75　ADBCC　DABAC　BDDAC　CBDAD
76. 这会毁坏太空服。
77. 展出是由一些放在木质盒子中的塑料食物构成。
78. 消防局队员们反应迅速，去"救援"小男孩。
79. 科学家正在琢磨这些树为什么会死亡。
80. 在此过程中，他们注意到一些树已经死亡。
81. He goes to work by bus every day.
82. I was playing basketball all this morning.
83. This movie is worth seeing.
84. It is much hotter today than yesterday.
85. The plane is going to take off soon.

附录 词 汇 表

A

a/an *art.* 一,一个
art. (一类事物中的)任何一个
prep. 每一
abandon *v.* 放弃,抛弃
ability *n.* 能力,智能,才能
able *a.* 有能力的,能干的
aboard *ad.* 在船(飞机,车)上
prep. 在船(飞机)上
about *ad.* 在周围,附近
ad. 大约,差不多
prep. 关于,对于
prep. 在……周围,在……附近
about to 即将
above *prep.* 上……上面,超过
a. 上面的,上述的
ad. 在上面
above all 首先,尤其
abuse *vt.* 虐待
absence *n.* 缺席,不在场
absolute *a.* 绝对的,完全的
absolutely *ad.* 完全地,极其
ad. 肯定地,绝对地
absorb *vt.* 吸收
academic *a.* 学院的,学术的
accelerate *v.* 加速,促进
accent *n.* 腔调,口音
n. 重音,重音符号
accept *v.* 接受,认可
acceptance *n.* 接受,接纳;承认
accident *n.* 事故
n. 意外的事,偶然的事
accompany *v.* 陪伴,伴随
v. 伴奏
accomplish *v.* 完成
accordance *n.* 一致
in accordance with 与……一致;按照,依照
according
according to 按照,根据
account *n.* 账,账目
v. 说明,解释
on account of 因为,由于
accumulate *vt.* 积累,积聚
vi. 累积,聚积
accurate *a.* 准确的,精确的
accuse *v.* 谴责
v. 指控,告发
accustomed *a.* 惯常的,习惯的
accustomed to 习惯于
ache *v./n.* 疼痛,酸痛
achieve *v.* 完成
v. 达到,达成,获得
achievement *n.* 完成,达到
n. 成就,成绩
acid *n.* 酸,酸性物质
a. 酸的
acquaintance *n.* 熟人,相识
acquire *v.* 取得,获得
acre *n.* 英亩
across *ad./prep.* 横越,横断
prep. 在……那边
act *n.* 行为,动作;(一)幕;法令,条例
v. 行动,举动;起作用;表演
act on 按照……行事
action *n.* 行动,动作
active *a.* 活动的,活跃的,活泼的
a. 敏捷的,积极的,主动的
activity *n.* 活动
actor *n.* 男演员
actress *n.* 女演员
actual *a.* 实际的,现实的
actually *ad.* 实际上
A. D. 公元
add *v.* 加,加上;增加,增进
addition *n.* 加法,增加
in addition to 除……之外
additional *a.* 附加的,另外的
address *n.* 地址,通讯处
n./v. 致词
v. 致函,写地址
adequate *a.* 足够的,恰当的
adjective *n./a.* 形容词
adjust *v.* 调节,调整
administration *n.* 管理,经营
n. 管理部门,行政机关,政府
admire *v.* 羡慕,赞赏,钦佩
admit *v.* 允许进入,接纳
v. 承认
adopt *v.* 收养
v./n. 采用,采纳,通过
adult *n.* 成人
advance *v.* 推进,促进
v./n. 前进,进展
advanced *a.* 前进的,先进的
advantage *n.* 优点,有利条件
n. 利益,好处
take advantage of 利用,趁……之机
adventure *n.* 冒险,惊险活动
adverb *n.* 副词
advertisement *n.* 广告
advice *n.* 忠告,意见
advise *v.* 忠告,劝告
v. 通知
affair *n.* 事,事情,事件
affect *vt.* 影响
affection *n.* 爱,感情
afford *v.* 担负得起,买得起,花得起(时间)
v. 供给,给予
afraid *a.* 怕的,害怕的
a. 惟恐的,担心的
Africa *n.* 非洲
African *a.* 非洲的
n. 非洲人
after *prep./conj.* 在……后
ad. 在后,后来
afternoon *n.* 下午
afterwards *ad.* 后来,以后
again *ad.* 再,再次
ad. 又,重新
against *prep.* 对(着),逆
prep. 反对,违反
prep. 靠,靠近
age *n.* 年龄
n. 时代
v. 变老
agent *n.* 代理人,代表
ago *ad.* 以前,……前
agree *v.* 同意,赞同;一致,适合
agree on (双方)同意,赞同
agreement *n.* 同意,一致;协定,
aggressive *a.* 挑衅的;放肆的;积极进取的
agriculture *n.* 农业
ahead *ad.* 前头,在前
ahead of 在……前面,先于
aid *v.* 援助,救援
n. 援助,救护;助手,辅助物
aim *v.* 志在,旨在(at);瞄准,针对(at)
n. 目标,目的
air *n.* 空气,大气,天空
v. 使通风
n. 神气,架子
aircraft *n.* 飞机,飞行器
airline *n.* 航空公司
n. (飞机的)航线

airplane *n.* 飞机
airport *n.* 航空站,机场
awkward *a.* 尴尬的
alarm *n.* 惊恐,忧虑;报警器
v. 使惊恐;向……报警
alcohol *n.* 酒精,乙醇
alike *a.* 相同的,相像的
alive *a.* 活着的
a. 活跃的,活泼的,热闹的
all *a.* 全部的,所有的
pron. 全部,一切
ad. 完全,都
after all 毕竟,虽然这样
all right 行,可以,顺利,良好
at all 完全,根本
all over 到处,遍及
in all 总共,共计
allow *v.* 允许
v. 承认
allow for 考虑到
almost *ad.* 几乎,差不多
alone *a.*/*ad.* 独自,单独
ad. 仅仅,只
along *ad.* 向前
prep. 沿着
aloud *ad.* 出声地,大声地
alphabet *n.* 字母表
already *ad.* 已,已经
also *ad.* 亦,也
alter *v.* 改变,变更
although *conj.* 虽然,即使
altogether *ad.* 完全,总之,全部
always *ad.* 总是,永远
a. m./A. M. 上午
amaze *v.* 使惊愕,使惊叹
ambition *n.* 雄心,野心
ambulance *n.* 救护车
America *n.* 美洲,美国
American *a.* 美洲的,美国的
n. 美国人
among *prep.* 在……之中,在……之间
amount *n.* 数量,数额,总数
v. 合计,相当于,等(to)
amuse *v.* 给……以消遣,给……以娱乐
analysis *n.* 分析,解析
analyze/analyse *v.* 分析,分解
ancestor *n.* 祖宗,祖先
anchor *n.* 锚
v. 抛锚,停泊
ancient *a.* 古代的,古老的
and *conj.* 和,而且
anger *n.* 愤怒,气愤
v. 使发怒,激怒
angle *n.* 角
n. 角度,观点
angry *a.* 愤怒的,生气的

animal *n.* 动物,野兽,牲畜
a. 动物的,野兽的
ankle *n.* 踝
announce *v.* 宣布,通告
v. 报告……的来到
annoy *v.* 使烦恼,使生气,打搅
annual *a.* 每年的,每年度的
another *a.* 另一,再一
pron. 另一个
one another 互相
one after another 一个接一个
answer *n.* 回答,答复,答案
v. 回答,答复,响应
anticipate *vt.* 预料,期望
anxiety *n.* 焦虑,挂虑
n. 渴望,热望
anxious *a.* 担心的,焦虑的
a. 渴望的
any *a.*(否定,疑问,条件句中)什么,一些
a. 任何的,任一的
pron. 无论哪个,无论哪些
anybody *pron.* 任何人,无论谁
pron. 重要人物
anyhow *ad.* 无论如何,不管怎样
anyone *pron.* 任何人,无论谁
anything *pron.* 无论什么事(物),任何事(物)
anyway *ad.* 无论如何
anywhere *ad.* 无论哪里
apart *ad.* 分离,隔开
ad. 相距,相隔
apartment *n.* 一套公寓房间
apologize/-ise *vi.* 道歉,认错
apology *n.* 道歉,歉意
apparent *a.* 明显的
appear *n.* 出现,出场,问世
v. 好像是,仿佛
appearance *n.* 出现,出场,露面
n. 外表,外观
appetite *n.* 食欲,胃口
apple *n.* 苹果,苹果树
application *n.* 申请,申请书
n. 运用,应用
apply *v.* 申请;运用,应用
appoint *v.* 任命,委派;约定
appointment *n.* 约会,约见;任命,选派
appreciate *v.* 感激,感谢
v. 评价,欣赏,赏识
approach *v.* 接近,走近
n. 途径,方法,探讨
appropriate *a.* 适合的,恰当的
approval *n.* 赞同,批准
approve *v.* 赞成,赞许,同意
v. 批准,审定,通过
approximately *ad.* 近似地,约
April *n.* 四月

area *n.* 面积;地区,范围,领域
arbitrary *a.* 随心所欲的,专断的
a. 任意(性)的
architecture *n.* 建筑学,建筑术
n. 建筑式样,建筑风格
argue *v.* 辩论,争论
v. 主张,论证
argument *n.* 辩论,论点,论据
arise *vi.* 出现,发生
vi. (from) 由……引起,起源于
arithmetic *n.* 算术
arm1 *n.* 手臂,臂状物;扶手,衣袖
arm2 *n.* (*pl.*) 武器,武装
v. 武装,装备
army *n.* 军队,军;大群
around *ad.* 周围,到处,在附近
prep. 在……周围,围着
prep. 在……各地
arouse *vt.* 引起,激起,唤起
vt. 唤醒
arrange *v.* 整理,布置
v. 安排,筹备
arrangement *n.* 安排;准备工作
arrest *v.*/*n.* 逮捕,扣留
arrival *n.* 到达,到来
arrive *v.* 到来,到达
v. 达成,得出
arrow *n.* 箭,箭状物
n. 箭头记号
art *n.* 艺术,美术
n. 技术,技艺
n. (*pl.*) 文科
article *n.* 文章
n. 东西
n. 冠词
artificial *a.* 人工的
artist *n.* 艺术家,美术家
as *ad.* 一样,同样
conj. 如……一样;正当;由于
prep. 作为,当作
as if/as though 好像,仿佛
as... as 与……一样
no as/so... as 不如……那样
as to 关于
ash *n.* 灰
ashamed *a.* 惭愧的,害臊的
Asia *n.* 亚洲
Asian *a.* 亚洲的
n. 亚洲人
aside *ad.* 一旁,一边
ask *v.* 问,求,请求,邀请,约请
ask for 请求,要求
ask after 询问,问候
asleep *a.* 睡着的
assemble *v.* 集合,集会
v. 装配,组装

assembly *n.* 集会,会议
n. 装配
assignment *n.* 分派的任务,指定的作业
n. 分配,指派
assist *v.* 帮助,协助
assistance *n.* 帮助,援助
assistant *n.* 助手,助教
a. 助理的
assume *v.* 假装;假定,设想;承担,采取
assure *v.* 保证,使确信
astonish *v.* 使惊讶,使吃惊
astronaut *n.* 宇航员
at *prep.* [表示地点,位置,场合] 在,于
prep. [表示时刻,时节,年龄] 在,当
prep. [表示目标,方向] 对,向
Atlantic *a.* 大西洋的
n. (the) 大西洋
atmosphere *n.* 空气,大气,大气层;气氛
atom *n.* 原子
attach *v.* 贴上,系上,附上;
v. 使依附,使隶属;使依恋
attack *v./n.* 攻击,进攻,抨击
attain *vt.* 获得;达到
attempt *v./n.* 试图,努力
attend *v.* 出席
v. 照顾,护理(to)
v. 注意,留意,专心于(to)
attention *n.* 注意,注意力
n. 立正
pay attention to 注意
attitude *n.* 态度,看法
n. 姿势
attract *v.* 吸引,招引,引诱
attraction *n.* 吸引,吸引力
n. 具有吸引力的事物(或人)
attractive *a.* 有吸引力的
audience *n.* 听众,观众,读者
August *n.* 八月
aunt *n.* 伯母,婶母,姑母,舅母,姨母
Australia *n.* 澳大利亚
author *n.* 作者
automatic *a.* 自动的
automobile/auto *n.* 汽车
autumn *n.* 秋
available *a.* 可利用的,可得到的
avenue *n.* 林荫路,大街
n. 途径,手段
average *n.* 平均,平均数
v. 平均,均分
a. 平均的
a. 通常的,一般的
avoid *v.* 避免,逃避
awake *a.* 醒着的
v. 唤醒,醒来,唤起
award *n.* 奖,奖品
v. 授予,奖给
aware *a.* 知道的,意识到的
away *ad.* 远离,离开
awful *a.* 使人畏惧的,可怕的,骇人的
ax(e) *n.* 斧子

B

baby *n.* 婴儿,孩子
back *n.* 背,背面,后面
ad. 向后,后退,回复
v. 后退
v. 支持
a. 后面的
back and forth 来回,往返
background *n.* 背景,经历
backward *ad.* 倒,向后
a. 向后的,倒行的
a. 落后的,迟钝的
bad *a.* 坏的,低劣的,错误的
a. 恶性的,严重的
a. 不舒服的,病的
badly *ad.* 坏,差,拙劣地
ad. 严重地,非常
badminton *n.* 羽毛球
bag *n.* 袋,提包,背包
baggage *n.* 行李
bake *v.* 烤,烘,焙
balance *v.* 称,平衡
v. 均衡,平衡
n. 差额,结余,余款
n. 天平
ball1 *n.* 球,球状物
ball2 *n.* 舞会
balloon *n.* 气球
banana *n.* 香蕉
band1 *n.* 乐队,军乐队
n. 一群,一伙
band2 *n.* 条,带
v. 缚,绑扎
bank1 *n.* 岸,堤
bank2 *n.* 银行
bar *n.* 棍,横木,闩
n. 障碍,妨碍
v. 闩上,阻挡,妨碍
n. 酒吧
barber *n.* 理发师
bare *a.* 赤裸的,光秃的,空的
a. 仅有的,勉强的
bargain *v.* 讨价还价
n. 便宜货
n. 契约,合同,交易
barn *n.* 谷仓,仓库
barrel *n.* 枪管,炮管
n. 桶
barrier *n.* 障碍,屏障
base *n.* 基础
n. 基地,根据地
based on 以……为基础
basic *a.* 基本的,基础的
basin *n.* 盆,脸盘
n. 盆地
basis *n.* 根据,基础
basket *n.* 篮子,篓
basketball *n.* 篮球
bat *n.* 蝙蝠
bath *n.* 洗澡,沐浴
n. 浴室,浴池,浴盆
bathe *v.* 洗澡,游泳
v. 浸,冲洗
bathroom *n.* 浴室
n. 盥洗室
battle *n.* 战斗,战役,斗争
bay *n.* 海湾,港湾
B.C. 公元前
be *v.* 是,就是,等于
v. 在,存在
beach *n.* 海滨,海滩
bean *n.* 豆,菜豆
bear1 *n.* 熊
bear2 *v.* 忍受,容忍
v. 负荷,负担
v. 结果实,生子女
beard *n.* 胡子
beast *n.* 兽,牲畜
n. 凶残的人
beat *v.* 打败,战胜
v./n. 打,敲
n. 拍子,节拍
v. 搅
v./n. 跳动,搏动
beautiful *a.* 美的
beauty *n.* 美,美丽
n. 美人,美丽的东西
because *conj.* 因为
because of 由于,因为
become *v.* 成为,变成
v. 适宜,同……相称
bed *n.* 床,床位
n. 苗圃,花坛
n. 河床,海底
bee *n.* 蜜蜂
beef *n.* 牛肉
beer *n.* 啤酒
before *prep./conj.* 在……之前
prep. 在……前面
ad. 从前,早些时候
beg *v.* 乞讨
v. 请求,恳求
begin *v.* 开始
begin with 从……开始
beginning *n.* 开端,开始
behalf *n.* 利益
on behalf of 代表,为了
behave *v.* 举动,举止,表现

v. 运转,开动
behavio(u)r n. 行为,举止
behind prep. 在……后面,落后于
ad. 在后,落后
belief n. 信仰,信条
n. 相信,信念
believe v. 相信,信仰
v. 认为
bell a. 钟,铃
belong v. 属,附属,隶属(to)
below prep. 在……下面,在……以下
ad. 在下,下面
belt n. 带,腰带
bench n. 长凳,条凳
n. 工作台,台,座
bend n. 弯曲,曲折处
v. 折弯,屈曲
beneath prep. 在……下方,在……之下
ad. 在下方
beneficial a. 有益的
benefit n. 利益,恩惠
v. 有利于,受益
beside prep. 在……旁边
prep. 和……相比
besides ad. 而且,还有
prep. 除……之外
best a. 最好的
ad. 最,最好
do one's best 尽力,努力
make the best of 充分利用,妥善处理
at best / at the best 最好,充其量
bet v. 赌,打赌
n. 打赌,赌注
better a. 较好的,更好的
ad. 更好
v. 改良,改善
n. 较佳者,较优者
had better 最好还是,应该
between prep. 在……中间,在……之间
beyond prep. 在……那边,在……以外
ad. 在那边,在远处
Bible n. 圣经
bicycle n. 自行车
big a. 大的
a. 重要的
bike n. 自行车
bill n. 账单,单子,招牌
billion n. 十亿
bind vt. 捆绑,捆扎
biology n. 生物学
bird n. 鸟
birth n. 出生
n. 出身
birthday n. 生日
biscuit n. 饼干
bit n. 一片,一点,一些
bite v./n. 咬,叮
n. 一口
bitter a. 苦的,痛苦的
black a./n. 黑,黑色
n. 黑人
blackboard n. 黑板
blame v. 责备,怪,怨
n. 责任,过失
blank a. 空白的,空着的
a. 茫然的,无表情的
n. 空白
n. 空白表格,空白处
blanket n. 毛毯,毯子
blind a. 盲的,瞎的,盲目的
v. 使失明,蒙蔽
block v. 阻塞,封锁
n. 木块,块料
n. 一排房屋,街段
blood n. 血,血液
n. 血统,血亲
n. 血气,气质
bloom v./n. 开花
n. 花,花朵
blow1 v. 吹,吹气,打气
v. 爆炸,爆裂
blow2 n. 打,殴打,打击
blue n./a. 蓝色,青色
board n. 板,木板,纸板
v. 上船(车,飞机)
n. 委员会
on board 在船(飞机)上
boast v. 夸口,夸耀(of/about)
n. 自夸,大话
boat n. 船,小船
body n. 身体;主体;尸体
n. 一堆,一群,一批
boil v. 沸腾,煮沸
bold a. 大胆的,冒失的
bolt n. 螺栓,插销
v. 闩门,关窗,拴住
bomb n. 炸弹
v. 轰炸
bond n. 联结,结合,约束
n. 契约,公债,债券
bone n. 骨,骨骼
book n. 书,书籍
v. 定,预定
boot n. 靴子
border n. 边缘,边界,边境
v. 交界,与……毗邻
bore v. 钻洞,打眼,钻探
born a. 天生的,生来的
borrow v. 借,借用
boss n. 老板,头儿
v. 指挥,发号施令
both pron. 二者,双方
a. 两,双
both … and … 既……又……
bother v. 打扰,麻烦
bottle n. 瓶子
v. 装瓶
bottom n. 底,底部
bound1 v./n. 跳,跳跃
bound2 a. 必定,一定
boundary n. 界线,边界
bow1 v./n. 鞠躬,点头
bow2 n. 弓,弓形;蝴蝶结
bowl n. 碗,钵
box1 n. 箱子,盒子
box2 v. 拳击,打耳光
boy n. 男孩,儿子
n. 男服务员,男仆
brain n. 大脑,骨髓;头脑,智能
brake v./n. 闸,刹车
branch n. 枝,树枝
n. 分支,分部
brand n. 商标,(商品的)牌子
v. 打烙印于
v. 铭刻
brass n. 黄铜,铜器
brave a. 勇敢的
bread n. 面包
break off v. 中止,中断
breadth n. 宽度,幅
break v. 打破,打碎,折断
v. 破坏,违反
n. (课间或工间)休息时间
v./n. 打断,中止
break away (from) 脱离,逃跑
break in 强行进入,闯入,打断,插嘴
break out 突然发生,爆发
break down 分解,瓦解
breakfast n. 早饭,早餐
breast n. 胸脯,乳房
breath n. 呼吸,气息
out of breath 喘不过气来,上气不接下气
breathe v. 吸入,呼吸
breed vt. 饲养
breeze n. 微风,轻风
brick n. 砖,砖状物
bride n. 新娘
bridge n. 桥,桥梁
brief a. 简短的,简洁的
v. 向……作简要的介绍
in brief 简要地说
bright a. 明亮的,光明的
a. 聪明的,伶俐的
a. 快活的,美好的
brilliant a. 辉煌的,灿烂的
a. 杰出的,有才华的
bring v. 拿来,带来
v. 产生,引起

bring about 带来,招致
bring down 减少,降低
bring up 抚养,培养
Britain *n.* 不列颠,英国
broadcast *n.*/*v.* 广播,播音
brother 兄弟,同胞,教友
brow *n.* 眉,眉毛;额
brown *n.* 棕色,烟色
brush *n.* 刷,毛刷,画笔
v. 刷,擦,擦亮
v. 擦过,掠过
bubble *n.* 泡,水泡,气泡
v. 吹泡,起泡
bucket *n.* 吊桶,水桶
build *v.* 修建,建造,建立
building *n.* 建筑物,大楼
bulb *n.* 球状物,灯泡
bulk *n.* 体积,容积
n. 大部分,主体
bullet *n.* 子弹,枪弹
bunch *n.* 束,捆,串
bundle *n.* 捆,包,束
burden *n.* 担子,负担
bureau *n.* 署,局
burn *v.* 燃烧,烧毁
v./*n.* 灼伤,烧伤
burn out 烧掉
burn up 烧尽
burst *n.*/*v.* 破裂,爆炸
v. 突然发生,突然发作
bury *v.* 埋,安葬
bus *n.* 公共汽车
trolley bus 电车
bush *n.* 灌木,灌木丛
business *n.* 行业,生意
n. 事务,业务,职责
busy *a.* 忙的,忙碌的
but *conj.* 可是,但是
conj./*prep.* 除……外
ad. 只,仅仅,不过
butter *n.* 黄油,奶油
v. 抹黄油
button *n.* 扣子,按钮
v. 扣紧,扣
buy *v.* 买,购买
by *prep.* 在……旁,靠近;被,由
prep. 在……以前,到……为止
prep. 经,沿,通过;按照,根据
prep. [表示方法,手段] 靠,用,通过
ad. 在旁,近旁,经过
by and by 不久以后,将来

C

cabbage *n.* 洋白菜,卷心菜
cabinet *n.* 橱柜;内阁
cable *n.* 电报
cafe *n.* 咖啡馆,小餐厅
cage *n.* 笼,鸟笼
cake *n.* 饼,糕
calculate *vt.* 计算
calendar *n.* 日历,月历
call *v.* 叫做,称为;叫,招呼;打电话
v. 拜访,访问
call for 要求,需要
call on/upon *v.* 访问,拜访
call off *v.* 取消
calm *a.* 平静的,镇静的,沉着的
v. (使)镇静,(使)镇定
n. 平静,风平浪静
camel *n.* 骆驼
camera *n.* 照相机,摄影机
camp *n.* 野营,营地
v. 设营,宿营
campaign *n.* 战役,运动
campus *n.* (大学)校园
can *v.* 能,会
v. 可以
Canada *n.* 加拿大
canal *n.* 运河,渠
cancel *vt.* 取消,撤销
cancer *n.* 癌
candidate *n.* 候选人,报考者
candle *n.* 蜡烛
n. 帆布,画布
cap *n.* 便帽,军帽
capable *a.* 有本领的,有能力的
capital *n.* 首都
n./*a.* 大写
n. 资本,资金
a. 主要的,基本的
captain *n.* 首领,队长
n. 船长,舰长
n. 上尉,上校
capture *v.* 捕获,捉拿
v. 夺得,攻占
car *n.* 汽车,车辆,车
carbon *n.* 碳
card *n.* 卡片,名片
n. 纸片
care *n.* 注意,小心;挂念,操心
v. 关心,计较;喜欢,愿意
care for 照管,关心;喜欢,意欲
take care of 照顾,照料;承担,处理,负责
career *n.* 生涯,经历
n. 专业,职业
careful *a.* 小心的,仔细的
careless *a.* 粗心的,草率的
cargo *n.* 船货,货物
carpenter *n.* 木工,木匠
carpet *n.* 地毯
carriage *n.* 马车,客车,车厢
carry *v.* 搬运,运送,携带
carry on 继续,坚持下去;从事,经营
carry out 执行,贯彻
cart *n.* 大车,手推车
case1 *n.* 事实,情况;案件,病历
in any case 无论如何,总之
in case 假如,以防
in case of 假如,万一
case2 *n.* 箱子,盒子
cash *n.* 现金,现款
v. 兑现,付现
cassette *n.* 盒式录音带
cast *v.* 投,掷,抛
v. 铸造;演员表
castle *n.* 城堡
casual *a.* 偶然的,碰巧的
a. 随便的,非正式的
a. 临时的
cat *n.* 猫
catch *v.* 捕,捉
v. 赶上
v. 感染传染病
catch on (to) 学会;懂得
catch up with 追上,赶上
cattle *n.* 牛
n. 牲口,家畜
cause *n.* 原因,理由,缘故
v. 引起
n. 事业,奋斗目标
cave *n.* 山洞,洞穴
cease *v.*/*n.* 停止
ceiling *n.* 天花板
celebrate *v.* 庆祝
cell *n.* 牢房,蜂房
n. 细胞
n. 电池
cent *n.* 分,分币
per cent 百分之……
central *a.* 中心的,中央的,中枢的
centre/center *n.* 中心,中央
v. 集中
century *n.* 世纪,百年
ceremony *n.* 仪式,典礼,礼节
certain *a.* 确实的,可靠的
a. 某一,某些
a. 一定的,必然的
certainly *ad.* 一定,必定,无疑
ad. 当然,行
certificate *n.* 证书,证明书
chain *n.* 链,链条
n. 一连串,连锁
v. 拴住
chair *n.* 椅子
chairman *n.* 主席,议长,会长
chalk *n.* 白垩,粉笔
challenge *n.* 挑战
champion *n.* 冠军
n. 捍卫者,拥护者

chance *n.* 机会,可能性
n. 偶然性,运气
v. 偶然发生,碰巧
by chance 偶然,碰巧
change *v./n.* 改变,变化
v. 更换,交换
n. 找头,零钱
channel *n.* 海峡,水道,沟渠
n. 渠道,频道
chapter *n.* 章,回
character *n.* 性格,品质
n. 特性,特征
n. 人物,角色
characteristic *a.* 特有的,独特的
n. 特征,特性
charge *n.* 指控;
vt. 指控
chart *n.* 图表,图
chase *v./n.* 追赶,追求
cheap *a.* 便宜的,贱的
a. 低劣的,不值钱的
cheat *vt.* 欺骗,骗取
vi. 行骗,作弊
n. 欺骗,欺诈行为
n. 骗子
check *v.* 制止,控制
v./n. 检查,核对
cheek *n.* 面颊
cheer *v./n.* 喝彩,欢呼
v. 使振作,使高兴
cheer up 使高兴,使振奋高兴起来,振作起来
cheerful *a.* 快乐的,高兴的
cheese *n.* 干酪,乳酪
chemical *a.* 化学的
n. 化学药品
chemist *n.* 化学家,药剂师
chemistry *n.* 化学
cheque *n.* 支票
cherry *n.* 樱桃,樱桃树
chess *n.* 棋
chest *n.* 柜子,橱
n. 胸腔,胸脯
chew *v.* 咀嚼
chicken *n.* 小鸡,小鸟
n. 鸡肉
chief *a.* 主要的,首要的
n. 领袖,首领
child *n.* 孩子,儿童,儿女
childhood *n.* 幼年,童年
chimney *n.* 烟囱,烟筒
chin *n.* 下巴
China *n.* 中国
Chinese *n.* 中国人,中文
a. 中国的
china *n.* 瓷器

chocolate *n.* 巧克力
choice *n.* 选择,选择机会
choose *v.* 选择,挑拣
v. 甘愿
Christmas *n.* 圣诞节
church *n.* 教堂,教会
cigarette *n.* 香烟,纸烟
cinema *n.* 电影院
circle *n.* 圆,圈,圆周
n. 圈子,集团
v. 环绕,盘旋
n. 周期,循环
circumstance *n.* 情形,环境,状况
citizen *n.* 公民,市民,居民
city *n.* 城市,都市
civil *a.* 公民的
a. 平民的,文职的
a. 国内的
a. 文明的,有教养的
civilize/civilise *v.* 使文明,开化
claim *v.* 声称,主张
v. 对……提出要求,索取
n. 要求
n. 主张,断言
clap *vi.* 鼓掌
class *n.* 种类,等级,阶级
n. 班,班级,年级
n. (一节)课
classical *a.* 经典的,古典的
classify *v.* 分类,分等
classmate *n.* 同班同学
classroom *n.* 教室
claw *n.* 爪,脚爪
clay *n.* 粘土
clean *a.* 清洁的,干净的
v. 弄清洁,扫清
clear *a.* 晴朗的,清澈的,明亮的
a./ad. 清楚,清晰,明白
v. 澄清,清除
clerk *n.* 办事员,职员,店员
clever *a.* 聪明的,伶俐的
a. 机敏的,精巧的
cliff *n.* 悬崖,崖
climate *n.* 气候
n. 风气,社会思潮
climb *v./n.* 爬,攀登
clock *n.* 钟
close *v./a.* 关,关闭
v./n. 结束,了结
a./ad. 接近,紧密
cloth *n.* 布,织物,衣料
n. (一块)布
clothe *v.* 给……穿衣
clothes *n.* (*pl.*) 衣服
cloud *n.* 云,云状物
n. 一大群

club *n.* 俱乐部,社
n. 棒,球棒
clue *n.* 线索,提示
coal *n.* 煤,煤块
coarse *a.* 粗的,粗糙的,粗劣的
a. 粗鲁的,粗俗的
coast *n.* 海岸,海滨
coat *n.* 外套,上衣
v. 涂上,包上
n. 涂层
cock *n.* 公鸡
n. 龙头,旋塞
coffee *n.* 咖啡
coin *n.* 硬币,货币
cold *a.* 冷的,冷淡的
n. 寒冷
n. 感冒
collar *n.* 衣领
colleague *n.* 同事,同僚
collect *v.* 收集,收(税等)
v. 领取,接走
collection *n.* 收藏,收集
n. 收藏品
collective *a.* 集体的,共同的
n. 团体,集体
college *n.* 学院,大学
colonel *n.* (陆军)上校
colony *n.* 殖民地
colo(u)r *n.* 颜色,色彩,颜料
column *n.* 柱,柱状物
n. 专栏
comb *n.* 梳子
v. 梳理
combination *n.* 结合,联合
combine *v.* 结合,联合,化合
come *v.* 来,来到
v. 出现,产生
come on 请,来吧,快点
come off 成功,奏效
come true 实现,达到
come up with 想出;提出
come to 苏醒
comfort *v./n.* 慰问,安慰
n. 安逸,舒适
comfortable *a.* 舒适的,舒服的,自在的
command *v./n.* 命令,指挥
n. 掌握,运用能力
commander *n.* 指挥员,司令
comment *n./v.* 解说,评论,意见
commerce *n.* 商业
commercial *a.* 商业的,商务的
commit *v.* 犯,干(错事)
committee *n.* 委员会,全体委员
common *a.* 普通的,通常的,平常的
a. 公共的,共同的
in common 共用,共有

communicate *vi*. 通讯,交流,交际
vt. 传达,传播
communism *n*. 共产主义
communist *n*. 共产党员
a. 共产主义的
community *n*. 社区,社会
companion *n*. 同伴,伴侣
companionship *n*. 伴侣关系;友谊;一群伙伴
company *n*. 公司,商号
n. 陪伴,同伴
n. 宾客,客人
keep company with 与……交往,与……结伴
comparative *a*. 比较的,相当的
compare *v*. 比较,相比
compare... to 把……比作
compass *n*. 罗盘,指南针
compel *v*. 强迫,逼迫
competent *a*. 有能力的,胜任的
competition *n*. 比赛,竞争
complain *v*. 抱怨
complete *a*. 完成的,完全的
v. 完成,结束
complex *a*. 复杂的,复合的
complicated *a*. 错综复杂的,麻烦的
compose *v*. 写作,作曲
v. 由……组成(of)
compound *a*. 复合的
n. 混合物,化合物
comprehension *n*. 理解(力),领悟
compromise *v*. & *n*. 妥协
computer *n*. 计算机,计算者
comrade *n*. 同志,朋友,同事
conceal *vt*. 隐藏,隐瞒
concentrate *vt*. 集中
vt. 聚集
vt. 浓缩
vi. 集中,专心
concept *n*. 概念
concern *n*. 关心,挂念
n. 关系,关联
vt. 涉及,有关于
vt. 使关心,使挂念
as/so far as... be concerned 就……而言
concerning *prep*. 关于
concert *n*. 音乐会,演奏会
conclude *v*. 结束,完结
v. 下结论,断定
v. 缔结,议定
conclusion *n*. 结束,终结
n. 结论
concrete *n*. 混凝土
a. 具体的,实质性的
condense *v*. 压缩,浓缩,精简
condition *n*. 状况,状态,情形
n. 条件
conduct *n*. 行为,品行
v. 引导,指挥
v. 传电,传热
conductor *n*. 领队,乐队指挥
n. 售票员,列车员
n. 导体
conference *n*. 会议,讨论会
confess *v*. 承认,坦白,忏悔
confident *a*. 确信的,有自信的
confine *v*. 限制,局限于
v. 管制,禁闭
confirm *vt*. 证实,肯定
vt. 进一步确定
vt. 批准,确认
conflict *n*. 战斗,斗争
n./*v*. 抵触,冲突
confuse *v*. 混淆,搞乱
congratulate *v*. 祝贺,贺喜
congress *n*. 大会
n. 国会,议会
conjunction *n*. 连接词
connect *v*. 连续,联系
connection *n*. 连结,联系,关系
conquer *v*. 征服,战胜
conquest *n*. 征服
conscience *n*. 良心,良知
conscious *a*. 有意识的
consent *v*./*n*. 同意,答应
consequence *n*. 后果
consequently *ad*. 因而,所以
conservative *a*. 保守的,守旧的
n. 保守的人
consider *v*. 考虑,细想
v. 认为,以为
considerable *a*. 相当的,可观的
considerate *a*. 考虑周到的,体谅的
consist *v*. 由……构成,由……组成(of)
v. 在于,存在(in)
consistent *a*. 一贯的;一致的
constant *a*. 不断的;始终如一的
constitute *vt*. 组成,构成,形成
constitution *n*. 章程,宪法
n. 体质,素质
n. 构造
construct *v*. 建设,建造
consult *v*. 商量,磋商
v. 请教,咨询
consume *vt*. 消耗;花费
contact *v*./*n*. 接触,联系,交往
contain *v*. 容纳,含有,装有
container *n*. 容器,集装箱
contemporary *a*. 现代的,当代的
n. 同代人,同辈
content1 *n*. 内容,(*pl*.)目录
n. 容量,含量
content2 *n*./*a*. 满足,甘愿
contest *v*. 竞争,比赛
continue *v*. 连续,继续
continuous *a*. 连续的,继续的,持续的
contract1 *n*. 契约,合同,包工
contract2 *v*. 收缩,紧缩
contradiction *n*. 矛盾
n. 反驳
contrary *a*. 相反的,矛盾的
on the contrary 相反,反之
contrast *n*. 对比,对照
contribute *v*. 捐助,捐献,投稿
contribute to 有助于
control *v*. 控制,操纵
v. 抑制
convenient *a*. 方便的
conventional *a*. 普通的,常见的
a. 习惯的,常规的
conversation *n*. (友好、随便的)谈话,会话
convert *vt*. 转化,转变
convey *vt*. 传送,传达
vt. 运送,输送
convince *v*. 使信服,使确信
cook *v*. 烹调,煮,烧
n. 炊事员,厨师
cool *a*. 凉的,凉爽的
a. 冷静的,沉着的,冷淡的
v. (使)冷却,(使)镇静
co-operate *v*. 合作,协作,相配合
cope *v*. 对付,应付(with)
copper *n*. 铜
n. 铜币,铜制品
copy *n*. 抄件,副本
v. 抄写,临摹
n. 本,册
cord *n*. 绳,索
cordial *a*. 诚恳的,亲切的,热诚的
core *n*. 心,核心
corn *n*. 谷物,庄稼,玉米
corner *n*. 角,角落
corporation *n*. 团体,公司
correct *a*. 正确的,恰当的,合适的
v. 改正,修正,矫正
correspond *v*. 相当于,对应,符合(to)
v. 通信
corresponding *a*. 相应的
corridor *n*. 走廊
cost *n*. 成本,费用,代价
v. 值,花费
at all costs 不惜任何代价,无论如何
costly *a*. 昂贵的,豪华的
cottage *n*. 村舍,别墅
cotton *n*. 棉花
n. 棉纱,棉制品

cough *v.*/*n.* 咳嗽
council *n.* 理事会,委员会,议事机构
count *v.* 数,计算
　v. 看做,认为
counter *n.* 柜台
　n. 计数器
　vt. 反对,对抗
　ad. 反方面地,对立地
country *n.* 国家
　n. 农村,乡间
countryside *n.* 乡下,农村
county *n.* 郡,县
couple *n.* 对,双,夫妇
courage *n.* 勇气,胆量
course *n.* 进程,过程,课程
　n. 一道菜
　of course 自然,当然,无疑
court *n.* 法院,法庭
　n. 宫廷,朝廷
　n. 院子,球场
cousin *n.* 堂(表)兄弟,堂(表)姐妹
cover *v.* 盖,覆
　v. 包括,涉及
　n. 覆盖物,套,封面
　cover up 掩饰,掩盖
cow *n.* 母牛,奶牛
crack *v.* (使)破裂,砸开
　n. 裂纹,龟裂
crash *v.*/*n.* 摔坏,坠毁
crawl *v.*/*n.* 爬行,蠕动,匍匐前进,缓慢行进
crazy *a.* 疯狂的,蠢的
cream *n.* 奶油
create *v.* 创造,创作
　v. 产生,制造,建立
creative *a.* 有创造力的,创造性的
creature *n.* 人,动物
creep *v.* 爬,爬行
crew *n.* 全体船员,全体乘务员
cricket *n.* 板球
　n. 蟋蟀
crime *n.* 罪,罪行
criminal *a.* 犯罪的,刑事的
　n. 罪犯,刑事犯
critic *n.* 批评家,评论家
critical *a.* 批评的,批判的
　a. 危急的,紧要的
criticism *n.* 批评,评论
criticize *v.* 批评,评论
crop *n.* 农作物,庄稼,收成
cross *n.* 十字形,十字架
　v. 越过,穿过
　n. 交叉,横穿
crowd *n.* 人群,群众
　v. 挤满,拥挤
crown *n.* 王冠,君权,君王
cruel *a.* 残酷的,残忍的
crush *n.*/*v.* 压碎,压坏
　v. 压服,压垮
cry *v.* 叫,喊
　v. 哭泣
　n. 叫喊,叫声,哭泣
crystal *n.* 水晶,晶体
　a. 水晶的,晶体的,透明的
culture *n.* 修养,教养
　n. 文化
cup *n.* 杯子,奖杯
　n. 一杯
cupboard *n.* 碗柜,小橱
cure *n.*/*v.* 治愈,医治
　v. 矫正,纠正
　n. 良药,疗法
curious *a.* 好奇的,爱打听的
　a. 稀奇的,莫明其妙的
current *n.* 流,水流,气流,电流
　a. 通用的,流行的,当前的
　n. 潮流,趋势
curse *n.*/*v.* 诅咒,咒骂
curtain *n.* 窗帘,幕(布)
cushion *n.* 垫子,坐垫
custom *n.* 习惯,风俗,惯例
　n. (*pl.*)海关,关税
customer *n.* 顾客,主顾
customs *n.* 海关
cut *n.*/*v.* 切,剪,割,削
　n./*v.* 删节,缩减,剪
　n. 伤口
　cut back 削减,减少
　cut down 削减,减少,降低
cycle *n.* 自行车,摩托车
　n. 循环,周期
　vi. 骑自行车,骑摩托车
　vi. 循环,作循环运动

D

daily *a.* 每日的,日常的
　ad. 每日,天天
dairy *n.* 牛奶场,奶店
damage *vt.* 毁坏,损害
　n. 毁坏,损害
　n. (*pl.*)损害赔偿金
dance *v.* 跳舞
　n. 舞蹈,舞会
danger *n.* 危险,威胁
　in danger 在危险中,垂危
　out of danger 脱离危险
dangerous *a.* 危险的,不安全的
dare *v.* 敢,胆敢
dark *a.* 暗的,黑暗的
　a. 深色的,黑色的
　n. 黑暗,暗处
darling *n.* 亲爱的人,宠儿
　a. 亲爱的,宠爱的
dash *v.*/*n.* 冲,猛冲,突进
　n. 破折号
data *n.* 数据,资料
date *n.* 日期,年代
　v. 注日期
　n./*v.* 约会
　out of date 过时的,陈旧的
daughter *n.* 女儿
dawn *n.* 黎明
　n. 开始
　vi. 破晓
　vi. 开始发展,出现
day *n.* 白昼,白天,(一)天
daylight *n.* 日光,白昼,黎明
dead *a.* 死的,无感觉的
deaf *a.* 聋的
　a. 不愿听的,装聋的
deal *v.* 处理,安排,应付(with)
　n. 交易,买卖,契约
　v. 做买卖,经营
　a good deal/a great deal 许多,大量,很多
dear *a.* 贵的
　a. 亲爱的,可爱的
　int. 啊,哎呀
death *n.* 死,死亡
debt *n.* 债,欠债
decade *n.* 十年
deceive *v.* 欺骗,蒙蔽
December *n.* 十二月
decide *v.* 决定,下决心
　v. 解决,裁决
decision *n.* 决定,决心,果断
deck *n.* 甲板,桥面,层面
declare *v.* 宣布,宣告
　v. 表明,声明
decorate *v.* 装饰,装潢,布置
decrease *v.*/*n.* 减少,减小
deduce *vt.* 推论,推断,演绎
deed *n.* 行为,行动
　n. 功绩,事迹
deep *a.* 深的,深刻的,深切的
　ad. 深深地
defeat *v.*/*n.* 战胜,挫败
defence/defense *n.* 防御,保卫
　n. (*pl.*)防务,工事
defend *v.* 保卫,防守
　v. 辩护
definite *a.* 明确的,确定的,限定的
definitely *ad.* 明确地,肯定地,当然
degree *n.* 度,程度
　n. 等级,学位
delay *v.*/*n.* 推迟,耽搁,延误
delegation *n.* 代表团
delicate *a.* 纤弱的,娇嫩的,易碎的
　a. 优美的,精美的,精致的

a. 微妙的,棘手的
delicious a. 美味的,芬芳的
delight n. 快乐,高兴
v. 使高兴,使欣喜
take delight in 以……为乐
deliver v. 投递,送交
vt. 发表
vt. 使分娩,接生
delivery n. 传递,传送,交付
demand n./v. 要求,需要
v. 质问,询问
democracy n. 民主,民主制,民主国家
demonstrate vt. 证实,表明
dense a. 密的,稠密的,浓厚的
deny vt. 否认,不承认
vt. 拒绝给予,拒绝(某人的)要求
depart v. 出发,离开
department n. 部门,系
depend v. 依靠,信任,信赖(on)
dependent a. (on, upon) 依靠的,依赖的
depress v. 压抑,降低
depth n. 深度,厚度
descend v. 下来,下降,传下
describe v. 描述,形容
description n. 描写,形容
desert n. 沙漠,不毛之地
deserve v. 应受,值得
design v./n. 计划,企图
n. 图案,花样
v. 设计,制图
desirable a. 合乎需要的,令人满意的
desire v./n. 愿望,欲望,要求
desk n. 书桌,服务台
despair v./n. 失望,绝望
desperate a. 绝望的,危急的
a. 不顾一切的,铤而走险的
despite prep. 不管,尽管
destination n. 目的地
destroy vt. 破坏,毁灭
vt. 消灭
destruction n. 破坏,毁灭
detail n. 细节,详情
n. 枝节,琐事
vt. 详述,详细说明
in detail 详细地
detect v. 察觉,发现
determination n. 决心,决定
determine v. 决心,决定
v. 确定,测定
develop v. 发展,进展
v. 发扬,开发
development n. 发展,进展,发达
n. 新事物,新发展
device n. 装置,设备,器具,仪器
devil n. 魔鬼
devote v. 奉献,献身,致力
diagram n. 图解,图表
dial n. 标度盘,钟面,拨号盘
v. 拨号,打电话
dialect n. 方言
dialogue n. 对话,对白
diameter n. 直径
diamond n. 钻石,金刚石
diary n. 日记,日记簿
dictate v. 听写,口授,口述
dictation n. 口授笔录,听写
dictionary n. 字典,词典
die v. 死亡,死
differ v. 不同,分歧
difference n. 差别,差异
n. 分歧,争论
different a. 差异的,不同的
difficult a. 困难的,艰难的
difficulty n. 困难,困境
n. 难事,难题
in difficulties 处境困难
dig v. 挖,掘
diligent a. 勤奋的,用功的
dim a. 暗淡的,模糊的,朦胧的
dinner n. 正餐,宴会
dip v. 浸,蘸
direct a./ad. 径直,直接,率直
v. 指引,指导
direction n. 方向,方位
n. 指导,指令,说明
directly ad. 直接地,直截了当地
ad. 立即,马上
director n. 主任,处长,局长
n. 导演
dirt n. 尘,土,污物
dirty a. 脏的
disadvantage n. 不利条件
disagree v. 意见分歧,不同意
v. 不一致,不符
disappear v. 消失,消散,失踪
disappoint vt. 使失望
disaster n. 灾害,灾祸,灾难
discharge n. 卸(货),解除
v./n. 排出,发射
v. 释放,遣散,解雇
discourage v. 使失去信心,使泄气
discover v. 发现
v. 暴露,显示
discovery n. 发现
discuss v. 讨论
discussion n. 讨论,议论
disease n. 疾病
disgust vt. 使厌恶
n. 厌恶
dish n. 碟,盘子
n. 菜肴
dishonour n. 不光彩,不名誉,耻辱
v. 使丢脸,凌辱
dislike n./v. 不喜欢,厌恶
dismiss vt. 驳回,对……不予受理
disorder n. 失调,疾病
display v./n. 陈列,展览,显示
dispute v. 争论,辩驳
n. 争论,争端
distance n. 距离,路程
n. 远处,远方
distant a. 在远处的,远隔的,久远的
distinction n. 区别,差别
distinguish v. 区别,辨别,辨认出
distress n. 苦恼,悲痛
n. 危难,不幸
v. 使苦恼,使痛苦
distribute v. 分配,分发,配给
v. 分布,散布
district n. 区,地区,行政区
disturb v. 扰乱,妨碍
v. 打扰,使不安
ditch n. 沟,渠,水沟
dive v./n. 潜水,跳水
v./n. 俯冲
divide v. 分,划分,隔开
v. 分配,分享,分担
division n. 分,分割,分裂
n. 除法
divorce v./n. 离婚,离异
v./n. 脱离,分离
do v. 做,干,办,从事
v. 完成,做完
v. 行,合适
How do you do! 你好!
do away with 废除,消灭
do without 没有……也行,将就
doctor n. 医生,大夫
n. 博士
dog n. 狗
dollar n. 美元,元
domestic n. 家庭的;国内的
donkey n. 驴
door n. 门
next door 隔壁的,在隔壁
out of doors 在户外
dormitory/dorm n. (集体)宿舍
dose n. 剂量,一服,一剂
dot n. 点,圆点,句点
v. 打点
double a. 两倍的,双重的
v. 加倍,翻一番
doubt n. 怀疑,疑问,疑惑
v. 怀疑,不相信
no doubt 无疑,必定
doubtful a. 怀疑的,不相信的
a. 可疑的,难料的
doubtless a. 无疑的,很可能的

down *ad.* 下,向下
prep. 下,顺……而下
downstairs *ad.* 在楼下,往楼下
a. 楼下的
dozen *n.* 一打,十二个
draft *n.* 草稿,草案,草图
v. 起草,草拟
drag *v.* 拖曳,拖拉
dramatic *a.* 戏剧性的;引人注目的
draw *v.* 拉,拖
v. 拔出,抽出,引出
v. 划,画
v. 吸,汲取,提取
drawer *n.* 抽屉
drawing *n.* 素描,图画
dream *n.* 梦,梦想,幻想
v. 做梦,幻想
dress *n.* 服装,女装,童装
v. 穿衣,打扮
dress up 穿上盛装,打扮得漂漂亮亮
drift *v./n.* 漂,漂流
drink *v.* 饮,喝,饮酒
n. 饮料,酒
drip *v.* 滴下,漏水
n. 滴,水滴,点滴
drive *v.* 驾驶,开动
v. 驱赶
v. 驱使,迫使
driver *n.* 司机
drop *n.* 滴,水滴,液滴
v. 滴下,落下,失落
drop by/in 顺便来访,非正式访问
drown *v.* 淹死,淹没
drug *n.* 药品,麻醉品,毒品
drum *n.* 鼓,鼓状物
dry *a.* 干的,干旱的
v. 使干燥,晒干
a. 口干的,干渴的
duck *n.* 鸭,鸭肉
due *a.* 预定(或应到)的
a. 应给的,应得的
a. 应有的,充分的,适当的
a. 应付的,到期的
due to 由于,因为
dull *a.* 愚笨的,迟钝的
a. 阴暗的,沉闷的,单调的
dumb *a.* 哑的,无声的
during *prep.* 在……期间,在……时候
dusk *n.* 黄昏,幽暗
dust *n.* 灰尘,尘土
v. 拂,掸
n. 垃圾,废品
duty *n.* 职务,义务,责任
n. 税,关税
off duty 下班
on duty 值班,当班
dye *v./n.* 染,染色
n. 染料

E

each *a./pron.* 各,各自,每
each other 互相
eager *a.* 热心的,渴望的
eagle *n.* 鹰
ear *n.* 耳朵,耳状物
n. 听力,听觉
early *a.* 早,早日的,及早的
ad. 早,初
a. 早期的,古代的
earn *v.* 赚得,赢得,获得
earnest *a.* 热切的,认真的,诚恳的
earth *n.* 地球,土壤,土地
on earth 究竟,到底
ease *n.* 容易,轻易
n. 安逸,安心
v. 减轻,放松,缓和
easily *ad.* 容易地,轻易地,顺利地
east *n./a.* 东,东方
ad. 在东方,向东方
eastern *a.* 东方的,东部的,朝东的
easy *a.* 容易的
a. 舒适的,安心的
eat *v.* 吃,喝(汤)
echo *n.* 回声,反响
economic *a.* 经济的
economy *n.* 经济,经济制度
n. 节约,节省
edge *n.* 刃,边缘,棱
v. 侧身移动,挤进
educate *v.* 教育,培养
education *n.* 教育,训练
effect *n.* 效果,作用,影响
in effect 实际上,事实上
effective *v.* 有效的,生效的
efficiency *n.* 效率
n. 功效
efficient *a.* 效率高的,有能力的
effort *n.* 努力,尽力
eg. 例如
egg *n.* 卵,蛋
eight *n./a.* 八
eighteen *n./a.* 十八
eighth *a.* 第八
n. 八分之一
eighty *n./a.* 八十
either *a./pron.* (两者中)任何一方,任何一个
ad. (与 not 连用)也(不)
either... or 或……或,不是……就是
elastic *a.* 弹性的,灵活的
n. 松紧带,橡皮圈
elder *a.* 年长的,资格老的
n. 长者,长辈
elect *v.* 推选,选举
election *n.* 选举
electric *a.* 电的,带电的,电动的
electrical *a.* 电的,电气科学的
electricity *n.* 电,电流,电学
electronic *a.* 电子的
element *n.* 元素
n. 要素,成分
elephant *n.* 象
elevator *n.* 电梯,升降机
eleven *n./a.* 十一
else *a.* 其他,另外,别的
ad. (与 or 连用)否则
elsewhere *ad.* 在别处
embarrass *v.* 使窘迫,使困惑,使为难
emerge *vi.* 出现,涌现
vi. (问题)冒出,(事实)暴露
emergency *n.* 紧急情况,突然事件
emit *vt.* 散发,放射
emotion *n.* 情感,情绪
emotional *a.* 感情的
emperor *n.* 皇帝
emphasis *n.* 强调
emphasize *vt.* 强调
empire *n.* 帝国
employ *v./v.* 雇佣
v. 用,使用
employee *n.* 雇员
employment *n.* 职业,就业,雇佣
empty *a.* 空的,空洞的
v. 倒空,搬空
enable *v.* 使能够
encounter *vt./n.* 遭遇,遇到
encourage *v.* 鼓励,助长,促进
end *n.* 端,尖,尾
v. 终止,结束
end up 结束,告终
in the end 最后,终于
endless *a.* 无限的,无穷的
endure *v.* 忍受,忍耐
v. 持久,持续
enemy *n.* 敌人,仇敌
energy *n.* 精力,气力,活力
n. 能,能量
enforce *v.* 实行,执行,强制
engage *v.* 雇佣,聘用
v. 使订婚
engine *n.* 发动机,引擎
n. 火车头,机车
engineer *n.* 工程师
engineering *n.* 工程(学)
England *n.* 英格兰,英国
English *n.* 英语,英国人
a. 英语的,英国的
enjoy *v.* 欣赏,喜爱

v. 享受,享有
enjoy oneself 过得快乐
enlarge *vt.* 扩大
vt. 放大
enormous *a.* 庞大的,巨大的
enough *a.* /*n.* 足够,充足
ad. 足够地
ensure *vt.* 保证,担保
enter *v.* 走进,进入;参加,加入;写入
v. 参加,加入;写入,登录
entertain *v.* 招待,款待
v. 使欢乐,使娱乐
enthusiasm *n.* 热心,热情,积极性
entire *a.* 完全的,全部的,完整的
entitle *v.* 给以权利,给以资格
entrance *n.* 入口,门口
n. 入场,入会,入学
entry *n.* 进入,入场
envelope *n.* 信封,信皮
environment *n.* 环境,周围状况,自然环境
envy *v.* /*n.* 妒忌,羡慕
equal *a.* 同等的,相等的,平等的
n. (地位等)相同的人,匹敌者
v. 等于,比得上
equation *n.* 方程(式),等式
equip *v.* 装备,设备
equipment *n.* 装备,设备,器材
era *n.* 时代,纪元
error *n.* 错误,过失
escape *n.* 逃跑,逃脱
v. 逃避,避免
especially *ad.* 特别,尤其,格外
essay *n.* 散文,随笔,短论
essential *a.* 必不可少的,必要的
establish *vt.* 建立,创办,设立
vt. 确立,使确认
estimate *v.* /*n.* 估计,估价,评价
etc. 等等
Europe *n.* 欧洲
European *a.* 欧洲的
n. 欧洲人
evaluate *vt.* 估价,评价
eve *n.* 前夜,前夕
even *ad.* 甚至,连……都
a. 平的,平坦的;平等的,均等的
even if/even though 即使,纵然
evening *n.* 晚上,傍晚,黄昏
event *n.* 事件,事变,大事
n. 比赛项目
at all events 无论如何,在任何情况下
eventually *ad.* 最后,终于
ever *ad.* 曾经,在任何时候
every *a.* 每,每个
everybody *pron.* 每人,人人
everyday *a.* 每天的,日常的
everyone *pron.* 每人,人人
everything *pron.* 事事,凡事,一切东西
everywhere *ad.* 到处,处处
evidence *n.* 证据,物证
evident *a.* 明显的,明白的
evil *a.* 坏的,邪恶的
exact *a.* 确切的,正确的,精确的
exactly *ad.* 确切地,精确地,恰好
exaggerate *vt.* 夸大,夸张
examination/exam *n.* 考试,测验
n. 检验,检查,审查
examine *v.* 检验,审查,调查
v. 考试
example *n.* 例,实例
n. 范例,榜样
for example 例如
exceed *v.* 超过,胜过
excellent *a.* 优秀的,杰出的,卓越的
except *prep.* 除……之外
except for 除了……以外
exception *n.* 除外,例外
excessive *a.* 过多的,过分的,极度的
exchange *v.* /*n.* 交换,调换
v. /*n.* 交流
excite *v.* 激动,使兴奋
v. 激发,刺激,唤起
exciting *a.* 令人兴奋的,令人激动的
exclaim *v.* 呼喊,惊叫,大声说
exclude *vt.* 把……排除在外,排斥
excuse *v.* 原谅
n. 借口,理由
execute *v.* 实行,执行,实施
v. 处死,处决
executive *a.* 执行的,实施的
exercise *n.* 习题,练习
v. 运用,行使,实行
v. /*n.* 锻炼,训练
exhaust *v.* 用尽,耗尽,竭力
v. 使衰竭,使精疲力竭
exhibit *v.* 展览,陈列,显示
n. 展览,展品
exhibition *n.* 展览会
n. 展览,显示
exist *v.* 在,存在
existence *n.* 存在,生存
exit *n.* 出口,太平门
n. 退场,退出
vi. 退出,离去
expect *v.* 期待,盼望
experience *n.* 经验,经历
v. 体验,经历
experiment *n.* /*v.* 试验,实验
expert *n.* 专家,能手
a. 专家的,内行的
explain *v.* 解释,说明
explanation *n.* 解释,说明
explode *v.* 爆炸,爆发,破裂
explore *v.* 探险,探索
explosion *n.* 爆炸,爆发
explosive *a.* 爆炸(性)的
n. 炸药
expose *vt.* 揭露
export *v.* /*n.* 出口,输出
express *v.* 表示,表达
a. 特快的,快速的
n. 快车,快运
expression *n.* 表示,表现
n. 措辞,词句
n. 表情,脸色
extend *vt.* 伸出
extensive *a.* 广博的,广泛的
extent *n.* 范围,程度
external *a.* 外部的
extra *a.* 额外的,附加的
extraordinary *a.* 非常的,非凡的,特别的
extreme *a.* 极端的
eye *n.* 眼睛
catch one's eye 引人注目
keep an eye on 留意,照看
eyesight *n.* 视力

F

fabric *n.* 织物,纺织品
face *n.* 脸,面,表面
v. 面临,面向
face to face 面对面地
face up to 大胆面向
make a face 做鬼脸
facility *n.* (*pl.*) 便利,设备,工具
n. 敏捷,熟练,灵巧
fact *n.* 事实,实际,真相
in fact 实际上,事实上
factor *n.* 因素,要素
factory *n.* 工厂,制造厂
fade *v.* 褪色,凋谢
v. 消失,淡薄
fail *v.* 失败,不及格
v. 没有,忘记
v. 衰退,减弱
failure *n.* 失败,不及格
n. 失败者
faint *v.* 发晕,昏过去
a. 微弱的,模糊的
fair1 *a.* 公平的,合理的
a. 相当的,尚好的
a. 晴朗的
fair2 *n.* 定期集市,交易会,博览会
fairly *ad.* 公平地,公正地
ad. 相当,完全
faith *n.* 信任,信用
n. 信念,信心,信仰
faithful *a.* 忠诚的,忠实的
fall *v.* /*n.* 落下,跌落,降落

v./n. 跌倒,坠落,陷落
n. 秋季
fall behind 落后
false a. 假的,虚伪的
a. 假造的,人造的
familiar a. 熟悉的,通晓的
a. 亲密的,交情好的
family n. 家,家庭,家属
n. 氏族,家族
n. 系,族,属
famine n. 饥荒,饥馑
famous a. 著名的
fan1 n. 扇子,风扇
fan2 n. 狂热爱好者,……谜
far a./ad. 远,遥远,久远
ad. ……得多
as far as/so far as 到……程度,就……而言
far from 决不,决非
fare n. 车费,船费
v. 过活,进展
farewell int. 再会,别了
n. 告别
farm n. 农场,农庄,牧场
v. 耕作,经营农场
farmer n. 农夫,农场主
farther ad. 更远,进一步
fashion n. 样子,方式
n. 流行,风尚,时髦
fashionable a. 流行的,时髦的
fast a./ad. 快,迅速
a./ad. 紧,牢
fasten v. 扣紧,结牢,闩上
fat n. 脂肪,肥肉
a. 肥胖的,多脂肪的
fatal a. 致命的,毁灭性的
fate n. 命运,毁灭
father n. 父亲
n. 神父
father-in-law n. 岳父,公公
fatigue n. 疲乏,劳累
fault n. 缺点,缺陷
n. 过失,过错
favo(u)r n. 好感,喜爱;恩惠,帮助
n./v. 赞成,支持
in favor of 赞成,支持
favo(u)rable a. 有利的,顺利的
a. 赞成的,称赞的
favo(u)rite n. 最喜爱的人(或物)
a. 最喜爱的
fear n./v. 恐惧,害怕,担心
fearful a. 吓人的,可怕的
feasible a. 可行的
feather n. 羽毛
feature n. 面貌,容貌
n. 特征,特色
February n. 二月
federal a. 联邦的,联盟的,联合的
fee n. 酬金,手续费,学费
feed v. 喂养,饲养
v. (牛、马)吃东西
feel v. 触,摸,感觉,感到
v. 认为,以为
v. 摸索,寻找(for)
feel like 想要
feeling n. 感觉,知觉
n. 情感,心情,情绪
be fed up with 对……极其厌倦
fell v. 砍伐
fellow n. 家伙,小伙子
n. 同辈,同事,伙伴
female n. 雌性的动物
n. 女子
a. 雌的,女(性)的
fence n. 篱笆,围栏,栅栏
fertile a. 肥沃的,富饶的
fertilizer n. 化肥,肥料
festival n. 音乐节,戏剧节
n. 节日,喜庆日
fetch v. (去)拿来,请来,带来
fever n. 发烧,发热,热病
n. 狂热,兴奋
few a. 不多的,少数的,几乎没有的
n. 很少,几乎没有
a few 少许,一些
quite a few 还不少,有相当数目
fibre/fiber n. 纤维,纤维质
field n. 原野,田野
n. 活动范围,领域界
fierce a. 凶猛的,凶恶的
a. 猛烈的,强烈的
fifteen n./a. 十五
fifteenth a. 第十五
fifth a. 第五
n. 五分之一
fifty n./a. 五十
fight v./n. 打仗,战斗,斗争
figure n. 外形,轮廓,体形
n. 图形,图表;数字,数值
n. 形象,人物
figure out 算出,估计,推测
file n. 文件夹,卷宗
fill v. 装满,充满,填充
fill in 填充,填写
fill out 填好,填写
film n. 电影,胶卷
n. 膜,薄层
filter n. 滤纸,过滤器
final a. 最后的,最终的,决定性的
finally ad. 最后,最终
financial a. 财政的,金融的
find v. 找,找到
v. 发现,发觉,感到
finding n. 调查(或研究)的结果
find out v. 发现,查明,找出
fine a. 美好的,优良的,优秀的
a. 晴朗的,明朗的
a. 细的,精细的,精致的
n./v. 罚金,罚款
finger n. 手指,指头
finish v. 完毕,结束,完成
fire n. 火,炉火
v./n. 开火,射击
catch fire 着火,烧着
on fire 烧着
fireman n. 消防队员
firm a. 坚固的,结实的,稳固的
a. 坚定的,坚决的,坚强的
n. 公司,商号
first a. 第一
ad. 最初,首先
at first 最初,首先
fish n. 鱼
v. 捕鱼,钓鱼
fisherman n. 渔夫
fist n. 拳头
fit a. 合适的,恰当的,合身的
v. 适合,适应,配合
a. 健壮的,健康的
five n./a. 五,五个
fix v. 固定,安装,装配
v. 整理,安排,修理
v. 确定,决定
flag n. 旗
flame n. 火焰,火苗
n. 热情,激情
flat1 a. 平坦的,扁平的
a. 平淡的,乏味的
flat2 n. 一套房间,公寓套房
flavo(u)r n. 滋味,风味,情趣
fleet n. 舰队,船队,机群
flesh n. 肉,果肉
n. 肉体,肌肤
flexible a. 柔软的,易弯曲的
flight n. 飞行,飞翔
n. 航班
n. 一段楼梯
float v. 浮动,漂浮
flock n. (一)群
flood n. 洪水,水灾
v. 泛滥,淹没
floor n. 地面,地板
n. 楼层,楼面
v. 铺地板
flour n. 面粉,粉状物
flourish v. 繁荣,茂盛,兴旺
flow v./n. 流,流动
flower n. 花,花卉

v. 开花
fluent *a.* 流利的,流畅的
fluid *a.* 流动的,流体的,液体的
n. 流体,液体
fly1 *v.* 飞,飞行
v. 放(风筝),驾驶(飞机)
v. 飘扬
fly2 *n.* 苍蝇
focus *vt.* 使聚焦;使集中
fog *n.* 雾
fold *v.* 折叠,合拢
n. 褶,褶痕
v. 包,笼罩
folk *n.* 人们
a. 民间的
follow *v.* 跟随,追逐,追求
v. 顺……走
v. 听从,遵循
v. 理解,听清楚
following *a.* 下列的,其次的,接着的
fond *a.* 喜爱的,爱好的
food *n.* 食物,粮食,养料
fool *n.* 笨蛋,傻瓜
v. 玩弄,愚弄
foolish *a.* 愚笨的,愚蠢的
foot *n.* 脚,足
n. 英尺
n. 最下部,底部
on foot 步行
football *n.* 足球,足球运动
footstep *n.* 脚步,脚步声
for *prep.* 为,为了,代替
prep. [表示目的,方向]向,对
prep. [表等值关系]换
prep. [表示时间,距离]达,计
conj. 由于,因为
prep. 对于,就……而言
forbid *vt.* 禁止
force *n.* 力,力量,力气
n. 暴力,武力
n. 军队,部队
v. 强迫,迫使
forecast *v./n.* 预测,预报
forehead *n.* 额,前额
foreign *a.* 外国的,对外的
a. 外国产的,外国来的
foreigner *n.* 外国人
forest *n.* 森林,森林地带
forever *ad.* 永远,总是
forget *v.* 忘记,遗忘
forgive *v.* 宽恕,饶恕
fork *n.* 叉,叉子
n. 分叉,岔口
form *n.* 形状,形式,方式
v. 形成,构成,组成
n. 类型,结构
n. 表格,格式
formal *a.* 正式的,礼仪上的
formation *n.* 形成,构成
n. 形成物,结构
former *a.* 在前的,以前的
formula *n.* 公式,程式
forth *ad.* 向前,向外
fortnight *n.* 两星期
fortunate *a.* 幸运的,侥幸的
fortunately *ad.* 幸运地;幸亏
fortune *n.* 命运,运气
n. 财富,财产
forty *n./a.* 四十
forward *a.* 前部的,向前的
a. 进步的,激进的
found *v.* 成立,建立,创办
foundation *n.* 成立,建立,创办
n. 地基,基础,根据
fountain *n.* 泉水,喷泉,喷水池
four *n./a.* 四
fourteen *n./a.* 十四
fourth *a.* 第四
n. 四分之一
fox *n.* 狐狸
fraction *n.* 碎片,小部分,一点儿
fragment *n.* 碎片,小部分,片断
frame *n.* 框架,框子
n. 骨架,体格
v. 装框子
framework *n.* 构架,框架,结构
France *n.* 法国
frank *a.* 坦白的,直率的
free *a.* 自由的,无约束的
a. 免费的,免除的
a. 自由开放的,畅通的
v. 使自由,解放
a. 空闲的,空余的
set free 释放
freedom *n.* 自由,自主
freeze *v.* 结冰,凝固
French *a.* 法国的,法语的
n. 法国人,法语
frequent *a.* 频繁的
frequently *ad.* 时常,往往
fresh *a.* 新的,新鲜的
a. 有生气的,健壮的
a. 清新的,凉爽的
a. 淡水的
Friday *n.* 星期五
friend *n.* 朋友,友人
make friends 交朋友,友好相处
friendly *a.* 友谊的,友好的
friendship *n.* 友好,友谊
frighten *v.* 吓唬,使惊恐
frog *n.* 蛙
from *prep.* [表示起点]从,自从
prep. [表示出处,来源]根据,按
prep. [表示原因,动机]由于,出于
prep. [表示去除,免除,阻止]
front *n./a.* 前部,前面
n. 前线,战线,阵线
v. 面向,面对
in front of 在……前面,面对
frontier *n.* 边界,边疆,国境
frost *n.* 霜,降霜;严寒
frown *n./v.* 皱眉头
fruit *n.* 水果,果实
n. 成果,结果
fry *v.* 油煎,油炸
fuel *n.* 燃料
fulfil(l) *v.* 完成,履行
full *a.* 满的,充满的
a./n. 完全,充分
fun *n.* 玩笑,乐趣
n. 有趣的人(或事)
make fun of 取笑,嘲弄
function *n.* 职责;功能;作用
fund *n.* 资金,基金,专款
fundamental *a.* 基本的
funeral *n.* 葬礼,丧葬
funny *a.* 滑稽的,可笑的,有趣的
a. 稀奇的,古怪的
fur *n.* 软毛
n. 毛皮,裘皮,皮衣
furnace *n.* 炉子,熔炉
furniture *n.* 家具
further *ad./a.* 更远,更往前
ad./a. 进一步
furthermore *ad.* 而且,此外
future *n./a.* 将来,未来
n. 前途,远景

G

gain *v.* 获得,赢得
v./n. 增加,增进,获利
gallon *n.* 加仑
game *n.* 游戏,玩耍
n. 比赛,运动会
n. 猎物,野味
gang *n.* 一帮,一群
gap *n.* 间隙,缺口
n. 隔阂,差距
garage *n.* 车库,飞机库
garden *n.* 花园,菜园
v. 从事园艺
gardener *n.* 园丁,花匠
gas *n.* 气体,煤气
n. 汽油
gasoline *n.* 汽油
gate *n.* 大门,城门
gather *v.* 聚集,集合
v. 采集,收集
gay *a.* 快乐的

a. 华丽的，艳丽的
gaze *vi.* /*n.* 凝视，注视
general *a.* 普通的，通用的
a. 总的，大体的
n. 将军，将官
in general 通常，一般来说
generally *ad.* 大概，通常，一般
generation *n.* 产生，发生
n. 代，世代
generator *n.* 发电机，发生器
generous *a.* 慷慨的，大方的
a. 宽厚的，宽宏大量的
genius *n.* 天才
gentle *a.* 和蔼的，文雅的，有礼貌的
gentleman *n.* 绅士，先生
gently *ad.* 文雅地，有礼貌地
ad. 轻轻地
genuine *a.* 真正的，真诚的
geometry *n.* 几何学
germ *n.* 微生物，细菌，病菌
German *n.* 德国人，德语
a. 德国(人)的，德语的
Germany *n.* 德意志，德国
gesture *n.* 姿势，手势，姿态
get *v.* 获得，得到
v. 使，使得
v. 变得，成为
v. 到达，抵达
get along with (与……)和睦相处
get away 脱离，离开
get in 收获，到达，进站
get off 下车，从……下来，离开，动身，开始
get together 集会，聚会
get up 起床，起立
get along 相处
ghost *n.* 鬼魂，幽灵
giant *n.* 巨人
a. 大的，巨大的
gift *n.* 赠品，礼物
n. 天赋，才能
girl *n.* 少女，女孩，姑娘
give *v.* 给，提供，授予
v. 举行，举办
v. 交给，托付
v. 传授，进行，做
give away 泄露，暴露，出卖，赠送，捐献
give in 投降，让步，认输，交上去，呈上
give up 放弃，辞去，投降，屈服
glad *a.* 高兴的，愉快的
glance *v.* 看一眼，看一看
n. 一看，一瞥
glass *n.* 玻璃，玻璃杯
n. 镜
n. (*pl.*) 眼镜
glimpse *n.* /*v.* 一瞥，瞥见
globe *n.* 地球，地球仪，球体
glorious *a.* 壮丽的，辉煌的
a. 光荣的
glory *n.* 光荣，荣誉
glove *n.* 手套
glow *v.* 发热，发光，发红
n. 白热
glue *n.* 胶，胶水
go *v.* 去，离去，走
v. 开动，运行，进行
v. 变成，成为
go down 下降；减少
go on 继续，持续发生
go over 浏览，读一遍，检查复习，重说(读，看)
go up 上升；增加
go after 追逐，追求
go ahead 开始，前进，领先
go by 经过，放过，过去，依照，遵守
goal *n.* 终点，球门
n. 目标，目的
goat *n.* 山羊
God *n.* 上帝，神
gold *n.* 金，黄金，金币
a. 金的，金制的
golden *a.* 金色的
a. 黄金的，金制的
good *a.* 好的，美好的，善良的
a. 有效的，有益的
n. 好处，利益
for good 永久地，一劳永逸地
good for 有效，适用，胜任
goodbye int. 再见
goods *n.* 货物，商品
n. 财产
goose *n.* 鹅
govern *v.* 统治，管理
government *n.* 政府，内阁
n. 管理，支配
n. 政治，政体
governor *n.* 地方长官，总督，州长
graceful *a.* 优美的；得体的
grade *n.* 等级，级别，年级
n. 分数
v. 分等，分级
gradual *a.* 逐渐的，逐步的
gradually *ad.* 逐渐地
graduate *n.* 毕业生
v. 毕业
a. 毕了业的，研究生的
grain *n.* 谷物，谷类
n. 颗粒，细粒
grammar *n.* 语法，语法书
grand *a.* 重大的，主要的
a. 宏大的，盛大的
a. 伟大的，崇高的
granddaughter *n.* 孙女，外孙女
grandfather *n.* 祖父，外祖父
grandmother *n.* 祖母，外祖母
grandson *n.* 孙子，外孙
grant *v.* 同意，准予
v. 给予，授予
grape *n.* 葡萄
graph *n.* (曲线)图，图解
grasp *v.* 掌握，理解
v. 抓紧，抓住
grass *n.* 草，牧草
grateful *a.* 感激的，感谢的
gratitude *n.* 感激，感谢
great *a.* 大的，伟大的
a. 重大的，极大的，十足的
a. 美妙的
greatly *ad.* 大大地，非常
greedy *a.* 贪吃的，嘴馋的
a. 贪婪的，渴望的
Greek *n.* 希腊人，希腊语
a. 希腊(人)的
green *n.* /*a.* 绿色
a. 生的，未成熟的
a. 缺乏经验的，生疏的
greet *v.* 致敬，致意，迎接
v. 扑(鼻)，入(耳)，触(目)
greeting *n.* 致敬，问候，祝贺
grey/gray *n.* /*a.* 灰色
grip *v.* /*n.* 紧握，抓紧
groan *v.* /*n.* 呻吟
grocer *n.* 食品商，杂货商
gross *a.* 总的，毛(重)的
ground *n.* 地面，土地
n. 场所，场地
n. 根据，理由
group *n.* 群，小组
v. 分组，聚集
grow *v.* 生长，发育
v. 增长，发展
v. 渐渐变得
v. 种植，栽培
grown-up *a.* 成长的，成熟的，成人的
n. 成年人
growth *n.* 生长，增长，发展
guarantee *n.* 保证，保证书
v. 保证，担保
guard *v.* /*n.* 守卫，保卫，提防
n. 哨兵，警卫
on guard 警惕，提防
guess *v.* /*n.* 推测，猜测
v. 以为，相信
guest *n.* 客人，宾客，旅客
guidance *n.* 引导，指导
guide *n.* 向导，导游者
v. /*n.* 引导，指导

n. 入门书，手册
guilty *a.* 有罪的，犯罪的
a. 自觉有罪的，负疚的
gulf *n.* 海湾
gum *n.* 树胶，口香糖
gun *n.* 枪，炮
gymnasium/gym *n.* 体育馆，健身房

H

habit *n.* 习惯，习性，脾性
hair *n.* 毛发，头发，汗毛
half *n./a./ad.* 半，一半
in half 成两半
hall *n.* 穿堂，门厅，大厅
n. 会堂，礼堂，办公大楼
halt *v./n.* 止步，停住，停止
hammer *n.* 锤，榔头
v. 锤击，敲打
hand *n.* 手，指针
v. 交出，传递
n. 人手，职工，船员
on the one hand..., on the other hand 一方面……，另一方面
by hand 用手
hand down 传下来，传给，往下递
hand in 交上，递交
hand in hand 手拉着手联合，连在一起
handful *n.* 一把，少数
handkerchief *n.* 手帕
handle *n.* 手柄，把手，拉手
v. 触，摸，抚弄
v. 处理，操纵，应付
handsome *a.* 漂亮的，俊俏的
a. 慷慨的，可观的
handwriting *n.* 笔迹，手迹
handy *a.* 手边的，近便的
hang *v.* 吊，悬挂
v. 吊死，绞死
hang up 挂断(电话)
happen *v.* 发生
v. 碰巧
happiness *n.* 幸福，幸运
happy *a.* 幸福的，快乐的，乐意的
harbo(u)r *n.* 港口，海港
n. 避难所，藏身处
hard *a.* 硬，坚硬
a. 困难的，艰苦的
ad. 努力地，猛烈地
harden *v.* 硬化，变硬
hardly *ad.* 几乎不，简直不，仅仅
hardship *n.* 艰难，困苦
hardware *n.* 五金，金属制品
n. 硬件
harm *n./v.* 损害，伤害，危害
harmony *n.* 和谐，和睦，融洽
harvest *n./v.* 收获，收割
n. 成果，后果
haste *n.* 匆忙，急速
v. 赶快，赶忙
hat *n.* 帽子
hate *v./n.* 恨，憎恨
v. 不喜欢，不愿
hatred *n.* 憎恶，憎恨，怨恨
have *v.* 有，具有
v. 体会，经受
v. 从事，进行
v. 使，让
v. 吃，喝，吸(烟)
have to/have got to 不得不，必须
have... back 要回，收回……
hay *n.* 干草
hazard *n.* 危险，危害
he *pron.* 他
head *n.* 头，头顶
n. 首脑，首长
v. 率领，带头
head for (使)朝……行进
headache *n.* 头痛
headmaster *n.* 校长
headquarters *n.* 司令部，指挥部
health *n.* 健康，卫生
healthy *a.* 健康，健壮的
a. 有益健康的，合乎卫生的
heap *n.* (一)堆，大量，许多
v. 堆，堆积
hear *v.* 听见，听说，得知
v. 倾听，听取
hear of 听到；听说
heart *n.* 心，心脏
n. 中心，要点
n. 内心，心肠
at heart 有内心，实质上
by heart 牢记，凭记忆
heart and soul 全心全意地
heat *n.* 热，热烈，激烈
v. 加热，发热
heaven *n.* 天堂，天国
n. 天，天空
heavy *a.* 重的，沉重的，繁重的
a. 大量的，猛烈的
hedge *n.* 篱笆，树篱
heel *n.* 脚跟，鞋跟
height *n.* 高，高度
n. 高处，高地，顶点
helicopter *n.* 直升飞机
hello int. 喂
help *v./n.* 帮助，援助
help out 帮助；帮助(某人)摆脱困境
can not help 禁不住，忍不住
help oneself 自取所需(食物等)
helpful *a.* 有帮助的，有益的
hen *n.* 母鸡，雌禽
hence *adv.* 因此
her *pron.* 她(宾格)
pron. 她的
here *ad.* 这里，到这里
ad. 在这一点上，这时
here and there 到处，处处
hero *n.* 英雄，勇士
n. 男主角，男主人公
heroine *n.* 女英雄，女主角
heroic *a.* 英雄的，英勇的
hers *pron.* 她的(东西)
herself *pron.* 她自己，她亲自
hesitate *v.* 犹豫，踌躇
hide *a.* 隐藏，隐瞒，躲藏
high *a.* 高的，高度的，高级的，高尚的
ad. 高
highly *ad.* 高度地，很，非常
highway *n.* 公路，大路
hill *n.* 小山，丘陵
hillside *n.* (小山)山腰，山坡
him *pron.* 他(宾格)
himself *pron.* 他自己，他亲自
hint *v./n.* 暗示，示意
hire *v./n.* 雇佣，租借
his *pron.* 他的
pron. 他的(东西)
history *n.* 历史
n. 来历，经历，履历
hit *v./n.* 打击，击中，碰撞
v. 达到，完成
hobby *n.* 业余爱好，嗜好，兴趣
hold *v.* 拿住，握住，持有，掌握
v. 举行，召开(会议)
v. 合用，适用，有效
v. 包含，容纳
n. 船舱
hold back 抑制，阻止
get hold of 抓住，掌握
hold up 举起，支撑，承载，阻挡，使停止
hole *n.* 洞，窟窿
holiday *n.* 假日，假期，休假
hollow *a.* 空的，中空的
a. 空洞的，空虚的
holy *a.* 神圣的，圣洁的
home *n.* 家，家乡，本国
a. 家的，家乡的，本国的
ad. 在家，回家
at home 在家，在国内
honest *a.* 诚实的，老实的，正直的
hono(u)r *n.* 荣誉，光荣，敬意
v. 尊敬，给以荣誉
in honor of 向……表敬意，为庆祝……，为纪念……
hono(u)rable *a.* 光荣的，荣誉的
a. 可尊敬的

hook *n.* 钩,钩状物
hope *v./n.* 希望,期望
hopeful *a.* 有希望的,怀有希望的
hopeless *a.* 没有希望的,绝望的
horn *n.* 角,触角
n. 号,喇叭
horror *n.* 恐怖,战栗
horsepower *n.* 马力
hospital *n.* 医院
host *n.* 主人,旅店老板
n. 节目主持人
hostile *a.* 敌对的
hot *a.* 热的
a. 辣的
a. 热烈的,激烈的
hotel *n.* 旅馆
hour *n.* 小时
n. 钟点,时刻
n. 课时,工作时间
house *n.* 房子,住宅
v. 供宿,留宿
household *n.* 户,家庭
housewife *n.* 家庭主妇
how *ad.* 怎么,怎样
ad. 多少,多么
how about ……如何,……怎么样
however *conj.* 然而,可是,不过
ad. 无论,不管
human *a.* 人的,人类的
humble *a.* 低下的,卑贱的
a. 恭顺的,谦卑的
v. 降低,贬抑
humid *a.* 湿的,湿气重的
humo(u)rous *a.* 幽默的,诙谐的
hundred *n./a.* 百
hunger *n.* 饥饿
n. 渴望
hungry *a.* 饥饿的
hunt *v./n.* 打猎,狩猎
v. 寻找,搜索
hurry *v./n.* 赶忙,匆忙,慌忙
hurry up(使)赶快迅速完成
in a hurry 匆忙,立即
hurt *v.* 伤害,刺痛,伤……感情
husband *n.* 丈夫
hydrogen *n.* 氢

I

I *pron.* 我
ice *n.* 冰
n. 冷饮
ice-cream *n.* 冰淇淋
idea *n.* 想法,念头
n. 概念,观念
n. 意见,主意
ideal *a.* 理想的,称心如意的
a. 理想主义的,唯心论的
n. 理想
identify *vt.* 认出,识别
idle *a.* 闲着的,闲置的
a. 无用的,无效的
v. 空虚,虚度
if *conj.* 如果,假使
conj. 是不是
in only 要是……就
ignore *vt.* 不顾,不理,忽视
ill *a.* 有病的
a. 坏的,恶意的
ad. 坏,不利地
illegal *a.* 不合法的,非法的
illness *n.* 病,疾病
image *n.* 像,肖像,形象
n. 影像,图像
imaginary *a.* 想像的,虚构的
imagination *n.* 想像,空想,想像力
imagine *v.* 想象,设想,料想
imitate *v.* 模仿,仿效
immediate *a.* 立即的,即时的
a. 直接的,最接近的
immense *a.* 巨大的,广大的
immigrant *n.* 移民,侨民
impact *n.* 影响,冲击
impatient *a.* 不耐烦的,急躁的
implication *n.* 含义,暗示,暗指
imply *v.* 意指,暗示
import *v./n.* 输入,进口
n.(*pl.*)进口商品,进口物资
importance *n.* 重要,重要性
important *a.* 重要的,重大的
a. 有地位的,显要的
impossible *a.* 不可能的,做不到的
impress *vt.* 给……深刻的印象
impression *n.* 印象,感想
n. 印记,压痕
impressive *a.* 给人以深刻印象的
improve *v.* 改善,改进
v. 好转,进步
improvement *n.* 改进,改良,增进
n. 改进措施
in *prep.* [表示场所,位置]在……里,在……中
prep. [表示时间]在……期间,在……以后
prep. [表示工具,方式]以……方式
prep. [表示状态,情况]在……之中,处于
prep. [表示范围,领域,方向]在……之内,在……方面
ad. 向里,向内
inch *n.* 英寸
incident *n.* 小事件,政治事件,事变
include *v.* 包含,包括,计入
income *n.* 收入,所得,进款
increase *v./n.* 增加,增长,增进
indeed *ad.* 的确,确实
ad. 多么,真的
independence *n.* 独立,自立,自主
independent *a.* 独立的,自立的,自主的
India *n.* 印度
Indian *n.* 印度人,印第安人
a. 印度(人)的,印第安人的
indicate *v.* 指示,表示,暗示
indication *n.* 迹象
indirect *a.* 间接的,迂回的
individual *n.* 个人,个体
a. 个别的,单独的
indoor(s) *a./ad.* 室内,户内
industrial *a.* 工业的,产业的
industry *n.* 工业,产业
inevitable *a.* 必然的,不可避免的
infant *n.* 婴儿,幼儿
infect *vt.* 传染,感染
infer *vt.* 推断,推论
inferior *a.* 次的,低劣的
influence *n.* 影响,感化力
n. 势力,权势
vt. 影响,感化
inform *v.* 通知,告诉,报告
v. 告发,告密
information *n.* 信息,资料,情报
inhabitant *n.* 居民,住户
inherit *v.* 继承
injection *n.* 注射,注入,喷射
injure *v.* 损害,损伤,伤害
ink *n.* 墨水
inn *n.* 小旅馆,客栈
inner *a.* 内部的,里面的,内心的
innocent *a.* 清白的,无罪的
insect *n.* 虫,昆虫
inside *n.* 内部,里面,内侧
a. 内部的,里面的,内幕的
ad. 在内部,在里面
prep. 在……里,在……内
insist *v.* 坚持,坚决主张,强烈要求
inspect *v.* 检查,调查,视察
inspire *v.* 使产生灵感
v. 鼓舞,感动
install *v.* 装置,安装
instance *n.* 例,例证,实例
for instance 举例说,比如
instant *a.* 立刻的,立即的
a. 紧急的,迫切的
n. 瞬间,时刻
instead *ad.* 代替,顶替
instead of 代替
instinct *n.* 本能,直觉,天性
institute *n.* 学会,研究所,学院
v. 设立,设置,制定
instruct *v.* 教,教授

v. 指示,指令
instruction n. (常 pl.)命令,指示,用法,说明
n. 教学,教导
instrument n. 工具,仪器,乐器
insult v./n. 侮辱,凌辱
insurance n. 保险,保险费
insure v. 保险,替……保险
v. 保证
intellectual n. 知识分子
intelligence n. 智力,理解力
n. 情报,消息,报道
intelligent a. 聪明的,明智的
intend v. 想要,打算,企图
intensive a. 加强的;集中的
intention n. 意图,意向,目的
intentional a. 故意的,有意识的
interest n. 兴趣,关心,注意
v. 使发生兴趣
n. 利息,利益
interesting a. 有趣的,引人入胜的
interfere v. 干涉,干扰,妨碍
interference n. 干涉,干扰,妨碍
intermediate a. 中间的,居间的
internal a. 内部的
international a. 国际的,世界的
interrupt v. 打断,打扰
v. 断绝,中断
interval n. 间隔,间歇,(工间)休息
interview n. 接见,会见,面试
intimate a. 亲密的,密切的
into prep. 到……里,进入
prep. 成为
introduce v. 介绍
v. 引进,传入
introduction n. 介绍,引进,传入
n. 引论,导言,绪论
n. 入门,初步
invasion n. 侵入,侵略
invent v. 发明,创造
invention n. 发明,创造
inventor n. 发明者,发明家,创造者
invest v. 投资
investigate v. 调查,调查研究
investment n. 投资,投资额
invitation n. 请柬
n. 邀请,招待
invite v. 邀请,招待
involve v. 卷入,陷入,连累
v. 包含,含有
inward a. 里面的,内在的,向内的
iron n. 铁
n. 烙铁,熨斗
v. 熨平,烫(衣)
island n. 岛
isolate v. 隔离,孤立
it pron. 它
Italian a. 意大利的
n. 意大利人,意大利语
item n. 条,项目,条款
n. 一则(新闻)
its pron. 它的
itself pron. 它自己,它本身

J

jacket n. 短上衣,夹克衫
jam n. 果酱
January n. 一月
Japan n. 日本
Japanese a. 日本的
n. 日本人,日语
jar 罐,坛
jaw n. 颌,颚
jazz n. 爵士乐
jealous a. 妒忌的
jewel n. 宝石
n. 宝石饰物
job n. 工作,职业
n. 一件工作,活儿
join v. 接合,结合,连结
v. 参加,加入
joint n. 关节,骨节
n. 接合处,接缝
a. 联合的,共同的,连接的
joke n. 笑话,玩笑
vi. 说笑话,开玩笑
journal n. 日报,期刊
n. 日志,日记
journey n. 旅行,旅程
joy n. 欢乐,喜悦
n. 乐事,乐趣
judge n. 审判员,法官
n. 评判员,裁判
v. 评价,鉴定
v. 认为,断定,判断
v. 审判,裁判,裁决
judg(e)ment n. 审判,判决
n. 判断力,识别力
n. 意见,看法,判断
judging by 根据……来判断
juice n. 汁,液
July n. 七月
jump v./n. 跳跃,跳动
n. 猛增
June n. 六月
junior a. 年少的,年幼的
a. 后进的,下级的
just ad. 正好,恰好
ad. 刚刚,刚才
a. 公正的,公平的
ad. 只是,仅仅是,只不过
justice n. 公道,公平
n. 审判,司法
justify vt. 证明……正当(或有理),为……辩护

K

keen a. 锋利的,尖锐的
a. 敏捷的,敏锐的
a. 热心的,渴望的
keep v. 保留,保存
v. 保持,继续
v. 保守,遵守
v. 防守,保卫
v. 抑制,防止
v. 扣留,留住
v. 赡养,饲养
keep from 阻止,克制
keep on 继续,保持
keep up (使)继续下去,(使)不停止
keep up with 跟上
key n. 钥匙
n. 答案,解答
n. 键,琴键
a. 主要的,关键的
kick n./v. 踢
kid1 n. 小孩,儿童
kid2 v. 戏弄,取笑
kill v. 杀死,消灭
v. 破坏,毁灭
v. 消磨(时间)
kilogram(me)/kilo n. 公斤,千克
kilometre n. 公里,千米
kind n. 种类
a. 仁慈的,和善的,亲切的
kindness n. 仁慈,好意
n. 友好行为
king n. 国王
kingdom n. 王国
n. 领域
kiss v./n. 接吻
kitchen n. 厨房
knee n. 膝,膝盖
kneel v. 跪,下跪
knife n. 刀,餐刀
v. 用刀切,用匕首刺
knock n./v. 敲,敲打,碰撞
knock down 撞倒,击倒
knot n. 结
n. 节疤
know v. 知道,了解,懂得
v. 认识,熟悉
v. 识别,认出
knowledge n. 知识,学识
n. 知道,了解

L

laboratory/lab n. 实验室,研究室
labo(u)r n. 工作,劳动
v. 劳动,苦干
n. 劳力,劳方

lack *n.* 缺乏,没有
v. 缺乏,缺少
ladder *n.* 梯子
lady *n.* 夫人,小姐,女士
lag *v.*/*n.* 落后,滞后
lake *n.* 湖
lamp *n.* 灯
land *n.* 陆地,土地
n. 国土,国家
v. 登陆,着陆
landlord *n.* 房东,地主
lane *n.* 小路,小巷
n. 行车道
language *n.* 语言
lap *n.* 膝盖
large *a.* 大的,广大的
a. 大规模的,众多的
largely *ad.* 大部分,基本上
laser *n.* 激光
last1 *a.* 最后的
ad. 最后,最近
at last 最终,终于
last2 *v.* 持续,持久
late *ad.*/*a.* 迟,迟到
a. 晚的,晚期的
lately *ad.* 近来,最近
latter *a.* 后面的,后者的
n. 后者
laugh *v.*/*n.* 笑
laugh at 讥笑,嘲笑
laughter *n.* 笑,笑声
launch *v.* 发射,下水
v. 开始,发起
laundry *n.* 洗衣房
lavatory *n.* 盥洗室,厕所
law *n.* 法律,法规
n. 规律,法则,定律
lawn *n.* 草地,草坪
lawyer *n.* 律师
lay *v.* 放,搁
v. 下(蛋)
v. 铺设,敷设
lay down 放下 拟订 铺设
layer *n.* 层
lazy *a.* 懒惰的
lead1 *v.* 领导,率领,领先
v. 引导,带领
lead to 通向,导致,引起
lead2 *n.* 铅
leading *a.* 指导的,领导的
a. 第一位的,最主要的
leader *n.* 领袖,领导者
leadership *n.* 领导
leaf *n.* 叶,叶子
n. 页,张
league *n.* 同盟,联盟

leak *n.* 漏洞
v. 渗漏,泄漏
lean *v.* 倾斜,屈身
v. 倚,靠,依赖
leap *v.* 跳跃,跳过
n. 跳跃,飞跃
learn *v.* 学习,学会
v. 听到,获悉
learned *a.* 有学问的,博学的
learning *n.* 学习,学问
least *a.* 最小的,最少的
ad. 最少,最小
at least 最低限度
leather *n.* 皮革,皮革制品
leave1 *v.* 离开,动身
v. 留下,剩下,忘带
v. 让,听任
leave behind 丢弃;留下,忘带
leave... to 交托,委托
leave2 *n.* 许可,同意
n. 告假,休假
lecture *n.*/*v.* 演讲,讲课
left *a.*/*n.* 左,左面,左边
leg *n.* 腿,腿脚
legal *a.* 法律(上)的
a. 合法的,法定的
leisure *n.* 空闲,闲暇
lemon *n.* 柠檬
lend *v.* 出借,借给
length *n.* 长,长度
lens *n.* 透镜,镜头
less *a.*/*ad.* 较少,更少
lessen *v.* 减少,变少
lesson *n.* 课,课程,功课
n. 教训
lest *conj.* 惟恐,以免,免得
let *v.* 让,允许
v. 出租
v. 放任,听任
let in 让……进入,放……进来
let out 放出,发出
let down 放下,降低使失望
letter *n.* 信,函件
n. 字母
level *n.* 水平,水准
v. 弄平,铺平
a. 水平的
liable *a.* 有……倾向的,易于……的 (to)
liberal *a.* 慷慨的,大方的
a. 丰富的,充足的
a. 自由的,思想开明的
liberate *v.* 解放,释放
library *n.* 图书馆,(个人)藏书
n. 丛书,文库
license/licence *v.* 准许,许可,认可
n. 执照,许可证

lid *n.* 盖
lie1 *v.* 躺,平放,处于
v. 位于,在于 (in)
lie2 *n.* 谎言
v. 说谎
life *n.* 生命,寿命,一生
n. 生活,生计
lifetime *n.* 一生,终生
lift *v.* 提起,举起
v. 消散,(云雾)升起
n. 电梯,升降机
light1 *n.* 光,光亮,光线
n. 灯,灯光
v. 点,点燃
v. 照亮,照耀
light2 *a.* 轻的
a. 轻捷的,轻快的
a. 淡(色)的
lightning *n.* 闪电
a. 闪电般的,快速的
like1 *v.* 喜爱,喜欢
like2 prep. 像,同……一样
a. 同样的,想象的
likely *a.* 可能的,有希望的
ad. 大概,多半
likewise *ad.* 同样,照样
ad. 也,而且
lime *n.* 石灰
limit *n.* 界限,限度,范围
v. 限制,限定
limitation *n.* 限制,限定,局限性
line *n.* 线,线条,界线
n. 行,行列
v. 排队,排列
n. 航线,交通线,通讯线
in line 成一直线,排成一行
line up 排队,使排成一行
link *n.* 环,链环
v. 连结,联系
lion *n.* 狮子
lip *n.* 嘴唇
liquid *n.* 液体
a. 液体的,液态的
liquor *n.* 酒
list *n.* 表,目录,名单
v. 列表,列入
listen *v.* 听,听从
literature *n.* 文学,文学作品
n. 文献,图书资料
litre/liter *n.* 公升
little *a.* 小的,幼小的
a. 矮小,渺小
a./*n.* 不多,没有多少
ad. 不大,不太
a little 一些,少许 稍许,一点儿
quite a little 相当多,不少

live1 *v.* 住,居住
v. 生活,过活,生存
live on/by 靠……生活,以……为食
live2 *a.* 活的,有生命的
lively *a.* 活泼的,活跃的
a. 逼真
liver *n.* 肝,肝脏
living *a.* 活的,现存的
living-room *n.* 起居室
load *v.* 装,装载,装填
n. 负荷,负担
n. (一)担,(一)车
loaf *n.* 一条面包,一只面包
loan *n.* 贷款
v./*n.* 借出
local *a.* 地方的,当地的
a. 局部的
locate *v.* 找出,查出
v. 设置在,位于
lock *n.* 锁
v. 上锁,锁住
lodge *v.* 住宿,投宿
log *n.* 圆木,木料
logic *n.* 逻辑,逻辑学
logical *a.* 逻辑(上)的,符合逻辑的
lonely *a.* 孤独的,寂寞的
a. 荒凉的,人迹稀少的
long *a.* 长的,远的
a. 长期的
v. 渴望,极想 (for)
long for 渴望
before long 不久以后
as long as/so long as 只要,如果,既然
no longer 不再,已不
look *v.*/*n.* 看,注视
v. 好像,显得
n. 脸色,外表
look after 照顾,关心,照料
look at 看,注视
look back 回顾,回头看
look for 寻找,寻求
look forward to 盼望,期待
look into 调查,观察
look over 把……看一遍,过目
look up 查找,寻找,查出
look down upon 蔑视,看不起
loose *a.* 松的,宽的,松散的
lorry *n.* 卡车,运货汽车
lose *v.* 丢,丢失,丧失
v. 失败,输
v. 迷(路)
loss *n.* 丧失,丢失
n. 亏损,损失
lot *n.* 许多
a lot 大量,许多 (of)
非常,相当
loud *a.* 响亮的,大声的
a. 吵闹的,喧嚣的
loudspeaker *n.* 扬声器,扩音器
love *n.*/*v.* 爱,热爱,爱戴
v. 爱好,喜欢
fall in love 相爱,爱上 (with)
lovely *a.* 可爱的,秀丽的
a. 令人愉快的,美好的
lover *n.* 爱好者
n. 情人
low *a.* 低的,矮的
a. 低级的,下层的,卑贱的
a. 低声的
lower *a.* 较低的,下级的,下游的
v. 放低,降低
loyal *a.* 忠诚的,忠贞的
loyalty *n.* 忠诚,忠心
luck *n.* 运气
n. 好运,侥幸
lucky *a.* 幸运的,侥幸的
luggage *n.* 行李
lump *n.* 块,团
lunch *n.* 午餐
lung *n.* 肺
luxury *n.* 奢侈,奢侈品

M

machine *n.* 机器,机械
machinery *n.* (总称)机械,机器
mad *a.* 疯的,神经错乱的
a. 狂热的,着迷的
magazine *n.* 杂志,期刊
magic *n.* 戏法,魔术,魔法
a. 魔术的,有魔力的
magnificent *a.* 壮丽的,宏伟的
maid *n.* 侍女,女仆
mail *n.* 邮件,邮政
v. 邮寄
main *a.* 主要的,总的
n. 总管道,干线
mainly *ad.* 主要地,大体上
mainland *n.* 大陆,本土
maintain *v.* 保养,维修
v. 维持,保持,继续
major1 *a.* 较大的,主要的
v. 主修 (in)
n. 主科,(某)专业学生
major2 *n.* 少校
majority *n.* 多数,过半数
make *v.* 制,制造,建造
v. 使,迫使
v. (使)成为,(使)变成
v. 获得,挣(钱)
v. 总计,等于
make for 走向,冲向
make out 开列,书写
看出,辨认出 理解,了解
make up 拼凑,组成,构成,编造(故事,谎言等)弥补,赔偿
male *a.* 男(性)的
man *n.* 男人
n. 人,人类
manage *v.* 管理,经营,处理
v. 设法,对付
management *n.* 管理,经营
manager *n.* 经理,管理人
mankind *n.* 人类
manner *n.* 方式,方法
n. 态度,举止
n. (*pl.*)礼貌,规矩
manual *a.* 用手的,手工的,体力的
many *a.* 许多的
n. 许多
a good many/a great many 大量的,许多
map *n.* 图,地图
march *v.*/*n.* 行进,行军
n. 进行曲
March *n.* 三月
margin *n.* 页边空白,边缘
mark *n.* 记号,标记,痕迹
n. 分数
v. 记分,打分
v. 作标记,标志
market *n.* 集市,市场
marriage *n.* 结婚,婚姻
n. 结婚仪式
married *a.* 已婚的,夫妇的
marry *v.* 结婚,嫁,娶
mask *n.* 面具,面罩,口罩
n. 假面具,伪装
vt. 用面具遮住,遮盖
vt. 掩饰,掩盖
mass *n.* 团,块,堆
n. (*pl.*)群众,民众
n. 众多,大量
master *n.* 主人,雇主
n. 能手,名家,大师
v. 掌握,精通
n. (M-)硕士
match1 *n.* 火柴
match2 *n.* 比赛,竞赛
n. 对手,敌手
v. 匹配,相配
mate *n.* 伙伴,配偶
material *n.* 材料,原料,资料
a. 物质的,实物的,具体的
mathematics/maths *n.* 数学
matter *n.* 物质,物体
n. 事情,情况,事态
n. 毛病,麻烦事
v. 要紧,有关系

no matter 无论,不管
mature *a.* 成熟的
maximum *n.* 最大量,最高值
a. 最大的,最高的
May *n.* 五月
may *v.* 可能,或许
v. 可以,不妨
v. 祝,愿
maybe *ad.* 或许,大概
mayor *n.* 市长
me *pron.* 我(宾格)
meal *n.* 一餐,一顿饭,膳食
mean *v.* 意指,意味着
v. 意欲,打算
meaning *n.* 意思,意义,含义
means *n.* 方法,手段,工具
by means of 用,凭借
meantime *n.* 其时,其间
ad. 同时,当时
meanwhile *n.* 其时,其间
ad. 同时,当时
measure *n.* 量度,测量
n. 措施,办法
v. 量,测量
measurement *n.* 测量,度量
meat *n.* 肉,食用肉类
mechanic *n.* 技工,机械工人
medical *a.* 医学的,医疗的,医药的
medicine *n.* 内服药,医药
n. 医学,医术
medium *a.* 中等的,适中的
n. 中间,适中
n. 媒介,媒介物,传导体
meet *v.* 遇见,碰上
v. 会见,迎接
v. 会合,相会,开会
v. 满足,符合
meeting *n.* 会议,集会
member *n.* 成员,会员
memorial *a.* 记忆的,纪念的
n. 纪念物,纪念碑,纪念馆
memory *n.* 记忆力,记忆,回忆
in memory of 纪念
mend *v.* 修补,修理,缝补
mental *a.* 思想的,精神的
a. 智力的,脑力的
mention *v.* 提及,说起,讲述
menu *n.* 菜单
merchant *n.* 商人,零售商
mercy *n.* 仁慈,怜悯,宽恕
mere *a.* 纯粹的,仅仅的
merely *ad.* 仅仅,只不过
merry *a.* 欢乐的,兴高采烈的
message *n.* 通讯,消息,音信
metal *n.* 金属,金属制品
method *n.* 方法,办法
metre/meter *n.* 公尺,米
microphone *n.* 麦克风,扩音器
microscope *n.* 显微镜
middle *n.* 中间,当中
a. 中间的,中部的
midnight *n.* 午夜,子夜
might *aux. v.* [may 的过去式]
aux. v. 可能,会
mild *a.* 温暖的,暖和的
a. 温和的,温柔的
mile *n.* 英里
military *a.* 军队的,军事的,军用的
milk *n.* 乳,牛奶
v. 挤奶
mill *n.* 磨房,磨粉机
n. 制造厂,工厂
million *n./a.* 百万
mind *n.* 头脑,精神
n. 理智,智能
n. 想法,意见,心情
v. 留心,当心,注意
v. 介意,在乎
make up one's mind 决定,下决心
never mind 不要紧,没关系
keep in mind 记住
mine1 *pron.* 我的(东西)
mine2 *n.* 矿,矿山,矿井
v. 采掘,开矿
mineral *n.* 矿物,矿石
a. 矿物的,矿质的
minister *n.* 部长,大臣
ministry *n.* 部
minor *a.* 较小的,较少的,较次要的
n. 兼修学科
v. 兼修(in)
minority *n.* 少数,少数派,少数民族
minus *a.* 减的,负的
prep. 减去
n. 减号,负号
minute1 *n.* 分,分钟
n. 一会儿,片刻
minute2 *a.* 微细的,微小的,详细的
miracle *n.* 奇迹,令人惊奇的人(或事)
mirror *n.* 镜子
miserable *a.* 悲惨的,痛苦的
misleading *a.* 使人产生误解的,引人歧途的
miss1 *n.* 小姐
n. (M-)……小姐
miss2 *v.* 未击中,没达到
v. 未看到,未听到,没赶上
v. 遗漏,省去
v. 惦念
missing *a.* 失去的,失踪的
mission *n.* 使节,代表团
n. 使命,任务,天职
mist *n.* 薄雾,霭
mistake *n.* 错误,过失,误会
v. 误解,弄错,错认
mister *n.* 先生
n. (M-)……先生
misunderstand *v.* 误解,误会,曲解
mix *v.* 混合,掺和
v. 混淆,搞混
mix up 混合,混淆,搞糊涂
mixture *n.* 混合,混合物
mode *n.* 方式,样式
model *n.* 样式
n. 模型,原型,模特
n. 模范,典型
moderate *a.* 中等的,适度的
a. 温和的,稳健的
modern *a.* 现代的,近代的,新式的
modest *a.* 端庄的,朴素的
a. 谦虚的,谦逊的
moist *a.* 湿润的,潮湿的
moisture *n.* 潮湿,湿气,湿度
molecule *n.* 分子
moment *n.* 片刻,瞬间,时刻
Monday *n.* 星期一
money *n.* 货币,金钱
monitor *n.* 监听器,监视器,检测器
n. (学校的)班长
v. 监听/监视
v. 检测
monkey *n.* 猴子
month *n.* 月,月份
monthly *a./ad.* 每月,按月
n. 月刊
monument *n.* 纪念碑,纪念馆
mood *n.* 心境,情绪
n. 语气
moon *n.* 月亮,月球,卫星
moral *a.* 道德的,道义的,有道德的
n. 寓意,教育意义
more *a.* 更多的,较多的
n. 更多的人(东西)
ad. 更,更多
more or less 或多或少,多少有点
no more 不再
moreover *conj./ad.* 再者,加之,而且
morning *n.* 早晨,上午
mosquito *n.* 蚊子
most *a.* 最多的,最大的
ad. 最,非常,极
n. 大多数,大部分
at most/at the most 最多,至多
make the most of 充分利用
mostly *ad.* 主要的,多半,基本上
mother *n.* 母亲,妈妈
motion *vi.* 打手势;点(或摇)头示意
motive *n.* 动机,目的

motor *n.* 发动机,电动机,马达
mo(u)ld *n.* 模子,模型,铸模
v. 造型,浇铸
Mount *n.* (用于山名前)山,峰
mountain *n.* 山
mouse *n.* 鼠,耗子
mouth *n.* 嘴,口
move *v.* 移动,搬动,迁移
v. 感动
n. 行动
movement *n.* 运动,活动,移动
movie *n.* 电影,电影院
Mr. *n.* ……先生
Mrs. *n.* ……夫人
Ms. *n.* ……女士
much *n./a.* 许多,大量
ad. 非常
ad. 更,……得多
mud *n.* 泥,泥浆
multiply *v.* 乘
v. 增加,繁殖
murder *v./n.* 谋杀,凶杀
muscle *n.* 肌肉,体力
museum *n.* 博物馆,展览馆
music *n.* 音乐,乐曲
musical *a.* 音乐的,悦耳的
a. 喜欢音乐的,有音乐才能的
musician *n.* 音乐家,乐师
must *v.* 必须,应当
v. 很可能,谅必
mutual *a.* 相互的,共同的
my *pron.* 我的
myself *pron.* 我自己
mysterious *a.* 神秘的,可疑的,难理解的
mystery *n.* 神秘,神秘的事

N

nail *n.* 钉
n. 指甲,爪
v. 钉,钉住
naked *a.* 裸体的,毫无遮掩的
name *n.* 名字,名称,名义
v. 命名,取名
v. 说出,指出
name after 以……名字命名
narrow *a.* 狭的,狭窄的,狭隘的
nation *n.* 国家,民族
national *a.* 国家的,国立的,民族的
nationality *n.* 国籍,民族
native *n.* 土著,当地人
a. 本国的,本地的,土生的
natural *a.* 自然界的,自然的
a. 天赋的,固有的
nature *n.* 自然,自然界
n. 性质,本性,天性
naval *a.* 海军的,军舰的
navy *n.* 海军
near *ad./a.* 近,接近
prep. 在……近旁,靠近
nearby *a./ad.* 附近
prep. 在……附近
nearly *ad.* 差不多,几乎
neat *a.* 整洁的,简洁的
a. 优美的,精致的
necessarily *ad.* 必定,必然,当然
necessary *a.* 必须的,必要的,必然的
n. 必需品
necessity *n.* 必要(性),(迫切)需要
n. (常 *pl.*)必需品
neck *n.* 颈,脖子
need *n.* 必要,需要
v. 需要,必须
needle *n.* 针,指针,针状物
negative *a.* 否定的,消极的,反面的
neglect *v./n.* 疏忽,忽视,忽略
Negro *n.* 黑人
a. 黑人的
neighbo(u)r *n.* 邻居
neighbo(u)rhood *n.* 邻近,附近,周围
neither *a./pron.* 两者都不,(两者)没有一个
neither... nor 既不……也不
nephew *n.* 侄子,外甥
nerve *n.* 神经
n. 勇气,胆量
nervous *a.* 神经的
a. 神经过敏的,紧张不安的
nest *n.* 巢,窝
net1 *n.* 网,网状物
v. 用网捕,使落网
net2 *a.* 净的,纯净的
neutral *a.* 中立的,中性的
never *ad.* 从不,永不,决不
nevertheless *conj.* 然而,不过
ad. 仍然,不过
new *a.* 新的,新近的
a. 不熟悉的,没经验的
news *n.* 新闻,消息
newspaper *n.* 报纸
next *ad.* 其次,然后
a. 紧接的,其次的,贴近的
nice *a.* 好的,美的,令人愉快的
niece *n.* 侄女,外甥女
night *n.* 夜,夜间
nine *n.* 九
nineteen *n./a.* 十九
ninety *n./a.* 九十
ninth *a.* 第九
n. 九分之一
no *a.* 没有,并非,不许
ad. 不,不是
noble *a.* 高尚的,贵族的
nobody *n.* 没有人,谁也不
nod *v./n.* 点头,点头招呼
v./n. 打盹,瞌睡
noise *n.* 噪声,吵嚷声,杂音
noisy *a.* 吵闹的
none *pron.* 谁也不,哪个都不,一点也不
nonsense *n.* 胡说,废话
noon *n.* 正午,中午
nor *conj.* 也不,又不
normal *a.* 正常的,标准的,正规的
north *a./n.* 北,北方
ad. 在北方,向北方
northeast *a./n.* 东北,东北部
ad. 向东北,在东北
northern *a.* 北的,北方的
northwest *a./n.* 西北,西北部
ad. 向西北,在西北
nose *n.* 鼻子
not *ad.* 不
note *n.* 笔记,记录,便条
n. 注解,注释,评论
v. 注意
n. 钞票,纸币
notebook *n.* 笔记本
nothing *n.* 没有东西,什么也没有
n. 无,零,小事
ad. 毫不,满不是
nothing but 除了……以外没有什么;仅仅,只不过
notice *n.* 注意,认识
v. 看到,注意到
n. 通知,通告,布告
noun *n.* 名词
novel *n.* 长篇小说
November *n.* 十一月
now *ad.* 现在,目前,如今
ad. 当时,于是,接着
just now 刚才,一会儿以前
now that 既然
nuclear *a.* 核的,核心的,原子核的
nuisance *n.* 麻烦事,讨厌的人(或事)
number *n.* 数,数字,号码
v. 编号,加号码
a number of 一些,许多
numerous *a.* 众多的,大批的,无数的
nurse *n.* 护士,保姆,保育员
v. 护理,养育,喂奶
nursery *n.* 托儿所,保育室
nut *n.* 坚果
nylon *n.* 尼龙

O

obey *v.* 服从,遵从
v. 听由,听从摆布
object *n.* 物体
n. 对象,目的
v. 反对(to)
n. 宾语

objection *n.* 反对,异议
objective *n.* 目标
a. 客观的
oblige *vt.* 迫使
vt. 施恩于,帮……的忙
vt. 使感激
observation *n.* 观察,监视
observe *v.* 遵守,奉行
v. 观察,注意到,看到
observer *n.* 观察员,观察家
obstacle *n.* 障碍,干扰
obtain *v.* 获得,得到
obvious *a.* 明显的,显而易见的
occasion *n.* 场合,时节,时刻
occasional *a.* 偶然的,不时的
occupation *n.* 占领
n. 职业,工作
occupy *v.* 占,占领,占据
occur *v.* 发生,出现
v. 想起,想到
ocean *n.* 海洋
o'clock ……点钟
October *n.* 十月
odd *a.* 奇数的,单的
a. 奇怪的,古怪的
of *prep.* [表示从属关系]……的
prep. [表示部分、选择]
prep. [表示行为主体或对象]
prep. [表示同位关系]
prep. [表示性质,内容,状况]
prep. [表示分离,除去,剥夺]
prep. [表示位置,距离]
off *ad.* 离,距,(离)开
ad. 去掉,休止,完,光
prep. 从,离
off and on 断断续续,不时地
offend *v.* 冒犯,触犯,得罪
v. 使不快,使恼火
offer *v.*/*n.* 提供,提出,提议
office *n.* 办公室,办事处
n. 职务,公职
n. 部,处,局
officer *n.* 工作人员,公务员
n. 军官
official *n.* 官员,行政人员
a. 官方的,正式的,公务的
often *ad.* 常常,屡次
oh *int.* 哦!
oil *n.* 油,石油
v. 涂油,上油
okay/O.K. *a.*/*ad.* 对,好,行
n. 同意
old *a.* 老的,旧的,以前的
a. ……岁的
omit *v.* 省略,省去
v. 遗漏,忽略
on *prep.* 在……上
prep. 靠,根据,由于
prep. 在……时候,在……后
prep. 关于,有关
prep. 向前,(继续)下去
prep. (是)……的成员,在……供职
prep. 在从事……中,处于……情况
and so on 等等
once *ad.* 一次,一度,曾经
conj. 一旦
n. 一次
at once 立刻,马上
once more 再一次,又一次
all at once 突然,同时,一起
once in a while 间或,偶尔
one *n.* 一,一个
pron. 一个人,任何人
oneself *pron.* 自己,自身,亲自
by oneself 独自地,单独
onion *n.* 洋葱(头)
only *ad.* 只,仅仅
a. 唯一的
conj. 可是,不过
not only...but(also) 不仅……而且
onto *prep.* 到……之上,在……之上
open *v.* 打开
v. 开始,开张,开放
a. 开着的,开放的
a. 公开的,坦率的
a. 开阔的,空旷的
opening *n.* 开,开始,开端
a. 开始的,开幕的
opera *n.* 歌剧
operate *n.* 操作,运转
v. 动手术,开刀
operation *n.* 操作,工作,运转
n. 手术
operator *n.* 操作人员,(电话)接线员
opinion *n.* 意见,主张,看法
opponent *n.* 敌手;对手,反对者
opportunity *n.* 机会
oppose *v.* 反对,反抗
opposite *a.* 对的,对立的,相反的
n. 对立物,对立面
prep. 在……对面
optimistic *a.* 乐观(主义)的
optional *a.* 可以任选的,非强制的
or *conj.* 或,或者
conj. 即
conj. 否则
oral *a.* 口头的,口的
orange *n.* 橙,桔
orbit *n.* 轨道
n. 作轨道运行
order *v.*/*n.* 命令
n. 顺序,次序
n. 等级
n. 秩序,治安
n. 定货,订货单
v. 定制,订购
in order to 以便,为了
in order 整齐,秩序井然
in order that 以便
orderly *a.* 整齐的,有秩序的
ordinary *a.* 平常的,普通的
a. 平凡的,平庸的
ore *n.* 矿石,矿砂
organ *n.* 器官
n. 风琴
organization *n.* 组织,体制
n. 团体,机构
organize *v.* 组织,编组
origin *n.* 起源,由来
original *a.* 起初的,原来的
a. 独创的,新颖的
other *a.* 另外的,别的
pron. 别的东西,别人
every other 每隔一个的
otherwise *ad.* 否则,不然
ad. 除此以外,在其他方面
ad. 别样,以另外方式
ought to *v.* 应该,应当
ounce *n.* 盎司,英两
our *pron.* 我们的
ours *pron.* 我们的(东西)
ourselves *pron.* 我们自己
out *ad.* 在外,向外,出
ad. 熄灭,完结,过去
outcome *n.* 结果
out of 在……外,离开,
从……里,出于,由于,缺乏,没有
out-dated *a.* 过时的
outdoor(s) *a.* 户外的,野外的
ad. 户外,野外
outer *a.* 外部的,外层的
outlet *n.* 出口,出路
output *n.* 产量,产品
outside *a.*/*n.* 外部
ad. 向外,在外
prep. 在……外
outstanding *a.* 突出的,显著的
outward(s) *ad.* 在外,向外
a. 外面的,外表的
oven *n.* 炉,灶,烘箱
over *prep.* 在……上方,高于,超过
prep./*ad.* 越过
ad. 完了,结束
prep. 到处,遍及
overcoat *n.* 外衣,大衣
overcome *v.* 克服,战胜
overlook *vt.* 俯瞰,眺望
vt. 看漏,忽略

vt. 宽容
overnight a./ad. 一夜间,一下子
oversea(s) a. 海外的
overtake v. 追上,赶上,超过
owe v. 欠,应向……付出
v. 得感谢,应归功于
owing to 由于,因为
own v. 拥有
a. 自己的
owner n. 物主,所有者
ownership n. 所有(权),所有制
ox n. 牛,公牛
oxygen n. 氧

P

pace n. 步子,步速
pacific n. (P-) 太平洋
pack v. 包装,打包
v. 塞满,挤满
n. (一)包,(一)群,(一)副
package n. 包,盒
packet n. 小包,小盒
pad n. 垫,衬垫
n. 便笺本,便条纸簿
page n. 页
pain n. 痛苦,疼痛
n. (pl.) 努力,劳苦
take pains 尽心,煞费苦心
painful a. 痛苦的,疼痛的
paint v. 涂,涂漆
v. 画
v. 描绘,描述
n. 油漆,颜料
painter n. 画家,油漆工
painting n. 绘画,油画,画法
pair n. (一)对,(一)双,(一)副
v. 配对,成对
n. 夫妇
palace n. 宫殿
pale a. 苍白的,浅的,淡的
palm1 n. 手掌
palm2 n. 棕榈
pan n. 平底锅
paper n. 纸
n. 报纸
n. (pl.) 文件
n. 论文,文章
n. 试卷
parade n. 游行,检阅
paragraph n. 段,节
parallel a. 平行的,与……平行的(to)
parcel n. 包裹,邮包
v. 打包
pardon n. 原谅,请再说一遍
v. 原谅,饶恕,赦免
parent n. 父,母
park n. 公园
v. 停放(汽车等)
n. 停车场
parliament n. 国会,议会
part n. 部分,份儿
n. 角色,作用
v. 使分开,分离,分别
n. 零件
take part in 参加,参与
particle n. 粒子,微粒
participate vi. 参与,参加
particularly ad. 特别地,尤其地
partly ad. 在一定程度上,部分地,不完全地
partner n. 伙伴,舞伴
party n. 党,政党
n. 聚会
n. 一方,当事人
pass v. 经过,走过
v. 传,传递
v. 通过(考试)等
n. 通行证,护照
n. 关隘
pass away 去世,逝世
pass by 旁走过;忽视
pass on 传递
passage n. 通过,经过
n. 通路,走廊
n. 段落,节
passenger n. 乘客,旅客
passion n. 激情
passive a. 被动的,消极的
passport n. 护照
past a. 过去的
n. 过去
prep. 过,经过
paste n. 糨糊
v. 粘,贴
pat v. 轻拍,抚摸
patch n. 小片,小块,补丁
v. 补,修补
path n. 小路,路线,途径
patience n. 耐心,忍耐
patient a. 有耐心的,能忍耐的
n. 病人,患者
pattern n. 模式,式样
n. 图案,花样
pause vi./n. 暂停,中止
paw n. 爪
pay v. 付款,交纳
n. 工资,薪饷
pay back 偿还,回报
pay off 还清(债),给清工资后遣散
pay up 全部付清
payment n. 支付,付款
pea n. 豌豆
peace n. 和平,平静
peaceful a. 平静的,爱好和平的
peak n. 峰,山峰
pear n. 梨,梨树
peasant n. 农民
peculiar a. 特殊的,独特的,古怪的
pen n. 钢笔
penetrate v. 穿透,渗入,看穿
penny n. 便士,一分
people n. 人,人们,人民
n. 民族
per prep. 每
perceive v. 察觉,感知
v. 理解,领悟
percent/per cent n. 百分之……
percentage n. 百分比
perfect a. 完善的,完美的
a. 完全的,十足的
perform v. 做,施行,完成
v. 表演,演出
performance n. 表演,演出
n. 执行,完成
perhaps ad. 也许,恐怕,大概
period n. 期间,一段时间
n. 时期,时代
n. 句点
permanent a. 永久的,持久的
permission n. 许可,允许
permit v. 允许,许可
n. 执照,许可证
persist v. 坚持
person n. 人
n. 人称
in person 亲自
personal a. 个人的,私人的
a. 本人的,亲身的
perspective n. 前景,前途
n. 观点,看法
persuade vt. 说服,劝服
vt. 使相信
pet n. 爱畜,宠儿
a. 宠爱的,表示亲昵的
petrol n. 汽油
petroleum n. 石油
phase n. 阶段,时期
philosopher n. 哲人
philosophy n. 哲学
phone n. 电话
v. 打电话
photograph/photo n. 照片
phrase n. 短语,词组,用语
physical a. 物质的,有形的
a. 肉体的,身体的
a. 自然科学的,物理的
physicist n. 物理学家
physics n. 物理学
piano n. 钢琴

pick *v.* 拾,采,摘
v. 挑选
pick out 选出,挑出
pick up 拣起,拾起(车船等)中途搭(人),中途带(货)
picnic *n.* 郊游野餐,户外用餐
vi. 去野餐
picture *n.* 画,图片
n. 照片
n. 电影
pie *n.* 馅饼
piece *n.* (一)件,(一)片,(一)篇
n. 碎块,片断
v. 拼合,修补
pig *n.* 猪
pigeon *n.* 鸽
pile *n.* 堆
v. 堆,迭,堆积
pill *n.* 药丸
pillar *n.* 柱,支柱
pillow *n.* 枕头
pilot *n.* 驾驶员,飞行员
n. 领港员,引入员
pin *n.* 大头针
n. 别针,徽章
n. 销,栓
v. 钉住,别住
pinch *v.*/*n.* 拧,捏,挟
pine *n.* 松树
pink *n.*/*a.* 粉红
pint *n.* 品脱
pioneer *n.* 先驱者,开拓者
pipe *n.* 管子,导管
n. 烟斗
pit *n.* 坑,窖
pity *v.*/*n.* 怜悯,惋惜
n. 可惜的事,憾事
place *n.* 地方,地点,位置
v. 放,置
n. 职位,职责
n. 住所,寓所
v. 安排,任命
take place 发生,进行
take the place of 代替
in place of 代替
in place 在适当的位置
out of place 不得其所的,不适当的
plain1 *n.* 平原
plain2 *a.* 平易的,易懂的
a. 简单的,朴素的
plan *v.*/*n.* 计划,打算
n. 平面图
v. 设计
plane *n.* 飞机
n. 平面
planet *n.* 行星
plant *n.* 植物
n. 工厂
v. 种植,栽培
plantation *n.* 种植园
plastic *n.* (pl.)塑料
plate *n.* 盘子,盆子
n. 板,钢板
v. 镀,电镀
play *v.* 玩,游玩
v. 演奏,表演
n. 游戏,娱乐
n. 剧,剧本,
n. 活动,作用
play with 以……为消遣,玩弄
player *n.* (球迷)运动员,游戏的人
n. 演奏者
playground *n.* 运动场,游戏场
pleasant *a.* 令人愉快的,舒适的
please int. 请
v. 使愉快,使满意
v. 喜欢,愿意
pleasure *n.* 愉快,欢乐
n. 乐事,乐趣
plentiful *a.* 丰富的,富裕的
plenty *n.* 丰富,富裕
plot *n.* 一块地
n. 计策,阴谋
n. 情节
v. 策划
plough/plow *n.* 犁
v. 犁,耕
plug *n.* 插头,塞子
plunge *v.* 跳入,(使)投入,(使)陷入
v. 猛冲
plural *n.*/*a.* 复数
plus *a.* 表示加的,正的
prep. 加,加上
n. 加号,正号
P. M./p. m. 下午,午后
pocket *n.* 衣袋
a. 袖珍的
poem *n.* 诗
poet *n.* 诗人
poetry *n.* 诗,诗歌
point *v.* 指
n. 尖端,头
n. 点,小数点
n. 论点,观点,要点
come to the point 说到要点,扼要地说
point out 指出,指明
poison *n.* 毒物,毒药
v. 放毒,毒害
poisonous *a.* 有毒的
pole1 *n.* 柱,杆
pole2 *n.* 地极,磁极
police *n.* 警察,警察局
policeman *n.* 警察
policy *n.* 政策,方针
polish *v.* 擦亮,抛光
n. 擦光剂,上光蜡
polite *a.* 有礼貌的,客气的
a. 斯文的,有教养的
political *a.* 政治的
politician *n.* 政客,政治家
politics *n.* 政治
pollute *v.* 污染,玷污
pollution *n.* 污染
pond *n.* 池塘
pool *n.* 水潭,池子,水塘
poor *a.* 穷的
a. 可怜的
a. 低劣的,不好的
pop1 *n.* 呼的一声
pop2 *a.* 流行的,通俗的
popular *a.* 广受欢迎的,有名的
a. 通俗的,流行的,大众的
population *n.* 人口
pork *n.* 猪肉
port *n.* 港口
porter *n.* 搬运工人
portion *n.* 部分,份儿
portrait *n.* 肖像,画像
position *n.* 位置
n. 职位,职务
n. 姿势,姿态
positive *a.* 确定的,肯定的
a. 正面的,积极的
possess *v.* 拥有,占有
n. 拥有(物)
possibility *n.* 可能性
possible *a.* 可能的,做得到的
a. 合理的
possibly *ad.* 可能地,也许,或者
post1 *n.* (支)柱
v. 贴出,宣布,公告
post2 *n.* 邮政
v. 邮寄,投寄
post office 邮局
post3 *n.* 哨所,岗位,职位
postage *n.* 邮费,邮资
postman *n.* 邮递员
postpone *v.* 推迟,延期
pot *n.* 壶,罐,盆
potato *n.* 马铃薯
potential *n.* 潜力
pound *n.* 磅
n. 英镑
pour *v.* 灌,倒,注
v. 倾泻,流出
poverty *n.* 贫困,贫穷
powder *n.* 粉末,药粉

powerful *a.* 强大的,有力的,有权的
practical *a.* 实际的,实用的
practically *ad.* 几乎,实际上
practice *n.* 实践,实施
n. 练习,实习
n. 业务,开业
in practice 在实践中,实际上
out of practice 久不练习,荒疏
practise/practice *v.* 实践,实行
v. 练习,实习
v. 开业,从事
praise *v.* 称赞,表扬
n. 称赞,赞美
pray *v.* 祈祷,祈求
v. 请求,恳求
precious *a.* 珍贵的,贵重的
precise *a.* 精确的,准确的
predict *vt.* 预言,预测
prefer *v.* 更喜欢,宁愿
preliminary *a.* 预备的,初步的
premier *n.* 首相,总理
preparation *n.* 准备,预备
n. 制剂,制备品
preposition *n.* 介词
preserve *vt.* 维护
prescribe *v.* (医生)开(药),嘱咐(疗法)
v. 规定,指定
presence *n.* 出席,在场
n. 在,存在
present1 *a.* 出席的,在场的
a. 目前的,现在的
n. 目前,现在
at present 目前,现在
present2 *n.* 礼物,礼品
present3 *v.* 赠送,给予
v. 提出,呈递,出示
v. 介绍,引见
president *n.* 主席,总统,校长,会长
press *v.* 压,挤,按
n. 报刊,出版界
pressure *n.* 压力,紧张
pretend *v.* 假装,假托
pretty *a.* 漂亮的,俊俏的
ad. 相当地
prevail *v.* 取胜,占优势
v. 流行,盛行
prevent *v.* 预防,防止
previous *a.* 先的,前的,以前的
a. 在……之前(to)
price *n.* 价格,价钱
n. 代价
pride *n.* 骄傲,自豪,自满
n. 自尊心
primarily *ad.* 主要地,首先
primary *a.* 首要的,主要的,基本的
a. 最初的,初级的
primitive *a.* 原始的
prince *n.* 王子,亲王
princess *n.* 公主,王妃
principal *a.* 主要的,首要的
n. 负责人,校长
principle *n.* 原理,原则
n. 主义,信念
print *v.* 印刷,出版
n. 印刷品,字体
v. 洗印
prior to *prep.* 在……之前
prison *n.* 监狱
prisoner *n.* 囚徒
private *a.* 私人的,私有的,私立的
a. 秘密的,私下的
privilege *n.* 优惠,特许,特权
v. 给予优惠,给予特权
prize *n.* 奖,奖金,奖品
v. 珍视,珍惜
probable *a.* 有希望的,可能的
a. 也许的,大概的
probably *ad.* 或许,大概,很可能
problem *n.* 问题,难题
procedure *n.* 程序,手续
proceed *v.* 继续进行
process *n.* 过程,历程
v. 加工,处理
produce *v.* 生产,制造,产生
v. 显示,出示
v. 上演,演出
n. 产品
product *n.* 产品,产物
production *n.* 生产,产量
n. 产品,作品
profession *n.* 职业,自由职业
professor *n.* 教授
profit *n.* 收益,利润,益处
v. 得利,获益
program(me) *n.* 计划,规划,大纲
n. 节目,节目单
progress *n./v.* 前进,进步,进展
progressive *a.* 进步的,前进的,发展的
prohibit *vt.* 禁止,不准
project *n.* 计划,方案,工程,项目
v. 设计,规划
v. 投射,放映
promise *v.* 答应,允诺
n. 承诺,诺言
v. 有……可能,有希望
n. 希望,出息
promote *vt.* 促进,发扬
vt. 提升,提拔
vt. 增进,助长
prompt *a.* 敏捷的,迅速的,即刻的
v. 促使,推动
pronoun *n.* 代词
pronounce *v.* 发音
v. 宣告,宣布
pronunciation *v.* 发音
proof *n.* 证明,证据
proper *a.* 适当的,恰当的
a. 特有的,固有的
property *n.* 财产,资产,所有物
n. 性质,特性
proportion *n.* 部分,份儿
n. 比例,比重
proposal *n.* 提议,建议
n. 求婚
propose *vt.* 提议,建议
vi. 求婚
prospect *n.* 展望,前景
prosperity *n.* 繁荣,兴旺
prosperous *a.* 繁荣的,兴旺的
protect *v.* 保护,保卫
protein *n.* 蛋白质
protest *v./n.* 抗议,反对
proud *a.* 骄傲的,自豪的
a. 引以自豪的
prove *v.* 证明,证实
v. 检验,鉴定
v. 结果是,表明是
provide *v.* 提供,供给
v. 规定
provided *conj.* 只要,假如
province *n.* 省
provision *n.* (pl.)给养,口粮
n. 准备,预备
psychological *a.* 心理的
public *a.* 公共的,公用的
a. 公开的,公然的
n. 公众,大众
publication *n.* 出版,出版物
publish *v.* 发表,公布
v. 出版
pull *v./n.* 拉,拖,牵
pull down 拆毁,拉倒
pull into 驶人,到达
pull on 穿上,戴上
pull out 拔出,抽出,取出(车,船等)驶出
pulse *n.* 脉搏,脉冲
punctual *a.* 准时的
punish *vt.* 惩罚,处罚
pupil *n.* 学生,小学生
n. 瞳孔
purchase *vt.* 买,购买
n. 购买,购买的物品
pure *a.* 纯的,纯洁的
a. 纯理论的,抽象的
a. 完全的,十足的
purpose *n.* 目的,意图;用途;效果
on purpose 故意,有意

pursue *vt.* 从事;追求
push *v./n.* 推,推进,促进
put *v.* 放,置
put off 推迟,拖延
put on 穿上,戴上,上演,增加(体重)
put forward 提出
put out 熄灭,消灭,关(灯),生产,出版,发布
put up 举起,升起,提(价),为……提供食宿,投宿建造,搭起,支起张贴
puzzle *n.* 难题,谜,迷惑
v. 使迷惑

Q

qualify *v.* 取得资格,使合格
quality *n.* 质,质量
n. 品质,特性
quantity *n.* 量,数量
n. 大量
quarrel *v./n.* 争吵,吵架
quarter *n.* 四分之一,一刻钟
n. 地区,区域
n. (*pl.*)住处
queen *n.* 女王,皇后,王后
question *n.* 问,问题,议题
v. 怀疑
queue *n.* 行列,长队
v. 排长队
quick *a.* 快的,迅速的
a. 敏捷的,伶俐的
a. 性急的,敏锐的
quicken *v.* 加快,加速
quiet *a./n.* 安静,平静,安定
v. 使安静,平定
quit *v.* 离开,退出
v. 停止,辞职
quite *ad.* 完全,十分
ad. 相当,颇
quotation *n.* 引语,语录
quote *v.* 引用,援引

R

rabbit *n.* 兔子
race1 *n.* 种族,人种,种类
race2 *v./n.* 比赛,赛跑
racial *a.* 种的,种族的
rack *n.* 搁板,行李架
radar *n.* 雷达
radio *n.* 无线电,收音机,无线电通讯
v. 用无线电通讯
rag *n.* 破布,碎布
rail *n.* 栏杆,围栏
n. 铁轨
railway *n.* 铁路
rain *n.* 雨
v. 下雨
rainbow *n.* 虹,彩虹
rainy *a.* 下雨的,多雨的
raise *v.* 举起,提高,提升
v. 抚养,饲养
v. 建立,树立
range *n.* 范围,距离,领域
n. 排列,连续,(山)脉
n. 炉灶
rank *n.* 排,行列
n. 等级,地位
v. 评价,分等,归类
rapid *a.* 快的,急速的
rare *a.* 稀有的,难得的,珍奇的
a. 稀薄的,稀疏的
ad. 很少,难得,非常地
rarely *ad.* 很少,难得
rat *n.* 鼠
rate *n.* 速率,比率;
n. 等级
at any rate 无论如何,至少
rather *ad.* 有些,相当;宁可,宁愿
rather than 而不,不顾
would rather 宁可,宁愿
ratio *n.* 比率,比
raw *a.* 生的,未煮熟的
a. 未加工过的
ray *n.* 线,光线,射线
reach *v.* 伸手,够到,触到
v. 到,到达
n. 能达到的范围
react *v.* 反应,起作用
reaction *n.* 反应,反作用(力)
read *v.* 朗读,阅读
v. 辨认,观察
reader *n.* 读者
n. 课本,读本
reading *n.* 阅读,读书
n. 读物,选读
ready *a.* 准备好的,现成的
a. 乐意的,情愿的
real *a.* 真的,真实的
a. 实际的,现实的
reality *n.* 现实,实际
realize/realise *v.* 认识到,体会到
v. 实现
really *ad.* 确实,实在
ad. 真正地,果然
realm *n.* 王国,国土
rear *n.* 后部,尾部
a. 后方的,背后的
reason *n.* 理由,原因
n. 理性,理智
v. 推论,推理
reasonable *a.* 合理的,讲理的,公道的
rebel *v.* 反抗,反叛,起义
n. 叛逆者,起义者
recall *v.* 回想,想起
v. 撤销,收回
receipt *n.* 收据,收条
n. 收到,接到
receive *v.* 收到,接到
v. 接待,接见
v. 受到,蒙受
receiver *n.* 话筒,受话器
recent *a.* 最近的,近来的
recently *ad.* 最近,新近
reception *n.* 接见,接待,招待会
recite *v.* 背诵,朗诵
recognition *n.* 认出
n. 承认
recognize *v.* 认出,识别,承认
recommend *v.* 劝告,建议
v. 介绍,推荐
recommendation *n.* 介绍信;推荐;介绍
record *n.* 唱片
v./n. 记录,记载
n. 最高记录
n. 经历,履历
recorder *n.* 记录者,录音机
recover *vi.* 恢复,痊愈
red *a.* 红色的
n. 红色,红颜料
reduce *v.* 缩小,减小,减低
v. 使成为,简化,还原
reduction *n.* 减少,缩小
refer *v.* 参考,查阅,查询
v. 提到,引用,指(to)
v. 提交,上呈
reference *n.* 参考,查阅
refine *v.* 精炼,精制,提纯
reflection *n.* 映像,倒影
reform *v./n.* 改革,改造,改良
refresh *v.* 提神,振作,使清新
refrigerator *n.* 冰箱,冷冻机,冷藏库
refusal *n.* 拒绝,推辞
regard *v.* 考虑,认为,看作
n. (*pl.*)敬重,敬意,问候
v. 注视,注重,留意
regardless *a.* 不管(of)
region *n.* 地区,区域
n. 范围
register *n./v.* 登记,注册,挂号
n. 登记本,注册簿
v. 记录
regret *v./n.* 遗憾,懊悔,抱歉
regular *a.* 定时的,定期的;规则的,规矩的
a. 正规的,正式的
a. 匀称的,整齐的
v. 驾驭,约束
reinforce *v.* 增援,加强
reject *v.* 拒绝,谢绝,驳回
relate *v.* 叙述,讲述
v. 联系,关联
relation *n.* 亲属,亲戚

n. 关系,联系
relative n. 亲属,亲戚
a. 相对的,比较的
relax v. (使)松弛,放松
release v. 释放,放出
reliable a. 可靠的
relief n. 缓解,消除
n. 救济,援救
relieve v. 缓解,消除,减少
v. 换班,换岗
religion n. 宗教,信仰
religious a. 宗教的,信教的,虔诚的
reluctant a. 不愿的,勉强的
rely v. 依靠,信赖,依仗(on)
remain v. 剩下,余留
v. 留待,尚需
v. 仍然是,依旧是
remark n. 评语,意见
n. 评论,谈论
n. 注意,觉察
remarkable a. 值得注意的
a. 显著的,异常的
remedy n. 药品
n. 治疗措施,补救办法
v. 治疗,补救
remember v. 记住,记得
v. 转达问候
remind v. 提醒,使想起(of)
remove v. 排除,消除,去掉
v. 搬迁,移动,运走
rent n. 租金
v. 租,租赁
repair v./n. 修理,修复
v. 补救,纠正
repeat v. 重复,重说,重做
v. 背,背诵
repeatedly ad. 重复地,再三地
replace v. 放回
v. 替换,取代
reply n./v. 答复,回答
v. 回答,以……作答
report v./n. 报告,汇报,报道
n. 传说,传闻
reporter n. 记者,报道者,通讯员
represent v. 表示,阐明,说明
v. 描写,表现,象征
v. 代理,代表
republic n. 共和国,共和政体
republican a. 共和的
reputation n. 名声,声望
request n./v. 请求,要求
require v. 需要
rescue v./n. 营救,救援
research v./n. 研究,调查
resemble v. 相似,像
reservoir n. 水库,蓄水池
residence n. 住处,住宅
resident n. 居民
resign v. 辞去,辞职
resist v. 抵抗,反抗
v. 忍住,抵制
resistance n. 抵抗,反抗
n. 抵抗力,阻力,电阻
resolve v./n. 决心,决意
v. 解决,解答
v. 议决,决议
resource n. (pl.)资源
n. 应变之才,谋略
respect v./n. 尊敬,尊重
n. (pl.)敬意,问候
respective a. 各自的,各个的
respond v. 回答,答复
v. 响应,起反应(to)
response n. 反应;回答
responsibility n. 责任,职责
responsible a. 应负责的,有责任的
rest1 n./v. 休息,静止
v. 放,靠
v. 信赖,依赖,依据(on/in)
rest2 n. (the-)其余的人(或物)
restaurant n. 饭店
restless a. 不安的,坐立不定的
restore v. 归还,放回
v. 修复,恢复
restrict v. 限制,约束
result n. 结果,成果,成绩
v. 产生于,来自(from)
result in 结果是;导致
as a result 由于,因此
resume n. 简历
retain v. 保持,保留
retire v. 退下,离开
v. 退休,引退
retreat v. 撤退,退却
return v./n. 归,回,归还
v. 回答,反驳
in return 作为回报,作为报答
reveal v. 揭示,揭露,展现
review v./n. 复习,回顾
v./n. 评论
revise v. 修订,修正
v. 复习
revolt v./n. 反抗,起义
revolution n. 革命
n. 旋转,转数
revolutionary a. 革命的,革新的
n. 革命者
reward n. 酬谢,报酬,奖金
v. 酬谢,报答,奖酬
rib n. 肋骨,肋状物
ribbon n. 带,缎带,丝带
rice n. 稻,米
rich a. 富的,富饶的,丰富的
a. 富丽的,浓艳的
rid v. 使摆脱,使去掉(of)
get rid of 摆脱,除去
ride v./n. 骑,乘
ridge n. 岭,山脉
n. 屋脊,鼻梁
ridiculous a. 荒谬的,可笑的
rifle n. 步枪
right a./ad. 正确,恰当
a./n. 右,右面
n. 权利
ad. 完全,正好
ad. 直接,马上
ring1 n. 戒指
n. 圆圈,环
ring2 v. 敲钟,打铃
n. 铃声,钟声,(打)电话
ripe a. 成熟的
rise v./n. 上升,上涨,增长
v. 起床,起立
n. 起源,发生
risk n. 风险
v. 冒风险
rival v. 竞争,与……抗衡
a. 竞争的
n. 竞争对手
river n. 江,河
road n. 路,道路,途径
on the road 在旅途中
roar vi. 吼叫,怒号,咆哮
vi. 轰鸣
roast v. 烤,炙,烘
rob v. 抢劫,盗取
robot n. 机器人
rock v. 摇
n. 岩,岩石
rocket n. 火箭
rod n. 杆,棍,棒
role n. 角色,任务,作用
roll v. 滚动,转动
v. 卷,绕
n. 卷,卷装物,面包卷
n. 名单,名册
Roman a. 罗马的,罗马数字的
roof n. 屋顶
room n. 房间,室
n. 余地,空间
root n. 根
n. 根源,来源
rope n. 绳,索
rose n. 玫瑰,蔷薇
rotten a. 腐烂的,腐朽的
rough a. 粗糙的
a. 粗野的,粗鲁的
round a. 圆的

prep. 围绕
ad. 在周围
v. 使成圆形
rouse *v*. 惊起,唤起,唤醒
route *n*. 路线,航线
routine *a*. 常规的;例行的
row1 *n*. (一)排,(一)行
row2 *v*. 划(船等),荡桨
royal *a*. 王室的,皇家的
rub *v*. 擦,摩擦
rub out 擦掉,拭去
rubber *n*. 橡皮,橡胶
n. 橡胶制品,胶鞋
a. 橡胶的
rubbish *n*. 废物,垃圾
n. 废话
rude *a*. 粗鲁的,不礼貌的
a. 粗糙的,简陋的
rug *n*. 小地毯
n. 围毯
ruin *v*. 毁坏,破坏
n. 毁灭,崩溃
n. (*pl*.)废墟,遗址
rule *n*./*v*. 统治,支配
n. 规则,规章,规律
n. 惯例,常规
ruler *n*. 统治者,支配者
n. 尺子,直尺
rumour *n*. 传闻,谣言
run *v*. 奔,跑,逃跑
v. 流,淌
v. 蔓延,伸展
v. 经营,管理
v. 运转,开动
run into 偶然遇到,撞见,碰撞
run out 用完;耗尽
rural *a*. 农村的
rush *v*./*n*. 冲,奔,急速流动
Russian *a*. 俄罗斯的
n. 俄语,俄罗斯人
rust *v*. 生锈
n. 锈

S

sack *n*. 袋,麻袋
sacrifice *n*. 牺牲,牺牲品
n. 祭品,供物
v. 献祭,牺牲
sad *a*. 忧愁的,悲哀的
saddle *n*. 鞍子,马鞍
safe *a*. 安全的,牢靠的
n. 保险箱
safety *n*. 安全
sail *n*. 帆,航行
v. 航行,开航
sailor *n*. 水手,海员
sake *n*. 缘故,理由
salad *n*. 色拉,凉拌菜
salary *n*. 薪金,薪俸
sale *n*. 出卖,出售
n. 贱卖,大减价
n. 销数,销售额
on sale 上市,出售,减价,贱卖
salesman *n*. 售货员,推销员
salt *n*. 盐,盐类
v. 盐渍,腌
same *a*. 相同的,一样的
pron. 同样的人,同样的事情
all the same 仍然,照样地
sample *n*. 样品,标本
v. 抽样,取样
sand *n*. 沙,(*pl*.)沙滩
sandwich 三明治,夹肉面包
satellite *n*. 卫星,人造卫星
satisfactory *a*. 令人满意的
Saturday *n*. 星期六
saucer *n*. 茶托,碟子
sausage *n*. 香肠,腊肠
save *v*. 救,拯救
v. 储蓄,贮存
v. 节省,节约
save up 储蓄
saving *n*. 储蓄
n. (*pl*.)储蓄金,存款
saw *v*. 锯,锯开
n. 锯子,锯床
say *v*. 说,讲
n. 发言,发言权
v. 比方说,大约
scale *n*. 标度,刻度;天平,无平盘;音阶
n. 鱼鳞,鳞片;天平,无平盘
n. 天平,无平盘;标尺,比例尺
n. 音阶
scar *n*. 疤,瘢痕
scarce *a*. 稀少的,罕见的
a. 缺乏的,不足的
scarcely *ad*. 几乎不,勉强
scare *v*. 惊吓,受惊
n. 惊慌,惊恐
scatter *vt*. 撒,撒播
vt. 使散开,驱散
vt. 分散,消散
scene *n*. 景色,景象
n. (戏)一场
n. 布景
schedule *n*. 时间表,时刻表,日程安排表
v. 安排,排定
on schedule 按时间表,准时
scheme *n*. 计划,方案
scholar *n*. 学者
scholarship *n*. 奖学金
school *n*. 学校,学院,系
primary school 小学
science *n*. 科学
scientific *a*. 科学的
scientist *n*. 科学家
scissors *n*. 剪子
scold *v*. 训斥,责骂
score *n*. 得分,分数
v. 记分,得分
n. 二十
scout *n*. 侦察员,侦察机
scrape *v*. 擦,刮去
scratch *v*. 搔,抓,扒
n. 搔,抓,抓痕
scream *v*./*n*. 尖叫,嚎叫
screen *v*. 遮蔽,包庇,庇护
n. 屏风,幕,屏幕
screw *n*. 螺钉,螺丝
v. 拧,拧紧
sea *n*. 海,海洋
seal *n*. 封口,封腊,封条
n. 印,戳
v. 封,密封
search *v*./*n*. 搜索,寻找,探查
season *n*. 季,季节,时节
seat *n*. 席位,座位
n. 底座
n. 所在地
v. 使……就座
second *a*. 第二
n. 秒
secondary *a*. 第二的,中级的
secret *a*. 秘密的,机密的
n. 秘密,奥秘
in secret 秘密地,私下地
secretary *n*. 书记
n. 秘书
section *n*. 章节,部分,地区
secure *a*. 安全的,可靠的
v. 得到,获得
v. 防护,保卫
security *n*. 安全
see *v*. 看见;理解,明白;会见,见面
v. 获悉,知道
see off 给……送行
see through 看穿,识破
see to 负责,照料,注意,留心
seed *n*. 种子
v. 播种
seek *v*. 寻找,探求
v. 试图,企图
seem *v*. 好像,仿佛
seize *v*. 抓住,捉住
v. 夺取,占领
seldom *ad*. 很少,不常
select *v*. 选择,挑选
a. 精选的,选择的
selection *n*. 选择,挑选

self *n.* 自我,自己,本身
selfish *a.* 自私的,利己的
sell *v.* 卖,出售
semester *n.* 学期
send *v.* 送,寄
v. 派遣,打发
send for 派人请,召唤,索取
send in 呈报,提交,送来
senior *a.* 年长的,资格老的,地位高的
sense *v.* 感觉到,意识到
n. 感官,官能
n. 辨别力,感觉
n. 意义,意思
in a sense 从某种意义上说
sensible *a.* 懂事的,明智的
sensitive *a.* 有感觉的,敏感的
sentence *n.* 句子
n./*v.* 判决,宣判
separate *a.* 分离的,分开的
v. 分离,分开
September *n.* 九月
series *n.* 一系列,一连串,序列
serious *a.* 严肃的,庄重的
a. 严重的,危急的
a. 认真的
servant *n.* 仆人
serve *v.* 服务,尽责
v. 侍候,招待
v. 适用,适合
service *n.* 服务,帮助,服侍
set *v.* 放,安置
v. (太阳)落山
n. 一套,一付
a. 固定的,规定的
set aside 留出
set out 动身,出发,开始
set up 建立,设立,树立,资助,使自立,扶持
settle *v.* 安定,安顿
v. 停息,定居
v. 解决,调停
v. 结算,支付
settle down 定居,过安定的生活
seven *n.*/*a.* 七
seventeen *n.*/*a.* 十七
seventh *a.* 第七
n. 七分之一
seventy *n.*/*a.* 七十
several *a.* 若干,数个
severe *a.* 严厉的,严格的
a. 严重的,凛冽的
sew *v.* 缝,缝纫
sex *n.* 性别,性
shade *n.* 荫,阴影
n. 遮光物,罩
v. 遮蔽,遮光
shadow *n.* 影子,阴影
n. 暗处,阴暗
shake *v.* 摇,摇动
v. 震动,颤抖
shall *v.* 将,将要
v. 必须,应该
shallow *a.* 浅的,肤浅的
n. 浅滩,浅处
shame *n.* 羞愧,耻辱
shape *n.* 形状,外形
v. 形成,成形
share *v.* 均分,分配;分享,分担
n. 份子,份额,股份
sharp *a.* 尖锐的,锋利的;急转的,突然的
a. 尖声的,刺耳的;敏锐的,灵敏的
a. 线条分明的,鲜明的
shave *v.* 剃,刮,削
n. 刮脸
she *pron.* 她
shed1 *n.* 棚,车库
shed2 *v.* 脱落,脱去;流出,流下
sheep *n.* 羊,绵羊
sheet *n.* 被单;(一)张,(一)片
n. 大片
shelf *n.* 架子
shell *n.* 壳,贝壳
shelter *n.* 躲避处,掩蔽部
v./*n.* 掩蔽,庇护
shield *n.* 盾,屏障
v. 防护,保护
shift *v.*/*n.* 转移,移动,转变
shine *v.* 发光,照耀;使发光,擦亮
n. 光泽,光
ship *n.* 船,舰
v. 航运,装运,运送
shirt *n.* 衬衫
shiver *vi.* 发抖
shock *n.* 冲击,震动,震惊
n. 电击,触电
v. 使震动,使震惊
shoe *n.* 鞋
shoot *v.* 发射,射(门)
n. 枝条,嫩枝,苗
v. 疾驰而过
v. 发芽,长高
shop *n.* 商店,店铺
v. 购物
shore *n.* 海滨,湖滨
short *a.* 短的,矮的
a. 缺乏的,不足的
n. (*pl.*) 短裤
shortage *n.* 不足,缺少
shortcoming *n.* 短处,缺点
shortly *ad.* 立即,马上
shot *n.* 开枪,射击
n. 射门,投篮
n. 弹丸,炮弹,子弹
should *v.* [过去将来] 将
v. [假设] 万一,竟然
v. [义务,责任] 应当,应该
v. [说话者意愿] 就该
v. [可能,推测] 可能,该
shoulder *n.* 肩,肩膀
shout *v.* 呼喊,呼叫
n. 呼喊,叫声
show *v.* 展示,显示
v. 指示,指出
v. 说明,证明
n. 展出,陈列
show in 领入
show off 炫耀
shower *n.* 阵雨,暴雨
n. (一)阵,(一)大批
shrink *v.* 起皱,收缩
v. 退缩,畏缩(from)
shut *v.* 关,关闭
shut out 排除
shy *a.* 害羞的,腼腆的
a. 易受惊的,胆怯的
sick *a.* 有病的,患病的
a. 恶心的,想吐的
side *n.* 旁边,侧面
n. 一边,一侧,一方
side by side 肩并肩,一个挨一个
sigh *v.*/n 叹气,叹息
sight *n.* 视力,视觉
n. 望见,瞥见
in sight 被见到,在望
catch sight of 发现,突然看见
out of sight 在看不见的地方
sightseeing *n.* 观光,游览
sign *n.* 符号,标记,招牌
v. 签(名),签署
signal *n.* 信号,暗号
v. 发信号,打信号
signature *n.* 签名,签字
significance *n.* 意义
silence *n.* 寂静,沉默
v. 使寂静,使沉默
silent *a.* 寂静的,沉默的
silk *n.* 丝,绸
silly *a.* 愚蠢的
silver *n.* 银,银器,银币
similar *a.* 类似的,相似的
simple *a.* 简单的,朴素的
simplicity *n.* 简单,简易
n. 朴素
simply *ad.* 简单地;完全,简直;仅仅,不过
ad. 完全,简直;仅仅,只不过
since *prep.*/*conj.* 自从,从……以来
conj. 因为,既然
ad. 后来,从那以后

sincere *a.* 诚恳的,真诚的
sing *v.* 唱,唱歌,鸣叫
single *a.* 单人的,单身的
a. 单一的,单个的
sink *v.* 下落,下沉
sir *n.* 先生
n. (S-)(用于姓名前)……爵士
sister *n.* 姐妹
sit *v.* 坐,使就座
sit up 迟睡,熬夜
site *n.* 场所,地点
situation *n.* 形势,局面
six *n.*/*a.* 六
sixteen *n.*/*a.* 十六
sixteenth *a.* 第十六
sixth *a.* 第六
n. 六分之一
sixty *n.*/*a.* 六十
size *n.* 大小,尺寸
n. 号码,尺码
skate *n.* 冰鞋
v. 溜冰,滑冰
sketch *n.* 素描,速写,略图
v. 速写,写生
skil(l)ful *a.* 灵巧的,娴熟的
skill *n.* 技巧,熟练
n. 技能,手艺
skilled *a.* 有技能的,熟练的
skim *vt.* 撇(去)
vt. 掠过,擦过
vt. 浏览,略读
skin *n.* 皮,皮肤
skirt *n.* 裙子
n. 边缘,郊区
sky *n.* 天空
slam *v.* 砰地关上
slave *n.* 奴隶,苦工
sleep *v.*/*n.* 睡眠
sleeve *n.* 袖子
slender *a.* 细长的,苗条的
a. 微小的,微薄的
slide *v.*/*n.* 滑,滑动
slight *a.* 轻微的,微小的
a. 纤细的,瘦弱的
slip *v.* 滑,滑倒
v. 溜走
n. 疏忽,笔误,口误
slippery *a.* 滑的
slogan *n.* 标语,口号
slope *n.* 坡,斜坡
n. 倾斜,斜度
v. 倾斜
slow *a.* 慢的,缓慢的,迟钝的
v. 放慢,减速
slow down 放慢速度
small *a.* 小的,少的

smart *a.* 聪明的,伶俐的
a. 漂亮的,时髦的
smell *n.* 气味
n. 嗅觉
v. 嗅,闻
smile *v.*/*n.* 微笑
smoke *n.* 烟,烟尘
v./*n.* 吸烟,抽烟
v. 冒烟,冒气
smooth *a.* 光滑的,平滑的
a. 平稳的,顺利的
snake *n.* 蛇
snatch *v.*/*n.* 攫取,抢夺
snow *n.* 雪
v. 下雪
so *conj.* 因此,那么
ad. 那么,如此
ad. 非常,很
ad. 这样,那样
so... as to 如此……以至于,如此……以便
so for 以便,为的是
so... that 如此……以至于
soak *v.* 浸泡,浸湿,湿透
soap *n.* 肥皂
so-called *a.* 所谓的,号称的
social *a.* 社会的
a. 社交的,交际的
socialism *n.* 社会主义
socialist *n.* 社会主义者,社会党人
a. 社会主义的
society *n.* 社会
n. 协会,会
n. 社交界,上流社会
sock *n.* (*pl.*)短袜
soda *n.* 苏打,汽水
soft *a.* 柔软的,温柔的,柔和的
a. 细嫩的,光滑的
soil *n.* 土壤,土地
soldier *n.* 士兵,军人
sole1 *n.* 脚底,鞋底
sole2 *a.* 单独的,唯一的
solemn *a.* 庄严的,严肃的,隆重的
solid *n.*/*a.* 固体
a. 实心的,结实的
a. 稳固的,可靠的
solution *n.* 解答,解决办法
n. 溶解,溶液
solve *v.* 解答,解决
some *pron.*/*a.* 一些,有些
ad. 大约
somebody *pron.* 某人,有人
somehow *ad.* 不知怎么地
ad. 以某种方法
someone *pron.* 有人,某人
something *pron.* 某物,某事

sometime *ad.* 曾经,在某时候
sometimes *ad.* 间或,有时
somewhat *ad.* 稍微,有点
somewhere *ad.* 某地
son *n.* 儿子
song *n.* 歌声
n. 歌曲
soon *ad.* 不久
ad. 早,快
as soon as 一……就
so sooner... than 一……就
sooner or later 迟早,早晚
sore *a.* 疼痛的,痛心的
n. 痛处,疮口
sorrow *n.* 悲伤,悲哀
sorry *a.* 难过的,悔恨的,对不起的
sort *n.* 种类,类别
v. 分类,整理
soul *n.* 灵魂,心灵
n. 精神,精力
sound1 *n.* 声音,声响
v. 发声,响
v. 听起来
sound2 *a.* 健康的,健全的
a. 彻底的,充分的
a. 正当的,有根据的
soup *n.* 汤
sour *a.* 酸的,酸腐的
a. 脾气坏的,刻薄的
source *n.* 源,源泉
n. 来源,根源
south *n.*/*a.* 南,南部
southeast *n.*/*a.* 东南,东南部
southern *a.* 南方,南的
southwest *n.*/*a.* 西南,西南部
sow *v.* 播种
space *n.* 太空,宇宙
n. 空间,距离
v. 留间隔,隔开
spade *n.* 铁锹,铲子
Spanish *a.* 西班牙的
n. 西班牙语
spare *a.* 多余的,备用的
v. 让给,抽出(时间)
spark *n.* 火花,火星
v. 发火花,发电花
speak *v.* 说话,讲
v. 发言,演说
speaker *n.* 说话者,演讲者
n. 讲某种语言的人
n. 扬声器
special *a.* 专门的,特殊的
a. 附加的,额外的
specialist *n.* 专家
specific *a.* 明确的;具体的
specimen *n.* 标本,样本

speech *n.* 讲话,演说
n. 言语,语言
speed *n.* 速度,速率
n. 快,迅速
v. 急行,飞驰
spell *v.* 拼写
spelling *n.* 拼法,拼写
spend *v.* 花费,消耗
v. 度过,消磨
sphere *n.* 球,球体
n. 范围,领域
spider *n.* 蜘蛛
spill *v.* 溢出,流出
n. 摔下,跌下
spin *v./n.* 旋转,自转
v. 纺,纺织
v. 结网,吐丝
spirit *n.* 精神,心灵
n. (*pl.*) 情绪,心情
n. 气魄,勇气
n. (*pl.*) 酒精,烈酒
spiritual *a.* 精神(上)的,心灵的
spit *v.* 唾,吐痰
n. 唾液
spite *n.* 恶意,怨恨
in spite of 不顾,不管
splendid *a.* 辉煌的,壮丽的
a. 极好的
split *v.* 劈开,裂开
n. 裂缝,裂口
spoil *v.* 搞糟,损坏
v. 宠坏,溺爱
sponsor *n.* 发起人,主办者
v. 发起,主办
spoon *n.* 匙,汤匙
sport *n.* 运动
sportsman *n.* 运动员
spot *n.* 地点,场所
n. 点,斑点,污点
v. 认出,认清
v. 玷污,弄脏
v. 用点做记号
on the spot 当场,在现场
spread *vt.* 摊开,伸开
vt. 涂,敷
vt. 散布,传播
vi. 传开,蔓延
n. 传播,蔓延
spring1 *v.* 涌出,涌上
v. 生长,发生,出现
spring2 *n.* 春季,春天
v./n. 跳,跃
n. 弹簧,弹性,发条
n. 泉,源泉
spurt *n.* 靴刺,马刺
n. 刺激,刺激物

square *n.* 广场
n./a. 正方(形),平方
squeeze *v.* 压榨,挤
stable1 *a.* 稳定的,安定的
stable2 *n.* 马厩,马棚
stack *n.* (草)堆,一堆
stadium *n.* 体育场
staff *n.* 杆,棒
n. 参谋,参谋部
n. 工作人员,全体职员
v. 配备工作人员
stage *n.* 阶段,时期
n. 舞台,戏剧
stain *n.* 污点,瑕疵
v. 着色,染色
stair *n.* (*pl.*) 楼梯
stake *n.* 桩,标桩
stale *a.* 陈旧的,陈腐的
stamp *n.* 邮票
n. 戳子,图章
v./n. 跺脚,践踏
v. 盖章,盖印
stand *v.* 站立
v. 坐落,位于
v. 经受,忍受
n. 台,座
stand up 站起,竖起
stand by 站在旁边,袖手旁观 站在一起,支持,帮助
standard *n.* 标准,规格
star *n.* 星,恒星
n. 明星,名人
stare *v.* 盯,凝视
start *v./n.* 开始,着手
v./n. 动身,出发
v./n. 吃惊,惊起
starve *v.* 饿死,饿得慌
state *n.* 国家,州
n. 情况,状态
v. 声明,陈述
statement *n.* 陈述
statesman *n.* 政治家,国务活动家
station *n.* 车站
n. 站,局,所
status *n.* 地位
n. 身份,地位
stay *v.* 停留,逗留,作客
stay up 不睡觉,熬夜
steady *a.* 稳定的,不变的
a. 稳固的,平稳的
v. 使稳固
steal *v.* 偷,窃取
v. 偷偷地做,巧取
steam *n.* 汽,蒸汽
v. 蒸发,蒸(食物)
v. 用蒸汽开动

steamer *n.* 汽船,轮船
steel *n.* 钢
steer *v.* 驾驶,掌舵
stem *n.* 茎,干
step *n.* 脚步,脚步声
n. 台阶,梯级
v. 举步,走
n. 步骤,措施
stick1 *n.* 棍,棒,手杖
stick2 *v.* 刺,戳,扎
v. 粘贴
stick to 坚持,忠于,信守
stiff *a.* 硬的,僵直的
a. 生硬的,死板的
still *ad.* 还,仍旧
a./ad. 静,静止
ad. 还要,更
stimulate *v.* 刺激,使兴奋
v. 鼓励,鼓舞
sting *v.* 刺,蜇,叮
v. (被)刺痛
n. 刺(痛),剧痛
stocking *n.* (*pl.*) 长袜
stomach *n.* 胃
stone *n.* 石,石料
stoop *n./v.* 弯腰,俯身
stop *n.* 停车站
v./n. 停止,中止
v. 阻止,堵塞
v. 逗留,歇宿
store *v./n.* 贮藏,贮存
n. 商店,店铺
n. 贮存品,备用品
storey/story *n.* 楼层
storm *n.* 暴风雨
story *n.* 故事,小说
n. 传说,事迹
stove *n.* 炉子,火炉
straight *a.* 直的,平直的
ad. 直接,一直
a./ad. 正直,直率
a. 整齐的,有条理的
strange *a.* 奇怪的,奇异的
a. 陌生的,生疏的
stranger *n.* 陌生人,生客
n. 外地人,外国人
strap *n.* 带,皮带
v. 捆扎
strategy *n.* 战略,策略
straw *n.* 稻草,麦秆
stream *n.* 小河,溪流
v. 流,流出
street *n.* 街道,马路
strength *n.* 力,力量
strengthen *v.* 加强,巩固
stress *n.* 压力,紧迫

v. 强调,着重
strict a. 严格的
a. 严谨的,精确的
strike v./n. 罢工
v. 打,击
v. 敲响,报点
string n. 一串,一行,一列
n. 弦,线,绳
stroke n. 击,敲
n. (报时)钟声
strong a. 强壮的,强大的,强烈的
structure n. 结构,构造
n. 建筑物
vt. 建造,建立
struggle v./n. 斗争,奋斗,努力
student n. 学生,学者
study v./n. 学习,研究
stuff n. 材料,原料,东西
v. 填满,塞满
stun vt. 使震惊,使目瞪口呆
stupid a. 愚蠢的,迟钝的
style n. 风格,文体
n. 时式,时髦
subject n. 主题,题目
n. 学科,科目
n. 主语
submarine n. 潜水艇
submit v. 屈服,服从
v. 呈送,提交
subsequent a. 随后的,后来的
substitute n. 代用品,代替者
v. 代,代替
subtract v. 减,减去
suburb v. 郊外,近郊
subway n. 地下铁道
succeed v. 成功
v. 继承,接替
success n. 成功,成就
successful a. 成功的
succession n. 连续,系列
successive a. 接连的,连续的
such a. 这样的,这种的
pron. 这样的人,这样的事物
such as 像……那样的,诸如,例如
sudden a. 突然的,意想不到的
all of a sudden 突然
suffer v. 受苦,受难,受罪
v. 经历,遭受,忍受
sufficient a. 充分的,足够的
sugar n. 糖
suggest v. 建议,提出
v. 使想起,暗示
suggestion n. 建议,意见
suit n. (一套)西服
v. 适合,合适
n. 起诉,诉讼
suitable a. 合适的
sulphur/sulfur n. 硫
sum n. 总数,总和
n. 金额
sum up 总结,概括
summarize v. 概括,总结
summary n. 摘要,概要
summer n. 夏天,夏季
sun n. 太阳,阳光
Sunday n. 星期日
sunlight n. 日光,阳光
sunrise n. 日出
sunset n. 日落
sunshine n. 日光,日照
super a. 极好的,超级的
superior n./a. 上级
a. 更好的,较好的
a. 优秀的,优越的
supermarket n. 超级市场
supper n. 晚饭
supply v./n. 供给,供应
v. 补充,补足
support v./n. 支持,支援,拥护
v./n. 供养,赡养
n. 支柱
suppose v. 猜想,料想
v. 假定,以为
supreme a. 最高的
sure a. 确信的,有把握的
a. 一定的,必然的
a. 稳当的,可靠的
make sure 查明,弄确实
surface n. 面,表面
n. 外表,外观
surgery n. 外科,外科手术
n. 手术室
surprise n. 诧异,惊奇
v. 使诧异,使惊奇
v./n. 突然袭击,奇袭
surrender v. 投降
v. 交出,放弃
surround v. 围绕,包围
surroundings n. 周围事物,环境
survey v./n. 俯瞰,审察
v./n. 测量,勘查
survive v. 比……长命
v. 幸免于,幸存
suspect n. 嫌疑犯
v. 疑心,怀疑
suspicion n. 怀疑,疑心
swallow1 v. 吞下,咽下
swallow2 n. 燕子
sway v. 摇晃,摇动
swear v. 宣誓,发誓
v. 诅咒,骂人
sweat n. 汗
v. 出汗
sweep v. 扫,打扫
v. 冲走,席卷
sweet a. 甜的,香的
n. 甜食,糖果
a. 可爱的,温柔的
swell v. 膨胀,增大,隆起
swift a./ad. 快,迅速
swim v./n. 游泳
v. 眩晕
v. 浸,泡
swing v. 摇摆,摇荡
v. 回转,转回
n. 秋千
switch n. 电闸,开关
v./n. 转变,转向
sword n. 剑,刀
symbol n. 象征,符号,标志
sympathetic a. 同情的,共鸣的
sympathize v. 同情,怜悯
v. 共鸣,同感
sympathy n. 同情(心),赞同,同感
synthetic a. 合成的,人造的
system n. 系统,体系
n. 制度,体制

T

table n. 桌子
n. 表格,目录
tag n. 标签,货签
tail n. 尾巴
n. 尾部,后部
tailor v. 缝制
n. 裁缝
take v. 拿,取,握
v. 拿走,带去
v. 需要,花费
v. 接受,获得
v. 认为,当作
v. 做(一次动作)
take off 拿走,脱下,起飞
take one's time 慢慢来;不着急
take over 占用;接管
take up 开始从事,着手处理
tale n. 故事,传说
talent n. 才能,天资
n. 人才
talk v. 谈,讲
n. 讲话,演讲
v. 讨论,议论
tall a. 高的
tame v. 驯养
a. 驯服的,易于驾驭的
tank n. 箱,罐,槽
n. 坦克
tap1 n. 旋塞,龙头,塞子
tap2 v./n. 轻叩,轻拍

tape n. 带子,磁带
tape recorder 磁带录音机
target n. 靶子,目标
task n. 任务,工作
taste v. 品,尝
n. 滋味
n. 味觉
n. 趣味,口味,鉴赏力
v. 味道像,有……味道
tax v. 征税
n. 税
v. 加负担,使劳累
taxi n. 出租汽车
tea n. 茶叶,茶
n. 茶点
teach v. 教,教书,教训
teacher n. 教师
team n. 小队,小组
tear n. 眼泪
in tears 流着泪,含泪,哭
technical a. 技术的,工艺的
technician n. 技术员,技师
technique n. 技巧,手艺
n. 技术,工艺
technology n. 工艺,技术
tedious a. 冗长的,乏味的
teenager n. (13—19岁的)少年
telegram n. 电报
telephone n. 电话
v. 打电话
telescope n. 望远镜
television/TV n. 电视,电视机
tell v. 告诉,讲述
v. 吩咐,命令
v. 泄露,吐露
v. 辨别,区别(from)
temper n. 情绪,脾气
n. 韧度,回火色
temperature n. 温度
n. 发烧
temple n. 庙,寺
temporary a. 暂时的
tempt vt. 引诱
temptation n. 诱惑,引诱
ten n./a. 十
tend1 v. 趋于,倾向
tend2 v. 照料,看护
tendency n. 倾向,趋势
tender a. 温柔的,温厚的
a. 脆弱的,敏感的
tennis n. 网球
tense1 n. 时态
tense2 a. 拉紧的,紧张的
tension n. 紧张
tent n. 帐篷
tenth a. 第十
n. 十分之一
term n. 学期
n. 期,期限
n. 词,措词,术语
n. (pl.)条件,条款
terrible a. 可怕的,令人生畏的
a. 极度的,厉害的
a. 坏透的,很糟的
territory n. 领土,地区
n. 领域,范围
terror n. 恐怖
n. 恐怖的人(事)
test v./n. 测验,试验,检验
text n. 课文
n. 原文,本文,正文
textbook n. 教科书,课本
textile n./a. 纺织品
than conj. 比
thank v. 感谢
n. (pl.)感谢,谢忱
thanks to 由于,多亏
that a./pron. 那,那个
pron. [引出定语从句]……的
conj. [引出名词从句]
ad. 那样,那么
that is 就是说,即
the art. [定冠词]
theatre/theater n. 剧院
their pron. 他们的
theirs pron. 他们的(东西)
them pron. 他们(宾格)
themselves pron. 他们自己
then ad. 在那时,当时
ad. 那么,因而
ad. 然后,于是
ad. 另外,而且
theory n. 理论,学说
there ad. 在那里,往那里
ad. [作引导词]
ad. 在那一点上,在那方面
ad. [放在句首,用以加强语气]
therefore conj. 因此
ad. 结果
thermometer n. 温度计
these pron./a. 这些
they pron. 他们
thick a. 粗的,厚的,稠的,浓的
ad. 厚,浓,密
thief n. 贼
thin a. 细的,薄的,稀的,瘦的
v. 变细,变薄
thing n. 物,东西
n. 事,事情
think v. 想,思索
v. 认为
v. 考虑,打算
think of 想到,想起
think over 仔细考虑
third a. 第三
n. 三分之一
thirsty a. 口渴的
a. (for)渴望的,渴求的
thirteen n./a. 十三
thirty n. 三十
this pron. 这
thorough a. 彻底的,完全的
a. 仔细周到的,精细的
those a. 那些
pron. 那些,那些人
though conj. 虽然
ad. 可是,然而
thought n. 思想,思维,思考
n. 想法,观念
thoughtful a. 深思的,沉思的
a. 体贴的,关心的
thousand n./a. 一千
thread n. 线
v. 穿线,穿过
n. 线索,思路
threat n. 威胁,危险迹象
threaten v. 威胁,恫吓
v. 快要来临,有……征兆
three n./a. 三
thrive v. 兴旺,繁荣
throat n. 咽喉,嗓子
through prep./ad. 通过,穿过
ad. 自始至终
throughout prep. 贯穿,遍及
ad. 到处,全部
throw v. 投,扔,抛
throw away 扔掉,抛弃
thumb n. 拇指
thunder n. 雷,轰隆声
v. 打雷,轰隆响
Thursday n. 星期四
thus ad. 如此,这样
ad. 因而,从而
ticket n. 票,门票,车票
n. 票签,标签
tide n. 潮汐,潮
n. 潮流,趋势
tidy v. 整理,收拾
a. 整洁的,整齐的
tie n. 领带
v. 系,捆
n. 纽带,联系
tiger n. 虎
tight a. 紧的,紧身的
ad. 紧紧地
a. 密封的,紧密的
till conj./prep. 到……为止,直到
time n. 时间,时刻

n. 次,回
n. 时代,时期
n. 倍,乘
from time to time 时常
in no time 立即,马上
on time 准时
once upon a time 从前
ahead of time 提前
at a time 每次,一次
in time 及时地,适时地
tin n. 罐头
n. 锡
tiny a. 微小的,细小的
tip1 n. 尖,顶端
tip2 n. 小费
v. 给小费
tired a. 疲劳的,厌倦的
tissue n. 织物,薄纸
title n. 书名,题目
n. 头衔,称号
to prep. [表示方向] 向,往
prep. [表示终点,程度,范围] 到
part. [不定式符号]
prep. [用于间接宾语前] 给
prep. [表示对比,比例,选择] 比,对
toast n. 烤面包片,吐司
v. 烤(面包片等)
tobacco n. 烟草,烟叶
today n./ad. 今天,现在
toe n. 脚趾,足尖
together ad. 共同,一起
toilet n. 厕所,盥洗室
tomato n. 西红柿
tomorrow n./ad. 明天
ton n. 吨
tone n. 音,音调,声调
n. 腔调,语气
tongue n. 舌,舌头
n. 语音
tonight n./ad. 今晚
too ad. 也,又
ad. 太,过于
tool n. 工具
tooth n. 牙齿
n. 齿,齿状物
top n. 顶,顶部
a. 最高的
on top of 在……之上
topic n. 论题,题目
torch n. 火炬,火把
n. 手电筒
tortoise n. 龟
torture v./n. 拷问,拷打
n. 折磨,痛苦
total n. 总数,合计
a. 总的,完全的
v. 合计,总计
touch v. 触,摸,碰
v. 触动,感动
n. 接触,联系
keep in touch 保持联系
touch on 关系到,涉及
tough a. 坚韧的,难嚼烂的
a. 结实的,能吃苦耐劳的
a. 艰巨的,困难的
tour v./n. 旅游,旅行
tourist n. 旅游者,观光者
toward(s) prep. [表示运动,方向] 向
prep. [表示关系] 对于
prep. [表示时间] 将近
towel n. 毛巾
tower n. 塔
town n. 市镇
toy n. 玩具
trace n. 痕迹,踪迹
v. 跟踪,查找
tractor n. 拖拉机,牵引车
trade n. 贸易,商业
n. 行业,职业
tradition n. 传统,惯例
traffic n. 交通,交通量
tragedy n. 悲剧
n. 惨事,灾难
train n. 列车
v. 培训
training n. 训练
transform v. 转变,变形,变革
transistor n. 晶体管,晶体管收音机
translate v. 翻译
translation n. 翻译,译
n. 译文,译本
transparent a. 透明的
transport v./n. 运输,搬运
trap n. 陷阱,圈套
v. 诱捕,使中圈套
travel v./n. 旅行
tray n. 盘,托盘
treasure n. 财宝,财富
n. 宝贝,珍宝
v. 珍视,珍惜
treat v. 对待,处理
v. 医疗,治疗
v./n. 款待,请客
treatment n. 治疗,疗法
n. 对待,待遇
tree n. 树
tremble v. 颤抖,颤动
tremendous a. 巨大的
trend n. 倾向,趋势
trial n. 审讯
n. 试验
triangle n. 三角,三角形
trick n. 诡计,花招
v. 哄骗,欺骗
trim v./n. 整理,修剪,装饰
trip v. 绊倒,失足
n. 旅行,远足
triumph n. 胜利,成功
v. 得胜,战胜
troop n. (pl.) 部队,军队
trouble n. 苦恼,麻烦,困难
v. 麻烦,打扰
n. 辛苦,费心
trousers n. 裤子
truck n. 卡车,载重汽车
true a. 真实的,确实的
a. 忠实的,可靠的
trunk n. 大衣箱,(汽车后部)行李箱
n. 树干,躯干
trust v./n. 信任,信赖
v./n. 委托,信托
truth n. 真实,真相
n. 真理
try v. 试图,努力
v. 试验,试用
v. 审讯,审理
tube n. 管,软管
n. 电子管,显像管
n. 地下铁道
tuck v. 卷起
v. 塞进
Tuesday n. 星期二
tune n. 调子,曲调
n. 和谐,协调
v. 调整,调节
tunnel n. 隧道,山洞
turn v./n. 翻,旋转,转动
v./n. 扭转,转向
n. 轮流,轮班
v. 变化,改变
turn away 将……拒之门外
turn off 关,关闭,拐弯,叉开
turn on 打开,拧开
turn out 结果;证明是
in turn 依次,轮流
turn into (使)变成
turnip n. 萝卜,芜菁
twelfth a. 第十二
twelve n./a. 十二
twentieth a. 第二十
twenty n./a. 二十
twice ad. 两次,两倍
twin n. 孪生子,双生子
a. 成双的,孪生的
twist v./n. 搓,捻
v./n. 拧,扭
n. 扭转,扭弯
two n./a. 二

type *n.* 型式,类型
v. 打字
typewriter *n.* 打字机
typical *a.* 典型的,有代表性的
typist *n.* 打字员
tyre/tire *n.* 轮胎

U

ugly *a.* 丑的,丑陋的
a. 丑恶的,讨厌的
ultimate *a.* 最后的,最终的
umbrella *n.* 伞
unable *a.* 不能的,不会的
uncertain *a.* 不确定的
uncle *n.* 伯父,叔父,舅父,姑夫,姨父
under *prep.* 在……下面
prep. 少于,低于
prep. 在……情况下,在……中
undergo *v.* 遭受,经历
underground *a.* 地下的,秘密的
n. 地下铁道
underline *vt.* 强调
vt. 在……下面划线
underneath *prep.* 在……下面
ad. 在下面
understand *v.* 懂,理解
v. 揣测,认为
understanding *n.* 理解,理解力
n. 谅解
undertake *v.* 接受,承担
undo *v.* 松开,解开
undoubtedly *ad.* 无疑,必定
uneasy *a.* 局促的;不安的;不安适的
unexpected *a.* 想不到的,意外的
unfair *a.* 不公平的,不公道的
unfortunate *a.* 不幸的,令人遗憾的
uniform *n.* 制服,军服
a. 一致的,一律的
union *n.* 结合,组合,联合
n. 协会,工会,联盟
unit *n.* 单元,单位
n. 部件,元件,装置
unite *v.* 统一,结合,合并
v. 联合,团结
the United States/US 美国
the United Nations 联合国
universe *n.* 宇宙,万物
university *n.* 综合大学
unknown *a.* 未知的,不知名的
unless *conj.* 如果不,除非
unlike *a.* 不同的,不相似的
prep. 不像,和……不同
unload *vt.* 卸,从……卸下货物
vi. 卸货
until *prep.*/*conj.* 到……为止,直到
unusual *a.* 不平常的,稀有的,例外的
up *prep.*/*ad.* 向上
ad. 起床,起来
ad. [从静止到活动]……起来
ad. [从活动到结束]……完,……光
up to 从事于,忙于直到
该由……,轮到……
upon *prep.* 在……上
upper *a.* 上的,上部的,较高的
upright *a.* 直立的,竖立的
a. 正直的,诚实的
upset *v.* 弄翻,打翻
v. 扰乱,打乱,使不安
upstairs *a.*/*ad.* 在楼上,往楼上
up-to-date *a.* 时新的,新式的
a. 跟上时代的
upward *a.* 向上的
ad. [-(s)] 向上,往上,……以上
urban *a.* 城市的
urge *v.* 鼓励,促进
urgent *a.* 紧迫的,催促的
us *pron.* 我们(宾格)
use *v.* 用,使用,消耗
n. 使用,用法,用途
make use of 利用
put to use 使用,利用
use up 用光,花完
used1 to *v.* 过去惯常,过去经常
used2 *a.* 习惯于(to)
a. 用旧了的,旧的
useful *a.* 有用的,有益的,有帮助的
useless *a.* 无用的,无价值的
usual *a.* 通常的,惯常的
as usual 像往常一样,照例
usually *ad.* 通常
utilize *v.* 利用
utmost *a.* 最远的,最大的,极度的
n. 极限,极度,最大可能

V

vacant *a.* 空的,未占用的
vacation *n.* 休假,假期
vague *a.* 不明确的,含糊的,暧昧的
vain *n.* 徒劳,白费
a. 自负的,虚荣的
in vain 徒劳,白费,无效
valley *n.* 谷,山谷
valuable *a.* 有价值的,贵重的
value *n.* 价值,实用性,重要性
v. 评价,估计
vanish *v.* 消失,消散
vanity *n.* 虚荣心,浮华
vapo(u)r *n.* 汽,蒸汽
variety *n.* 多样性,变化
n. 变种,品种
n. 种类,种种
various *a.* 各种各样的,不同的
a. 多方面的,多种的
vary *v.* 变化,改变
vast *a.* 巨大的,广阔的
a. 大量的,巨额的
vegetable *n.* 植物,蔬菜
vehicle *n.* 车辆,交通工具
venture *v.*/*n.* 冒险,拚,闯
v. 敢于,大胆表示
n. 冒险(事业)
verb *n.* 动词
very *ad.* 很,非常
ad. 真正地,完全
a. [加强名词的语气]正是那个,恰好的
a. 真正的,真实的
vessel *n.* 船舶
n. 容器,器皿
veteran *n.* 老手,老兵
vice *n.* 罪恶,恶习,不道德行为
n. 缺点,毛病
victim *n.* 牺牲品,受害者
victorious *a.* 胜利的,得胜的
victory *n.* 胜利
view *n.* 观察,视域,眼界
n. 观点,见解,看法
n. 景色,风景
v. 看待,考虑,观察
viewpoint *n.* 观点
village *n.* 村,村庄
vinegar *n.* 醋
violence *n.* 强暴,暴力,暴行
n. 激烈,猛烈
violent *a.* 猛烈的,强烈的,剧烈的
violet *n.* 紫罗兰
violin *n.* 小提琴
virtually *ad.* 实际上,事实上
vision *n.* 视觉,视力
n. 幻想,幻影
visit *v.*/*n.* 访问,参观,作客
v. 常去
visitor *n.* 客人,来宾,参观者
vital *a.* 重要的,致命的
vitamin *n.* 维生素
vivid *a.* 鲜艳的
a. 生动的,栩栩如生的
vocabulary *n.* 词汇(量)
n. 词(汇)表
voice *n.* 嗓音,声音
n. 嗓子,发声能力
n. 语态
volcano *n.* 火山
volleyball *n.* 排球
volume *n.* (一)卷,(一)册
n. 体积,容积
n. 音量,响度
voluntary *a.* 自愿的,志愿的
vote *n.* 选票,选票数
v./*n.* 选举,表决

voyage *n.* 航海，航程

W

wage1 *n.* (*pl.*) 工资，报酬
wage2 *v.* 进行，开展
wag(g)on *n.* 运货马车，运货车
waist *n.* 腰，腰部
wait *v.* 等候
v. 侍候(on)
n. 等候，等待时间
waiter *n.* 侍者，服务员
wake *v.* 醒来，唤醒
v. 使觉悟，激发，引起
waken *v.* 醒，弄醒，唤醒
walk *v./n.* 步行，散步
n. 人行道，散步场所
wall *n.* 墙壁，围墙
v. 筑墙围住，用墙隔开
wander *v.* 徘徊，漫步
v. 迷路，迷失
v. 离开正道，离题
want *v.* 想要，需要
v. 缺乏，缺少
n. 必需品
n. 缺乏，需要
war *n.* 战争，战斗
warm *a.* 暖的，温暖的
a. 热忱的，热心的
v. 使暖和
warm up 变热
warmth *n.* 暖和，温暖
n. 热忱，热烈
warn *v.* 警告，告诫
wash *v./n.* 洗，冲洗
v. (浪涛)冲刷，拍打
n. 洗涤物，衣服
waste *a.* 荒废的，没用的
v./n. 浪费，消耗
n. 废物，废品
watch *v.* 观看，注视
v./n. 看管，监视
n. 表，手表
v. 窥伺，等待(for)
water *n.* 水
v. 浇，灌
waterproof *a.* 耐水的，防水的
wave *n.* 波浪，波
n. 飘扬，起伏
v. 挥舞，摇动
wax *n.* 蜡，蜂蜡
v. 打蜡
way *n.* 道路，路程
n. 方法，手段，方式
n. 习惯，作风
stand/be in sb.'s way 阻碍；妨碍
be the way 顺便提一下，另外
make way 开路，让路，通过……方式，前进，行进
we *pron.* 我们
weak *a.* 虚弱的，软弱的
a. 薄弱的，差的
weakness *n.* 衰弱，软弱
n. 弱点，缺点
wealth *n.* 财富，财产
n. 丰富，大量
wealthy *a.* 富裕的，富有的，富庶的
weapon *n.* 武器，兵器
wear *v.* 穿戴，佩带
v. 磨损，用旧
wear off 逐渐消逝
weather *n.* 天气，气象
weave *n.* 编，编织
wedding *n.* 婚礼
Wednesday *n.* 星期三
weed *n.* 杂草，野草
v. 除草，锄草
week *n.* 星期，周
weekday *n.* 平常日，工作日
weekend *n.* 周末
weekly *a.* 每周的，一周一次的
n. 周刊，周报
weep *v.* 哭泣，流泪
v. 悲叹，哀悼，为……伤心(for)
weigh *v.* 称，量
v. 重，重达
v. 考虑，权衡
weight *n.* 重量，体重
welcome *a.* 受欢迎的
v./n. 欢迎
int. 欢迎
welfare *n.* 福利
well1 *n.* 井，水井
well2 *ad.* 好
a. 健康的，良好的
int. 好啦
ad. 有理由地，恰当地
as well 同样，也
as well as 既……又，除……之外(还)
west *n./a.* 西，西部，西方
ad. 向西
western *a.* 西的，西方的
westward(s) *a./ad.* 向西
wet *a.* 湿的；下雨的，多雨的
v. 沾湿，弄湿
what *pron./a.* 什么
a. (表示感叹)多么，何等
pron. [引出定语从句]所……的事物(或人)
what about (对于)……怎么样
what if 如果……将会怎样，即使……又有什么要紧
whatever *pron.* [引出状语从句]无论什么
pron. [引出名词从句]凡是……的，无论什么
a. 不管怎样的，无论什么样的
wheat *n.* 小麦
wheel *n.* 轮，车轮
when *ad.* 什么时候，何时
ad. [引出定语从句]……的时候，那时
conj. 当……时；在那时，然后
whenever *ad.* 无论何时，随时
pron. 每当
where *ad.* 在哪里，往哪里
pron. 哪里，什么地方
ad. 从[状语从句]在……的地方
ad. [定语从句]……的地方
wherever *ad.* 无论在哪里，无论到哪里
ad. 究竟在哪里，究竟到哪里
whether *conj.* 是否，会不会
conj. 不管，无论
whether... or 是……还是，不管……还是
which *pron./a.* 哪一个，哪一些
pron. [引出定语从句]……的
pron. [引出非限制性定语从句]那一个，那一些
whichever *pron./a.* 无论哪个，无论哪些
while *conj.* 当……的时候
conj. 虽然，尽管
n. 一会儿，一段时间
v. 消磨
once in a while 偶尔，有时
whip *n.* 鞭子
v. 抽打，鞭策
v. 搅打，打成泡沫
whisper *v./n.* 耳语，私语
whistle *v.* 吹口哨，鸣笛
n. 口哨声，汽笛声
n. 哨子，汽笛
white *n./a.* 白色
who *pron.* 谁
pron. [引出定语从句]……的
pron. [引出非限制性定语从句]他，她，他们
whoever *pron.* [引出名词从句]谁
pron. 无论谁，不管谁
whole *n./a.* 全部，全体，完整
wholly *ad.* 完全，一概
whom *pron.* 谁(宾格)
whose *pron.* 谁的
pron. [引出定语从句]那个(人)的，那些(人)的
why *ad.* 为什么
ad. [引出定语从句]为什么……的
int. 咳，哎呀
wicked *a.* 坏的，不道德的居心不良的
wide *a.* 宽阔的，广泛的
ad. 完全地，充分地

widen *vt.* 加宽,放宽
vi. 变宽
widespread *a.* 分布(或散布)广的,普遍的
widow *n.* 寡妇
width *n.* 宽度,幅
n. 广阔,宽阔
wife *n.* 妻子
wild *a.* 野生的,未驯化的
a. 荒芜的,荒凉的
a. 野蛮的,放肆的
a. 疯狂的,狂热的
will *v.* 将,会;愿,要
n. 决心,意志;遗嘱
willing *a.* 自愿的,心甘情愿的
win *v.* 赢得,获胜
v. 达到,赶上
wind1 *v.* 绕,缠,弯曲
wind2 *n.* 风
window *n.* 窗,窗户
wine *n.* 葡萄酒,果酒
wing *n.* 翼,翅膀
winner *n.* 得胜者,获奖者
winter *n.* 冬季
wipe *v.*/*n.* 擦,抹,揩
wipe out 消灭,毁灭
wire *n.* 铁丝,电线
n. 电信,电报
wisdom *n.* 智慧,明智
wise *a.* 智慧的,聪明的
wish *v.*/*n.* 祝,祝愿
v. 希望,想要
n. 希望,愿望
wit *n.* 智力,才智
with *prep.* 跟……一起
prep. 用
prep. 具有,带有
prep. 关于,就……而言
prep. 因,由于
prep. 随着
withdraw *v.* 收回,撤销,撤退
vi. 缩回,退出,撤退
within *prep.* 在……里面,在……以内
ad. 以内
without *prep.* 没有,毫无
witness *n.* 目击者,见证人
v. 目击,目睹
wolf *n.* 狼
woman *n.* 妇女,女人
wonder *n.* 惊奇,惊异
n. 奇迹,奇事
v. 诧异,奇怪
v. 纳闷,想知道
no wonder 难怪,怪不得
wonderful *a.* 惊人的,奇妙的,极好的
wood *n.* 小森林,树林
n. 木头,木材
wooden *a.* 木制的
a. 木头似的,呆笨的
wool *n.* 羊毛
n. 毛线,毛织品
wool(l)en 羊毛的,羊毛制的
word *n.* 词,单词
n. 言语,话
n. 诺言,保证
n. 音信,消息
in a word 总而言之
in other words 换句话说,也就是说
keep one's word 守信用
work *v.*/*n.* 工作,劳动
n. 著作,作品;成果,制品
v. 运转,开动
out of work 失业
at work 在工作,忙于
work out 解决,算出,设计出,制定出
worker *n.* 工人,工作者
workman *n.* 工人
works *n.* 工厂
workshop *n.* 工场,车间
world *n.* 世界,地球
n. ……界,领域
n. 世间,人间
n. 全世界,世人
world-wide *a.* 全世界的
worm *n.* 虫,蠕虫
worn *a.* 破烂的,损坏的
worry *v.*/*n.* 发愁,担忧,烦恼
worse *a.*/*ad.* 更坏,更差
worship *n.* 礼拜,礼拜仪式
worst *a.*/*ad.* 最坏,最差
at (the) worst 在最坏的情况下
worth *a.* 值……钱,值得……的
n. 价值
worthless *a.* 无价值的,无用的
worthwhile *a.* 值得的
worthy *a.* 有价值的,可尊敬的
a. 值得的,配得上的(of)
would *v.* 愿,想,要;总是,总会
wound *n.* 创伤,伤口
v. 受伤,伤害
wrap *v.* 卷,包,缠绕
n. 披肩,围巾
wreck *n.* 失事,海难
n. 沉船,残骸
v. (船等)失事,遇难
wrist *n.* 腕,腕关节
write *v.* 写,写作;写作,函告
writer *n.* 作者,作家
wrong *a.* 错误的,有毛病的
ad. 错,不对

X

x-ray *n.* 射线,X光

Y

yard1 *n.* 院子,场地
yard2 *n.* 码
yawn *v.* 打阿欠
n. 呵欠
year *n.* 年,年度
yearly *a.*/*ad.* 每年,一年一度
yell *v.* 叫喊
yellow *n.*/*a.* 黄色
yes *ad.* 是的
yesterday *n.*/*ad.* 昨天
yet *ad.* 还,仍然
ad. 已经
conj. 然而,可是
ad. 更
yield *v.* 生产,出产
n. 产量,收获量
v. 让步,屈服
you *pron.* 你,你们
young *a.* 年轻的
n. 青年人
your *pron.* 你的,你们的
yours *pron.* 你的(东西),你们的(东西)
yourself *pron.* 你自己,你本身
youth *n.* 青春,青年时期
n. 青年,青年人

Z

zero *n.* 零,零点,零度
zone *n.* 地带,区域
v. 分区,划分地带
zoo *n.* 动物园